# Lecture Notes in Computer Science    16318

Founding Editors

Gerhard Goos
Juris Hartmanis

Editorial Board Members

Elisa Bertino, *Purdue University, West Lafayette, IN, USA*
Wen Gao, *Peking University, Beijing, China*
Bernhard Steffen, *TU Dortmund University, Dortmund, Germany*
Moti Yung, *Columbia University, New York, NY, USA*

The series Lecture Notes in Computer Science (LNCS), including its subseries Lecture Notes in Artificial Intelligence (LNAI) and Lecture Notes in Bioinformatics (LNBI), has established itself as a medium for the publication of new developments in computer science and information technology research, teaching, and education.

LNCS enjoys close cooperation with the computer science R & D community, the series counts many renowned academics among its volume editors and paper authors, and collaborates with prestigious societies. Its mission is to serve this international community by providing an invaluable service, mainly focused on the publication of conference and workshop proceedings and postproceedings. LNCS commenced publication in 1973.

Tong Chen · Jinge Wu · Kun Yuan ·
Xiaohan Xing · Yuning Du · Jinman Kim ·
Nicolas Padoy · Hongliang Ren · Nassir Navab ·
Long Bai
Editors

# Efficient Medical Artificial Intelligence

First International Workshop, EMA4MICCAI 2025
Held in Conjunction with MICCAI 2025
Daejeon, South Korea, September 23, 2025
Proceedings

 Springer

*Editors*
Tong Chen 
University of Sydney
Sydney, NSW, Australia

Kun Yuan 
Technical University of Munich
Munich, Germany

Yuning Du 
University of Edinburgh
Edinburgh, UK

Nicolas Padoy 
University of Strasbourg
Strasbourg, France

Nassir Navab 
Technical University of Munich
Munich, Germany

Jinge Wu 
University College London
London, UK

Xiaohan Xing 
Stanford University
Stanford, CA, USA

Jinman Kim 
University of Sydney
Sydney, NSW, Australia

Hongliang Ren 
The Chinese University of Hong Kong
Sha Tin, Hong Kong

Long Bai 
The Chinese University of Hong Kong
Sha Tin, Hong Kong

ISSN 0302-9743     ISSN 1611-3349  (electronic)
Lecture Notes in Computer Science
ISBN 978-3-032-13960-3     ISBN 978-3-032-13961-0  (eBook)
https://doi.org/10.1007/978-3-032-13961-0



This Springer imprint is published by the registered company Springer Nature Switzerland AG
The registered company address is: Gewerbestrasse 11, 6330 Cham, Switzerland

If disposing of this product, please recycle the paper.

# Preface

The Efficient Medical Artificial Intelligence (EMA4MICCAI) Workshop aims to address the critical need for computationally efficient and resource-conscious Artificial Intelligence (AI) solutions in medical applications. As medical AI models grow in complexity and deployment scales, challenges such as high computational costs, energy consumption, high annotation expenses, and latency in real-time clinical environments have emerged as significant barriers to widespread adoption. EMA focuses on advancing research and fostering discussion around innovative strategies to enhance the efficiency, scalability, and accessibility of medical AI, while maintaining or improving performance and reliability.

While the MICCAI community has extensively explored medical AI development and application, the computational efficiency of these solutions remains underrepresented. EMA directly addresses this gap by focusing on the practical challenges and opportunities for optimizing medical AI training and deployment procedures for real-world use. By integrating computational efficiency into the conversation, EMA contributes to the MICCAI mission of advancing healthcare through innovative and deployable technologies.

The EMA4MICCAI Workshop focuses on advancing computational efficiency in medical AI by exploring innovative techniques such as lightweight model architectures, resource-conscious deployment strategies, and energy-efficient computing. Key themes include optimizing deep learning models for medical imaging and diagnostics, enabling scalable and privacy-preserving federated learning, leveraging edge and embedded systems for real-time clinical applications, and benchmarking efficiency metrics to drive sustainable AI development in healthcare. By addressing these themes, the workshop aims to bridge the gap between cutting-edge AI research and practical, deployable solutions in medical environments.

For the first edition of EMA4MICCAI, we received a total of 40 paper submissions, covering a broad spectrum of topics in efficient medical AI. After a thorough peer-review process, 36 full papers were accepted for presentation. Each manuscript underwent a rigorous double-blind review, with at least three expert reviewers assigned to every submission. The review assignments were handled automatically, with strict conflict-of-interest checks in place to prevent recent collaborations or institutional overlaps. Our reviewers were selected from a global pool of leading researchers with recognized expertise in the field, ensuring a fair and high-quality evaluation process. Following the completion of the reviews, final decisions were made by the program chairs, based solely on the reviewers' assessments and recommendations. All decisions were final and were made with the goal of maintaining scientific integrity and quality throughout.

Additionally, the workshop organizing committee granted awards to the best submissions at EMA4MICCAI 2025. The Best Paper Award, Best Paper Award Honorable Mention, and Best Student Paper Award were selected via a double-blind rating procedure where each committee member rated the shortlisted papers. The top three papers with the highest scores were then selected by the committee. The Best Oral Presentation Award and the Best Poster Award were determined through on-site evaluation. Members of the organizing committee scored the oral presentations and posters, and the candidate with the highest average score received each award. We are confident that the careful selection process applied at EMA4MICCAI 2025, combined with the overall strength of the submissions, has resulted in a collection of high-impact, technically sound, and timely contributions to both the MICCAI community and the growing research domain of efficient medical AI.

We would like to express our sincere appreciation to all authors for their valuable submissions and to our reviewers for their professionalism, thoughtful feedback, and commitment to upholding academic standards throughout the review process.

October 2025

Tong Chen
Jinge Wu
Kun Yuan
Xiaohan Xing
Yuning Du
Jinman Kim
Nicolas Padoy
Hongliang Ren
Nassir Navab
Long Bai

# Organization

## Organizing Chairs

| | |
|---|---|
| Long Bai | The Chinese University of Hong Kong, China |
| Tong Chen | The University of Sydney, Australia |
| Yuning Du | The University of Edinburgh, UK |
| Jinman Kim | The University of Sydney, Australia |
| Nassir Navab | Technical University of Munich, Germany |
| Nicolas Padoy | University of Strasbourg, France |
| Hongliang Ren | The Chinese University of Hong Kong, China |
| Jinge Wu | University College London, UK |
| Xiaohan Xing | Stanford University, USA |
| Kun Yuan | Technical University of Munich, Germany |

## Program Committee

| | |
|---|---|
| Ruicheng Ao | Hong Kong University of Science and Technology (Guangzhou), China |
| Yuan Bi | Technical University of Munich & Munich Center for Machine Learning, Germany |
| Boyu Chen | University College London, UK |
| Keqi Chen | University of Strasbourg, France |
| Beilei Cui | The Chinese University of Hong Kong, China |
| Chengliang Dai | Imperial College London, UK |
| Wenzhen Dong | The Chinese University of Hong Kong, China |
| Zhicheng He | National University of Singapore, Singapore |
| Yiming Huang | The Chinese University of Hong Kong, China |
| Yunsoo Kim | University College London, UK |
| Feng Li | Technical University of Munich & Munich Center for Machine Learning, Germany |
| Ruochen Li | Technical University of Munich, Germany |
| Shi Li | University of Strasbourg, France |
| Wei Li | Shanghai Jiao Tong University, China |
| Yanheng Li | City University of Hong Kong, China |
| Zexi Li | University of Oxford, UK |
| Zhihua Liu | The University of Edinburgh, UK |
| Zihao Luo | The University of Sydney, Australia |

| | |
|---|---|
| Boyi Ma | University of Toronto, Canada |
| Xinyu Ma | Macao Polytechnic University, China |
| Chi Kit Ng | The Chinese University of Hong Kong, China |
| Bo Peng | University College London, UK |
| Yaling Shen | Monash University, Australia |
| Zechao Sun | University of Adelaide, Australia |
| Rui Tang | Hong Kong University of Science and Technology (Guangzhou), China |
| An Wang | The Chinese University of Hong Kong, China |
| Guankun Wang | The Chinese University of Hong Kong, China |
| Hongqiu Wang | Hong Kong University of Science and Technology (Guangzhou), China |
| Jie Wang | The Chinese University of Hong Kong, China |
| Jingsong Wang | Shandong University, China |
| Junyi Wang | The Chinese University of Hong Kong, China |
| Wenyang Wang | The University of Sydney, Australia |
| Yu Wang | University College London, UK |
| Yunheng Wu | Nagoya University, Japan |
| Shilong Yao | City University of Hong Kong, China |
| Jieming Yu | Hong Kong University of Science and Technology, China |
| Weiyi Zhang | The Hong Kong Polytechnic University, China |
| Yanguang Zhao | National University of Singapore, Singapore |

# Contents

# Beyond One-Hot Encoding? Journey Into Compact Encoding for Large Multi-Class Segmentation

Aaron Kujawa$^{(\boxtimes)}$ (iD), Thomas Booth (iD), and Tom Vercauteren (iD)

King's College London, London, UK
`aaron.kujawa@kcl.ac.uk`

**Abstract.** This work presents novel methods to reduce computational and memory requirements for medical image segmentation with a large number of classes. We curiously observe challenges in maintaining state-of-the art segmentation performance with all of the explored options. Standard learning-based methods typically employ one-hot encoding of class labels. The computational complexity and memory requirements thus increase linearly with the number of classes. We propose a family of binary encoding approaches instead of one-hot encoding to reduce the computational complexity and memory requirements to logarithmic in the number of classes. In addition to vanilla binary encoding, we investigate the effects of error-correcting output codes (ECOCs), class weighting, hard/soft decoding, class-to-codeword assignment, and label embedding trees. We apply the methods to the use case of whole brain parcellation with 108 classes based on 3D MRI images. While binary encodings have proven efficient in so-called *extreme classification* problems in computer vision, we faced challenges in reaching state-of-the-art segmentation quality with binary encodings. Compared to one-hot encoding (Dice Similarity Coefficient (DSC) = 82.4(2.8)), we report reduced segmentation performance with the binary segmentation approaches, achieving DSCs in the range from 39.3 to 73.8. Informative negative results all too often go unpublished. We hope that this work inspires future research of compact encoding strategies for large multi-class segmentation tasks.

**Keywords:** Multi-class segmentation · One-hot encoding · Extreme classification · Error-correcting output codes · Negative results

## 1 Introduction

Deep learning models for semantic segmentation tasks typically rely on one-hot encoding of class labels. The computational complexity of calculating the class probabilities and the memory required to store them is linear in the number of

**Supplementary Information** The online version contains supplementary material available at https://doi.org/10.1007/978-3-032-13961-0_1.

classes. For the segmentation of high resolution 3D medical images, this linear dependence can lead to excessive resource requirements. While the number of classes for many semantic segmentation tasks in the medical imaging field is often small, an increasing number of applications require a high number of classes. For example, whole brain parcellation (WBP) protocols can include hundreds of distinct classes [4,14]. Another example is TotalSegmentator, a family of foundation models for segmentation of 100+ structures in CT and MRI images [1,29].

This has led to the development of mitigation strategies such as patch-based methods which extract smaller sub-volumes at the cost of losing spatial context [6,8,12,16,18,18,19,25,26]. Other approaches reduce these resource requirements by merging related label pairs during model training and inference [11,15,23,24]. Model compression, quantization, and related techniques [17] can also help but the expected gains are not commensurate with the linear class number scaling.

Here, to address the linear increase of resources, we explore a family of different approaches that relies on binary encoding of class labels and thereby frames the original *multi-class* segmentation task as a *multi-task* segmentation problem. Each task is a binary segmentation task that corresponds to one bit of the binary representation of the class label. Each voxel will thus typically be associated with several positive bits. The complexity of this approach is reduced and becomes logarithmic in the number of classes.

To date, binary encoding strategies employed in computer vision have mostly focused on so-called *extreme classification* tasks where large numbers of classes are expected [2]. Error Correcting Output Codes (ECOCs) have been explored as an efficient way of improving classification performance, improve speed of convergence, and include prior information about the class taxonomy [7,9,10,21,22]. These works are motivated by the use of lower dimensional output embeddings to encourage the identification and exploitation of intrinsic class relationships. Instead, our work focuses on the increased computational and memory requirements associated with a large output space.

To the best of our knowledge, this work presents the first investigation of binary encoding strategies in the context of semantic 3D medical image segmentation. Curiously, we find that vanilla binary encoding reduces the segmentation performance compared to one-hot encoding. Our analysis shows that misclassified voxels occur mostly at structure boundaries and predominantly affect small structures. We assess the effect of ECOCs, class weighting, hard and soft decoding of output codes, class-to-codeword assignment, and the use of label embedding trees. While, these strategies did not improve segmentation performance, the negative results presented here serve as a starting point for future research.

## 2   Methods and Materials

We use nnU-Net [13], which is recognised as a strong baseline, as a common backbone and implement our proposed output encodings as bespoke final layers with corresponding loss functions.

## 2.1 Standard One-Hot Encoding with Multi-Class Learning

The standard method of one-hot encoding was used as a reference standard. In the U-Net architecture, the final $1 \times 1 \times 1$ convolution maps the feature vectors to $N_C$ output channels, where $N_C$ is the number of classes. A softmax operation yields probability distributions along the class dimension for each voxel. At training time, the sum of Dice loss and cross-entropy (Dice+CE) loss is applied. The Dice loss is defined as $L_D = \frac{1}{N_C} \sum_c 1 - \frac{2\sum_i p_{c,i} g_{c,i}}{\sum_i p_{c,i} + \sum_i g_{c,i}}$ where $p_{c,i}$ is the predicted probability of class $c$ and voxel $i$, and $g_{c,i}$ is the corresponding value of the one-hot encoded ground-truth label. The cross-entropy loss is defined as $L_X = \sum_i \frac{1}{\sum_i w_{g_i}} (-w_{g_i} \log(p_{g_i,i}))$ where the index $g_i$ is the ground truth ordinal class label at voxel $i$ and $w_{g_i}$ is the corresponding class weight. At inference time, the class with the highest probability is chosen as the predicted output class (argmax operation).

## 2.2 Vanilla Binary Encoding with *multi-Label* learning

This method encodes the class labels in a binary representation. At least $N_B = \lceil \log_2(N_C) \rceil$ bits are required to represent $N_C$ classes. For example, $N_B = 7$ binary bits are sufficient to represent up to 128 classes, where each class is represented by a binary number between 0000000 and 1111111. The CNN's final $1 \times 1 \times 1$ convolution maps the feature vector to $N_B$ output channels, rather than $N_C$ output channels used for standard one-hot encoding. A sigmoid function is applied to each of the output channels to convert output logits to the range $(0,1)$. Each of the output channels is considered as the probabilistic model output of a binary segmentation task, where the output values $p_{c,i}$ represent the probability of the corresponding ground truth bit $g_{c,i}$ to be 1: $p_{c,i} = P(g_{c,i} = 1)$. The same loss function (Dice+CE) with $N_C = 2$ was used to supervise each of the binary output channels. This method reduces the size of the output tensor size by a factor of $N_C/N_B$.

**Hard Decoding.** At inference time, hard decoding was employed, i.e., a threshold of 0.5 was applied to the output values $p_{c,i}$ to obtain a binary number. A lookup-table was used to map the binary numbers to the original ordinal class labels. Binary numbers that did not exist in the code book were mapped to the background. In the case of vanilla binary encoding, soft decoding as described in Sect. 2.3 is equivalent to hard decoding. Therefore, no separate experiment was conducted.

## 2.3 Hamming-Based Error Correcting Encoding

Hamming codes are a family of linear error-correcting codes [20]. Error-correction is achieved by the introduction of so-called parity bits in addition to the data bits used in vanilla binary encoding. For example, Hamming(7,4) encodes 4 data bits into 7 bits by adding 3 parity bits. A generator matrix $\mathbf{G}$ can be used to

Hamming(7,4) encode data bits $\mathbf{d} = (d_0, d_1, d_2, d_3)$ as Hamming encoded bits $\mathbf{h} = \mathbf{G}^T\mathbf{d} = (h_1, \ldots, h_7)$. To apply Hamming(7,4) encoding to binary numbers with more than 4 data bits, the binary number can be split into multiple chunks of 4 data bits and each chunk can be encoded and decoded separately. The number of required bits is thus at least $N_{\mathrm{Hamm}} = 7\lceil \frac{1}{4}\log_2(N_C)\rceil$. Other ECOCs could be used, for example Hamming(15,7) to avoid chunking. However, here we stick to Hamming(7,4) encoding as the simplest starting point. The CNN is then trained to predict the encoded bits using a $1 \times 1 \times 1$ convolution with one output channel for each encoded bit. At training time, a sigmoid operation is applied to each of the output channels and supervised separately with the corresponding Hamming encoded ground truths using the Dice+CE loss with $N_C = 2$.

**Hard Error-Correcting Decoding.** At inference time, hard error-correcting decoding is achieved by applying a sigmoid operation to the output logits, followed by thresholding at 0.5 to obtain an encoded binary prediction. For each of the 4-bit chunks, error-correcting decoding is performed by calculation of a so-called syndrome vector $\mathbf{z}$, through a modulo 2 binary matrix multiplication with a parity check matrix $\mathbf{P}$, which indicates the erroneous bit. Flipping/negating the erroneous bit of $\mathbf{r}$ results in the corrected Hamming code which can be decoded through another binary matrix multiplication. Finally, ordinal labels can by restored by means of a look-up table.

**Soft Error-Correction Decoding.** With soft error-correction decoding, the corrected Hamming code is obtained as that Hamming code of the code book with the smallest $L_2$-distance to the model output. With a naive implementation, this approach is computationally expensive and has no memory-saving advantage compared to standard one-hot encoding. It was applied as a means to assess the impact of hard decoding on the segmentation quality knowing that memory efficient soft decoding approaches existing for a range of ECOCs [20].

### 2.4   Binary-Tree Encoding, Learning, and Decoding

The method explained in this section and illustrated in Fig. 1 is inspired by [3] and aims at increasing the consistency of output channels by conditioning the weights of the $1 \times 1 \times 1$ convolution on the bits of the other channels. Specifically, for $N_B = \lceil \log_2(N_C) \rceil$ output channels with indices $k \in 0, \ldots, N_B - 1$, the weights $\mathbf{w}_k$ of the $1 \times 1 \times 1$ convolution that are associated with output channel $k$ are conditioned on all preceding output channels $\{j|j < k\}$. As shown in Fig. 1, this approach can be visualized as a binary tree with $N_B$ levels. While there is only one set of weights for the first output channel, for subsequent channels a different set of weights is applied for each combination of preceding output bits:

$$\mathbf{w}_k = \begin{cases} \mathbf{w}_0 & \text{if } k = 0 \\ \mathbf{w}_k^{b_0,\ldots,b_{k-1}} & \text{otherwise} \end{cases} \tag{1}$$

Hence, for output channel $k$ there are $2^k$ sets of weights, only one of which is selected during each forward pass and updated during the backward pass (training only). At training time, the preceding bits $b_0, ..., b_{k-1}$ are given by the ground truth, whereas at inference time, $b_0, ..., b_{k-1}$ are given by the discretized (sigmoid operation followed by thresholding) network prediction and therefore need to be predicted sequentially.

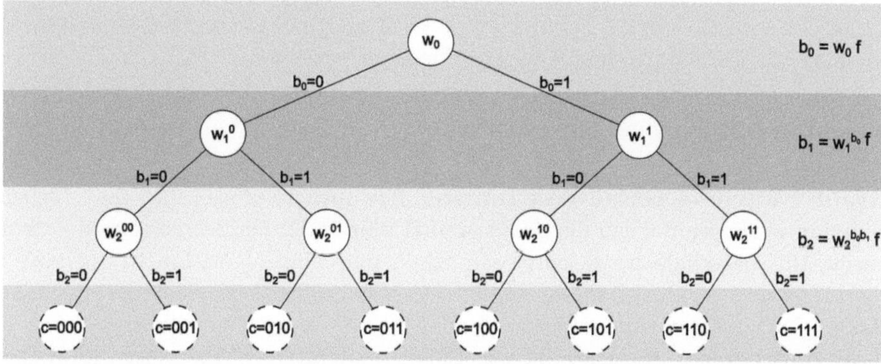


**Fig. 1.** Binary tree representing the hierarchy of codeword bits. Weight vectors $\mathbf{w}_i$ for $i > 0$ are determined by preceding bits which are determined by the ground truth during training and by the model prediction during inference. The dashed nodes at the bottom of the tree represent the class associated with the path taken from the root node.

**Implementation Details.** Due to the conditioning on preceding bits, the weights also depend on the spatial location $i$. Typically, implementations of convolutions do not feature a dependence of input weights on spatial location that could be exploited to condition the weights on preceding bits. However, $1 \times 1 \times 1$ convolutions are a linear mapping from a feature vector at a single location $i$ to the output vector $b_k(i)$ at that location and can therefore be expressed as a matrix multiplication.

Inclusion of the convolution bias parameter $\mathbf{w}_{k,\text{bias}}$ in the weight parameters $\mathbf{w}_k$ requires appending a 1 at the end of the feature vector $\mathbf{f}$. For matrix multiplication, efficient algorithms exist that allow to incorporate the spatial dependence of the weights: $\mathbf{w}_k \rightarrow \mathbf{w}_k(i)$. Here we apply the `gather_mm` function of the Deep Graph Library (DGL) [27].

## 2.5 Class to Binary Code Assignment

The assignment between classes and (encoded) binary numbers is a bijective mapping called a *code book*. The choice of the code book has been shown to significantly influence performance in classification tasks [10]. The performance resulting from a code book can depend on 1) the minimum distance $\rho$ between codewords, 2) the degree of correlation between output channels, and 3) the difficulty of the binary sub-problems. A high minimum distance $\rho$ between codewords leads to better error correction capability. Low correlation between output channels discourages simultaneous errors in multiple output channels. A codeword-to-class assignment that leads to binary output maps which are easier to learn can lead to improved performance. For example, a binary output map with a balanced number of foreground and background voxels may be easier to learn. On the other hand, a binary map with multiple foreground structures of complex shapes may present a more difficult sub-problem.

**Random.** As a baseline, a random codeword-to-class assignment was applied.

**Graph Matching Based Assignment** The authors of [10] find that "generalization is superior when encoding similar classes by similar codewords". Following this observation, we employ a graph matching algorithm to optimize a class-to-code assignment with respect to the Hamming distance between similar classes. We consider two classes as similar if we encounter neighboring voxels of those two classes in the training set. This is motivated by the observation that most errors by models trained with random class-to-code assignment are made at the boundary between structures (see Sect. 3). Thus, the first graph which represents the similarity between classes is an undirected connected graph with $N_C$ nodes representing the classes. Two nodes $c_1$ and $c_2$ are connected only if neighboring voxels of both classes are encountered in at least one instance of the training set. The second graph represents the codeword similarity. Each node represents one of $N_H = 2^{N_B}$ valid codewords, where $N_B$ is the number of data bits (excluding parity bits). Edge weights between nodes are set to 1 if the Hamming distance between codewords is larger than an empirically determined threshold that minimized the Hamming distance between connected classes, otherwise the edge was removed. The pygmtools python library [28] was applied to perform the matching between the two graphs.

## 2.6  Dataset

We evaluate the methods on a subset of 585 multi-parametric MRI scans included in the BraTS (Brain Tumor Segmentation) 2021 dataset. Each scan includes 4 modalities: a) native T1-weighted (T1), b) post-contrast T1-weighted (T1Gd), c) T2-weighted (T2), and d) T2 Fluid Attenuated Inversion Recovery (T2-FLAIR). The BraTS preprocessing pipeline was replaced with a custom preprocessing pipeline without skull-stripping to prevent the unintentional removal of brain tissue near the skull which is problematic for the whole brain segmentation task. To this end, corresponding unprocessed image volumes were retrieved from The Cancer Imaging Archive (TCIA) [5]. The reference pseudo-ground-truth labels for model training and evaluation were created as a combination of manual segmentations of tumor sub-regions contained in the BraTS 2021 dataset and pseudo-ground truth segmentations generated with the GIF algorithm [4].

## 3   Results

Results of all experiments are shown in Table 1. Curiously, compared to traditional one-hot encoding, methods that rely on binary encoding (with and without Hamming error-correction) result in a significant reduction in DSC. Use of the binary tree output head further reduces the DSC.

**Table 1.** Average Dice Similarity Coefficient (DSC) obtained in all experiments. The reported values are obtained by first calculating the average DSCs over all structures on a case-by-case basis, and then taking the average over all cases. The GPU memory was obtained experimentally for the reported number of output channels by running 1 training epoch with nnU-Net [13].

| # | encoding | loss | head | output channels | decoding | class-to- codeword assignment | avg. Dice | Mem. [GiB] |
|---|---|---|---|---|---|---|---|---|
| 1 | one-hot | multi-channel Dice+CE | 1x1x1 conv | $N_C = 108$ | - | - | 82.4 (2.8) | 26.7 |
| 2 | vanilla bin. | binary Dice+CE | 1x1x1 conv | $N_B = 7$ | hard | random | 72.7 (3.3) | 12.08 |
| 3 | Hamming | binary Dice+CE | 1x1x1 conv | $N_H = 14$ | hard | random | 73.7 (3.2) | 12.21 |
| 4 | Hamming | weighted binary CE | 1x1x1 conv | $N_H = 14$ | hard | random | 71.9 (3.3) | 12.21 |
| 5 | Hamming | weighted binary CE | 1x1x1 conv | $N_H = 14$ | soft | random | 73.8 (3.3) | - |
| 6 | Hamming | weighted binary CE | 1x1x1 conv | $N_H = 14$ | hard | graph- matching | 72.4 (2.9) | 12.21 |
| 7 | vanilla bin. | binary Dice+CE | tree | $N_B = 7$ | hard | random | 39.3 (1.5) | - |

We note that one-hot encoding outperforms the other encoding strategies significantly for small structures such as *inferior lateral ventricles* or *vessels* while the differences in DSC for larger structures such as *cerebellum* or *cerebral white matter* are small, except for the binary-tree encoding strategy which significantly under-performs for the majority of classes.

Figure 2 shows a comparison of label map predictions with one-hot encoding and vanilla binary encoding and highlights the main binary encoding artifact that affects voxels at structure boundaries. Figure 3 shows that classes of small volume have significantly lower DSC when binary encoding is used, while classes of larger volume are less affected. Use of a weighted binary CE loss function (experiments 4–6 of Table 1) did not lead to significant improvements.

## 4   Discussion

This work investigates the impact of different binary encodings on segmentation performance and associated requirements. Despite positive results published in the computer vision literature, we find that, when applied to medical image segmentation, these strategies lead to decreased performance compared to one-hot encoding. Attempts to improve the segmentation performance with ECOCs, spatial weighting, soft decoding, similarity preserving class-to-codeword assignments, or predictions conditioned on preceding output bits did not yield significant improvements over the vanilla binary encoding strategy.

Our analysis shows that binary encoding results in a higher number of misclassifications in the vicinity of structure boundaries. In terms of DSC, small

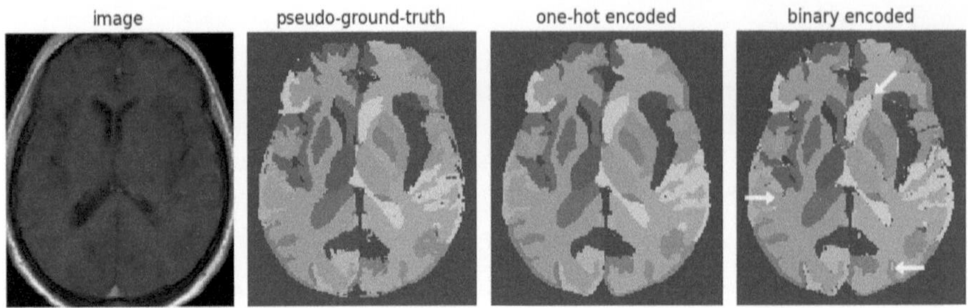


**Fig. 2.** Comparison of predicted segmentations with one-hot encoding and vanilla binary encoding. Both encoding strategies yield sensible predictions. However, the white arrows point out examples of misclassified pixels at structure boundaries as a result of the binary encoding strategy.

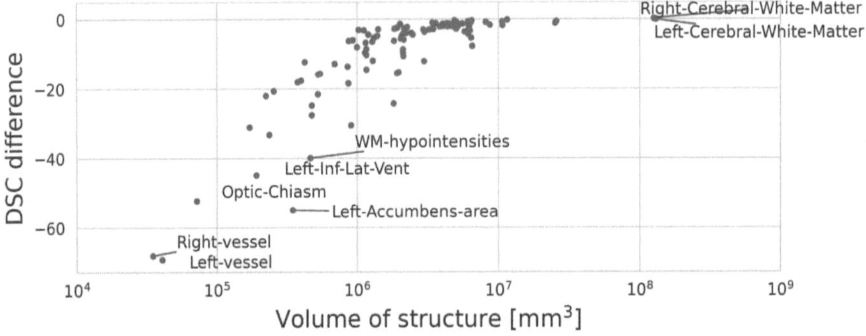


**Fig. 3.** Comparison between one-hot encoding and vanilla binary encoding. The difference in average DSC between both encoding strategies shows that small structures experience the largest drop in DSC.

structures are affected the most. These mis-classifications are a result of the independence of predictions made by each of the bit-wise output heads. The binary tree approach presented in this work was applied to reduce the mis-classifications by conditioning the weights of the final CNN layer on the predictions of previous output heads. However, a further DSC reduction was observed. Although the binary tree approach did not yield satisfactory segmentation performance, we speculate that a method that enforces consistency between predicted output heads is required to close the segmentation quality gap with one-hot encoding.

We hope that our informative negative results can serve as a stepping stone for the community to develop novel strategies for large multi-class segmentation.

**Acknowledgments.** This work was supported by the MRC [MR/X502923/1] and core funding from the Wellcome/EPSRC [WT203148/Z/16/Z; NS/A000049/1]. For the purpose of open access, the authors have applied a CC-BY public copyright license to any Author Accepted Manuscript version arising from this submission.

**Disclosure of Interests.** TV is co-founder and shareholder of Hypervision Surgical. The authors have no other relevant interests to declare.

# References


1. Akinci D'Antonoli, T., et al.: TotalSegmentator MRI: robust sequence-independent segmentation of multiple anatomic structures in MRI. Radiology **314**(2), e241613 (2025)
2. Bengio, S., Dembczynski, K., Joachims, T., Kloft, M., Varma, M.: Extreme classification (dagstuhl seminar 18291). Dagstuhl Reports **8**(7) (2019)
3. Bengio, S., Weston, J., Grangier, D.: Label embedding trees for large multi-class tasks. Adv. Neural Inf. Process. Syst. **23** (2010)
4. Cardoso, M.J., et al.: Geodesic information flows: spatially-variant graphs and their application to segmentation and fusion. IEEE Trans. Med. Imaging **34**(9), 1976–1988 (2015)
5. Clark, K., et al.: The cancer imaging archive (TCIA): maintaining and operating a public information repository. J. Digit. Imaging **26**, 1045–1057 (2013)
6. Coupé, P., et al.: AssemblyNet: a novel deep decision-making process for whole brain MRI segmentation. In: Shen, D., Liu, T., Peters, T.M., Staib, L.H., Essert, C., Zhou, S., Yap, P.-T., Khan, A. (eds.) MICCAI 2019. LNCS, vol. 11766, pp. 466–474. Springer, Cham (2019). https://doi.org/10.1007/978-3-030-32248-9_52
7. Dietterich, T.G., Bakiri, G.: Solving multiclass learning problems via error-correcting output codes. J. Artif. Intell. Res. **2**, 263–286 (1994)
8. Dolz, J., Desrosiers, C., Ayed, I.B.: 3D fully convolutional networks for subcortical segmentation in MRI: a large-scale study. Neuroimage **170**, 456–470 (2018)
9. Evron, I., Moroshko, E., Crammer, K.: Efficient loss-based decoding on graphs for extreme classification. Adv. Neural Inf. Process. Syst. **31** (2018)
10. Evron, I., Onn, O., Weiss, T., Azeroual, H., Soudry, D.: The role of codeword-to-class assignments in error-correcting codes: an empirical study. In: International Conference on Artificial Intelligence and Statistics, pp. 8053–8077. PMLR (2023)
11. Henschel, L., Conjeti, S., Estrada, S., Diers, K., Fischl, B., Reuter, M.: Fastsurfer-a fast and accurate deep learning based neuroimaging pipeline. Neuroimage **219**, 117012 (2020)
12. Huo, Y., et al.: 3D whole brain segmentation using spatially localized atlas network tiles. Neuroimage **194**, 105–119 (2019)
13. Isensee, F., Jaeger, P.F., Kohl, S.A., Petersen, J., Maier-Hein, K.H.: nnU-Net: a self-configuring method for deep learning-based biomedical image segmentation. Nat. Methods **18**(2), 203–211 (2021)
14. Klein, A., Tourville, J.: 101 labeled brain images and a consistent human cortical labeling protocol. Front. Neurosci. **6**, 171 (2012)
15. Kujawa, A., Dorent, R., Ourselin, S., Vercauteren, T.: Label merge-and-split: a graph-colouring approach for memory-efficient brain parcellation. In: International Conference on Medical Image Computing and Computer-Assisted Intervention, pp. 350–360. Springer (2024)

16. Li, W., Wang, G., Fidon, L., Ourselin, S., Cardoso, M.J., Vercauteren, T.: On the compactness, efficiency, and representation of 3d convolutional networks: brain parcellation as a pretext task. In: Niethammer, M., Styner, M., Aylward, S., Zhu, H., Oguz, I., Yap, P.-T., Shen, D. (eds.) IPMI 2017. LNCS, vol. 10265, pp. 348–360. Springer, Cham (2017). https://doi.org/10.1007/978-3-319-59050-9_28
17. Li, Z., Li, H., Meng, L.: Model compression for deep neural networks: a survey. Computers **12**(3), 60 (2023)
18. Mehta, R., Majumdar, A., Sivaswamy, J.: BrainSegNet: a convolutional neural network architecture for automated segmentation of human brain structures. J. Med. Imaging **4**(2), 024003–024003 (2017)
19. Moeskops, P., Viergever, M.A., Mendrik, A.M., De Vries, L.S., Benders, M.J., Išgum, I.: Automatic segmentation of MR brain images with a convolutional neural network. IEEE Trans. Med. Imaging **35**(5), 1252–1261 (2016)
20. Proakis, J.G., Salehi, M.: Digital communications. McGraw-hill, 5th edn. (2008)
21. Radoi, A.: Semantic segmentation of RGB-NIR images with error-correcting output codes. In: 2018 International Conference on Communications (COMM), pp. 135–138. IEEE (2018)
22. Rodríguez, P., Bautista, M.A., Gonzalez, J., Escalera, S.: Beyond one-hot encoding: lower dimensional target embedding. Image Vision Comput. **75**, 21–31 (2018)
23. Roy, A.G., Conjeti, S., Navab, N., Wachinger, C., Initiative, A.D.N., et al.: Quick-NAT: a fully convolutional network for quick and accurate segmentation of neuroanatomy. Neuroimage **186**, 713–727 (2019)
24. Roy, A.G., Conjeti, S., Sheet, D., Katouzian, A., Navab, N., Wachinger, C.: Error corrective boosting for learning fully convolutional networks with limited data. In: Descoteaux, M., Maier-Hein, L., Franz, A., Jannin, P., Collins, D.L., Duchesne, S. (eds.) MICCAI 2017. LNCS, vol. 10435, pp. 231–239. Springer, Cham (2017). https://doi.org/10.1007/978-3-319-66179-7_27
25. Roy, S., Kügler, D., Reuter, M.: Are 2.5 D approaches superior to 3D deep networks in whole brain segmentation? In: International Conference on Medical Imaging with Deep Learning, pp. 988–1004. PMLR (2022)
26. Wachinger, C., Reuter, M., Klein, T.: DeepNAT: deep convolutional neural network for segmenting neuroanatomy. Neuroimage **170**, 434–445 (2018)
27. Wang, M., et al.: Deep graph library: a graph-centric, highly-performant package for graph neural networks. arXiv preprint arXiv:1909.01315 (2019)
28. Wang, R., et al.: Pygmtools: a python graph matching toolkit. J. Mach. Learn. Res. **25**, 1–7 (2024)
29. Wasserthal, J., et al.: TotalSegmentator: robust segmentation of 104 anatomic structures in CT images. Radiol. Artif. Intell. **5**(5) (2023)

# BrainNetMLP: An Efficient and Effective Baseline for Functional Brain Network Classification


Jiacheng Hou, Zhenjie Song, and Ercan Engin Kuruoglu[(✉)]

Tsinghua Shenzhen International Graduate School, Tsinghua University, Tsinghua, China
kuruoglu@sz.tsinghua.edu.cn



**Abstract.** Recent studies have made great progress in functional brain network analysis by modeling the brain as a network of Regions of Interest (ROIs) and leveraging their connections to understand brain functionality and classify brain disorders. Various deep learning architectures, including Convolutional Neural Networks, Graph Neural Networks, and the recent Transformer, have been developed. However, despite the increasing complexity of these models, the performance gain has not been as salient. Furthermore, the escalating model complexity will exacerbate the gap between theoretical research and real-world deployment. To mitigate this gap, we revisit the simplest deep learning architecture, the Multi-Layer Perceptron (MLP), and propose a pure MLP-based method, named BrainNetMLP for functional brain network classification. Specifically, BrainNetMLP incorporates a dual-branch structure to jointly capture spatial connectivity and temporal dynamics in spectral domain, enabling spatiotemporal feature fusion for precise classification. Besides, considering the fully-connected property of MLPs, we also propose an Edge-Degree Guided Pruning technique to remove redundant parameters of MLPs, further improving the efficiency. We evaluate our proposed BrainNetMLP on two public and popular brain network classification datasets, the Human Connectome Project (HCP) and the Autism Brain Imaging Data Exchange (ABIDE). Experimental results demonstrate pure MLP-based methods can achieve state-of-the-art accuracy and efficiency, revealing the potential of MLP-based models as more efficient yet effective alternatives in functional brain network classification. The code is available at https://github.com/JayceonHo/BrainNetMLP

**Keywords:** Functional brain network classification · rs-fMRI · MLP · Transformer · Neural network pruning


---

J. Hou and Z. Song—Equal contribution.

---


**Supplementary Information** The online version contains supplementary material available at https://doi.org/10.1007/978-3-032-13961-0_2.

# 1   Introduction

The human brain is an extremely complex system composed of numerous interacting regions. Investigating the organization and understanding the connectivity between different regions has long been a central goal of neuroscience, which is valuable in clinical analysis, diagnosis, and the corresponding treatment [2,3,23]. For this reason, tremendous effort has been put into investigating the functional brain network. Among various brain networks, the Functional Connectivity (FC) network based on resting-state functional Magnetic Resonance Imaging (rs-fMRI) data is common and widely adopted. Given a specific atlas, Regions of Interest (ROIs) can be separated from rs-fMRI images and defined as nodes. The average Blood-Oxygen Level Dependent (BOLD) signal on each region is then extracted, and the statistical dependence between different regions is modeled as edges [17,18]. In this way, a brain functional network is built, and the analysis of it can effectively assist the prediction of neurological disorder [1,12].

With the success of deep learning, various deep learning models have been adapted and applied to classify different brain functional networks, such as Convolutional Neural Networks (CNN), Graph Neural Networks (GNN), and Transformer [13,14,25]. Among them, the Transformer has been favored mostly because of its strength in capturing long-range correlation of different ROIs [1,12,20]. However, as shown in Fig. 1, in comparison to the surge of model complexity, the performance gain of transformers is relatively marginal. Moreover, the increased complexity will hinder the real-world application.

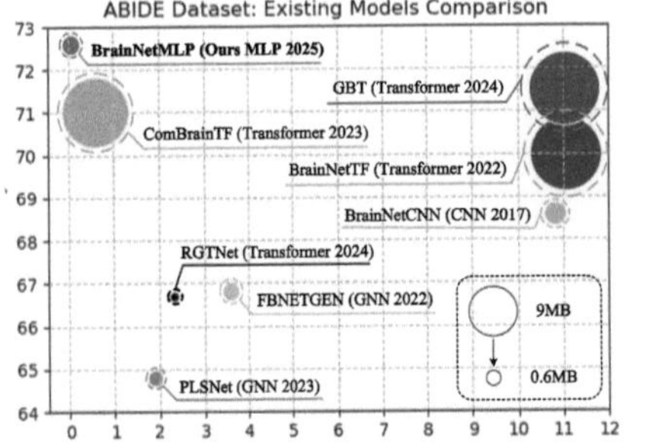

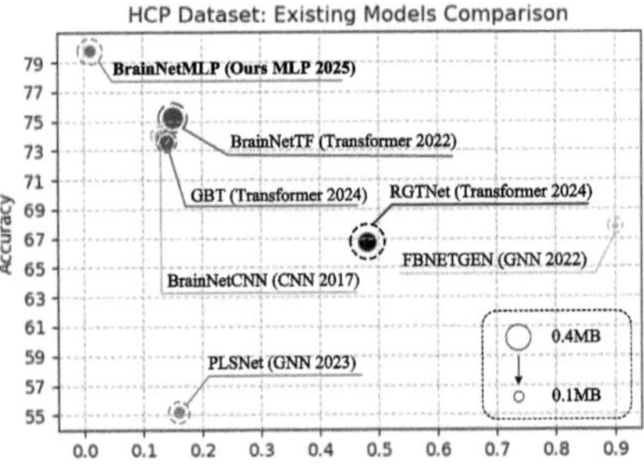


**Fig. 1.** Comparison of the existing state-of-the-art models and our proposed BrainNetMLP model on ABIDE dataset and HCP dataset. The size of the circles corresponds to the size of the models.

Recently, the Multiple Layer Perceptron (MLP), a classical machine learning model, has been revisited, and a series of MLP-based models emerged as efficient yet effective alternatives to transformers in varying tasks [8,19,22]. Compared to transformers, MLPs possess several inherent merits, such as lower computational complexity and fewer parameters, which are desired properties in brain network classification, especially when dealing with large-scale networks. Furthermore, owing to its fully connected structure, like transformers, the MLP model is also able to learn the underlying relationship between distant ROIs.

Motivated by this, we propose a pure MLP-based method, named Brain-NetMLP. BrainNetMLP is a dual-branch architecture that incorporates two types of MLPs, named the Spatial Connectivity Mixer (SCMixer) and Spectrum ROI Mixer (SRMixer), to separately extract the discriminative features from FC and the filtered spectrum of the raw BOLD signals. The SCMixer leverages the symmetric property of the Pearson functional network to save computation and employs an MLP to globally learn ROI connectivity. Then, different from previous methods [1, 4, 16], we adopt spectral information in our designed SRMixer to utilize the temporal dynamics via spectral filtering and learning. The learned spatial and spectral features are fused to collaboratively classify the brain connectome. By exploiting the spatial connectivity of ROIs, their spectral dynamics, and the spatiotemporal correlation, high classification accuracy is attained.

Additionally, considering the fully-connected property of MLPs, we propose an unstructural pruning technique, named Edge Degree Guided Pruning (EDGP) method. It prunes redundant parameters based on both the learnable weight and the edge degree calculated from the network to improve biological plausibility, yielding more comprehensive and effective pruning results.

- We propose an efficient yet effective method, BrainNetMLP, for functional brain network classification, which is the first pure MLP-based method and demands much fewer computation (*i.e.*, $10\times$ less FLOPs) and parameters (*i.e.*, $2\times$ fewer parameters) compared with existing transformer models.
- BrainNetMLP not only leverages spatial connectivity information but also exploits effective spectral components of the brain network signal, thereby collaboratively capturing the spatiotemporal dynamics for precise analysis.
- To further improve efficiency, we propose an Edge Degree Guided Pruning method to produce more efficient variants of our BrainNetMLP.

## 2   Method

In functional brain network classification, we begin by separating each rs-fMRI brain scan into $N$ ROIs. Subsequently, we construct the FC matrix $\mathbf{X} \in \mathbb{R}^{N \times N}$ based on the average BOLD time series $\mathbf{T} \in \mathbb{R}^{L \times N}$, where $L$ signifies the length of each time series. Each element within this matrix represents the Pearson correlation coefficient estimated between pairs of ROIs. The goal of the classification model is to predict the label $y$ (*e.g.*, the clinical diagnosis) from the given connectome $\mathbf{X}$ and time series $\mathbf{T}$ of the subject. The model pipeline is depicted in Fig. 2, and we follow the pruning after training scheme [15] to produce more efficient versions of BrainNetMLP for real-world deployment.

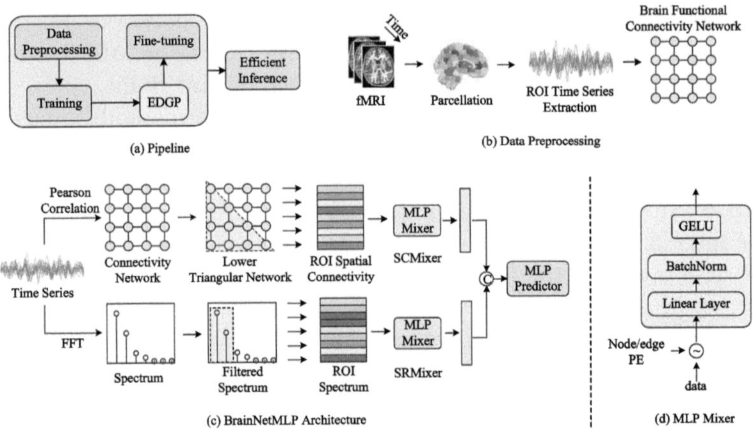



**Fig. 2.** (a) the whole pipeline (b) the data preprocessing scheme (c) the structure of our BrainNetMLP (d) the structure of the MLP Mixer.

## 2.1  Spatial Connectivity Mixer

Previous transformer models [1,11,20] directly treat the connectome $\mathbf{X}$ as a feature matrix. In these works, one dimension of $\mathbf{X}$ is regarded as tokens, and the other dimension is regarded as channels. Although the transformer structure allows token and channel mixing by the self-attention and feed-forward layer separately, we argue that this separate processing scheme is neither efficient nor necessary. In essence, each element in $\mathbf{X}$ represents the correlation between two ROIs, the meaning of which is quite different from the features of transformers in computer vision (*e.g.*, images and videos) [6,7,9] and natural language processing (*e.g.*, texts) [27,28]. Thus, it is unnecessary to separately process elements of $\mathbf{X}$ by different modules. Based on this observation, the MLP structure becomes a good choice, as it can simultaneously and globally process all elements in the input. On the other hand, there is an important property of $\mathbf{X}$ that has long been ignored by previous transformer-based brain network classification models [1,12,16], that is the symmetry of $\mathbf{X}$. The Pearson correlation is a commutable operation, which means $\mathbf{X}[i,j] = \mathbf{X}[j,i]$. Making use of this property can undoubtedly reduce the amount of computation. With these beliefs, in our designed SCMixer, we first extract the lower triangular (or upper triangular) matrix $\mathbf{X}_{lower}$ from $\mathbf{X}$. Then it is flattened to a one-dimensional vector $\boldsymbol{u} \in \mathbb{R}^{\frac{N(N+1)}{2}}$:

$$\mathbf{X}_{lower} = \mathrm{TriExact}(\mathbf{X}),$$
$$\boldsymbol{u} = \mathrm{Flatten}(\mathbf{X}_{lower}), \tag{1}$$

where "TriExtract" and "Flatten" represent the operations to extract the lower triangular matrix and flatten the matrix to a 1D vector.

In this way, the dimensionality of the to-be-processed feature (*i.e.*, $\frac{N(N+1)}{2}$) is reduced to nearly half of the whole connectivity matrix (*i.e.*, $N \times N$), which greatly saves computational resources. Besides, due to the symmetry property of $\mathbf{X}$, there is theoretically no loss of valid information. Then, a simple MLP Mixer (denoted by $f_{con}$) is applied to $\boldsymbol{u}$ for connectivity feature extraction:

$$\boldsymbol{x}_c = f_{con}(\boldsymbol{u} + \boldsymbol{p}_{edge}), \tag{2}$$

where $\boldsymbol{p}_{edge}$ represents the positional embedding for each brain connectivity [26]. Generally, $f_{con}$ plays the role of a learnable dimensionality reduction function, aiming to extract useful connectivity information and abandon non-discriminative connectivity information.

## 2.2   Spectrum ROIs Mixer

Besides the spatial connectivity information, an increasing number of works found that the network dynamics are also crucial [4,24], as the human brain network is evolving with the change of mental states. A straightforward way to capture the dynamics is to leverage the time series $\mathbf{T}$. However, due to the noise and variance in different collection sites [12], we find that directly using $\mathbf{T}$ for analysis would easily cause over-fitting. Hence, we choose to leverage the spectrum of $\mathbf{T}$, which is usually a more noise-robust feature representation. Specifically, in our developed SRMixer, we firstly apply the Fast Fourier Transform (FFT) on the temporal dimension of $\mathbf{T}$ as:

$$\mathbf{S}_{real} = \text{FFT}(\mathbf{T}), \tag{3}$$

where $\mathbf{S}_{real}$ represents half of the extracted spectrum (as the result of the FFT for real number is symmetric). Then, we implement the low-pass filtering on $\mathbf{S}_{real}$ to filter out the noise, as the noise is usually high-frequency components, which can be expressed by:

$$\mathbf{S}_{real}^{low} = \mathcal{B}_{low}^{k}(\mathbf{S}_{real}), \tag{4}$$

where $\mathcal{B}_{low}^{k}$ represents the low-pass filter, allowing only the first $k$ frequency components to pass. Then, the amplitude of $\mathbf{S}_{real}^{low}$ is sent to an MLP Mixer (denoted by $f_{roi}$) for spectrum ROIs learning as:

$$\mathbf{X}_r = f_{roi}(|\mathbf{S}_{real}^{low}| + \boldsymbol{p}_{rois}), \tag{5}$$

where $\mathbf{X}_r \in \mathbb{R}^{\frac{L \times H}{2}}$ denotes the learned spectrum features; $\boldsymbol{p}_{rois}$ symbolizes the positional embedding for every ROI. Next, we average the spectrum features of different ROIs to obtain a more compact and comprehensive ROI feature representation as:

$$\boldsymbol{x}_r = \text{Mean}(\mathbf{X}_r), \tag{6}$$

where $\boldsymbol{x}_r$ represents the averaged spectrum features of ROIs.

## 2.3   Feature Fusion and Pruning

After obtaining $\boldsymbol{x}_c$ and $\boldsymbol{x}_r$ from the spatial connectivity and ROIs spectrum, we employ a simple non-linear projection layer (denoted by $\mathcal{P}$) as a predictor to jointly estimate the label $\hat{y}$ as:

$$\hat{y} = \mathcal{P}(\text{GELU}(\text{Norm}([\boldsymbol{x}_c, \boldsymbol{x}_r]))), \tag{7}$$

where "GELU" and "Norm" represent the activation function [5] and normalization layers; [ . ,. ] indicates the concatenation operation. Then, we employ the cross-entropy loss function as the objective function. We do not adopt additional loss functions to maintain the simplicity of BrainNetMLP in implementation and comparison. After training, we apply pruning to obtain more efficient variants.

Most of the parameters in BrainNetMLP stem from the SCMixer. Although we extract the triangular matrix to reduce the dimension of the feature to $\frac{N(N+1)}{2}$, when $N$ is large (*e.g.*, for large-scale brain networks), it will still lead to high complexity in computation and memory. To further decrease the complexity, we propose an unstructural pruning method, named Edge Degree Guided Pruning (EDGP), which computes an importance score $s_{i,j}$ for each parameter in the SCMixer based on the $\mathcal{L}_1$ norm and Edge Degree (ED) by:

$$s_{i,j} = \|w_{i,j}\|_1 + ED(e_i) \cdot \lambda, \tag{8}$$

where $\lambda$ is a coefficient to ensure the same numerical scale between $\|w_{i,j}\|_1$ and $ED(e_i)$. $w_{i,j}$ and $e_i$ respectively denote the parameter in the linear layer of SCMixer and the element in $\boldsymbol{u}$. $ED(e_i)$ is defined as the sum of node degrees connected by $e_i$. By this means, $s_{i,j}$ can be constrained by the brain network topology, rather than solely by the amplitude of the learned weight, as nodes with high degree are usually regarded as important [10, 29]. Based on the calculated importance weights, parameters $w_{i,j}$ with smaller $s_{i,j}$ can be cut to make room for storage and benefit speedup techniques (*e.g.*, sparse matrix multiplication).

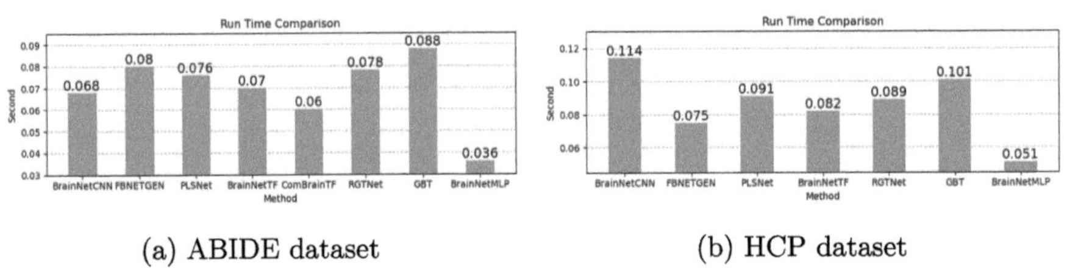

(a) ABIDE dataset                              (b) HCP dataset

**Fig. 3.** Runtime comparison between our method and the other compared methods, for classifying a subject's rs-fMRI scans.

**Table 1.** Quantitative performance comparison with baselines on HCP and ABIDE datasets (Mean±standard deviation). The best is shown in bold black.

| Method | Structure | Dataset: ABIDE | | | | Dataset: HCP | | | |
|---|---|---|---|---|---|---|---|---|---|
| | | Accuracy | AUCROC | Specificity | Sensitivity | Accuracy | AUCROC | Specificity | Sensitivity |
| VanillaCNN | CNN | 65.6±1.7 | 72.6±2.0 | 66.1±1.7 | 68.9±4.2 | 71.4±2.1 | 79.3±2.8 | 74.2±3.1 | 68.9±3.8 |
| BrainNetCNN [13] | CNN | 68.6±1.2 | 69.9±5.0 | 68.5±6.9 | 71.7±5.9 | 74.0±1.8 | 82.6±2.2 | 72.5±10.4 | **77.0±11.6** |
| STGCN* [4] | GNN | - | - | - | - | 77.7±3.2 | 86.9±2.5 | 82.5±4.3 | 72.2±3.3 |
| BrainGNN [14] | GNN | 60.1±2.6 | 65.6±0.9 | 43.5±9.4 | **77.1±6.2** | 62.5±3.1 | 65.4±4.0 | 73.0±13.0 | 49.3±14.4 |
| FBNETGEN [11] | GNN | 66.8±1.9 | 74.8±1.0 | 72.5±5.1 | 62.2±7.0 | 67.8±4.7 | 74.6±3.7 | 70.8±5.3 | 64.9±3.9 |
| PLSNet [21] | GNN | 64.8±1.1 | 71.8±2.3 | 67.1±2.5 | 64.2±2.7 | 55.2±4.6 | 58.5 ±4.3 | 63.2±6.7 | 46.8±9.3 |
| BrainNetTF [12] | Transformer | 70.0±2.3 | 79.1±1.1 | 68.3±4.7 | 72.7±1.0 | 75.2±2.1 | 82.5±1.6 | 81.0±6.1 | 69.6±6.4 |
| ComBrainTF* [1] | Transformer | 71.0±1.5 | 77.2±0.6 | 70.9±4.3 | 72.6±3.8 | - | - | - | - |
| RGTNet [20] | Transformer | 66.7±2.8 | 73.4±1.2 | 67.5 ±1.8 | 65.6±5.6 | 63.6±1.2 | 68.4±1.7 | 69.7±4.4 | 56.2±3.3 |
| GBT [16] | Transformer | 71.5±2.1 | **79.2±0.4** | 69.5±4.3 | 72.9±3.5 | 73.6±2.3 | 81.4±2.6 | 80.1±7.2 | 66.7±9.0 |
| Ours + 20% pruning | MLP | 72.2±1.9 | 78.6±0.1 | 71.5±2.3 | 73.9±1.9 | **80.0±1.7** | 87.8±1.6 | **84.2±4.3** | 76.2±2.4 |
| Ours + 50% pruning | MLP | 72.4±1.7 | 79.1±0.1 | **72.9±2.7** | 72.5±2.6 | 76.8±2.9 | 86.0±2.7 | 84.1±6.2 | 68.9±13.2 |
| Ours + no pruning | MLP | **72.6±1.7** | 78.4±0.1 | 72.5±2.7 | 73.7±1.4 | 79.8±1.7 | **88.1±1.5** | 83.1+3.4 | 76.8±4.1 |

* STGCN and ComBrainTF require fixed adjacency matrices and community priors, which are not provided in the ABIDE and HCP datasets.

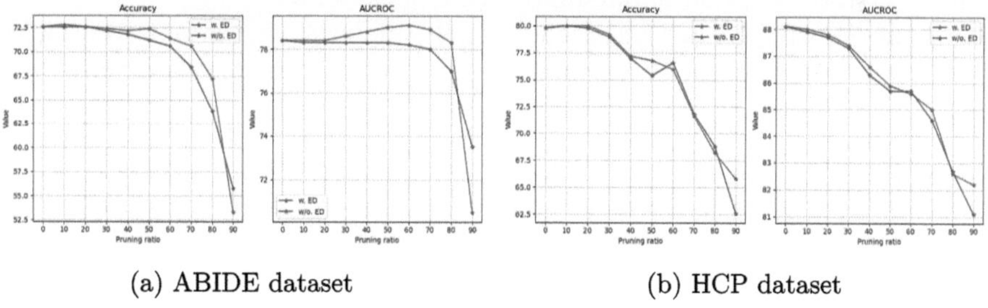

(a) ABIDE dataset                    (b) HCP dataset

**Fig. 4.** Pruning results in different ratios with and without ED.

# 3   Experimental Results

## 3.1   Quantitative Comparison

**Performance Comparison.** We compare the performance quantitatively in Table 1, where it can be seen that BrainNetMLP achieves state-of-the-art performance on both datasets. Specifically, on the ABIDE dataset, BrainNetMLP improves the accuracy by around 1.1% and realizes comparative AUCROC compared with the second-best model. On the HCP dataset, BrainNetMLP yields a 2.1% improvement in accuracy and a 1.2% increase in AUCROC, observably outperforming the second-best model. This can be attributed to the additionally incorporated spectral information in BrainNetMLP, which has been ignored by the existing methods (*e.g.*, GBT and BrainNetTF). The experimental settings can be found in our supplementary material.

**Complexity comparison.** As compared in Fig. 1, the consumed computational cost (FLOPs) and the number of learnable parameters are all signifi-

**Table 2.** Ablation study on the architecture of our proposed BrainNetMLP.

| Method | Dataset: ABIDE | | | | Dataset: HCP | | | |
|---|---|---|---|---|---|---|---|---|
| | Accuracy | AUCROC | Specificity | Sensitivity | Accuracy | AUCROC | Specificity | Sensitivity |
| w/o. SCMixer | 52.2±1.5 | 51.9±2.3 | 34.0±8.0 | **74.0±7.5** | 61.6±2.9 | 66.0±3.0 | 62.2±2.8 | 62.1±6.5 |
| w/o. SRMixer | 62.0±6.1 | 75.0±1.8 | **77.0±17.5** | 48.5±27.6 | 77.6±2.9 | 86.4±1.4 | 82.0±1.3 | 73.6±6.5 |
| w/o. filtering* | 71.8±1.5 | 78.4±0.3 | 71.7±1.6 | 73.5±2.2 | 78.6±1.9 | 87.6±1.6 | 81.1±2.4 | 76.8±5.0 |
| Full model | **72.6±1.7** | **78.4±0.1** | 72.5±2.7 | 73.7±1.4 | **79.8±1.7** | **88.1±1.5** | **83.1±3.4** | **76.8±4.1** |

* filtering means only removing the low-pass filter $\mathcal{B}_{low}^{k}$ in SRMixer. The best is shown in bold black.

cantly fewer than the state-of-the-art transformers. Moreover, with the expansion of the network (*i.e.*, from 22 ROIs per network in the HCP dataset to 200 ROIs per network in the ABIDE dataset), unlike the rapid increase of complexity in the GBT ($0.14\text{G}/0.21\text{M} \rightarrow 11.04\text{G}/8.89\text{M}$) and BrainNetTF ($0.15\text{G}/0.4\text{M} \rightarrow 11.06\text{G}/9.08\text{M}$), our BrainNetMLP exhibits more advanced scalability ($0.01\text{G}/0.14\text{M} \rightarrow 0.06\text{G}/0.65\text{M}$). The detailed FLOPs and the number of parameters can be found in our supplementary material.

**Runtime comparison.** Due to the model simplicity, as shown in Fig. 3, the inference speed of our method is much faster than all other methods, and only one third/a half time consumed for classifying an functional brain network. Note that the functional brain network is estimated from rs-fMRI images spanning across a period of time (*e.g.*, 100 time steps in ABIDE and 1000 time steps in HCP), so the time spent for HCP dataset is longer than that of ABIDE dataset.

## 3.2   Ablation Study

**Ablation Study on ED.** We test the model performance in accuracy and AUCROC under different pruning ratios (from 0% to 90%) with and without our added edge degree criterion. The results are shown in Fig. 4. It can be found that the pruning performance can be elevated with the aid of ED, which even produces the best performance at a pruning ratio of 50% on the ABIDE dataset. This demonstrates the existence of spurious connections in the ABIDE dataset, and ED can assist in discovering these connections, while pure $\mathcal{L}_1$ norm cannot. Since only 22 important ROIs and their connections are used in the HCP dataset, the performance gain of ED is not obvious.

**Ablation study on model architecture.** To investigate the effectiveness of each module, we remove them from the full model. As reported in Table 2, on both datasets, no matter which component is removed, the overall performance is worse than the full model. Notably, on the ABIDE dataset, solely employing SCMixer or SRMixer can achieve the best specificity and sensitivity, which shows SCMixer and SRMixer can respectively help decreasing the rate of false alarms and miss detections. As a result, it can be observed that adaptively combining them complementarily improves the overall performance of the full model. More ablation studies can be found in the y material.

# 4    Conclusion

In this paper, we propose the first MLP-only method, named BrainNetMLP, for functional brain network classification. Owing to the simplicity of the MLP structure, it is superior in efficiency and scalability, with more than one order of magnitude reduction in computational complexity compared with the state-of-the-art transformer models. Besides, we design a dual-branch architecture, which utilizes spatial connectivity and spectral features with adaptive feature fusion. As a result, BrainNetMLP produces advanced classification performance on the ABIDE and HCP datasets. Moreover, we propose a brain topology-aware pruning method to further save parameters for the real-world deployment. The experimental results illustrate the significant untapped potential of the MLP structure in functional brain network classification and outline an efficient yet effective alternative to the transformers.

**Acknowledgments.** This work is supported by Shenzhen Science and Technology Innovation Commission under Grant JCYJ20220530143002005, Shenzhen Ubiquitous Data Enabling Key Lab under Grant ZDSYS20220527171406015, and Tsinghua Shenzhen International Graduate School Start-up fund under Grant QD2022024C.

**Disclosure of Interests.** The authors have no competing interests to declare that are relevant to the content of this article.

# References


1. Bannadabhavi, A., Lee, S., Deng, W., Ying, R., Li, X.: Community-aware transformer for autism prediction in FMRI connectome. In: MICCAI, pp. 287–297. Springer (2023)
2. Deco, G., Jirsa, V.K., McIntosh, A.R.: Emerging concepts for the dynamical organization of resting-state activity in the brain. Nat. Rev. Neurosci. **12**(1), 43–56 (2011)
3. Fornito, A., Zalesky, A., Bullmore, E.: Fundamentals of Brain Network Analysis. Academic Press (2016)
4. Gadgil, S., Zhao, Q., Pfefferbaum, A., Sullivan, E.V., Adeli, E., Pohl, K.M.: Spatio-temporal graph convolution for resting-state FMRI analysis. In: MICCAI, pp. 528–538. Springer (2020)
5. Hendrycks, D., Gimpel, K.: Gaussian error linear units (GELUS). arXiv preprint arXiv:1606.08415 (2016)
6. Hou, J., Ji, Z., Yang, J., Wang, C., Zheng, F.: Mcd-net: toward rgb-d video inpainting in real-world scenes. IEEE Trans. Image Process. **33**, 1095–1108 (2024)
7. Hou, J., Ji, Z., Yang, J., Zheng, F.: Bidirectional error-aware fusion network for video inpainting. IEEE Trans. Circuits Syst. Video Technol. (2024)
8. Hu, Y., You, H., Wang, Z., Wang, Z., Zhou, E., Gao, Y.: Graph-MLP: node classification without message passing in graph. arXiv preprint arXiv:2106.04051 (2021)
9. Ji, Z., Su, Y., Zhang, Y., Hou, J., Pang, Y., Han, J.: Raformer: redundancy-aware transformer for video wire inpainting. IEEE Trans. Image Process. (2025)

10. Joyce, K.E., Laurienti, P.J., Burdette, J.H., Hayasaka, S.: A new measure of centrality for brain networks. PLoS ONE **5**(8), e12200 (2010)
11. Kan, X., Cui, H., Lukemire, J., Guo, Y., Yang, C.: Fbnetgen: task-aware GNN-based FMRI analysis via functional brain network generation. In: MIDL, pp. 618–637. PMLR (2022)
12. Kan, X., Dai, W., Cui, H., Zhang, Z., Guo, Y., Yang, C.: Brain network transformer. NIPS **35**, 25586–25599 (2022)
13. Kawahara, J., et al.: Brainnetcnn: convolutional neural networks for brain networks; towards predicting neurodevelopment. Neuroimage **146**, 1038–1049 (2017)
14. Li, X., et al.: Braingnn: interpretable brain graph neural network for FMRI analysis. bioRxiv (2020)
15. Liu, Z., Sun, M., Zhou, T., Huang, G., Darrell, T.: Rethinking the value of network pruning. arXiv preprint arXiv:1810.05270 (2018)
16. Peng, Z., He, Z., Jiang, Y., Wang, P., Yuan, Y.: GBT: geometric-oriented brain transformer for autism diagnosis. In: MICCAI, pp. 142–152 (2024)
17. Simpson, S.L., Bowman, F.D., Laurienti, P.J.: Analyzing complex functional brain networks: fusing statistics and network science to understand the brain. Stat. Surv. **7**, 1 (2013)
18. Smith, S.M., et al.: Network modelling methods for fmri. Neuroimage **54**(2), 875–891 (2011)
19. Tolstikhin, I.O., et al.: MLP-mixer: an all-MLP architecture for vision. NIPS **34**, 24261–24272 (2021)
20. Wang, Y., Long, H., Bo, T., Zheng, J.: Residual graph transformer for autism spectrum disorder prediction. Comput. Methods Programs Biomed. **247**, 108065 (2024)
21. Wang, Y., Long, H., Zhou, Q., Bo, T., Zheng, J.: Plsnet: position-aware GCN-based autism spectrum disorder diagnosis via fc learning and ROIS sifting. Comput. Biol. Med. **163**, 107184 (2023)
22. Wang, Z., Jiang, W., Zhu, Y.M., Yuan, L., Song, Y., Liu, W.: Dynamixer: a vision MLP architecture with dynamic mixing. In: ICLR, pp. 22691–22701. PMLR (2022)
23. Wig, G.S., Schlaggar, B.L., Petersen, S.E.: Concepts and principles in the analysis of brain networks. Ann. N. Y. Acad. Sci. **1224**(1), 126–146 (2011)
24. Yan, J., et al.: Multi-head gagnn: a multi-head guided attention graph neural network for modeling spatio-temporal patterns of holistic brain functional networks. In: MICCAI, pp. 564–573. Springer (2021)
25. Yan, Y., Hou, J., Song, Z., Kuruoglu, E.E.: Signal processing over time-varying graphs: a systematic review. arXiv preprint arXiv:2412.00462 (2024)
26. Yang, Y., Mao, Y., Liu, X., Liu, X.: Brainmae: a region-aware self-supervised learning framework for brain signals. arXiv preprint arXiv:2406.17086 (2024)
27. Yu, J., Li, J., Yu, Z., Huang, Q.: Multimodal transformer with multi-view visual representation for image captioning. IEEE Trans. Circuits Syst. Video Technol. **30**(12), 4467–4480 (2019)
28. Zhang, J., Chang, W.C., Yu, H.F., Dhillon, I.: Fast multi-resolution transformer fine-tuning for extreme multi-label text classification. NIPS **34**, 7267–7280 (2021)
29. Zhang, J., Luo, Y.: Degree centrality, betweenness centrality, and closeness centrality in social network. In: International Conference on Modelling, Simulation and Applied Mathematics, pp. 300–303. Atlantis Press (2017)

# Conquering the Retina: Bringing Visual in-Context Learning to OCT

Alessio Negrini and Simon Reiß[✉][iD]

Karlsruhe Institute of Technology, 76131 Karlsruhe, Germany
`simon.reiss@kit.edu`

**Abstract.** Recent advancements in medical image analysis have led to the development of highly specialized models tailored to specific clinical tasks. These models have demonstrated exceptional performance and remain a crucial research direction. Yet, their applicability is limited to predefined tasks, requiring expertise and extensive resources for development and adaptation. In contrast, generalist models offer a different form of utility: allowing medical practitioners to define tasks on the fly without the need for task-specific model development. In this work, we explore how to train generalist models for the domain of retinal optical coherence tomography using visual in-context learning (VICL), *i.e.*, training models to generalize across tasks based on a few examples provided at inference time. To facilitate rigorous assessment, we propose a broad evaluation protocol tailored to VICL in OCT. We extensively evaluate a state-of-the-art medical VICL approach on multiple retinal OCT datasets, establishing a first baseline to highlight the potential and current limitations of in-context learning for OCT. To foster further research and practical adoption, we openly release our code (https://github.com/negralessio/thesis-visual-in-context-learning *both authors contributed equally to this work*).

**Keywords:** Visual in-Context Learning · Retinal OCT · Generalization

## 1  Introduction

Medical image analysis has been pushed forward significantly through the adaptation of deep neural nets [6,7,12]. Through the curation of datasets, the successive annotation by medical experts and supervised training of neural models, tasks such as classification-, segmentation- or even style-transfer tasks can be addressed with increasing accuracy. While this progress is leading to solutions which fulfill the high standards of medical applications, each new task to be solved at the same time requires going through the costly steps of data collection, annotation and model training. To circumvent this, some works in literature propose to design the neural architectures and training strategies such that they are extensible to new contexts, *i.e.*, new tasks to be addressed at test time without


T. Chen et al. (Eds.): EMA4MICCAI 2025 Workshops, LNCS 16318, pp. 21–30, 2026.
https://doi.org/10.1007/978-3-032-13961-0_3

model re-training [5,11], so called visual in-context learning models. This shift enables medical practitioners to solve highly individual use-cases by providing new context information at test time.

The design of architectures and training objectives for visual in-context learning are currently heavily researched open questions [1,2,5,11,13]. In our work, we start by exploring the data- and annotation requirements for training, *i.e.*, whether a set of images and segmentation annotations are a suitable enough starting point to train an in-context learning model. Specifically, we investigate this in the medical image domain of retinal optical coherence tomography (OCT). We then setup an evaluation protocol to benchmark trained visual in-context learning models in their efficacy in adapting to new, unseen tasks without re-training and we investigate the boundaries of the model's transfer capabilities by testing the adaptation to unseen tasks *and* unseen data distributions, so called domain generalization. In our exploration, we heavily utilize the Neuralizer architecture [5] and train it on retinal OCTs leading to our *Retinalizer* models. We further enable the models to draw multi-class predictions and explore the effect of a simple and effective *random recoloring task-augmentation* to improve the generalization capabilities of trained in-context learners. Our extensive – and to our best knowledge – first exploration into visual in-context learning for OCT allows a first glimpse of the potential of generalist models in the domain of optical coherence tomography. Our contributions summarize to:

- We investigate visual in-context learning for retinal optical coherence tomography for the first time by using image- and segmentation data only.
- We propose a design to draw multi-class predictions from a medical visual in-context learning model and a color-based task-augmentation technique.
- We extensively evaluate generalization efficacy of trained models to unseen tasks and unseen data distributions in optical coherence tomography.

## 2   Visual in-Context Learning as Conditional Prediction

In visual in-context learning, a model $\theta(\cdot, \cdot)$ is trained, which based on a task-specific context set $C$ can transform a query image $Q$ into a task-specific output via $\theta(C, Q) = O$. As such, in case the context set $C$ conditions the model to the task of segmentation, the model should yield a segmentation of $Q$. To inform the model $\theta$ how $Q$ has to be transformed, visual in-context learning utilizes example images of the task to be solved in $C$. For convenient and coherent provision of this task information to the model, all tasks are formulated as image-to-image tasks (*i.e.*, in- and output are both RGB images), which leads to a context set $C \in \mathbb{R}^{n \times 2 \times 3 \times width \times height}$, where $n$ specifies the number of image-pair examples to describe the task. This formulation does not only allow tasks such as denoising or inpainting, which naturally are image-to-image tasks, but also tasks like semantic segmentation: Instead of predicting a 1-hot class vector for each pixel the model predicts a color value, with class-color associations defined in the image-pairs of the context set $C$.

This unified interface of defining all tasks in terms of image-to-image processing enables predictions with context sets $C^{unseen}$, which contain tasks not observed in training. As such, the predictive capabilities of $\theta$ to generalize to unseen context sets is the target measure to evaluate in visual in-context learning.

## 3 From Neuralizer to Retinalizer

Training a visual in-context learning model that can generalize to new tasks generally requires a large dataset containing many tasks to pre-train on [1,5]. As vessel for medical visual in-context learning, we utilize the network architecture Neuralizer [5]. Neuralizer allows for in-context learning by introducing Pairwise-Conv-Avg blocks, which enable processing context sets of varying size $n$ into a Unet architecture [12]. As the name suggests, Neuralizer is originally trained on neuro images. Next, we outline our data pre-processing and training strategy to bring such a visual in-context learning model to the domain of optical coherence tomography, which due to the focus on the retina in OCT, we term *Retinalizer*.

### 3.1 Base Optical Coherence Tomography Datasets

To get hold of enough data to train visual in-context learners, we make use of publicly available datasets from the OCT community, namely the DUKE dataset family for cyst- and retinal layer segmentation, the UMN dataset with diabetic macular edema fluid annotations, the RETOUCH dataset family for multi fluid segmentation with its diversity of three OCT device vendors and the OCTDL dataset, which covers OCT scans of diverse medical conditions in the retina.

**DUKE** [4] contains OCT scans which are annotated with diabetic macular edema (DME) fluids and, for a second set of scans also with the different anatomical layers of the retina. DME labeled scans amount to 610 of which 532 contain healthy retinas, while the layer segmentation portion includes 110 scans.

**UMN** [10] also contains pixel-wise annotations of fluid accumulations in patients with DME. However, it has no severe class imbalance as it contains 725 samples in total, taken from 29 patients with 25 scans per subject. It includes 405 segmentation masks of which ca. 56% depict healthy retinal sections.

**RETOUCH** [3] contains scans with manual annotations for retinal fluids acquired with devices of three different OCT manufactures: Topcon, Cirrus and Spectralis. Retinal fluids are subdivided into Intra-retinal fluid, Sub-retinal fluid and Pigment Epithelial Detachment. Of the $6,936$ scans in the dataset $3,563$ (ca. 50%) are healthy, in the remaining scans $2,068$ (ca. 30%) contain one fluid class, $1,013$ (ca. 15%) contain two and 292 (ca. 5%) contain all three classes.

**OCTDL** [9] consists of around $1,618$ scans with ca. 16% showing healthy retinas, while the rest show manifestations of diverse diseases. As the scans come with classification labels, in our study, we use it to represent the diversity in OCT without directly utilizing the label information. Specifically, OCTDL builds the basis of image-content tasks, where in- and output images depict retinal scans.

## 3.2   Heterogeneous Task Enrichment

In addition to a large set of images, visual in-context training requires a diverse set of pre-training tasks exceeding merely segmenting retinal layers and fluids. To enable training on such a task diversity, we propose to enrich the data by deriving additional tasks: semantic-, transformation- and generative tasks.

**Semantic tasks** are based on the binary- and multi-class segmentation annotations of the base OCT datasets. As such, we pre-compute the tasks *semantic edge detection*, where semantic regions are delimited by thin lines, *semantic skeletons*, which indicate the medial axes of segments and *coarse semantic segmentation*, which encompasses the semantic hull of each segment as crude approximate segmentation. We also use the original *segmentation tasks*, which leads to four *semantic task types* for four pixel-wise labeled datasets, *i.e.*, 16 semantic tasks.

**Transformation tasks** are based on OCTDL, where a single scan serves as basis for both input and output. We setup four transformation tasks, the first two are rotation tasks where the input image is transformed with a *rotation* by either $90°$ or $270°$, the rotated image serves as output. Similarly, in the *image inversion task*, the intensity values $v$ of the input scan are inverted by $255 - v$, yielding the corresponding output. The *image revert task* is its counterpart, where the input and output are switched. In total, this amounts to four additional tasks.

**Generative tasks** are based on OCTDL as well, but center around reconstructing the original scan from manipulated input scans. One such task is *Gaussian denoising* where the input is a heavily noised version of the output scan. In the *image super resolution* task, a scan is down-scaled to a lower resolution which is taken as manipulated input. The task aims to reconstruct information from the low resolution image to the original, higher resolution image. Finally, the *image in-painting* task takes an image with a masked region as input, the original image is the output. Thus, in total we have 23 tasks as seen in Fig. 1.

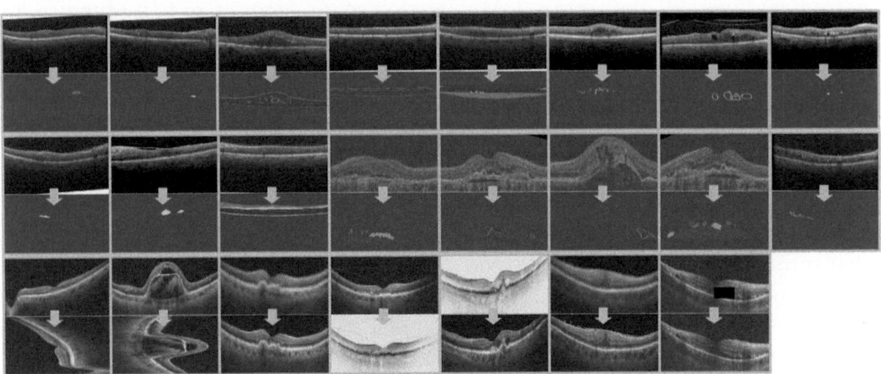

**Fig. 1.** Examples for seen tasks. Input-output pairs grouped into orange boxes. (Color figure online)

### 3.3   Visual in-Context Training for Optical Coherence Tomography

With datasets and a broad set of pre-training tasks in place, the visual in-context model can be trained. Accommodating the properties of OCT datasets and tasks, we adapted key components in the training strategy, which we describe next.

**Batch Sampling and Optimization.** To ensure, that the model does not predominantly focus on tasks which have a high number of samples during training, we utilize task balancing, *i.e.*, tasks with fewer samples are over-sampled, while populous tasks are under-sampled. This is necessary due to the imbalance in sample size of the tasks, which itself stems from our utilization of multiple datasets. Further, in optimization we deviate from the Neuralizer training strategy to define task-specific loss functions [5] and instead reduce complexity during training by using a single reconstruction loss function:

$$\mathcal{L}_{\mathrm{MSE}} = \frac{1}{|B|} \sum_{i=1}^{|B|} \|y_i - \theta(C_i, Q_i)\|_2^2 \, , \tag{1}$$

with the mini-batch $B$, $y_i$ indicating the ground-truth at batch index $i$ for the input $Q_i$ under the task-specific context set $C_i$ in the batch.

**Enabling Multi-class Predictions.** Out-of-the-box, the Neuralizer architecture does not allow for multi-class predictions, as it was designed for binary semantic prediction. To address this, we define multi-class problems, *e.g.*, segmentation of multiple types of retinal fluid by predicting differently colored segments. To map the network prediction for semantic tasks back to the original classes, we extract all unique colors $v_c$ from the context set and compute the euclidean distance to each individual pixel-prediction $v_p$:

$$d(v_p, v_c) = \|v_p - v_c\|_2 \quad \forall v_c \in C \, . \tag{2}$$

Each pixel vector $v_p$ in the prediction is then replaced with the color $v_c$ from the context set that has the lowest distance: $v_p \doteq argmin_{v_c} \, d(v_p, v_c) \; \forall v_c \in C$.

**Random Recoloring Augmentation for Task-adaptiveness.** A high diversity in tasks during training is key for visual in-context learning. Therefore, as in standard image processing, where diversity and quantity of training samples are increased through image augmentations such as rotation, cropping or color jitter, we aim to explore the effect of a task-augmentation for visual in-context learning. Specifically, we holistically augment the context set $C$ and expected output $O$. To this end, we apply a random recoloring augmentation on all semantic tasks, where coherently in $C$ and $O$, we randomly draw new colors for each present class and substitute the new class colors on the fly during training.

### 3.4   A Visual in-Context Learning Testbed for OCT

To get a clear view on the capabilities of visual in-context learners a clear evaluation protocol is key. In this section we outline quantitative evaluation scenarios and baselines to rigorously measure model efficacy for previously unseen tasks.

**Evaluation of Task Adaptation Capabilities.** To investigate how well a visual in-context model is able to adapt to new tasks, *i.e.*, tasks not present in training, we define additional unseen tasks. For a broad investigation of how different such unseen tasks can be with respect to seen tasks, they are created to have varying degrees of discrepancies with them. The tasks we define are *binary layer segmentation*, where all layers of the DUKE dataset are merged into a single layer to be segmented, *retinal boundary detection*, which we define as task to detect the outermost boundaries of the retina region and finally the task *random recolored multi fluid segmentation*, where we chose randomly new colors for each fluid type. We further define the tasks of *salt and pepper denoising, i.e.*, a new type of noise to be removed, $2\times$ *in-painting*, where we task the model to in-paint two patches in an image and *out-painting* where the model needs to fill a masked out frame at the border of the image.

In addition, on the RETOUCH dataset, we further evaluate the generalization capability of visual in-context models to new data distributions by training on data from two vendors and exclusively evaluate on data of the third, held out vendor in testing. In these so called domain generalization experiments, the model needs to adapt to new unseen tasks and to new data distributions without information about them at training time. These experiments are three-fold as we hold out data from the vendors Topcon, Cirrus and Spectralis, successively.

We split all data into train, val and test sets (60/20/20). The VICL models are developed on train and val using the seen tasks, results are reported on unseen tasks in the test set. As metrics, we report mean Intersection over Union (IoU) for segmentation, for sparse semantic structures such as boundaries we use the F-1 Score, generative tasks are evaluated with Mean Average Error (MAE).

**Table 1.** Generalization performance for models solving previously unseen tasks.

| Task | Metric | Copy | Neuralizer | Retinalizer | Retinalizer Rec. | Single-task |
|---|---|---|---|---|---|---|
| D-Layer Bin. Seg. | IoU ↑ | 67.74 ± 18.0 | 41.43 ± 1.0 | 62.99 ± 3.9 | **81.94 ± 4.9** | 98.15 ± 0.7 |
| R-Rec. Fluid Seg. | IoU ↑ | 31.84 ± 10.1 | 5.81 ± 12.6 | 38.53 ± 13.1 | **53.64 ± 15.7** | 46.73 ± 15.8 |
| D-Layer Boundary | F-1 ↑ | 51.88 ± 2.9 | 49.73 ± 0.0 | 53.46 ± 3.1 | **60.69 ± 1.9** | 65.58 ± 6.9 |
| O-2× in-painting | MAE ↓ | 0.143 ± 0.026 | 0.305 ± 0.0360 | 0.010 ± 0.004 | **0.008 ± 0.003** | 0.007 ± 0.003 |
| R-2× in-painting | MAE ↓ | 0.115 ± 0.031 | 0.293 ± 0.047 | 0.013 ± 0.005 | **0.009 ± 0.005** | 0.004 ± 0.002 |
| O-Outpainting | MAE ↓ | 0.143 ± 0.025 | 0.304 ± 0.036 | 0.014 ± 0.003 | **0.013 ± 0.003** | 0.009 ± 0.002 |
| R-Outpainting | MAE ↓ | 0.113 ± 0.030 | 0.294 ± 0.047 | 0.017 ± 0.005 | **0.014 ± 0.004** | 0.006 ± 0.001 |
| O-S&P Denoising | MAE ↓ | 0.143 ± 0.027 | 0.305 ± 0.037 | **0.017 ± 0.004** | 0.028 ± 0.007 | 0.001 ± 0.001 |
| R-S&P Denoising | MAE ↓ | 0.114 ± 0.030 | 0.292 ± 0.047 | **0.022 ± 0.018** | 0.037 ± 0.020 | 0.001 ± 0.000 |

**Baselines.** Here, we briefly outline the baseline methods we compare to when evaluating visual in-context learning models in the above scenarios.

Copy chooses one of the output images from the context set $C$ and returns it as 'prediction'. This is a naive lower bound that trained models should exceed.

Neuralizer is a model by Czolbe *et al.*, trained on neural imaging and evaluated on OCT data. Models trained in the OCT domain should outperform this model.

<u>Retinalizer</u> is our re-trained model using the same architecture as Neuralizer, but trained on OCT as outlined in Sect. 3.1, Sect. 3.2 and Sect. 3.3.
<u>Retinalizer Rec.</u> is a similarly trained model as Retinalizer, with the distinction, that random recoloring augmentation is enabled during training.
<u>Single-task</u> baselines are multiple models with the architecture of Neuralizer, but trained in a supervised fashion on each task individually. As such each model was trained on the respective unseen tasks and thus presents a loose upper bound.

**Table 2.** Domain generalization results on unseen RETOUCH tasks.

| Task | Metric | Copy | Retinalizer | Retinalizer Rec. | Single-task |
|---|---|---|---|---|---|
| *Domain generalization to RETOUCH-spectralis* | | | | | |
| R-Rec. Fluid Seg. | IoU ↑ | $31.09 \pm 9.6$ | $31.89 \pm 10.1$ | $\mathbf{39.80 \pm 10.4}$ | $37.56 \pm 11.4$ |
| R-2× in-painting | MAE ↓ | $0.144 \pm 0.030$ | $0.014 \pm 0.004$ | $\mathbf{0.013 \pm 0.004}$ | $0.007 \pm 0.002$ |
| R-Outpainting | MAE ↓ | $0.143 \pm 0.029$ | $0.020 \pm 0.003$ | $\mathbf{0.019 \pm 0.004}$ | $0.010 \pm 0.002$ |
| R-S&P Denoising | MAE ↓ | $0.144 \pm 0.028$ | $0.036 \pm 0.012$ | $\mathbf{0.031 \pm 0.011}$ | $0.002 \pm 0.000$ |
| *Domain generalization to RETOUCH-topcon* | | | | | |
| R-Rec. Fluid Seg. | IoU ↑ | $35.25 \pm 12.0$ | $38.75 \pm 11.4$ | $\mathbf{40.77 \pm 10.7}$ | $40.88 \pm 12.1$ |
| R-2× in-painting | MAE ↓ | $0.071 \pm 0.021$ | $\mathbf{0.016 \pm 0.010}$ | $0.017 \pm 0.009$ | $0.005 \pm 0.002$ |
| R-Outpainting | MAE ↓ | $0.071 \pm 0.022$ | $0.027 \pm 0.011$ | $\mathbf{0.027 \pm 0.009}$ | $0.006 \pm 0.001$ |
| R-S&P Denoising | MAE ↓ | $0.072 \pm 0.023$ | $\mathbf{0.033 \pm 0.009}$ | $0.033 \pm 0.015$ | $0.003 \pm 0.000$ |
| *Domain generalization to RETOUCH-cirrus* | | | | | |
| R-Rec. Fluid Seg. | IoU ↑ | $37.25 \pm 10.6$ | $\mathbf{44.91 \pm 16.6}$ | $42.58 \pm 13.6$ | $45.72 \pm 16.0$ |
| R-2× in-painting | MAE ↓ | $0.085 \pm 0.017$ | $0.011 \pm 0.002$ | $\mathbf{0.010 \pm 0.002}$ | $0.005 \pm 0.001$ |
| R-Outpainting | MAE ↓ | $0.085 \pm 0.017$ | $\mathbf{0.014 \pm 0.002}$ | $0.015 \pm 0.002$ | $0.007 \pm 0.001$ |
| R-S&P Denoising | MAE ↓ | $0.086 \pm 0.017$ | $0.071 \pm 0.009$ | $\mathbf{0.029 \pm 0.004}$ | $0.001 \pm 0.000$ |

**Implementation Details.** We train the Retinalizer models on $3 \times 192 \times 192$ images, with batch size 5 and context set size $|C| = 6$. We further alter the sampling process of the context set for semantic tasks such that at least 2 of the image-pairs include non-empty masks. We use a learning rate of 0.0002, Adam [8] with $(\beta_1, \beta_2) = (0.5, 0.999)$ and train 16 epochs on a RTX 2080 Ti.

## 4    Experimental Results

**Quantitative Results.** In Table 1, we see the results of the models when adapting to unseen OCT tasks. First off, we see the varying difficulty of the tasks by the loose bounds set with the Copy and Single-task baselines, *e.g.*, the binary segmentation tasks is very simple, as the copy baseline already achieves a high IoU. Yet, we see, that only the Retinalizer model with the proposed color augmentation is able to exceed this naive baseline and coherently predict the merged retinal layers with an IoU of 81.94%. Handling different color-prompts in the retinal recoloring multi fluid segmentation task is done best by the same model, which is expected, as during training, *Retinalizer Rec.* has been exposed to different semantic color variations. Here, it even surpasses the Single-task baseline, indicating that a broad pre-training on diverse tasks may in itself already have a positive effect. Finding fine-grained structures, such as retinal boundaries is a challenging task for the models, which might hint at an architectural shortcoming, still, the Retinalizer Rec. model achieves the closest score to the Single-task model with 60.69% F-1. Moving to the generative tasks, we can see that Retinalizer with and without recoloring augmentation lead to the best results, with generally quite similar reconstruction errors. Most of the time, the recoloring augmentation has a positive effect, merely for salt and pepper denoising it leads to slightly worse results, indicating, its main effects unfold for semantic tasks.

Moving to domain generalization experiments in Table 2, we can, for the majority of tasks confirm, that the recoloring augmentation has a positive effect and improes generalization to new data distributions. Only in the setting when adapting to Cirrus the augmentation strategy produces slightly lower segmentation scores as compared to Retinalizer. These results hint at bridging domain gaps via in-context learning to be a promising research direction.

**Qualitative Results.** In Fig. 2, we see the inference results of different trained models. The Neuralizer model, not trained on OCTs, as expected can not be used to faithfully address tasks on the retina, further all predictions are predominantly red, as the model is originally trained to predict one channel outputs. Our trained Retinalizer is able to predict semantic regions, which correspond to the correct regions to segment. Yet, it tries to infer these regions by *interpolating* between outputs of seen tasks, *i.e.*, it tries to generalize through seen task interpolation. When we add the recoloring augmentation to Retinalizer, we see, that it can much better generalize to unseen tasks, as variance in colorization of segmentation tasks was already introduced during training, enabling a swift adaptation. Similar behavior can be seen for Layer Boundary detection. For the reconstructive task in the bottom row of the figure, all models produce similarly washed out predictions, indicating that for generative pixel-prediction, an exten-

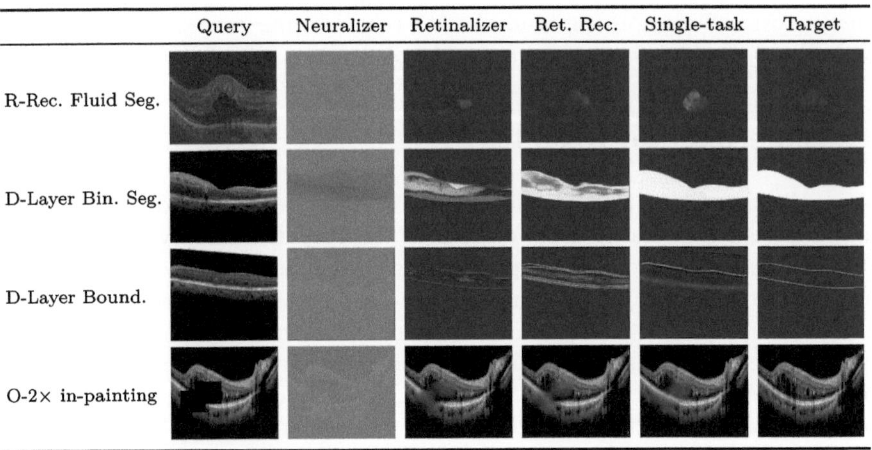

**Fig. 2.** Qualitative predictions of baselines and our Retinalizers on unseen tasks.

sion of the MSE loss we train with and further integrate an adversarial objective might lead to more faithful generated OCTs.

## 5   Conclusion

In this work, we brought the first visual in-context learning models to the domain of OCT, enabling to solve diverse and individualized retinal tasks, while overcoming the severe restrictions of small amount of available data and a small compute budget. We showed, that simply from OCT segmentation datasets, we can train models addressing a diverse set of tasks from semantic- to generative tasks and adapt to new unseen tasks and data distributions on the fly at test time. A limitation is, that in general the metric scores do not yet reach specialist model performance. Thus, in future work we aim at expanding the number of pre-training tasks and build further task-augmentations beside our recoloring strategy which we believe to be key for better adaptation to unseen tasks.

**Acknowledgments.** This work was supported by funding from the pilot program Core-Informatics of the Helmholtz Association (HGF).

**Disclosure of Interests.** The authors have no competing interests to declare that are relevant to the content of this article.

## References

1. Bai, Y., et al.: Sequential modeling enables scalable learning for large vision models. In: Proceedings of the IEEE/CVF Conference on Computer Vision and Pattern Recognition, pp. 22861–22872 (2024)
2. Bar, A., Gandelsman, Y., Darrell, T., Globerson, A., Efros, A.: Visual prompting via image inpainting. Adv. Neural Inf. Process. Syst. **35**, 25005–25017 (2022)
3. Bogunović, H., et al.: Retouch: The retinal oct fluid detection and segmentation benchmark and challenge. IEEE Trans. Med. Imaging **38**(8), 1858–1874 (2019)
4. Chiu, S.J., Allingham, M.J., Mettu, P.S., Cousins, S.W., Izatt, J.A., Farsiu, S.: Kernel regression based segmentation of optical coherence tomography images with diabetic macular edema. Biomed. Opt. Express **6**(4), 1172–1194 (2015)
5. Czolbe, S., Dalca, A.V.: Neuralizer: general neuroimage analysis without retraining. In: Proceedings of the IEEE/CVF Conference on Computer Vision and Pattern Recognition, pp. 6217–6230 (2023)
6. Huang, Z., et al.: Stu-net: scalable and transferable medical image segmentation models empowered by large-scale supervised pre-training. arXiv preprint arXiv:2304.06716 (2023)
7. Isensee, F., Jaeger, P.F., Kohl, S.A., Petersen, J., Maier-Hein, K.H.: nnu-net: a self-configuring method for deep learning-based biomedical image segmentation. Nat. Methods **18**(2), 203–211 (2021)
8. Kingma, D.P., Ba, J.: Adam: a method for stochastic optimization. arXiv e-prints pp. arXiv–1412 (2014)
9. Kulyabin, M., et al.: Octdl: optical coherence tomography dataset for image-based deep learning methods. Scientific Data **11**(1), 365 (2024)

10. Rashno, A., et al.: Fully automated segmentation of fluid/cyst regions in optical coherence tomography images with diabetic macular edema using neutrosophic sets and graph algorithms. IEEE Trans. Biomed. Eng. **65**(5), 989–1001 (2017)
11. Ren, S., et al.: Medical vision generalist: unifying medical imaging tasks in context. arXiv preprint arXiv:2406.05565 (2024)
12. Ronneberger, O., Fischer, P., Brox, T.: U-Net: convolutional networks for biomedical image segmentation. In: Navab, N., Hornegger, J., Wells, W., Frangi, A. (eds.) Medical Image Computing and Computer-Assisted Intervention – MICCAI 2015. MICCAI 2015. LNCS, vol. 9351, pp. 234–241. Springer, Cham (2015). https://doi.org/10.1007/978-3-319-24574-4_28
13. Wang, X., Wang, W., Cao, Y., Shen, C., Huang, T.: Images speak in images: a generalist painter for in-context visual learning. In: Proceedings of the IEEE/CVF Conference on Computer Vision and Pattern Recognition, pp. 6830–6839 (2023)

# Electrocardiogram Feature Extraction: A Quantitative Comparison of Signal Reconstruction Using Traditional and Autoencoder Methods


Roy R. M. van Mierlo[✉], Freek J. A. Relouw, and Natal A. W. van Riel

Department of Biomedical Engineering, Eindhoven University of Technology, Eindhoven, The Netherlands
{r.r.m.v.mierlo,f.j.a.relouw,n.a.w.v.riel}@tue.nl



**Abstract.** This work focuses on comparing ECG feature extraction methods to enable a two-step approach for diagnostic modeling. Traditional feature extraction methods rely on handcrafted features extracted from fiducial points within the ECG waveform, such as the P-wave, QRS complex, and T-wave. However, these methods often fail to capture the full complexity of the signal. Recent advances in end-to-end deep learning enable automatic feature extraction, but at the cost of large datasets and substantial computational resources. Alternatively, an autoencoder is trained to reconstruct ECG signals by compressing the waveform into a latent space representation, which forces the model to learn and retain the most critical morphological features. This latent representation could subsequently be used as input for secondary lightweight machine learning models. This work evaluates the information retention of an LSTM autoencoder by comparing its reconstruction performance with that of a traditional fiducial point-based method. The median root mean square error (RMSE) for reconstruction from fiducial points is 0.223, while the autoencoder achieves a notably lower median RMSE of 0.033. Additionally, a quality score analysis shows that the optimal trade-off between latent space size and performance is achieved at a latent space size of 11. The autoencoder approach offers a promising alternative to traditional feature extraction techniques and a computationally efficient alternative to end-to-end predictive deep learning.

The source code is publicly available at https://github.com/Computational-Biology-TUe/ae_waveform_compression.

**Keywords:** Electrocardiogram (ECG) Analysis · Deep Learning · Machine Learning · Autoencoder · Feature Extraction · Biomedical Signal Processing · Computational Efficiency


---


R.R.M. van Mierlo, F.J.A. Relouw — Shared first authorship.

# 1   Introduction

Electrocardiogram (ECG) waveforms are a vital source of information for assessing a patient's cardiovascular status and are routinely collected in high-care clinical settings such as intensive care units and operating rooms [1]. However, the complexity of high-frequency patient monitor signals, combined with time constraints in high-care clinical settings, often leads to these signals not being used to their full potential. Efficient extraction of clinically relevant features from ECG signals is essential for enhancing diagnostic accuracy [2–4]. Automation of this feature extraction process has the potential to significantly improve the utilization of ECG data in clinical predictive models, facilitating early detection of potential patient deterioration and enabling timely intervention [5].

Traditionally, ECG analysis relies on handcrafted features derived from fiducial points within the waveform, such as the P-wave, QRS complex, and T-wave [6]. These features are associated with key physiological events, such as atrial depolarization (P-wave), ventricular depolarization (QRS complex), and ventricular repolarization (T-wave). By measuring intervals and amplitudes associated with these fiducial points, clinicians can assess cardiac abnormalities, such as arrhythmias and other irregularities [7]. Despite their clinical relevance, these traditional methods have limitations. They often overlook more subtle or complex variations in the waveform, potentially missing valuable information necessary for accurate diagnosis.

Recent advances in deep learning have sought to address these limitations by enabling automatic feature extraction from raw ECG data [8–11], bypassing the need for manual fiducial point identification. However, end-to-end deep learning models require large datasets and substantial computational resources, making them challenging to implement in clinical practice. Furthermore, the multitude of architectures and hyperparameters introduces difficulties regarding reproducibility and generalizability of results.

To overcome these challenges, several recent studies have focused on two-step approaches for ECG signal feature extraction and predictive modeling. In the first step, an autoencoder network is trained to reconstruct ECG signals, learning the intricate details of the waveform's morphology through a latent space bottleneck [12–14]. This step compresses the ECG signal into a more compact representation, capturing essential features of the waveform. In the second step, this latent space representation is fed into a secondary machine learning model for further predictive tasks and diagnostic applications [15–20]. When separating these two tasks of feature extraction and prediction with lightweight machine learning models, this two-step approach offers a more efficient and reproducible alternative to end-to-end deep learning models by reducing data requirements and computational complexity.

This work focused on the first step in the aforementioned two-step approach and aims to quantify the performance of autoencoder-based ECG feature extraction. Thus far, it was unclear whether autoencoders outperform traditional clinically used features in their ability to retain information from the original ECG waveform. Autoencoder-based feature extraction was compared with the traditional fiducial point feature extraction method in terms of their ability to compress, preserve, and uncover latent waveform information. Their performance was evaluated by comparing their ability to reconstruct ECG signals from their respective feature sets. Our results demonstrate that the autoencoder method outperforms the traditional approach, highlighting its ability to preserve more comprehensive morphological information. This cements its viability as an ECG feature extraction approach.

## 2   Methods

In this work, two distinct ECG feature extraction methods are compared: a traditional method that extracts fiducial points based on ECG delineation and an LSTM-autoencoder-based method (Fig. 1). The aim is to quantitatively and qualitatively assess information capture based on compression rate and reconstruction capabilities. Gaussian-based interpolation was used as the traditional signal reconstruction method, which outperformed multiple other established interpolation strategies like Akima spline interpolation and Piecewise Cubic Hermite Interpolating Polynomial (PCHIP) interpolation. LSTM-autoencoder models were chosen over inferiorly performing 1D-CNN-based approaches [14, 22].

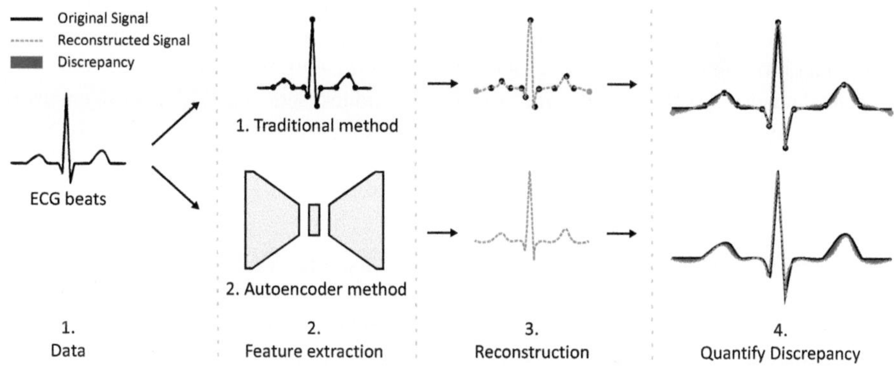


**Fig. 1.** Visualization of the workflow. The traditional method (top) extracts 11 fiducial points with ECG delineation and uses these to reconstruct the ECG waveform using a Gaussian-based interpolation technique. The autoencoder-based reconstruction method (bottom) encodes the ECG signal into a latent space representation and then decodes it to reconstruct the signal. The reconstructed signals from both methods are compared to the original ECG, and the root mean squared error (RMSE) is calculated to quantitatively assess reconstruction accuracy.

### 2.1   Data

The ECG waveform data used in this study were sourced from the VitalDB dataset [21], a large open-source collection of high-resolution physiological signals recorded from surgical patients. The dataset consists of 6,354 patients undergoing non-cardiac surgeries (general, thoracic, urologic, and gynecologic) at Seoul National University Hospital, Republic of Korea. The ECG signals were recorded at a sampling frequency of 500 Hz.

34        R. R. M. van Mierlo et al.

## 2.2  Preprocessing

ECG signals were standardized using Z-score normalization. Baseline wander was removed with a zero-phase high-pass Butterworth filter (cutoff frequency: 1 Hz) and a low-pass Butterworth filter (cutoff frequency: 30 Hz), both with a fourth-order design. Signals were segmented into 20-s ECG samples, which were again Z-score normalized. R-peaks were detected using Neurokit 2.0 [22], and samples with missing values, extreme heart rates (<30 bpm or > 180 bpm), or other anomalies (e.g., RMS successive differences > 150 ms, standard deviation/beat count > 1.63) were excluded.

ECG wave delineation was performed using Neurokit 2.0 to extract fiducial points (P, Q, S, and T peaks, and the onsets/offsets of P, R, and T waves). Inputs for the traditional reconstruction method were ten median fiducial point values (x and y coordinates) over the 20-s sample and relative to the R-peak.

A single median beat was constructed from each 20-s sample by extracting 640 ms segments (80% of the duration of one heartbeat with an average heart rate of 75 bpm) around the detected R-peaks, where one-third of the beat lies before, and two-thirds lie behind the R-peak. At a 500 Hz sampling frequency, this produced median samples of size 320. These beat segments serve as the input for the autoencoder networks, as well as the label to compare reconstruction outputs with for both methods.

The dataset was split into training, validation, and test sets in a 97-2-1 ratio, ensuring no indirect data leakage by keeping patient samples together within a single split.

## 2.3  Traditional ECG Reconstruction

To ensure smooth, nonlinear transitions between discrete fiducial points, a Gaussian-based interpolation method was employed. Given two adjacent fiducial points, $(x_1, y_1)$ and $(x_2, y_2)$, interpolation was performed over the integer range $[x_1, x_2]$. The transition was modeled using a Gaussian function with peak amplitude:

$$a = \max(y_1, y_2) \tag{1}$$

centered at $\mu = x_2$ if $y_2 > y_1$, or at $\mu = x_1$ otherwise. The interpolated values were computed as:

$$y(x) = a\exp\left(-\frac{(x - \mu)^2}{2\sigma^2}\right) \tag{2}$$

where $\sigma$ is a tunable parameter controlling the steepness of the transition. To ensure interpolation remained bounded by the original values, a linear rescaling was applied:

$$y(x) = \frac{(y(x) - y_0)(y_2 - y_1)}{y_f - y_0} + y_1, \text{ if } y_2 > y_1 \tag{3}$$

$$y(x) = \frac{(y(x) - y_f)(y_1 - y_2)}{y_0 - y_f} + y_2, \text{ otherwise} \tag{4}$$

where $y_0$ and $y_f$ correspond to the first and last computed Gaussian values.

The baseline value of a wave segment was computed as the mean of all its on- and offset fiducial points (P, R, T waves). This baseline ensured physiological consistency by setting a reference level to which the outer ends of the reconstructed ECG returned.

Bayesian optimization using Gaussian process regression was performed over 1000 steps to optimize the $\sigma$ parameters for the twelve reconstructed wave segments on the validation set. The predefined parameter search space was limited to integer values between and including 1 and 5.

## 2.4  Autoencoder-Based ECG Reconstruction

A deep LSTM-based autoencoder was used for sequence-based dimensionality reduction and ECG reconstruction [14, 23]. The model consisted of an encoder-decoder structure, where both components used stacked LSTM layers to capture temporal dependencies. The encoder processed the input sequence $x \in \mathbb{R}^{T \times 1}$ (where $T$ is the sequence length) through three LSTM layers with progressively smaller hidden sizes (128, 64, $d$, where $d$ represents the latent space size) and dropout layers between them (rate $= 0.2$). The latent representation was obtained from the final hidden state of the deepest LSTM layer. The decoder reconstructed the waveform by repeating the latent vector across the temporal dimension and passing it through three LSTM layers with hidden sizes in reverse order. A final linear layer mapped the output to a single-channel time-series representation, yielding the reconstructed ECG waveform $\hat{x}$.

Model training was performed using Python 3.11 with PyTorch 2.0.1 + cu118 on an 8-core Intel i7-9700 CPU and an NVIDIA GeForce RTX 2060 GPU (6.4 GB memory). The Adam optimizer was used with a learning rate of 0.001 and a batch size of 128. The loss function was defined as the mean squared error (MSE):

$$MSE = \frac{1}{N} \sum_{i=1}^{N} \sum_{t=0}^{T} (\hat{x}_{ti} - x_{ti})^2 \tag{5}$$

with N the batch size.

Multiple models were trained with $d$ varying from 2 to 24, each with multiple random initializations to evaluate encoding and reconstruction capabilities. Models were validated every 200 training steps to assess performance on unseen data.

## 2.5  Reconstruction Performance

Reconstruction performance on the test set was compared for the traditional and autoencoder methods using root mean squared error (RMSE) and quality score (QS) [24]. The QS aims to find the most optimal consideration on the trade-off between reconstruction accuracy and latent space size ($d$) and is defined as the compression rate divided by the percentage root mean square difference (PRD).

$$RMSE = \frac{1}{N} \sqrt{\sum_{t=0}^{T} (\hat{x}_t - x_t)^2} \tag{6}$$

$$PRD = 100 \times \sqrt{\frac{\sum_{t=0}^{T} (\hat{x}_t - x_t)^2}{\sum_{t=0}^{T} x_t^2}} \tag{7}$$

$$QS = \frac{T}{d \times PRD} \qquad (8)$$

## 3   Results

After preprocessing, the dataset consisted of 3,014,476 ECG median beat samples.

The initial analysis of the autoencoder method focused on the relationship between RMSE and latent space size ($d$) through the QS (Fig. 2). The RMSE follows a nonlinear decreasing trend with increasing $d$, which leveled off at $d = 16$. Two distinct peaks are observed in the QS at $d = 4$ and $d = 11$. To facilitate further comparison, the best performing models for $d = 20$ and $d = 10$ were selected for additional analysis, as they align with the number of traditional fiducial point-based features.

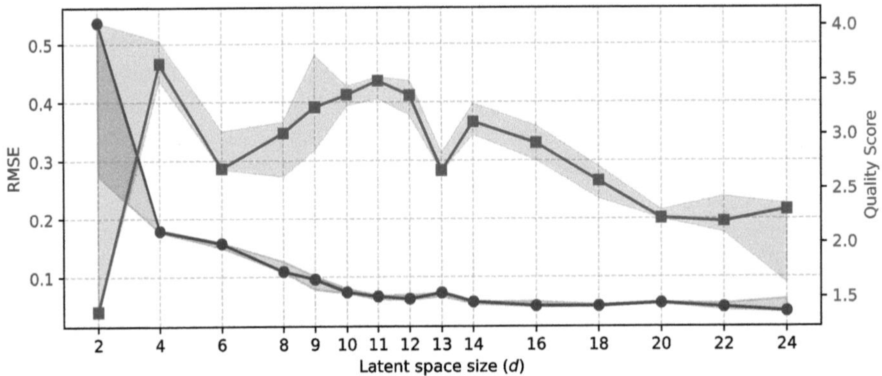

**Fig. 2.** RMSE (blue dots) and Quality Score (red cubes) for the reconstruction using LSTM autoencoder models with different latent space sizes. Points show median values, and shaded areas indicate IQR values for trained models with five different weight initializations. (Colour figure online)

Subsequently, the performance of the traditional reconstruction method and the two autoencoder models was evaluated with respect to global and local error distributions.

Table 1 quantifies the global errors by showing the RMSE and QS metrics across the test dataset for each reconstruction method. It is noteworthy that the classical reconstruction method relying on fiducial points exhibited significantly higher reconstruction errors compared to both autoencoder models. The $d = 20$ model yielded superior RMSE compared to $d = 10$ model, while conversely, the $d = 10$ model yielded a superior QS compared to the $d = 20$ model.

Figure 3 illustrates that the classical method particularly struggled to capture morphological information around the Q and S peaks, as well as the ST-segment and the region following the T peak. In contrast, the autoencoder demonstrated much more consistent reconstruction performance across the entire ECG segment, with minor deviations observed only around the Q and S peaks.

**Table 1.** RMSE and Quality Score (QS) for the different methods on the test dataset, with best performances in bold. All RMSE and QS differences are statistically significant (p < 0.05, Wilcoxon signed-rank test). Holm–Bonferroni correction was applied for multiple comparisons.

|  |  | Traditional Method (10 x,y coordinates) | LSTM Autoencoder ($d = 20$) | LSTM Autoencoder ($d=10$) |
|---|---|---|---|---|
| RMSE | mean (SD) | 0.334 (0.347) | **0.046 (0.039)** | 0.070 (0.052) |
|  | median [Q1-Q3] | 0.223 [0.151–0.415] | **0.033 [0.026–0.047]** | 0.054 [0.042–0.078] |
| QS | mean (SD) | 0.776 (0.478) | 4.890 (2.340) | **6.079 (2.973)** |
|  | median [Q1-Q3] | 0.741 [0.377–1.081] | 5.110 [3.167–6.579] | **6.149 [3.729–8.179]** |

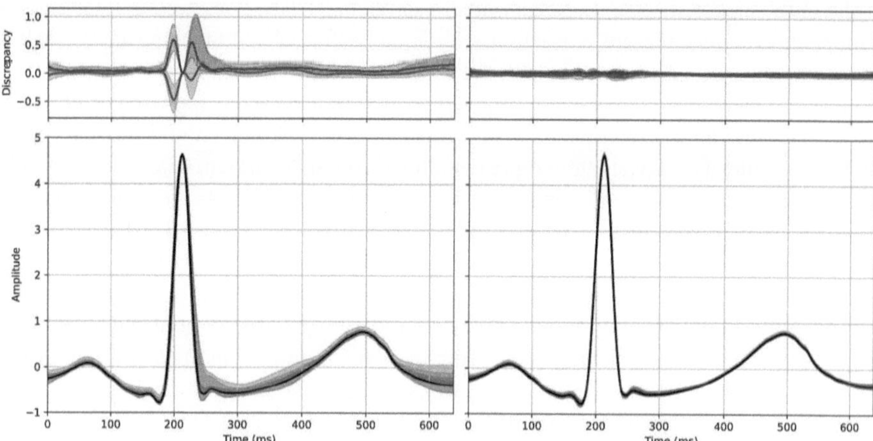

**Fig. 3.** Local error (red) and absolute error (blue) distributions on the test dataset for the traditional method (left column) and the autoencoder method with latent space size $d = 20$ (right column). Top: Discrepancy quantification with lines indicating median and shaded areas indicating IQR values. Bottom: Localization of discrepancies along the median ECG waveform in the test dataset (black). Dark shaded area indicates median, while light shaded area indicates IQR values. (Colour figure online)

## 4  Discussion

In this work, an autoencoder-based approach for ECG signal feature extraction was compared to a traditional fiducial point-based feature extraction method. The results demonstrate that the autoencoder method outperforms the fiducial point approach, achieving a more accurate reconstruction of ECG morphology. This confirms that the autoencoder is capable of capturing more intricate morphological features within the same feature set size as the traditional method, cementing the relevance of autoencoder-based approaches for improved waveform feature extraction.

An obvious limitation of this study is that the reconstruction performance is inherently dependent on the model that is selected to decode latent features. It can be argued that the Gaussian-based model used to reconstruct an ECG from the traditional fiducial points is not optimal. However, it should be noted that multiple different established interpolation strategies, like Akima spline interpolation and Piecewise Cubic Hermite Interpolating Polynomial (PCHIP) interpolation, performed worse than the Gaussian-based method. Meanwhile, the same can be argued for the LSTM autoencoder model structure. Despite this, it should be considered that this work was not an exercise in finding the optimal decoder structures, but rather a proof of principle of autoencoder-based feature extraction.

While improved reconstruction performance is a crucial first step, further research is needed to assess whether the additional morphological detail captured by the autoencoder improves downstream clinical diagnostic models. In addition, the tradeoff between interpretability of features and extraction and reconstruction performance should be considered when making decisions for downstream predictive tasks. Nonetheless, the ability of the autoencoder to encode richer waveform characteristics suggests its potential as a more informative feature extraction technique, potentially enhancing tasks such as arrhythmia classification or early deterioration detection.

Beyond reconstruction accuracy, the advantages of a two-step approach of ECG feature extraction and consecutive lightweight predictive modeling should be highlighted. By first learning a compact latent representation through an autoencoder, clinically relevant features can be efficiently extracted without relying on large-scale end-to-end deep learning predictive models. This not only reduces the computational burden and data requirements but also simplifies model interpretability and reproducibility. The second step, where the latent representation is used in downstream models, allows for flexible integration into existing clinical decision-support systems without requiring high-performance hardware or extensive hyperparameter tuning. This makes the approach particularly well-suited for deployment in resource-constrained environments such as smaller hospitals, ambulatory monitoring, or wearable device applications.

Furthermore, the generalizability of this autoencoder feature extraction method could extend beyond ECG signals. Many other physiological waveforms, such as arterial blood pressure (ABP), central venous pressure (CVP), and photoplethysmogram (PPG) signals, exhibit complex morphologies that are not fully captured by traditional feature extraction techniques. The advantage of the autoencoder-based method operating without prior knowledge is especially present for CVP signals that can show large variations in morphology. Applying the same two-step approach to these signals and combining modalities in downstream models could enhance predictive models for cardiovascular risk assessment, hemodynamic instability detection, and continuous patient monitoring even further.

This method bridges the gap between classical feature engineering and end-to-end deep learning, providing a scalable and interpretable alternative that balances accuracy, efficiency, and clinical feasibility.

## 5 Conclusion

This study demonstrates that an autoencoder-based approach outperforms traditional fiducial point-based methods for ECG signal reconstruction, capturing more detailed morphological features within the same feature set size. While further investigation is needed to assess its impact on clinical diagnostic performance, the autoencoder method offers advantages in terms of reduced computational costs, data requirements, and model optimization challenges compared to end-to-end deep learning prediction tasks. This approach could also be easily extended to multiple ECG leads and other waveform modalities, providing a valuable tool for resource-limited environments.

**Disclosure of Interests.**   The authors have no competing interests to declare that are relevant to the content of this article.

# References


1. Brady, W.J., Truwit, J.D.: Critical decisions in emergency and acute care electrocardiography. Critical Decisions in Emergency and Acute Care Electrocardiography, pp. 1–492 (2009)
2. Singh, A.K., Krishnan, S.: ECG signal feature extraction trends in methods and applications. Biomed. Eng. Online **22**, 1–36 (2023)
3. Martis, R.J., Acharya, U.R., Adeli, H.: Current methods in electrocardiogram characterization. Comput. Biol. Med. **48**, 133–149 (2014)
4. Monfredi, O.J., et al.: Continuous ECG monitoring should be the heart of bedside AI-based predictive analytics monitoring for early detection of clinical deterioration. J. Electrocardiol. **76**, 35–38 (2023)
5. Mathis, M.R., et al.: Prediction of postoperative deterioration in cardiac surgery patients using electronic health record and physiologic waveform data. Anesthesiology **137**, 586–601 (2022)
6. Sattar, Y., Chhabra, L.: Electrocardiogram. StatPearls (2023)
7. Tabassum, T., Islam, M.: An approach of cardiac disease prediction by analyzing ECG signal. In: 2016 3rd International Conference on Electrical Engineering and Information and Communication Technology, iCEEiCT 2016 (2017)
8. Narotamo, H., Dias, M., Santos, R., Carreiro, A.V., Gamboa, H., Silveira, M.: Deep learning for ECG classification: a comparative study of 1D and 2D representations and multimodal fusion approaches. Biomed. Signal Process. Control **93**, 106141 (2024)
9. Liu, X., Wang, H., Li, Z., Qin, L.: Deep learning in ECG diagnosis: a review. Knowl. Based Syst. **227**, 107187 (2021)
10. Kwon, J. et al.: Artificial intelligence for detecting electrolyte imbalance using electrocardiography. Ann. Noninvasive Electrocardiol. **26** (2021)
11. An, J.N., et al.: Development of deep learning algorithm for detecting dyskalemia based on electrocardiogram. Sci. Rep. **14**, 1–9 (2024)
12. Yildirim, O., Tan, R.S., Acharya, U.R.: An efficient compression of ECG signals using deep convolutional autoencoders. Cogn. Syst. Res. **52**, 198–211 (2018)
13. Jang, J.H., Kim, T.Y., Lim, H.S., Yoon, D.: Unsupervised feature learning for electrocardiogram data using the convolutional variational autoencoder. PLoS ONE **16**, e0260612 (2021)
14. Farady, I., Patel, V., Kuo, C.C., Lin, C.Y.: ECG Anomaly Detection with LSTM-Autoencoder for Heartbeat Analysis. Digest of Technical Papers - IEEE International Conference on Consumer Electronics (2024)
15. Zhang, S., Fang, Y., Ren, Y.: ECG autoencoder based on low-rank attention. Sci. Rep. **14**, 1–10 (2024)
16. Shan, L., et al.: Abnormal ECG detection based on an adversarial autoencoder. Front. Physiol. **13**, 961724 (2022)
17. Sieliwonczyk, E., et al.: Unsupervised electrocardiogram feature extraction using deep learning empowers discovery of genetic and phenotypic determinants of cardiac electrophysiology. Eur Heart J. **45** (2024)

18. Akkus, M., Karabatak, M., Tekin, R.: Classification of ECG Signals Encrypted with CNN Based Autoencoder with LSTM. 12th International Symposium on Digital Forensics and Security, ISDFS 2024 (2024)
19. Yu, H., Lu, Y., Zheng, S.: Inferring spatial–temporal dynamics of ECG signals with deep neural networks for cardiovascular diseases diagnosis. Biomed. Signal Process. Control **97**, 106668 (2024)
20. Sun, C., Liu, C., Wang, X., Liu, Y., Zhao, S.: Coronary artery disease detection based on a novel multi-modal deep-coding method using ECG and PCG signals. Sensors **24**, 6939 (2024)
21. Lee, H.C., Park, Y., Yoon, S.B., Yang, S.M., Park, D.,Jung, C.W.: VitalDB, a high-fidelity multi-parameter vital signs database in surgical patients. Sci Data. **9** (2022)
22. Makowski, D., et al.: NeuroKit2: a Python toolbox for neurophysiological signal processing. Behav. Res. Methods **53**, 1689–1696 (2021)
23. Roy, M., Majumder, S., Halder, A., Biswas, U.: ECG-NET: a deep LSTM autoencoder for detecting anomalous ECG. Eng. Appl. Artif. Intell. **124**, 106484 (2023)
24. Blanco-Velasco, M., Cruz-Roldán, F., Godino-Llorente, J.I., Blanco-Velasco, J., Armiens-Aparicio, C., López-Ferreras, F.: On the use of PRD and CR parameters for ECG compression. Med. Eng. Phys. **27**, 798–802 (2005)

# Improving Few-Shot-Segmentation of New Structures in Volumetric Medical Images by Support Set Optimization

Yekutiel Uliel[1], Alina Ryabtsev[1], Assaf Hoogi[2], and Leo Joskowicz[1](✉)

[1] School of Computer Science and Engineering, The Hebrew University of Jerusalem, Jerusalem, Israel
josko@cs.huji.ac.il
[2] School of Computer Science, Ariel University, Ariel, Israel

**Abstract.** Few-Shot Learning (FSL) offers a promising solution to the high annotation costs in medical image analysis by suggesting a solution for handling limited labeled data. In the typical FSL setup, a pre-trained model uses a small, annotated support set to segment a new, unlabeled query image. However, performance can be highly variable due to overfit, as the limited support set may not be representative of the query. We propose a novel method to improve FSL performance for image segmentation tasks by dynamically optimizing the support set based on representative features extracted from the query image. The query-aware choice of more representative support set exploits overfitting to effectively overfit to the query image and improve model performance without re-training or additional annotations. We validate our approach on the task of liver lesions detection and segmentation in contrast-enhanced abdominal CT scans (103 scans, 2,442 lesions). The method improved the F1 score by 8.5% (from 0.59 to 0.64) on a support set of 13 scans, with respect to simple support selection policies that do not consider the query. Our results demonstrate that query-aware support set optimization significantly enhances FSL performance for small structures.

**Keywords:** Few-Shot Learning · Deep Learning · Annotation Efficiency · Small Structures Detection and Segmentation

## 1 Introduction

Deep learning (DL) models developed for medical image analysis tasks hold the promise of high impact in Radiology [1]. However, DL models require large, annotated datasets to train them, which requires expert annotators and is time-consuming [2].

Various approaches have been proposed to address this issue, such as semi-supervised learning [3–7], active learning [8–10], and meta-learning [11]. Few-Shot-Learning (FSL), often an instance of meta-learning, typically uses a pretrained model and a small set of labeled examples, called the support set, to perform inference on a query image for a new task [12]. The FSL models are designed to capture the task definition from the support set examples and apply it to generate a prediction for the query sample.

© The Author(s), under exclusive license to Springer Nature Switzerland AG 2026
T. Chen et al. (Eds.): EMA4MICCAI 2025 Workshops, LNCS 16318, pp. 41–50, 2026.
https://doi.org/10.1007/978-3-032-13961-0_5

Medical few-shot-segmentation (FSS) is a specific case of FSL. It inputs a query image and a labeled support set of an unseen structure and outputs a classification of the pixels/voxel in the query image using a pre-trained model and the support set. It is label-efficient because it only requires the annotation of the support set, which is usually small. Recent medical FSS models include SENet [13], ALPNet [14] and UniverSeg [15]. UniverSeg, pre-trained on 22,000 images from different modalities achieved state-of-the-art performance on various anatomical structures. However, since it relies on a small support set that is not always representative of the query it may yield high variability and poor results for small structures, e.g. lesions [16].

Our hypothesis is that the variability stems from overfitting to the small support set, that causes the model to perform well on similar queries but poorly on queries that are not. By matching the support set closely to the query, we increase the similarity, and intentionally overfit to the query itself, reducing the variance and improving the results.

In this paper, we present a new method to optimize the support set in FSS whose aim is to improve its alignment with the query image. The method leverages task- and structure-specific knowledge to extract representative features from the query and use them to tailor the support set without modifying or re-training the pre-trained model. We demonstrate our method using UniverSeg as the FSS model, for the task of liver lesions detection and segmentation in contrast-enhanced CT (CECT) scans.

The contributions of this paper are: 1) a novel FSL based query-aware strategy that optimizes the support set to become more representative of the query. This strategy turns model overfitting - traditionally seen as a limitation - into an advantage, improving the performance on new queries; 2) a fully automated pipeline that is customized to realize this strategy for the task of liver lesions detection; 3) a representative classification of query liver CECT scans that does not require expert annotation to compute; 4) a query-aware support set optimization technique for liver lesions detection; 5) Experimental validation of the proposed method on a clinical liver lesions dataset.

## 2  Methods

We present a new method to tune the performance of a FSS model for the detection and segmentation of small structures in volumetric images not included in the pre-trained FSS model. The key idea is to optimize the support set according to information that is extracted from the query scan while avoiding expert annotation.

Our method, shown in Fig. 1, is a pipeline that inputs a set of expert annotated scans as support set and a query scan, and outputs the segmentation for the query scan using an FSS model. It consists of three steps: 1) extract representative features of the query at hand without expert annotation; 2) optimize the support set for the required task according to the representation that was extracted for the query; 3) compute the segmentation mask for the query with a pre-trained FSS model using the optimized support set.

To demonstrate our method on the new task of detecting liver lesions in abdominal CECT scans, we implemented a variant of the above pipeline, by the following steps: 1) represent the query at hand as either few-lesion or many-lesion type by self-supervision or rough manual annotation; 2) Optimize the distribution of lesions across the support set according to the query type; Include more patches of high lesion area in the support set in case of a many-lesion type query, or fewer such patches in the case of a few-lesion type query; 3) compute the segmentation mask using the FSS model with the query scan and the optimized support set. Lesions are detected on the output mask.

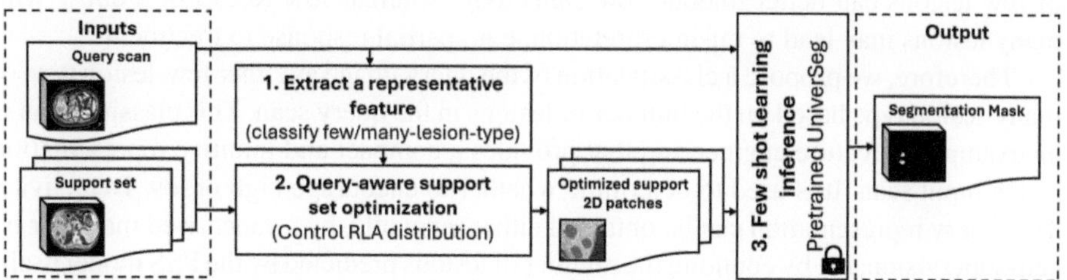


**Fig. 1.** Overview of the pipeline and its realization for the liver lesions detection (task-related items appear in parentheses). The inputs are the query scan and the support set. First, representative features are extracted from the query scan. Next, the features are used to generate a matching support set of patches. The resulting patches and the query are then input to a pretrained FSS model. The output is the query segmentation mask.

This implementation of the pipeline is customized for enhanced lesion detection scores. The key idea behind it is to differentiate scans with few and many lesions by:

– Use the Recall as a detection figure-of-merit for scans with many lesions.
– Use the Precision as a detection figure-of-merit for scans with few lesions.
– Promote either a higher Recall or Precision at the expense of the other according to the figure-of-merit of the query scan; Namely, optimize the support set examples to include more lesions in case of a query with many lesions that prioritizes Recall, or less lesions in case of a query with few lesions that prioritizes Precision.

We detail steps 1 and 2 of the pipeline next. For step 3, we perform intensity clipping and min-max normalization before inference with the pretrained UniverSeg FSS model.

### 2.1  Extraction of the Representative Query Features

The first step involves extracting features that capture key characteristics of the query scan for the specific task. These can be obtained by various means such as unsupervised methods, self-supervision, pretrained models or explicit annotation of the query that requires less time or less expertise than full annotation. For the task of liver lesions detection, we focus on the latter to realize this step.

For this task, we desire high Recall (low false negative rate) and high Precision (low false positive rate). In the low-data regime, a compromise between the two is often required. The optimal balance is guided by the clinical context, which indicates the relative importance of avoiding false positives (FP) and false negatives (FN).

Let the *Detectivity* be defined as the ratio between the Recall and the Precision:

$$Detectivity = \frac{Recall}{Precision} = \frac{TP + FP}{TP + FN} \tag{1}$$

This measure captures the Recall-Precision tradeoff: the model's tendency to risk FP versus FN, with respect to the number of true positives (TP). For liver lesions detection, a query of many lesions is more tolerant to low Precision, i.e., it prioritizes high Detectivity, whereas a query with few lesions would suffer strongly from low Precision that may modify clinical decisions and require expensive expert review. On the other hand, a query of few lesions can better tolerate low Detectivity whereas low Recall of a query with many lesions may lead to misinterpretation, e.g., partial response to treatment.

Therefore, we propose a classification of the query image as either few-lesion type or many-lesion type based on the number of lesions in the query scan. This classification is an example of feature engineering that provides a compact and intuitive representation of the input scan. It is used to determine whether to encourage high or low Detectivity. This query representation can be obtained either manually, by a supervised model or by self-supervision, i.e. by counting the number of lesions predicted by the FSS model itself. Note that obtaining such classification is less demanding than the actual segmentation of the liver lesions, as it can be obtained with low-cost annotation methods, i.e., bounding box or a non-expert annotation.

## 2.2 Query-Aware Optimization of the Support Set

We propose a method to control the Detectivity by biassing the distribution of the support set as an alternative to controlling the Recall-Precision tradeoff by a hyper-parameter or by modifying the pretrained model. This is achieved by first converting the few labelled scans into 2D patches and then selecting a subset with a patch reduction policy, a function that inputs the support set and returns a fixed size subset of the most relevant patches. A policy is defined as query-aware if it also inputs the representation of the query scan and considers it to generate the subset. The model infers according to the distribution present in the generated subset, thus an educated choice of the policy dictates the results without directly processing the input scans. This method controls the results while avoiding any training or fine-tuning of the model that is often undesired either due to risk of violating its training assumptions or due to lack of expertise.

For liver lesions detection, we focus on the distribution of lesion area across the support patches as defined by the relative lesion area ($RLA$):

$$RLA = \frac{lesionarea}{liverarea} \tag{2}$$

where the lesion and liver areas are computed for each patch in pixels and the liver area is computed from the segmentation mask produced by TotalSegmentor [17].

We draw a subset of the available selection of support patches of non-zero RLA. The probability of drawing a patch to be included in the support subset depends on its RLA according to a predefined policy. Different policies applied to a given set of support scans will take form as different distributions of RLA across the support subset. For example, the policy can control the median of the RLA. Since we hypothesize that including examples with high RLA promotes high Detectivity, setting a higher RLA median realizes a policy that targets many-lesion type queries, and similarly a low RLA median targets few-lesion type queries.

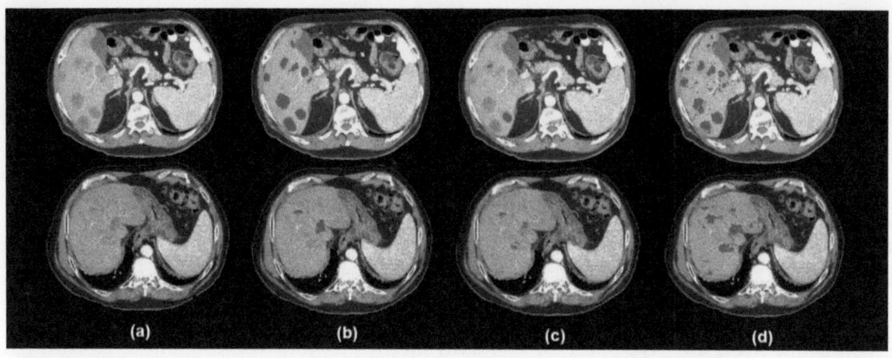

**Fig. 2.** Examples of lesion segmentations: (a) axial slices of a many-lesion (top) and few-lesion-type (bottom) query scans with 31 and 2 lesions respectively; (b) ground-truth lesion segmentation; (c) segmentation with policy $P_{few}$ that targets few-lesion-type queries: Recall, Precision, F1 and Dice score were 0.55, 1.00, 0.71 and 0.25 (top), and 1.00, 0.4, 0.57 and 0.38 (bottom); (d) segmentation with policy $P_{many}$ that targets many-lesion-type queries: Recall, Precision, F1 and Dice score were 1.00, 0.84, 0.91 and 0.57 (top) and 1.00, 0.13, 0.22 and 0.17 (bottom).

## 3 Experimental Results

**Dataset.** Our experimental dataset comprised 103 venous-phase abdominal CT scans acquired using Philips Brilliance iCT, Canon Aquilion Prime SP, and GE Optima 660 scanners. These scans were collected during routine clinical treatment of 45 unique patients diagnosed with liver metastases (source: Hadassah University Medical Center).

To evaluate our method, the dataset was randomly partitioned into two subsets: a support set ($DSUPPORT$) containing 13 scans of distinct patients, and a query set ($DQUERY$) containing the rest (90 scans, 45 patients). $DQUERY$ was further divided into two disjoint subsets based on ground-truth (GT) lesion annotations: $DMANY$ (27 scans, 16 patients), consisting of scans classified as many-lesion-type, defined as having more than 10 clinically significant lesions (diameter > 10 mm), and $DFEW$ (63 scans, 37 patients), containing the complementary few-lesion-type scans. This stratification enables separate evaluation of the performance on queries of either type.

**Annotation.** An expert radiologist created GT lesion annotations for the dataset, resulting in 2,442 liver lesions ($23.7 \pm 27.0$ lesions per scan), of which 850 are significant.

**Table 1.** Recall, Precision, F1 and Dice scores (mean $\pm$ std) for the policies $P_{few}$ and $P_{many}$ that target few- and many-lesion-type queries respectively. The scores are listed for three query sets.

| Policy/ | $P_{few}$/ | $P_{few}$/ | $P_{few}$/ | $P_{many}$/ | $P_{many}$/ | $P_{many}$/ |
|---|---|---|---|---|---|---|
| Query set | $DFEW$ | $DMANY$ | $DQUERY$ | $DFEW$ | $DMANY$ | $DQUERY$ |
| Recall | $0.60 \pm 0.39$ | $0.52 \pm 0.20$ | $0.58 \pm 0.34$ | $0.96 \pm 0.16$ | $0.94 \pm 0.09$ | $0.95 \pm 0.14$ |
| Precision | $0.78 \pm 0.37$ | $0.95 \pm 0.08$ | $0.83 \pm 0.32$ | $0.25 \pm 0.23$ | $0.77 \pm 0.17$ | $0.40 \pm 0.32$ |
| F1 | $0.56 \pm 0.39$ | $0.65 \pm 0.17$ | $0.59 \pm 0.34$ | $0.34 \pm 0.26$ | $0.83 \pm 0.11$ | $0.49 \pm 0.32$ |
| Dice | $0.60 \pm 0.35$ | $0.29 \pm 0.16$ | $0.50 \pm 0.34$ | $0.63 \pm 0.24$ | $0.56 \pm 0.14$ | $0.61 \pm 0.22$ |

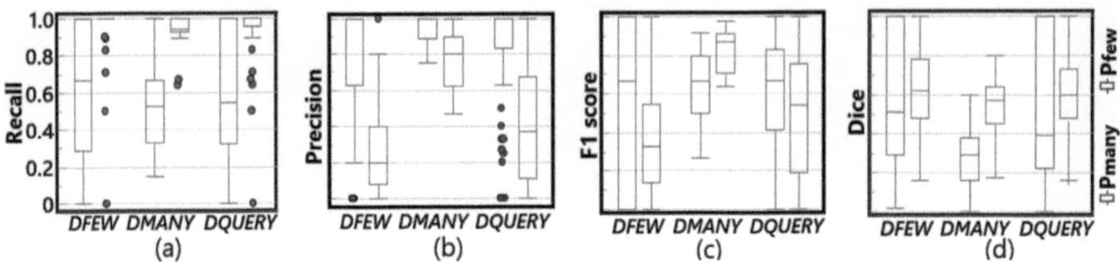

**Fig. 3.** Box plots of the Recall (a), Precision (b), F1 (c), Dice (d) scores for two non-query-aware policies, $P_{few}$ and $P_{many}$ (color) that target few- or many-lesion-type queries across query sets.

**Evaluation Metrics.** We use four standard metrics as follows. Precision, Recall, and F1 score were calculated for significant lesions. A lesion is defined as TP if there is nonzero overlap between its computed and the GT masks. Otherwise, it is a FP if in the computed mask but not on the GT, and FN if it is in the GT mask and not in the computed mask. The Dice score was calculated for TP lesions only.

**Studies.** We designed and conducted four studies as follows. Study 1 quantifies the effect of the query classification into few- and many-lesions type. Study 2 demonstrates our method for liver lesions detection. Study 3 is a sensitivity analysis study designed to estimate the penalty of query classification errors on the method's performance. Study 4 explores the relationship between the model's lesions detection accuracy and various support patches selection policies.

**Study 1: Query Classification.** We quantify the performance of the UniverSeg model on a 13-shot FSS task. We converted *DSUPPORT* into a $128 \times 128 \times 1$ patches set with 1/2 stride. We used two different reduction policies, $P_{few}$ and $P_{many}$, that target few- and many-lesions-type queries respectively, to draw 450 patches as a support set. For each policy we used the outcome support set to infer on *DQUERY*, *DFEW* and *DMANY*.

Figure 2 shows examples of the model results; Table 1 lists them; Fig. 3 shows them as box plots; Note in Fig. 3 that Precision or Recall degenerate to unity for most queries with either $P_{few}$ or $P_{many}$ respectively. And so, we use F1 as a detection figure-of-merit that shows each policy excels on a different type of queries.

Figure 4b shows the trends of F1 versus the number of lesions in the query for $P_{few}$ and $P_{many}$. The slope of this trend depends on the policy and explains which of few- or many-lesion-type classes will better fit each policy. The excess variability of results for few-lesion-type queries (seen in Table 1 and Fig. 2) is further explained by Fig. 4a., as the fewer positive lesions there are in the GT or the output mask, the more discrete Recall or Precision become respectively, adding quantization error on top of the mean trend.

**Study 2: Performance on the Liver Lesions Detection Task.** We estimate the performance of the pipeline described in Fig. 1. We used a query-aware policy, $P_{combined}$, to select the support patches. $P_{combined}$ selects patches drawn by either of the non-query-aware policies $P_{few}$ or $P_{many}$ for each query according to its type, hence its name. The results are juxtaposed against the F1 scores obtained by the two non-query-aware policies. Lists the results. $P_{combined}$ reproduces the F1 scores of the better non-query-aware policy for *DFEW* and *DMANY* and surpasses both on the overall *DQUERY* (Table 2).

**Table 2.** Results of the F1 score of our method ($P_{combined}$) across query sets with classification errors occurrence determined by the error parameter $\eta$. The results for the non-query-aware policies $P_{few}$ and $P_{many}$ that target few- or many-lesion-type queries respectively are also presented.

| Query set | $P_{few}$ | $P_{many}$ | Pcombined ($\eta = 0$, ideal) | Pcombined ($\eta = 5$) | Pcombined ($\eta = 10$) |
|---|---|---|---|---|---|
| *DFEW* | $0.56 \pm 0.39$ | $0.34 \pm 0.26$ | $0.56 \pm 0.39$ | $0.56 \pm 0.38$ | **$0.57 \pm 0.37$** |
| *DMANY* | $0.65 \pm 0.17$ | **$0.83 \pm 0.11$** | **$0.83 \pm 0.11$** | $0.81 \pm 0.14$ | $0.74 \pm 0.17$ |
| *DQUERY* | $0.59 \pm 0.34$ | $0.49 \pm 0.32$ | **$0.64 \pm 0.35$** | $0.64 \pm 0.35$ | $0.62 \pm 0.33$ |

**Study 3: The Effect of Classification Errors.** We repeated Study 2, this time introducing classification errors to account for the penalty of relying on low-cost annotation (or self-supervision) of the query to drive the pipeline.

The query was classified by roughly estimating the number of lesions included in it and comparing it to a predefined threshold. The classification errors were modeled by perturbating the accurate count of lesions with random noise:

$$c_{query} = \begin{cases} few - lesion - type & \left(1 + \frac{a}{10}\right) \cdot (n_{lesions} + a) \leq 10 \\ many - lesion - type & else \end{cases} \tag{3}$$

where $c_{query}$ is the result class for the query, $n_{lesions}$ is the number of significant lesions present in the GT annotation, $a$ is an additive noise random parameter uniformly drawn from $[-\eta, \eta]$, and $\left(1 + \frac{a}{10}\right)$ is a multiplicative noise term.

Setting $\eta = 0$ results in unrealistic perfect classification; increasing it results in misclassification of some queries. The value of $\eta$ enables sensitivity analysis of the detection scores to classification errors as their occurrence is dictated by it.

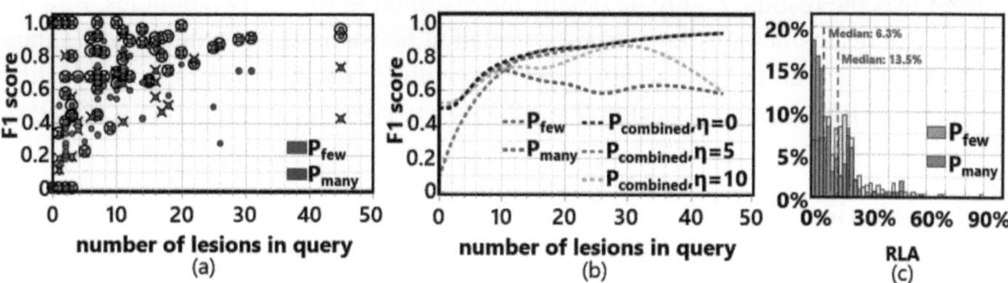


**Fig. 4.** (a) Plot of the F1 score as a function of the number of lesions in the query scan for our method $P_{combined}$ and the non-query-aware policies $P_{few}$ and $P_{many}$ that target few- and many-lesions-type queries respectively. Each dot represents a query scan. Circled results were reproduced by $P_{combined}$ with $\eta = 0$, crossed dots were reproduced with $\eta = 10$; (b) trendlines (spline $\lambda = 0.428$) of F1 score against the number of lesions in the query for different policies and $\eta$ values; (c) Distribution of the RLA across the support patches for each of the non-query-aware policies.

**Table 3.** F1 score of the seven reduction policies on few- and many-type-lesions, and on the overall query set. Each policy is characterized by the RLA median of the support patches it yielded and the mean Detectivity it yielded on the overall query set. The non-query-aware policies $P_{few}$ and $P_{many}$ are marked. The correlation between RLA median and the F1 score is reported.

| RLA median (%) | Few-lesions-type | Many-lesions-type | Both types (mean Detectivity) |
|---|---|---|---|
| 6.3 ($P_{few}$) | $0.56 \pm 0.39$ | $0.65 \pm 0.17$ | $0.59 \pm 0.34$ (0.80) |
| 6.4 | $0.57 \pm 0.38$ | $0.60 \pm 0.21$ | $0.60 \pm 0.33$ (1.04) |
| 12.8 | $0.31 \pm 0.24$ | $0.83 \pm 0.09$ | $0.45 \pm 0.31$ (2.95) |
| 13.2 | $0.36 \pm 0.27$ | $0.82 \pm 0.10$ | $0.49 \pm 0.31$ (3.15) |
| 13.5 ($P_{many}$) | $0.34 \pm 0.26$ | $0.83 \pm 0.11$ | $0.49 \pm 0.32$ (3.53) |
| 16.0 | $0.38 \pm 0.28$ | $0.87 \pm 0.08$ | $0.52 \pm 0.33$ (2.44) |
| 23.9 | $0.26 \pm 0.26$ | $0.89 \pm 0.06$ | $0.50 \pm 0.33$ (3.00) |
| Correlation with RLA median | $-87.1\%$ | $87.5\%$ | $-61.2\%$ (70%) |

lists the results for $\eta$ ranging from 0 (ideal, expensive) to 10. Figure 4a and 4b show the plots. Classification errors result in the selection of a sub-optimal support set for queries and become more common as $\eta$ increases. The added value of our method over the non-query-aware policies it combines stands even with the introduction of a noise as high as $\eta = 10$ (errors observed even on queries with 45 lesions – considered pessimistic). We believe that the observed immunity to errors is due to the small penalty of misclassification near the threshold where errors are more likely to occur.

**Study 4: Support Set Optimization based on the RLA Median.** We quantify the performance of seven support-set selection policies on the model detection accuracy. Table 3 lists the results. Figure 4c details the distribution for the two policies, $P_{few}$ and $P_{many}$. The results demonstrate strong correlation between RLA median and F1 mean on *DMANY*, as well as strong anti-correlation with F1 mean on *DFEW*. This justifies the choice of RLA median as a simple mechanism to control the detection for each type.

## 4   Conclusion

Medical FSS models accept the query- and support-set simultaneously thus allowing us to peek at the query, extract features and utilize its representation to our benefit at inference time. A small set of support scans, limits the variety of cases the network considers and thus increases the risk of overfit. We exploited this risk to our benefit, by matching the support set distribution to the query type, and effectively overfitting to the required query. We demonstrated this approach on the task of liver lesions detection and were able improve F1 score by 5–8.5% with respect to the non-query-aware policies based on the quality of query classification. Future work is planned to refine and automate the computation of the representations of the support- and query-sets to enhance and generalize this method further.

## 5   Disclosure of Interests.

The authors have no competing interests to declare that are relevant to the content of this article.

## References


1. Razzak, M.I., Naz, S., Zaib, A.: Deep learning for medical image processing: overview, challenges and the future. In: Dey, N., Ashour, A., Borra, S. (eds.) Classification in BioApps. LNCVB, vol. 26, pp. 323–350. Springer, Cham (2018). https://doi.org/10.1007/978-3-319-65981-7_12
2. Nemoto, T., et al.: Effects of sample size and data augmentation on U-Net-based automatic segmentation of various organs. Radiol. Phys. Technol. **14**(3), 318–327 (2021)
3. Wu, Y., Xu, M., Ge, Z., Cai, J., Zhang, L.: Semi-supervised left atrium segmentation with mutual consistency training. In: de Bruijne, M., et al. (eds.) Medical Image Computing and Computer Assisted Intervention – MICCAI 2021. MICCAI 2021. LNCS, vol. 12902, pp. 297–306. Springer, Cham (2021). https://doi.org/10.1007/978-3-030-87196-3_28
4. Luo, X., Chen, J., Song, T., Wang, G.: Semi-supervised medical image segmentation through dual-task consistency. In: Proceedings of the AAAI Conference on Artificial Intelligence, vol. 35, no. 10, pp. 8801–8809 (2021)
5. Yu, L., Wang, S., Li, X., Fu, C.W., Heng, P.A.: Uncertainty-aware self-ensembling model for semi-supervised 3D left atrium segmentation. In: Shen, D., et al (eds.) Medical Image Computing and Computer Assisted Intervention – MICCAI 2019. MICCAI 2019. LNCS, vol. 11765, pp. 605–613. Springer Cham (2019). https://doi.org/10.1007/978-3-030-32245-8_67
6. Wu, Y., et al.: Mutual consistency learning for semi-supervised medical image segmentation. Med. Image Anal. **81**, 102530 (2022)
7. Shen, Z., Cao, P., Yang, H., Liu, X., Yang, J., Zaiane, O.: Co-training with high-confidence pseudo labels for semi-supervised medical image segmentation. Proc. 32$^{nd}$ Int. Joint Conference on Artificial Intelligence, pp. 4199–4207. AAAI Organization, California (2023)
8. Bangert, P., Moon, H., Woo, J.O., Didari, S., Hao, H.: Active learning performance in labeling radiology images: is 90% effective? Front. Radiol. **1**, 748968 (2021)
9. Budd, S., Robinson, E., Kainz, B.: A survey on active learning and human-in-the-loop deep learning for medical image analysis. Med. Image Anal. **71**, 102062 (2021)
10. Gaillochet, M., Desrosiers, C., Lombaert, H.: TAAL: test-time augmentation for active learning in medical image segmentation. In: Nguyen, H.V., Huang, S.X., Xue, Y. (eds.) Data Augmentation, Labelling, and Imperfections. DALI 2022. LNCS, vol. 13567, pp. 43–53. Springer, Cham (2022). https://doi.org/10.1007/978-3-031-17027-0_5
11. Khadka, R., et al.: Meta-learning with implicit gradients in a few-shot setting for medical image segmentation. Comput. Biol. Med. **143**, 105227 (2022)
12. Parnami, A, Lee, M.: Learning from few examples: a summary of approaches to Few-Shot Learning. arXiv abs/2203.04291 (2022)
13. Roy, A., Siddiqui, S., Pölsterl, S., Navab, N., Wachinger, C.: 'Squeeze & excite' guided few-shot segmentation of volumetric images. Med. Image Anal. **59**, 101587 (2020)
14. Ouyang, C., Biffi, C., Chen, C., Kart, T., Qiu, H., Rueckert, D.: Self-supervised learning for Few-Shot medical image segmentation. IEEE Trans. Med. Imaging **41**(7), 1837–1848 (2022)
15. Butoi, V.I., Ortiz, J.J.G., Ma, T., Sabuncu, M.R., Guttag, J.V., Dalca A.V.: UniverSeg: universal medical image segmentation. In: Proceedings of the IEEE/CVF Int. Conf. on Computer Vision (ICCV), pp. 21381–21394. IEEE Computer Society, Los Alamitos, CA, USA (2023)

16. Ryabtsev, A., Lederman, R., Sosna, J., Joskowicz, L.: Streamlining the annotation process by radiologists of volumetric medical images with few-shot learning. Int. J. Comput. Aided Radiol. Surg. (2025). https://doi.org/10.1007/s11548-025-03457-3
17. Wasserthal, J., et al.: TotalSegmentator: robust segmentation of 104 anatomic structures in CT images. Radiol. Artif. Intell. **5**(5), e230024 (2023)

# Towards Radar-Driven Speech Therapy: Multimodal Training with Ultrasound, Audio, and Radar for Unimodal Phonetic Segment Classification

Ilhan Aytutuldu$^{(\boxtimes)}$ , Yakup Genc , and Yusuf Sinan Akgul

Department of Computer Engineering, Gebze Technical University, Kocaeli, Turkey
{iaytutuldu,yakup.genc,akgul}@gtu.edu.tr

**Abstract.** This paper addresses the task of phonetic segment classification, a fundamental challenge in speech therapy, and proposes a method that utilizes joint embeddings learned from ultrasound tongue imaging (UTI), audio, and mmWave radar data. To create embeddings, we compiled a collection of raw mmWave radar signals synchronized with ultrasound images and audio, focusing on specific consonants. The embeddings are derived from artificial neural network models trained on this dataset. Additionally, recent advances have introduced jointly trained models that, while leveraging multiple data sources during training, are designed to operate with only a single modality at inference, enhancing practicality without sacrificing performance. During inference, our model, USRadioAI, solely utilizes radar data, excluding UTI and audio, hence improving practicality for potential speech therapy applications. Experimental results show that USRadioAI performs as well as approaches that use both audio and UTI, while outperforming those that rely only on a single modality, such as radar, audio, or UTI, in real-time phonetic classification.

**Keywords:** Millimeter-Wave (mmWave) Radar · Phonetic Classification · Speech Therapy · Ultrasound Tongue Imaging (UTI)

## 1  Introduction

Phonetic segment classification is a fundamental challenge in speech therapy and linguistics, where each phonetic segment is assigned to a predefined class based on audio or imaging data [14]. Traditional unimodal approaches, relying solely on audio or articulatory data, have shown effectiveness in many speech and language processing (SLP) applications [11,16,19]. However, audio-based models struggle with acoustically similar phonemes and noise robustness, while

**Supplementary Information** The online version contains supplementary material available at https://doi.org/10.1007/978-3-032-13961-0_6.


T. Chen et al. (Eds.): EMA4MICCAI 2025 Workshops, LNCS 16318, pp. 51–60, 2026.
https://doi.org/10.1007/978-3-032-13961-0_6

articulatory data, such as ultrasound tongue imaging (UTI), provides valuable complementary insights into speech production, improving classification accuracy [3].

Despite its advantages, UTI-based methods face practical limitations [7,17], including high costs, the need for specialized equipment, and user discomfort during prolonged use [1]. To address these challenges, multimodal approaches that integrate articulatory data with audio have been explored [20]. These methods, such as combining UTI or video-based lip movement analysis with audio, enhance phonetic classification by capturing both internal and external speech articulation [4,9]. However, while UTI provides internal articulatory details [15,18], its practical constraints limit widespread adoption [8]. Similarly, video-based lip movement analysis, though useful for capturing external articulators, lacks information on internal speech dynamics, restricting its effectiveness in fully modeling speech production.

Millimeter-wave (mmWave) radar has been widely adopted in human movement analysis, including applications such as motion tracking, action recognition, and gait analysis [2,5]. Recently, it has also emerged as a promising approach for both audio and articulatory data acquisition in SLP [6,12,13]. It enables contactless and privacy-preserving tracking of speech signals and articulatory movements, including the jaw, lips, teeth, tongue, and vocal cords. Despite its advantages, its potential for phonetic segment classification remains under-explored.

This paper proposes a multimodal learning approach that integrates mmWave radar, ultrasound tongue imaging (UTI), and audio data to improve phonetic segment classification. Our method leverages the strengths of each modality during training while ensuring that the model operates using only mmWave radar at inference, eliminating the need for UTI or audio input. To achieve this, we construct a joint embedding space that captures articulatory and acoustic features, allowing the model to generalize phonetic representations effectively.

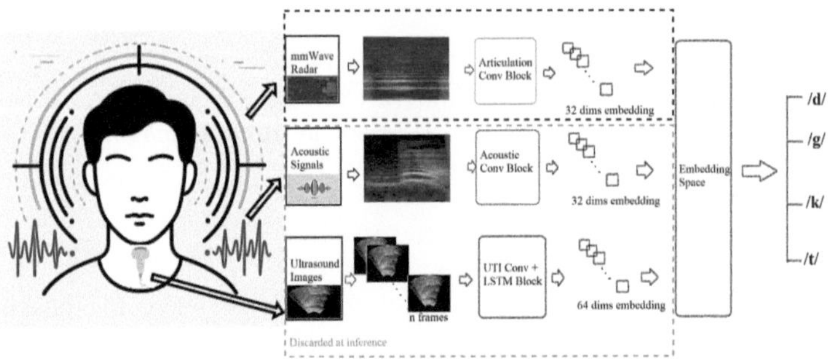


**Fig. 1.** System overview of a multimodal speech and language processing framework integrating mmWave radar, audio signals, and ultrasound tongue imaging (UTI). During training, each modality undergoes feature extraction through convolutional and LSTM-based blocks to generate embeddings, which are mapped into a shared embedding space for phoneme classification.

## 2  Joint Embedding and Radar-Driven Classification

We introduce USRadioAI, a radar-driven approach that leverages a joint embedding space for phonetic segment classification. To construct this embedding space, we employ mmWave radar, audio, and UTI data within the introduced deep neural network, called MMnet (Fig. 1). The MMnet model, in its design, requires a device equipped with mmWave sensing capabilities, a microphone, and a UTI device to extract features and map them into the joint embedding space.

### 2.1  Joint Embedding Space

To develop a robust phonetic segment classification system, we implemented neural network architectures, each designed to extract meaningful representations from different sensing modalities. Figure 2 illustrates two key architectures contributing to the phonetics embedding space.

The first network (Fig. 2a) integrates spatiotemporal features by employing Convolutional Neural Networks (CNNs) for feature extraction, followed by TimeDistributed layers and BiDirectional Long Short-Term Memory (BiLSTM) networks to capture sequential dependencies. This model processes ultrasound tongue imaging (UTI) data and generates a 64-dimensional embedding, encapsulating articulatory movements. The second network (Fig. 2b) focuses on mmWave radar (top) and acoustic sensing (bottom), using stacked CNN layers to extract spectro-temporal patterns and producing a 32-dimensional embedding.

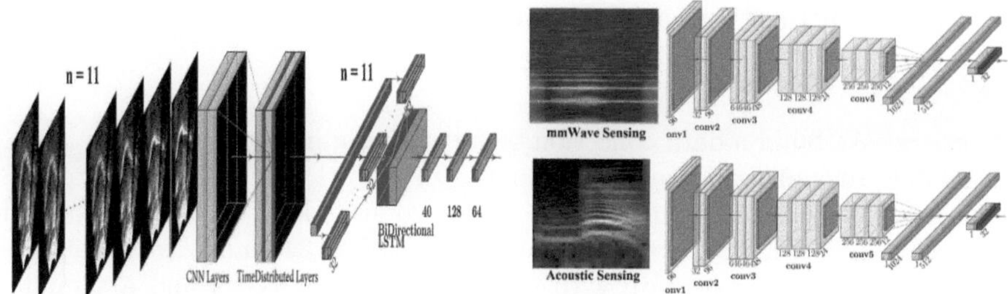


(a) This network finally employs dense layers to produce a 64-dimensional embedding from the data, encompassing UTI.

(b) 32-dimensional embedding generated for mmWave and acoustic sensing.

**Fig. 2.** The sub-components of the phonetics embedding space (MMnet).

### 2.2  Radar-Driven Classification

During training, we create a joint embedding space that captures shared features across radar, audio, and UTI data. However, at inference, we only extract

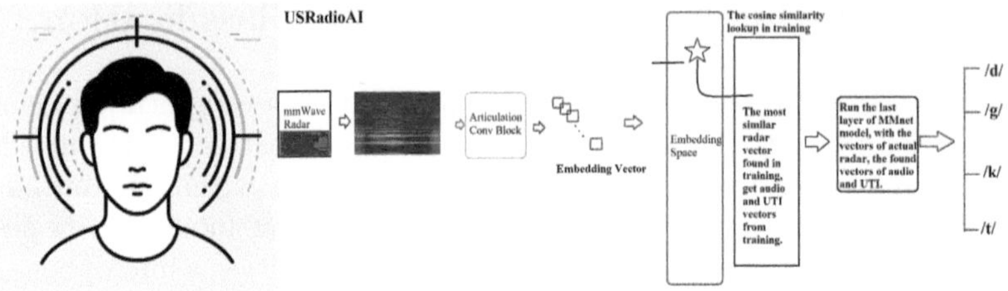


**Fig. 3.** USRadioAI's inference process, where radar embeddings are matched to the closest training embeddings using cosine similarity. Missing audio and UTI representations are inferred, enhancing feature extraction and phonetic classification with radar-only input.

embeddings from radar, using the trained network to process mmWave sensing separately.

During inference, USRadioAI estimates the missing audio and UTI data by finding the radar embeddings most similar to the joint embedding space. Specifically, we compare the extracted radar embeddings to those stored in the embedding space during training and select the closest matches by cosine similarity [3]. These matched embeddings provide the corresponding audio and UTI representations, allowing us to reconstruct the missing modalities (Fig. 3). The inferred representations are then combined with real-time radar data, enhancing feature extraction and improving the robustness of phonetic classification.

## 3   Implementation and Experiments

### 3.1   Data Collection

*Hardware:* We build a data collection setup[1], as seen in Fig. 4, to gather multimodal data to train, validate, and evaluate USRadioAI. We collect synchronized audio with Shure Beta 58a microphone, sampled at 48 kHZ, and UTI data with [10], radar data using a Texas Instruments (TI) IWR1843 mmWave radar. The radar is configured to operate with a bandwidth of 3.89 GHz and a sampling rate of 25600 Hz. For synchronization, the ultrasound device runs continuously for the entire session (around 2 min) while being synchronized with audio. The mmWave radar starts separately, with a ping sound played at the beginning of each capture to align recordings. This allows for offline synchronization using the known signal. A ping sound is played at the beginning of each capture to cue the speaker and align the ultrasound device with radar recording. The video[2] illustrates this process. Note that our experiments were conducted in an actual speech therapy room actively used for clinical purposes.

---

[1] Please find the publicly available assets on GitHub at the following: https://github.com/iaytutu1/EMA4MICCAI2025.

[2] See a sample from our setup on GitHub: CollectionSetup.mp4.

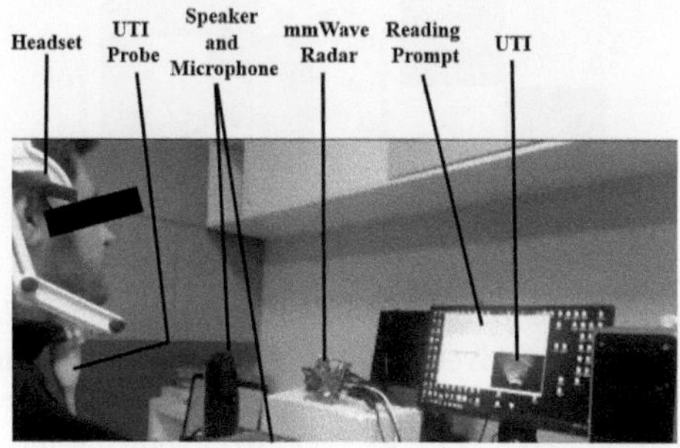


**Fig. 4.** Data Collection Setup.

The processing pipeline converts raw mmWave radar ADC data into spectrograms. The data is loaded, padded, and structured into frames, then aligned using DCA1000 processing. After averaging across channels and flattening, the signal undergoes Short-Time Fourier Transform, generating a decibel-scaled spectrogram for time-frequency analysis.

*Participants:* We engage 6 participants, comprising only native speakers, to perform phonetic readings. The participants in our study are native speakers, consisting of two women and four men, ranging in age from 18 to 65. All participants exhibit normal speech abilities without any speaking difficulties. In our experimental setup, speech data from five speakers were utilized for training, while an additional speaker, unseen during training, was exclusively designated for testing to evaluate the model's generalization capability. A total of 2,400 utterances were articulated, incorporating four distinct phonetic consonants (represented by /d/, /g/, /k/, /t/ in International Phonetic Alphabet). An auditory cue (a ping sound) was played for each data capture, asking the participant to speak the utterance immediately after the sound ended. During data collection, participants were positioned approximately 50 cm away from the radio device. They read each word at a regular speaking volume while minimizing excessive movement to ensure data quality.

### 3.2   UTI-Based Classification Using UTI Data for both Training and Inference

We investigated phonetic segment classification using UTI. Certain phonemes, like /k/ and /g/ or /t/ and /d/, share similar articulatory patterns, making them difficult to distinguish in UTI images.

Initially, a four-class classification task (/k/, /g/, /t/, /d/) yielded inconsistent results (Fig. 5(a)), suggesting that UTI-based models struggle to differentiate voiced and unvoiced phoneme pairs. Reformulating the task as a binary classification (velar vs. alveolar) significantly improved performance (Fig. 5(b)), indicating that while UTI alone may not enable fine-grained phoneme classification, it effectively distinguishes broader articulatory categories. This experiment

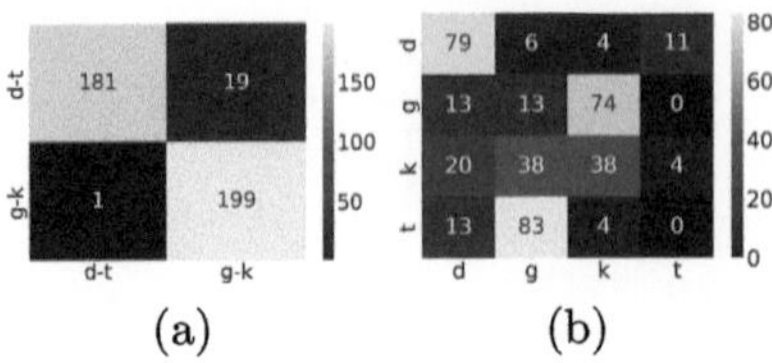

(a)          (b)

**Fig. 5.** Confusion matrices for phoneme classification using UTI. (a) Binary classification task (velar: /k/, /g/ vs. alveolar: /d/, /t/) demonstrating improved accuracy, confirming the effectiveness of UTI in distinguishing broader articulatory categories. (b) Four-class classification task (/k/, /g/, /t/, /d/) showing inconsistent performance due to similar articulatory patterns.

highlights the importance of multimodal approaches, where additional information, such as acoustic or radar data, could enhance phoneme discrimination beyond what is possible with UTI alone.

## 3.3  Unimodal vs. Multimodal Classification

This section presents model implementations, experimental results, and performance comparisons, highlighting the advantages of our phonetic segment classification approach over existing methods.

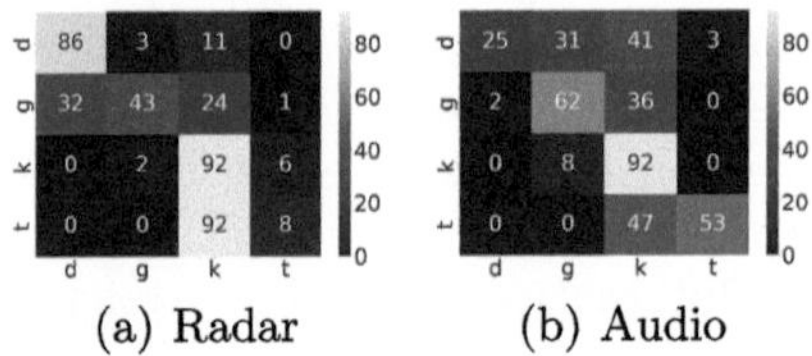

(a) Radar          (b) Audio

**Fig. 6.** Comparison of phoneme classification using (a) radar and (b) audio.

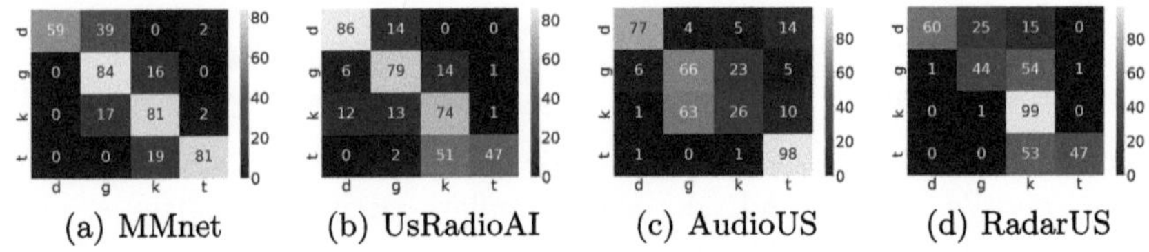

(a) MMnet          (b) UsRadioAI          (c) AudioUS          (d) RadarUS

**Fig. 7.** The results of our proposed architectures on test data show that the MMnet model outperforms in the classification task of phonetics segments.

The classification results highlight distinct advantages of only audio and only radar phoneme recognition. Radar struggles to differentiate /k/ and /t/ since both are voiceless and lack vocal cord vibrations, making it difficult to distinguish their articulatory movements (Fig. 6(a)). However, radar performs better in distinguishing /k/ and /g/, as it captures subtle articulatory differences that UTI struggles with. In contrast (Fig. 6(b)), audio excels at differentiating voiceless phonemes, as it captures aspiration and high-frequency bursts, making it more effective for /k/ and /t/ classification. However, radar outperforms audio in recognizing voiced phonemes like /d/ and /g/, as it tracks articulatory motion more effectively, while audio tends to confuse them due to their similar spectral features.

*Incorporating UTI with Audio (Fig. 6(b) vs. Fig. 7(c)):* This significantly impacts phoneme classification, both improving and introducing new challenges. One key improvement is in distinguishing /t/ and /k/, where audio alone struggled, but UTI helps reduce misclassification due to its ability to track tongue movement. However, the addition of UTI negatively affects /k/ and /g/ classification, as UTI struggles to differentiate these phonemes due to their similar dorsal tongue positioning. While audio alone handled /k/ and /g/ better, adding UTI increases confusion between them. These findings indicate that while multimodal fusion enhances classification for some phonemes, it can also introduce new ambiguities, highlighting the need for careful modality selection and feature integration.

**Table 1.** Accuracy and modalities for phoneme classification with our proposed architectures.

| Test Accuracy | Model | Training | | | Inference | | |
|---|---|---|---|---|---|---|---|
| | | UTI | Audio | mmWave | UTI | Audio | mmWave |
| 0.33 | US | + | | | + | | |
| 0.57 | Radar | | | + | | | + |
| 0.58 | Audio | | + | | | + | |
| 0.60 | RadioAudio | | + | + | | + | + |
| 0.62 | RadioUS | + | | + | + | | + |
| 0.67 | AudioUS | + | + | | + | + | |
| 0.71 | USRadioAI | + | + | + | | | + |
| 0.76 | MMnet | + | + | + | + | + | + |

*Incorporating UTI with Radar (Fig. 6(a) vs. Fig. 7(d)):* This significantly (5%) improves phoneme classification performance, particularly for /k/ and /t/, which were difficult to distinguish using radar alone (Table 1). This suggests that UTI effectively captures tongue movement, compensating for radar's limitations in tracking voiceless phonemes. Additionally, /d/ and /g/, which were frequently confused in the radar-driven model, show improved separation when UTI is added, indicating that articulatory data enhances classification of voiced phonemes. However, the inclusion of UTI also introduces new errors, particularly increasing misclassifications of /d/ with other phonemes. This highlights the need for careful fusion of modalities, as while UTI enhances some distinctions, it may also introduce noise in certain cases.

*Comparing MMNet and USRadioAI: Accuracy vs. Practicality:* MMNet achieves the highest accuracy at 76%, benefiting from the combined power of UTI, audio, and radar during both training and inference (Table 1, Fig. 8). However, this requires multiple devices, making it less practical for real-world deployment. In contrast, USRadioAI—trained with all modalities but running only on radar— offers a much more practical and cost-effective solution while still achieving 71% accuracy. This marks a significant improvement over the radar-only model, which lags behind at 57%, demonstrating the power of multimodal training even when only radar is used at inference. Although USRadioAI performs slightly lower than MMNet, the trade-off in practicality makes it an ideal choice for real-world applications, eliminating the need for multiple devices while still ensuring robust classification performance.

Our results align with the literature, where some studies relied solely on UTI [14], while others integrated video and audio for fusion [3,21], despite differences in datasets.

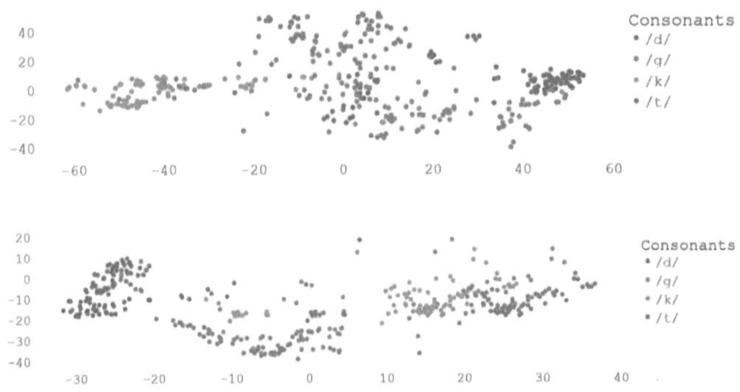

**Fig. 8.** We used t-SNE to project the final classification layer's output vectors into 2D space for visualization. MMnet (top) and USRadioAI (bottom).

## 4   Conclusions

While the proposed system demonstrates promising results in radar-driven phonetic classification, it offers key strengths in privacy, portability, and multimodal training strategies. However, limitations such as the small dataset size and limited speaker diversity highlight areas for further improvement. Future work will focus on expanding dataset diversity, enhancing model robustness, and implementing radar-based gamification features to maximize the clinical applicability and user engagement of speech therapy applications.

**Acknowledgments.** This work was supported by the Health Institutes of Türkiye (TUSEB) C-YZ Project (No. 33944) and by Gebze Technical University Scientific Research Projects (No. 2023-A-102-04). The authors like to thank both institutions for their financial support. The authors also thank Assoc. Prof. Ramazan Sertan Özdemir, Assoc. Prof. Talat Bulut, and Research Assistant Ezgi Apaydın from the Department of Speech and Language Therapy and MEDKOM Research Group at Medipol University for their kind support in data collection.

**Disclosure of Interests.** The authors have no competing interests to declare that are relevant to the content of this article.

# References


1. Annand, C.T., et al.: Using ultrasound imaging to create augmented visual biofeedback for articulatory practice. In: INTERSPEECH, pp. 974–975 (2019)
2. Aytutuldu, I., Bilici, Z., Genc, Y., Akgul, Y.S.: Indoor human counting based on range-doppler spectrum in the presence of material penetration and occlusion. In: 2024 6th International Conference on Communications, Signal Processing, and their Applications (ICCSPA), pp. 1–5. IEEE (2024)
3. Aytutuldu, I., Genc, Y., Akgul, Y.S.: Audio-only phonetic segment classification using embeddings learned from audio and ultrasound tongue imaging data. IEEE/ACM Trans. Audio Speech Lang. Process. (2024)
4. Beeson, R., Richmond, K.: Silent speech recognition with articulator positions estimated from tongue ultrasound and lip video. In: Interspeech 2023, pp. 1149–1153. ISCA (2023)
5. Bilici, Z., Aytutuldu, I., Genc, Y., Akgul, Y.S.: mmWave frequency modulated continuous wave radar-based human action recognition. In: 2024 32nd Signal Processing and Communications Applications Conference (SIU), pp. 1–4. IEEE (2024)
6. Chen, F., Li, S., Zhang, Y., Wang, J.: Detection of the vibration signal from human vocal folds using a 94-ghz millimeter-wave radar. Sensors **17**(3), 543 (2017)
7. Chen, T., et al.: Ultrasound image-to-video synthesis via latent dynamic diffusion models. In: proceedings of Medical Image Computing and Computer Assisted Intervention – MICCAI 2024. LNCS, vol. 15004. Springer, Cham (2024). https://doi.org/10.1007/978-3-031-72083-3_71
8. Cleland, J.: Ultrasound tongue imaging in research and practice with people with cleft palate±cleft lip. Cleft Palate Craniofacial J. 10556656231202448 (2023)
9. Eshky, A., Cleland, J., Ribeiro, M.S., Sugden, E., Richmond, K., Renals, S.: Automatic audiovisual synchronisation for ultrasound tongue imaging. Speech Commun. **132**, 83–95 (2021)
10. Instruments, A.: Articulate assistant advanced user guide: Version 2.16. Articulate Instruments Ltd (2012)
11. Loizou, P.C.: Speech Enhancement: Theory and Practice. CRC Press, Boca Raton (2007)
12. Ozturk, M.Z., Wu, C., Wang, B., Liu, K.R.: Sound recovery from radio signals. In: ICASSP 2021-2021 IEEE International Conference on Acoustics, Speech and Signal Processing (ICASSP), pp. 8022–8026. IEEE (2021)
13. Ozturk, M.Z., Wu, C., Wang, B., Liu, K.R.: Radiomic: sound sensing via radio signals. IEEE Internet Things J. **10**(5), 4431–4448 (2022)

14. Ribeiro, M.S., Eshky, A., Richmond, K., Renals, S.: Speaker-independent classification of phonetic segments from raw ultrasound in child speech. In: ICASSP 2019-2019 IEEE International Conference on Acoustics, Speech and Signal Processing (ICASSP), pp. 1328–1332. IEEE (2019)
15. Tatulli, E., Hueber, T.: Feature extraction using multimodal convolutional neural networks for visual speech recognition. In: 2017 IEEE International Conference on Acoustics, Speech and Signal Processing (ICASSP), pp. 2971–2975. IEEE (2017)
16. Wang, D., Brown, G.J.: Computational Auditory Scene Analysis: Principles, Algorithms, and Applications. Wiley-IEEE press, Hoboken (2006)
17. Wu, H., et al.: Towards multi-modality fusion and prototype-based feature refinement for clinically significant prostate cancer classification in transrectal ultrasound. In: proceedings of Medical Image Computing and Computer Assisted Intervention – MICCAI 2024. LNCS, vol. 15005. Springer, Heidelberg (2024)
18. Xu, K., Roussel, P., Csapó, T.G., Denby, B.: Convolutional neural network-based automatic classification of midsagittal tongue gestural targets using b-mode ultrasound images. J. Acoust. Soc. Am. **141**(6), EL531–EL537 (2017)
19. Xu, Y., Du, J., Dai, L.R., Lee, C.H.: A regression approach to speech enhancement based on deep neural networks. IEEE/ACM Trans. Audio Speech Lang. Process. **23**(1), 7–19 (2014)
20. Zheng, R.C., Ai, Y., Ling, Z.H.: Incorporating ultrasound tongue images for audio-visual speech enhancement. IEEE/ACM Trans. Audio Speech Lang. Process. **32**, 1430–1444 (2024). https://doi.org/10.1109/TASLP.2024.3361376
21. Zheng, R.C., Ai, Y., Ling, Z.H.: Incorporating ultrasound tongue images for audio-visual speech enhancement. IEEE/ACM Trans. Audio Speech Lang. Process. (2024)

# EU-Net: Efficient Training of U-Net for Biomedical Image Segmentation


Lujia Zhong[1,2], Shuo Huang[1,3], and Yonggang Shi[1,2,3(✉)]

[1] Stevens Neuroimaging and Informatics Institute, Keck School of Medicine, University of Southern California (USC), Los Angeles, CA 90033, USA
[2] Ming Hsieh Department of Electrical and Computer Engineering, Viterbi School of Engineering, University of Southern California (USC), Los Angeles, CA 90089, USA
[3] Alfred E. Mann Department of Biomedical Engineering, Viterbi School of Engineering, University of Southern California (USC), Los Angeles, CA 90089, USA
yshi@loni.usc.edu



**Abstract.** Deep learning has revolutionized many fields, including computer vision, natural language processing, medical imaging, etc., through its ability to process complex data and learn discriminative representations. However, training deep learning models often requires substantial computational resources, leading to high energy consumption and unignorable environmental impact. The urgency of developing training-efficient methods to alleviate such influence is increasing, especially as the scaling laws are widely adopted in various research domains, requiring increasing computation to train a stronger model. In this work, building on the principles of backpropagation sparsification, we propose EU-Net, an efficient way of training U-Net in terms of backpropagation FLOPs and time consumption, and demonstrate its efficacy on multiple biomedical image segmentation tasks. Unlike previous methods that rely on top-k selection to keep the most important gradients, our approach adopts Bernoulli random subsampling with an interleaved subsampling schedule, achieving a balance of gradient direction and computation efficiency. We also mathematically prove the guaranteed convergence of our method under common optimization assumptions. We validate our approach on 20 biomedical segmentation tasks, demonstrating its ability to handle diverse data distributions and scales while maintaining computational efficiency. Experimental results show that our approach reduces the backpropagation FLOPs by 40% and time consumption by 20% while keeping comparable and even improved model performance compared to normal training. Code is available at https://github.com/lujiazho/EU-Net.

**Keywords:** Efficient Training · Backpropagation Sparsification · Gradient Subsampling · U-Net


## 1 Introduction

The rapid advancement of deep learning has come at a steep environmental and computational cost. Training state-of-the-art models like OpenAI's GPT-4 [1], vision-language systems [3,6,19], and video generation models [4,14,17]



T. Chen et al. (Eds.): EMA4MICCAI 2025 Workshops, LNCS 16318, pp. 61–71, 2026.
https://doi.org/10.1007/978-3-032-13961-0_7

demands billions of petaFLOPs, translating to unignorable financial costs and significant carbon emissions [15,21,24,25]. This inefficiency harms both sustainable AI development and the pace of research. Recent efforts in natural language modeling like DeepSeek-R1 [9] and sparse attention [28] demonstrate that optimized training frameworks can achieve competitive performance with drastically reduced costs, underscoring the power and urgency of efficiency solutions. Similar initiatives are equally crucial in the biomedical image processing domain, particularly given the widespread adoption of U-Net architecture and its versatility in adapting to even general computer vision tasks. This shows potential for advancing efficient training methodologies that not only optimize performance but also substantially reduce the carbon footprint.

While techniques like initialization [7,10], normalization [13,26], and decorrelation [2,5] improve training efficiency by accelerating model convergence, sparsification remains a major technique for directly reducing computational overhead. Prior sparsification approaches, such as gradient pruning [18,20,23,27] and gradient approximation [8,22,29,31], often suffer from narrow applicability, accuracy trade-offs, or hardware-specific dependencies, limiting their utility for real-world deployment. While ssProp [30] addresses these gaps through PyTorch-compatible channel-wise sparsity, its generality to medical image segmentation hasn't been proved, which usually involves small datasets and requires dense gradient during backpropagation compared to classification tasks. Besides, Top-K strategies are commonly used by sparsification works [20,22], including ssProp [30], which even introduce additional overhead for training speed.

In this work, we propose EU-Net, a novel subsampling strategy for CNN architecture with hardware-agnostic implementation by utilizing PyTorch native functions. Hence, our method can be applied to any U-Net architecture that involves CNN modules on any machine. Unlike ssProp, our subsampling schedule adapts to gradient magnitudes based on iteration instead of epoch to stabilize the training. Besides, we replace the top-K selection with Bernoulli random subsampling to further improve the training speed, enabling biased-gradients correction interleavedly without sacrificing critical learning signals for weights update direction. We further provide a theoretical analysis proving convergence guarantees under non-convex optimization assumptions. Extensive experiments on biomedical segmentation datasets demonstrate that our approach reduces backward-pass FLOPs by 40% and time consumption by 20% while maintaining and even improving model performance, validating its efficacy for sustainable, high-performance biomedical AI development.

## 2    Method

In this work, we introduce efficient training for U-Net (EU-Net) on biomedical segmentation tasks by subsampling back-propagation gradients during training. Inspired by ssProp [30], we keep the channel-level sparsification technique because of its generality, making it adaptable to any task and architecture that involves convolutional neural networks. The overall workflow is illustrated in

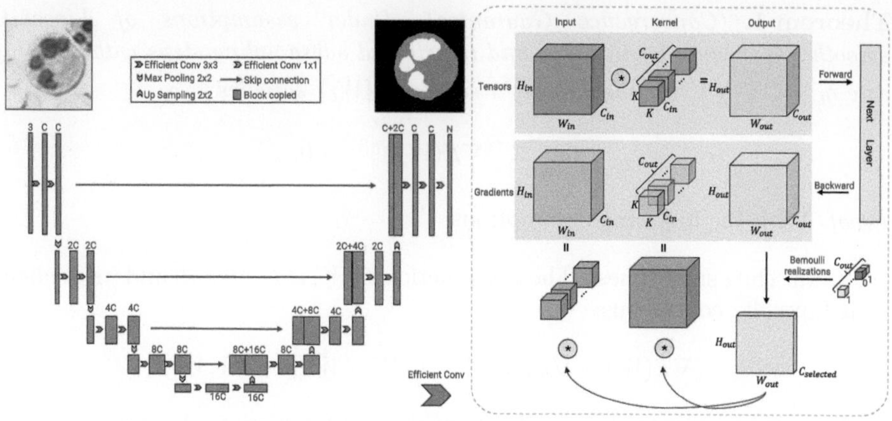

**Fig. 1.** Overall workflow of proposed EU-Net. Left: a common U-Net architecture with convolution layers being replaced by our efficient CNN module. Right: proposed efficient convolution layer, where the backward gradients are subsampled according to Bernoulli distribution. Backward operations are simplified using a convolution sign for clarity.

Fig. 1, where the batch size $Bt$ is omitted for clarity without losing generality. Given one layer of CNN, we denote the gradient map of the output as $grad\_O$ in the shape of $(Bt, C_{out}, H_{out}, W_{out})$. The ssProp calculates channel importance by taking absolute values on $grad\_O$ and averaging over all dimensions except the output channel, ending up with an importance vector in the shape of $(C_{out})$. Then, the top-K algorithm is applied to select the most important K channels for gradient propagation and the other channels are discarded. However, the summation, absolute operation, and sorting algorithm are applied for each CNN layer throughout the entire training process, introducing additional computational overhead. Therefore, we adopt a Bernoulli random subsampling strategy to discard a subset of channels of $grad\_O$. We empirically found that random subsampling performs well when combined with gradient direction correction through iteration-interleaved subsampling. We choose the subsampling rate $p = 0.2$, i.e. only 20% of the channels are retained in each subsampling step.

As for the subsampling scheduling, we adopt an iteration-based interleaving scheduler, which means that, for each CNN layer, we utilize normal training with full gradients for odd iterations (1, 3, ...) and randomly sample 20% gradients channel-wisely for backpropagation and discard the rest for even iterations (2, 4, ...). In this way, the gradient direction correction can be timely applied to stabilize the training, making the subsampling period independent of the dataset scales.

Besides, we mathematically show that our method has a convergence guarantee under common non-convex optimization assumptions.

**Theorem 1.** *(Convergence Guarantee). Under assumptions of Lipschitz smoothness, bounded gradients, and interleaved subsampling steps with learning rate $\eta_t = \mathcal{O}\left(\frac{1}{\sqrt{t}}\right)$, the model weight sequence $\{W_t\}$ satisfies:*

$$\lim_{T\to\infty} \mathbb{E}\left[\|\nabla\mathcal{L}(W_T)\|^2\right] = 0.$$

*Proof.* With the following assumptions:

1. $L$-Lipschitz smoothness. The loss function $\mathcal{L}(W)$ is $L$-smooth and its gradient is Lipschitz continuous:

$$\|\nabla\mathcal{L}(W) - \nabla\mathcal{L}(W')\| \le L\|W - W'\|, \quad \forall W, Wn'.$$

2. Bounded gradients. The gradients of the loss function are bounded:

$$\exists G > 0, \quad \forall W, \quad \|\nabla\mathcal{L}(W)\| \le G.$$

3. Subsampled gradients. With subsampling rate $p \in (0, 1)$ subject to Bernoulli distribution, the gradient estimates $\hat{g}_t$ satisfy the following properties:

$$\mathbb{E}_t[\hat{g}_t] = p\nabla\mathcal{L}(W_t) \quad \text{and} \quad \mathbb{E}_t[\|\hat{g}_t\|^2] \le pG^2.$$

In fact, the quadratic upper bound holds for any iteration $t$ of stochastic gradient descent (SGD):

$$\mathcal{L}(W_{t+1}) \le \mathcal{L}(W_t) - \eta_t\langle\nabla\mathcal{L}(W_t), g_t\rangle + \frac{L\eta_t^2}{2}\|g_t\|^2.$$

where $g_t$ stands for $\nabla\mathcal{L}(W_t)$ and $\hat{g}_t$ for full steps and subsampled steps, respectively. By applying conditional and total expectation, we have:

$$\mathbb{E}[\mathcal{L}(W_{t+1}) - \mathcal{L}(W_t)] \le \begin{cases} -\eta_t\mathbb{E}[\|\nabla\mathcal{L}(W_t)\|^2] + \frac{L\eta_t^2}{2}\mathbb{E}[\|\nabla\mathcal{L}(W_t)\|^2], & \text{if full,} \\[2mm] -\eta_t p\mathbb{E}[\|\nabla\mathcal{L}(W_t)\|^2] + \frac{L\eta_t^2}{2}pG^2, & \text{if subsampled.} \end{cases}$$

By telescoping the sum over T iterations and simplifying, we have:

$$\sum_{t\in T_{\text{full}}} \mathbb{E}\|\nabla\mathcal{L}(W_t)\|^2 + p\sum_{t\in T_{\text{sub}}} \mathbb{E}\|\nabla\mathcal{L}(W_t)\|^2 \le \frac{\mathcal{L}(W_1) - \mathcal{L}^*}{\eta_t} + \frac{L\eta_t TG^2}{4}(1 + p).$$

where $T_{\text{full}} = T_{\text{sub}} = \frac{T}{2}$ and $\mathcal{L}^*$ indicates the optimal loss; the left-hand side (LHS) has the lower bound $p\sum_{t=1}^{T} \mathbb{E}\|\nabla\mathcal{L}(W_t)\|^2$. Choosing learning rate $\eta_t = \frac{\eta_0}{\sqrt{t}}$ and take the minimum of the LHS:

$$\min_{t \in [T]} \mathbb{E}\|\nabla \mathcal{L}(W_t)\|^2 \leq \frac{\mathcal{L}(W_1) - \mathcal{L}^*}{\eta_0 \frac{T}{\sqrt{t}} p} + \frac{L\eta_0(1+p)G^2}{4p\sqrt{t}} \overset{t \to T}{=} \mathcal{O}\left(\frac{1}{\sqrt{T}}\right).$$

Thus, as $T \to \infty$, $\mathcal{O}(1/\sqrt{T}) \to 0$, proving:

$$\lim_{T \to \infty} \mathbb{E}\left[\|\nabla \mathcal{L}(W_T)\|^2\right] = 0.$$

Therefore, our interleaved subsampling method eventually converges to a stationary point with rate $\mathcal{O}(1/\sqrt{T})$. The full steps correct the gradient direction while the subsampling steps reduce computation without destabilizing the process. We empirically show that the convergence theorem still holds for the Adam optimizer with a small constant learning rate in the experiment section.

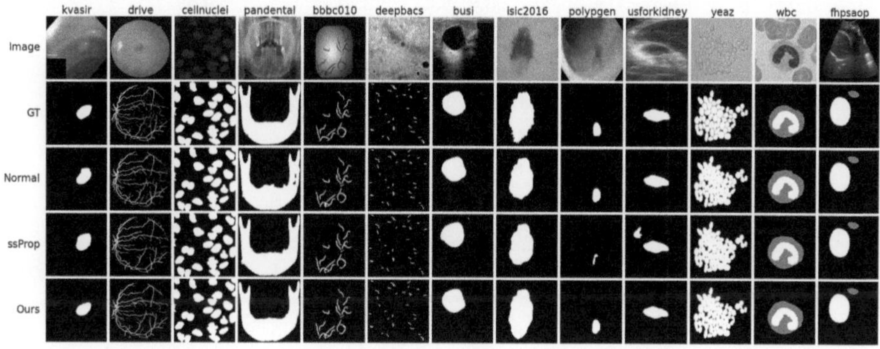


**Fig. 2.** Qualitative comparison. The last two columns are multi-class datasets.

## 3    Experiments

### 3.1    Implementation

We adopt the PyTorch built-in backward implementation to make it compatible with any model architecture and physical machine. We demonstrate the efficacy of our method on 20 biomedical datasets with varying scales and class numbers from MedSegBench [16], using two different U-Net backbones of ResNet-18 and ResNet-50 [11]. All models are trained for 200 epochs with three different seeds without data augmentation and initialization from pre-trained models for simplicity. Implementations of models follow [12]. For both binary and multiclass segmentation tasks, we set spatial image sizes of (256, 256) and use optimizers of Adam with learning rate of 1e-3 and default hyperparameters. Following [16], we use dice Loss and cross-entropy loss, respectively, for binary and multiclass segmentation tasks. We use pixel $F_1$ score and intersection over union (IOU) for model performance evaluation; use backpropagation time and FLOPs for efficiency evaluation. All experiments are conducted with a single 48G NVIDIA RTX A6000 GPU. The computation of the backward FLOPs consumption follow the calculation formula as described in ssProp [30].

**Table 1.** Performance metrics (F1 and IOU) on binary segmentaion tasks under ssProp and normal configurations. Each cell contains metric value for U-Net with backbones of ResNet18/ResNet50. The unerve stands for ultrasoundnerve.

| Dataset | Backbone | F1 (%) | IOU (%) | Time (min) | FLOPs (Quad.) |
|---|---|---|---|---|---|
| deepbacs | ResNet-18/50 | 90.8/90.8 | 83.2/83.1 | **0.3/0.5** | 0.17/0.27 |
|  | ssProp-18/50 | **91.1/90.8** | **83.8/83.1** | 0.3/0.6 | **0.10/0.16** |
| drive | ResNet-18/50 | 77.5/77.3 | 63.4/63.1 | **0.3/0.5** | 0.18/0.29 |
|  | ssProp-18/50 | **78.0/77.3** | **64.1/63.2** | 0.3/0.6 | **0.11/0.17** |
| bbbc010 | ResNet-18/50 | 90.7/90.8 | 83.3/83.3 | **1.0/1.4** | 0.69/1.11 |
|  | ssProp-18/50 | **91.1/91.0** | **83.9/83.7** | 1.1/1.5 | **0.41/0.67** |
| pandental | ResNet-18/50 | 96.0/**96.1** | 92.3/**92.5** | **0.9/1.5** | 0.80/1.28 |
|  | ssProp-18/50 | **96.0**/95.9 | **92.4**/92.2 | 0.9/1.5 | **0.48/0.77** |
| nuclei | ResNet-18/50 | 20.3/17.1 | 11.6/9.6 | **1.1/1.7** | 0.97/1.56 |
|  | ssProp-18/50 | **21.8/18.5** | **12.6/10.5** | 1.1/1.8 | **0.58/0.94** |
| busi | ResNet-18/50 | **68.8/66.6** | **60.2/56.6** | 4.4/6.8 | 4.44/7.17 |
|  | ssProp-18/50 | 67.0/64.1 | 57.0/53.4 | 4.6/7.1 | **2.67/4.31** |
| cellnuclei | ResNet-18/50 | **91.0/91.2** | **84.1/84.4** | 4.6/7.1 | 4.65/7.47 |
|  | ssProp-18/50 | 89.8/90.1 | 82.5/82.9 | 4.8/7.4 | **2.79/4.50** |
| yeaz | ResNet-18/50 | **94.8/94.8** | **90.3/90.2** | 3.5/5.5 | 3.54/5.71 |
|  | ssProp-18/50 | 94.5/94.3 | 89.7/89.4 | 3.6/5.7 | **2.13/3.43** |
| kvasir | ResNet-18/50 | 71.4/70.9 | **62.9/61.9** | **6.8/10.6** | 6.94/11.16 |
|  | ssProp-18/50 | **71.9/71.5** | 62.8/61.8 | 7.0/11.0 | **4.17/6.71** |
| cystoidfluid | ResNet-18/50 | **85.0/85.0** | **75.6**/75.4 | **6.8/10.6** | 6.97/11.20 |
|  | ssProp-18/50 | 84.8/**85.0** | 75.3/**75.6** | 7.1/11.1 | **4.19/6.74** |
| isic2016 | ResNet-18/50 | **88.7/88.3** | **81.5/81.0** | 7.9/12.2 | 8.03/12.91 |
|  | ssProp-18/50 | 88.0/87.5 | 80.7/80.1 | 8.2/12.8 | **4.83/7.76** |
| brifiseg | ResNet-18/50 | 76.5/75.8 | 62.8/62.0 | **9.7/15.1** | 9.88/15.93 |
|  | ssProp-18/50 | **77.1/77.5** | **63.6/64.1** | 10.1/15.9 | **5.94/9.58** |
| polypgen | ResNet-18/50 | 53.8/**53.2** | **46.1/45.7** | **9.4/15.0** | 9.75/15.68 |
|  | ssProp-18/50 | **54.2**/48.9 | 46.0/40.8 | 9.8/15.6 | **5.86/9.43** |
| unerve | ResNet-18/50 | 78.4/**78.5** | 67.0/**67.2** | **15.8/25.1** | 16.23/26.18 |
|  | ssProp-18/50 | **78.5**/78.1 | **67.4**/66.8 | 16.5/26.3 | **9.76/15.74** |
| usforkidney | ResNet-18/50 | **98.0/97.8** | **96.2/95.8** | **30.9/49.1** | 31.55/50.89 |
|  | ssProp-18/50 | 97.8/97.7 | 95.7/95.5 | 32.3/51.4 | **18.97/30.61** |
| covid19radio | ResNet-18/50 | 99.1/99.1 | 98.2/98.2 | **142.3/226.3** | 145.59/234.87 |
|  | ssProp-18/50 | **99.1/99.1** | **98.2/98.2** | 148.8/237.1 | **87.53/141.27** |

**Table 2.** Performance metrics (F1 and IOU) on binary segmentaion tasks under ours and normal configurations. Each cell contains metric value for U-Net with backbones of ResNet18/ResNet50. The unerve stands for ultrasoundnerve.

| Dataset | Backbone | F1 (%) | IOU (%) | Time (min) | FLOPs (Quad.) |
|---|---|---|---|---|---|
| deepbacs | ResNet-18/50 | 90.8/90.8 | 83.2/83.1 | **0.3/0.5** | 0.17/0.27 |
|  | Ours-18/50 | **91.1/90.8** | **83.7/83.1** | 0.3/0.6 | **0.10/0.16** |
| drive | ResNet-18/50 | 77.5/77.3 | 63.4/63.1 | **0.3/0.5** | 0.18/0.29 |
|  | Ours-18/50 | **78.0/77.5** | **64.0/63.4** | 0.3/0.7 | **0.11/0.17** |
| bbbc010 | ResNet-18/50 | 90.7/90.8 | 83.3/83.3 | **1.0/1.4** | 0.69/1.11 |
|  | Ours-18/50 | **91.0/91.1** | **83.7/83.8** | 1.2/1.5 | **0.41/0.67** |
| pandental | ResNet-18/50 | **96.0/96.1** | **92.3/92.5** | 0.9/1.5 | 0.80/1.28 |
|  | Ours-18/50 | 95.9/95.9 | 92.2/92.1 | **0.8/1.2** | **0.48/0.77** |
| nuclei | ResNet-18/50 | 20.3/17.1 | 11.6/9.6 | 1.1/1.7 | 0.97/1.56 |
|  | Ours-18/50 | **21.4/19.1** | **12.4/10.9** | **1.0/1.4** | **0.58/0.94** |
| busi | ResNet-18/50 | 68.8/66.6 | 60.2/56.6 | 4.4/6.8 | 4.44/7.17 |
|  | Ours-18/50 | **69.7/69.0** | **60.6/60.5** | **3.8/5.7** | **2.67/4.31** |
| cellnuclei | ResNet-18/50 | **91.0/91.2** | **84.1/84.4** | 4.6/7.1 | 4.65/7.47 |
|  | Ours-18/50 | 90.9/91.0 | 84.0/84.2 | **3.9/5.9** | **2.79/4.50** |
| yeaz | ResNet-18/50 | 94.8/94.8 | 90.3/90.2 | 3.5/5.5 | 3.54/5.71 |
|  | Ours-18/50 | **94.8/94.9** | **90.3/90.3** | **2.9/4.4** | **2.13/3.43** |
| kvasir | ResNet-18/50 | 71.4/70.9 | 62.9/61.9 | 6.8/10.6 | 6.94/11.16 |
|  | Ours-18/50 | **73.0/73.9** | **64.2/64.7** | **5.7/8.6** | **4.17/6.71** |
| cystoidfluid | ResNet-18/50 | **85.0/**85.0 | **75.6/**75.4 | 6.8/10.6 | 6.97/11.20 |
|  | Ours-18/50 | 84.9/**85.2** | 75.5/**75.8** | **5.7/8.7** | **4.19/6.74** |
| isic2016 | ResNet-18/50 | 88.7/88.3 | 81.5/81.0 | 7.9/12.2 | 8.03/12.91 |
|  | Ours-18/50 | **88.9/88.4** | **81.6/81.0** | **6.5/9.9** | **4.83/7.76** |
| brifiseg | ResNet-18/50 | 76.5/75.8 | 62.8/62.0 | 9.7/15.1 | 9.88/15.93 |
|  | Ours-18/50 | **76.9/77.0** | **63.4/63.5** | **8.0/12.2** | **5.94/9.58** |
| polypgen | ResNet-18/50 | 53.8/53.2 | 46.1/45.7 | 9.4/15.0 | 9.75/15.68 |
|  | Ours-18/50 | **55.0/56.6** | **46.8/48.8** | **7.8/12.0** | **5.86/9.43** |
| unerve | ResNet-18/50 | 78.4/**78.5** | 67.0/**67.2** | 15.8/25.1 | 16.23/26.18 |
|  | Ours-18/50 | **78.5/**77.8 | **67.2/**66.4 | **13.1/20.2** | **9.76/15.74** |
| usforkidney | ResNet-18/50 | 98.0/97.8 | **96.2/95.8** | 30.9/49.1 | 31.55/50.89 |
|  | Ours-18/50 | **98.0/97.8** | 96.1/95.7 | **25.5/39.3** | **18.97/30.61** |
| covid19radio | ResNet-18/50 | 99.1/99.1 | 98.2/98.2 | 142.3/226.3 | 145.59/234.87 |
|  | Ours-18/50 | **99.1/99.1** | **98.2/98.2** | **116.2/179.2** | **87.53/141.27** |

**Table 3.** Performance metrics (F1 and IOU) on multi-class segmentaion tasks under ssProp and normal configurations. Each cell contains metric value for U-Net with backbones of ResNet18/ResNet50.

| Dataset | Backbone | F1 (%) | IOU (%) | Time (min) | FLOPs (Quad.) |
|---|---|---|---|---|---|
| monusac | ResNet-18/50 | 50.7/48.7 | 46.6/44.7 | **2.4/3.2** | 1.88/3.01 |
| | ssProp-18/50 | **56.1/56.5** | **52.9/53.3** | 2.4/3.3 | **1.13/1.81** |
| wbc | ResNet-18/50 | **95.9**/95.9 | **92.6/92.6** | **2.8/4.3** | 2.78/4.47 |
| | ssProp-18/50 | 95.7/**95.9** | 92.2/92.5 | 2.8/4.5 | **1.67/2.69** |
| abdomenus | ResNet-18/50 | 61.9/**63.9** | 59.9/62.7 | **5.6/8.6** | 5.66/9.09 |
| | ssProp-18/50 | **63.9**/63.8 | **62.7/62.7** | 5.7/9.0 | **3.40/5.47** |
| fhpsaop | ResNet-18/50 | **98.0/97.8** | **96.2/95.8** | **27.2/43.0** | 27.60/44.48 |
| | ssProp-18/50 | 97.7/97.6 | 95.6/95.4 | 27.8/44.5 | **16.60/26.75** |

**Table 4.** Performance metrics (F1 and IOU) on multi-class segmentaion tasks under ours and normal configurations. Each cell contains metric value for U-Net with backbones of ResNet18/ResNet50.

| Dataset | Backbone | F1 (%) | IOU (%) | Time (min) | FLOPs (Quad.) |
|---|---|---|---|---|---|
| monusac | ResNet-18/50 | 50.7/48.7 | 46.6/44.7 | **2.4/3.2** | 1.88/3.01 |
| | Ours-18/50 | **56.8/51.5** | **53.4/47.9** | 2.6/2.9 | **1.13/1.81** |
| wbc | ResNet-18/50 | 95.9/95.9 | 92.6/92.6 | 2.8/4.3 | 2.78/4.47 |
| | Ours-18/50 | **96.0/96.3** | **92.7/93.2** | **2.5/3.7** | **1.67/2.69** |
| abdomenus | ResNet-18/50 | 61.9/63.9 | 59.9/62.7 | 5.6/8.6 | 5.66/9.09 |
| | Ours-18/50 | **63.4/63.9** | **62.1/62.8** | **4.6/7.0** | **3.40/5.47** |
| fhpsaop | ResNet-18/50 | **98.0/97.8** | **96.2/95.8** | 27.2/43.0 | 27.60/44.48 |
| | Ours-18/50 | 97.8/97.7 | 95.8/95.6 | **22.0/33.9** | **16.60/26.75** |

## 3.2  Results

We conduct comprehensive experiments to compare with ssProp and demonstrate the superiority of our methods. All numbers shown in tables are average among three runs with different seeds. Table 1 and Table 2 show the results on binary segmentation tasks of ssProp and ours, respectively. Because of the nature of epoch-level interleaving schedule, the ssProp sometimes leads to unstable and significantly downgraded performance on datasets such as `polygen` and `busi`, as shown in Table 1. This situation can be visually seen as demonstrated in Fig. 2. Besides, because of the overhead introduced by the top-K selection, which requires sorting in each layer of the model for each iteration during training, ssProp even increases the backpropagation time compared to the baseline U-Net. As shown in Table 2, our method has more stable performances across different tasks, leading to highly comparable accuracies (similar or even improved) to the same baseline, and we achieve 40% backward FLOPs and 20% time reduction at the same time. This conclusion still holds for multiclass segmentation tasks as shown in Table 3 and Table 4 for ssProp and our method, respectively. Based on these, we bring the backpropagation sparsification to a more practical level with more trustable performance and faster training for biomedical segmentation tasks, while reducing the backward FLOPs needs and potential carbon footprint by a large margin.

## 4    Conclusion

In conclusion, we propose a simple and effective subsampling strategy for efficient training of U-Net. Our method simultaneously saves 40% FLOPs and 20% time during backpropagation while maintaining comparable and even improved model performance. We validate our method both theoretically and empirically on extensive biomedical segmentation tasks with varying scales, distributions, and class numbers. More importantly, our method possesses generality and wide applicability, meaning that EU-Net can be applied to any deep learning architecture with CNN modules on any machine that supports PyTorch to reduce the carbon footprint introduced during biomedical AI development.

**Acknowledgments.** This work was supported by the National Institute of Health (NIH) under grants R01EB022744, RF1AG077578, RF1AG064584, U19AG078109, and P30AG066530.

**Disclosure of Interests.** The authors have no competing interests to declare that are relevant to the content of this article.

## References


1. Achiam, J., et al.: Gpt-4 technical report. arXiv preprint arXiv:2303.08774 (2023)
2. Ahmad, N.: Correlations are ruining your gradient descent. arXiv preprint arXiv:2407.10780 (2024)
3. Alayrac, J.B., et al.: Flamingo: a visual language model for few-shot learning. Adv. Neural. Inf. Process. Syst. **35**, 23716–23736 (2022)
4. Blattmann, A., et al.: Stable video diffusion: scaling latent video diffusion models to large datasets. arXiv preprint arXiv:2311.15127 (2023)
5. Dalm, S., Offergeld, J., Ahmad, N., van Gerven, M.: Efficient deep learning with decorrelated backpropagation. arXiv preprint arXiv:2405.02385 (2024)
6. Esser, P., et al.: Scaling rectified flow transformers for high-resolution image synthesis. In: Forty-first International Conference on Machine Learning (2024)
7. Glorot, X., Bengio, Y.: Understanding the difficulty of training deep feedforward neural networks. In: Proceedings of the Thirteenth International Conference on Artificial Intelligence and Statistics, pp. 249–256. JMLR Workshop and Conference Proceedings (2010)
8. Goli, N., Aamodt, T.M.: Resprop: reuse sparsified backpropagation. In: Proceedings of the IEEE/CVF Conference on Computer Vision and Pattern Recognition, pp. 1548–1558 (2020)

9. Guo, D., et al.: Deepseek-r1: incentivizing reasoning capability in llms via reinforcement learning. arXiv preprint arXiv:2501.12948 (2025)
10. He, K., Zhang, X., Ren, S., Sun, J.: Delving deep into rectifiers: surpassing human-level performance on imagenet classification. In: Proceedings of the IEEE International Conference on Computer Vision, pp. 1026–1034 (2015)
11. He, K., Zhang, X., Ren, S., Sun, J.: Deep residual learning for image recognition. In: Proceedings of the IEEE Conference on Computer Vision and Pattern Recognition, pp. 770–778 (2016)
12. Iakubovskii, P.: Segmentation models pytorch (2019). https://github.com/qubvel/segmentation_models.pytorch
13. Ioffe, S., Szegedy, C.: Batch normalization: accelerating deep network training by reducing internal covariate shift. In: International Conference on Machine Learning, pp. 448–456. PMLR (2015)
14. Kong, W., et al.: Hunyuanvideo: a systematic framework for large video generative models. arXiv preprint arXiv:2412.03603 (2024)
15. Kuo, C.C.J., Madni, A.M.: Green learning: introduction, examples and outlook. J. Vis. Commun. Image Represent. **90**, 103685 (2023)
16. Kuş, Z., Aydin, M.: Medsegbench: a comprehensive benchmark for medical image segmentation in diverse data modalities. Sci. Data **11**(1), 1283 (2024)
17. Liu, Y., et al.: Sora: a review on background, technology, limitations, and opportunities of large vision models. arXiv preprint arXiv:2402.17177 (2024)
18. Raihan, M.A., Aamodt, T.: Sparse weight activation training. Adv. Neural. Inf. Process. Syst. **33**, 15625–15638 (2020)
19. Rombach, R., Blattmann, A., Lorenz, D., Esser, P., Ommer, B.: High-resolution image synthesis with latent diffusion models. In: Proceedings of the IEEE/CVF Conference on Computer Vision and Pattern Recognition, pp. 10684–10695 (2022)
20. Sun, X., Ren, X., Ma, S., Wang, H.: meprop: Sparsified back propagation for accelerated deep learning with reduced overfitting. In: International Conference on Machine Learning, pp. 3299–3308. PMLR (2017)
21. de Vries, A.: The growing energy footprint of artificial intelligence. Joule **7**(10), 2191–2194 (2023)
22. Wang, Z., Nelaturu, S.H., Amarasinghe, S.: Accelerated cnn training through gradient approximation. In: 2019 2nd Workshop on Energy Efficient Machine Learning and Cognitive Computing for Embedded Applications (EMC2), pp. 31–35. IEEE (2019)
23. Wei, B., Sun, X., Ren, X., Xu, J.: Minimal effort back propagation for convolutional neural networks. arXiv preprint arXiv:1709.05804 (2017)
24. Wu, C.J., Acun, B., Raghavendra, R., Hazelwood, K.: Beyond efficiency: scaling AI sustainably. IEEE Micro (2024)
25. Wu, C.J., et al.: Sustainable AI: environmental implications, challenges and opportunities. Proc. Mach. Learn. Syst. **4**, 795–813 (2022)
26. Wu, Y., He, K.: Group normalization. In: Proceedings of the European Conference on Computer Vision (ECCV), pp. 3–19 (2018)
27. Ye, X., et al.: Accelerating CNN training by pruning activation gradients. In: Vedaldi, A., Bischof, H., Brox, T., Frahm, J.-M. (eds.) ECCV 2020. LNCS, vol. 12370, pp. 322–338. Springer, Cham (2020). https://doi.org/10.1007/978-3-030-58595-2_20
28. Yuan, J., et al.: Native sparse attention: hardware-aligned and natively trainable sparse attention (2025). https://arxiv.org/abs/2502.11089
29. Zhang, Z., Yang, P., Ren, X., Su, Q., Sun, X.: Memorized sparse backpropagation. Neurocomputing **415**, 397–407 (2020)

30. Zhong, L., Huang, S., Shi, Y.: ssprop: energy-efficient training for convolutional neural networks with scheduled sparse back propagation. arXiv preprint arXiv:2408.12561 (2024)
31. Zhou, X., Zhang, W., Chen, Z., Diao, S., Zhang, T.: Efficient neural network training via forward and backward propagation sparsification. Adv. Neural. Inf. Process. Syst. **34**, 15216–15229 (2021)

# Multi-scale Spatial Context with Learnable High-Frequency Augmentation for Polyp Segmentation

Min Wang[1], Yanzhou Su[1], Yiqing Shen[2], and Wen Wang[3(✉)]

[1] University of Electronic Science and Technology of China, Chengdu, China
[2] Johns Hopkins University, Baltimore, USA
[3] Tianmushan Laboratory, Hangzhou, China
`wenwang.uestc@vip.163.com`

**Abstract.** Accurate polyp segmentation is important for early colorectal cancer detection and effective treatment planning. However, existing methods struggle to precisely segment polyps with diverse morphologies, varying sizes, and ambiguous boundaries because they cannot simultaneously capture the contextual information in both the spatial and frequency domains. To address these limitations, we propose a novel segmentation network that synergistically combines multi-scale spatial context and learnable high-frequency domain augmentation. Specifically, our architecture introduces two major innovations: (1) a multi-scale dilated convolution module that efficiently aggregates multi-scale features through parallel dilated convolutions in the spatial domain, and (2) a high-frequency augmentation that selectively enhances high-frequency components such as edges and textures of polyps via learning FFT spectrum soft masks in the frequency domain. Importantly, these proposed two components are fully differentiable and easily pluggable, making them broadly applicable to different medical image segmentation backbones. Experimental results on five public polyp datasets demonstrate that our approach not only captures global structure effectively but also preserves fine-grained boundary details, outperforming state-of-the-art methods with consistent cross-dataset performance while maintaining superior computational efficiency.

**Keywords:** Deep Learning · Polyp Segmentation · Multi-scale Context · High-frequency Enhancement

## 1 Introduction

Colorectal cancer (CRC) ranks among the leading causes of cancer-related mortality worldwide [13]. Early detection and removal of colorectal polyps, which are precursor lesions to CRC, can reduce both the incidence and death rates. While endoscopic screening remains the golden standard for polyp detection, its effectiveness and efficiency heavily depend on physicians' expertise. Deep


T. Chen et al. (Eds.): EMA4MICCAI 2025 Workshops, LNCS 16318, pp. 72–82, 2026.
https://doi.org/10.1007/978-3-032-13961-0_8

learning methods, such as convolutional neural networks (CNNs) and Transformers, enable automatic polyp delineation in supporting clinical decision-making [2,4,8,9,16]. These methods commonly employ multi-scale feature extraction, such as pyramid pooling [31] and atrous spatial pyramid pooling (ASPP) [3], to address the diverse morphologies of polyps while capturing their spatial global context [8].

Nevertheless, these methods suffer a trade-off: emphasizing large receptive fields to capture semantic and structural information comes at the cost of boundary precision and fine detail preservation [25,28,29]. This limitation becomes more pronounced when segmenting small or irregularly shaped polyps, which are common in clinical practice. Recent research has explored high-frequency augmentation to address this challenge [15,19,22,27], either by amplifying high-frequency components in the frequency domain [11,15], or by enhancing edge textures in the spatial domain [4,9,33]. However, existing approaches tend to focus on either multi-scale spatial context modeling or high-frequency detail augmentation, but rarely achieve both simultaneously Additionally, frequency domain information is typically implemented as a fixed pre-processing step rather than as a learnable component, limiting adaptability to diverse polyp appearances Furthermore, state-of-the-art segmentation architectures such as Segment Anything Model (SAM) [10,14] generally require substantial computational resources, hindering real-time clinical deployment.

To bridge the gap, we propose a novel polyp segmentation method that seamlessly integrates multi-scale spatial context extraction with high-frequency augmentation. Specifically, our network incorporates an atrous convolutionâĂŞbased multi-scale feature extraction module alongside a learnable high-frequency enhancement module. The former captures polyp structures and textures at various scales in the spatial domain, while the latter applies a learnable soft-thresholding mechanism in the frequency domain to selectively boost high-frequency components, emphasizing boundaries and subtle details. This integration enables our method to maintain robust global semantic understanding while effectively preserving local edge information.

Our main contributions are three-fold, summarized as follows. Firstly, we propose a robust polyp segmentation network, integrating multi-scale atrous convolutions with a learnable high-frequency augmentation to facilitate precise delineation of polyps across a variety of sizes and shapes. Secondly, we propose a novel soft-thresholding mechanism to selectively amplify high-frequency information. It can effectively enhance boundaries and local details, particularly for small or irregular polyps. Finally, extensive experiments are conducted on multiple polyp segmentation benchmarks, demonstrating the state-of-the-art performance of the proposed method in practical clinical applications.

## 2   Methods

**Method Overview.** The overall architecture of the proposed polyp segmentation network is illustrated in Fig. 1. Our network aims to address the challenges of capturing global contextual information while preserving fine bound-

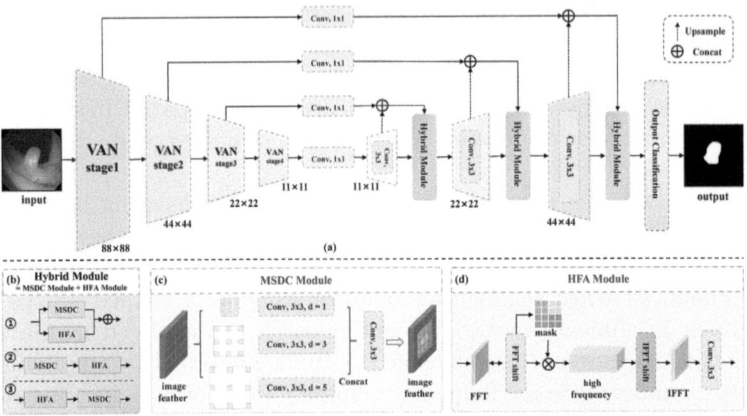

**Fig. 1.** Overall architecture of the proposed network.

ary details essential for accurate polyp delineation. Given an endoscopic image dataset $\mathbf{X} = \{\mathbf{x}_1, \ldots, \mathbf{x}_N\}$ with its corresponding binary segmentation ground truth $\mathbf{Y} = \{\mathbf{y}_1, \ldots, \mathbf{y}_N\}$, our network maps each input image $\mathbf{x} \in \mathbf{R}^{H \times W \times 3}$ to a binary semantic segmentation map $\mathbf{y} \in \{0, 1\}^{H \times W}$, where $H$ and $W$ denote the height and width of the image, respectively. The proposed network consists of three primary components: (1) an image encoder for multi-scale spatial feature extraction, (2) a mask decoder for progressive feature refinement, and (3) a module for enhancing multi-scale representations and high-frequency feature representations. For the image encoder backbone, we adopt the Visual Attention Network (VAN) [5], due to its efficient attention mechanisms and hierarchical feature representation capabilities. Specifically, the encoder extracts multi-level features that capture polyps of various morphologies, sizes, and appearances across different scales. The mask decoder follows a top-down pathway that progressively refines the encoded feature maps through bilinear upsampling. This process enables the fusion of high-level semantic information with low-level detailed features, facilitating comprehensive polyp characterization. At each stage of the mask decoder, the feature maps are first passed through a multi-scale atrous convolution, followed by a learnable high-frequency enhancement module that selectively amplifies boundary details and texture information in the frequency domain via adaptive FFT spectrum soft masks.

## 2.1  Multi-scale Dilated Convolution

To capture the diverse shapes and sizes of polyps effectively, we proposed a simplified Atrous Spatial Pyramid Pooling (ASPP) [3], which we designate as Multi-Scale Dilated Convolution (MSDC), as is shown in Fig. 1(c). Our MSDC consists of three parallel convolutional branches, each employing a $3 \times 3$ convolution with different dilation rates $\{d_1, d_2, d_3\}$. Each branch incorporates batch normalization followed by ReLU activation to enhance feature discrimination and mitigate gradient issues:

$$\mathbf{F}_i = \text{ReLU}(\text{BN}(\text{Conv}_{3\times3}(\mathbf{X}, d_i))), \quad d_i \in \{1, 3, 5\}. \tag{1}$$

Here, $\text{Conv}_{3\times3}$ denotes a $3 \times 3$ convolution operation with dilation rate $d_i$, BN indicates batch normalization, and $\mathbf{F}_i$ is the output of the i-th branch. The outputs from these parallel branches are concatenated along the channel dimension and subsequently integrated through a $1 \times 1$ convolution to fuse these multi-scale features:

$$\mathbf{F}_o = \text{Conv}_{1\times1}\Big([\mathbf{F}_1, \mathbf{F}_2, \mathbf{F}_3]\Big), \tag{2}$$

where $[\cdot]$ denotes concatenation. To preserve the original feature information and facilitate gradient propagation, we implement a residual connection by adding the input $\mathbf{X}$ back to $\mathbf{F}_o$. Additionally, we introduce a learnable parameter $\beta$, initialized to 1 and broadcast across spatial dimensions, which dynamically adjusts the contribution of the multi-scale features $i.e.$, $\mathbf{F}_{\text{context}} = \beta \cdot \mathbf{F}_o + \mathbf{X}$.

## 2.2   Learnable High-Frequency Augmentation

While the Multi-Scale Dilated Convolution effectively captures global context, it may inadvertently smooth boundary details. To address this limitation, we introduce a learnable High-Frequency Augmentation (HFA) module to amplify high-frequency components such as edge and texture information selectively. The architecture of HFA is illustrated in Fig. 1(d).

**FFT and Shift.** The HFA module begins by decomposing the input feature map $\mathbf{X}$ into its frequency components using the two-dimensional Fast Fourier Transform (FFT). This transformation is applied to each channel independently $\mathbf{X}^{\text{fft}} = \text{fftshift}(\mathcal{F}(\mathbf{X}))$, where $\mathcal{F}(\mathbf{X})$ represents the 2D Fourier transform of $\mathbf{X}$ and $\text{fftshift}(\cdot)$ repositions the zero-frequency component to the center of the spectrum. This re-centering facilitates a radial-based frequency mask, enabling more intuitive frequency selection.

**Adaptive Soft Frequency Masking.** Unlike conventional fixed frequency filters, we propose a learnable soft masking mechanism that adapts to the specific characteristics of polyp structures. It generates a continuous-valued mask $\mathbf{M}$ over the frequency plane using learnable parameters, depicted as

$$\mathbf{M}(u, v) = \sigma\Big(s\left(\text{dist}^2(u, v) - c\right)\Big), \tag{3}$$

where $\sigma(\cdot)$ denotes the sigmoid function, and $\text{dist}^2(u, v)$ is the squared Euclidean distance from the frequency-domain coordinate $(u, v)$ to the center of the spectrum, and $c$ and $s$ are learnable parameters controlling the frequency threshold and transition sharpness, respectively. The center parameter $c$ determines the frequency threshold above which components are emphasized, effectively separating low from high frequencies. Based on the size of the features, we initialize $c$ with stage-specific values (64.0, 225.0, and 961.0) corresponding to the squared distances $8^2$, $15^2$ and $31^2$ for each decoder stage. This scale-adaptive initialization ensures appropriate frequency selection across different feature resolutions. The sharpness parameter $s$, initialized to 10.0, controls the smoothness of transition between suppressed and emphasized frequencies. Higher values of $s$ create a more abrupt transition, approximating a hard threshold, while lower values produce a more gradual change.

**High-Frequency Component Extraction and Enhancement.** After generating the frequency mask, we apply it to the shifted Fourier spectrum through element-wise multiplication ($\odot$), attenuating low-frequency components while preserving high-frequency details. The resulting frequency representation is then transformed back to the spatial domain using inverse operations, formulated by $\mathbf{X}^{\text{high}} = \mathcal{F}^{-1}(\text{ifftshift}(\mathbf{X}^{\text{fft}} \odot \mathbf{M}))$, where ifftshift reverses the earlier frequency shift, and $\mathcal{F}^{-1}$ represents the inverse Fourier transform. To ensure numerical stability and maintain real-valued feature maps, we retain only the real part of $\mathbf{X}^{\text{high}}$ for subsequent processing. The extracted high-frequency components are selectively integrated with the original features through an adaptive fusion *i.e.*, $\mathbf{F}_{\text{freq}} = \mathbf{X} + \alpha \cdot \mathbf{X}^{\text{high}}$, where $\alpha$ is a learnable scaling parameter initialized to 1.0 that modulates the contribution of high-frequency information. It can preserve the original mid- and low-frequency content while selectively enhancing high-frequency details such as polyp boundaries and texture variations.

### 2.3   Hybrid Module Integration

Our network employs a novel integration strategy that synergistically combines MSDC and HFA modules either in a parallel or sequential manner, as illustrated in Fig. 1(b). The default integration strategy implements a parallel processing paradigm where both the MSDC and HFA modules process the same input feature map $\mathbf{X}$ independently. Their outputs are then combined through element-wise addition, namely $\mathbf{F}_{\text{out}} = \mathbf{F}_{\text{context}} + \mathbf{F}_{\text{freq}}$, where $\mathbf{F}_{\text{context}}$ is the multi-scale output from the MSDC module, and $\mathbf{F}_{\text{freq}}$ is the high-frequency-enhanced representation from the HFA module. We also explore sequential integration strategies where the MSDC and HFA modules are applied consecutively. This integration approach offers alternative information flow patterns that may better suit certain polyp morphologies or backbone architectures. Two primary sequential configurations are proposed. First, in context-first integration, the MSDC module first processes the input to extract multi-scale contextual features, which are subsequently refined by the HFA module:

$$\mathbf{F}_{\text{mid}} = \mathbf{F}_{\text{context}}(\mathbf{X}), \quad \text{then} \quad \mathbf{F}_{\text{out}} = \mathbf{F}_{\text{freq}}(\mathbf{F}_{\text{mid}}), \tag{4}$$

which is designed to be effective for recovering boundary details that may have been attenuated during multi-scale feature extraction. The HFA module selectively enhances high-frequency components in the already contextually rich representation, effectively restoring fine structural details while maintaining semantic coherence. Conversely, the frequency-first approach applies the HFA module initially to enhance boundary information, followed by multi-scale contextual modeling:

$$\mathbf{F}_{\text{mid}} = \mathbf{F}_{\text{freq}}(\mathbf{X}), \quad \text{then} \quad \mathbf{F}_{\text{out}} = \mathbf{F}_{\text{context}}(\mathbf{F}_{\text{mid}}). \tag{5}$$

This strategy enables the MSDC module to incorporate already-enhanced boundary information into its multi-scale feature extraction process. By emphasizing high-frequency components before contextual modeling, this approach can be advantageous for small polyps or those with subtle textural variations, where boundary information is particularly critical for accurate segmentation.

## 3  Experiments

**Implementation Details and Datasets.** All experiments are implemented with the PyTorch framework on one Tesla A100 GPU. The encoder of our network is based on VAN [5], and we initialize the model with pre-trained weights from ImageNet. The other components of the network are initialized randomly, with an initial learning rate of 1e-4. For network optimization, we use the AdamW optimizer with a weight decay of 1e-4, a batch size of 16 and a total epoch number of 120. For evaluation metric, we follow previous work [4,9] by using mDice and mIoU. We leverage five datasets, namely Kvasir [7], CVC-ClinicDB [1], CVC-ColonDB [21], CVC-T [23], and ETIS [17]. Following previous work [4,9], we used a portion of images from CVC-ClinicDB and Kvasir for training, consisting of 550 and 900 images, respectively. Thus, the training set consisted of a total number of 1450 images, and the remaining data from these two datasets were used as the test set. In addition, the remaining three datasets were used to evaluate the model's cross-dataset generalization performance, consisting of 60, 380, and 196 images, respectively.

**Comparisons with State-of-the-Arts.** We quantitatively evaluate our method (denoted as "Prop") against recent polyp segmentation counterparts in Table 1. Our approach demonstrates consistently strong performance across all datasets, showcasing its generalization capability. On the Kvasir dataset, our method achieves a competitive mDice score of 0.921, while on CVC-T, it attains 0.907 mDice, outperforming most competing approaches. Although not always achieving the highest performance on individual datasets, our method maintains top-tier accuracy across all benchmarks, including ClinicDB (0.925 mDice), ColonDB (0.784 mDice), and ETIS (0.784 mDice); and our method can also be integrated into other methods to achieve future performance boost. This consistent cross-dataset performance distinguishes our approach from other methods that excel on specific datasets but exhibit performance drops when applied to different polyp appearance distributions. We also evaluate the model complexity in

**Table 1.** Quantitative comparison of polyp segmentation performance.

| Model | CVC-ClinicDB | | Kvasir | | CVC-T | | CVC-ColonDB | | ETIS | |
|---|---|---|---|---|---|---|---|---|---|---|
| | mDice | mIoU | mDice | mIoU | mDice | mIoU | mDice | mIoU | mDice | mIoU |
| UNet [16] | 0.823 | 0.755 | 0.818 | 0.746 | 0.710 | 0.627 | 0.512 | 0.444 | 0.398 | 0.335 |
| PraNet [4] | 0.899 | 0.849 | 0.898 | 0.840 | 0.871 | 0.797 | 0.709 | 0.640 | 0.628 | 0.567 |
| ResUNet++ [8] | 0.846 | 0.786 | 0.807 | 0.727 | 0.687 | 0.598 | 0.588 | 0.497 | 0.337 | 0.275 |
| SANet [26] | 0.916 | 0.859 | 0.904 | 0.847 | 0.888 | 0.815 | 0.752 | 0.669 | 0.750 | 0.654 |
| MSNet [32] | 0.915 | 0.866 | 0.902 | 0.847 | 0.862 | 0.796 | 0.747 | 0.668 | 0.720 | 0.650 |
| UACANet-S [9] | 0.916 | 0.870 | 0.905 | 0.852 | 0.902 | 0.837 | 0.783 | 0.704 | 0.694 | 0.615 |
| UACANet-L [9] | 0.926 | 0.880 | 0.912 | 0.859 | 0.910 | 0.849 | 0.751 | 0.678 | 0.766 | 0.689 |
| Polyp-PVT [2] | 0.937 | 0.889 | 0.917 | 0.864 | 0.900 | 0.833 | 0.808 | 0.727 | 0.787 | 0.706 |
| CaraNet [12] | 0.921 | 0.876 | 0.913 | 0.859 | 0.902 | 0.836 | 0.775 | 0.700 | 0.740 | 0.660 |
| LDNet [30] | 0.923 | 0.872 | 0.912 | 0.855 | 0.893 | 0.826 | 0.794 | 0.715 | 0.778 | 0.707 |
| FastFPN [20] | 0.923 | 0.873 | 0.913 | 0.863 | 0.909 | 0.844 | 0.785 | 0.710 | 0.777 | 0.698 |
| SSFormer [24] | 0.916 | 0.873 | 0.925 | 0.878 | 0.887 | 0.821 | 0.772 | 0.697 | 0.767 | 0.698 |
| Prop | 0.925 | 0.876 | 0.921 | 0.870 | 0.907 | 0.843 | 0.784 | 0.702 | 0.784 | 0.699 |

**Table 2.** Ablation study. We explore multiple fusion strategies for combining the multi-scale context branch ($\mathbf{F}_{context}$) with the high-frequency branch ($\mathbf{F}_{freq}$). Here, "Seq. ($\mathbf{F}_{context} \rightarrow \mathbf{F}_{freq}$)" stands for applying the multi-scale branch first, followed by frequency enhancement; "Seq. ($\mathbf{F}_{freq} \rightarrow \mathbf{F}_{context}$)" reverses that order; and "Prop (parallel)" indicates simultaneous processing. The best scores for each dataset are in bold.

| Model | CVC-ClinicDB | | Kvasir | | CVC-T | | CVC-ColonDB | | ETIS | |
|---|---|---|---|---|---|---|---|---|---|---|
| | mDice | mIoU | mDice | mIoU | mDice | mIoU | mDice | mIoU | mDice | mIoU |
| Baseline | 0.911 | 0.859 | 0.901 | 0.847 | 0.877 | 0.809 | 0.774 | 0.695 | 0.764 | 0.676 |
| $\mathbf{F}_{context}$ | 0.913 | 0.863 | 0.913 | 0.858 | 0.902 | 0.837 | 0.789 | 0.712 | 0.767 | 0.682 |
| $\mathbf{F}_{freq}$ | 0.916 | 0.867 | 0.910 | 0.856 | 0.898 | 0.832 | 0.793 | 0.713 | 0.782 | 0.706 |
| Seq. ($\mathbf{F}_{context} \rightarrow \mathbf{F}_{freq}$) | 0.921 | 0.872 | 0.919 | 0.868 | 0.903 | 0.840 | 0.782 | 0.708 | **0.799** | **0.712** |
| Seq. ($\mathbf{F}_{freq} \rightarrow \mathbf{F}_{context}$) | **0.929** | **0.883** | 0.913 | 0.860 | 0.905 | 0.842 | **0.784** | 0.707 | 0.777 | 0.694 |
| Prop (parallel) | 0.925 | 0.876 | **0.921** | **0.870** | **0.907** | **0.843** | **0.784** | **0.702** | 0.784 | 0.699 |

Table 3 in terms of Multiply-Accumulate Operations (MACs), number of parameters (M), and frames-per-second (FPS). Despite incorporating both multi-scale and high-frequency processing branches, our network maintains relatively low computational requirements (2.72 G MACs, 4.01 M parameters), while maintaining one of the highest throughput (63.11). This efficiency can be attributed to our lightweight VAN-b0 backbone and the computationally efficient design of our high-frequency enhancement module, which introduces minimal additional parameters while improving polyp boundary delineation.

**Ablation Study.** Table 2 presents the ablation study of six configurations, illustrating how the multi-scale context branch ($\mathbf{F}_{context}$) and the high-frequency

**Table 3.** Model complexity comparison.

| Method | MACs (G) | Params (M) | FPS |
|---|---|---|---|
| ResUNet++ [8] | 134.12 | 14.48 | 25.25 |
| PraNet [4] | 13.15 | 32.55 | 44.42 |
| HarDMSEG [6] | 11.39 | 33.34 | 58.02 |
| UACANet-S [9] | 12.04 | 26.90 | 28.53 |
| UACANet-L [9] | 59.85 | 69.16 | 25.72 |
| SANet [26] | 11.32 | 23.90 | 34.94 |
| MSNet [32] | 17.03 | 29.74 | 44.34 |
| CaraNet [12] | 21.76 | 46.64 | 26.97 |
| LDNet [30] | 66.57 | 33.38 | 21.45 |
| SSFormer [24] | 19.10 | 29.57 | 52.38 |
| FAPN [18] | 12.83 | 27.02 | 38.06 |
| FastFPN [20] | **2.63** | 4.55 | 60.32 |
| PolypPVT [2] | 10.1 | 25.11 | 44.69 |
| Prop | 2.72 | **4.01** | **63.11** |

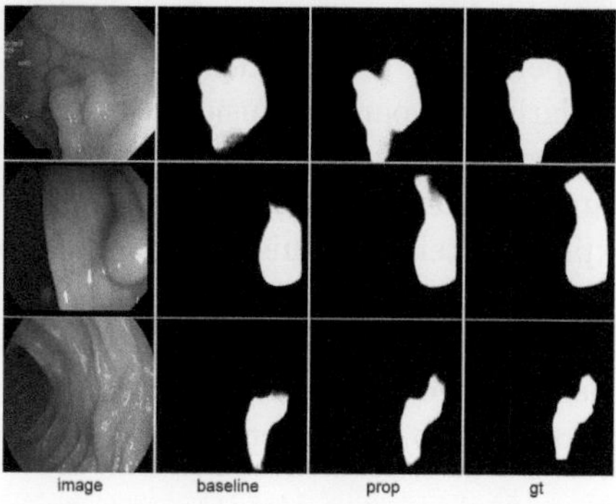


**Fig. 2.** Illustrative example of segmentation results.

branch ($\mathbf{F}_{\text{freq}}$) complement each other. Specifically, we evaluate: (1) *Baseline*, which lacks both modules; (2) *Only Context* ($\mathbf{F}_{\text{context}}$ alone); (3) *Only Frequency* ($\mathbf{F}_{\text{freq}}$ alone); (4) *Context $\rightarrow$ Frequency* (sequential); (5) *Frequency $\rightarrow$ Context* (sequential); and (6) *Proposed (Parallel)*. While the baseline already achieves moderate mDice (*i.e.*, 0.910 on Kvasir), it lacks explicit mechanisms for large receptive fields or boundary enhancement. Adding $\mathbf{F}_{\text{context}}$ alone brings consistent improvements by capturing multi-scale semantics, whereas using only $\mathbf{F}_{\text{freq}}$ similarly boosts performance by preserving fine-grained edges. For sequential fusion, $\mathbf{F}_{\text{context}} \rightarrow \mathbf{F}_{\text{freq}}$ delivers stable gains (*i.e.*, mDice of 0.921 on ClinicDB, 0.799 on ETIS), while the reverse order $\mathbf{F}_{\text{freq}} \rightarrow \mathbf{F}_{\text{context}}$ achieves the highest ClinicDB score of 0.929 but marginally lower results on ETIS. In contrast, our parallel strategy strikes a strong overall balance, notably achieving mDice of 0.925 on ClinicDB and 0.907 on CVC-T without sacrificing performance on the harder ETIS set. These findings confirm that (i) each branch independently benefits the baseline, (ii) combining them further improves segmentation quality, and (iii) parallel fusion provides a robust yet flexible solution for harmonizing global context and boundary fidelity in polyp segmentation. As illustrated in Fig. 2, our method ("Prop") yields clearer and more accurate polyp boundaries compared to the baseline approach. In particular, subtle morphological details along the polyp edges are better preserved, demonstrating the efficacy of high-frequency enhancement in our design.

## 4    Conclusion

In this paper, we propose a novel polyp segmentation framework that integrates multi-scale context extraction with learnable high-frequency enhancement. By jointly leveraging atrous convolutions for global semantic coverage and a differentiable soft mask for high-frequency enhancement, our method achieves robust performance across multiple publicly available datasets. Extensive experiments and ablation studies on five public datasets demonstrate that each module independently contributes to the final accuracy, and their combination, particularly via parallel fusion, effectively balances coarse-scale information and fine-grained edge details. Moreover, our design is architecturally flexible, allowing easy integration into various encoder-decoder paradigms. Future work may explore extending this approach to other medical image segmentation tasks where preserving boundary details while capturing global context is essential.

**Disclosure of Interests.** The authors have no competing interests to declare that are relevant to the content of this article.

# References


1. Bernal, J., Sánchez, F.J., Fernández-Esparrach, G., Gil, D., Rodríguez, C., Vilariño, F.: Wm-dova maps for accurate polyp highlighting in colonoscopy: validation vs. saliency maps from physicians. CMIG **43**, 99–111 (2015)
2. Bo, D., Wenhai, W., Jinpeng, L., Deng-Ping, F.: Polyp-pvt: polyp segmentation with pyramid vision transformers. arXiv preprint arXiv:2108.06932v3 (2021)
3. Chen, L.C., Papandreou, G., Kokkinos, I., Murphy, K., Yuille, A.L.: Deeplab: semantic image segmentation with deep convolutional nets, atrous convolution, and fully connected crfs. IEEE Trans. Pattern Anal. Mach. Intell. **40**(4), 834–848 (2017)
4. Fan, D.-P., et al.: PraNet: parallel reverse attention network for polyp segmentation. In: Martel, A.L., et al. (eds.) MICCAI 2020. LNCS, vol. 12266, pp. 263–273. Springer, Cham (2020). https://doi.org/10.1007/978-3-030-59725-2_26
5. Guo, M.H., Lu, C.Z., Liu, Z.N., Cheng, M.M., Hu, S.M.: Visual attention network. Comput. Visual Media **9**(4), 733–752 (2023)
6. Huang, C.H., Wu, H.Y., Lin, Y.L.: Hardnet-mseg: a simple encoder-decoder polyp segmentation neural network that achieves over 0.9 mean dice and 86 fps (2021)
7. Jha, D., et al.: Kvasir-SEG: a segmented polyp dataset. In: Ro, M., et al. (eds.) MMM 2020. LNCS, vol. 11962, pp. 451–462. Springer, Cham (2020). https://doi.org/10.1007/978-3-030-37734-2_37
8. Jha, D., et al.: Resunet++: an advanced architecture for medical image segmentation. In: ISM, pp. 225–2255. IEEE (2019)
9. Kim, T., Lee, H., Kim, D.: Uacanet: uncertainty augmented context attention for polyp segmentation. In: Proceedings of the 29th ACM International Conference on Multimedia, pp. 2167–2175 (2021)
10. Kirillov, A., et al.: Segment anything. arXiv preprint arXiv:2304.02643 (2023)
11. Li, Y., Zhou, H., Liu, N., Shen, Y.: Stain normalization and augmentation in frequency space for histology analysis. In: 2023 IEEE International Conference on Bioinformatics and Biomedicine (BIBM), pp. 2031–2035. IEEE (2023)
12. Lou, A., Guan, S., Ko, H., Loew, M.H.: Caranet: context axial reverse attention network for segmentation of small medical objects, pp. 81–92. SPIE (2022)
13. Mei, J., et al.: A survey on deep learning for polyp segmentation: techniques, challenges and future trends. Visual Intell. **3**(1), 1 (2025)
14. Ravi, N., Gabeur, V., Hu, Y.T., et al.: Sam 2: segment anything in images and videos. arXiv preprint arXiv:2408.00714 (2024)
15. Ren, J., Zhang, X., Zhang, L.: Hifiseg: high-frequency information enhanced polyp segmentation with global-local vision transformer. IEEE Access (2025)

16. Ronneberger, O., Fischer, P., Brox, T.: U-net: convolutional networks for biomedical image segmentation. In: Navab, N., Hornegger, J., Wells, W.M., Frangi, A.F. (eds.) MICCAI 2015. LNCS, vol. 9351, pp. 234–241. Springer, Cham (2015). https://doi.org/10.1007/978-3-319-24574-4_28

17. Silva, J., Histace, A., Romain, O., Dray, X., Granado, B.: Toward embedded detection of polyps in wce images for early diagnosis of colorectal cancer. IJCARS 9(2), 283–293 (2014)

18. Su, Y., Cheng, J., Yi, M., Liu, H.: FAPN: feature augmented pyramid network for polyp segmentation. Biomed. Signal Process. Control 78, 103903 (2022)

19. Su, Y., et al.: Fednet: feature decoupled network for polyp segmentation from endoscopy images. Biomed. Signal Process. Control 83, 104699 (2023)

20. Su, Y., Xie, Q., Ye, J., He, J., Cheng, J.: An accurate polyp segmentation framework via feature secondary fusion. In: 2023 IEEE 20th International Symposium on Biomedical Imaging (ISBI), pp. 1–5. IEEE (2023)

21. Tajbakhsh, N., Gurudu, S.R., Liang, J.: Automated polyp detection in colonoscopy videos using shape and context information. TMI 35(2), 630–644 (2015)

22. Tang, R., et al.: A frequency attention-embedded network for polyp segmentation. Sci. Rep. 15(1), 4961 (2025)

23. Vázquez, D., et al.: A benchmark for endoluminal scene segmentation of colonoscopy images. JHE (2017)

24. Wang, J., Huang, Q., Tang, F., Meng, J., Su, J., Song, S.: Stepwise feature fusion: local guides global. In: Medical Image Computing and Computer Assisted Intervention–MICCAI 2022: 25th International Conference, Singapore, 18–22 September 2022, Proceedings, Part III, pp. 110–120. Springer, Heidelberg (2022). https://doi.org/10.1007/978-3-031-16437-8_11

25. Wang, P., Zheng, W., Chen, T., Wang, Z.: Anti-oversmoothing in deep vision transformers via the fourier domain analysis: from theory to practice. arXiv preprint arXiv:2203.05962 (2022)

26. Wei, J., Hu, Y., Zhang, R., Li, Z., Zhou, S.K., Cui, S.: Shallow attention network for polyp segmentation. In: de Bruijne, M., et al. (eds.) MICCAI 2021. LNCS, vol. 12901, pp. 699–708. Springer, Cham (2021). https://doi.org/10.1007/978-3-030-87193-2_66

27. Xu, W., Xu, R., Wang, C., Li, X., Xu, S., Guo, L.: Pstnet: enhanced polyp segmentation with multi-scale alignment and frequency domain integration. IEEE J. Biomed. Health Inf. (2024)

28. Zhang, G., Zhang, Y., Zhang, T., Li, B., Pu, S.: PHA: patch-wise high-frequency augmentation for transformer-based person re-identification. In: Proceedings of the IEEE/CVF Conference on Computer Vision and Pattern Recognition, pp. 14133–14142 (2023)

29. Zhang, L., Li, X., Arnab, A., Yang, K., Tong, Y., Torr, P.H.: Dual graph convolutional network for semantic segmentation. arXiv preprint arXiv:1909.06121 (2019)

30. Zhang, R., et al.: Lesion-aware dynamic kernel for polyp segmentation. In: Medical Image Computing and Computer Assisted Intervention–MICCAI 2022: 25th International Conference, Singapore, 18–22 September 2022, Proceedings, Part III, pp. 99–109. Springer, Heidelberg (2022). https://doi.org/10.1007/978-3-031-16437-8_10

31. Zhao, H., Shi, J., Qi, X., Wang, X., Jia, J.: Pyramid scene parsing network. In: Proceedings of the IEEE Conference on Computer Vision and Pattern Recognition, pp. 2881–2890 (2017)

32. Zhao, X., Zhang, L., Lu, H.: Automatic polyp segmentation via multi-scale subtraction network. In: de Bruijne, M., et al. (eds.) MICCAI 2021. LNCS, vol. 12901, pp. 120–130. Springer, Cham (2021). https://doi.org/10.1007/978-3-030-87193-2_12
33. Zhou, T., Zhang, Y., Chen, G., Zhou, Y., Wu, Y., Fan, D.P.: Edge-aware feature aggregation network for polyp segmentation. Mach. Intell. Res. **22**(1), 101–116 (2025)

# EL-UNet: An Efficient and Lightweight U-Net with Multi-scale Attention for Medical Image Segmentation


Yulong Xiao[1] , Sibo Ju[1], Zongjie Weng[2], Yang Sun[3], and Xiangwen Liao[1(✉)]

[1] College of Computer and Data Science, Fuzhou University, Fuzhou, China
`liaoxw@fzu.edu.cn`
[2] Department of Medical Ultrasonics, Fujian Maternity and Child Health Hospital,
College of Clinical Medicine for Obstetrics and Gynecology and Pediatrics, Fujian
Medical University, Fuzhou, China
[3] Department of Gynecology, Clinical Oncology School of Fujian Medical University,
Fujian Cancer Hospital, Fuzhou, China



**Abstract.** Medical image segmentation plays a vital role in intelligent healthcare, with the U-Net architecture widely recognized for its strong performance. However, many U-Net variants remain impractical for mobile and real-time applications due to their large parameter counts and high computational demands, and they often underperform in multiscale feature representation and generalization. To overcome these limitations, we introduce EL-UNet, a lightweight model that preserves U-Net's architectural strengths while improving both efficiency and accuracy. EL-UNet incorporates an Attentive Multi-Scale Block (AMSB), which unites multiscale convolutions with channel and spatial attention, to better capture critical features of small structures and complex backgrounds. A novel gated skip connection further mitigates semantic discrepancies between encoder and decoder features. By adopting depthwise separable convolutions and a streamlined channel design, EL-UNet substantially reduces the parameter count and computational overhead. Experiments on multiple public datasets demonstrate that EL-UNet outperforms recent U-Net variants in precision, mIoU, and Dice metrics, achieving an optimal balance between resource efficiency and segmentation performance.

**Keywords:** Medical Image Segmentation · Multi-scale · Attention · Lightweight U-Net


## 1 Introduction

Medical image segmentation is a fundamental task in medical image analysis and plays a critical role in the early diagnosis of diseases. It directly affects the accuracy of treatment and the reliability of efficacy assessment. In recent years, deep learning techniques, especially convolutional neural networks [1], have advanced


© The Author(s), under exclusive license to Springer Nature Switzerland AG 2026
T. Chen et al. (Eds.): EMA4MICCAI 2025 Workshops, LNCS 16318, pp. 83–92, 2026.
https://doi.org/10.1007/978-3-032-13961-0_9

rapidly and empowered medical image segmentation. Among them, U-Net [2] has become a representative CNN architecture and, along with its many variants, has been a central focus in medical image segmentation research over the past few years.

In the integration of multi-scale feature representation and attention mechanisms, the Feature Pyramid Network (FPN) [3] employs a top-down pathway and lateral connections to construct high-level semantic features across all scales, and has been widely adopted. Attention U-Net [4] introduces an attention gating mechanism to suppress redundant information during the fusion of high- and low-level features in the U-Net framework, enhancing the representation of target regions and improving the sensitivity to small structures. Recently, novel approaches have emerged—such as the VM-UNet [5] proposed by Ruan et al., which constructs a segmentation model based on state space models (SSM). Inspired by VM-UNet, Wu et al. proposed H-vmuNet [6], which utilizes higher-order 2D selective scanning to reduce information redundancy through more sophisticated feature interactions. However, existing U-Net models and their variants still face several critical challenges. Most models are overly complex and difficult to deploy. They often lack sufficient multi-scale feature representation capabilities and exhibit either inadequate or redundant use of attention mechanisms.

It is evident that future research will focus on designing segmentation networks that are structurally efficient, expressive, easy to deploy, and capable of strong generalization. In response to these challenges, this study proposes a lightweight, high-performance U-shaped segmentation network—EL-UNet (Efficient and Light UNet). By integrating multi-scale cascaded structures with attention mechanisms, we introduce a novel Attentive Multi-Scale Block (AMSB). Specifically, after modeling features at various semantic scales, channel and spatial attention mechanisms are employed to generate attention guidance maps, helping the model focus on multi-scale features and key regions. To achieve lightweight and deployable design, we adopt depthwise separable convolutions and further optimize the encoder-decoder structure. Compared to standard convolutions, depthwise separable convolutions significantly reduce computational complexity. Additionally, we propose a novel gated skip connection module that dynamically integrates features between the encoder and decoder, largely mitigating semantic inconsistency between shallow and deep layers.

The main contributions of this study are summarized as follows:

1. We propose the AMSB module, which integrates multi-scale cascaded convolutions and dual attention to enhance semantic representation.
2. A gated skip connection is designed to improve feature fusion between encoder and decoder, mitigating semantic inconsistency.
3. Lightweight strategies such as depthwise separable convolutions are employed to reduce complexity while maintaining performance.
4. Extensive experiments on multiple datasets validate the effectiveness and efficiency of EL-UNet compared to state-of-the-art methods.

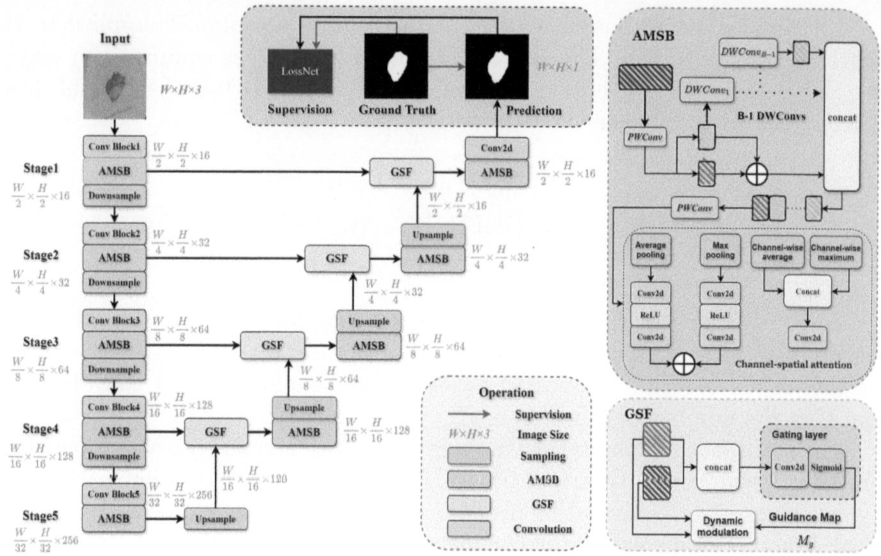

**Fig. 1.** The overview of EL-UNet. In the AMSB and GSF sections of the figure, the squares with diagonal fillings of different colors represent the image features of different stages or different parts.

## 2  Methodology

### 2.1  Architecture Overview

The EL-UNet architecture (Fig. 1) follows a five-stage U-shaped encoder–decoder with channel sizes [16, 32, 64, 128, 256]. Each stage integrates an AMSB module, combining parallel depthwise separable convolutions and channel-spatial attention to extract multi-scale features and enhance focus on key regions. To reduce semantic gaps, gated skip connections replace traditional ones. Lightweight designs are applied throughout to balance efficiency and segmentation performance.

### 2.2  Attentive Multi-scale Block

To enhance the representation of multi-scale semantic features while maintaining a lightweight architecture, we propose the Attentive Multi-Scale Block (AMSB).

Following channel compression performed by pointwise convolution, the feature map $\mathbf{F}_c \in \mathbb{R}^{(C/B) \times H \times W}$ is evenly divided into a primary path $P_0$ (even-indexed channels) and auxiliary paths $S_0, S_1, \ldots, S_{B-2}$ (odd-indexed channels). The primary path retains the essential semantic information, while each auxiliary branch undergoes a depthwise convolutional transformation to model hierarchical receptive fields. The aggregated output $\mathbf{F}_{ms}$ is formulated as:

$$\mathbf{F}_{ms} = \text{Concat}\left(P_0 \oplus S_0,\ \text{DWConv}_1(S_0),\ \ldots,\ \text{DWConv}_{(B-1)}(S_{B-2})\right) \quad (1)$$

where $\oplus$ denotes element-wise addition.

To enhance discriminability, the channel-spatial attention is applied to the aggregated feature map. The channel attention map $\mathbf{M}_c$ is computed by applying global average pooling and max pooling, followed by two shared multilayer perceptrons with nonlinear activation, formulated as:

$$\mathbf{M}_c = \sigma(F_{avg} + F_{max}),$$

$$\begin{cases} F_{avg} = W_2 \left(\text{ReLU}\left(W_1 \cdot \text{AvgPool}(X)\right)\right) \\ F_{max} = W_2 \left(\text{ReLU}\left(W_1 \cdot \text{MaxPool}(X)\right)\right) \end{cases} \tag{2}$$

Here, $\sigma(\cdot)$ denotes the sigmoid activation function, $X$ represents the input feature map after the multi-scale cascaded structure, $W_1$ and $W_2$ are the shared weights of the two fully connected layers (implemented via $1 \times 1$ convolutions), and $C$ is the number of channels in $X$.

The input feature map is then modulated by the channel-wise attention $\mathbf{M}_c$ to produce the intermediate output $\mathbf{F}'$. Following this, spatial attention is computed by applying a $7 \times 7$ convolution over the concatenated average-pooled and max-pooled feature maps across the channel dimension:

$$\mathbf{M}_s = \sigma\left(\text{Conv}_{7\times7}\left(\left[\frac{1}{C}\sum_{i=1}^{C}\mathbf{F}'_i;\ \max_{1\leq i \leq C}\mathbf{F}'_i\right]\right)\right) \tag{3}$$

This dual attention mechanism enables the model to focus on informative features both channel-wise and spatially, facilitating rich semantic representation while maintaining computational efficiency, which is crucial for accurately segmenting complex or low-contrast medical images.

## 2.3  Gated Skip Fusion

In encoder–decoder architectures, skip connections bridge low-level spatial features and high-level semantic cues. To better integrate multi-scale information while avoiding feature interference, we propose a lightweight Gated Skip Fusion (GSF) mechanism.

At each decoder stage, the upsampled decoder feature $\mathbf{F}_{\text{dec}}$ is projected via a $1 \times 1$ transposed convolution and concatenated with the corresponding encoder feature $\mathbf{F}_{\text{enc}}$. A spatial gating map $\mathbf{M}_{\text{gate}} \in [0, 1]^{H \times W}$ is then learned through a convolutional attention module to weigh the importance of each spatial location. The fusion is performed as:

$$\mathbf{F}_{\text{out}} = \mathbf{F}_{\text{enc}} \odot \mathbf{M}_{\text{gate}} + \text{Conv}_{1\times1}^{T}(\mathbf{F}_{\text{dec}}) \odot (1 - \mathbf{M}_{\text{gate}}) \tag{4}$$

This formulation enables adaptive modulation of skip connections, enhancing the preservation of fine structures and suppressing noisy activations. We apply GSF at each decoder level to facilitate spatial–semantic alignment across scales, yielding more accurate and robust segmentation, especially for small or blurry targets.

### 2.4   Loss Function

To enhance both segmentation accuracy and robustness, we adopt a hybrid loss function that combines Binary Cross-Entropy (BCE) and Dice loss. BCE is designed to evaluate the pixel-wise classification quality, while Dice loss effectively measures the overlap between predicted masks and ground truth, which is especially useful in imbalanced data scenarios.

The total loss is formulated as follows:

$$\mathcal{L}_{\text{total}} = \lambda_1 \mathcal{L}_{\text{BCE}} + \lambda_2 \mathcal{L}_{\text{Dice}}, \tag{5}$$

where the individual components are defined by:

$$\mathcal{L}_{\text{BCE}} = -\frac{1}{N} \sum_{i=1}^{N} \left[ y_i \log(\hat{y}_i) + (1 - y_i) \log(1 - \hat{y}_i) \right], \tag{6}$$

$$\mathcal{L}_{\text{Dice}} = 1 - \frac{2 \sum_{i=1}^{N} y_i \hat{y}_i + \varepsilon}{\sum_{i=1}^{N} y_i + \sum_{i=1}^{N} \hat{y}_i + \varepsilon}. \tag{7}$$

Here, $N$ denotes the total number of pixels, $y_i$ is the ground truth label, and $\hat{y}_i$ represents the predicted probability for the $i$-th pixel. A small constant $\varepsilon$ is added to avoid division by zero. By default, the weighting coefficients $\lambda_1$ and $\lambda_2$ are set to 1 to equally balance the influence of both loss components during training.

## 3   Experiments

### 3.1   Datasets

We evaluate EL-UNet on four public medical segmentation datasets: DDTI [7], TN3K [8], QaTa-COV19-v2 [9], and ISIC2018 [10], covering diverse diseases and imaging modalities such as ultrasound, chest CT, and dermoscopy. This diversity enables a comprehensive assessment of the model's generalization across varying textures, lesion types, and data scales. To ensure consistency, all images were resized to $256 \times 256$ and standardized to RGB (images) or grayscale (masks). A 7:3 train-validation split was used for balanced performance evaluation.

### 3.2   Implementation Details

Experiments were conducted on two NVIDIA RTX 4090 GPUs using PyTorch. We used AdamW with PolynomialLR schedulers. The initial learning rate and weight decay were 0.01, with a batch size of 8 and 300 epochs. Each dataset was trained 8 times, and results were averaged to ensure reliability and generalizability.

## 3.3   Comparison with the State-of-the-Art Methods

To comprehensively evaluate the performance of EL-UNet, we selected 8 representative models widely adopted in recent medical image segmentation studies. These include classical architectures such as U-Net [2], FPN [3], and Attention U-Net [4], as well as more advanced designs like VM-UNet [5] and HSH-UNet [11]. Furthermore, several ultra-lightweight models, including EGE-UNet [12] and LB-UNet [13], were also incorporated for comparison.

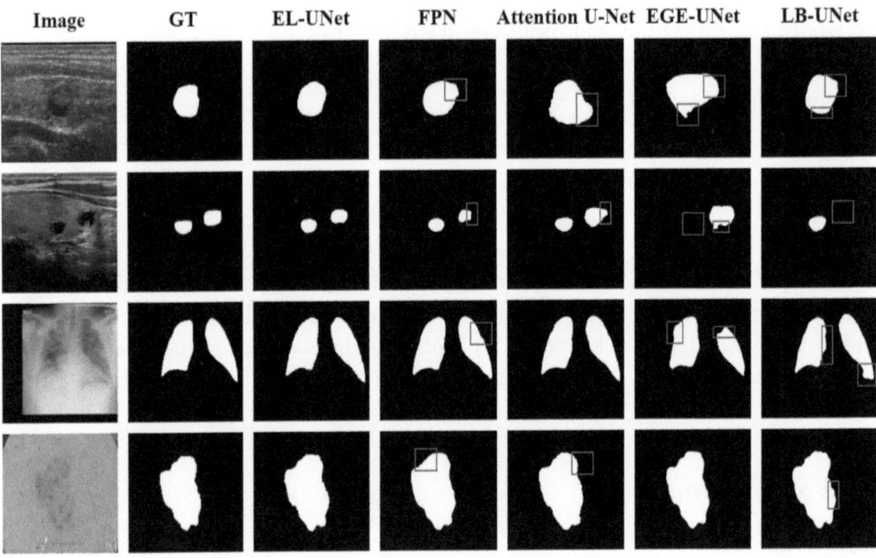

**Fig. 2.** Several visualization results on four datasets. From top to bottom, each row corresponds to DDTI, TN3K, QaTa-COV19-v2, and ISIC2018.

As summarized in Table 1, EL-UNet consistently outperforms state-of-the-art models on four benchmarks. On two thyroid ultrasound datasets, Compared with traditional models such as U-Net and Attention U-Net, EL-UNet improves the mIoU by 7.02% and 4.03% on the first dataset, and by 3.65% and 3.23% on the second dataset. When compared to current lightweight models like EGE-UNet, EL-UNet achieves improvements of up to 10.33% in mIoU and 7.94% in DSC. On QaTa-COV19-v2, it improves mIoU by at least 2.95% over lightweight models, and still outperforms large-scale VM-UNet by 2.89% mIoU and 1.85% DSC. On ISIC2018, EL-UNet maintains near-top performance. With strong generalization and efficiency, it is well-suited for diverse segmentation tasks. Visualization results (Fig. 2) further confirm its ability to handle blurry boundaries and varied lesion types.

Table 2 further presents the computational complexity comparison. EL-UNet contains only 545.3K parameters and limits its FLOPs to 1.117G. Although not

**Table 1.** Quantitative results on four datasets. Bold numbers indicate the best performance, while underlined numbers denote the second-best.

| Dataset | Model | ACC ↑ | DSC ↑ | mIoU ↑ | PRE ↑ | SEN ↑ | SPE ↑ |
|---|---|---|---|---|---|---|---|
| DDTI | U-Net [2] | 92.60 | 74.67 | 59.58 | 78.36 | 71.33 | **96.44** |
| | FPN [3] | 91.45 | 72.76 | 57.20 | 71.07 | 74.61 | 94.48 |
| | Attention U-Net [4] | 93.15 | 76.97 | 62.57 | <u>79.16</u> | 74.96 | <u>96.43</u> |
| | EGE-UNet [12] | 91.55 | 72.01 | 56.27 | 73.10 | 71.02 | 95.26 |
| | LB-UNet [13] | 92.64 | 75.92 | 61.21 | 75.95 | 76.02 | 95.63 |
| | VM-UNet [5] | 89.53 | 66.58 | 50.14 | 65.61 | 67.75 | 93.47 |
| | HSH-UNet [11] | 90.67 | 68.01 | 51.56 | 66.77 | 69.57 | 94.20 |
| | H-vmunet [6] | **93.92** | <u>78.76</u> | <u>64.96</u> | 78.72 | <u>78.90</u> | 96.42 |
| | EL-UNet(ours) | <u>93.87</u> | **79.95** | **66.60** | **80.09** | **79.95** | 96.39 |
| TN3K | U-Net [2] | 96.78 | 85.53 | 74.72 | 87.17 | 83.98 | 98.41 |
| | FPN [3] | 96.80 | 85.61 | 74.84 | 87.56 | 83.82 | <u>98.47</u> |
| | Attention U-Net [4] | 96.84 | 85.81 | 75.14 | 87.38 | 84.30 | 98.44 |
| | EGE-UNet [12] | 96.79 | 86.67 | 76.48 | 86.94 | 86.42 | 98.22 |
| | LB-UNet [13] | 96.79 | 85.66 | 74.92 | 86.81 | 84.55 | 98.36 |
| | VM-UNet [5] | 96.53 | 85.53 | 74.73 | 85.99 | 85.09 | 98.10 |
| | HSH-UNet [11] | 96.42 | 85.40 | 74.53 | 84.61 | 86.22 | 97.83 |
| | H-vmunet [6] | <u>96.99</u> | <u>87.58</u> | <u>77.91</u> | <u>87.87</u> | **87.32** | 98.33 |
| | EL-UNet(ours) | **97.28** | **87.87** | **78.37** | **88.94** | <u>86.83</u> | **98.62** |
| QaTa-COV19-v2 | U-Net [2] | 96.84 | 86.77 | 76.63 | 85.98 | 87.59 | <u>98.08</u> |
| | FPN [3] | 96.43 | 84.81 | 73.63 | 85.42 | 84.23 | 98.07 |
| | Attention U-Net [4] | <u>96.91</u> | <u>87.04</u> | <u>77.05</u> | **86.43** | 87.66 | **98.15** |
| | EGE-UNet [12] | 96.39 | 85.14 | 74.13 | 83.10 | 87.29 | 97.61 |
| | LB-UNet [13] | 96.58 | 85.87 | 75.24 | 84.02 | <u>87.80</u> | 97.76 |
| | VM-UNet [5] | 96.59 | 85.91 | 75.30 | 84.18 | 87.70 | 97.78 |
| | HSH-UNet [11] | 96.45 | 84.94 | 73.83 | 83.13 | 86.89 | 97.70 |
| | H-vmunet [6] | 96.68 | 85.82 | 75.16 | 84.52 | 87.16 | 97.92 |
| | EL-UNet(ours) | **97.04** | **87.76** | **78.19** | <u>86.12</u> | **89.47** | 98.06 |
| ISIC2018 | U-Net [2] | 94.27 | 87.69 | 78.01 | 89.15 | 86.19 | 96.76 |
| | FPN [3] | 93.97 | 86.90 | 76.84 | 89.23 | 84.70 | <u>96.84</u> |
| | Attention U-Net [4] | 94.01 | 87.13 | 77.19 | 88.40 | 85.92 | 96.51 |
| | EGE-UNet [12] | 94.44 | 88.12 | 78.77 | 88.87 | 87.42 | 96.60 |
| | LB-UNet [13] | <u>94.67</u> | <u>88.62</u> | <u>79.56</u> | <u>89.38</u> | 87.89 | 96.77 |
| | VM-UNet [5] | 94.34 | 88.08 | 78.69 | 87.64 | **88.52** | 96.14 |
| | HSH-UNet [11] | 93.52 | 86.23 | 75.80 | 86.55 | 85.92 | 95.87 |
| | H-vmunet [6] | 93.91 | 87.19 | 77.29 | 86.58 | 87.81 | 95.80 |
| | EL-UNet(ours) | **94.80** | **88.88** | **79.98** | **89.77** | <u>88.06</u> | **96.88** |

the most lightweight model, it achieves a favorable trade-off between accuracy and efficiency. In terms of inference speed, EL-UNet reaches 106.45 FPS, outperforming other lightweight models while maintaining remarkable stability with minimal runtime fluctuation. These results suggest that EL-UNet achieves an excellent balance between segmentation performance and computational cost, making it suitable for real-time and resource-constrained clinical scenarios.

**Table 2.** Comparison of Model Parameters, GFLOPs, and FPS.

| Model | Params ↓ | GFLOPs ↓ | FPS ↑ |
|---|---|---|---|
| U-Net [2] | 7.764M | 13.714 | 103.28 |
| FPN [3] | 16.701M | 7.524 | 83.72 |
| Attention U-Net [4] | 7.853M | 14.001 | 92.68 |
| EGE-UNet [12] | 0.0458M | **0.072** | 61.15 |
| LB-UNet [13] | **0.0385M** | 0.098 | 99.38 |
| VM-UNet [5] | 22.038M | 4.112 | 56.23 |
| HSH-UNet [11] | 18.037M | 9.362 | 4.21 |
| H-vmunet [6] | 6.438M | 0.742 | 3.98 |
| EL-UNet(ours) | 0.5453M | 1.117 | **106.45** |

### 3.4   Ablation Study

As shown in Table 3, we conducted three groups of ablation experiments: the baseline model, the model with only the AMSB module, and the model with only the GSF module. The baseline model adopts a 5-layer U-shaped segmentation architecture and employs standard convolutions to extract features in both the encoder and decoder. It is evident that the Baseline + AMSB method enhances the model's ability to express multi-scale features and guides it to focus on key regions, thereby improving adaptability to target contours and texture variations while effectively suppressing background interference. Meanwhile, the Baseline + GSF approach optimizes the integration of contextual information, enabling the model to accurately reconstruct high-resolution image outputs during decoding. Therefore, our EL-UNet integrates both the AMSB and GSF modules, achieving an optimal balance in terms of accuracy, robustness, and generalization capability.

**Table 3.** Ablation study of each module.

| Dataset | Baseline | AMSB | GSF | ACC ↑ | DSC ↑ | mIoU ↑ | PRE ↑ | SEN ↑ | SPE ↑ |
|---|---|---|---|---|---|---|---|---|---|
| DDTI | ✓ | | | 92.85 | 76.12 | 60.37 | 77.95 | 75.48 | 95.61 |
| | ✓ | ✓ | | 93.76 | 79.43 | 65.89 | **80.15** | 78.89 | **96.45** |
| | ✓ | | ✓ | 93.21 | 78.10 | 63.42 | 79.02 | 77.30 | 96.01 |
| | ✓ | ✓ | ✓ | **93.87** | **79.95** | **66.60** | 80.09 | **79.95** | 96.39 |
| ISIC2018 | ✓ | | | 94.21 | 86.32 | 77.01 | 87.52 | 84.99 | 96.31 |
| | ✓ | ✓ | | 94.66 | 88.01 | 79.11 | 88.86 | 87.20 | 96.80 |
| | ✓ | | ✓ | 94.53 | 87.62 | 78.49 | 89.01 | 86.58 | 96.65 |
| | ✓ | ✓ | ✓ | **94.80** | **88.88** | **79.98** | **89.77** | **88.06** | **96.88** |

## 4   Conclusion

This paper presents a novel lightweight U-Net variant named EL-UNet, designed to address the challenge of balancing segmentation performance with model efficiency in existing architectures. EL-UNet retains the fundamental U-shaped encoder-decoder structure while integrating multi-scale parallel convolutional modules and attention mechanisms to better focus on key regions of medical images at both local and global levels. Additionally, a novel gated skip connection mechanism is proposed to alleviate semantic inconsistencies between shallow and deep feature representations. Experimental results on four datasets demonstrate that EL-UNet not only significantly improves segmentation performance but also maintains a lightweight model structure, making it an effective solution that balances segmentation accuracy and computational efficiency.

## References


1. Shelhamer, E., Long, J., Darrell, T.: Fully convolutional networks for semantic segmentation. IEEE Trans. Pattern Anal. Mach. Intell. **39**(4), 640–651 (2017). https://doi.org/10.1109/TPAMI.2016.2572683
2. Ronneberger, O., Fischer, P., Brox, T.: U-net: convolutional networks for biomedical image segmentation. In: Navab, N., Hornegger, J., Wells, W.M., Frangi, A.F. (eds.) MICCAI 2015. LNCS, vol. 9351, pp. 234–241. Springer, Cham (2015). https://doi.org/10.1007/978-3-319-24574-4_28
3. Lin, T.Y., Dollár, P., Girshick, R., He, K., Hariharan, B., Belongie, S.: Feature pyramid networks for object detection. In: 2017 IEEE Conference on Computer Vision and Pattern Recognition (CVPR), pp. 936–944 (2017). https://doi.org/10.1109/CVPR.2017.106
4. Oktay, O., et al.: Attention u-net: learning where to look for the pancreas. In: Proceedings of the Medical Imaging with Deep Learning (MIDL) (2018)
5. Ruan, J., Li, J., Xiang, S.: Vm-unet: vision mamba unet for medical image segmentation (2024). https://arxiv.org/abs/2402.02491
6. Wu, R., Liu, Y., Liang, P., Chang, Q.: H-vmunet: high-order vision mamba unet for medical image segmentation. Neurocomputing 129447 (2025). https://doi.org/10.1016/j.neucom.2025.129447

7. Pedraza, L., Vargas, C., Narváez, F., et al.: An open access thyroid ultrasound image database. In: Proceedings of SPIE 9287, 10th International Symposium on Medical Information Processing and Analysis, p. 92870W (2015). https://doi.org/10.1117/12.2073532

8. Gong, H., Chen, G., Wang, R., et al.: Multi-task learning for thyroid nodule segmentation with thyroid region prior. In: 2021 IEEE 18th International Symposium on Biomedical Imaging (ISBI), pp. 257–261. IEEE (2021)

9. Degerli, A., Ahishali, M., Kiranyaz, S., et al.: Reliable covid-19 detection using chest x-ray images. In: 2021 IEEE International Conference on Image Processing (ICIP), Anchorage, AK, USA, pp. 185–189. IEEE (2021). https://doi.org/10.1109/ICIP42928.2021.9506442

10. Codella, N.C.F., Nguyen, Q.T., Halicek, M., et al.: Skin lesion analysis toward melanoma detection: a challenge at the 2017 international symposium on biomedical imaging (isbi), hosted by the international skin imaging collaboration (isic). In: 2018 IEEE 15th International Symposium on Biomedical Imaging (ISBI 2018), pp. 168–172. IEEE (2018)

11. Ruoxi, W., Lv, H., Liang, P., et al.: Hsh-unet: hybrid selective high order interactive u-shaped model for automated skin lesion segmentation. Comput. Biol. Med. **168**, 107798 (2024). https://doi.org/10.1016/j.compbiomed.2023.107798

12. Ruan, J., Xie, M., Gao, J., Liu, T., Fu, Y.: Ege-unet: an efficient group enhanced unet for skin lesion segmentation. In: Greenspan, H,. et al. (eds.) Medical Image Computing and Computer Assisted Intervention – MICCAI 2023. LNCS, vol. 14223, pp. 473–483. Springer, Cham (2023). https://doi.org/10.1007/978-3-031-43901-8_46

13. Xu, J., Tong, L.: Lb-unet: a lightweight boundary-assisted unet for skin lesion segmentation. In: Medical Image Computing and Computer Assisted Intervention – MICCAI 2024, pp. 361–371. Springer, Cham (2024). https://doi.org/10.1007/978-3-031-72114-4_35

# SwiM-UNet: A Lightweight Hybrid Swin Transformer-Vision Mamba U-Net with a Novel Adapter Design


Yeonwoo Noh[1], Seyong Jin[2], Jiwon Kim[3], Yunyoung Chang[4], Minwoo Lee[5], and Wonjong Noh[6(✉)]

[1] College of Medicine, Gachon University, Incheon, Korea
nyw0207@gachon.ac.kr
[2] Artificial Intelligence, Sejong University, Seoul, Korea
[3] Convergence Engineering for Artificial Intelligence, Sejong University, Seoul, Korea
[4] School of Artificial Intelligence, Gachon University, Seongnam, Korea
[5] Neurology, Hallym University Sacred Heart Hospital, Anyang, Korea
[6] School of Software, Hallym University, Chuncheon, Korea
wonjong.noh@hallym.ac.kr



**Abstract.** For medical image segmentation, transformer-based models have exhibited superior segmentation performance. However, their high computational complexity continues to pose a major challenge. In contrast, Mamba offers a more computationally efficient alternative; however, its performance remains inferior to that of transformers. This study proposes a U-Net-based novel lightweight hybrid model, SwiM-UNet, which is the first Mamba transformer hybrid model specifically designed to process 3D data. Specifically, efficient TSMamba (eTS-Mamba) is utilized in the initial stages of the U-Net architecture to efficiently manage computational overhead, while efficient Swin transformers (eSwin) are employed in the later stages to effectively capture long-range dependencies and local contextual information. In addition, this model strategically integrates both the Mamba and Swin transformer architectures using a Mamba–Swin adapter (MS-adapter) to leverage their complementary advantages. The proposed MS-adapter consists of three sub-adapters that play different roles in emphasizing local information between eTSMamba and eSwin modules and gates that balance the sub-adapters. This model also employs a low-rank MLP in the encoder and applies channel reduction in the decoder to enhance computational efficiency. We conducted performance evaluations using the publicly available BraTS2023 dataset and confirmed that the proposed model outperformed state-of-the-art benchmark models while significantly reducing computational complexity.


**Keywords:** Adaptor · Brain Tumor Segmentation · Hybrid Model · Lightweight Model · Mamba · Swin Transformer · UNet


© The Author(s), under exclusive license to Springer Nature Switzerland AG 2026
T. Chen et al. (Eds.): EMA4MICCAI 2025 Workshops, LNCS 16318, pp. 93–102, 2026.
https://doi.org/10.1007/978-3-032-13961-0_10

## 1   Introduction

With the rapid advancement of artificial intelligence (AI), medical imaging—
particularly brain tumor segmentation—has emerged as one of the most challenging and actively researched areas. The success of AI in medical imaging has
been facilitated by the emergence of advanced architectures, ranging from convolutional neural networks (CNNs) to transformers, along with U-Net models.

Various types of transformers [5,10,18], including vision transformers (ViTs)
[1] and Swin transformers [12], have been introduced to enhance the performance
of computer vision tasks. Notably, the Swin Transformer, which incorporates a
shifted-window mechanism, was utilized in the winning model of the 2023 BraTS
challenge [4]. The attention mechanism in transformers is highly effective for
capturing global context and long-range dependencies within images, enabling
them to achieve high performance in brain tumor segmentation in recent years.
However, despite these advantages, transformers suffer from a major drawback:
their computational complexity increases substantially owing to their attention
mechanisms, particularly when processing large images.

To address this challenge, a novel architecture known as MAMBA [7] was
introduced. Mamba is an architecture that utilizes a state-space model (SSM)
[8] instead of the traditional attention mechanism, resulting in superior computational efficiency compared with transformers, particularly when processing long-sequence data. Recently, besides a Vision Mamba [17], other Mamba
approaches [3,11,14] have also been explored. Despite its enhanced efficiency,
Mamba has a notable limitation in that its performance is generally inferior to
that of transformers.

Owing to the performance limitations when using Mamba alone, active
research has been conducted on hybrid models that integrate other architectures. Zhou et al. [16] combined Mamba with CNN to leverage the strengths of
both architectures. This method incorporated cascade residual multi-scale convolutions, which employ filters of varying sizes to effectively capture tumors at
multiple scales. Hatamizadeh et al. [9] proposed the MambaVision model, which
employs residual convolution blocks in the initial stages for fast feature extraction while incorporating both Mamba and transformer in the later stages. Zhang
et al. [15] proposed the HMT-UNet model, which integrates the MambaVision
structure into both the encoder and decoder of a U-Net architecture. However,
both MambaVision [9] and HMT-UNet [15] are limited to processing only 2D
data. To address this limitation, Cao et al. [2] proposed the MedSegMamba
model, a CNN-Mamba hybrid model that accepts 3D data as input. However,
as Mamba is a relatively recent development, research on hybrid models that
combine Mamba with other architectures remains limited.

## 2   The Proposed Model: SwiM-UNet

We propose the lightweight SwiM-UNet model consisting of three components:
1) An encoder that incorporates efficient TSMamba (eTSMamba) blocks in the

early stages, efficient Swin transformer (eSwin) blocks in the later stages, and an MS-adapter between them. 2) A CNN-based decoder predicts segmentation results. 3) Skip connections that link the encoder and decoder. Here, we assume the four-stage U-Net architecture as a basic backbone. The overall architecture is shown in Fig. 1.

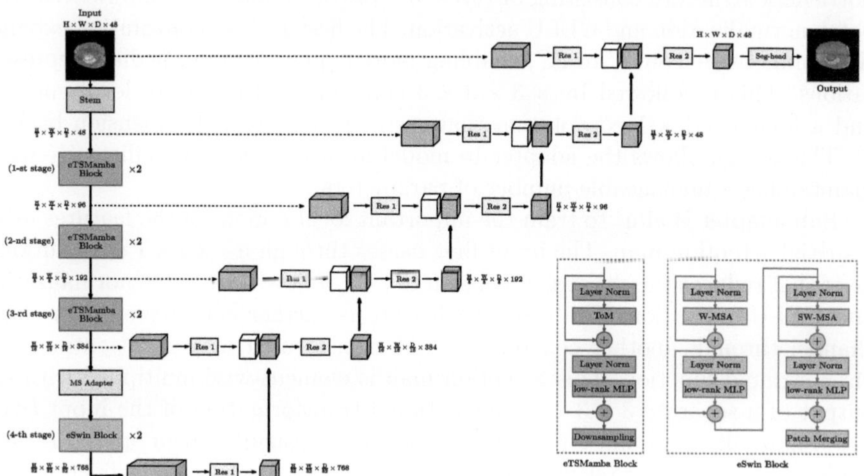

**Fig. 1.** Overall architecture of the proposed SwiM-UNet model.

## 2.1 Encoder

The encoder uses a preprocessed 3D brain MRI volume as the input. The first component of the encoder is the stem layer, which consists of a depth-wise convolution with a kernel size of $7 \times 7 \times 7$, padding of $3 \times 3 \times 3$, and a stride value of $2 \times 2 \times 2$. When an input with size $C \times D \times H \times W$ passes through the stem layer, the output size is $48 \times \frac{D}{2} \times \frac{H}{2} \times \frac{W}{2}$. The output of the stem layer was processed using the proposed eTSMamba blocks and eSwin blocks. These two types of blocks are modified version of the conventional TSMamba Block proposed by Xing et al. [14] and the conventional Swin Transformer Block introduced by Hatamizadeh et al. [10]. Here, we replaced the MLP structure with the low-rank MLP to enhance the computational efficiency. Specifically, the input feature map is first projected into a lower-dimensional space using a $1 \times 1 \times 1$ convolution with reduced rank $(r = \frac{C}{8})$, and then expanded to the desired MLP dimension with another $1 \times 1 \times 1$ convolution. This structure significantly reduces the number of parameters and FLOPs, especially in deeper layers with large channel sizes, while retaining the non-linear transformation capacity through the GELU activation.

**The Proposed Adapter Model.** The output obtained after passing through all the eTSMamba blocks is then fed into the MS-adapter, as shown in Fig. 2. The proposed MS-adapter consists of three sub-adapters and gates, each designed to enhance the feature representation in different ways.

Sub-adapter A is designed to enhance local feature representations by increasing the model's capacity to capture fine-grained spatial patterns. It follows a bottleneck structure consisting of three 3D convolutional layers interleaved with batch normalization and GELU activation. The first $1 \times 1 \times 1$ convolution expands the channel size from $C$ to $2C$, enabling more expressive intermediate representations. This is followed by a $3 \times 3 \times 3$ convolution to capture local context, and a final $1 \times 1 \times 1$ convolution that restores the channel dimension back to $C$. This design allows the adapter to model local dependencies efficiently while maintaining a manageable number of parameters.

Sub-adapter B aims to train the important local regions of the features using a spatial attention map. The input first passes through a $1 \times 1 \times 1$ convolutional layer that reduces the channel dimension to $C/4$, followed by batch normalization and GELU activation. The resulting feature is further compressed to a single channel through another convolution and transformed into an attention map via a sigmoid function. This attention map is element-wise multiplied with the output of a separate $3 \times 3 \times 3$ convolutional transformation of the input (with batch normalization and GELU activation), emphasizing salient spatial regions while suppressing less relevant areas. Through this mechanism, salient regions are adaptively emphasized while irrelevant areas are suppressed.

Sub-adapter C is designed to capture multi-scale contextual features by aggregating information from different receptive field sizes. The input is processed in parallel through three branches: (i) a $3 \times 3 \times 3$ average pooling layer, (ii) a $5 \times 5 \times 5$ max pooling layer, and (iii) a $7 \times 7 \times 7$ average pooling layer. Each branch uses a stride of 1 and padding values that preserve the spatial resolution. The outputs from the branches are concatenated with the original input to form a enhanced multi-scale feature representation. This concatenated feature is then passed through two consecutive convolutional layers (each followed by batch normalization and GELU activation) to reduce the channel dimension back to $C$, enabling effective integration of multi-scale features.

The gate module adaptively balances the contribution of the sub-adapter-transformed features and the original features. Consequently, the network can selectively suppress or enhance the adapter's influence based on the current input content and context. The gate module consists of a 3D adaptive average pooling layer with an output size of $1 \times 1 \times 1$, followed by a 3D convolutional layer with a kernel size of $1 \times 1 \times 1$ and a sigmoid activation. The feature transformation through the gate module is given by:

$$G = \text{Conv3d}\left(\text{AdaptiveAvgPool3d}(x)\right)$$
$$Gate_{out} = \sigma(G) \cdot \text{Adapter}(x) + (1 - \sigma(G)) \cdot x \tag{1}$$

To further enhance flexibility, each sub-adapter can be modulated by a dedicated gate. This multi-gate mechanism enables the network to control the contribution of each sub-adapter independently, facilitating more precise and dynamic feature adaptation.

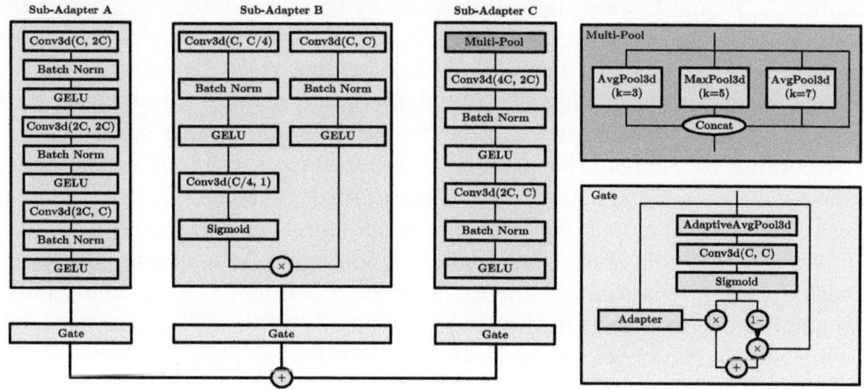

**Fig. 2.** The architectures of the proposed MS-adapter.

## 2.2 Decoder

The decoder utilizes skip connections to link with the encoder, enabling the transfer of feature representations between corresponding layers. These feature representations were first processed through Residual Block 1, which consisted of a $3 \times 3 \times 3$ 3D convolutional layer, instance normalization, and Leaky ReLU (LReLU) activation. The feature processed by the residual block is then concatenated with the output from the previous stage. After concatenation, the output passes through Residual Block 2, which is essential for computational efficiency. Unlike previous works such as Swin UNETR [10] and SegMamba [14], Residual Block 2 adopts a bottleneck structure with channel reduction ($2C \rightarrow \frac{C}{4} \rightarrow C$) and GELU activation for improved efficiency. The final output of the decoder passes through the segmentation head, which consists of a $1 \times 1 \times 1$ convolutional layer followed by a sigmoid activation function. It completes the segmentation task.

## 3   Experiments

**Dataset.** In this study, we used the publicly available BraTS2023 dataset (https://www.kaggle.com/datasets/shakilrana/brats-2023-adult-glioma), which comprises 1251 3D brain MRI volumes. Each MRI volume has a size of $240 \times 240 \times 155$, divided into four modalities: native (T1), T1-weighted (T1Gd), T2-weighted (T2), and T2 Fluid Attenuated Inversion Recovery (T2-FLAIR). We divided the dataset into training, validation, and test sets in a ratio of 7:1:2. Segmentation targets were classified into three types: whole tumor (WT), tumor core (TC), and enhancing tumor (ET).

**Ablation Study of MS-Adapter.** Ablation studies were performed on the MS-adapter. Here, the baseline model is one that only has the proposed eTS-Mamba and eSwin blocks and does not have the adapter module. First, sub-adapters A, B, and C were applied individually to compare their respective contributions to model performance. The sub-adapter that yielded the best results was subsequently combined with a gating mechanism to further assess its impact. Second, models incorporating all sub-adapters—A, B, and C—simultaneously were compared, both with and without the addition of a gating mechanism.

According to Table 1, the number of parameters and FLOPs increased in the order of sub-adapters A, C, and B, respectively. The addition of the gating mechanism to each sub-adapter resulted in only a marginal increase in both the number of parameters and FLOPs. Simultaneous use of sub-adapters A, B, and C with gating mechanism exhibited the highest parameter count and FLOPs. The number of parameters in the model increased by 73.452% compared to the baseline model. Nevertheless, the increase in FLOPs was limited to only 6.503%.

**Table 1.** Ablation study of MS-adapter: computational complexity.

| A | B | C | Gate | Parameters | FLOPs |
|---|---|---|---|---|---|
| × | × | × | × | 41.02M | 233.74G |
| ✓ | × | × | × | 57.54M | 242.20G |
| × | ✓ | × | × | 45.04M | 235.80G |
| × | × | ✓ | × | 50.16M | 238.42G |
| × | × | ✓ | ✓ | 50.16M | 238.42G |
| ✓ | ✓ | ✓ | × | 70.71M | 248.94G |
| ✓ | ✓ | ✓ | ✓ | 71.15M | 248.94G |

Table 2 compares the segmentation performance in terms of the Dice score and HD95, respectively. Regarding Dice score, applying only a single sub-adapter did not yield an improvement in the Dice score. The simultaneous application of sub-adapters A, B, and C with the gate mechanism led to the highest Dice score. Regarding HD95, the application of any sub-adapter resulted in a lower HD95. Similar to the Dice score, the lowest HD95 was observed when all sub-adapters were used simultaneously with the gate mechanism. In summary, compared with the baseline, only a single sub-adapter provides a marginal performance enhancement. However, when all sub-adapters and gate modules were implemented, the performance improvement became more substantial. That is, the sub-adapter modules have a complementary relationship regarding performance improvement, especially for local lesions such as TC and ET.

**Comparison with SOTA.** We compared the proposed model with the following: 1) VT-UNet [13] is a transformer-based U-Net architecture tailored for

**Table 2.** Ablation study of MS-adapter: Dice score and HD95

| A | B | C | Gate | Dice Score (% ↑) | | | | HD95 (mm ↓) | | | |
|---|---|---|---|---|---|---|---|---|---|---|---|
| | | | | WT | TC | ET | Mean | WT | TC | ET | Mean |
| × | × | × | × | 0.933 | 0.890 | 0.855 | 0.893 | 4.314 | 4.510 | 4.753 | 4.526 |
| ✓ | × | × | × | **0.934** | 0.890 | 0.854 | 0.893 | **3.872** | 4.371 | 4.731 | 4.325 |
| × | ✓ | × | × | 0.933 | 0.887 | 0.848 | 0.889 | 4.029 | 4.528 | 4.594 | 4.384 |
| × | × | ✓ | × | **0.934** | 0.891 | 0.855 | 0.893 | 3.943 | 4.194 | 4.844 | 4.327 |
| × | × | ✓ | ✓ | 0.933 | 0.890 | 0.854 | 0.892 | 4.112 | 4.476 | 4.528 | 4.372 |
| ✓ | ✓ | ✓ | × | 0.933 | **0.897** | 0.858 | 0.896 | 4.153 | 4.033 | 4.425 | 4.204 |
| ✓ | ✓ | ✓ | ✓ | **0.934** | **0.897** | **0.860** | **0.897** | 4.157 | **4.015** | **4.353** | **4.175** |

3D medical image segmentation, 2) nnMamba [6] is an SSM based architecture designed for efficient and scalable 3D biomedical image segmentation, 3) SegMamba [14] uses only conventional TSMamba blocks, 4) Swin UNETR [10] employs only conventional Swin transformer blocks and 5) MedSegMamba [2], a hybrid Mamba-CNN model, was designed to process 3D data.

First, we compared the computational complexity in terms of the number of parameters and FLOPs, as shown in Table 3. Among the compared models, MedSegMamba [2] had the largest number of parameters, while VT-UNet [13] exhibited the highest FLOPs among all models. The nnMamba [6] had the lowest number of parameters, whereas the proposed SwiM-UNet exhibited the lowest FLOPs. In particular, the proposed SwiM-UNet achieved 65.727% lower FLOPs compared to SegMamba [14] having the second lowest FLOPs. This reduction was achieved by incorporating a low-rank MLP into the TSMamba blocks and applying channel reduction in the decoder.

**Table 3.** Comparison of computational complexity across different models.

| Methods | Paramters | FLOPs |
|---|---|---|
| VT-UNet [13] | 20.75M | 1,651.63G |
| Swin UNETR [10] | 69.62M | 780.22G |
| nnMamba [6] | **17.89M** | 1,109.24G |
| SegMamba [14] | 58.90M | 726.34G |
| MedSegMamba [2] | 84.47M | 1,257.54G |
| SwiM-UNet (proposed) | 71.15M | **248.94G** |

Second, we compared the segmentation performance, as shown in Table 4. The proposed SwiM-UNet outperformed the other models by achieving the highest Dice score. The proposed model also achieved the lowest mean HD95 among the compared models. In particular, it demonstrated superior performance in segmenting fine-grained lesions such as TC and ET. Although VT-UNet and the MedSegMamba exhibited the highest FLOPs, the proposed model demonstrates an improvement in segmentation performance while reducing FLOPs by 84.928% and 80.204% compared with VT-UNet and MedSegMamba, respectively. Several factors contribute to this outcome: 1) The combination of transformers and Mamba, which utilize different feature extraction methods, resulted in a more robust feature representation. 2) Incorporating Mamba into transformer-based models have enhanced the generalization performance and mitigated overfitting. 3) The integration of the transformer's powerful feature representation with Mamba's efficient sequential processing has contributed to improved model performance.

In summary, compared to the SOTA models, the proposed SwiM-UNet achieved the best trade-off in terms of computational efficiency and performance, which is shown in Fig. 3.

**Table 4.** Comparison of segmentation performance across different models.

| Methods | Dice Score (%, ↑) | | | | HD95 (mm, ↓) | | | |
|---|---|---|---|---|---|---|---|---|
| | WT | TC | ET | Mean | WT | TC | ET | Mean |
| VT-UNet [13] | 0.930 | 0.893 | 0.850 | 0.891 | 4.093 | 4.205 | 4.670 | 4.323 |
| Swin UNETR [10] | 0.929 | 0.877 | 0.842 | 0.883 | 4.315 | 5.026 | 5.200 | 4.847 |
| nnMamba [6] | 0.930 | 0.892 | 0.846 | 0.889 | **3.780** | 4.217 | 4.602 | 4.200 |
| SegMamba [14] | 0.917 | 0.873 | 0.843 | 0.878 | 5.317 | 4.898 | 5.226 | 5.087 |
| MedSegMamba [2] | 0.930 | 0.893 | 0.850 | 0.891 | 4.093 | 4.205 | 4.670 | 4.323 |
| SwiM-UNet (proposed) | **0.934** | **0.897** | **0.860** | **0.897** | 4.157 | **4.015** | **4.353** | **4.175** |

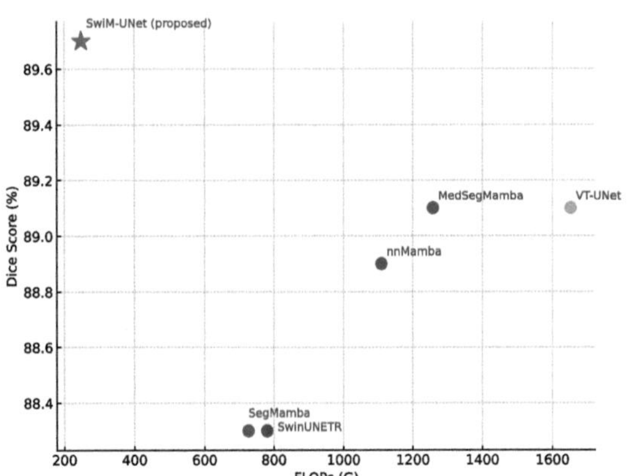


**Fig. 3.** Comparison between the proposed SwiM-UNet and other models.

## 4    Conclusion

In this study, we presented a novel lightweight Mamba–transformer hybrid model, SwiM-UNet. It integrated the proposed eTSMamba block and eSwin block which incorporate low-rank MLPs and MS-adapter. Here, the eTSMamba blocks were employed in the early stages to maximize computational efficiency, whereas the eSwin blocks were employed in the later stages to effectively capture long-range dependencies and the local context. The proposed MS-adapter consists of three sub-adapters that emphasize local information in different manners between Mamba and Swin transformer, along with gating mechanisms that balance the contributions of the sub-adapters. We also incorporated a channel reduction into the residual blocks of the decoder to reduce the number of parateters and FLOPs. The performance evaluation confirmed that the proposed SwiM-UNet outperformed SOTA benchmark models in terms of Dice score and HD95 while also exhibiting much lower computational complexity. In future work, we plan to explore parameter-efficient techniques to further reduce the number of model parameters without sacrificing performance. Additionally, we intend to incorporate medical domain knowledge—such as tumor-specific priors and multi-modal fusion strategies—into the model design to enhance its robustness in real-world applications.

**Acknowledgments.** This research was supported by the Bio&Medical Technology Development Program of the National Research Foundation (NRF) funded by the Korean government (MSIT) (No. RS-2023-00223501).

**Disclosure of Interests.** The authors have no competing interests to declare that are relevant to the content of this article.

## References


1. Alexey, D.: An image is worth 16x16 words: transformers for image recognition at scale. arXiv preprint arXiv: 2010.11929 (2020)
2. Cao, A., Li, Z., Jomsky, J., Laine, A.F., Guo, J.: Medsegmamba: 3d cnn-mamba hybrid architecture for brain segmentation. arXiv preprint arXiv:2409.08307 (2024)
3. Dang, T.D.Q., Nguyen, H.H., Tiulpin, A.: Log-vmamba: local-global vision mamba for medical image segmentation. In: Proceedings of the Asian Conference on Computer Vision, pp. 548–565 (2024)
4. Ferreira, A., et al.: How we won brats 2023 adult glioma challenge? Just faking it! enhanced synthetic data augmentation and model ensemble for brain tumour segmentation. arXiv preprint arXiv:2402.17317 (2024)
5. Ghazouani, F., Vera, P., Ruan, S.: Efficient brain tumor segmentation using swin transformer and enhanced local self-attention. Int. J. Comput. Assist. Radiol. Surg. **19**(2), 273–281 (2024)
6. Gong, H., et al.: nnmamba: 3d biomedical image segmentation, classification and landmark detection with state space model. In: 2025 IEEE 22nd International Symposium on Biomedical Imaging (ISBI), pp. 1–5. IEEE (2025)

7. Gu, A., Dao, T.: Mamba: linear-time sequence modeling with selective state spaces. arXiv preprint arXiv:2312.00752 (2023)

8. Gu, A., Goel, K., Ré, C.: Efficiently modeling long sequences with structured state spaces. arXiv preprint arXiv:2111.00396 (2021)

9. Hatamizadeh, A., Kautz, J.: Mambavision: a hybrid mamba-transformer vision backbone. arXiv preprint arXiv:2407.08083 (2024)

10. Hatamizadeh, A., Nath, V., Tang, Y., Yang, D., Roth, H.R., Xu, D.: Swin unetr: swin transformers for semantic segmentation of brain tumors in mri images. In: International MICCAI Brainlesion Workshop, pp. 272–284. Springer, Heidelberg (2021). https://doi.org/10.1007/978-3-031-08999-2_22

11. Lai, Y., Cao, A., Gao, Y., Shang, J., Li, Z., Guo, J.: Advancing efficient brain tumor multi-class classification–new insights from the vision mamba model in transfer learning. arXiv preprint arXiv:2410.21872 (2024)

12. Liu, Z., et al.: Swin transformer: hierarchical vision transformer using shifted windows. In: Proceedings of the IEEE/CVF International Conference on Computer Vision, pp. 10012–10022 (2021)

13. Peiris, H., Hayat, M., Chen, Z., Egan, G., Harandi, M.: A robust volumetric transformer for accurate 3d tumor segmentation. In: International Conference on Medical Image Computing and Computer-Assisted Intervention, pp. 162–172. Springer, Heidelberg (2022). https://doi.org/10.1007/978-3-031-16443-9_16

14. Xing, Z., Ye, T., Yang, Y., Liu, G., Zhu, L.: Segmamba: long-range sequential modeling mamba for 3d medical image segmentation. In: International Conference on Medical Image Computing and Computer-Assisted Intervention, pp. 578–588. Springer, Heidelberg (2024). https://doi.org/10.1007/978-3-031-72111-3_54

15. Zhang, M., Chen, Z., Ge, Y., Tao, X.: Hmt-unet: a hybird mamba-transformer vision unet for medical image segmentation. arXiv preprint arXiv:2408.11289 (2024)

16. Zhou, R., Wang, J., Xia, G., Xing, J., Shen, H., Shen, X.: Cascade residual multiscale convolution and mamba-structured unet for advanced brain tumor image segmentation. Entropy **26**(5), 385 (2024)

17. Zhu, L., Liao, B., Zhang, Q., Wang, X., Liu, W., Wang, X.: Vision mamba: efficient visual representation learning with bidirectional state space model (2024)

18. ZongRen, L., Silamu, W., Yuzhen, W., Zhe, W.: Densetrans: multimodal brain tumor segmentation using swin transformer. IEEE Access **11**, 42895–42908 (2023)

# Federated and Continual Learning of AI Models from Routine Clinical Data Under Privacy Constraints

Varghese Alex Kollerathu[1]([✉]), Vineet Vinay Bhombore[1], Rahul Ramesh[1], Abhinandan Tejani[1], Matthias Wolf[2], and Gerardo Hermosillo Valadez[2]

[1] Siemens Healthineers, Bengaluru, India
{varghese.kollerathu,vineet.vinay-bhombore,rahul.ramesh,
abhinandan.tejani}@siemens-healthineers.com
[2] Siemens Healthineers, Malvern, PA, USA
{mwolf,gerardo.hermosillovaladez}@siemens-healthineers.com

**Abstract.** Lung cancer remains one of the most prevalent cancers world-wide and has a low overall five-year survival rate, making early detection a critical clinical priority. The advent of AI-based Computer-Aided Detection (CAD) systems for lung cancer has significantly reduced the workload of radiologists. Traditionally, these AI models are trained on curated datasets that are extensively annotated and reviewed by multiple radiologists. In modern clinical workflows, radiologists frequently interact with AI-generated results to aid interpretation and streamline reading and reporting processes. These routine interactions offer a valuable opportunity to enhance AI algorithms further. However, regulatory frameworks such as HIPAA and GDPR restrict the centralized sharing of patient data due to privacy concerns, limiting the ability to aggregate and retrain models centrally. To overcome this challenge, we adopt a decentralized learning framework that preserves patient privacy. Our approach leverages data generated during routine interpretation of thoracic CT scans to retrain an existing lung nodule detection model. We propose an AI/ML-based methodology designed to address the inherent noise in annotations generated during routine clinical readings. To further improve efficiency, we incorporate a negative mining strategy during retraining, which reduces computational overhead and enables faster model updates. We evaluate the retrained model on a Lung Cancer Screening dataset (n = 1128). Compared to the baseline AI model, our decentralized model achieves improvements in sensitivity of 6.90%, 6.98%, 5.65%, 4.05%, 3.55%, 3.87%, and 3.32% at 1/8, 1/4, 1/2, 1, 2, 4, and 8 false positives per scan, respectively. These results demonstrate a scalable, efficient, and privacy-preserving approach to continuously improve AI algorithms using data generated during routine clinical practice.

**Keywords:** Federated Learning · Routine Reading · Lung Nodules · Continual Learning


T. Chen et al. (Eds.): EMA4MICCAI 2025 Workshops, LNCS 16318, pp. 103–111, 2026.
https://doi.org/10.1007/978-3-032-13961-0_11

# 1    Introduction

Lung cancer accounted for an estimated 1.8 million deaths in 2020 according to the World Health Organization (WHO) [7] and an estimated 2.2 million diagnoses each year. Furthermore, lung cancer is associated with a low overall survival rate, therefore timely diagnosis of lung cancer plays a vital role in increasing survival rates [13]. The high prevalence of lung cancer increases the burden on radiologists. Computer Aided Detection (CAD) systems have been developed to aid radiologists by reducing the reading time and subsequently the time required to diagnose lung cancer [1,4,11].

Typically, a CAD system used to detect lung cancer is a multistage approach [2] consisting of a candidate generator, followed by a false positive reduction network and a nodule-type detector. The datasets used to train CAD algorithms for lung cancer (LUNA [10], NLST [12]) are read by multiple experts and the ground truth is derived by obtaining consensus among them.

Due to factors such as difference in patient population or country-specific guidelines, algorithms trained using these datasets are prone to perform below the expected level. Given this context, in a clinical setting, radiologists interact with the results generated by AI algorithms as part of their clinical routine. These interactions include

- Accepting CAD findings,
- Editing CAD findings for example correcting the dimensions of the detected finding and
- Rejecting CAD findings.

These interactions could be used to retrain and improve existing CAD systems. However, data regulations such as HIPAA and GDPR prevent the collection of such data due to patient privacy concerns.

Decentralized learning techniques such as Federated Learning (FL) are the apt choice for circumventing data regulations in a privacy-preserving manner. For example, an AI model was built for breast cancer classification using federated learning by collaborating with seven clinical sites [9]. Similarly, data from 71 sites were used to build a model in a decentralized fashion to segment gliomas into its subcomponents, [8]. [3] explores the application of federated learning to identify COVID-19-related lung abnormalities in chest CT scans.

Although previous work in FL has illustrated promising results in the domain of healthcare, an area which is relatively less explored is the efficacy of models (re)trained using data arising from routine reading. Data obtained from routine clinical reading presents additional challenges, such as:

1. Data is read by a single expert.
2. Not all nodules or lesions are reported by radiologists; typically, only those considered to be clinically significant are reported. Moreover, the criteria for clinical significance can vary depending on regional guidelines and the reporting protocols adopted by individual hospitals.

3. Findings arising from routine reading could be associated with single or multiple pathological conditions. For example, a radiologist looking for lung nodules may also report the presence of comorbidities such as emphysema or atelectasis.
4. Experts during their routine reading are only required to detect the presence of pathological conditions. This leads to a situation where the data arising from a clinical site have over and under representation of the "lesion" and "not a lesion class" respectively.

The first two factors mentioned above make routine clinical data noisy in nature when compared to publicly available dataset. Our major contribution in this article is the methodology to minimize noise arising from the annotations and how to continually re-train and improve existing AI algorithms.

In this article, we simulated continual retraining of a LungCAD false positive reduction network (Post Classifier) in a decentralized fashion using data arising from routine reading. The section below provides further information on the data and the training strategy. In Sect. 3, a lung cancer screening dataset is used to compare the gains attained upon using the proposed training strategy. Finally, the manuscript ends with Sect. 4 which presents the conclusion and the next steps.

## 2    Materials and Methods

### 2.1    Model

In this work, annotations from routine reading data were used to retrain the post-classifier network in LungCAD. The model is a proprietary 3-D Convolutional Neural Network (CNN) with 31 convolutional layers with residual connections. The candidates generated by the Candidate Generation model are the input to the model, and the model returns the posterior probability of each of them being a nodule.

### 2.2    Training the Base Model

Prior to re-training the model on routine reading, the model was trained on dataset (*clean*) arising from 2000 patients which was annotated by multiple expert readers. The parameters of the model were updated by minimizing the binary cross-entropy loss. Performance on the validation data (**v_data**) was used to determine the base model ($BM$). This model is part of the Lung CAD portfolio offered by Siemens Healthineers and has received regulatory clearance from multiple authorities, underscoring its clinical maturity and readiness for deployment in real-world settings. This model acts as the first initial model/global model for downstream Decentralized Learning.

### 2.3  Data Collection and Preparation from Clinical Routine

Thoracic CT volumes were acquired from a collaborating site after obtaining the appropriate approvals and clearances. The inclusion criteria for the dataset were volumes with slice thickness $\leq 2.5\,$mm of complete chest from adult population. The distribution of the data according to the original equipment manufacturer (OEM) is shown in Table 1(a). Each data point within the data set was read by one of the three radiologists. Table 1(b) provides information on the number of cases read by each of the radiologist and their years of experience.

To emulate a clinical scenario, each volume in the data set was presented to a radiologist to perform a routine reading. The impact of noise arising from the annotations due to routine reading was minimized by using a proprietary ensemble composed of AI/ML models. Briefly, the ensemble consists of deep learning models and machine learning algorithms, such as isolation forests. The base model and variants of it form the deep learning components in the ensemble. The one class classifiers,i.e. the isolation forest in the ensemble, were trained solely on lung nodule features extracted from deep learning models. The results of the one-class classifiers, the posterior probability of the deep learning model, and the uncertainty of the predictions made in the model are used in unison to determine if the incoming finding from routine readings exhibits characteristics similar to a lung nodule (inlier). A finding is considered as an inlier if atleast 3 out of the 4 entities in ensemble individually term the incoming measurement as a nodule. This design choice makes the ensemble highly specific in nature and thereby aids in reducing the noise in the annotations. The findings considered as inliers by the ensemble were then used to retrain the algorithm, Fig. 1. Table 1(b) shows the number of data points from each radiologist used for training the model.

### 2.4  Simulating Decentralized Learning

To simulate decentralized learning, we made use of 3 clients which was obtained by splitting the routine data based on the reader (R1, R2, R3) to form the clients. The number of communication rounds for Federated Learning was set at 5. In each communication round, a client was initialized with the global model and trained for 25 epochs. The learning rate and optimizer used were $5\,\mathrm{e}^{-4}$ and RMSProp respectively. The parameters of the model were learned by minimizing two distinct losses namely cosine distillation ($CD$) loss with respect to the base model ($BM$) and binary cross-entropy (BCE), Eq. 1. In Eq. 1, $CM$ denotes current model. In our experiments, $W_1$ and $W_2$ were set to 0.5 (Fig. 2).

$$loss = W_1 \cdot CD(BM, CM) + W_2 \cdot BCE(CM) \tag{1}$$

Additionally, at the start of each epoch only data points that were wrongly classified by the model were used to train the model. This design choice leads to shorter training times and thereby enables one to reduce resource utilization at clinical sites when deployed.

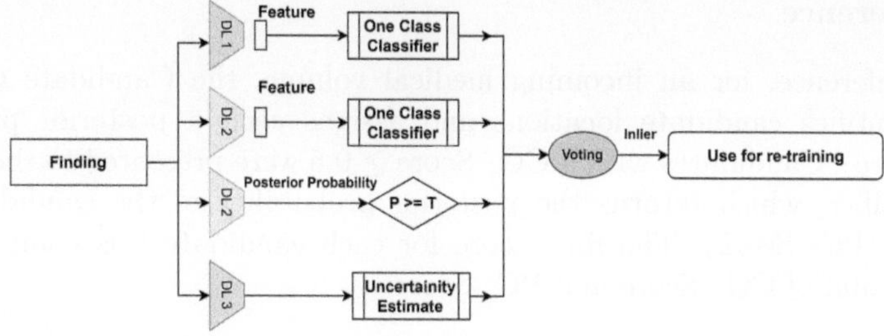



**Fig. 1.** Overall pipeline of the proprietary ensemble. Multiple deep learning models and machine learning algorithms constitute the ensemble. The ensemble reduces noise and bias arising from routine reading annotations.

**Table 1.** Dataset characteristics: distribution across OEM and radiologist expertise.

a) **Distribution by OEM**

| Manufacturer | # Datapoints |
|---|---|
| GE | 731 |
| Siemens | 208 |
| Others | 189 |

(b) **Distribution by Radiologist**

| User | Exp. | Vol. | Findings | Inliers |
|---|---|---|---|---|
| 1 | 15 | 428 | 1702 | 963 |
| 2 | 21 | 566 | 3339 | 2058 |
| 3 | 19 | 134 | 378 | 279 |

At the end of each communication round, models from each client that demonstrate the best performance on the central and clean validation dataset (v_data) were aggregated to create the new global model, Eq. 2. In our experiments, we set $w_n$ to 1.

$$\text{Global Model} = \frac{\sum_{n=1}^{3} w_n \cdot \text{Model}_n}{\sum_{n=1}^{3} w_n} \tag{2}$$

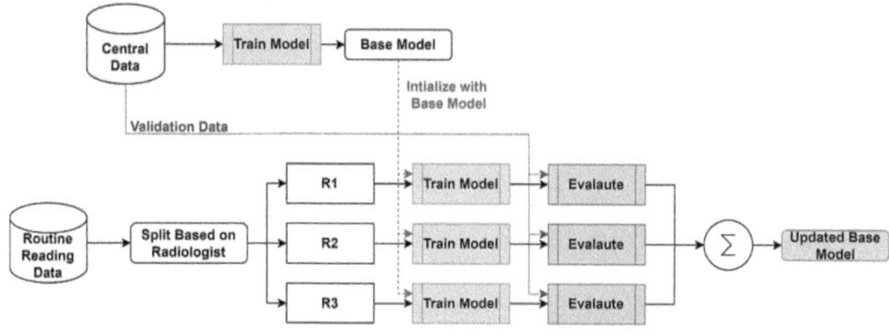



**Fig. 2.** Pipeline used to train the model in a decentralized routine-reading setup. Central data is used to obtain a base model. Data from three readers is split into clients, each initialized with the base model. After local training, models are validated centrally; the best-performing ones are ensembled to form an updated base.

### 2.5  Inference

During inference, for an incoming medical volume, the Candidate Generator (CG) identifies candidate locations and assigns each a posterior probability (CG_Score). Candidates with a CG_Score $\geq 0.5$ were presented to the updated post-classifier, which returns the posterior probability of the candidate being a nodule (PC_Score). The final score for each candidate was computed as a weighted sum of CG_Score and PC_Score.

## 3  Results and Discussion

### 3.1  Test Data

We used data from the HANSE lung cancer screening trial [6] to evaluate the performance of our models. The data set is multicentric and includes a total of 946 patients. Initially, an experienced radiologist reviewed the dataset, after which a third-party computer-aided detection (CAD) tool was employed to detect, segment, and classify pulmonary nodules. All findings generated by the CAD algorithm were subsequently reviewed by the radiologist. More details on the dataset and the creation of the ground truth can be found in [5]. The distribution of the types of nodules and its size range is shown in Table 2.

**Table 2.** Data characteristics of the Test Data (n = 1128)

| Type of Nodule | 0–3 mm | 3 mm–30 mm | >30 mm |
|---|---|---|---|
| Solid | 1167 | 3089 | 14 |
| Sub-Solid | 92 | 1304 | 9 |
| Calcified | 477 | 505 | 0 |

In this article, we evaluate models on solid nodules within the range of 4 mm to 30 mm and sub-solid nodules in the range of 6 mm to 30 mm. The number of solid and sub-solid nodules the models were evaluated on were 2278 and 578 respectively.

### 3.2  Performance on Test Data

In this section, we compare the performance of the proposed approach against the base model and the model trained using vanilla decentralized learning. The proposed approach differs from vanilla decentralized learning in the following ways:

- In each of the sub-sequent epoch, the model is only trained on the misclassified entities,
- The parameters of model are learnt by minimizing a dual cost function, and

– At the end of each communication round, performance metrics such as weighted loss is used to determine the set of models from each client which needs to be aggregated to form the new global model.

Figures 3 a,b and c illustrate the performance of the proposed solution (green curve) on various cohorts in the test data. Table 3 presents the Area Under the Free-response Receiver Operating Characteristic (FROC) curve at various false positive rates per scan for all evaluated models. From the results, we observe that the proposed solution performs better than the base model and the vanilla federated learning approach. In terms of detecting solid nodules, both alternative approaches outperform the base model. As shown in Fig. 3a, at higher false positives per scan ($\geq 2.5$), the performance of the vanilla federated learning approach becomes comparable to that of the base model. However, the proposed solution consistently outperforms the base model across all false positive rates (1/8, 1/4, 1/2, 1, 2, 4, and 8 FPs/scan).

For subsolid nodule detection, as illustrated in Fig. 3b, the vanilla federated learning approach performs worse than the base model across the entire range of FPs/scan. In contrast, the proposed solution maintains performance comparable to the base model up to 1 FP/scan. We believe that the guardrails incorporated in terms of dual loss, and evaluating the models on the centralized data to determine models to be aggregated aid in reducing model drift. On the entire test data (solid 4 mm–30 mm, and subsolid 6 mm–30 mm), the proposed approach performs better than the base model and vanilla federated learning approach, Fig. 3c.

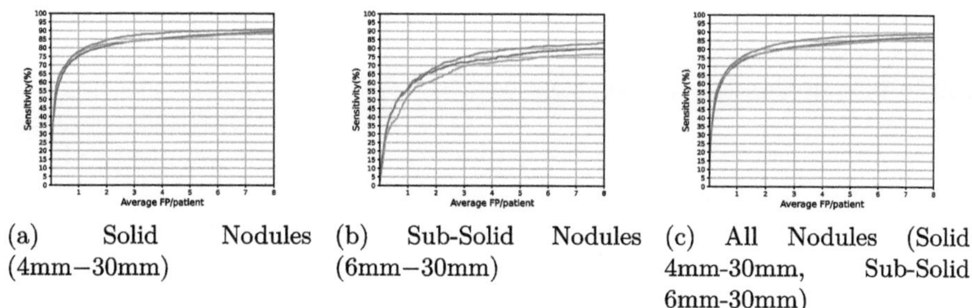

(a)    Solid    Nodules (4mm−30mm)

(b)    Sub-Solid    Nodules (6mm−30mm)

(c)    All    Nodules    (Solid 4mm-30mm,    Sub-Solid 6mm-30mm)

**Fig. 3.** Comparison between the base model (blue), vanilla FL (orange) and the proposed approach (green) on the test data (n = 1128 SUIDs). a) Performance on Solid Nodules (2278 nodules), b) Performance on Sub-Solid Nodules (578 nodules), and c) Performance on Solid+Sub-Solid Nodules (2856 nodules). (Color figure online)

**Table 3.** Comparison of AUC curves for the Base Model, Vanilla FL, and Proposed Approach on the HANSE dataset (n = 1128) across various false positives per scan. Detection restricted to 4–30 mm solid and 6–30 mm sub-solid nodules.

| Type | N | Model | AUC @ | | | | | | |
|---|---|---|---|---|---|---|---|---|---|
| | | | 1/8 | 1/4 | 1/2 | 1 | 2 | 4 | 8 |
| Solid | 2278 | Base Model | 0.033 | 0.096 | 0.251 | 0.609 | 1.397 | 3.070 | 6.580 |
| | | Vanilla FL | 0.034 | 0.104 | 0.270 | 0.639 | 1.442 | 3.119 | 6.601 |
| | | Proposed Approach | 0.036 | 0.104 | 0.267 | 0.638 | 1.454 | 3.195 | 6.795 |
| Sub-Solid | 578 | Base Model | 0.013 | 0.047 | 0.146 | 0.406 | 1.036 | 2.467 | 5.591 |
| | | Vanilla FL | 0.009 | 0.038 | 0.123 | 0.345 | 0.930 | 2.301 | 5.299 |
| | | Proposed Approach | 0.011 | 0.046 | 0.147 | 0.406 | 1.048 | 2.542 | 5.792 |
| All Nodules | 2856 | Base Model | 0.029 | 0.086 | 0.230 | 0.568 | 1.324 | 2.948 | 6.380 |
| | | Vanilla FL | 0.029 | 0.091 | 0.240 | 0.580 | 1.339 | 2.953 | 6.338 |
| | | Proposed Approach | 0.031 | 0.092 | 0.243 | 0.591 | 1.371 | 3.062 | 6.592 |

## 4    Conclusion

In this work, we showcase how an existing AI based solution can be improved via decentralized learning using data arising from routine clinical reads. We simulated decentralized learning creating clients based on the medical expert who read the case.

A highly specific ensemble consisting of machine learning and deep learning models was utilized to reduce the noise arising from routine clinical annotations. To reduce resource usage and accelerate model updates, training was performed only on misclassified data points. During the training phase, model drift arising due to bias in the data arising from each site was minimized by utilizing dual loss function.

On a lung cancer screening test dataset (n = 1128), the proposed solution demonstrates improved performance compared to both the vanilla federated learning approach and the base model. This result is encouraging, as it provides a foundation for continuously training AI models in a decentralized manner using annotations generated from routine clinical data. We believe that collaborating with multiple clinical sites using the technique mentioned in the paper would have a greater impact on model performance. Thus, as the next step, the plan is to collaborate with other clinical sites and sites performing Lung Cancer Screening to further enhance the performance of the model.

## References


1. AlMohammad, B., Brennan, P.C., Mello-Thoms, C.: A review of lung cancer screening and the role of computer-aided detection. Clin. Radiol. **72**(6), 433–442 (2017)
2. Cao, H., et al.: A two-stage convolutional neural networks for lung nodule detection. IEEE J. Biomed. Health Inform. **24**(7), 2006–2015 (2020)

3. Dou, Q., et al.: Federated deep learning for detecting Covid-19 lung abnormalities in CT: a privacy-preserving multinational validation study. NPJ Digit. Med. **4**(1), 60 (2021)
4. Juan, J., et al.: Computer-assisted diagnosis for an early identification of lung cancer in chest X rays (2023)
5. Kondrashova, R., et al.: Comparison of AI software tools for automated detection, quantification and categorization of pulmonary nodules in the HANSE LCS trial. Sci. Rep. **14**(1), 27809 (2024)
6. Kondrashova, R., Vogel-Claussen, J.: Lungenkrebsscreening: neue horizonte. Die Radiol. **64**(6), 456–462 (2024)
7. World Health Organization. Lung cancer (2023)
8. Pati, S., et al.: Federated learning enables big data for rare cancer boundary detection. Nat. Commun. **13**(1), 7346 (2022)
9. Roth, H.R., et al.: Federated learning for breast density classification: a real-world implementation. In: Albarqouni, S., et al. (eds.) DART/DCL -2020. LNCS, vol. 12444, pp. 181–191. Springer, Cham (2020). https://doi.org/10.1007/978-3-030-60548-3_18
10. Setio, A.A.A., et al.: Validation, comparison, and combination of algorithms for automatic detection of pulmonary nodules in computed tomography images: the luna16 challenge. Med. Image Anal. **42**, 1–13 (2017)
11. Shariaty, F., Mousavi, M.: Application of cad systems for the automatic detection of lung nodules. Inform. Med. Unlock. **15**, 100173 (2019)
12. National Lung Screening Trial Research Team. Data from the national lung screening trial (NLST) (n.d)
13. Suchsland, M.Z., et al.: How timely is diagnosis of lung cancer? cohort study of individuals with lung cancer presenting in ambulatory care in the united states. Cancers **14**, 5756 (2022)

# From $\mathcal{O}(n^2)$ to $\mathcal{O}(n)$ Parameters: Quantum Self-attention in Vision Transformers for Biomedical Image Classification


Thomas Boucher[1,2,4]($\boxtimes$) (ID), John Whittle[1,3,4] (ID),
and Evangelos B. Mazomenos[1,2] (ID)

[1] UCL Hawkes Institute, University College London, London, UK
`{thomas.boucher.23,e.mazomenos}@ucl.ac.uk`
[2] Department of Medical Physics and Biomedical Engineering, University College London, London, UK
[3] Department of Anaesthesia and Peri-operative Medicine, University College London Hospitals NHS Foundation Trust, London, UK
[4] Human Physiology and Performance Laboratory (HPPL), Centre for Peri-operative Medicine, Department of Targeted Intervention, Division of Surgery and Interventional Science, University College London, London, UK
`thomas.boucher.23@ucl.ac.uk`



**Abstract.** We demonstrate that quantum vision transformers (QViTs), vision transformers (ViTs) with self-attention (SA) mechanisms replaced by quantum self-attention (QSA) mechanisms, can match state-of-the-art (SOTA) biomedical image classifiers while using 99.99% fewer parameters. QSAs are produced by replacing linear SA layers with parameterised quantum neural networks (QNNs), producing a QSA mechanism and reducing parameter scaling from $\mathcal{O}(n^2)$ to $\mathcal{O}(n)$. On RetinaMNIST, our ultra parameter-efficient QViT outperforms 13/14 SOTA methods including CNNs and ViTs, achieving 56.5% accuracy, just 0.88% below the top MedMamba model while using 99.99% fewer parameters (1K vs 14.5M) and 89% fewer GFLOPs. We present the first investigation of knowledge distillation (KD) from classical to quantum vision transformers in biomedical image classification, showing that QViTs maintain comparable performance to classical ViTs across eight diverse datasets spanning multiple modalities, with improved QSA parameter-efficiency. Our higher-qubit architecture benefitted more from KD pre-training, suggesting a scaling relationship between QSA parameters and KD effectiveness. These findings establish QSA as a practical architectural choice toward parameter-efficient biomedical image analysis (Code available at https://github.com/surgical-vision/QViT-KD.git).

**Keywords:** Biomedical Image Classification · Quantum Self-Attention · Vision Transformers · Knowledge Distillation · Parameter Efficiency



© The Author(s), under exclusive license to Springer Nature Switzerland AG 2026
T. Chen et al. (Eds.): EMA4MICCAI 2025 Workshops, LNCS 16318, pp. 112–122, 2026.
https://doi.org/10.1007/978-3-032-13961-0_12

# 1   Introduction

Vision transformers (ViTs) [5] have emerged as a transformative architecture in computer vision. By treating images as sequences of patches, and leveraging self-attention (SA) to capture long-range dependencies and intricate patterns within image data, ViTs have demonstrated exceptional performance for biomedical classification tasks, often surpassing convolutional neural networks (CNNs) [15]. However, their computational demands, with $\mathcal{O}(n^2)$ parameter scaling in SA layers, limit deployment in resource-constrained clinical settings.

Quantum machine learning (QML) offers a fundamentally different approach to the efficiency challenge. By leveraging quantum neural networks (QNNs) that exploit quantum mechanical phenomena within complex Hilbert spaces, QML achieves rich, parameter-efficient feature representations unattainable in classical Euclidean spaces. QML has recently witnessed significant advancements, with a surge of applications in biomedical image analysis [17], where the enhanced representational power enables QNNs to capture intricate data patterns with dramatically improved parameter efficiency, leading to more effective machine learning, particularly for supervised tasks [8].

Quantum vision transformers (QViTs) merge ViTs and QML by replacing the parameter-heavy linear projections in ViT's SA mechanisms with QNNs, creating quantum self-attention (QSA) mechanisms. This architectural substitution reduces the SA mechanism's parameter scaling from $\mathcal{O}(n^2)$ to $\mathcal{O}(n)$ while maintaining representational power within the expressive complex Hilbert space. Whilst research into QViTs is still in its nascent stages, recent work has shown these architectures can compete with classical models despite using vastly fewer parameters [3].

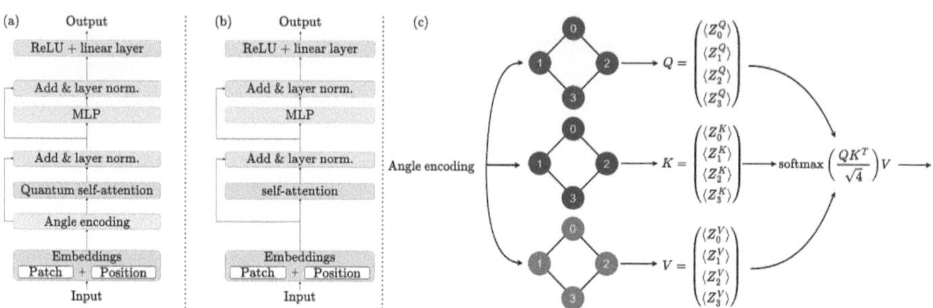

**Fig. 1.** (a) The QViT architecture, utilising QSA following angle-encoding in place of classical SA, (b) the respective ViT architecture, (c) a visualisation of the QSA with angle encoding and our chosen ansatz.

Knowledge distillation (KD), which transfers rich knowledge from large teacher models to efficient students [10], offers a compelling direction to further improve QViT performance, that is unexplored in the literature. While KD has proven effective for enhancing classical ViTs [18], its application to enhancing QViTs remains uninvestigated. This gap is particularly significant in biomedical imaging, where model efficiency is crucial for potential clinical deployment. We systematically compare the performance of QViTs against classical ViTs across eight datasets encompassing distinct imaging modalities, a variety of binary and multi-class classification tasks, and an ordinal regression task. We evaluate the performance of models trained both from scratch and with KD pre-training from a high-quality classical teacher model, under a range of training conditions.

We make the following contributions: (1) we present the first investigation into the efficacy of pre-training parameter-efficient QViTs with KD for biomedical image classification, revealing that effectiveness scales with parameters in the QSA; (2) we demonstrate that QViTs compete with ViTs of equivalent parameter number (Fig. 1(a), (b)) both with and without KD pre-training across eight diverse datasets spanning multiple modalities and classification tasks, whilst utilising more parameter-efficient QSA; (3) we show that extremely parameter-efficient QViTs are capable of outperforming state-of-the-art (SOTA) classical models, achieving near-best accuracy on RetinaMNIST with a 99.99% reduction in parameters compared to MedMamba, illustrating the potential to produce high-performance, parameter-efficient biomedical image classifiers by replacing SA with more parameter-efficient QSA (Fig. 1(c)), and through combining QViTs with KD for effective QML.

## 2    Primer: Quantum Networks

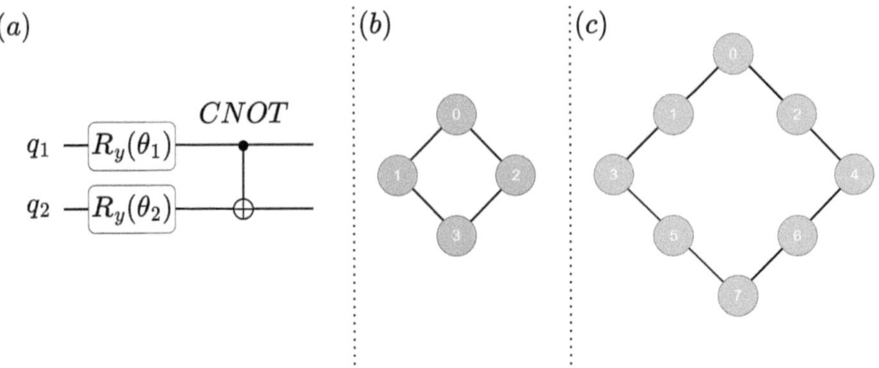


**Fig. 2.** (a) The ansatz we use, applied to qubit pairs ($q_1$, $q_2$), (b) the four-qubit and (c) the eight qubit QNNs structure we use, with paired qubits connected by lines.

Quantum networks are comprised of qubits, which represent a continuous superposition of quantum states. These states are parametrised by complex probability amplitudes of unit norm:

$$|\psi\rangle = \alpha|0\rangle + \beta|1\rangle = \begin{bmatrix} \alpha \\ \beta \end{bmatrix} \in \mathbb{H}, \quad \alpha, \beta \in \mathbb{C}, \quad |\alpha|^2 + |\beta|^2 = 1, \tag{1}$$

where $\mathbb{H}$ is a Hilbert space. This allows qubits to occupy an infinite number of states, enhancing their representational power compared to a bit, which is binary. Quantum states are transformed by unitary operations, which are also essential for encoding classical data onto quantum networks via a quantum feature map $x \in \mathbb{R} \rightarrow |\psi(x)\rangle \in \mathbb{H}$. For an $n$-qubit network initialised in a state $|0\rangle^n = \bigotimes_{i=1}^{n} |0\rangle$, this encoding is a unitary transformation $U_\psi(x)|0\rangle^n = |\psi(x)\rangle$. We use angle encoding, which encodes $n$ classical bits onto $n$ qubits. For $x \in \mathbb{R}^n$:

$$U_\psi = \bigotimes_{i=1}^{n} U_{x_i}, \quad U_{x_i} := \begin{bmatrix} cos(x_i/2) & -sin(x_i/2) \\ sin(x_i/2) & cos(x_i/2) \end{bmatrix} \tag{2}$$

This is chosen for its efficiency and high performance in quantum classifiers [7]. This encoded state can then be transformed by further parametrised unitary operations $U(\Theta)|\psi(x)\rangle = |\psi'(x)\rangle$, $U(\Theta) \in U(n)$. A specific sequence of parametrised unitary operations is an ansatz, which is typically designed to act on qubit pairs. We use a particularly parameter-efficient ansatz, visualised in Fig. 2(a), that is shown to be effective with angle encoding for classification tasks [11]. This ansatz applies a parametrised unitary operation $R_y(\theta_i)$ to each qubit for $i = 1, 2$, followed by a controlled-NOT (CNOT):

$$R_y(\theta_i) := \begin{bmatrix} cos(\theta_i/2) & -sin(\theta_i/2) \\ sin(\theta_i/2) & cos(\theta_i/2) \end{bmatrix}, \quad \text{CNOT} := \begin{bmatrix} 1 & 0 & 0 & 0 \\ 0 & 1 & 0 & 0 \\ 0 & 0 & 0 & 1 \\ 0 & 0 & 1 & 0 \end{bmatrix}, \tag{3}$$

where CNOT, defined by $\text{CNOT}\,(|q_1\rangle \otimes |q_2\rangle) := |q_1\rangle \otimes |(q_1 \oplus q_2)\,\text{mod}\,2\rangle$, entangles the two qubits, creating a joint state which is essential for quantum algorithms to achieve computational advantages over classical methods [12].

To extract classical information from the network, a unitary operation $Z$ is used to measure the expectation value $\langle Z \rangle$ of each qubit, defined by:

$$\langle Z \rangle := \langle \psi | Z | \psi \rangle = \begin{bmatrix} \alpha & \beta \end{bmatrix} \begin{bmatrix} 1 & 0 \\ 0 & -1 \end{bmatrix} \begin{bmatrix} \alpha \\ \beta \end{bmatrix} = |\alpha|^2 - |\beta|^2 \in \mathbb{R}. \tag{4}$$

Performing this measurement for each qubit produces a vector $y \in \mathbb{R}^n$.

# 3   Methods

## 3.1   Architecture Design

We use the QSA architecture of [2], where QNNs replace the linear projection layers for key, query, and value in the SA to produce a QSA mechanism. In this study, $n$-qubit QNNs (Fig. 2(b, c)) replace $n \rightarrow n$ linear projections, and the resulting QViTs are compared to the original ViTs. While both maintain $\mathcal{O}(n^2)$ computational complexity, they differ fundamentally in parameter scaling: QSAs require only $\mathcal{O}(n)$ parameters ($6n$ with our ansatz) vs $\mathcal{O}(n^2)$ for ViTs (specifically $3n^2$). This comparison methodology follows standard practice for assessing quantum advantage for low qubit configurations [9].

For both architectures, patch embeddings are extracted using convolutions and combined with positional embeddings. These embeddings are processed by the SA mechanism, followed by a multilayer perceptron, before passing through a rectified linear unit (ReLU) and final linear layer for classification.

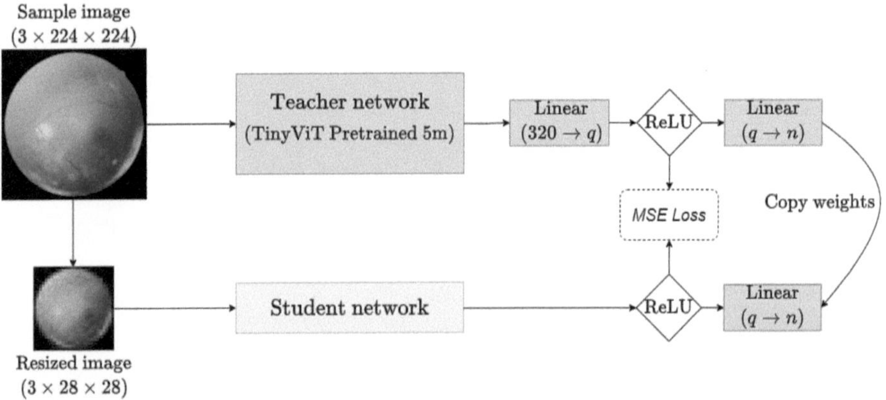


**Fig. 3.** The KD architecture for a sample image from RetinaMNIST with a 28 × 28 input student network, where $q$ is the number of qubits, $n$ is number of target classes. The student is optimised to minimise the MSE loss between the teacher's and student's intermediate logits. Following KD training, the teacher's final linear layer weights are copied to the student's final layer. For 224 × 224 inputs, the resizing step is skipped.

## 3.2   Knowledge Distillation Framework

We use the ImageNet-pre-trained TinyViT model [18] (5M parameters) as our teacher network, fine-tuning it independently on each dataset to create task-specific teachers. Its moderate size makes it suitable for distilling to extremely parameter-efficient students [4].

To enable effective knowledge transfer between classical and quantum models, we modified TinyViT's classification head by replacing the original linear layer with two linear layers: the first mapping to the number of qubits $(n)$, and the second mapping to the number of output classes, with a ReLU activation function in-between. This intermediate layer provides compatible targets for distillation, as the quantum student naturally produces $n$-dimensional outputs from its $n$-qubit measurements. During KD pre-training, students learn to match the teacher's intermediate representations over 50 epochs with Adam optimiser (learning rate $1 \times 10^{-3}$, batch size 32), and using MSE loss, which has been shown to be most effective for KD [13].

Following KD, we transfer the teacher's final linear layer weights directly to the student, leveraging the aligned intermediate representations. This approach outperformed direct logit distillation, improving accuracy by 9.31% for ViT and 14.1% for QViT. The complete KD architecture is visualised in Fig. 3.

### 3.3  Experimental Setup

We evaluate three configurations evaluating 4-qubit models on $28 \times 28$ images ($2 \times 2$ patches) and $224 \times 224$ images ($16 \times 16$ patches), and 8-qubit models on $224 \times 224$ images ($16 \times 16$ patches). The specific qubit topologies (Fig. 2(b, c)) match IBM and Rigetti quantum processor connectivity, ensuring our simulated results translate to real hardware.

**Table 1.** The details of the eight datasets used in this research.

| Name | Modality | Classes | Train/Val/Test |
|---|---|---|---|
| BreastMNIST | Breast Ultrasound | 2 | 546/78/156 |
| RetinaMNIST | Fundus Camera | 5 | 1,080/120/400 |
| PneumoniaMNIST | Chest X-Ray | 2 | 4,708/524/624 |
| DermaMNIST | Dermatoscope | 7 | 7,007/1,003/2,005 |
| BloodMNIST | Blood Cell Microscope | 8 | 11,959/1,712/3,421 |
| OrganCMNIST | Abdominal CT | 11 | 13,000/2,392/8,268 |
| PathMNIST | Colon Pathology | 9 | 89,996/10,004/7,180 |
| OASIS | Brain MRI | 4 | 5320/896/512 |

**Training Protocol:** Following [19], we use Adam optimiser with initial learning rate $1 \times 10^{-3}$, decaying by $10\times$ at epochs 50 and 75, batch size 32, and 100 total epochs. Models are evaluated both trained from scratch (QViT/ViT) and with 50 epochs of KD pre-training before fine-tuning (QViT-KD/ViT-KD).

**Datasets:** We evaluate across eight biomedical imaging tasks (Table 1): seven from MedMNIST [19] spanning multiple modalities and classification types with predefined train/validation/test sets, plus OASIS [16] for Alzheimer's progression classification. For OASIS, axial slices were used as input, with only slices between the 100th and 160th slice considered for each patient. We used a subset of the full dataset for a better balance between the four classes and for time efficiency. Our dataset selection ensures robust evaluation across binary and multi-class classification, and an ordinal regression task (RetinaMNIST).

**Implementation:** All experiments utilised PennyLane [1] with PyTorch for quantum circuit simulation on a single NVIDIA GeForce RTX 4090 GPU.

## 4    Results

Our primary findings, detailed in Table 2, demonstrate that replacing SA with QSA can achieve high performance with improved parameter efficiency.

**QViTs are Competitive with Classical ViTs:** When trained from scratch, QViTs consistently perform on par with their classical ViT counterparts that share the same structural design but have quadratically more parameters in their SA mechanism. For instance, across the four-qubit configurations (ViT_28 vs. QViT_28 and ViT_224 vs. QViT_224), the quantum models achieve comparable or slightly better average performance (48 SA parameters vs. 24 QSA parameters). This trend continues in the eight-qubit setting, where the ViT model's larger parameter count in its attention block (192 SA parameters vs. 48 QSA parameters) does not translate to a consistent performance advantage.

**SOTA-Level Performance with Extreme Parameter Efficiency:** The most striking result is the performance of our 4-qubit QViT_28 on the RetinaMNIST dataset. This model, with only 1K total parameters, achieved 56.5% accuracy, outperforming 13/14 SOTA classifiers, including various ResNets, ViTs, and all but one MedMamba variant [20]. This near-SOTA performance was achieved with just a 0.88% accuracy gap to the top MedMamba model, while using 99.99% fewer parameters (1K vs. 14.5M) and requiring 89% fewer GFLOPs. This result powerfully illustrates the potential of QSA to contribute to SOTA models with significant parameter-efficiency.

**Table 2.** Performance comparison of QViT and ViT. Top score in each metric for each dataset is in bold.

| Methods | BreastMNIST | | RetinaMNIST | | PneumoniaMNIST | | DermaMNIST | |
|---|---|---|---|---|---|---|---|---|
| | AUC | ACC | AUC | ACC | AUC | ACC | AUC | ACC |
| Trained from Scratch | | | | | | | | |
| ViT_28 | 0.733 | **0.821** | 0.690 | 0.468 | 0.931 | 0.846 | 0.863 | 0.694 |
| ViT_224 | 0.709 | 0.744 | 0.696 | 0.528 | 0.931 | 0.849 | 0.870 | 0.691 |
| ViT_224 (8 qubits) | 0.749 | 0.814 | 0.705 | 0.510 | 0.949 | 0.830 | **0.900** | **0.729** |
| QViT_28 | **0.788** | 0.801 | **0.748** | **0.565** | 0.904 | **0.862** | 0.857 | 0.695 |
| QViT_224 | 0.735 | 0.763 | 0.683 | 0.525 | **0.944** | 0.856 | 0.862 | 0.696 |
| QViT_224 (8 qubits) | 0.675 | 0.731 | 0.722 | 0.523 | 0.940 | 0.827 | 0.883 | 0.702 |
| Knowledge Distillation Pretraining | | | | | | | | |
| ViT-KD_28 | 0.770 | 0.756 | 0.701 | 0.518 | 0.935 | 0.824 | 0.865 | 0.696 |
| ViT-KD_224 | 0.681 | 0.731 | 0.708 | 0.488 | 0.938 | 0.825 | 0.857 | 0.685 |
| ViT-KD_224 (8 qubits) | 0.647 | 0.731 | 0.699 | 0.500 | 0.937 | 0.814 | **0.896** | **0.725** |
| QViT-KD_28 | 0.636 | 0.750 | **0.744** | **0.535** | 0.938 | **0.864** | 0.849 | 0.693 |
| QViT-KD_224 | 0.714 | 0.763 | 0.720 | 0.510 | **0.943** | 0.840 | 0.860 | 0.701 |
| QViT-KD_224 (8 qubits) | **0.786** | **0.808** | 0.722 | 0.515 | 0.933 | 0.830 | 0.890 | 0.719 |
| TinyViT (Teacher) | 0.900 | 0.904 | 0.790 | 0.618 | 0.988 | 0.886 | 0.933 | 0.823 |

| Methods | BloodMNIST | | OrganCMNIST | | PathMNIST | | OASIS | |
|---|---|---|---|---|---|---|---|---|
| | AUC | ACC | AUC | ACC | AUC | ACC | AUC | ACC |
| Trained from Scratch | | | | | | | | |
| ViT_28 | 0.979 | 0.844 | 0.912 | 0.574 | 0.932 | 0.686 | **0.822** | **0.701** |
| ViT_224 | 0.976 | 0.835 | 0.938 | 0.627 | 0.944 | 0.687 | 0.603 | 0.400 |
| ViT_224 (8 qubits) | **0.996** | **0.944** | **0.977** | **0.792** | **0.970** | **0.813** | 0.785 | 0.684 |
| QViT_28 | 0.968 | 0.812 | 0.923 | 0.618 | 0.934 | 0.684 | 0.812 | 0.693 |
| QViT_224 | 0.969 | 0.815 | 0.947 | 0.633 | 0.933 | 0.650 | 0.785 | 0.678 |
| QViT_224 (8 qubits) | 0.972 | 0.816 | 0.965 | 0.719 | 0.930 | 0.762 | 0.767 | 0.682 |
| Knowledge Distillation Pretraining | | | | | | | | |
| ViT-KD_28 | 0.976 | 0.839 | 0.914 | 0.613 | 0.942 | 0.709 | 0.810 | 0.693 |
| ViT-KD_224 | 0.981 | 0.863 | 0.906 | 0.555 | 0.942 | 0.682 | 0.749 | 0.652 |
| ViT-KD_224 (8 qubits) | **0.995** | **0.939** | **0.978** | **0.798** | 0.959 | 0.789 | **0.824** | **0.697** |
| QViT-KD_28 | 0.972 | 0.824 | 0.928 | 0.612 | 0.921 | 0.660 | 0.764 | 0.641 |
| QViT-KD_224 | 0.971 | 0.815 | 0.917 | 0.613 | 0.939 | 0.712 | 0.763 | 0.656 |
| QViT-KD_224 (8 qubits) | **0.995** | 0.937 | 0.974 | 0.788 | **0.970** | **0.822** | 0.777 | 0.684 |
| TinyViT (Teacher) | 0.999 | 0.989 | 0.997 | 0.956 | 0.990 | 0.889 | 0.983 | 0.965 |

**Knowledge Distillation Effectiveness Scales with Quantum Capacity:** Our investigation into classical-to-quantum KD reveals a nuanced relationship between QSA capacity and KD effectiveness. For the low-parameter QSA 4-qubit models, KD pre-training did not yield a performance benefit and in some cases was detrimental compared to training from scratch. However, for the 8-qubit QViT, which has double the quantum parameters in its QSA mechanism, KD pre-training provided a clear performance boost, improving average accuracy from 0.720 to 0.748 and bringing its performance in line with its 8-qubit ViT counterpart. This suggests that a minimum level of parametric capacity in the QSA mechanism is necessary for the student QViT to effectively absorb the distilled knowledge from a complex classical teacher.

## 5   Discussion

Our research establishes QViTs as a compelling architecture for biomedical image classification, demonstrating that replacing classical SA with QSA in ViTs can yield models that are competitive with SOTA methods while being orders of magnitude more parameter-efficient.

The central insight from our work is the relationship between a QSA's parametric capacity and its ability to benefit from KD. 4-qubit models failed to benefit from KD, with QViT-KD_28 performing 2.65% and 2.64% worse than its scratch-trained counterpart for ROC AUC and accuracy, and QViT-KD_224 performing marginally worse also. This aligns with classical findings that student models require sufficient capacity to learn from teachers [4]. However, eight-qubit QViTs showed marked improvement with KD, achieving 0.876 and 0.748 average AUC and accuracy compared to 0.857 and 0.720 without pre-training. The successful application of KD on our 8-qubit QViT provides the first evidence in this domain that as the capacity of the QSA mechanism increases, so does its potential to leverage pre-training from larger classical models. As developing quantum hardware enables higher stable qubit counts, this relationship suggests a clear scaling path, where larger QViTs combined with KD should yield increasingly competitive performance while maintaining parameter efficiency.

A current and practical limitation of our work is the reliance on classical simulation of quantum circuits, where computational cost scales exponentially ($\mathcal{O}(2^n)$) with the number of qubits $n$. This restricted our experiments to 4- and 8-qubit QNNs, which naturally limits the maximal performance achievable. However, this represents an engineering bottleneck rather than a fundamental limitation. The distributed architecture of the QSA is well-suited for near-term networked quantum processors [14], and breakthroughs in fault-tolerant quantum computing [6] promise stable 100+ qubit systems, and facilitating the deployment of more powerful QViTs to clinical settings in the fear future.

Our work provides a strong proof-of-concept for the utility of QSAs within ViTs for biomedical image analysis. By achieving near-SOTA performance on RetinaMNIST with a 99.99% parameter reduction, and demonstrating that KD can benefit QViTs with appropriate QSA parameter number, we have shown that QSA offers a practical path toward developing ultra-efficient yet powerful hybrid classical-quantum models. This is particularly relevant for deployment in resource-constrained clinical settings where computational efficiency is paramount. Our results lay the groundwork for developing the next generation of hybrid quantum-classical models for SOTA, parameter-efficient biomedical image analysis.

**Acknowledgments.** This work was supported by the EPSRC under the UCL Centre for Doctoral Training in Intelligent, Integrated Imaging in Healthcare (i4health) [EP/S021930/1] and the Human-centred Machine Intelligence to optimise Robotic Surgical Training (HuMIRoS) project [EP/Z534754/1]; the International Anesthesia Research Society Mentored Research grant; and the NIHR University College London Hospitals Biomedical Research Centre.

**Disclosure of Interests.** The authors have no competing interests.

# References


1. Bergholm, V., et al.: PennyLane: automatic differentiation of hybrid quantum-classical computations. arXiv preprint arXiv:1811.04968 (2022)
2. Cara, M.C., et al.: Quantum vision transformers for quark-gluon classification. Axioms (2024)
3. Cherrat, E.A., Kerenidis, I., Mathur, N., Landman, J., Strahm, M., Li, Y.Y.: Quantum vision transformers. Quantum **8**, 1265 (2024)
4. Cho, J.H., Hariharan, B.: On the efficacy of knowledge distillation. In: Proceedings of the IEEE/CVF ICCV, pp. 4794–4802 (2019)
5. Dosovitskiy, A., et al.: An image is worth 16×16 words: transformers for image recognition at scale. arXiv preprint arXiv:2010.11929 (2021)
6. Google Quantum AI and Collaborators: Quantum error correction below the surface code threshold. Nature (2024)
7. Grant, E., et al.: Hierarchical quantum classifiers. NPJ Quantum Inf. **4**(1), 65 (2018)
8. Havlíček, V., et al.: Supervised learning with quantum-enhanced feature spaces. Nature **567**(7747), 209–212 (2019)
9. Herrmann, N., et al.: Quantum utility–definition and assessment of a practical quantum advantage. In: 2023 IEEE QSW, pp. 162–174. IEEE (2023)
10. Hinton, G., Vinyals, O., Dean, J.: Distilling the knowledge in a neural network. arXiv preprint arXiv:1503.02531 (2015)
11. Hur, T., Kim, L., Park, D.K.: Quantum convolutional neural network for classical data classification. Quant. Mach. Intell. **4**(1), 3 (2022)
12. Jozsa, R., Linden, N.: On the role of entanglement in quantum-computational speed-up. Proc. R. Soc. Lond., Ser. A Math. Phys. Eng. Sci. **459**(2036), 2011–2032 (2003)
13. Kim, T., Oh, J., Kim, N., Cho, S., Yun, S.Y.: Comparing Kullback-Leibler divergence and mean squared error loss in knowledge distillation, pp. 2628–2635. IJCAI (2021)
14. Main, D., et al.: Distributed quantum computing across an optical network link. Nature 1–6 (2025)
15. Manzari, O.N., Ahmadabadi, H., Kashiani, H., Shokouhi, S.B., Ayatollahi, A.: MedViT: a robust vision transformer for generalized medical image classification. Comput. Biol. Med. **157**, 106791 (2023)

16. Marcus, D.S., Wang, T.H., Parker, J., Csernansky, J.G., Morris, J.C., Buckner, R.L.: Open access series of imaging studies (OASIS): cross-sectional MRI data in young, middle aged, nondemented, and demented older adults. JoCN **19**(9), 1498–1507 (2007)
17. Wei, L., et al.: Quantum machine learning in medical image analysis: a survey. Neurocomputing **525**, 42–53 (2023)
18. Wu, K., et al.: TinyViT: fast pretraining distillation for small vision transformers. In: ECCV, pp. 68–85 (2022)
19. Yang, J., et al.: MedMNIST v2-a large-scale lightweight benchmark for 2D and 3D biomedical image classification. Sci. Data **10**(1), 41 (2023)
20. Yue, Y., Li, Z.: MedMamba: vision mamba for medical image classification. arXiv preprint arXiv:2403.03849 (2024)

# Human-in-the-Loop Active Learning
# for Real-Time Endoscopic Diagnostics
# on Edge Devices


Shabir Ahmad[1(✉)] [iD], Sheeraz Ahmad[1], Sujeong Kim[1], Behraj Khan[2,3] [iD],
Tahir Qasim Syed[2] [iD], and Junwon Chung[1,4(✉)]

[1] Center of AI for Medical Instruments (CAIMI Pvt., Ltd.), Incheon,
Republic of Korea
{shabir,sheeraz_ahmad,ksj,luke_chung}@caimi.co.kr
[2] Institute of Business Administration, Karachi, Pakistan
[3] National University of Computer and Emerging Sciences, Karachi, Pakistan
[4] Gachon Gil Hospital, Incheon, Republic of Korea



**Abstract.** Early diagnosis of gastrointestinal (GI) conditions through
endoscopy can drastically improve patient outcomes. However, the accuracy and consistency of endoscopic interpretation often vary with operator expertise, and existing AI-assisted solutions remain too resource-
intensive for deployment on low-powered clinical devices. In this work, we
propose a lightweight, human-in-the-loop (HITL) active learning framework that incrementally fine-tunes a compact deep learning model based
on expert feedback collected during clinical deployment. Initially trained
on a limited subset of annotated endoscopy images, our model is optimized for real-time inference on edge hardware (Jetson Nano). During
deployment, expert feedback on erroneous predictions is collected and
used for periodic fine-tuning without increasing model complexity. Our
system supports continual improvement, maintains fixed model size, and
demonstrates enhanced diagnostic performance in both sensitivity and
precision, thus offering a robust, adaptive solution for AI-assisted endoscopic diagnostics in resource-constrained environments.

**Keywords:** Edge devices · Real-time image processing · Active
learning · Human-in-the-loop · Model optimization


## 1  Introduction

Artificial intelligence (AI)-based computer-aided detection (CADe) systems have
become increasingly prevalent in gastrointestinal (GI) endoscopy, offering the
potential to enhance lesion detection accuracy and reduce operator dependency
during routine examinations. Recent advances in deep learning have demonstrated promising results in real-time detection of polyps, neoplasms, and other
abnormalities from colonoscopic and gastroscopic images [3,9,13]. These systems have shown significant improvements in diagnostic accuracy, with meta-
analyses confirming their superiority over traditional methods in several contexts


© The Author(s), under exclusive license to Springer Nature Switzerland AG 2026
T. Chen et al. (Eds.): EMA4MICCAI 2025 Workshops, LNCS 16318, pp. 123–132, 2026.
https://doi.org/10.1007/978-3-032-13961-0_13

124     S. Ahmad et al.

[2,12]. However, despite these advancements, challenges remain in deploying such models effectively within clinical settings, particularly in resource-constrained environments. These include limited generalizability due to non-diverse training datasets, hardware and integration demands, and ethical and regulatory hurdles [2,13]. The development of lightweight, cost-effective, and clinically validated AI systems, along with efforts toward workflow integration and physician training, remains essential for broad clinical adoption [3,9].

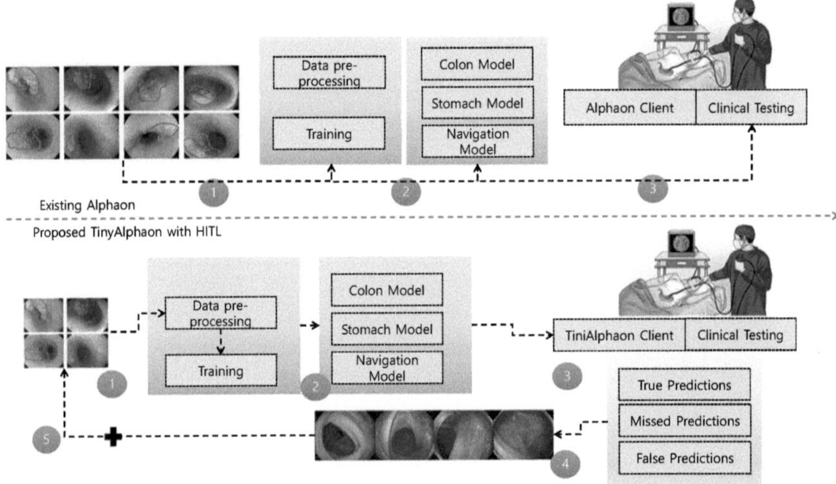


**Fig. 1.** Overview of the HITL (Human-in-the-Loop) learning pipeline for gastrointestinal diagnosis. In our existing Alphaon (above the separator arrow), A high-capacity model is trained on large annotated datasets and deployed on a full-fledged computer. In our current work (below the separator line), a lightweight model is then trained on curated subsets and deployed on edge devices (TiniAlphaon). Expert feedback from clinical usage is used to iteratively fine-tune the model, improving performance without increasing complexity.

Existing studies [1,9] have primarily focused on training high-capacity convolutional neural networks on large-scale annotated datasets to achieve high detection sensitivity and specificity. For instance, Lee et al. [9] reported a YOLOv5-based colonic neoplasm detection model trained on over 50,000 colonoscopy images, which achieved a sensitivity of 88.8% and a precision of 90.7% on both internal and external test sets. While such performance is clinically meaningful, the model's practical deployment required workstation-level hardware with a discrete GPU, which limits its usability in compact or low-cost endoscopic units [1]. Furthermore, many existing CADe solutions, such as GI Genius, CAD EYE, Endo Mind, and Alphaon, rely on workstation-level hardware with discrete GPUs, which limits their practical use in compact or resource-constrained endoscopy units [5,7,15]. Although these systems demonstrate strong performance in controlled environments, they are typically deployed with fixed architectures that cannot adapt to real-time clinical feedback or evolving data distributions.

To overcome these limitations, we present a novel lightweight CADe system, named TiniAlphaon, designed for real-time inference on embedded edge hardware. The system is based on a compressed version of the YOLOv8-Tiny architecture and trained on a curated subset of 10,000 diverse GI endoscopy images. It is optimized for execution on NVIDIA Jetson, an edge device with limited computational resources. TiniAlphaon integrates a clinician-facing graphical user interface (GUI) and supports seamless PACS connectivity, thereby enabling deployment in real-world clinical settings without the need for external computing infrastructure.

While model compression ensures real-time operation, it introduces a higher rate of false positives, which may increase the cognitive load on clinicians and undermine their trust in the system [6,14,16]. To address this, we propose a human-in-the-loop (HITL) active learning mechanism [8] that enables clinicians to flag erroneous predictions during or after the procedure. These flagged samples are subsequently verified, labeled, and used for iterative fine-tuning of the model. Importantly, this feedback loop is designed to improve diagnostic performance without increasing the model's complexity or inference latency. Recent studies have demonstrated the efficacy of adaptive learning paradigms, such as active learning and semi-supervised fine-tuning, in enhancing medical image analysis [4]. However, integrating these approaches into deployable embedded systems suitable for clinical practice remains a significant challenge [10,11].

The proposed HITL pipeline was deployed at Gachon Gil Medical Center between May 15 and June 5, where it was used in routine clinical procedures. Weekly fine-tuning was performed using expert-verified feedback samples, resulting in a progressive improvement in model sensitivity. After three update cycles, the HITL-enhanced TiniAlphaon model matched the detection accuracy of the earlier high-complexity model while maintaining its lightweight and real-time properties. These results underscore the feasibility of adaptive, resource-efficient AI systems for endoscopic diagnostics, particularly in settings where scalability and hardware cost are critical considerations. The main contributions of this work are:

- We propose a lightweight CADe system, TiniAlphaon, designed for real-time deployment on edge devices such as Jetson Nano, enabling AI-powered endoscopic diagnostics without requiring server-level computation.
- We develop a human-in-the-loop (HITL) learning mechanism that allows expert feedback during deployment to be integrated into periodic fine-tuning cycles without increasing model complexity.
- We demonstrate that fine-tuning on a curated subset and iterative expert feedback enables the lightweight model to match the diagnostic performance of a high-complexity model trained on a full dataset.

– We conduct a real-world clinical deployment at Gachon Gil Medical Center, showcasing the practical feasibility, responsiveness, and adaptability of our system in a hospital environment.

## 2   Material and Methods

Our proposed architecture is composed of three integrated components: (1) a lightweight client system for real-time inference, (2) a cloud-based HITL + AL server for expert feedback processing and model fine-tuning, and (3) an update module to push new weights to deployed devices.

### 2.1   Detailed Design

– **Client System:** A trained YOLOv8-Tiny-based model is deployed on an NVIDIA Jetson Nano embedded system. It includes a Qt/C++ GUI to visualize endoscopic streams and overlay detection results in real-time. The client is connected to the endoscopy device via a capture card and integrated with a local PACS system for test scheduling and patient data retrieval. During each session, clinicians can capture snapshots and manually flag incorrect predictions (e.g., false positives or missed detections).
– **HITL + AL Server:** Post-examination, feedback data including flagged images, annotations, and logs are uploaded to Microsoft Azure Server. These samples are filtered using uncertainty sampling and manually verified by domain experts. The verified samples are then added to a feedback pool used for periodic model fine-tuning. The AL server, in addition to the above, also hosts a Restful API server which provides medical records of patients, registered doctors and ensure unauthorized access.
– **Model Update Module:** A weekly update scheduler fine-tunes the model using a small learning rate and LoRA-based adapter tuning. The updated model is validated on a test set and pushed back to all Jetson devices via secure API endpoints.

Figure 1 illustrates the complete architecture, highlighting data flow, feedback loop, and update cycle.

### 2.2   Formulation

We define the real-time model as $f_\theta : \mathcal{X} \rightarrow \mathcal{Y}$, where: - $\mathcal{X}$ is the space of input endoscopic frames, - $\mathcal{Y}$ is the space of predicted bounding boxes and lesion classes, - $\theta$ represents the model parameters deployed on the edge device.

At time $t$, the model infers $\hat{y}_t = f_{\theta_t}(x_t)$. Feedback is obtained when a clinician flags the prediction $\hat{y}_t$ as incorrect. This creates a feedback pair $(x_t, y_t^*)$, where $y_t^*$ is the corrected label.

The model is updated every $\Delta T$ time units using a small batch $\mathcal{F} = \{(x_i, y_i^*)\}_{i=1}^{N}$ of expert-verified feedback samples. The fine-tuning objective is:

$$\theta_{t+\Delta T} = \arg\min_{\theta} \left[ \mathcal{L}(\theta) = \frac{1}{N} \sum_{i=1}^{N} \ell(f_\theta(x_i), y_i^*) + \lambda \cdot \Omega(\theta, \theta_t) \right]$$

where: - $\ell$ is the detection/classification loss (e.g., CIoU + cross-entropy), - $\Omega(\theta, \theta_t)$ is a regularization term (e.g., Elastic Weight Consolidation or LoRA distance), - $\lambda$ controls how strictly the model retains prior knowledge.

This formulation ensures that the model incrementally adapts without catastrophic forgetting, while keeping computation tractable for embedded hardware.

### 2.3   Implementation Details

Our training and deployment pipeline is developed to support a seamless integration between clinical environments and edge devices, ensuring real-time performance and continuous model improvement. The training is conducted on an internal Linux server equipped with 4 NVIDIA RTX 3060 GPUs. Models are developed and trained using PyTorch, and once converged, they are exported to ONNX format and deployed on the NVIDIA Jetson Nano, referred to as *TiniAlphaon* in our setup.

The endoscopy AI pipeline is implemented in C++ for low-level inference operations and optimized execution. The front-end user interface is built using QML (Qt Quick), enabling a lightweight and responsive GUI on edge hardware. Image preprocessing and augmentation are performed using OpenCV, while model quantization and inference are accelerated using TensorRT and ONNX Runtime.

For clinical feedback collection and model updates, we host an Azure-based virtual server with a Flask web server. The server exposes multiple API endpoints, the most critical being `/postdata`, which allows uploading of endoscopy frames post-procedure. These frames are annotated by clinicians when mispredictions occur, enabling us to collect both false and true predictions. This feedback data is incorporated into the training pipeline on the server, where the updated model is periodically redeployed to all edge devices using an automated sync mechanism.

## 3   Experiments

### 3.1   Dataset Description

For this study, we compiled a comprehensive gastrointestinal (GI) endoscopy dataset comprising over 25,000 labeled images, aggregated from multiple internal hospitals and validated by expert endoscopists. The dataset was stratified into three primary categories:

**Table 1.** Technology Stack for Development, Deployment, and Feedback Loop

| Component | Technology Used |
| --- | --- |
| Model Training | PyTorch, Linux server (4x RTX 3060 GPUs) |
| Model Export | ONNX |
| Model Quantization & Inference | TensorRT, ONNX Runtime |
| Image Preprocessing | OpenCV |
| Edge Deployment | Jetson Nano (TiniAlphaon) |
| Front-End UI | QML (Qt Quick) |
| Server Backend | Flask (Python), Azure Virtual Machine |
| Data API Endpoint | /postdata |
| Annotation Feedback | Clinician-annotated samples (via Flask API) |
| Retraining Loop | Periodic update on central server |

- **Colonoscopy Dataset:** A total of 10,000 colonoscopy images were carefully selected. These include both polyp-containing and normal images, with annotations for bounding boxes around lesions.
- **Stomach Dataset:** 10,000 images capturing gastric abnormalities such as ulcers and gastritis, as well as healthy stomach regions. Annotation was performed by board-certified endoscopists.
- **Navigation Dataset:** An additional 5,000 images representing anatomical landmarks and spatial navigation views inside the stomach were used for auxiliary model validation.

All datasets were pre-processed to a unified resolution of $512\times512$, and bounding box annotations were manually validated by certified GI specialists. Images containing motion blur or low visibility were excluded to maintain training quality.

### 3.2 Evaluation Metrics

We adopted standard metrics for evaluating diagnostic performance:

$$\text{Sensitivity (Recall)} = \frac{TP}{TP + FN} \tag{1}$$

$$\text{Precision} = \frac{TP}{TP + FP} \tag{2}$$

$$\text{Specificity} = \frac{TN}{TN + FP} \tag{3}$$

$$\text{Accuracy} = \frac{TP + TN}{TP + TN + FP + FN} \tag{4}$$

where $TP$ is true positives, $FP$ false positives, $FN$ false negatives, and $TN$ true negatives.

## 3.3   Deployment Models and Inference Optimization

We trained two model architectures: YOLOv8-Tiny and EfficientDet-D0, both optimized for real-time inference on edge hardware. For deployment, each model was quantized to TensorRT INT8 of NVIDIA Jetson AGX Xavier's integrated VOLTA GPU.

Table 1 summarizes the average inference latency and detection performance across both models. Despite the aggressive quantization, sensitivity and specificity metrics were preserved with minimal degradation.

The average inference latency per image was 10 ms for YOLOv8 and 12 ms for EfficientDet, achieving frame rates of 20–25 FPS in clinical test scenarios with real-time video feeds.

**Table 2.** Model inference speed and accuracy after quantization

| Model | Latency (ms) | FPS | Sensitivity | Precision |
|---|---|---|---|---|
| YOLOv8-Tiny (FP8) | 10 | 25 | 0.88 | 0.89 |
| EfficientDet-D0 (FP8) | 12 | 20 | 0.87 | 0.91 |

Quantization was performed using NVIDIA's TensorRT calibration toolkit with representative calibration datasets. All models were deployed with a Flask-based inference pipeline connected to a Qt/C++ clinical interface and PACS export functionality.

## 3.4   Human-in-the-Loop Evaluation and Feedback Integration

The system was deployed in a clinical setting at Gachon Gil Medical Center, South Korea, over a period of three weeks (May 15 – June 5). Each week, the TiniAlphaon system was used during routine endoscopic procedures, and feedback was collected from expert endoscopists for all misclassified samples (false positives and false negatives).

During each deployment phase, approximately 100 patients were screened per week. After each cycle, erroneous frames flagged by clinicians were annotated and used to fine-tune the model using low-rank adaptation (LoRA) modules. Crucially, model complexity and inference latency remained constant across all iterations.

- **Week 1:** 100 patient tests, 5,000 new feedback samples collected. FP rate: 20%, FN rate: 23.2%.
- **Week 2:** Additional 100 tests, fine-tuned on Week 1 data. FP dropped to 12%, FN to 14.3%.
- **Week 3:** Same number of tests, final model shows FP: 10%, FN: 10%.

**Table 3.** Weekly Evaluation of HITL Alphaon Deployment in Clinical Setting

| Week | Patients Tested | FP Rate (%) | FN Rate (%) | Expert Feedback Samples | Sensitivity (%) | Specificity (%) |
|---|---|---|---|---|---|---|
| 1 | 100 | 20.3 | 23.2 | 5,000 | 88.4 | 91.1 |
| 2 | 100 | 12.1 | 14.3 | 5,000 | 91.6 | 93.8 |
| 3 | 100 | 10.2 | 10.5 | 5,000 | 93.9 | 95.2 |

As seen in Table 2, the integration of human-in-the-loop feedback resulted in consistent performance gains with each successive fine-tuning iteration. By week 3, the false positive and false negative rates had dropped to under 11%, closely matching the performance of the original high-complexity model trained on the full 50,000-sample dataset [4], but without increasing computational demand (Table 3).

These results underscore the clinical viability of the HITL-enhanced TiniAlphaon system as a lightweight, adaptive, and efficient alternative to traditional server-grade CADe solutions.

## 3.5   Summary

These results demonstrate the system's capacity to learn incrementally from clinical data, reduce diagnostic error rates, and maintain real-time performance on embedded hardware. The HITL mechanism proves effective for adapting lightweight models to new patient populations without requiring architecture changes or full retraining.

## 4   Conclusion

This study presented a lightweight, adaptive diagnostic system for endoscopic imaging that integrates a human-in-the-loop (HITL) learning mechanism with real-time deployment on edge devices. The proposed framework departs from conventional CADe architectures by emphasizing efficiency, adaptability, and clinician-guided improvement. Rather than relying on large-scale pretraining and static inference models, we demonstrate that performance can be continuously refined through expert feedback collected during real-world use. Through a three-week clinical deployment, the system achieved measurable gains in diagnostic accuracy while preserving its compact form factor and low-latency operation. By incorporating periodic fine-tuning from expert-verified feedback, the model progressively reduced false detections and achieved sensitivity and specificity levels comparable to those of higher-capacity models. Importantly, these improvements were obtained without increasing the model's complexity or compromising runtime efficiency, highlighting the viability of feedback-driven optimization in constrained clinical environments. The findings suggest that adaptive learning strategies, when paired with lightweight architectures and edge-based deployment, can offer a scalable path forward for AI-assisted diagnostics. As clinical demands continue to evolve and data diversity grows, systems that can respond to local feedback without retraining from scratch may prove critical to widespread adoption. Future work will focus on validating this approach across multiple institutions and exploring techniques to balance adaptation with long-term stability, ensuring both clinical trust and regulatory robustness.

**Acknowledgments.** This research was supported by Tech Incubator Program Startup (TIPS) grant funded by the Korea Technology and information Promotion Agency for Small and Medium Enterprises (TIPA) (grant number: 00224027)

**Disclosure of Interests.** The authors have no competing interests to declare that are relevant to the content of this article.

# References


1. Anonymous: Automatic detection of colorectal polyps from narrow-band imaging colonoscopy based on an improved deep-learning model. In: 2024 11th International Conference on Biomedical and Bioinformatics Engineering (2024). https://doi.org/10.1145/3707127.3707133
2. Bin, L., Chen, H., Liu, J.: Artificial intelligence–assisted capsule endoscopy for detecting lesions in Crohn's disease: systematic review and meta-analysis. Front. Artif. Intell. **8**(42), 1–12 (2025). https://doi.org/10.3389/frai.2025.00123
3. Bin, L., Zhang, W., Chen, R.: Integration of artificial intelligence enhanced capsule endoscopy in clinical practice. Digest. Dis. Sci. (2025). https://doi.org/10.1007/s10620-025-07932-3
4. Budd, S., Robinson, E.C., Kainz, B.: A survey on active learning and human-in-the-loop deep learning for medical image analysis. Med. Image Anal. **71**, 102062 (2021)
5. Giordano, A., Romero-Mascarell, C., González-Suárez, B., Guarner-Argente, C.: Integration of artificial intelligence-enhanced capsule endoscopy in clinical practice: a review of market-available tools for clinical practice. Digest. Dis. Sci. 1–11 (2025)
6. Hassan, C., Repici, A., Sharma, P., et al.: The role of artificial intelligence in colorectal cancer screening: lesion detection and lesion characterization. Ther. Adv. Gastroenterol. **15**, 17562848221134368 (2022). https://doi.org/10.1177/17562848221134368
7. Hirasawa, T., et al.: Current status and future perspective of artificial intelligence applications in endoscopic diagnosis and management of gastric cancer. Dig. Endosc. **33**(2), 263–272 (2021)
8. Kumar, S., Datta, S., Singh, V., Datta, D., Singh, S.K., Sharma, R.: Applications, challenges, and future directions of human-in-the-loop learning. IEEE Access (2024)
9. Lee, H., et al.: Validation of artificial intelligence computer-aided detection of colonic neoplasm in colonoscopy. Diagnostics **14**(23), 2762 (2024)
10. Li, S., Qi, L., Yu, Q., Huo, J., Shi, Y., Gao, Y.: Stitching, fine-tuning, re-training: a SAM-enabled framework for semi-supervised 3d medical image segmentation. IEEE Trans. Med. Imaging (2025)
11. Logan, Y.Y., Prabhushankar, M., AlRegib, G.: DECAL: DEployable clinical active learning. arXiv preprint arXiv:2206.10120 (2022)

12. Mehta, A., et al.: Effectiveness of artificial intelligence-assisted colonoscopy in early diagnosis of colorectal cancer: a systematic review. Int. J. Surg. **109**(4), 946–952 (2023)
13. Misawa, M., Mori, Y., Kudo, S.E.: Current status of artificial intelligence use in colonoscopy. Digestion **106**(2), 85–96 (2025). https://doi.org/10.1159/000534567
14. Chung, G.E., et al.: A prospective comparison of two computer aided detection systems with different false positive rates in colonoscopy. npj Digit. Med. **7**(1), 366 (2024). Nature Publishing Group UK London
15. Troya, J., et al.: Direct comparison of multiple computer-aided polyp detection systems. Endoscopy **56**(01), 63–69 (2024)
16. Wang, Y., Liu, Z., Li, Y., et al.: Artificial intelligence in colonoscopy: is it time to take a step forward? Cancers **15**(8), 2193 (2023). https://doi.org/10.3390/cancers15082193

# Triple Expert Adaptation Networks
# with Adaptive Prompt Selection
# for Multi-modal Medical Image Fusion


Cong Wang[(✉)], Kang Wang, and Yang Yang

Department of Radiology and Biomedical Imaging, University of California, San Francisco,
San Francisco, CA 94107, USA
`{cong.wang,kang.wang,yang.yang4}@ucsf.edu`



**Abstract.** Multi-modal medical image fusion seeks to integrate complementary information from heterogeneous imaging modalities to enhance clinical diagnostics. However, it faces challenges in reconciling channel-wise feature conflicts, spatial misalignments, and redundant feature propagation. In this paper, we propose a Triple Expert Adaptation Network (TEA-Net) to address these limitations through three domain-specific fusion mechanisms: Channel Expert Adaptation Fusion (CEAF), Low-Rank Expert Adaptation Fusion (LoR-EAF), and Spatial Expert Adaptation Fusion (SEAF). The CEAF employs globally dynamic channel attention to resolve intensity conflicts across different modalities. The LoR-EAF focuses on modulating the most relevant interactions between modalities in low-rank to compress extraneous information. The SEAF integrates large-kernel convolutions with cross-modality interactions to align features across different modalities. To boost fusion, we introduce an adaptive prompt selection module that utilizes learnable prompts to guide fusion among experts. Experiments on publicly available datasets demonstrate the superiority of our TEA-Net over state-of-the-art methods. The source codes are available at https://github.com/supersupercong/TEA-Net.



**Keywords:** Medical Image Fusion · Channel Expert Adaptation Fusion · Low-rank Expert Adaptation Fusion · Spatial Expert Adaptation Fusion · Adaptive Prompt Selection


## 1  Introduction

Medical imaging technologies have transformed modern healthcare by offering non-invasive insights into the human body's anatomical and functional processes. Among the leading modalities, Magnetic Resonance Imaging (MRI) excels in soft tissue contrast and multi-planar resolution, Computed Tomography (CT) provides superior visualization of bony structures and acute pathologies, while Positron Emission Tomography (PET) and Single-Photon Emission Computed



T. Chen et al. (Eds.): EMA4MICCAI 2025 Workshops, LNCS 16318, pp. 133–142, 2026.
https://doi.org/10.1007/978-3-032-13961-0_14

Tomography (SPECT) capture critical metabolic and physiological information for oncology and neurology. Despite their strengths, each modality has limitations: MRI lacks sensitivity to calcifications, CT offers limited soft tissue differentiation, and PET/SPECT has poor spatial resolution. Consequently, multi-modal image fusion has emerged as a vital technique, combining heterogeneous information from various imaging sources to enable comprehensive clinical decision-making, such as tumor boundary delineation.

Traditional fusion methods [8,9,12,15,21] often struggle to preserve modality-specific features while suppressing redundant or noisy components. Recent convolutional neural networks and transformer-based architectures have been introduced to address these challenges [4,7,11,17,18]. However, three critical issues persist: 1) Channel-wise feature conflict due to inconsistent intensity distributions across modalities, 2) Redundant feature propagation resulting from overlapping information in multi-modal representations, and 3) Spatial misalignment between different modalities. These limitations often lead to suboptimal fusion quality, thereby compromising diagnostic backgrounds.

To address the above challenges, we propose a Triple Expert Adaptation Network (TEA-Net), which systematically coordinates three specialized modules: Channel Expert Adaptation Fusion (CEAF), Low-Rank Expert Adaptation Fusion (LoR-EAF), and Spatial Expert Adaptation Fusion (SEAF). The CEAF learns global channel features that dynamically emphasize modality-specific discriminative features while suppressing conflicting responses. The LoR-EAF modulates the most relevant interactions between different modalities in low-rank to compress extraneous information. The SEAF employs large kernel convolutions coupled with cross-modality interaction to resolve spatial misalignments. To further boost fusion, we propose adaptive prompt selection that generates learnable prompts to select more useful expert features for fusion.

Our contributions can be summarized as follows:

- We propose the TEA-Net that integrates channel, low-rank, and spatial expert fusion to enhance the preservation of modality-specific features, resolve spatial misalignments, and reduce redundant feature propagation.
- We propose adaptive prompt selection that integrates kinds of experts by adaptively learning optimal selection parameters to prompt for better fusion.
- Experimental results demonstrate that our proposed TEA-Net outperforms state-of-the-art approaches on publicly available datasets.

## 2    Method

### 2.1    Overall Framework

Our framework (Fig. 1(a)) processes inputs from two different modalities. These images undergo feature extraction and triple expert adaptation blocks including Channel Expert Adaptation Fusion, Low-Rank Expert Adaptation Fusion, and Spatial Expert Adaptation Fusion, culminating in fused image reconstruction. To further enhance fusion, we propose Adaptive Prompt Selection, which

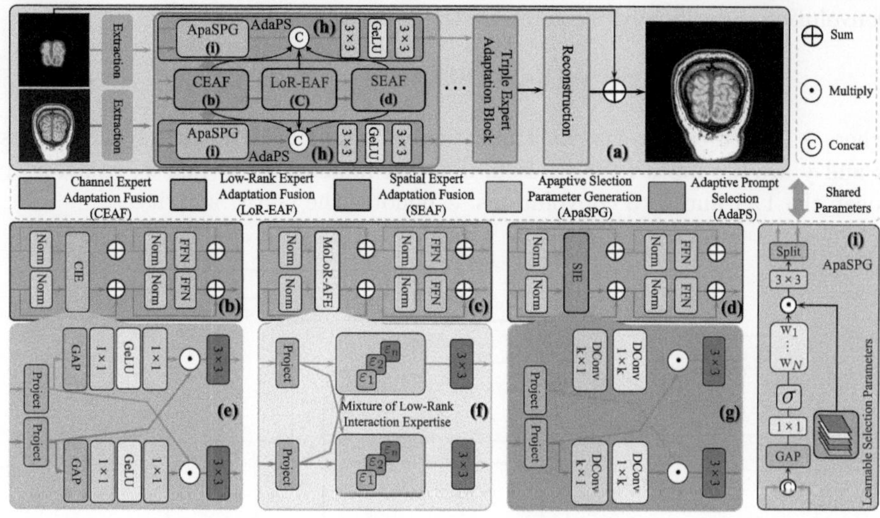

**Fig. 1.** Overall framework. Our TEA-Net processes inputs from two different modalities. These images undergo feature extraction and selection expert adaptation fusion, culminating in the reconstruction of fused images. The selection expert adaptation fusion encompasses Channel Expert Adaptation Fusion (CEAF), Low-Rank Expert Adaptation Fusion (LoR-EAF), and Spatial Expert Adaptation Fusion (SEAF). These modules enhance the preservation of modality-specific features, resolve spatial misalignments, and reduce redundant feature propagation. To further boost fusion, we propose Adaptive Prompt Selection, which generates learnable prompt parameters to select more useful features among these three experts for fusion.

autonomously selects more useful features from different experts by learning learnable prompts. Since our model mutually fuses the features of both modalities, we describe the fusion process in the general case below.

## 2.2   Channel Expert Adaptation Fusion

We observe that fusion from the perspective of the channel is crucial for fusion, as integrating global information may yield better results. Thus, we propose Channel Expert Adaptation Fusion (CEAF) for feature fusion, as shown in Fig. 1(b). Our CEAF contains a channel interaction expertise (Fig. 1(e)) with layer normalization [1] and a feed-forward network (FFN) [3].

*Channel Interaction Expertise.* Our Channel Interaction Expertise (CIE) first employs Global Adaptive Pooling (GAP) to extract global channel-wise features from one modality. The feature is then processed by a $1 \times 1$ convolution, GeLU activation, and another $1 \times 1$ convolution, and subsequently gated by the feature from another modality. Finally, the gated features undergo another $3 \times 3$

convolution. Specifically, we compute the process as follows:

$$\mathbf{z} = \mathtt{W}_3\Big(\mathtt{W}_1\varphi\mathtt{W}_1\big(\mathtt{GAP}(\mathbf{P}^x\mathbf{x})\big)\odot\mathbf{P}^y\mathbf{y}\Big), \tag{1}$$

where $\odot$ is the element-wise multiplication, $\mathbf{P}^x$ and $\mathbf{P}^y$ are linear (project) layers. $\mathbf{x}$ and $\mathbf{y}$ are the input features from different modalities. $\mathtt{W}_1$ and $\mathtt{W}_3$ respectively mean the $1\times1$ and $3\times3$ convolutions. $\varphi$ denotes the GeLU activity.

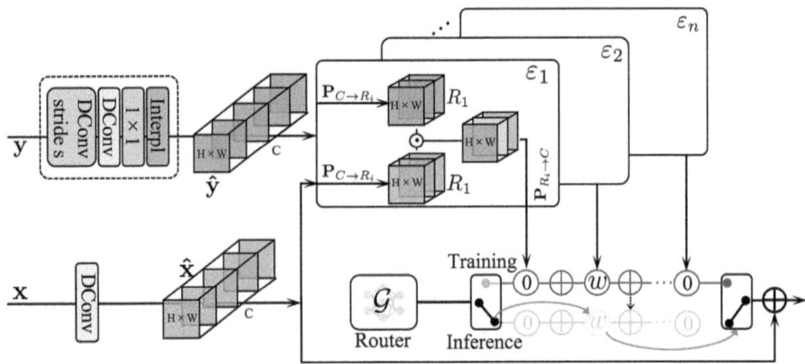


**Fig. 2.** Mixture of Low-Rank Interaction Expertise. During the training phase, our method learns from various experts. However, during inference, only the selected top-$k$ experts are utilized for computation, thereby enhancing efficiency.

## 2.3   Low-Rank Expert Adaptation Fusion

We propose to modulate the most relevant interactions between different modalities in low-rank to compress useless information for better fusion. Our Low-Rank Expert Adaptation Fusion (LoR-EAF), motivated by [20], contains a Mixture of Low-Rank Adaptation Fusion Expertise (MoLoR-AFE) to efficiently model relevant global informative features between different modalities and an FFN [3] for boosting feature representations, as shown in Fig. 1(c). In the MoLoR-AFE, we propose a Mixture of Low-Rank Interaction Expertise to model the interaction between different modalities in low-rank, as shown in Fig. 2.

*Mixture of Low-Rank Interaction Expertise.* We employ a $3 \times 3$ convolution to project features $\mathbf{x}$ and $\mathbf{y} \in \mathbb{R}^{H\times W\times C}$ from different modalities. To efficiently aggregate pixel-wise cross-channel context, a recursive strided convolution is applied $t$ times, followed by a refinement and upsampling step. This process constructs the feature pyramid, denoted as $\hat{\mathbf{y}} \in \mathbb{R}^{H\times W\times C}$. The process is formulated as follows:

$$|p|_{\downarrow h\times w} = \mathtt{W}^d_{k\times k,\ s}(...(\mathtt{W}^d_{k\times k,\ s}(\mathbf{y})) \tag{2}$$

$$\hat{\mathbf{y}} = |\ \mathbf{P}_{C\to C}(\mathtt{W}^d_3(|p|_{\downarrow h\times w}))\ |_{\uparrow H\times W}, \tag{3}$$

where $\mathsf{W}^d_{k \times k, s}$ refers to a depth-wise convolution with a kernel size of $k$ and a stride of $s$. The term $\mathbf{P}_{C \to C}$ represents a linear layer, and $p$ signifies the contextual feature pyramid. At the same time, a depth-wise convolution extracts the context $\hat{\mathbf{x}}$ in a parallel manner before feeding both the extracted features into the mixture of low-rank interaction expertise.

To explore the inter-dependencies among different modalities while reducing redundancy, we utilize low-rank for the inputs while exploring to model global relationships. As shown in Fig. 2, a single low-rank expert ($\mathcal{E}$) takes the spatial features $\hat{\mathbf{x}}$ and encoded pixel-wise contextual cues $\hat{\mathbf{y}}$ as inputs and is formulated as:

$$\mathcal{E}_i(\hat{\mathbf{x}}, \hat{\mathbf{y}}) = \mathbf{P}_{R_i \to C}(\mathbf{P}_{C \to R_i}\hat{\mathbf{x}} \odot \mathbf{P}_{C \to R_i}\hat{\mathbf{y}}), \tag{4}$$

where the $\mathbf{P}_{C \to R_i}$ compresses the encoded features in channel dimension into their low-rank approximations $R_i$, where $i \in \{1, \dots, n\}$. Then, $\mathbf{P}_{R_i \to C}$ restores the features to their original dimension $C$.

We also employ a dynamic strategy that utilizes a mixture of low-rank experts. A routing network ($\mathcal{G}$) systematically navigates the search space to determine the optimal low-rank expert, considering both the input and network depth. Following [14], the final output $\mathbf{z}$ of the mixture of low-rank experts is as follows:

$$\mathbf{z} = \mathsf{W}_3\left( \sum_i^n \mathcal{G}(\hat{\mathbf{x}})\mathcal{E}_i(\hat{\mathbf{x}}, \hat{\mathbf{y}}) + \hat{\mathbf{x}} \right), \tag{5}$$

where $\mathcal{G}(\cdot)$ represents the learned routing function, and $\mathcal{E}_i(\cdot)$ indicates the output of the $i$-th expert. The router function $\mathcal{G}(\cdot)$ boosts computational efficiency by focusing on the top-$k$ low-rank experts.

### 2.4  Spatial Expert Adaptation Fusion

Inspired by previous works [5, 19, 20], we design Spatial Expert Adaptation Fusion (SEAF), which contains Spatial Interaction Expertise (SIE) and an FFN [3].

*Spatial Interaction Expertise.* Our SIE (Fig. 1(g)) employs a striped depth-wise convolution with a large kernel within $k \times k$ window to sequentially convolve the features with those from one modality. The convolved results are then interacted with features from another modality. Finally, the features undergo processing through a $3 \times 3$ convolution. Specifically, we compute the spatial-wise interaction as follows:

$$\mathbf{z} = \mathsf{W}_3\left( \mathsf{W}^d_{k \times k, \ s}(\mathbf{P}^x\mathbf{x}) \odot \mathbf{P}^y\mathbf{y} \right). \tag{6}$$

**Table 1.** Results on three publicly available datasets. **Bold**/<u>underline</u> show the best/second-best values.

| Method | PET | | | | CT | | | | SPECT | | | |
|---|---|---|---|---|---|---|---|---|---|---|---|---|
| | SCD ↑ | VIF ↑ | Qabf ↑ | SSIM ↑ | SCD ↑ | VIF ↑ | Qabf ↑ | SSIM ↑ | SCD ↑ | VIF ↑ | Qabf ↑ | SSIM ↑ |
| EMFusion [17] | 0.943 | 0.685 | <u>0.783</u> | 1.221 | 1.190 | <u>0.552</u> | 0.475 | <u>1.266</u> | 0.885 | 0.665 | 0.692 | <u>1.212</u> |
| MSRPAN [4] | 1.017 | 0.581 | **0.799** | 1.182 | 1.319 | 0.436 | 0.455 | 1.261 | 0.960 | 0.525 | 0.560 | 1.153 |
| SwinFusion [11] | **1.642** | <u>0.703</u> | 0.683 | 0.725 | <u>1.537</u> | 0.522 | 0.545 | 0.579 | **1.678** | 0.744 | <u>0.720</u> | 0.684 |
| Zero [7] | 0.950 | 0.635 | 0.774 | 1.162 | 0.768 | 0.320 | <u>0.582</u> | 1.199 | 1.046 | 0.582 | 0.681 | 1.180 |
| U2Fusion [18] | 0.947 | 0.460 | 0.292 | 0.494 | 0.309 | 0.074 | 0.489 | 0.042 | 0.865 | 0.419 | 0.696 | 0.479 |
| CDDFuse [22] | <u>1.481</u> | 0.650 | 0.765 | <u>1.227</u> | **1.589** | 0.526 | 0.530 | 1.224 | 0.995 | <u>0.786</u> | 0.719 | 1.169 |
| PSLPT [16] | 0.888 | 0.548 | 0.373 | 0.815 | 0.675 | 0.502 | 0.432 | 0.810 | 0.850 | 0.359 | 0.325 | 0.933 |
| **TEA-Net (Ours)** | 1.474 | **0.795** | 0.740 | **1.259** | 1.532 | **0.557** | **0.601** | **1.329** | <u>1.457</u> | **0.801** | **0.742** | **1.244** |

## 2.5 Adaptive Prompt Selection

To better fuse these three experts, we propose the Adaptive Prompt Selection (AdaPS) to encode expert-specific context in selection parameters, as shown in Fig. 1(h). Inspired by [13], our approach develops learnable selection parameters that interact with input, enriching them through different experts. Given adaptive selection-parameters $\mathbf{S_{AdaSPG}} \in \mathbb{R}^{H \times W \times C}$ and features $\mathbf{F_{concat}} \in \mathbb{R}^{H \times W \times C}$ concatenated by the output features of CEAF, LoR-EAF, and SEAF, the process of adaptive selection fusion is defined as:

$$\mathbf{x}, \mathbf{y} = \mathtt{Split}\left( \mathtt{W}_3 \varphi \mathtt{W}_3 \Big( \mathtt{Concat}\left[\mathbf{S_{AdaSPG}}, \mathbf{F_{concat}}\right] \Big) \right), \tag{7}$$

where $\mathbf{x}$ and $\mathbf{y}$ are the outputs of AdaPS that are sent to the next triple expert adaptation block.

*Adaptive Selection Parameter Generation.* Adaptive Selection Parameter Generation (AdaSPG) generates selection weights from input features from different modalities by applying GAP, creating a feature vector, which then passes through a channel-downscaling convolution layer, yielding a compact feature vector. The softmax operation generates selection-weights $w \in \mathbb{R}^N$, followed by a $3 \times 3$ convolution layer:

$$\mathbf{S_{AdaSPG}} = \mathtt{W}_3 \left( \sum_{c=1}^{N} w_i \mathbf{S}_c \right), \quad w_i = \mathtt{Softmax}\left( \mathtt{W}_1 \Big( \mathtt{GAP}(\mathtt{Concat}[\mathbf{x}, \mathbf{y}]) \Big) \right). \tag{8}$$

Here we use parameter-shared AdaSPG in one triple expert adaptation block, as we observe that such a design helps produce better performance, as discussed in Table 3.

## 3 Experiments

### 3.1 Datasets and Benchmarks

We employ medical images from the Harvard Medical website, comprising pairs such as MRI-CT, MRI-PET, and MRI-SPECT as our datasets. We compare our TEA-Net with learning-based SOTA multi-modal fusion techniques.

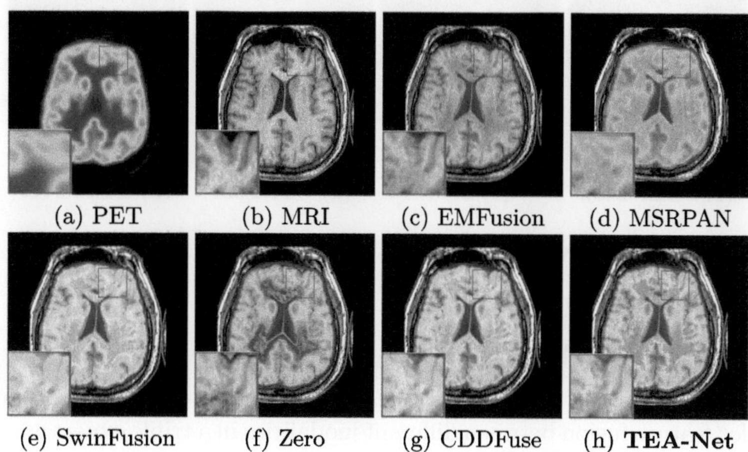

(a) PET        (b) MRI        (c) EMFusion        (d) MSRPAN

(e) SwinFusion        (f) Zero        (g) CDDFuse        (h) **TEA-Net**

**Fig. 3.** Visual comparison on MRI-PET datasets.

### 3.2 Implementation Details

We train our TEA-Net for 200 epochs with a batch size of 1. We use Adam [6] as the optimizer to update the parameters of our TEA-Net. The initial learning rate is set to $5 \times 10^{-4}$ and gradually reduced to $5 \times 10^{-8}$ using the CosineAnnealingLR scheduler [10]. The training images are cropped to $256 \times 256$ pixels. Consistent with established norms [2], we use two input images and the fused image to calculate a composite loss function comprising L1, SSIM, and gradient losses. There are 6 triple expert adaptation blocks in our TEA-Net. For the reconstruction part, we use the reconstruction process used in [23].

### 3.3 Comparison with SOTA Methods

We report the experimental results compared with state-of-the-art approaches in Table 1 on the widely-used dataset in terms of SCD, VIF, Qabf, and SSIM. Our proposed TEA-Net outperforms existing SOTAs across almost all metrics, demonstrating the superiority of our TEA-Net in medical image fusion. Figures 3 and 4 present qualitative comparisons on the MRI-PET and MRI-SPECT datasets, respectively. As can be seen, our TEA-Net exhibits superior visual quality, a finding corroborated by the experimental metrics.

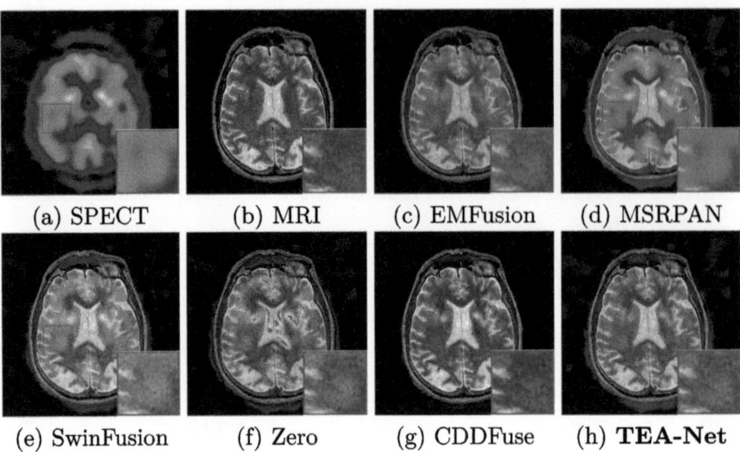



**Fig. 4.** Visual comparison on MRI-SPECT datasets.

## 3.4 Ablation Study

*Effect on Triple Expert Adaptation Block.* As we propose CEAF, LoR-EAF, and SEAF for feature fusion between different modalities in a triple expert adaptation block, we need to examine their effectiveness. Table 2 shows that removing either the CEAF, LoR-EAF, or SEAF results in a model performance drop slightly, indicating that all of the proposed various expert mining modules effectively enhance the quality of medical image fusion.

*Effect on Adaptive Prompt Selection.* We design the adaptive prompt selection to better mine useful information from different expert modules for improving fusion quality. Hence, it is of great interest to analyze how it affects the model performance. Table 3 shows that disabling the selection module, i.e., Table 3(a), will result in a model drop slightly. We also replace the adaptive prompt selection module by designing independent learnable parameters or independent input rather than concatenation between them. The results show neither of them is better than our proposed shared parameters when concatenation them as input.

**Table 2.** Ablation study on triple expert adaptation block.

| ID | Experiments | PET | | CT | | SPECT | |
|---|---|---|---|---|---|---|---|
| | | SCD ↑ | Qabf ↑ | Qabf ↑ | SSIM ↑ | VIF ↑ | Qabf ↑ |
| (a) | w/o Channel Expert Adaptation Fusion | 1.453 | 0.738 | 0.597 | 1.328 | 0.786 | 0.736 |
| (b) | w/o Low-rank Expert Adaptation Fusion | 1.468 | 0.741 | 0.601 | 1.328 | 0.787 | 0.740 |
| (c) | w/o Spatial Expert Adaptation Fusion | 1.442 | 0.739 | 0.594 | 1.329 | 0.787 | 0.737 |
| (d) | Full Model (Ours) | **1.474** | 0.740 | **0.601** | **1.329** | **0.801** | **0.742** |

**Table 3.** Ablation study on adaptive prompt selection. Independent $\mathbf{x}$ and $\mathbf{y}$ means that we respectively input $\mathbf{x}$ and $\mathbf{y}$ to parameters-independent AdaPS in Eq. (8).

| ID | Formulation of Input | Types of Parameters | PET | | CT | SPECT | | |
|---|---|---|---|---|---|---|---|---|
| | | | SCD ↑ | Qabf ↑ | Qabf ↑ | SSIM ↑ | VIF ↑ | Qabf ↑ |
| (a) | – | – | 1.476 | 0.738 | 0.600 | 1.328 | 0.781 | 0.736 |
| (b) | Concat[$\mathbf{x}$, $\mathbf{y}$] | Independent | 1.449 | 0.740 | 0.598 | 1.328 | 0.784 | 0.736 |
| (c) | Independent $\mathbf{x}$, and $\mathbf{y}$ | Independent | 1.455 | 0.739 | 0.598 | 1.328 | 0.786 | 0.737 |
| (d) | Concat[$\mathbf{x}$, $\mathbf{y}$] | Shared | 1.474 | **0.740** | **0.601** | **1.329** | **0.801** | **0.742** |

# 4   Conclusion

In this paper, we have proposed a Triple Expert Adaptation Network (TEA-Net) for multi-modal medical image fusion. By systematically coordinating the Channel Expert Adaptation Fusion, Low-Rank Expert Adaptation Fusion, and Spatial Expert Adaptation Fusion, TEA-Net effectively enhances modality-specific feature preservation, resolves spatial misalignments, and mitigates redundant features. We have proposed an adaptive prompt selection mechanism to dynamically select better features generated by different experts for better fusion. Experiments have shown that our TEA-Net performs better than state-of-the-art approaches.

# References


1. Ba, J.L., Kiros, J.R., Hinton, G.E.: Layer normalization. arXiv preprint arXiv:1607.06450 (2016)
2. Cao, K., et al.: Shuffle mamba: state space models with random shuffle for multi-modal image fusion. arXiv preprint arXiv:2409.01728 (2024)
3. Chen, Z., Zhang, Y., Gu, J., Kong, L., Yang, X., Yu, F.: Dual aggregation transformer for image super-resolution. In: Proceedings of the IEEE/CVF International Conference on Computer Vision (2023)
4. Fu, J., Li, W., Du, J., Huang, Y.: A multiscale residual pyramid attention network for medical image fusion. Biomed. Signal Process. Control **66**, 102488 (2021)
5. Hou, Q., Lu, C.Z., Cheng, M.M., Feng, J.: Conv2Former: a simple transformer-style convnet for visual recognition. In: Proceedings of the IEEE Conference on Computer Vision and Pattern Recognition (2022)
6. Kingma, D.P., Ba, J.: Adam: a method for stochastic optimization. In: ICLR (2015)
7. Lahoud, F., Süsstrunk, S.: Zero-learning fast medical image fusion. In: 2019 22th International Conference on Information Fusion (FUSION), pp. 1–8 (2019)
8. Li, H., Manjunath, B., Mitra, S.K.: Multisensor image fusion using the wavelet transform. Graph. Models Image Process. **57**(3), 235–245 (1995)
9. Li, S., Kwok, J.T., Wang, Y.: Combination of images with diverse focuses using the spatial frequency. Inf. Fusion **2**(3), 169–176 (2001)
10. Loshchilov, I., Hutter, F.: SGDR: stochastic gradient descent with warm restarts. In: ICLR (2017)

11. Ma, J., Tang, L., Fan, F., Huang, J., Mei, X., Ma, Y.: SwinFusion: cross-domain long-range learning for general image fusion via swin transformer. IEEE/CAA J. Autom. Sinica **9**(7), 1200–1217 (2022)
12. Nunez, J., Otazu, X., Fors, O., Prades, A., Pala, V., Arbiol, R.: Multiresolution-based image fusion with additive wavelet decomposition. IEEE Trans. Geosci. Remote Sens. **37**(3), 1204–1211 (1999)
13. Potlapalli, V., Zamir, S.W., Khan, S., Khan, F.: PromptIR: prompting for all-in-one image restoration. In: Thirty-Seventh Conference on Neural Information Processing Systems (2023)
14. Shazeer, N., et al.: Outrageously large neural networks: the sparsely-gated mixture-of-experts layer. arXiv preprint arXiv:1701.06538 (2017)
15. Toet, A.: Image fusion by a ratio of low-pass pyramid. Pattern Recogn. Lett. **9**(4), 245–253 (1989)
16. Wang, W., Deng, L.J., Vivone, G.: A general image fusion framework using multi-task semi-supervised learning. Inf. Fusion **108**, 102414 (2024)
17. Xu, H., Ma, J.: EMFusion: an unsupervised enhanced medical image fusion network. Inf. Fusion **76**, 177–186 (2021)
18. Xu, H., Ma, J., Jiang, J., Guo, X., Ling, H.: U2Fusion: a unified unsupervised image fusion network. IEEE Trans. Pattern Anal. Mach. Intell. **44**(1), 502–518 (2020)
19. Yang, J., Li, C., Gao, J.: Focal modulation networks. arXiv (2022)
20. Zamfir, E., Wu, Z., Mehta, N., Zhang, Y., Timofte, R.: See more details: efficient image super-resolution by experts mining. In: Forty-First International Conference on Machine Learning (2024)
21. Zhang, Z., Blum, R.S.: A categorization of multiscale-decomposition-based image fusion schemes with a performance study for a digital camera application. Proc. IEEE **87**(8), 1315–1326 (1999)
22. Zhao, Z., et al.: CDDFuse: correlation-driven dual-branch feature decomposition for multi-modality image fusion. In: Proceedings of the IEEE/CVF Conference on Computer Vision and Pattern Recognition, pp. 5906–5916 (2023)
23. Zheng, N., et al.: Probing synergistic high-order interaction in infrared and visible image fusion. In: IEEE/CVF Conference on Computer Vision and Pattern Recognition, CVPR 2024, Seattle, WA, USA, 16–22 June 2024, pp. 26374–26385 (2024)

# Towards Efficient and Privacy-Preserving Medical Image Segmentation: A Point-Driven Source-Free Active Adaptation Framework


Hongqiu Wang[1], Jialu Li[1], Zhaohu Xing[1], Haipeng Zhou[1], Xiangde Luo[2], and Lei Zhu[1,3(✉)]

[1] Hong Kong University of Science and Technology (Guangzhou), Guangzhou, China
`leizhu@ust.hk`
[2] West China Hospital, Sichuan University, Chengdu, China
[3] The Hong Kong University of Science and Technology, Sai Kung, Hong Kong



**Abstract.** Medical image segmentation remains a cornerstone for precision diagnosis and therapeutic planning in clinical workflows. However, deep learning models trained on development datasets often suffer from limited generalizability, exhibiting poor performance when deployed across different clinical centers due to domain shifts (such as variations in imaging protocols). It raises privacy concerns when sensitive patient data needs to be shared across institutions. Meanwhile, the increasing prevalence of high-resolution medical images (e.g., ultra-wide-field retinal scans) exacerbates the challenge of manual annotation, which is labor-intensive. To address the need for efficient and privacy-preserving model adaptation and deployment, we propose a Point-Driven Source-Free Active Domain Adaptation Framework. This framework enables significant performance improvement in high-resolution medical image segmentation across multiple datasets. Notably, it achieves this without accessing source domain data, relying only on annotating a minimal number of pixels. By bridging the gap between algorithm generalization and clinical practicality, our framework offers a privacy-compliant solution for deploying medical image segmentation models across heterogeneous healthcare environments, highlighting its potential for cost-effective and secure precision medicine. Furthermore, we provide our insights into the limitations of current paradigms and outline promising directions for future research in efficient medical AI.

**Keywords:** Medical image segmentation · High-resolution imaging · Source-free domain adaptation · Active learning · Point supervision


---


H. Wang, J. Li, and Z. Xing—Contributed equally to this work.




T. Chen et al. (Eds.): EMA4MICCAI 2025 Workshops, LNCS 16318, pp. 143–153, 2026.
https://doi.org/10.1007/978-3-032-13961-0_15

# 1   Introduction

Medical image segmentation is fundamental to precision medicine, underpinning accurate diagnosis and personalized treatment planning [6,13,23,27]. Despite the transformative impact of deep learning [1,2,19,21,25,26], models trained on data from a single institution often fail to generalize effectively across diverse clinical settings [7]. This shortfall stems from inherent domain shifts—differences in imaging hardware, acquisition protocols, and patient demographics—that create mismatches between training and target domains [24]. For example, a segmentation model optimized on one center's data may exhibit substantial performance drops when applied to another due to subtle variations in image contrast, resolution, or noise, leading to unreliable clinical decisions.

The proliferation of high-resolution imaging technologies—such as Ultra-Wide-Field (UWF) retinal scans—further compounds these challenges [20,22]. UWF imaging has emerged as a critical tool for detecting peripheral retinal diseases by capturing expansive ocular structures [12], but its high-resolution, wide-field datasets pose unique annotation burdens. Manually labeling UWF images at the pixel level is extremely time-consuming (requiring hundreds of hours per dataset) and costly [18]. It also raises privacy concerns when sensitive patient data needs to be shared across institutions. These barriers are especially pronounced in cross-center deployment, where heterogeneous imaging pipelines and strict data regulations hinder the development of AI models.

While recent advancements in source-free domain adaptation (SFDA) have shown promise in mitigating domain shifts without explicit source data, their reliance on feature alignment or pseudo-labels often falls short in challenging scenarios like UWF vessel segmentation. To address this gap, we build on the source-free active domain adaptation (SFADA) paradigm and introduce a Grid-Dither Sampling (GDS) strategy—an efficient, training-free mechanism that identifies and selects approximately 1% of informative pixels for annotation, far sparser than the 5% patches typically required by prior methods. By strategically sampling critical points using a combination of grid-based spatial coverage and dithered uncertainty estimation, GDS ensures that minimal annotations capture the most representative features for learning. Experiment results demonstrate that our approach achieves comparable or superior performance to state-of-the-art methods requiring 5× more labeled pixels on multi-center UWF datasets, showcasing its efficacy in balancing annotation cost and segmentation accuracy.

Beyond methodological innovation, our work contributes actionable insights into sparse supervision for high-resolution medical imaging. In the discussion, we delve into the trade-offs between pixel selection density and operation efficacy, highlighting how GDS strategy can be generalized to other modalities. We also outline promising future directions. By grounding our framework in the real-world challenges of UWF imaging while emphasizing broader applicability, we aim to catalyze research at the intersection of efficient learning and privacy preservation in medical image analysis.

The main contributions are summarized as follows:

- We pioneer the exploration of sparse point supervision in Ultra-Wide-Field (UWF) retinal vessel segmentation in the Source-Free Active Domain Adaptation (SFADA) paradigm for high-resolution medical imaging.
- We propose a novel training-free active learning strategy that synergistically combines grid-based spatial coverage and random-guided dithering to identify representative pixels, achieving competitive performance with 1% labeled pixels (vs. 5% in prior methods).
- Experimental results demonstrate our framework achieves state-of-the-art accuracy on the existing Multi-center UWF Vessel Segmentation (MU-VS) dataset, with score improvement over existing methods while reducing annotation costs. We further provide insights into sparse supervision trade-offs and outline actionable directions for efficient medical AI.

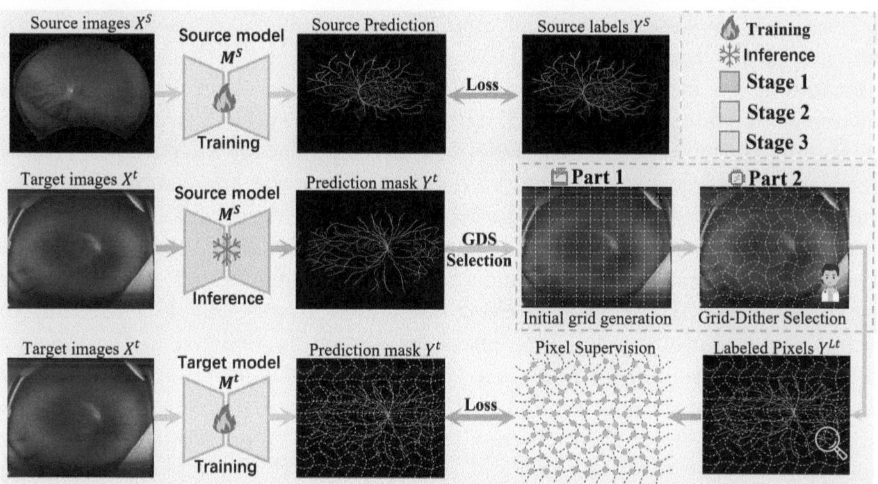


**Fig. 1.** Pipeline of the proposed point-driven SFADA method, including the GDS selection strategy. The first row illustrates the source model $M^s$ training process; the second row represents the selection and active annotation of the valuable target domain pixels based on the GDS strategy; and the third row represents the target model $M^t$ fine-tuning process.

## 2   Methodology

### 2.1   Preliminary of SFADA

Given the input image $x$, medical image segmentation task is to predict a pixel-wise segmentation mask $y$ using the segmentation model $M$. To maintain data privacy and security, SFADA methods prohibit direct access to the source domain images along with their corresponding annotations $(x^s, y^s)$. Previous method [20] proposed to recommend valuable UWF image patches for annotation based on the predictions by the frozen source domain model $\mathcal{M}^s$. In this work, we propose a training-free strategy to select a small quantity of target pixels for manual annotation $N_t^{AL} = \alpha \cdot N_t$, where $\alpha$ signifies the selection ratio and $N_t$ is the count of all target pixels, and the quantity of selected pixels is fewer than the total target pixels. Moreover, the labels of these selected pixels $N_t^{AL}$ are denoted as $Y^{Lt}$. The purpose of our work is to enhance the target domain segmentation model $\mathcal{M}^t$ with fewer quantities of annotated pixels $Y^{Lt}$.

## 2.2  Point-Driven SFADA Framework

Performing full annotation for UWF images could be a time-consuming task for clinicians, primarily attributed to the high-resolution nature of UWF images. The recent SFADA method [20] proposes to enhance target domain segmentation performance by selecting a small quantity of valuable patches for annotation, which typically relies on pre-trained source models and focuses on patch-level annotation, yet still imposes a relatively huge workload on clinicians. Hence, we explore a training-free **Grid-Dither Sampling (GDS)** strategy that both eliminates the need for source data and enables efficient selection of valuable pixels for annotation. Specifically, GDS prioritizes the annotation of a set of representative pixels, which are directly used for point-wise fine-tuning.

Figure 1 depicts the pipeline of our proposed point-driven SFADA method. The initial row in grey color illustrates the first stage of our pipeline, where we utilize source UWF images along with their masks $(X^s, Y^s)$ to train the source segmentation model $\mathcal{M}^s$. The second stage is depicted in the blue row of Fig. 1. The Grid-Dither Sampling (GDS) strategy is proposed to correct the knowledge bias of the source model $\mathcal{M}^s$ by recommending diverse target domain pixels for active annotation, thereby improving the target model segmentation performance. The third row in Fig. 1 illustrates the third stage of our pipeline, where the actively annotated pixel labels $Y^{Lt}$ are used for target-domain model $\mathcal{M}^t$ fine-tuning with the combination of cross-entropy loss and Dice loss.

## 2.3  Grid-Dither Sampling (GDS) Selection

Although the source-domain model $\mathcal{M}^s$ could predict preliminary vessel masks for the target-domain UWF image $X^t$. However, due to the domain gaps between different centers, the source model $\mathcal{M}^s$ could inevitably suffer different degrees of performance degradation in the target center. Existing methods focus on selecting valuable images or patches for annotation. To further enhance target-domain segmentation performance, the GDS selection strategy is proposed to bridge the vessel segmentation knowledge gap by selecting diverse target-domain pixels, thereby improving the performance of the target-domain model.

As illustrated in Fig. 1, the proposed GDS strategy includes the following two phases: $P_1$ for the initial grid generation and $P_2$ for the selection of the jitter pixels. First, we initialize a uniform position grid $\mathcal{G}$ based on the coordinate system of the pixel points in each target-domain image $x^t$:

$$\mathcal{G} = \{g_1, g_2, \ldots, g_{N^2}\}, \quad g_k = \left(\frac{j}{N-1}, \frac{i}{N-1}\right), \quad i, j \in \{1, \ldots, N\} \quad (1)$$

where $g_k$ denotes the k-th point coordinate in the grid set $\mathcal{G}$, $N$ denotes the edge length of the grid $\mathcal{G}$ which determines the grid resolution, $i$ represents the row index of the grid, $j$ represents the column index of the grid.

Moreover, we introduce random perturbations $p_k$ of magnitude $\epsilon$ on each grid point to alleviate the issue of overly fixed sampling locations with grid sampling, introducing more varied pixel points for annotation:

$$p_k = g_k + \delta_k, \quad \delta_k = (\delta_{x_k}, \delta_{y_k}), \quad \delta_{x_k}, \delta_{y_k} \sim \mathcal{U}(-\epsilon, \epsilon). \quad (2)$$

where $p_k$ represents the coordinate vector of the target point after adding the disturbance; $\delta_k$ represents the two-dimensional random disturbance vector acting on $g_k$; $\delta_{x_k}$ represents the disturbance component in the x direction, which obeys the uniform distribution $\mathcal{U}(-\epsilon, \epsilon)$; $\delta_{y_k}$ represents the disturbance component in the y direction, which obeys the uniform distribution $\mathcal{U}(-\epsilon, \epsilon)$; $\epsilon$ represents the disturbance amplitude parameter. Then we select pixels in the jittered grid $\mathcal{G}$ for annotation to supplement the segmentation knowledge of the target domain.

**Table 1.** Quantitative analysis of the Multi-center UWF-SLO Vessel Segmentation (MU-VS) dataset, including categories and image resolution.

| Dataset | Amount of data | Categories | Resolution | Public available |
|---|---|---|---|---|
| PRIME-FP20 [4] | 15 | DR | 4000 × 4000 | yes |
| Center A | 30 | Normal, RVO | 3900 × 3072 | yes |
| Center B | 30 | DR, RVO, RP, RAO, CSC | 3900 × 3072 | yes |

## 3  Experiments and Results

### 3.1  Data Description

To evaluate our framework on high-resolution medical image analysis tasks, we conducted experiments using the Multi-center UWF Vessel Segmentation (MU-VS) dataset [20]. Following the common protocol, we adopted the publicly available PRIME-FP20 dataset [4] as the source domain for pre-training the segmentation model. The two other clinical datasets from distinct medical centers (Center A and Center B in Table 1) served as target domains to simulate real-world deployment scenarios.

## 3.2  Implementation Details

Following the established setting in [20], we maintained identical experimental settings across all comparisons. The MU-VS dataset was split into training/validation/test subsets at a 6:2:2 ratio. Input images (original 3900 × 3072) were uniformly resized to 1024 × 1024 for training. We employed an SGD optimizer with momentum = 0.9, batch size = 5, and initial learning rate = 0.03, exponentially decaying at rate = 0.9/iteration. While fully supervised training used 6000 iterations, subsequent fine-tuning completed in 3000 iterations. All methods adopted the same U-Net backbone [9] with consistent hyperparameters to ensure fair comparison.

## 3.3  Measurement Metrics

Building on prior research [8,18,20], we evaluate model performance using four commonly-used metrics: Dice score (Dice), Intersection-over-Union (IoU), Matthews Correlation Coefficient (MCC), and Bookmaker Informedness (BM).

**Table 2.** Comparison on Dice and IoU of our method and other state-of-the-art domain adaptation and active domain adaptation methods on the MU-VS dataset.

| Methods | Dice (mean±std, %) | | | IoU (mean±std, %) | | |
|---|---|---|---|---|---|---|
| | Center A | Center B | Overall | Center A | Center B | Overall |
| Lower bound | $54.76 \pm 2.73$ | $51.32 \pm 3.25$ | $53.04 \pm 2.99$ | $37.75 \pm 2.56$ | $34.58 \pm 2.91$ | $36.17 \pm 2.74$ |
| Upper bound | $62.00 \pm 1.32$ | $57.36 \pm 2.99$ | $59.68 \pm 2.16$ | $44.94 \pm 1.38$ | $40.27 \pm 2.96$ | $42.61 \pm 2.17$ |
| AdvEnt [15] | $56.29 \pm 1.35$ | $51.95 \pm 2.96$ | $54.12 \pm 2.16$ | $39.18 \pm 1.30$ | $35.14 \pm 2.72$ | $37.16 \pm 2.01$ |
| DPL [3] | $56.50 \pm 2.20$ | $52.58 \pm 2.92$ | $54.54 \pm 2.56$ | $39.40 \pm 2.12$ | $35.72 \pm 2.67$ | $37.56 \pm 2.40$ |
| CBMT [11] | $57.51 \pm 1.42$ | $52.95 \pm 2.79$ | $55.23 \pm 2.10$ | $40.38 \pm 1.39$ | $36.06 \pm 2.57$ | $38.22 \pm 1.98$ |
| CPR [5] | $57.79 \pm 2.01$ | $53.28 \pm 2.93$ | $55.54 \pm 2.47$ | $40.66 \pm 1.96$ | $36.36 \pm 2.71$ | $38.51 \pm 2.34$ |
| 5% pixels | | | | | | |
| Adversarial [14] | $58.79 \pm 1.73$ | $53.32 \pm 2.76$ | $56.06 \pm 2.25$ | $41.66 \pm 1.71$ | $36.40 \pm 2.56$ | $39.03 \pm 2.14$ |
| AADA [10] | $58.92 \pm 1.46$ | $53.38 \pm 2.84$ | $56.15 \pm 2.15$ | $41.78 \pm 1.46$ | $36.45 \pm 2.66$ | $39.12 \pm 2.06$ |
| MHPL [16] | $59.32 \pm 1.22$ | $53.58 \pm 2.99$ | $56.45 \pm 2.11$ | $42.18 \pm 1.23$ | $36.66 \pm 2.84$ | $39.42 \pm 2.04$ |
| STDR [17] | $59.51 \pm 1.54$ | $53.96 \pm 2.80$ | $56.73 \pm 2.17$ | $42.38 \pm 1.56$ | $37.00 \pm 2.67$ | $39.69 \pm 2.11$ |
| CUP [20] | $60.92 \pm 0.94$ | $54.92 \pm 2.81$ | $57.92 \pm 1.88$ | $43.81 \pm 0.98$ | $37.91 \pm 2.70$ | $40.86 \pm 1.84$ |
| 1% pixels | | | | | | |
| Ours | $60.58 \pm 1.80$ | $\mathbf{56.53 \pm 2.89}$ | $\mathbf{58.56 \pm 2.35}$ | $43.47 \pm 1.85$ | $\mathbf{39.46 \pm 2.84}$ | $\mathbf{41.47 \pm 2.35}$ |

## 3.4  Comparison with State-of-the-Art Methods

This section summarizes the experimental results presented in Tables 2 and 3, covering two medical centers. It includes performance comparisons between the lower bound (without fine-tuning), the upper bound (fine-tuning with full label access), and several state-of-the-art methods in domain adaptation and active domain adaptation. Figure 2 illustrates segmentation outputs for visual reference. Analysis of Tables 2 and 3 reveals substantial performance differences between the lower and upper bounds across multiple evaluation metrics.

**Unsupervised Domain Adaptation (UDA) Comparison.** We compare our method with several leading UDA techniques using consistent backbones. This comparison includes source-dependent methods such as AdvEnt [15], as well as source-free approaches like DPL [3], CBMT [11], and CPR [5]. As shown in Table 2, these methods achieve improvements over the lower bound (53.04% Dice). However, due to the lack of supervision with real labels, the improvements remain modest. In contrast, our method achieves a significantly higher overall Dice score of 58.56% with around 1% of annotated pixels, outperforming all methods. A similar trend is observed in Table 3, which presents the performance in terms of MCC and BM metrics. Compared to the lower bound (52.18% MCC and 49.61% BM), UDA methods show incremental gains, with MCC values ranging from 53.17% to 54.78% and BM values from 51.23% to 53.11%.

**Table 3.** Comparison on MCC and BM of our method and other state-of-the-art domain adaptation and active domain adaptation methods on the MU-VS dataset.

| | MCC (mean±std, %) | | | BM (mean±std, %) | | |
|---|---|---|---|---|---|---|
| Methods | Center A | Center B | Overall | Center A | Center B | Overall |
| Lower bound | 54.03 ± 2.54 | 50.33 ± 3.25 | 52.18 ± 2.90 | 48.95 ± 4.91 | 50.27 ± 4.74 | 49.61 ± 4.83 |
| Upper bound | 61.48 ± 1.29 | 56.58 ± 2.80 | 59.03 ± 2.05 | 55.71 ± 3.98 | 60.87 ± 4.23 | 58.29 ± 4.10 |
| AdvEnt [15] | 55.40 ± 1.38 | 50.94 ± 2.85 | 53.17 ± 2.11 | 51.18 ± 3.63 | 52.92 ± 4.64 | 52.05 ± 4.14 |
| DPL [3] | 55.69 ± 2.13 | 51.60 ± 2.79 | 53.65 ± 2.46 | 51.07 ± 4.39 | 51.39 ± 4.59 | 51.23 ± 4.49 |
| CBMT [11] | 56.79 ± 1.42 | 51.99 ± 2.67 | 54.39 ± 2.05 | 51.25 ± 2.84 | 52.34 ± 4.68 | 51.79 ± 3.76 |
| CPR [5] | 57.21 ± 1.93 | 52.35 ± 2.82 | 54.78 ± 2.38 | 50.88 ± 3.67 | 55.33 ± 4.73 | 53.11 ± 4.20 |
| 5% pixels | | | | | | |
| Adversarial [14] | 57.99 ± 1.79 | 52.39 ± 2.64 | 55.19 ± 2.22 | 53.27 ± 3.27 | 55.60 ± 4.31 | 54.44 ± 3.79 |
| AADA [10] | 58.03 ± 1.54 | 52.43 ± 2.70 | 55.23 ± 2.12 | 53.99 ± 3.00 | 54.63 ± 4.88 | 54.31 ± 3.94 |
| MHPL [16] | 58.38 ± 1.31 | 52.72 ± 2.89 | 55.55 ± 2.10 | 55.00 ± 2.74 | 56.91 ± 5.00 | 55.96 ± 3.87 |
| STDR [17] | 58.58 ± 1.64 | 53.07 ± 2.67 | 55.83 ± 2.16 | 55.08 ± 2.97 | 56.56 ± 4.78 | 55.82 ± 3.88 |
| CUP [20] | 59.94 ± 0.99 | 54.09 ± 2.67 | 57.02 ± 1.83 | 57.82 ± 3.06 | 57.95 ± 5.15 | 57.89 ± 4.10 |
| 1% pixels | | | | | | |
| Ours | **60.31** ± 1.47 | **55.65** ± 2.74 | **57.98** ± 2.11 | 53.06 ± 4.76 | 57.62 ± 4.24 | 55.34 ± 4.50 |

**Active Domain Adaptation (ADA) Comparison.** We conduct a comparative analysis against recent state-of-the-art ADA approaches, all comparison methods using the same backbones with 5% labeled patches, while ours uses around 1% pixels (10000 pixels in a 1024 * 1024 image). This includes Adversarial [14], AADA [10], MHPL [16], STDR [17], and the most recent CUP [20]. As shown in Tables 2 and 3, ADA methods generally outperform UDA techniques across all metrics. Among them, CUP [20] demonstrates strong performance, achieving 57.92% Dice, 40.86% IoU, 57.02% MCC, and 57.89% BM.

Despite these gains, our method still achieves the highest overall performance, even with just about 1% of labeled pixels. Specifically, it surpasses CUP [20] with an overall Dice score of 58.56%, IoU of 41.47%, MCC of 57.98%, and remains competitive with a BM score of 55.34%. These results underscore the effectiveness of our pixel-based framework combined with the GDS sampling strategy, offering superior performance with significantly fewer annotations.

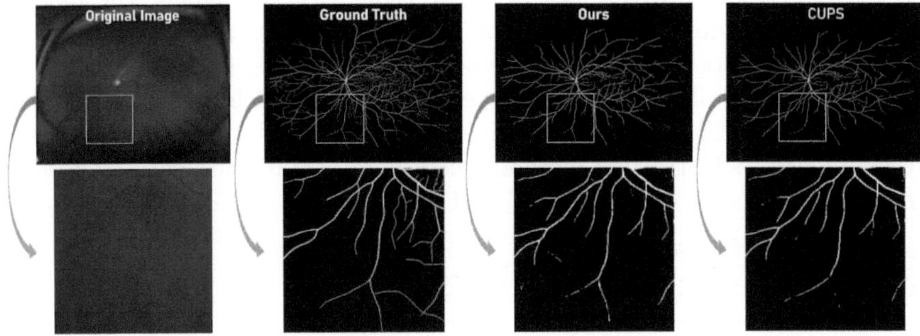


**Fig. 2.** Visual comparisons of our method and the leading active domain adaptation method. Our method can more accurately segment the vessels in the UWF image (please zoom in for more details).

## 3.5 Ablation Studies

We conduct ablation experiments to assess the impact of our Grid-Dither Sampling (GDS) strategy, comparing it against a baseline that uses random pixel selection. As shown in Tables 4 and 5, our method consistently outperforms the baseline across all metrics. Specifically, GDS improves the overall Dice from 57.80% to 58.56%, IoU from 40.71% to 41.47%, MCC from 57.35% to 57.98%, and BM from 53.10% to 55.34%. These results confirm the effectiveness of our targeted sampling strategy in enhancing segmentation performance.

**Table 4.** Ablation experiments on the MU-VS dataset with Dice and IoU.

| | Pixel-based Methods | | Dice (mean±std, %) | | | IoU (mean±std, %) | | |
|---|---|---|---|---|---|---|---|---|
| Methods | Random | GDS | Center A | Center B | Overall | Center A | Center B | Overall |
| Baseline | ✓ | - | $59.56 \pm 2.23$ | $56.03 \pm 2.95$ | $57.80 \pm 2.59$ | $42.44 \pm 2.25$ | $38.98 \pm 2.87$ | $40.71 \pm 2.56$ |
| Ours | - | ✓ | $\mathbf{60.58} \pm 1.80$ | $\mathbf{56.53} \pm 2.89$ | $\mathbf{58.56} \pm 2.35$ | $\mathbf{43.47} \pm 1.85$ | $\mathbf{39.46} \pm 2.84$ | $\mathbf{41.47} \pm 2.35$ |

**Table 5.** Ablation experiments on the MU-VS dataset with MCC and BM.

| Methods | Pixel-based Methods | | MCC (mean±std, %) | | | BM (mean±std, %) | | |
|---|---|---|---|---|---|---|---|---|
| | Random | GDS | Center A | Center B | Overall | Center A | Center B | Overall |
| Baseline | ✓ | - | $59.54 \pm 1.70$ | $55.15 \pm 2.79$ | $57.35 \pm 2.25$ | $50.98 \pm 4.99$ | $55.21 \pm 4.74$ | $53.10 \pm 4.87$ |
| Ours | - | ✓ | $\mathbf{60.31} \pm 1.47$ | $\mathbf{55.65} \pm 2.74$ | $\mathbf{57.98} \pm 2.11$ | $\mathbf{53.06} \pm 4.76$ | $\mathbf{57.62} \pm 4.24$ | $\mathbf{55.34} \pm 4.50$ |

## 4 Discussion

While our framework achieves competitive performance with only 1% labeled pixels—surpassing prior methods requiring 5% patch annotations—the current implementation primarily focuses on numerical efficiency rather than optimizing the annotation workflow itself. In point annotation, the scattered, intricate nature of vascular structures presents unique challenges compared to organ/tumor segmentation. This highlights the need for intuitive and effective interaction tools to streamline sparse point labeling in clinical workflows.

Future research could explore deep learning-based strategies to further enhance efficiency. For instance, active learning models could prioritize critical points and explore point-to-region growth mechanisms, where single-point annotations expand to local regions via geometric/feature similarity, transforming a single annotated point into a small labeled area. Such approaches could allow clinicians to annotate complex vessel networks with minimal input, potentially surpassing our current 1% pixel coverage with just a few strategic points.

## 5 Conclusion

This study introduces a point-driven source-free active domain adaptation framework to address the challenges of cross-center generalization and high annotation costs in medical image segmentation. By focusing on sparse pixel-level supervision and eliminating the need for source data, our approach achieves efficient and privacy-preserving model adaptation across heterogeneous datasets. Experimental results demonstrate its effectiveness in bridging algorithmic generalization and clinical practicality, offering a solution for deploying segmentation models in resource-constrained, privacy-sensitive environments. The insights gained here highlight the potential of lightweight supervision strategies in medical AI, exploring the potential and offering guidance for further research on cost-effective and secure cross-domain learning techniques.

**Acknowledgements.** This work is supported by the Guangdong Science and Technology Department (2024ZDZX2004).

**Disclosure of Interests.** The authors declare that they have no competing interests.

# References


1. Bai, L., Islam, M., Seenivasan, L., Ren, H.: Surgical-VQLA: transformer with gated vision-language embedding for visual question localized-answering in robotic surgery. In: 2023 IEEE International Conference on Robotics and Automation (ICRA), pp. 6859–6865. IEEE (2023)
2. Bai, L., Wang, G., Islam, M., Seenivasan, L., Wang, A., Ren, H.: Surgical-VQLA++: adversarial contrastive learning for calibrated robust visual question-localized answering in robotic surgery. Inf. Fusion **113**, 102602 (2025)
3. Chen, C., Liu, Q., Jin, Y., Dou, Q., Heng, P.-A.: Source-free domain adaptive fundus image segmentation with denoised pseudo-labeling. In: de Bruijne, M., et al. (eds.) MICCAI 2021. LNCS, vol. 12905, pp. 225–235. Springer, Cham (2021). https://doi.org/10.1007/978-3-030-87240-3_22
4. Ding, L., Kuriyan, A.E., Ramchandran, R.S., Wykoff, C.C., Sharma, G.: Weakly-supervised vessel detection in ultra-widefield fundus photography via iterative multi-modal registration and learning. IEEE Trans. Med. Imaging **40**(10), 2748–2758 (2020)
5. Huai, Z., Ding, X., Li, Y., Li, X.: Context-aware pseudo-label refinement for source-free domain adaptive fundus image segmentation. In: Greenspan, H., et al. (eds.) MICCAI 2023. LNCS, vol. 14226, pp. 618–628. Springer, Cham (2023). https://doi.org/10.1007/978-3-031-43990-2_58
6. Luo, X., et al.: Segrap 2023: a benchmark of organs-at-risk and gross tumor volume segmentation for radiotherapy planning of nasopharyngeal carcinoma. Med. Image Anal. **101**, 103447 (2025)
7. Luo, X., et al.: Generalizable magnetic resonance imaging-based nasopharyngeal carcinoma delineation: bridging gaps across multiple centers and raters with active learning. Int. J. Radiat. Oncol.* Biol.* Phys. **121**(5), 1384–1393 (2025)
8. Qiu, Z., Hu, Y., Chen, X., Zeng, D., Hu, Q., Liu, J.: Rethinking dual-stream super-resolution semantic learning in medical image segmentation. IEEE Trans. Pattern Anal. Mach. Intell. (2023)
9. Ronneberger, O., Fischer, P., Brox, T.: U-Net: convolutional networks for biomedical image segmentation. In: Navab, N., Hornegger, J., Wells, W.M., Frangi, A.F. (eds.) MICCAI 2015. LNCS, vol. 9351, pp. 234–241. Springer, Cham (2015). https://doi.org/10.1007/978-3-319-24574-4_28
10. Su, J.C., Tsai, Y.H., Sohn, K., Liu, B., Maji, S., Chandraker, M.: Active adversarial domain adaptation. In: WACV, pp. 739–748 (2020)
11. Tang, L., Li, K., He, C., Zhang, Y., Li, X.: Source-free domain adaptive fundus image segmentation with class-balanced mean teacher. In: Greenspan, H., et al. (eds.) MICCAI 2023. LNCS, vol. 14220, pp. 684–694. Springer, Cham (2023). https://doi.org/10.1007/978-3-031-43907-0_65
12. Tang, Q.Q., Yang, X.G., Wang, H.Q., Wu, D.W., Zhang, M.X.: Applications of deep learning for detecting ophthalmic diseases with ultrawide-field fundus images. Int. J. Ophthalmol. **17**(1), 188 (2024)
13. Tian, M., et al.: Delineation of clinical target volume and organs at risk in cervical cancer radiotherapy by deep learning networks. Med. Phys. **50**(10), 6354–6365 (2023)
14. Tsai, Y.H., Hung, W.C., Schulter, S., Sohn, K., Yang, M.H., Chandraker, M.: Learning to adapt structured output space for semantic segmentation. In: Proceedings of the IEEE Conference on Computer Vision and Pattern Recognition, pp. 7472–7481 (2018)

15. Vu, T.H., Jain, H., Bucher, M., Cord, M., Pérez, P.: ADVENT: adversarial entropy minimization for domain adaptation in semantic segmentation. In: CVPR, pp. 2517–2526 (2019)

16. Wang, F., Han, Z., Zhang, Z., He, R., Yin, Y.: MHPL: minimum happy points learning for active source free domain adaptation. In: Proceedings of the IEEE/CVF Conference on Computer Vision and Pattern Recognition, pp. 20008–20018 (2023)

17. Wang, H., et al.: Dual-reference source-free active domain adaptation for nasopharyngeal carcinoma tumor segmentation across multiple hospitals. IEEE Trans. Med. Imaging (2024)

18. Wang, H., et al.: Serp-mamba: advancing high-resolution retinal vessel segmentation with selective state-space model. IEEE Trans. Med. Imaging (2025)

19. Wang, H., Jin, Y., Zhu, L.: Dynamic interactive relation capturing via scene graph learning for robotic surgical report generation. arXiv preprint arXiv:2306.02651 (2023)

20. Wang, H., et al.: Advancing UWF-SLO vessel segmentation with source-free active domain adaptation and a novel multi-center dataset. In: Linguraru, M.G., et al. (eds.) MICCAI 2024. LNCS, vol. 15009, pp. 75–85. Springer, Cham (2024). https://doi.org/10.1007/978-3-031-72114-4_8

21. Wang, H., et al.: Classification for diabetic retinopathy by using staged convolutional neural network. In: 2022 Asia Conference on Algorithms, Computing and Machine Learning (CACML), pp. 228–233. IEEE (2022)

22. Wang, H., et al.: Non-invasive to invasive: enhancing FFA synthesis from CFP with a benchmark dataset and a novel network. In: Proceedings of the 1st International Workshop on Multimedia Computing for Health and Medicine, pp. 7–15 (2024)

23. Wang, H., et al.: Video-instrument synergistic network for referring video instrument segmentation in robotic surgery. IEEE Trans. Med. Imaging (2024)

24. Wang, H., Zhang, S., Luo, X., Liao, W., Zhu, L.: Advancing delineation of gross tumor volume based on magnetic resonance imaging by performing source-free domain adaptation in nasopharyngeal carcinoma. In: Qin, W., Zaki, N., Zhang, F., Wu, J., Yang, F., Li, C. (eds.) CMMCA 2023. LNCS, vol. 14243, pp. 71–80. Springer, Cham (2023). https://doi.org/10.1007/978-3-031-45087-7_8

25. Wu, H., Yang, Y., Aviles-Rivero, A.I., Ren, J., Chen, S., Chen, H., Zhu, L.: Semi-supervised video desnowing network via temporal decoupling experts and distribution-driven contrastive regularization. In: Leonardis, A., Ricci, E., Roth, S., Russakovsky, O., Sattler, T., Varol, G. (eds.) ECCV 2024. LNCS, vol. 15068, pp. 70–89. Springer, Cham (2024). https://doi.org/10.1007/978-3-031-72684-2_5

26. Wu, H., Yang, Y., Xu, H., Wang, W., Zhou, J., Zhu, L.: RainMamba: enhanced locality learning with state space models for video deraining. In: Proceedings of the 32nd ACM International Conference on Multimedia, pp. 7881–7890 (2024)

27. Xing, Z., Ye, T., Yang, Y., Liu, G., Zhu, L.: SegMamba: long-range sequential modeling mamba for 3D medical image segmentation. arXiv preprint arXiv:2401.13560 (2024)

# CSTNet: A Generative Framework for EEG-to-ECoG Mapping via Optimal Transport

Ruslan Kalimullin[1(✉)], Ekaterina Antipushina[1], Alexandra Razorenova[1,2], Georgiy Kormakov[1], and Nikolay Koshev[1,2]

[1] Skolkovo Institute of Science and Technology, Center for Neurobiology and Brain Rehabilitation, Moscow, Russia
`ruslan.kalimullin@skoltech.ru`
[2] LLC "LIFT Center", Moscow, Russia

**Abstract.** Electroencephalography (EEG) and electrocorticography (ECoG) are complementary neuroimaging techniques, balancing non-invasiveness (EEG) and high spatial resolution (ECoG). Conventional EEG inverse solutions face spatial blurring and mislocalization due to mathematical constraints. We propose **C**ortical **S**ignal **T**ransformation **Net**work (CSTNet), a deep learning framework that leverages Optimal Transport (OT) to directly map EEG scalp potentials to ECoG-equivalent cortical signals. Through OT-based geometric alignment of paired EEG-ECoG data, CSTNet bypasses explicit noise modeling assumptions while preserving cortical signal topology. This approach bridges EEG's safety with ECoG-like accuracy, advancing applications in epilepsy surgery planning and brain-computer interfaces.

**Keywords:** EEG · ECoG · EEG inverse problem · Optimal Transport · Deep Generative Modeling

## 1 Introduction

Current epilepsy surgery practices create an unprecedented treatment bottleneck, with limited annual procedures serving 10.1 million eligible candidates worldwide [6]. This massive gap stems from invasive ECoG monitoring requirements that carry substantial risks of complications [11,23], despite achieving seizure freedom in 53–65% of cases, when completed successfully [5,20]. The inherent limitations of traditional source localization methods create significant errors in epileptogenic zone identification, with EEG mislocalization propagating through ill-conditioned forward operators [11], necessitating direct invasive cortical recording for surgical planning.

CSTNet addresses this fundamental clinical challenge by enabling direct EEG-to-ECoG mapping with non-invasive precision equivalent to invasive monitoring. By circumventing error-prone two-step source estimation approaches, this


T. Chen et al. (Eds.): EMA4MICCAI 2025 Workshops, LNCS 16318, pp. 154–162, 2026.
https://doi.org/10.1007/978-3-032-13961-0_16

technology could dramatically expand surgical access for the 50 million people with epilepsy worldwide [7], particularly the 30% with drug-resistant forms [16] who currently face limited therapeutic options beyond invasive grid placement with its associated risks and resource demands.

Modeling brain electrophysiology involves three fundamental challenges: modeling quasi-static electromagnetic fields, resolving the inverse problem of source localization, and reconciling macroscopic measurements (EEG sensor measurements) with microscopic neural dynamics. Let $\Omega \subset \mathbb{R}^3$ denote the head volume with conductivity $\sigma(x)$ derived from multimodal imaging. Neural activity is modeled by primary current dipoles $J_s(x) = \sum_j \mathbf{j}_j \delta(x - x_j)$ confined to the cortical surface $C \subset \Omega$ [19]. This generates three key problems: the **Forward Problem** computes scalp EEG $\phi|_{\partial\Omega}$ and cortical ECoG $\psi|C$ from known current sources $J_s$ via Maxwell's equations; the **Inverse Problem** estimates $J_s$ from EEG measurements, which is ill-posed and thus requires regularization [10]; and the **EEG-to-ECoG Mapping** learns a direct mapping $T : \phi|\partial\Omega \to \psi|_C$, bypassing error-prone source estimation.

Notably, ECoG recordings $\psi|_C$ can be considered a close spatial and temporal approximation of the true cortical current distribution, due to their high signal-to-noise ratio and proximity to the cortical surface. In this sense, ECoG provides a more direct and reliable representation of brain activity compared to the latent source space $J_s$, which is discontinuous and not directly observable. Therefore, learning the EEG-to-ECoG mapping can be seen as a pragmatic and physiologically grounded alternative to solving the ill-posed inverse problem— enabling reconstruction of cortical dynamics in a more data-driven and stable manner.

Traditional approaches compound localization errors due to the ill-conditioned nature of the forward operator [1]. Current clinical practice relies on the placement of an invasive ECoG grid for planning epilepsy surgery, carrying substantial complication risks documented in national databases [22]. Our CST-Net enables noninvasive presurgical mapping with ECoG-level spatial resolution, potentially transforming epilepsy surgery accessibility by eliminating the need for invasive monitoring in many cases.

### 1.1    Current Solutions and Limitations

Traditional EEG source localization employs Minimum Norm Estimation (MNE) with L2 regularization, spreading point sources over 15–20 mm regions due to spatial blurring [12]. Beamforming methods fail in correlated source scenarios common in clinical data [18]. However, these approaches face fundamental limitations: error propagation through forward modeling, simplified head model assumptions, computational complexity and a lack of ground-truth validation.

Recent CNN-based approaches achieve 2.8 mm localization accuracy, but still require forward projection, inheriting error propagation problems [21]. Graph neural networks incorporate connectome information, but remain limited by the ill-posedness of the inverse problem [14]. As shown in Fig. 1, our CSTNet represents the first direct EEG-to-ECoG mapping.

## 1.2   EEG-to-ECoG as Manifold Alignment

Let $\mu \in \mathcal{P}(\partial\Omega)$ and $\nu \in \mathcal{P}(C)$ be EEG/ECoG signal distributions. The mapping task finds a transport map $T : \mu \to \nu$ preserving neurophysiological semantics despite the geometric mismatch between the spherical scalp and the convoluted cortical surface, non-linear skull attenuation, and cortical phase reversals invisible to EEG.

CSTNet addresses this through optimal transport on neuroanatomical manifolds. We minimize the Wasserstein distance:

$$W_c(\phi,\psi) = \inf_{\gamma \in \Pi(\phi,\psi)} \mathbb{E}[c(\phi,\psi)], \quad c(\phi,\psi) = \|G(\phi) - \psi\|^2 + \lambda d_{\mathrm{geo}}(x,y), \qquad (1)$$

where $d_{\mathrm{geo}}$ encodes geodesic distances on cortical surface $C$. The Kantorovich dual formulation via PatchGAN discriminator $D$ yields:

$$L_G = \lambda\|G(\phi) - \psi\|_1 + \mathbb{E}[D(G(\phi))] - \mathbb{E}[D(\psi)] - \lambda_{\mathrm{GP}}L_{\mathrm{GP}}. \qquad (2)$$

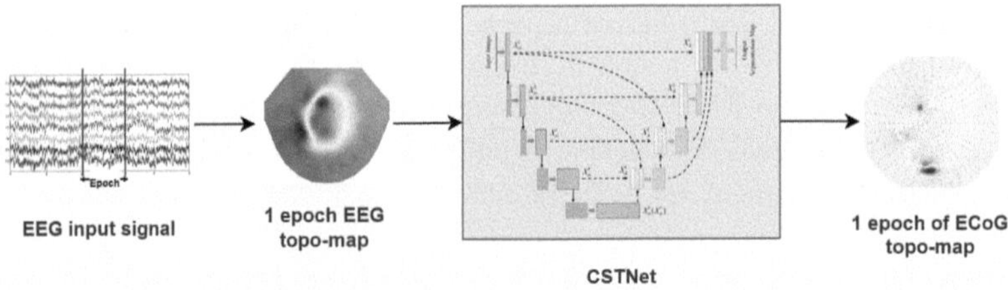


**Fig. 1.** CSTNet framework workflow: extracting EEG epoch, generating topomap, and processing through CSTNet to produce ECoG topomap.

## 2   Methodology

### 2.1   Data Generation

A realistic 3-D head model was constructed from the sample subject data provided by Yavich et al. [24]. Triangulated surfaces of the cortex (pial and white matter), skull and skin were extracted using FreeSurfer [8] and smoothed with `iso2mesh` (10 iterations, $\lambda = 0.3$) to maintain a geometric error below 1 mm [3]. The volume conductor was meshed into 261 565 linear tetrahedral elements with 42 684 vertices (mean edge length $\approx 1.2$ mm). Isotropic tissue conductivities were set to cortex (and skin) 0.33 S/m, and skull 0.01 S/m [2]. Source dipoles were placed at the centers of the boundary triangles on the upper part of the cortical mesh (400 possible locations) and oriented normal to the local surface [19]. Cortical potential sensors (ECoG) were co-located with these 400 triangles. Scalp

(EEG) sensors were uniformly distributed over the outer skin surface in the 128-channel 10–05 configuration.

For each of the 15 000 simulation runs, we first initialized a random number of active dipoles $n_{dipoles}$ (see Sect. 3) with currents uniformly sampled in range of 0.1–0.9 μA [17]. The forward problem was solved via Finite Element Method (FEM) with a preconditioned conjugate gradient solver [3]. The resulting EEG and ECoG scalp maps were rasterized into $256 \times 256$ float32 images and min–max normalized, as shown in Fig. 2.

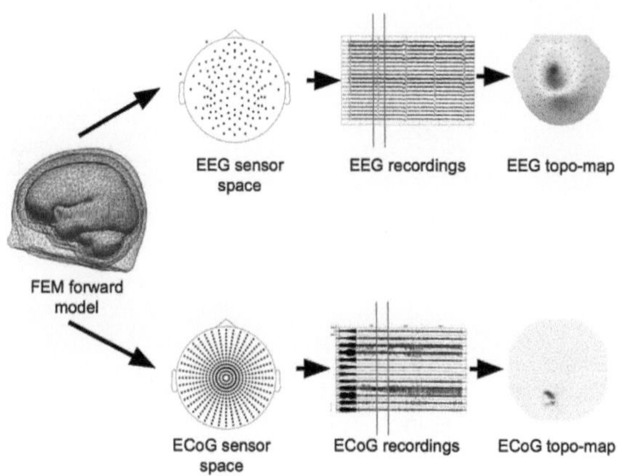


**Fig. 2.** Schematic overview of the EEG/ECoG data generation pipeline. **Top row:** EEG sensor configuration (10-05 system layout), simulated EEG time-series data (20 dB SNR), and corresponding topographic maps. **Center:** Four-layer finite element method (FEM) forward model comprising 1.04 million tetrahedral elements with tissue-specific conductivity profiles. **Bottom row:** ECoG sensor array (400-contact cortical grid), simulated ECoG recordings, and cortical surface activation maps.

### 2.2   CSTNet Architecture

CSTNet employs a Generator based on UNet 3+ architecture [13] for multi-scale feature fusion enabling simultaneous detection of primary and secondary foci, and a PatchGAN Discriminator [4] for fine-grained signal evaluation. Optimal transport integration geometrically aligns EEG and ECoG domains through Kantorovich dual formulation [15]. The discriminator approximates Kantorovich potentials:

$$\phi(G(x)) - D(G(x)), \quad \psi(y) = D(y), \tag{3}$$

yielding OT-regularized loss:

$$L_{OT} = \mathbb{E}[D(G(x))] - \mathbb{E}[D(y)] - \lambda_{GP}\mathbb{E}[(\|\nabla_{\hat{y}}D(\hat{y})\|_2 - 1)^2], \tag{4}$$

where $\hat{y} = \epsilon G(x) + (1 - \epsilon)y$, $\epsilon \sim U[0, 1]$.

The Generator loss combines L1 reconstruction ensuring structural fidelity and OT regularization preserving source accuracy:

$$L_G = \lambda_{L1} L_{L1} + \lambda_{OT} L_{OT}, \tag{5}$$

with empirically tuned weights $\lambda_{L1} = 25$, $\lambda_{OT} = 1$.

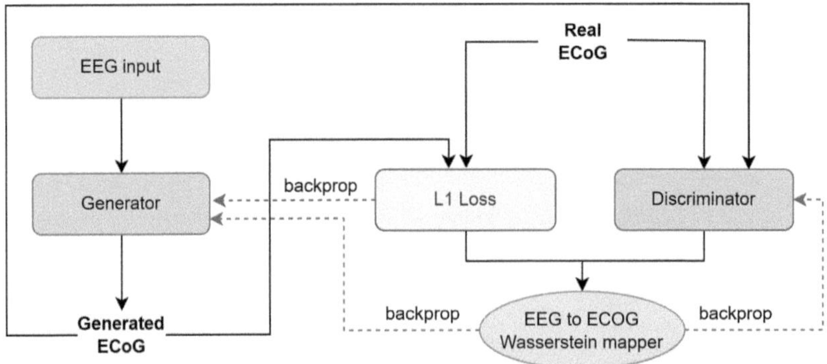


**Fig. 3.** CSTNet architecture: Generator transforms EEG to ECoG while discriminator evaluates authenticity, with Wasserstein distance integration for training stability.

We evaluated two configurations of the optimal transport cost function $c(\phi, \psi)$ in Eq. (1):

1. Standard CSTNet employs Euclidean cost: $c(\phi, \psi) = |G(\phi) - \psi|2 + \lambda dgeo(x, y)$
2. CSTNet-QC (Quadratic Cost) uses squared Euclidean distance: $c(\phi, \psi) = |G(\phi) - \psi|2^2 + \lambda dgeo(x, y)$

The quadratic cost in CSTNet-QC amplifies the penalty for large prediction errors, enhancing sensitivity to focal activations at the expense of increased smoothing for distributed sources. This design choice reflects the clinical priority for precise localization of epileptic foci, where accurate reconstruction of high-amplitude point sources is critical for surgical planning.

## 3    Experiments and Results

We conducted five experiments comparing CSTNet variants (with the standard architecture shown in Fig. 3 and using a quadratic transport cost) against conditional GAN (Pix2Pix), baseline UNet [21], and Variational Autoencoder architectures. All models were trained for 250 epochs with a learning rate of $1 \times 10^{-4}$ using the Adam optimizer. Training took approximately 8 h on an NVIDIA A100 × 8, with a 12 ms inference time enabling real-time applications. The dataset was split into train (70% ratio or 10,500 samples) test (15% ratio or 2,250 samples) and validation (15% ratio or 2,250 samples).

## 3.1    Quantitative Performance

Table 1 summarizes model performance using SSIM, MSE and L2 norm metrics. CSTNet achieves highest SSIM ($0.985 \pm 0.005$) and lowest MSE ($0.0004 \pm 0.0003$), outperforming UNet (0.982 SSIM) and likelihood-based approaches (0.956 SSIM).

**Table 1.** Validation Scores for Different Models

| Model | SSIM | MSE | L2 Norm |
|---|---|---|---|
| CSTNet | **$0.985 \pm 0.005$** | **$0.0004 \pm 0.0003$** | **$0.0189 \pm 0.0087$** |
| CSTNet-QC | $0.984 \pm 0.005$ | $0.0005 \pm 0.0003$ | $0.0201 \pm 0.0091$ |
| UNet Model | $0.982 \pm 0.016$ | $0.0008 \pm 0.0018$ | $0.0285 \pm 0.0134$ |
| VAE | $0.956 \pm 0.006$ | $0.0025 \pm 0.0009$ | $0.0498 \pm 0.0189$ |
| cGAN Model | $0.955 \pm 0.008$ | $0.0025 \pm 0.0010$ | $0.0512 \pm 0.0201$ |

## 3.2    Multifocal Activity Detection

The clinical significance lies in CSTNet's ability to detect multifocal activation patterns invisible to traditional methods. Figure 4 demonstrates three challenging validation cases: complex multifocal patterns with primary focus and secondary scattered activations, bilateral activation with interhemispheric spread, and dual-focus patterns with spatially separated sources.

CSTNet and CSTNet-QC successfully reconstruct both primary and all secondary foci with accurate spatial localization across all cases. Competing methods show critical limitations: cGAN captures primary foci but misses secondary regions, VAE demonstrates poor spatial specificity with artifacts, and UNet shows partial detection with reduced accuracy. This multifocal detection capability is crucial for epilepsy surgery planning, where missing secondary seizure onset zones leads to $>40\%$ surgical failure rates [9].

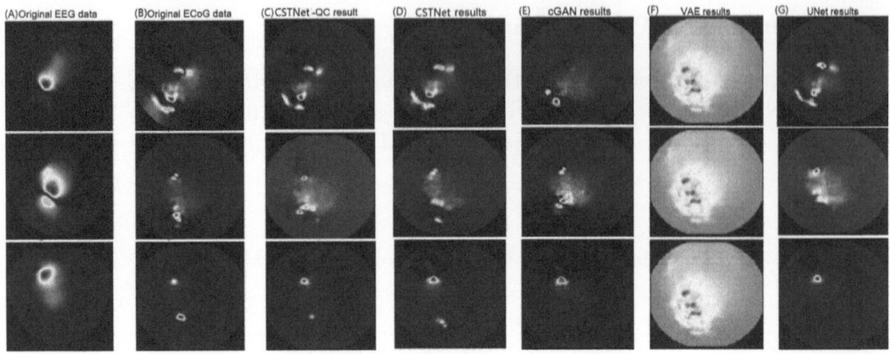

**Fig. 4.** Model performance on challenging multifocal validation cases. (A) Input EEG patterns, (B) Ground truth ECoG revealing complex multifocal patterns, (C-D) CSTNet variants accurately reconstructing primary and secondary foci, (E-G) Competing methods missing critical secondary activations. Only CSTNet successfully resolves multiple concurrent sources critical for surgical planning.

## 4   Conclusion

CSTNet pioneers EEG-to-ECoG mapping via optimal transport-regularized adversarial learning, achieving spatial precision enabling detection of multi-focal activation patterns invisible to traditional methods. The framework's key innovation lies in resolving multiple concurrent cortical sources from non-invasive EEG.

Unlike traditional approaches suffering from error propagation and spatial blurring, CSTNet directly learns EEG-to-ECoG transformation through optimal transport principles, eliminating intermediate source localization steps. This end-to-end approach bypasses fundamental inverse method limitations while achieving multi-focal detection capability crucial for epilepsy surgery planning. CSTNet enables identification of multiple seizure onset zones from non-invasive recordings, potentially improving surgical outcomes through comprehensive pre-operative mapping.

## 5   Discussion

### 5.1   Implications of Image-Based Representation

The decision to represent EEG and ECoG signals as rasterized topomaps fundamentally shapes CSTNet's capabilities and limitations. This design choice enables three critical advantages: (1) Convolutional architectures efficiently capture spatial relationships and activation patterns through learned filters; (2) The image format naturally accommodates cortical surface geometry during OT-based manifold alignment; and (3) Standard computer vision metrics (SSIM, MSE) provide unambiguous performance quantification. However, this approach introduces notable constraints: Temporal dynamics are implicitly encoded rather than explicitly modeled, potentially limiting performance on high-frequency oscillations (>30 Hz) critical for seizure localization. Additionally, the $256 \times 256$ resolution creates interpolation artifacts at gyral crowns where ECoG electrodes would physically contact folded cortex. Future work should explore hybrid spatiotemporal architectures that preserve the spatial advantages demonstrated here while incorporating explicit temporal modeling.

## 5.2   Limitations and Future Directions

While CSTNet demonstrates unprecedented spatial precision in synthetic validation, three fundamental limitations must be addressed for clinical translation. First, our FEM head model simplifies electrical properties by assuming isotropic skull conductivity (0.01 S/m), whereas real skulls exhibit anisotropic conductivity variations up to $10\times$ between compact and spongy bone layers [1]. Second, the cortical source model assumes discrete dipoles rather than distributed patches of synchronized pyramidal neurons, potentially over-simplifying epileptogenic zones. Third, the current framework processes static snapshots rather than continuous time-series, limiting utility for dynamic seizure propagation analysis.

Future work will focus on: (1) Incorporating patient-specific DTI-derived conductivity tensors to address electrical anisotropy; (2) Validating against intraoperative ECoG recordings from epilepsy patients (IRB approval pending); and (3) Extending to spatiotemporal domain with 3D-OT for seizure propagation mapping. The 12 ms inference time demonstrated here provides a computational foundation for real-time implementations. Importantly, the current simulation-based paradigm enables controlled validation impossible with clinical data alone - particularly for multifocal scenarios where ground truth is otherwise unattainable.

**Disclosure of Interests.** The authors have no competing interests to declare.

# References


1. Akalin Acar, Z., Makeig, S.: Effects of forward model errors on EEG source localization. Brain Topogr. **26**, 378–396 (2013)
2. Baumann, S.B., Wozny, D.R., Kelly, S.K., Meno, F.M.: Finite element volume conductor modeling: a geometric approach. IEEE Trans. Biomed. Eng. **44**(6), 531–535 (1997)
3. Dannhauer, M., Lanfer, B., Wolters, C.H., Knösche, T.R.: Automatic generation of finite-element meshes from 3D segmented medical images. Biomed. Eng./Biomedizinische Technik **56**(Suppl. 1) (2011)
4. Demir, U., Unal, G.: Patch-based image inpainting with generative adversarial networks. arXiv preprint arXiv:1803.07422 (2018)
5. Englot, D.J., Chang, E.F.: Rates and predictors of seizure freedom in resective epilepsy surgery: an update. Neurosurg. Rev. **37**, 389–405 (2014)
6. Englot, D.J., Ouyang, D., Garcia, P., Barbaro, N., Chang, E.: Epilepsy surgery trends in the united states, 1990–2008. Neurology **78**(16), 1200–1206 (2012)

7. Feigin, V.L., et al.: Global, regional, and national burden of epilepsy, 1990–2021: a systematic analysis for the global burden of disease study 2021. Lancet Public Health **10**(3), e203–e227 (2025)

8. Fischl, B.: Freesurfer. NeuroImage **62**(2), 774–781 (2012)

9. Gascoigne, S.J., et al.: Incomplete resection of the intracranial electroencephalographic seizure onset zone is not associated with postsurgical outcomes. Epilepsia **65**(9), e163–e169 (2024)

10. Grech, R., et al.: Review on solving the inverse problem in EEG source analysis. J. Neuroeng. Rehabil. **5**, 1–33 (2008)

11. Hallez, H., et al.: Review on solving the forward problem in EEG source analysis. J. Neuroeng. Rehabil. **4**, 1–29 (2007)

12. Hämäläinen, M.S., Ilmoniemi, R.J.: Interpreting magnetic fields of the brain: minimum norm estimates. Med. Biol. Eng. Comput. **32**(1), 35–42 (1994)

13. Huang, H., et al.: Unet 3+: A full-scale connected unet for medical image segmentation. In: ICASSP 2020-2020 IEEE International Conference on Acoustics, Speech and Signal Processing (ICASSP), pp. 1055–1059. IEEE (2020)

14. Li, Z., Hwang, K., Li, K., Wu, J., Ji, T.: Graph-generative neural network for EEG-based epileptic seizure detection via discovery of dynamic brain functional connectivity. Sci. Rep. **12**(1), 18998 (2022)

15. Liu, H., Gu, X., Samaras, D.: Wasserstein GAN with quadratic transport cost. In: Proceedings of the IEEE/CVF International Conference on Computer Vision, pp. 4832–4841 (2019)

16. Löscher, W., Potschka, H., Sisodiya, S.M., Vezzani, A.: Drug resistance in epilepsy: clinical impact, potential mechanisms, and new innovative treatment options. Pharmacol. Rev. **72**(3), 606–638 (2020)

17. Michel, C.M., Brunet, D.: EEG source imaging: a practical review of the analysis steps. Front. Neurol. **10**, 325 (2019)

18. Mosher, J.C., Leahy, R.M., Baillet, S.: EEG and meg source localization using beamforming methods. Clin. Neurophysiol. **79**(3), 37–53 (1999)

19. Nunez, P.L., Srinivasan, R.: Electric Fields of the Brain: The Neurophysics of EEG. Oxford University Press (2006)

20. Pereira Dalio, M.T.R., et al.: Long-term outcome of temporal lobe epilepsy surgery in 621 patients with hippocampal sclerosis: clinical and surgical prognostic factors. Front. Neurol. **13**, 833293 (2022)

21. Razorenova, A., Yavich, N., Malovichko, M., Fedorov, M., Koshev, N., Dylov, D.V.: Deep learning for non-invasive cortical potential imaging. In: International Workshop on Machine Learning in Clinical Neuroimaging, pp. 45–55. Springer (2020)

22. Rolston, J.D., Englot, D.J., Cornes, S., Chang, E.F.: Major and minor complications in extraoperative electrocorticography: a review of a national database. Epilepsy Res. **122**, 26–29 (2016)

23. Rolston, J.D., Ouyang, D., Englot, D.J., Wang, D.D., Chang, E.F.: National trends and complication rates for invasive extraoperative electrocorticography in the USA. J. Clin. Neurosci. **22**(5), 823–827 (2015)

24. Yavich, N., Koshev, N., Malovichko, M., Razorenova, A., Fedorov, M.: Conservative finite element modeling of EEG and meg on unstructured grids. IEEE Trans. Med. Imaging **41**(3), 647–656 (2021)

# Spiking MU-Net: Toward Low-Power and Efficient Microscopic Image Segmentation


Liangyi Wang[1(✉)], Yunheng Wu[1], Masahiro Oda[1,2], Yuichiro Hayashi[1], and Kensaku Mori[1,2,3(✉)]

[1] Graduate School of Informatics, Nagoya University, Nagoya, Japan
`liangywang@mori.m.is.nagoya-u.ac.jp`, `kensaku@is.nagoya-u.ac.jp`
[2] Information Technology Center, Nagoya University, Nagoya, Japan
[3] Research Center for Medical Bigdata, National Institute of Informatics, Tokyo, Japan



**Abstract.** In contemporary biomedical research, microscopic image segmentation has emerged as an indispensable analytical task. However, complex morphologies and diverse sizes of cellular structures make accurate cell segmentation challenging. Although deep learning based methods have shown great potential in microscopic image segmentation, they come with high computational complexity, reliance on extensive GPU resources, large parameter counts, and high power consumption. To address these challenges, this paper introduces a novel, computationally efficient framework that integrates the Mamba with Spiking Neural Networks (SNNs) for biomedical applications. Spiking MU-Net maintains accuracy comparable to state-of-the-art methods while significantly reducing computational load, parameter size, and power consumption. Specifically, (1) We propose a spiking neuron-based model that integrates Mamba and convolutional modules, enabling discrete, addition-only operations. This design significantly reduces computational overhead and parameter count, paving the way for real-time microscopy analysis. (2) Experiments on multiple cell datasets demonstrated that our method achieved high accuracy with a DSC of 83% while significantly reducing energy consumption to just 3.22mJ. (3) Our approach attained accuracy comparable to ANN-based networks, with a DSC improvement of 1.04%, while achieving the lowest energy consumption among SNN-based segmentation models, reducing parameters by 10.21M and energy by 0.29mJ.

**Keywords:** Image Segmentation · Spiking Neural Network · Vision Mamba


## 1 Introduction

Cell segmentation is essential in biomedical research by enabling extract structural and functional information from bio-samples, thereby facilitating new scientific discoveries [1]. To address the diverse and complex nature of cell morphology,



T. Chen et al. (Eds.): EMA4MICCAI 2025 Workshops, LNCS 16318, pp. 163–173, 2026.
https://doi.org/10.1007/978-3-032-13961-0_17

numerous high-precision machine learning methods have been proposed [2–4]. However, most of these methods emphasize precision while overlooking real-time performance—a critical factor for live-cell analysis, where low latency and fast inference are vital to capturing dynamic biological processes [5]. Although recent studies [6,7] have started to pay attention to low-power requirements in the field of cell analysis, the former still relies on manual prompts that require human interaction to annotate points or bounding boxes, while the latter demands additional resources for storing and managing a cell segmentation dictionary. This highlights the need for lightweight models that can be efficiently deployed on edge devices to perform high-precision, real-time, and unsupervised segmentation with minimal computational cost and power consumption [8].

In recent years, Spiking Neural Networks (SNNs) have attracted growing attention due to their low power consumption and inherent biological plausibility. Unlike Artificial Neural Networks (ANNs) based on the von Neumann architecture—which rely heavily on floating-point multiplications—SNNs transmit information via discrete spikes. This event-driven paradigm allows them to skip computations when inputs or activations are zero, with only a subset of spiking neurons activated to perform sparse synaptic accumulation [9]. SNNs have now been successfully deployed on neuromorphic hardware platforms [10], demonstrating significantly lower energy consumption compared to conventional ANNs, and highlighting their promising potential for energy-efficient computing.

Currently, image analysis using SNNs is primarily built upon two architectures: Convolutional Neural Networks (CNNs) and Transformers [11]. However, CNNs are inherently limited by their local receptive fields and fixed kernel sizes, making them less effective in capturing long-range dependencies [12]. In contrast, Transformer-based models excel at global modeling, but their self-attention mechanism introduces quadratic computational complexity when computing token relationships [13], leading to significant computational redundancy [14]. This leads to excessive computational overhead, especially for dense prediction tasks like medical image segmentation. To address the computational inefficiency of Transformers in modeling long-range dependencies, a novel architecture named Mamba [15] has recently been proposed in the natural language processing. It is based on State Space Models (SSMs) [16,17]. In addition to inheriting the SSM's ability to model long-term dependencies with linear complexity, Mamba introduces a core algorithm—the parallelized selective scan operation. This mechanism enables efficient temporal feature selection across channels, thereby further reducing computational overhead. Recently, Mamba has also been applied to medical image segmentation, such as VM-UNet [18].

Therefore, in this work, we propose a novel architecture named **Spiking MU-Net**. While current SSMs are typically built upon artificial neurons, they rely on dense vector-matrix multiplications, leading to high computational costs. We argue that dense operations undermine SSMs' goal of achieving linear complexity. To address this, we introduce spiking neurons into the Vision Mamba [19], combining efficient parallel training with event-driven sparse computation for significantly reduced energy consumption and complexity. In the context of cell segmentation, we further modify the architecture of VM-UNet [18], achieving improved accuracy while maintaining a lightweight parameter profile. To validate our architecture and its compatibility between the sequential computation nature of SSMs and the temporal dynamics of SNNs, we conduct experiments on both the NeuroIPS22 [20] and TNBC [21] datasets.

**Our Contributions are Summarized as Follows:**

1. We propose a model that integrates SNNs with Mamba-based U-net for segmentation, reducing energy consumption while maintaining precision.
2. We conduct experiments on the NeurIPS22-CellSeg and TNBC datasets, showcasing our model's competitiveness in cell segmentation tasks.

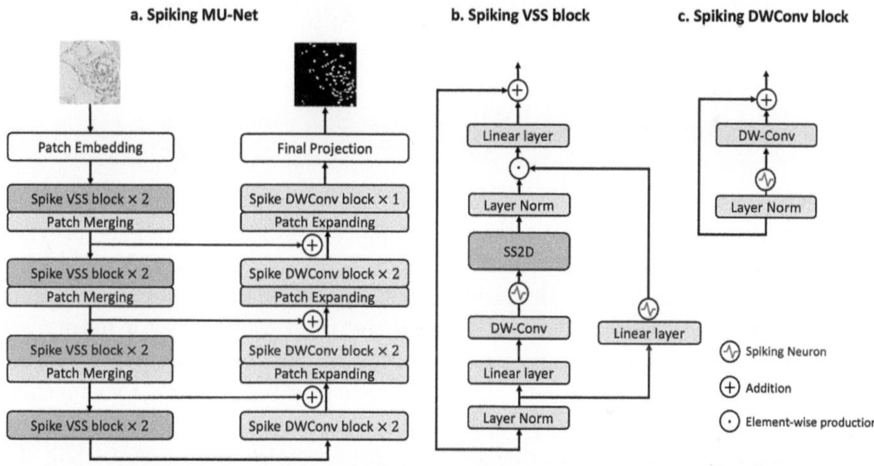


**Fig. 1.** (a) Overall architecture; (b) Spiking VSS block; (c) Spiking DWConv block.

# 2   Method

## 2.1   Preliminaries

**Mamba.** In Mamba [15], they map the input $\mathbf{X}_t$ into an input sequence $\mathbf{x}(t) = (x_0, \ldots, x_{L-1}) \in \mathbb{R}^L$, which is then projected into an output sequence $\mathbf{y}(t) = (y_0, \ldots, y_{L-1}) \in \mathbb{R}^L$ through an implicit latent state $\mathbf{h}(t) \in \mathbb{R}^N$ that captures the dynamic relationship between the output and input, where $L$ denotes the length of the output. The continuous computation process follows a linear Ordinary Differential Equation (ODE):

$$\mathbf{h}'(t) = \mathbf{A}\mathbf{h}(t) + \mathbf{B}\mathbf{x}(t), \quad \mathbf{y}(t) = \mathbf{C}\mathbf{h}(t), \tag{1}$$

where $t$ represents the time step, $\mathbf{A} \in \mathbb{R}^{N \times N}$ denotes the state matrix, and $\mathbf{B} \in \mathbb{R}^{N \times 1}$ and $\mathbf{C} \in \mathbb{R}^{N \times 1}$ are the projection parameters. To better adapt the model to real-world discretized data, Mamba introduce discretization rules. The $\bar{\mathbf{A}}$ and $\bar{\mathbf{B}}$ are the parameters after discretization. Equation (1) can be computed using convolution, as shown in Eq. (2), where $\bar{K}$ represents a structured convolutional kernel and $L$ denotes the length of the input sequence $\mathbf{x}$:

$$\mathbf{y} = \mathbf{x} * \bar{K}, \quad \bar{K} = \left( \overline{\mathbf{CB}}, \overline{\mathbf{CAB}}, \ldots, \overline{\mathbf{CA}^{L-1}\mathbf{B}} \right) \in \mathbb{R}^{L}. \tag{2}$$

**Spiking Neuron.** In SNNs, the core functionality is realized by spiking neurons. These neurons exhibit spatiotemporal dynamics and use spike-based communication to simulate biological neurons [22]. The Integrate-and-Fire (IF) neuron is the most widely used neuron. With $t$ denoting the time step, the IF neuron is:

$$\mathbf{U}[t] = \beta \mathbf{V}[t - 1] + \mathbf{X}[t], \tag{3}$$

$$\mathbf{S}[t] = \mathrm{Hea}(\mathbf{U}[t] - V_{\mathrm{th}}), \tag{4}$$

$$\mathbf{V}[t] = \begin{cases} \mathbf{U}[t] \cdot (1 - \mathbf{S}[t]) + V_{\mathrm{reset}} \cdot \mathbf{S}[t], & \text{hard reset} \\ \mathbf{U}[t] - V_{\mathrm{th}} \cdot \mathbf{S}[t], & \text{soft reset} \end{cases} \tag{5}$$

where $\mathbf{X}[t]$ represents the input at the current time step. $\mathbf{U}[t]$ denotes the leaky membrane potential, while $\mathbf{V}[t-1]$ is the membrane potential from the previous time step. Whether a spike $\mathbf{S}[t]$ is fired depends on the threshold $V_{\mathrm{th}}$, which is typically determined by the Heaviside function $\mathrm{Hea}(\cdot)$ and instead of original continuous value in forward. $V_{\mathrm{reset}}$ denotes the reset value after a hard reset. The reset mechanism for the membrane potential can be implemented in two ways: Eq. (5) describes the soft and hard reset method. These two methods reflect different memory mechanisms in spiking neurons, but both suffer from significant quantization errors due to the limitations of reset designs [23]. On the other hand, when processing static images, previous spiking neural network training methods involved repeating a single image for $t$ time steps for encoding, which increased the training cost due to repeated input of the same image.

### 2.2　Spiking MU-Net

The Fig. 1 shows the architecture of our Spiking MU-Net, which builds upon VM-UNet [18] by redesigning the decoder and integrating a novel spiking neuron.

**SFA Spiking Neuron.** In this study, we adopt the Spike Firing Approximation (SFA) Method developed by [24] for our model. SFA retains the spiking behavior of traditional IF neurons while mitigating redundant inputs across multiple time steps, thereby reducing the training complexity for static images. Specifically, this method introduces a new dimension $D$ to the spiking neuron, enabling integer-based firing within a single time step, while defining the neuronal state by current signal intensity to reduce information loss from the reset mechanism.

In the SFA method, the integer $D$ is normalized during training and converted to binary spikes during inference to preserve the spike-driven nature [24]. The SFA method can be formulated as follows:

$$a_D^l = \frac{1}{D} \sum_{d=1}^{D} \mathbf{S}^l[d], \tag{6}$$

$$\mathbf{S}_D^l = \mathrm{Fire}_D(\mathbf{U}^l) = \lfloor \mathrm{clip}\{\mathbf{U}^l, 0, D\} \rfloor, \tag{7}$$

$$\mathbf{X}^{l+1} = \mathbf{W}^{l+1} a_D^l = \mathbf{W}^{l+1} \frac{1}{D} \mathbf{S}_D^l = \left(\frac{1}{D} \mathbf{W}^{l+1}\right) \sum_{d=1}^{D} \mathbf{S}^l[d]. \tag{8}$$

The spike firing rate $a_D^l$ is the ratio of spike $\mathbf{S}^l[d]$ at $l$-th layer discharges $d$ to the total number of steps. $\mathbf{S}_D^l$ replaces the spike firing $\mathbf{S}[t]$ in Eq. (4). The function $\mathrm{Fire}_D(\cdot)$ represents an integer-valued activation function, while $D$ simulates the time steps. The operation $\mathrm{clip}\{\mathbf{U}^l, 0, D\}$ constrains the value of $\mathbf{U}^l$ within the range of 0 to $D$, meaning that $D$ is the maximum allowed integer activation value for spikes. And $\lfloor \cdot \rfloor$ is the floor function. The weight matrix $\mathbf{W}^{l+1}$, obtained from either the Conv or Mamba module, maps the spike-processed features $a_D^l$ through an accumulation operation. $\mathbf{X}^{l+1}$ denotes the spatial output to the spiking neurons in the $l+1$-th layer. Figure 2 shows that SFA [24] reduces training complexity compared to conventional spiking neurons on static tasks.

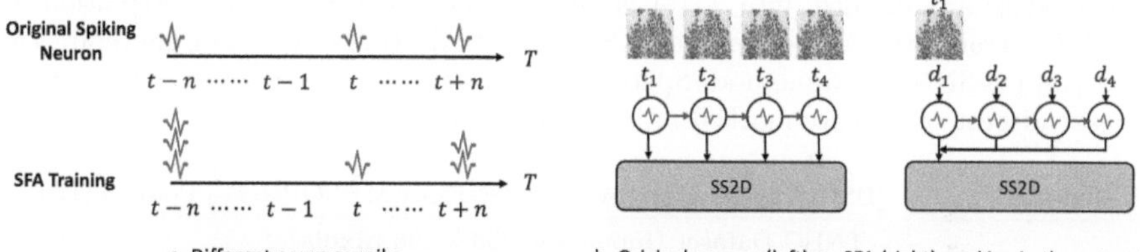


**Fig. 2.** The difference between the operation of SFA [24] and original spiking neurons.

**Spiking SS2D & Conv.** We first use spiking neurons to discretize the input image $x$ (with a size of $1/4, 1/4$) into spikes. This converts continuous signals into spike sequences to adapt to the computational model of SNNs. Subsequently, the spike sequence is fed into the SS2D module, which performs a one-dimensional spatial scanning convolution on the sparse spike input using a state space module. As shown in Eq. (2), the system conducts a stepwise weighted summation along the temporal dimension, where the convolution kernel $\bar{K}$ is constructed from the state transition matrix and applied to the input spike sequence, resulting in an interpretable additive convolution operation. Let the input feature map of the current module be $\mathbf{X}_{\mathrm{in}} \in \mathbb{R}^{C \times H \times W}$ and $\odot$ denotes the Hadamard product. The full computational process of this module is defined as follows:

$$\mathbf{X}_{\mathrm{out}} = \mathrm{LayerNorm}\left(\mathrm{SS2D}\left(SN\left(\mathrm{DWConv}\left(\mathbf{X}_{\mathrm{in}}\right)\right)\right)\right) \odot SN(\mathbf{X}_{\mathrm{in}}), \tag{9}$$

where DWConv($\cdot$) is depthwise convolution [25], $SN(\cdot)$ is the spiking neuron, and SS2D($\cdot$) is 2D-Selective-Scanmodule [26] for Mamba feature extraction. Similarly, the Conv blocks in the Decoder follow the same principle, as illustrated in Eq. (10). Binary values are enforced before being fed into the convolution layers, enabling additive operations between spikes and weight matrices. Spiking operations are skipped in the patch layer to preserve the semantic information.

**Decoder.** In the original VM-UNet, we observed that even with the integration of the Mamba module, the network could hardly be regarded as lightweight under the tiny configuration. This reveals a typical performance-efficiency trade-off. To address this issue, we redesigned the structure of the decoder. Specifically, we replaced the original Mamba modules with DWConv, reducing the number of parameters and alleviating the power consumption problems caused by large convolutional kernels. To compensate for the limitations of convolution in modeling long-range dependencies, the decoder further incorporates features extracted by the Mamba module to enhance the model's ability to capture global semantic information. Furthermore, to enhance training stability and mitigate the vanishing gradient problem, we introduced residual connections into the convolutional modules. The decoding process can be expressed by the following equation:

$$\mathbf{X}_{\text{out}} = \text{DWConv}\left(SN\left(\text{LayerNorm}(\mathbf{X}_{\text{in}})\right)\right) + \mathbf{X}_{\text{in}}. \tag{10}$$

**Table 1.** Comparison with previous models on **TNBC and NeurIPS22 Dataset**. Past models are divided into (1) CNN-based methods: U-Net [2], Attention U-Net [3] (2) Transformer-based methods: Swin-Unet [4] (3) Mamba-based method: VM-UNet [18] (4) SNN-based method: Spiking UNet [27] Spiking VM-UNet. The best and the second-best results are marked in bold and underline, respectively.

| Model | DSC(%) ↑ | IoU(%) ↑ | Acc(%) ↑ | Params(M) ↓ | OPs(G) ↓ | Power(mJ) ↓ |
|---|---|---|---|---|---|---|
| TNBC Dataset (Input Size $256 \times 256$ **pixels**) | | | | | | |
| Unet [2] | 81.54 | 68.83 | 95.89 | 34.53 | 65.59 | 301.71 |
| Att-UNet [3] | 81.80 | 69.20 | 95.94 | 34.88 | 66.7 | 306.82 |
| SwinUNet [4] | 74.94 | 59.92 | 93.97 | 27.18 | 7.72 | 35.51 |
| VM-UNet [18] | 82.14 | 69.69 | 95.91 | 27.43 | 4.09 | 18.81 |
| Spiking UNet [27] | 41.37 | 27.83 | 90.20 | 34.51 | 65.28 | 11.75 |
| Spiking VM-UNet | 81.45 | 68.71 | 95.87 | 25.59 | 4.08 | 3.51 |
| Ours | **83.18** | **71.21** | **96.22** | **15.38** | **2.49** | **3.22** |
| NeurIPS22 Dataset (Input Size $512 \times 512$ **pixels**) | | | | | | |
| Unet [2] | 66.47 | 49.78 | 81.03 | 34.53 | 262.34 | 1206.76 |
| Att-UNet [3] | 70.23 | 54.12 | 83.39 | 34.88 | 266.78 | 1227.18 |
| SwinUNet [4] | 72.02 | 56.27 | 81.57 | 27.18 | 30.88 | 142.05 |
| VM-UNet [18] | 77.15 | 62.79 | 87.28 | 27.43 | 16.38 | 75.35 |
| Spiking UNet [27] | 66.82 | 50.17 | 81.60 | 34.51 | 261.11 | 47.00 |
| Spiking VM-UNet | 76.64 | 62.13 | 86.72 | 25.59 | 16.32 | 16.73 |
| Ours | **78.08** | **64.04** | **88.32** | **15.38** | **9.94** | **15.58** |

## 3   Experiments

**Dataset.** To ensure comprehensive evaluation, we employed the NeurIPS22-CellSeg dataset [20], which was provided for the NeurIPS 2022 Cell Segmentation Challenge. This dataset includes diverse cell types captured under four microscopy modalities—brightfield (2040 × 1546 pixels), fluorescent (512 × 512 pixels), phase-contrast (600 × 600 pixels), and differential interference contrast (970 × 970 pixels)—providing a solid benchmark for evaluating model robustness across varying imaging conditions. It includes 1,000 training and 400 test images. To validate our model on histological data, we selected the Triple Negative Breast Cancer (TNBC) dataset [21], which captures interpatient variability in cellular structures between patients diagnosed with the cancer. This dataset comprises 50 images of size 512 × 512 pixels, with 4,022 annotated cells in total. We chose 10 images for testing.

**Metrics.** We adopt the evaluation metrics used in prior research [18], including Intersection over Union (IoU), Dice Similarity Coefficient (DSC) and Accuracy (Acc). For model performance, we consider three aspects: Parameters, Operations (OPs), and Energy Consumption. The energy consumption is calculated based on the energy costs of Multiply-Accumulate (MAC) and Accumulate (AC) operations [28]. The energy consumption of ANNs is computed as OPs times $E_{MAC}$, while that of SNNs is calculated as OPs times $E_{AC}$ times spiking firing rate, where the firing rate [29] refers to the average proportion of active spikes per neuron over time steps.

**Implementation Details.** We implemented experiments using the PyTorch framework [30] on an NVIDIA A100 GPU. All models were trained with a combination of BCE-Dice loss and the AdamW optimizer [31], with an initial learning rate of 0.01. In addition we use the CosineAnnealingLR scheduler [32]. For the TNBC dataset, each 512 × 512-pixel training image is evenly divided into four non-overlapping 256 × 256-pixel sub-images. This patch processing helps increase the training samples and focuses the model on local details. The images were resized to 512 × 512 pixels, with a batch size of 32, and the training lasted 500 epochs. Data augmentation included horizontal flipping and random 360-degree rotation, both with a probability of 0.5. We used pre-trained VMamba-S weights [26] on ImageNet-1k for the backbone (Fig. 3).

## 4   Results and Discussion

**Experiment Results.** For direct comparison, we convert VM-UNet into a spiking version (Spiking VM-UNet) using our adopted spiking neuron, since SNNs are mainly used for classification and detection. The proposed model demonstrates notable improvements in precision on both the TNBC and NeurIPS22 datasets. Specifically, it outperforms the second-best model on the TNBC dataset by 1.04%, 1.52%, and 0.31% across three key metrics, and 0.93%, 1.25%, and

1.07% on the NeurIPS22 dataset. Notably, adjusting the input size to $256 \times 256$ according to the original VM-UNet configuration yields an IoU of 65.51% on the NeurIPS dataset, which may be related to Mamba's ability to capture long-range dependencies. Besides, Spiking UNet performs particularly poorly on the TNBC dataset, mainly due to two factors: (1) limitations of the original architecture and (2) the inability of conventional spiking neurons to effectively handle static, small, and scattered objects. As shown in Table 1, Spiking MU-Net demonstrates significant advantages due to the unique sparse computational characteristics of spiking neurons. It reduces the parameters by half compared to the VM-UNet. Besides, the energy consumption is only 20% of that of the VM-UNet.

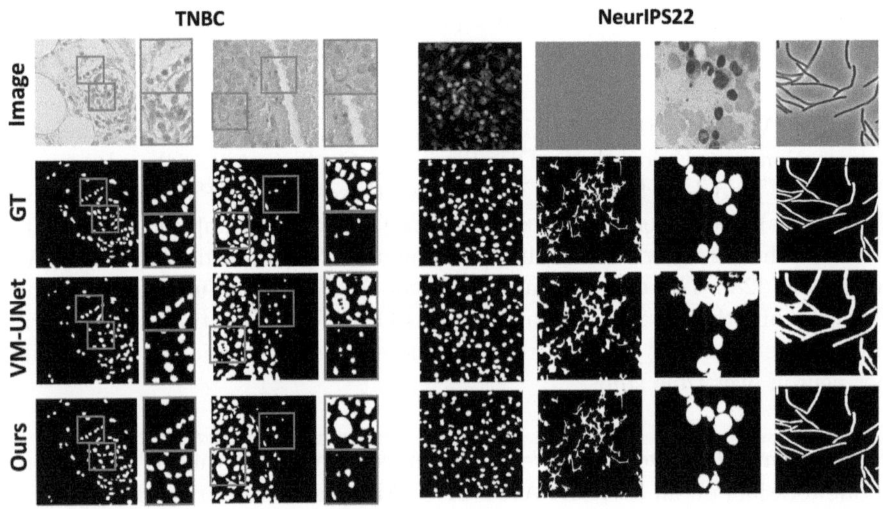

**Fig. 3.** Comparison between our model and the most competitive model on the TNBC and NeurIPS22 datasets.

**Ablation Study.** We compared CNN, Transformer, and Mamba by substituting the SS2D in Spiking MU-Net with $3 \times 3$ Conv or Transformer self-attention modules. All the experimental results are reported in Table 2. Our model shows an advantage across all evaluation metrics. From the results, we observe that the Parameters and OPs of the Self-Attention and the Mamba are relatively close. It is important to note that in our network, the Mamba module is only applied 8 blocks in the whole network, which limits the degree of difference in theoretical complexity. And during actual training with $512 \times 512$ pixels input and a batch size of 32, the Self-Attention model consumes up to **223.2 GB** of GPU memory, whereas the Mamba-based model requires only **41 GB**. This observation aligns with our earlier discussion: **Transformer attention has a quadratic complexity** $O(N^2)$ with respect to sequence length, while **Mamba exhibits linear**

**Table 2.** Ablation studies in Spiking VSS Block on the **TNBC** [21] dataset.

| Model | Params(M) ↓ | OPs(G)↓ | Power(mJ)↓ | DSC(%) ↑ | IoU(%) ↑ | Acc(%) ↑ |
|---|---|---|---|---|---|---|
| SS2D → Conv3 | 23.67 | 4.59 | 3.61 | 68.76 | 52.39 | 93.49 |
| SS2D → Self-Attention | 15.85 | 3.08 | 3.32 | 81.56 | 68.86 | 96.20 |
| w/o Spiking neuron | 15.45 | 2.51 | 11.55 | 82.54 | 70.27 | 96.07 |
| Ours | **15.38** | **2.49** | **3.22** | **83.18** | **71.21** | **96.22** |

**complexity** $O(N)$, leading to significantly improved memory efficiency. On the other hand, although spiking neurons exhibit comparable parameter counts and precision to networks using conventional activation functions, their event-driven nature ensures AC and significantly reduced power consumption.

## 5   Conclusion

In this work, we propose the Spiking MU-Net achieves reduced computation through Mamba's linear operations, fewer parameters via architectural redesign, and lower power consumption by utilising the Accumulated Consumption mechanism Spiking Neuron dynamics. However, the current model still has limitations in capturing complex image features. In the future, we will address this issue and further leverage temporal information.

**Acknowledgments.** This work was funded by grants from the JST Moonshot R&D Grant Number JPMJMS2033 and the JSPS KAKENHI Grant Numbers 24KJ1231 and 24H00720. Liangyi Wang was supported by the Nagoya University THERS Make New Standards program from MEXT. Yunheng Wu was supported by the Nagoya University CIBoG WISE program from MEXT.

**Disclosure of Interests.** Authors have no competing interests in the paper.

## References

1. Chen, Y., et al.: SELMA3D Challenge: Self-supervised learning for 3D light-sheet microscopy image segmentation. arXiv (2025). https://doi.org/10.48550/arXiv.2501.03880
2. Ronneberger, O., Fischer, P., Brox, T.: U-Net: convolutional networks for biomedical image segmentation. In: Navab, N., Hornegger, J., Wells, W.M., Frangi, A.F. (eds.) MICCAI 2015. LNCS, vol. 9351, pp. 234–241. Springer, Cham (2015). https://doi.org/10.1007/978-3-319-24574-4_28
3. Oktay, O., et al.: Attention U-Net: learning where to look for the pancreas. In: 1st Conference on Medical Imaging with Deep Learning (MIDL 2018) (2018)
4. Cao, H., et al.: Swin-Unet: Unet-like pure transformer for medical image segmentation. In: Karlinsky, L., Michaeli, T., Nishino, K. (eds.) Computer Vision – ECCV 2022 Workshops. LNCS, vol. 13803. Springer, Cham (2023). https://doi.org/10.1007/978-3-031-25066-8_9

5. Alieva, M., Wezenaar, A.K.L., Wehrens, E.J., Rios, A.C.: Bridging live-cell imaging and next-generation cancer treatment. Nat. Rev. Cancer **23**(11), 731–745 (2023). https://doi.org/10.1038/s41568-023-00610-5

6. Haro, C., et al.: SAMJ-IJ: an ImageJ/Fiji plugin for segment-anything models (SAMs) (2024). https://github.com/segment-anything-models-java/SAMJ-IJ. Accessed 09 June 2024

7. Wu, Y., et al.: A deployable microscopic image segmentation look-up table based on a dilated CNN. In: Proceedings of International Workshop on Medical Optical Imaging and Virtual Microscopy Image Analysis (MOMI), pp. 3–13. Springer (2024). https://doi.org/10.1007/978-3-031-12345-6_1

8. Archit, A., Freckmann, L., Nair, S., Khalid, N., Hilt, P., Rajashekar, V., et al.: Segment anything for microscopy. Nat. Methods **22**(3), 579–591 (2025). https://doi.org/10.1038/s41592-024-02580-4

9. Roy, K., Jaiswal, A., Panda, P.: Towards spike-based machine intelligence with neuromorphic computing. Nature **575**(7784), 607–617 (2019). https://doi.org/10.1038/s41586-019-1677-2

10. Pei, J., Deng, L., Song, S., Zhao, M., Zhang, Y., Wu, S., et al.: Towards artificial general intelligence with hybrid Tianjic chip architecture. Nature **572**(7767), 106–111 (2019). https://doi.org/10.1038/s41586-019-1424-8

11. Vaswani, A., Shazeer, N., Parmar, N., Uszkoreit, J., Jones, L., Gomez, A.N., et al.: Attention is all you need. Adv. Neural. Inf. Process. Syst. **30**, 5998–6008 (2017)

12. Hatamizadeh, A., Kautz, J.: MambaVision: a hybrid mamba-transformer vision backbone. In: Proceedings of IEEE Conference on Computer Vision and Pattern Recognition (CVPR), pp. 25261–25270 (2025). https://doi.org/10.1109/CVPR.2025.01234

13. Liu, Z., et al.: Swin transformer: hierarchical vision transformer using shifted windows. In: Proceedings of IEEE/CVF International Conference on Computer Vision, pp. 10012–10022 (2021). https://doi.org/10.1109/ICCV48922.2021.00986

14. Gallusser, B., Weigert, M.: TRACKASTRA: transformer-based cell tracking for live-cell microscopy. In: Leonardis, A., Ricci, E., Roth, S., Russakovsky, O., Sattler, T., Varol, G. (eds.) Computer Vision – ECCV 2024. LNCS, vol. 15134, Springer, Cham (2025). https://doi.org/10.1007/978-3-031-73116-7_27

15. Gu, A., Dao, T.: Mamba: Linear-Time Sequence Modeling with Selective State Spaces. arXiv (2023). https://doi.org/10.48550/arXiv.2312.00752

16. Mehta, H., Gupta, A., Cutkosky, A., Neyshabur, B.: Long Range Language Modeling via Gated State Spaces. arXiv (2022). https://doi.org/10.48550/arXiv.2206.13947

17. Wang, J., et al.: Selective structured state-spaces for long-form video understanding. In: Proceedings of IEEE/CVF Conference on Computer Vision and Pattern Recognition, pp. 6387–6397 (2023). https://doi.org/10.1109/CVPR52729.2023.00617

18. Ruan, J., Li, J., Xiang, S.: VM-UNet: Vision Mamba UNet for Medical Image Segmentation. arXiv (2024). https://doi.org/10.48550/arXiv.2402.02491

19. Zhu, L., et al.: Vision Mamba: Efficient Visual Representation Learning with Bidirectional State Space Model. arXiv (2024). https://doi.org/10.48550/arXiv.2401.09417

20. Ma, J., Xie, R., Ayyadhury, S., Ge, C., Gupta, A., Gupta, R., et al.: The multimodality cell segmentation challenge: toward universal solutions. Nat. Methods **21**(6), 1103–1113 (2024). https://doi.org/10.1038/s41592-024-02244-3

21. Naylor, P., Laé, M., Reyal, F., Walter, T.: Segmentation of nuclei in histopathology images by deep regression of the distance map. IEEE Trans. Med. Imaging **38**(2), 448–459 (2019). https://doi.org/10.1109/TMI.2018.2865709

22. Maass, W.: Networks of spiking neurons: the third generation of neural network models. Neural Netw. **10**(9), 1659–1671 (1997). https://doi.org/10.1016/S0893-6080(97)00011-7

23. Luo, X., Yao, M., Chou, Y., Xu, B., Li, G.: Integer-valued training and spike-driven inference spiking neural network for high-performance and energy-efficient object detection. In: Proceedings of European Conference on Computer Vision, pp. 253–272. Springer (2024). https://doi.org/10.1007/978-3-031-73411-3_15

24. Yao, M., Qiu, X., Hu, T., Hu, J., Chou, Y., Tian, K., et al.: Scaling spike-driven transformer with efficient spike firing approximation training. IEEE Trans. Pattern Anal. Mach. Intell. **47**(1), 123–135 (2025). https://doi.org/10.1109/TPAMI.2025.1234567

25. Chollet, F.: Xception: deep learning with depthwise separable convolutions. In: Proceedings of IEEE Conference on Computer Vision and Pattern Recognition, pp. 1800–1807 (2017). https://doi.org/10.1109/CVPR.2017.195

26. Liu, Y., Tian, Y., Zhao, Y., Yu, H., Xie, L., Wang, Y., et al.: VMamba: visual state space model. Adv. Neural. Inf. Process. Syst. **37**, 103031–103063 (2025)

27. Patel, K., Hunsberger, E., Batir, S., Eliasmith, C.: A Spiking Neural Network for Image Segmentation. arXiv (2021). https://doi.org/10.48550/arXiv.2106.08921

28. Horowitz, M.: 1.1 computing's energy problem (and what we can do about it). In: Proceedings of IEEE International Solid-State Circuits Conference (ISSCC), pp. 10–14 (2014). https://doi.org/10.1109/ISSCC.2014.6757323

29. Yao, M., et al.: Spike-Driven Transformer V2: Meta Spiking Neural Network Architecture Inspiring the Design of Next-Generation Neuromorphic Chips. arXiv (2024). https://doi.org/10.48550/arXiv.2404.03663

30. Imambi, S., Prakash, K.B., Kanagachidambaresan, G.R.: PyTorch. In: Prakash, K.B., Kanagachidambaresan, G.R. (eds.) Programming with TensorFlow. EICC, pp. 87–104. Springer, Cham (2021). https://doi.org/10.1007/978-3-030-57077-4_10

31. Loshchilov, I., Hutter, F.: Decoupled Weight Decay Regularization. arXiv (2017). https://doi.org/10.48550/arXiv.1711.05101

32. Loshchilov, I., Hutter, F.: SGDR: stochastic gradient descent with warm restarts. In: Proceedings of International Conference on Learning Representations (2017)

# SAM 2 in Robotic Surgery: An Empirical Evaluation for Robustness and Generalization in Surgical Video Segmentation


Jieming Yu[1,2,3], An Wang[1,2], Wenzhen Dong[1,2], Mengya Xu[1,3],
Mobarakol Islam[4], Jie Wang[2], Long Bai[1,2(✉)], and Hongliang Ren[1,2(✉)]

[1] Department of Electronic Engineering, The Chinese University of Hong Kong (CUHK), Hong Kong SAR, China
{jmyu,b.long}@link.cuhk.edu.hk, hlren@ee.cuhk.edu.hk
[2] Shenzhen Research Institute, CUHK, Shenzhen, China
[3] Department of Computer Science and Engineering, CUHK, Hong Kong SAR, China
[4] UCL Hawkes Institute, University College London, London, UK



**Abstract.** The recent Segment Anything Model 2 (SAM 2), has demonstrated remarkable foundational competence in semantic segmentation, with its memory mechanism and mask decoder further addressing challenges in video tracking and object occlusion, thereby achieving superior results in interactive segmentation for both natural images and videos. Building upon our previous empirical studies, we further explore the zero-shot segmentation performance of SAM 2 in robot-assisted surgery based on prompts, along with its robustness against real-world corruption. For static images, we employ two forms of prompts: 1-point and bounding box, while for video sequences, the 1-point prompt is applied to the initial frame. Through extensive experimentation on the MICCAI EndoVis 2017 and EndoVis 2018 benchmarks, SAM 2, when utilizing bounding box prompts, outperforms state-of-the-art (SOTA) methods in comparative evaluations. The results with point prompts also exhibit a substantial enhancement over SAM's capabilities, nearing or even surpassing existing unprompted SOTA methodologies. In addition, SAM 2 demonstrates improved inference speed and less performance degradation against various image corruption. Although slightly unsatisfactory results remain in specific edges or regions, SAM 2's robust adaptability to 1-point prompts underscores its potential for downstream surgical tasks with limited prompt requirements.


## 1 Introduction

Surgical instrument segmenting and tracking is a significant topic, with its rich representation contributing to the development of various downstream applications [5,17,26]. Unfortunately, due to a lack of large-scale surgical data, the efforts toward surgical foundational models are significantly lagging compared to general computer vision. Specifically, the acquisition and annotation of high-quality surgical data require expensive resources and human labor, while synthetic data training falls short of distribution diversity and real-world applications. The segmentation foundation models, which are trained on more than one billion masks, have made great progress in the field of natural image segmentation, but tend to fail in common medical scenarios because of the large domain gap [8,15]. To tackle this issue, researchers have adapted Segment Anything Model (SAM) [14] from general 2D vision to medical applications, capitalizing on the rich, diverse pre-trained data through Parameter-Efficient Fine-Tuning (PEFT) techniques such as adapters or low-rank adaptations (LoRA) [9]. For example, the Med-SAM-Adapter [27] leverages medical-specific domain knowledge to refine segmentation models effectively, via a simple yet effective adapter. Similarly, SAMed [29] employs a low-rank finetuning strategy on both the image encoder and the prompt encoder, alongside the mask decoder, for medical image segmentation tasks. Furthermore, a series of works have been proposed for automating prompts and fine-tuning SAM models to perform end-to-end semantic segmentation tasks in surgical scenarios, including two-stage strategy [28], text prompt [18], automating bounding box prompt [22], and feature matching [16].

The recently introduced SAM 2 [19] unifies video and image segmentation by treating images as single-frame videos. Leveraging its unique memory mechanism and mask decoder, SAM 2 demonstrates notable superiority in both effectiveness and efficiency over its predecessor. Moreover, SAM 2 is significantly faster than SAM, with approximately six times the speed in generating segmentation masks, which allows for more rapid processing and real-time applications. SAM 2 excels in handling dynamic scenes with fast-moving objects, thanks to its advanced memory management that tracks object trajectories across frames with precision. SAM 2 successfully manages complex scenarios characterized by detailed anatomical structures, motion, and occlusion, thereby enhancing the model's reliability across an extensive array of applications. Benefiting from SAM 2's robust capability in handling complex scenarios, it demonstrates significant potential in processing surgical scene data. Surgical scenes often involve intricate anatomical details, rapid changes in object positions, and frequent occlusions, all of which align well with the capabilities that SAM 2 has been shown to possess. Consequently, it is necessary to evaluate the performance of SAM 2 in medical contexts and its robustness under real-world corruption for further investigation.

In this work, we assess the generalizability of SAM 2 across various surgical scenarios. Specifically, our contributions and findings can be summarized as:

- We conduct a comprehensive empirical study on surgical images and videos based on SAM 2 to thoroughly evaluate its performance. For surgical images, we use the bounding box or 1-point as the prompt input; for videos, we prompt 1 point for each object in the first frame. The results indicate that SAM 2 overall outperforms its previous version.
- By using bounding boxes as prompts, SAM 2 has become the new state-of-the-art (SOTA) in the surgical domain. Surprisingly, in video segmentation, SAM

2, which applies the 1-point prompt only in the first frame, demonstrated superior performance compared to SAM with images using the 1-point prompt for every frame.

- We further evaluate the robustness of SAM 2 by analyzing its performance on synthetic surgical datasets with diverse levels of corruption and perturbations. Using bounding boxes as prompts, SAM 2 demonstrated strong resistance to real-world corruptions on images, with minimal performance degradation under challenges such as image compression, noise, and blur.

**Table 1.** Quantitative comparison of binary and instrument segmentation on EndoVis17 and EndoVis18 datasets. For SAM 2, we present the results in images and videos.

| Type | Method | Pub/Year(20-) | Arch. | EndoVis17 | | EndoVis18 | |
|---|---|---|---|---|---|---|---|
| | | | | Binary IoU | Instrument IoU | Binary IoU | Instrument IoU |
| Single-Task | Vanilla UNet | MICCAI15 | UNet | 75.44 | 15.80 | 68.89 | - |
| | TernausNet | ICMLA18 | UNet | 83.60 | 35.27 | - | 46.22 |
| | MF-TAPNet | MICCAI19 | UNet | 87.56 | 37.35 | - | 67.87 |
| | Islam et al. | RA-L19 | - | 84.50 | - | - | - |
| | ISINet | MICCAI21 | Res50 | - | 55.62 | - | 73.03 |
| | Wang et al. | MICCAI22 | UNet | - | - | 58.12 | - |
| Multi-Task | ST-MTL | MedIA21 | - | 83.49 | - | - | - |
| | AP-MTL | ICRA20 | - | 88.75 | - | - | - |
| | S-MTL | RA-L22 | - | - | - | - | 43.54 |
| | TraSeTR | ICRA22 | Res50 + Trfm | - | 60.40 | - | 76.20 |
| | S3Net | WACV23 | Res50 | - | 72.54 | - | 75.81 |
| Prompt-based | SAM (1 Point) | arxiv23 | ViT_h | 53.88 | 55.96* | 57.12 | 54.30* |
| | SAM (Box) | arxiv23 | ViT_h | 89.19 | **88.20*** | 89.35 | 81.09* |
| | SAM 2-Image (1 Point) | arxiv24 | ViT_h | 84.96 | 81.10* | 77.14 | 73.76* |
| | SAM 2-Image (Box) | arxiv24 | ViT_h | **90.97** | 86.92* | **90.18** | **81.97*** |
| | SAM 2-Video (1 Point) | arxiv24 | ViT_h | 62.45 | 58.74* | 65.19 | 57.59* |

* Categorical information directly inherits from associated prompts.

**Table 2.** Comparison of inference speed (fps) of SAM and SAM 2 on EndoVis18 [1]. Experiments are conducted on 1 RTX 3090 GPU, with Pytorch 2.4 and CUDA 12.1.

| Model | Point | Box |
|---|---|---|
| SAM | 2.95 | 3.04 |
| SAM 2 | 8.75 | 8.94 |

## 2   Surgical Instruments Segmentation with Prompts

**Implementation.** MICCAI EndoVis17 [2] and EndoVis18 [1] are used for our evaluation and we follow all the validation set splitting in [25]. For images, we utilize either 1-point or a bounding box as prompts. Specifically, for the object that has the same id in the same image, 1-point is the centroid of its mask while its bounding box is the smallest rectangle that fully encloses the mask, determined by the extreme coordinates of the mask pixels. For videos, we employ

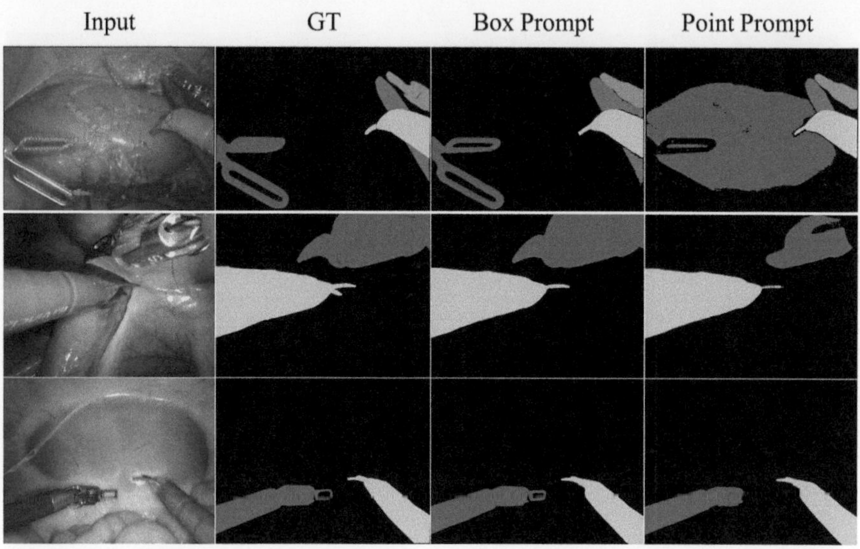

Fig. 1. Qualitative results of SAM 2 on five images of the surgical scene.

a single point from the initial frame as the prompt. The bounding box, which is a rectangular frame defined by its top-left and bottom-right coordinates to enclose an object, originates from manual annotations in our previous work [4], while the single point is derived by calculating the centroid of the corresponding mask. Since the output of SAM 2 does not contain class information, we directly assign the class information from the input prompt to the output mask to prevent poor performance caused by incorrect class information.

**Comparison Methods.** We follow the comparison methods in our previous version as follows: vanilla UNet [20], TernausNet [23], MF-TAPNet [13], Islam et al. [10], Wang et al. [24], ST-MTL [11], S-MTL [21], AP-MTL [12], ISINet [6], TraSeTR [30], and S3Net [3] for surgical binary and instrument-wise segmentation. The results of SAM are directly adopted from [25], and we use the SAM 2-Hiera-Large [14] model for our evaluation. It is important to note that a completely fair comparison cannot be achieved, as other existing methods do not require prompts during inference.

**Results and Analysis.** Overall, SAM 2 [19] demonstrates better performance compared to SAM [14] in Table 1 and 2. The results using the bounding box prompt maintain SOTA performance over previous unprompted methods, but its improvement on SAM [14] is not significant. In terms of the 1-point prompt, SAM 2 [19] exhibits substantial enhancements, with overall performance increasing by 20%–30%. Figure 1 presents several examples of the qualitative results of SAM 2 on surgical images. Furthermore, SAM 2 [19] boasts an inference speed

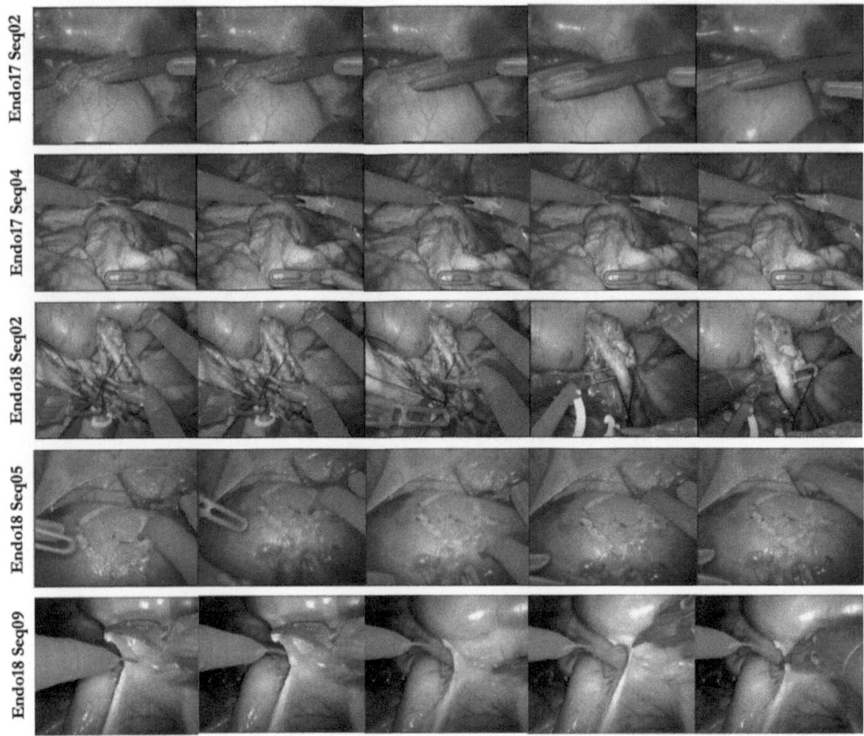

**Fig. 2.** Qualitative results of SAM 2 on five surgical video sequences.

that is more than twice as fast as that of SAM [14], which brings significant advantages to practical clinical applications. Doctors can simply click on the desired areas, and the model promptly provides accurate results for the corresponding targets in the images, facilitating medical diagnosis.

Additionally, in SAM 2, we compare the differences in the segmentation results between video and image when using a 1-point prompt. The performance of video segmentation, with only the first frame prompt, is lower than that of image segmentation. The results are consistent with the results presented in the SAM 2 technical report, since the image segmentation task will get more prompt information – the 1-point prompt will be applied at each frame. Despite this, the video segmentation results with the 1-point prompt in SAM 2 still outperform the previous SAM image segmentation results using the 1-point prompt, enabling satisfactory results for downstream applications. The qualitative results of SAM 2 on surgical video sequences are illustrated in Fig. 2.

**Table 3.** Quantitative results on various corrupted EndoVis18 validation data. The prompts used by SAM-Image Segmentation, SAM 2-Image Segmentation, and SAM 2-Video Segmentation are bounding box, bounding box, and point, respectively.

| Task | | Severity | Noise | | | | Blur | | | | | Weather | | | | | Digital | | | |
|---|---|---|---|---|---|---|---|---|---|---|---|---|---|---|---|---|---|---|---|---|
| | | | Gaussian | Shot | Impulse | Speckle | Defocus | Glass | Motion | Zoom | Gaussian | Snow | Frost | Fog | Bright | Spatter | Contrast | Pixel | JPEG | Saturate |
| SAM - Image Segmentation | Binary | 0 | 89.35 | | | | | | | | | | | | | | | | | |
| | | 1 | 77.69 | 80.18 | 80.43 | 83.28 | 82.01 | 80.53 | 82.99 | 80.30 | 85.40 | 84.08 | 83.12 | 85.38 | 87.43 | 86.69 | 85.76 | 81.12 | 58.77 | 86.64 |
| | | 2 | 73.92 | 76.07 | 76.15 | 81.65 | 80.21 | 79.20 | 80.22 | 77.55 | 81.69 | 80.69 | 80.34 | 84.65 | 87.27 | 84.21 | 84.90 | 79.32 | 56.04 | 84.85 |
| | | 3 | 69.21 | 71.74 | 73.02 | 77.74 | 76.96 | 72.64 | 75.50 | 75.27 | 78.31 | 79.58 | 78.90 | 83.62 | 87.23 | 82.50 | 83.36 | 73.81 | 56.25 | 86.84 |
| | | 4 | 63.80 | 65.41 | 67.29 | 75.28 | 73.79 | 72.38 | 69.60 | 73.22 | 75.23 | 76.33 | 78.38 | 82.28 | 87.06 | 83.12 | 77.12 | 70.82 | 57.59 | 83.21 |
| | | 5 | 57.07 | 60.61 | 61.61 | 71.83 | 69.85 | 69.59 | 66.25 | 71.58 | 66.96 | 77.66 | 76.82 | 78.84 | 86.43 | 79.62 | 66.58 | 68.55 | 56.77 | 81.26 |
| | Instrument | 0 | 81.09 | | | | | | | | | | | | | | | | | |
| | | 1 | 69.51 | 71.83 | 72.25 | 74.82 | 73.64 | 72.13 | 74.33 | 71.41 | 76.79 | 75.40 | 74.42 | 76.82 | 79.16 | 78.24 | 77.17 | 72.94 | 54.86 | 78.27 |
| | | 2 | 66.06 | 68.09 | 68.53 | 73.19 | 71.74 | 71.02 | 71.46 | 68.85 | 73.15 | 72.13 | 71.65 | 76.14 | 79.00 | 75.54 | 76.22 | 71.55 | 52.23 | 76.61 |
| | | 3 | 62.01 | 64.44 | 65.89 | 69.75 | 68.74 | 64.97 | 67.13 | 67.12 | 70.08 | 70.97 | 70.21 | 75.01 | 78.90 | 73.70 | 74.67 | 66.83 | 51.63 | 78.39 |
| | | 4 | 57.28 | 59.12 | 61.03 | 67.82 | 65.87 | 64.87 | 62.15 | 65.18 | 67.23 | 68.43 | 69.79 | 73.73 | 78.73 | 74.24 | 69.48 | 63.99 | 51.88 | 74.91 |
| | | 5 | 51.56 | 55.16 | 55.86 | 64.76 | 62.43 | 62.23 | 59.26 | 63.96 | 60.60 | 69.33 | 68.32 | 70.45 | 78.19 | 70.72 | 61.14 | 61.79 | 51.01 | 73.35 |
| SAM 2 - Image Segmentation | Binary | 0 | 90.18 | | | | | | | | | | | | | | | | | |
| | | 1 | 85.20 | 86.24 | 85.20 | 87.69 | 85.53 | 84.95 | 85.46 | 81.83 | 87.34 | 87.81 | 89.50 | 87.36 | 88.96 | 88.63 | 87.79 | 86.92 | 85.68 | 88.80 |
| | | 2 | 82.04 | 83.69 | 82.38 | 86.77 | 83.93 | 84.43 | 82.71 | 79.18 | 85.39 | 85.06 | 89.48 | 86.88 | 88.96 | 87.78 | 87.31 | 86.39 | 83.58 | 88.01 |
| | | 3 | 77.35 | 80.01 | 80.19 | 83.94 | 81.56 | 79.16 | 78.72 | 77.12 | 83.09 | 85.20 | 89.43 | 85.34 | 88.90 | 87.13 | 86.13 | 83.24 | 82.33 | 88.54 |
| | | 4 | 72.75 | 74.65 | 75.99 | 81.91 | 79.31 | 79.41 | 74.01 | 75.24 | 80.75 | 83.30 | 89.42 | 84.05 | 88.90 | 87.23 | 82.08 | 80.75 | 74.81 | 86.61 |
| | | 5 | 68.09 | 71.30 | 71.47 | 79.56 | 77.06 | 78.07 | 71.52 | 73.40 | 76.55 | 83.04 | 89.46 | 80.70 | 88.61 | 85.28 | 72.93 | 78.78 | 65.16 | 84.96 |
| | Instrument | 0 | 81.97 | | | | | | | | | | | | | | | | | |
| | | 1 | 76.61 | 77.56 | 76.58 | 79.24 | 76.99 | 76.47 | 76.95 | 72.99 | 78.96 | 79.33 | 81.21 | 78.93 | 80.73 | 80.39 | 79.39 | 78.39 | 77.00 | 80.50 |
| | | 2 | 73.76 | 75.25 | 74.19 | 78.29 | 75.37 | 75.97 | 74.21 | 70.30 | 76.69 | 76.40 | 81.12 | 78.20 | 80.75 | 79.50 | 78.71 | 77.88 | 74.91 | 79.62 |
| | | 3 | 69.65 | 72.02 | 72.20 | 75.57 | 72.85 | 70.72 | 70.14 | 68.64 | 74.25 | 76.74 | 81.00 | 76.72 | 80.73 | 78.76 | 77.44 | 74.78 | 73.72 | 80.39 |
| | | 4 | 65.68 | 67.47 | 68.61 | 73.97 | 70.63 | 70.98 | 65.88 | 67.00 | 72.04 | 74.71 | 81.00 | 75.61 | 80.79 | 78.75 | 73.72 | 72.39 | 67.18 | 78.45 |
| | | 5 | 61.44 | 64.25 | 64.34 | 71.99 | 68.53 | 69.52 | 63.56 | 65.70 | 68.24 | 74.76 | 81.04 | 72.62 | 80.55 | 76.66 | 65.79 | 70.83 | 58.93 | 77.10 |
| SAM 2 - Video Segmentation | Binary | 0 | 65.19 | | | | | | | | | | | | | | | | | |
| | | 1 | 60.36 | 58.86 | 23.57 | 63.22 | 55.76 | 71.84 | 60.07 | 53.31 | 62.74 | 50.52 | 70.92 | 58.47 | 65.10 | 72.62 | 62.87 | 60.63 | 57.53 | 64.71 |
| | | 2 | 43.53 | 60.07 | 26.01 | 54.63 | 52.33 | 64.71 | 50.44 | 64.93 | 55.77 | 45.60 | 71.82 | 66.17 | 72.26 | 68.72 | 63.42 | 66.21 | 49.61 | 63.37 |
| | | 3 | 31.64 | 40.17 | 34.03 | 52.60 | 48.08 | 57.57 | 47.44 | 60.00 | 53.22 | 43.29 | 69.59 | 59.88 | 70.37 | 65.78 | 51.68 | 42.22 | 51.51 | 68.40 |
| | | 4 | 20.54 | 23.87 | 30.87 | 46.71 | 57.18 | 61.08 | 53.64 | 58.31 | 50.67 | 44.38 | 70.52 | 56.90 | 72.30 | 58.02 | 50.86 | 42.24 | 47.94 | 45.04 |
| | | 5 | 18.45 | 18.73 | 21.75 | 33.14 | 55.21 | 57.92 | 46.85 | 57.40 | 34.01 | 43.38 | 70.42 | 38.73 | 64.67 | 60.73 | 25.44 | 37.81 | 39.39 | 57.04 |
| | Instrument | 0 | 57.59 | | | | | | | | | | | | | | | | | |
| | | 1 | 48.09 | 50.67 | 19.96 | 56.22 | 42.55 | 58.50 | 47.62 | 41.00 | 49.44 | 43.92 | 58.12 | 46.45 | 56.92 | 58.80 | 52.42 | 54.80 | 46.13 | 55.64 |
| | | 2 | 37.18 | 49.89 | 20.43 | 48.89 | 40.56 | 41.95 | 44.26 | 42.45 | 44.20 | 38.90 | 57.69 | 54.17 | 62.65 | 58.77 | 50.86 | 60.96 | 38.71 | 52.41 |
| | | 3 | 28.82 | 37.78 | 29.80 | 41.97 | 38.73 | 47.11 | 46.29 | 45.92 | 40.59 | 31.40 | 55.53 | 48.24 | 56.10 | 54.22 | 40.19 | 42.59 | 43.53 | 58.02 |
| | | 4 | 15.47 | 16.06 | 24.24 | 36.74 | 45.70 | 48.94 | 43.36 | 44.94 | 35.05 | 37.68 | 56.61 | 40.14 | 57.63 | 52.65 | 36.11 | 30.11 | 34.76 | 39.73 |
| | | 5 | 9.30 | 13.21 | 15.60 | 26.89 | 40.97 | 45.50 | 36.27 | 39.54 | 19.01 | 37.36 | 56.22 | 29.38 | 51.90 | 54.11 | 12.77 | 24.34 | 27.43 | 46.64 |

## 3   Robustness Under Data Corruption

**Implementation.** We introduce image perturbations to evaluate robustness against input variations and analyze performance discrepancies. According to the robustness evaluation benchmark [7], SAM [14] and SAM 2 [19] underwent assessment across 18 types of data corruptions spanning 5 severity levels, following the official implementations[1]. Specifically, these data corruptions are (i) *Blur* (defocus, glass, motion, zoom, Gaussian); (ii) *Digital* (contrast, pixel, jpeg); and (iii) *Noise* (Gaussian, Shot, Impulse, Speckle); (iv) *Weather* (snow, frost, fog, brightness); (v) Others (spatter, saturate). The exclusion of the *Elastic Transformation* was deemed necessary to ensure proper alignment between the input images and their corresponding masks.

**Results and Analysis.** The extent of data corruption correlates directly with the observable degradation in the performance of SAM [14] and SAM 2 [19], as illustrated in Table 3. Both SAM-Image Segmentation and SAM 2-Image Segmentation use bounding box prompts. Notably, considering that SAM 2 [19] inherently does not offer bounding boxes as the prompt interface for video segmentation, SAM 2-Video Segmentation consequently employs point prompts.

---

[1] https://github.com/hendrycks/robustness.

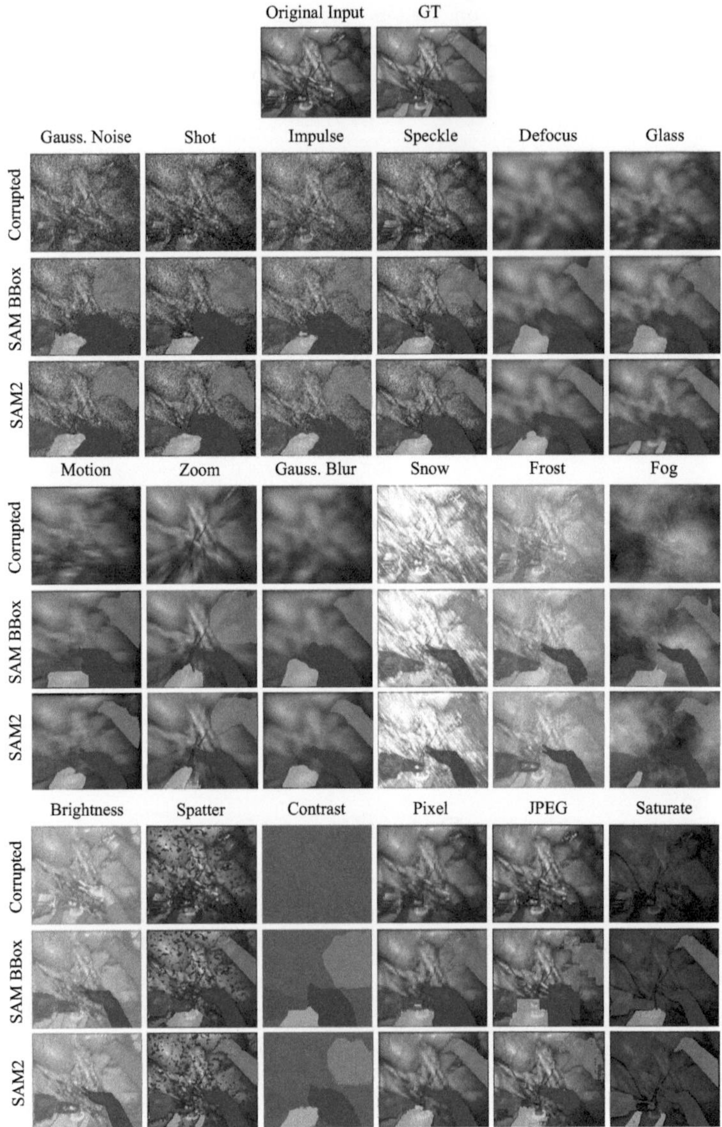


**Fig. 3.** Qualitative results of SAM 2 under 18 data corruptions of level-5 severity. Given that the implementation of specific transformations (e.g., spatter) relies on random functions, and the corrupted dataset in our previous version is no longer accessible, we have regenerated the corrupted images. While some types of images may exhibit slight variations, the overall statistical consistency ensures the reliability of our findings.

The robustness of SAM [14] and SAM 2 [19] can vary depending on the type of corruption, but generally, the performance tends to decline noticeably. Particularly, for SAM [14], *JPEG Compression* and *Gaussian Noise* exert the most pronounced effects on segmentation performance, whereas *Brightness* has minimal impact. When subjected to identical levels and types of corruption, SAM 2 demonstrates less performance degradation compared to SAM, indicating that SAM 2 exhibits greater robustness than SAM. However, SAM 2 and SAM maintained consistency in the most and least affected corruption types. Specifically, *Gaussian Noise*, *JPEG Compression*, and *Zoom* significantly affect the segmentation performance of SAM 2, whereas *Brightness* has a minor influence. SAM 2-Video Segmentation has the worst robustness. This is reflected in the fact that its performance degrades more than SAM-Image Segmentation and SAM 2-Image Segmentation when faced with corrupted images. Especially when faced with corrupted images with a severity level of 5, its performance drops sharply. This may be because point prompts, although more convenient, make the model unable to track tools well and cope with complex variations. Figure 3 displays an initial frame alongside several altered versions under severity level 5. It is evident from the images that SAM [14] and SAM 2 [19] experience significant performance degradation across most scenarios.

## 4    Conclusion

In this empirical study, we build upon prior work [25] by further investigating the zero-shot capabilities and data corruption robustness of SAM 2 [19] in semantic segmentation for robot-assisted surgery. Our analysis is primarily based on two types of prompts: single point and bounding box. Under the bounding box prompt, SAM 2 [19] maintains the exceptional performance observed in SAM [14], achieving SOTA results with slight improvements over SAM [14]. In contrast, the 1-point prompt results from SAM [14] exhibited subpar performance, making precise segmentation of surgical instruments challenging. However, SAM 2 [19] demonstrates high performance with the 1-point prompt, producing satisfactory inference results compared to previous work, even with this simple prompting approach, which significantly advances downstream applications. Furthermore, in video segmentation, although we only employ a single point from the initial frame as the prompt, SAM 2 [19] exhibits better results than SAM [14]'s image segmentation, which utilizes the 1-point prompt for each frame. When encountering various types of image quality corruption, SAM 2 [19] also demonstrates less performance degradation compared to SAM [14], highlighting its exceptional ability to handle complex scenarios, including occlusions, noise, blur, and other challenges in downstream tasks for robotic-assisted surgery.

Despite its advancements, SAM 2 [19] still faces notable limitations, such as suboptimal segmentation performance in challenging edge cases and specific regions. Future research could focus on developing fully automated, prompt-free methods to achieve precise and reliable segmentation in complex surgical environments. Another promising direction is enhancing SAM's ability to interpret and utilize textual representations of images, which may improve its overall functionality. Moreover, integrating SAM 2 with other vision-based models offers opportunities to advance segmentation capabilities further. Finally, extending SAM 2's generalizability to a broader range of surgical images and videos could significantly enhance its utility in robot-assisted surgery.

**Acknowledgements.** This work was supported by Hong Kong Research Grants Council (RGC) Collaborative Research Fund (CRF C4026-21GF), General Research Fund (GRF 14203323, GRF 14216022, and GRF 14211420), NSFC/RGC Joint Research Scheme N_CUHK420/22; Shenzhen-Hong Kong-Macau Technology Research Programme (Type C) STIC Grant 202108233000303.

# References


1. Allan, M., et al.: 2018 robotic scene segmentation challenge. arXiv preprint arXiv:2001.11190 (2020)
2. Allan, M., et al.: 2017 robotic instrument segmentation challenge. arXiv preprint arXiv:1902.06426 (2019)
3. Baby, B., et al.: From forks to forceps: a new framework for instance segmentation of surgical instruments. In: Proceedings of the IEEE/CVF Winter Conference on Applications of Computer Vision, pp. 6191–6201 (2023)
4. Bai, L., Islam, M., Seenivasan, L., Ren, H.: Surgical-vqla: transformer with gated vision-language embedding for visual question localized-answering in robotic surgery. In: 2023 IEEE International Conference on Robotics and Automation (ICRA), pp. 6859–6865. IEEE (2023)
5. Baste, J.M., et al.: Development of a precision multimodal surgical navigation system for lung robotic segmentectomy. J. Thorac. Dis. **10**(Suppl 10), S1195 (2018)
6. González, C., Bravo-Sánchez, L., Arbelaez, P.: ISINet: an instance-based approach for surgical instrument segmentation. In: Martel, A.L., et al. (eds.) MICCAI 2020. LNCS, vol. 12263, pp. 595–605. Springer, Cham (2020). https://doi.org/10.1007/978-3-030-59716-0_57
7. Hendrycks, D., Dietterich, T.: Benchmarking neural network robustness to common corruptions and perturbations. In: International Conference on Learning Representations (2019)
8. Hu, C., Li, X.: When SAM meets medical images: an investigation of segment anything model (SAM) on multi-phase liver tumor segmentation. arXiv preprint arXiv:2304.08506 (2023)
9. Hu, E.J., et al.: Lora: low-rank adaptation of large language models. arXiv preprint arXiv:2106.09685 (2021)
10. Islam, M., Atputharuban, D.A., Ramesh, R., Ren, H.: Real-time instrument segmentation in robotic surgery using auxiliary supervised deep adversarial learning. IEEE Robot. Autom. Lett. **4**(2), 2188–2195 (2019)
11. Islam, M., Vibashan, V., Lim, C.M., Ren, H.: ST-MTL: spatio-temporal multitask learning model to predict scanpath while tracking instruments in robotic surgery. Med. Image Anal. **67**, 101837 (2021)
12. Islam, M., Vibashan, V., Ren, H.: AP-MTL: attention pruned multi-task learning model for real-time instrument detection and segmentation in robot-assisted surgery. In: 2020 IEEE International Conference on Robotics and Automation (ICRA), pp. 8433–8439. IEEE (2020)
13. Jin, Y., Cheng, K., Dou, Q., Heng, P.-A.: Incorporating temporal prior from motion flow for instrument segmentation in minimally invasive surgery video. In: Shen, D., et al. (eds.) MICCAI 2019. LNCS, vol. 11768, pp. 440–448. Springer, Cham (2019). https://doi.org/10.1007/978-3-030-32254-0_49
14. Kirillov, A., et al.: Segment anything. arXiv preprint arXiv:2304.02643 (2023)

15. Ma, J., Wang, B.: Segment anything in medical images (2023)
16. Murali, A., Mascagni, P., Mutter, D., Padoy, N.: Cyclesam: one-shot surgical scene segmentation using cycle-consistent feature matching to prompt SAM. arXiv preprint arXiv:2407.06795 (2024)
17. Pakhomov, D., Navab, N.: Searching for efficient architecture for instrument segmentation in robotic surgery. In: Martel, A.L., et al. (eds.) MICCAI 2020. LNCS, vol. 12263, pp. 648–656. Springer, Cham (2020). https://doi.org/10.1007/978-3-030-59716-0_62
18. Paranjape, J.N., Nair, N.G., Sikder, S., Vedula, S.S., Patel, V.M.: Adaptivesam: towards efficient tuning of SAM for surgical scene segmentation. In: Annual Conference on Medical Image Understanding and Analysis, pp. 187–201. Springer (2024)
19. Ravi, N., et al.: Sam 2: segment anything in images and videos. arXiv preprint arXiv:2408.00714 (2024)
20. Ronneberger, O., Fischer, P., Brox, T.: U-Net: convolutional networks for biomedical image segmentation. In: Navab, N., Hornegger, J., Wells, W.M., Frangi, A.F. (eds.) MICCAI 2015. LNCS, vol. 9351, pp. 234–241. Springer, Cham (2015). https://doi.org/10.1007/978-3-319-24574-4_28
21. Seenivasan, L., Mitheran, S., Islam, M., Ren, H.: Global-reasoned multi-task learning model for surgical scene understanding. IEEE Robot. Autom. Lett. **7**(2), 3858–3865 (2022)
22. Sheng, Y., Bano, S., Clarkson, M.J., Islam, M.: Surgical-DeSAM: decoupling SAM for instrument segmentation in robotic surgery. Int. J. Comput. Assist. Radiol. Surg. 1–5 (2024)
23. Shvets, A.A., Rakhlin, A., Kalinin, A.A., Iglovikov, V.I.: Automatic instrument segmentation in robot-assisted surgery using deep learning. In: 2018 17th IEEE International Conference on Machine Learning and Applications (ICMLA), pp. 624–628 (2018)
24. Wang, A., Islam, M., Xu, M., Ren, H.: Rethinking surgical instrument segmentation: a background image can be all you need. In: International Conference on Medical Image Computing and Computer-Assisted Intervention, pp. 355–364. Springer (2022)
25. Wang, A., Islam, M., Xu, M., Zhang, Y., Ren, H.: Sam meets robotic surgery: an empirical study on generalization, robustness and adaptation. In: International Conference on Medical Image Computing and Computer-Assisted Intervention, pp. 234–244. Springer (2023)
26. Wang, G., Bai, L., Wu, Y., Chen, T., Ren, H.: Rethinking exemplars for continual semantic segmentation in endoscopy scenes: entropy-based mini-batch pseudo-replay. Comput. Biol. Med. **165**, 107412 (2023)
27. Wu, J., et al.: Medical SAM adapter: adapting segment anything model for medical image segmentation. arXiv preprint arXiv:2304.12620 (2023)
28. Yu, J., et al.: Adapting SAM for surgical instrument tracking and segmentation in endoscopic submucosal dissection videos. arXiv preprint arXiv:2404.10640 (2024)
29. Zhang, K., Liu, D.: Customized segment anything model for medical image segmentation. arXiv preprint arXiv:2304.13785 (2023)
30. Zhao, Z., Jin, Y., Heng, P.A.: Trasetr: track-to-segment transformer with contrastive query for instance-level instrument segmentation in robotic surgery. In: 2022 International Conference on Robotics and Automation (ICRA), pp. 11186–11193. IEEE (2022)

# EcoScale-Net: A Lightweight Multi-kernel Network for Long-Sequence 12-Lead ECG Classification


Dong-Hyeon Kang[1], Ju-Hyeon Nam[1], and Sang-Chul Lee[1,2(✉)]

[1] Department of Electrical and Computer Engineering, Inha University, Incheon, Republic of Korea
{orionis2001,jhnam0514}@inha.edu, sclee@inha.ac.kr
[2] DeepCardio, Incheon, Republic of Korea
sclee@deepcardio.com



**Abstract.** Accurate interpretation of 12-lead electrocardiograms (ECGs) is critical for early detection of cardiac abnormalities, yet manual reading is error-prone and existing CNN-based classifiers struggle to choose receptive-field sizes that generalize to the long sequences typical of ECGs. Omni-Scale CNN (OS-CNN) addresses this by enumerating prime-sized kernels inspired by Goldbach's conjecture to cover every scale, but its exhaustive design explodes computational cost and blocks deeper, wider models. We present ***Efficient Convolutional Omni-Scale Network (EcoScale-Net)***, a hierarchical variant that retains full receptive-field coverage while eliminating redundancy. At each stage, the maximum kernel length is capped to the scale still required after down-sampling, and $1 \times 1$ bottleneck convolutions inserted before and after every Omni-Scale block curtail channel growth and fuse multi-scale features. On the large-scale CODE-15% ECG dataset, EcoScale-Net reduces parameters by 90% and FLOPs by 99% compared with OS-CNN, while raising macro-averaged F1-score by 2.4%. These results demonstrate that EcoScale-Net delivers state-of-the-art accuracy for long-sequence ECG classification at a fraction of the computational cost, enabling real-time deployment on commodity hardware. Our EcoScale-Net code is available in GitHub Link.

**Keywords:** Deep Learning · Signal Processing · ECG Classification


## 1 Introduction

Cardiovascular disease is the leading global cause of death, and 12-lead electrocardiograms (ECGs) remain the most widely used non-invasive modality for detecting cardiac abnormalities. Manual interpretation, however, is error-prone owing to noise and inter-observer variability [1]. These constraints have accelerated interest in automated ECG analysis based on deep learning, a trend already validated in other medical-vision domains [2].



T. Chen et al. (Eds.): EMA4MICCAI 2025 Workshops, LNCS 16318, pp. 184–193, 2026.
https://doi.org/10.1007/978-3-032-13961-0_19

Early ECG classifiers combined convolutional neural networks (CNNs) with recurrent units to exploit both local morphology and long-range rhythm cues, achieving super-human accuracy in some tasks [3]. Subsequent work expanded to multi-lead, multi-label settings [4] and even image-based ECG interpretation [5]. Yet these architectures still depend on manually tuned kernel sizes or dilations, which scale poorly to the long sequences characteristic of ECG signals.

Omni-Scale CNN (OS-CNN) [6] sidesteps manual tuning by enumerating prime-sized kernels—via Goldbach's conjecture—to cover every receptive-field length. Unfortunately, this exhaustive design inflates parameters and FLOPs quadratically with input length, throttling model depth and width; follow-ups such as OSGAN [7] and TF-Net [8] inherit the same bottleneck.

To address these issues, we introduce **_Efficient Convolutional Omni-Scale Network (EcoScale-Net)_**, a hierarchical reformulation of OS-CNN that preserves full receptive-field coverage while eliminating redundancy. This straightforward architectural modification enables the proposed model to leverage Omni-Scale Convolution within a hierarchical framework, progressively reducing the required coverage range at deeper layers. This modification facilitates more comprehensive feature extraction and allows for a deeper and wider design than the OS-CNN. Evaluated on the large-scale CODE-15% dataset [9], EcoScale-Net cuts parameters by 90% and FLOPs by 99% relative to OS-CNN, while boosting macro-averaged F1-score by 2.4%—the best among all compared models. The contributions of this study are as follows:

- We introduce a novel structure (**_EcoScale-Net_**) aimed at efficiently configuring the kernel size for processing long signals such as ECG. Compared to OS-CNN, our method allows for a deeper and wider design using a hierarchical framework, leading to a reduction in parameters by over tenfold and FLOPs by more than 99%, while achieving a 2.4% performance enhancement.
- We demonstrate that applying convolution with a kernel size of 1 before and after each OS stage effectively prevents an explosive increase in channel dimensions while modeling the relationships of each receptive field.
- Despite having lower FLOPs and fewer parameters compared to most other models, it demonstrates the best performance in terms of the average F1-score among the various models we compared.

## 2   Method

### 2.1   Preliminary: Omni-Scale Convolution

Omni-Scale Convolution (OS-Conv) was introduced to avoid _manual_ kernel-size tuning in long signals. Its key idea is to enumerate prime-sized kernels so that every possible receptive-field (RF) length can be obtained by _adding_ three 1-D convolutions.

*Kernel Set.* Let $\mathbb{P}^{(j)}$ be the kernel set at OS stage $j$ ($j = 1, 2, 3$):

$$\mathbb{P}^{(j)} = \begin{cases} \{p \mid p \text{ is prime}, \ 1 \leq p \leq p_k\} & (j = 1, 2), \\ \{1, 2\} & (j = 3), \end{cases} \tag{1}$$

where $p_k$ is the *largest* prime allowed at the first two stages.

*Receptive-Field Coverage.* For $p^{(j)} \in \mathbb{P}^{(j)}$, the RF length produced by the three-stage stack is

$$S = p^{(1)} + p^{(2)} + p^{(3)} - 2. \tag{2}$$

Because any even number $e$ ($\leq 2p_k$) can be written as the sum of two primes ($p^{(1)} + p^{(2)}$) by Goldbach's conjecture, (2) yields

$$\mathbb{S} = \big\{e, \ e - 1 \mid e \in \mathbb{E}\big\}, \qquad \mathbb{E} = \{2, 4, \ldots, 2p_k\},$$

so *all* even and adjacent odd RF lengths up to $2p_k$ are covered.

*Computational Bottleneck.* Enumerating every prime up to $p_k$ incurs $O(\sum_{p \leq p_k} p) = O(p_k^2)$ parameters and FLOPs per stage; thus complexity grows *quadratically* with $p_k$ and linearly with sequence length. For long ECG sequences ($\sim$4k samples) this leads to impractical memory and time costs, preventing deeper or wider models. The remainder of this paper presents a hierarchical reformulation that keeps full RF coverage while eliminating this redundancy.

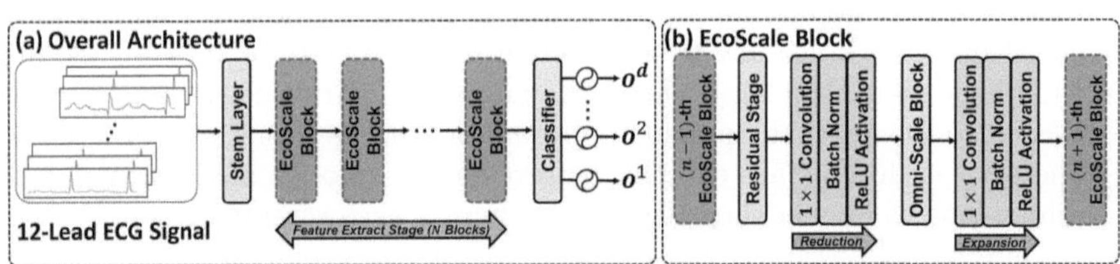


**Fig. 1.** (a) Overview of EcoScale-Net. (b) EcoScale Block which is main module for proposed approach.

## 2.2   Overall Architecture

Our main goal is to *efficiently configure the kernel size to cover the receptive field for signals with arbitrary lengths, leveraging the key advantage of OS convolution.* To achieve main goals and address such impractical issues for long-range 12-ECG, we propose the ***Efficient Convolutional Omni-Scale Network (EcoScale-Net)***, a lightweight reformulation of OS-CNN for multi-label ECG classification (Fig. 1). EcoScale-Net replaces OS-CNN's exhaustive kernel list with a *hierarchical* design and dual $1 \times 1$ bottlenecks, preserving full receptive-field (RF) coverage while cutting parameters and FLOPs. Note that we select same kernel selection strategy with OS-CNN (Algorithm 1). In this paper, we used ResNet-34 [10] as the backbone for the hierarchical architecture.

Let $\mathbf{X} = \{x_1, x_2, \ldots, x_{12}\} \in \mathbb{R}^{12 \times T}$ be the input 12-lead ECG signals where $T$ is the length of the ECG signals. Then, we extract the fundamental features $z_0$ from the input ECG signal $\mathbf{X}$ as follows:

$$z_0 = s(\mathbf{X}) \in \mathbb{R}^{C_0 \times L_0} \tag{3}$$

where $s(\cdot)$ denotes the stem layer, which consists of a convolution with a kernel size of 7 and a stride of 2, followed by batch normalization, ReLU, and max pooling for downsampling. And, $C_0$ and $L_0$ are the numbers of channels and time length of the stem feature $z_0$, respectively. Subsequently, the stem feature $z_0$ is processed through a feature extractor composed of $N$ stages. At $i$-th feature extractor stage, we can represent feature $z_i$ as follows:

$$\begin{cases} h_i = r_i(z_{i-1}) \in \mathbb{R}^{C_i \times L_i} \\ z_i = e_i(h_i) \in \mathbb{R}^{C_i \times L_i} \end{cases} \tag{4}$$

where $r_i(\cdot)$ and $e_i(\cdot)$ are the residual stage and EcoScale block, respectively. For convenience, we let $f_i = e_i \circ r_i$. And, $C_i$ and $L_i$ denote the number of channels and time length at $i$-th feature extractor stage, respectively. The feature $z_N \in \mathbb{R}^{C_N \times L_N}$, which is processed through the final $N$-th stage, is then fed into a classifier $g(\cdot)$ comprising Global Average Pooling (GAP) and a fully connected layer to produce the final prediction $p = g(z_N) \in \mathbb{R}^M$ where $M$ is the number of classes contained in datasets. This overall process can be formally described as follows:

$$\underbrace{p}_{\text{Final Prediction}} = ( \underbrace{g}_{\text{Classifier}} \circ \underbrace{\overset{N}{\underset{i=1}{\bigcirc}} f_i}_{\text{Feature Extractor with } N \text{ stages}} \circ \underbrace{s}_{\text{Stem Layer}} )(\mathbf{X}) \tag{5}$$

where $\overset{N}{\underset{i=1}{\bigcirc}} f_i = f_N \circ f_{N-1} \circ \cdots \circ f_2 \circ f_1$. And, we use the binary cross entropy (BCE) loss $\mathcal{L}_{\text{bce}}$ to optimize the parameters of stem layer $s$, feature extractor $f_i$ for $i = 1, \ldots, N$, and classifier $g$ as follows:

$$\mathcal{L}(p, t) = \sum_{m=1}^{M} \mathcal{L}_{BCE}(p^m, t^m) \tag{6}$$

where $t$ denotes the ground truth label corresponding to $p$. Hence, $t^m$ is $m$-th class label.

---

**Algorithm 1** Selection of kernel sizes

---

**Input:** length to cover $L$
**Output:** Set of kernel sizes $\{1, 2, ..., p_k\}$
**Step 1: Calculate the minimum prime number $p_k$ such that $2 \cdot p_k > L$**
$p_k \leftarrow$ Find minimum prime $p_k$ satisfying $2 \cdot p_k > L$ (Find the prime number such that $2 \cdot p_k$ exceeds the cover length $L$)
**Step 2: Generate the prime number set up to $p_k$**
Prime Set $\leftarrow \{1, 2, 3, ..., p_k\}$ where each number is prime     (Collect all prime numbers up to $p_k$)
**return** Set of kernel sizes

---

### 2.3  EcoScale Residual Block

*Hierarchical RF Cascading.* StageÂăi covers an effective signal length $l_i = L_{i-1}/d_i$ ($d_i$=cumulative down-sampling factor). We choose the smallest prime $p_k^{(i)}$ satisfying $2p_k^{(i)} > l_i$ and set the stage kernel set $\mathbb{P}^{(i)} = \{p \leq p_k^{(i)} \mid p \text{ is prime}\} \cup \{1, 2\}$. Thus deeper stages use *smaller* maximum kernels, avoiding redundant large filters while retaining complete RF coverage.

*Channel-Efficient Fusion.* Each block applies

$$\text{conv}_{1\times1} \rightarrow (\text{parallel OS-Conv}) \rightarrow \text{concat} \rightarrow \text{conv}_{1\times1},$$

where the first $1 \times 1$ bottleneck reduces channels to $C_i/2$ and the second restores them, preventing the quadratic channel explosion observed in vanilla OS-CNN.

### 2.4  Complexity Analysis and Receptive Field of EcoScale-Net

While EcoScale-Net enhances computational efficiency by hierarchically reducing the length to be covered, we conducted an analysis to demonstrate its efficiency compared to OS-CNN, even when maintaining the same feature length. Using the prime number theory ($\sum_{x \in \{1,2,3,5,7,...,p_k\}} x \approx \frac{p_k^2}{\ln(p_k)}$), we can theoretically compare the parameter counts of OS-CNN and EcoScale-Net. For convenience, we consider only the first stage and the number of channels of the input feature signal is $C_i$. Then, the ratio of number of parameters between OS-CNN and

EcoScale-Net can be represented as follows:

$$\frac{(1 \times C_i \times \frac{C_i}{2}) + \sum_{x \in \{1,2,3,5,7,\ldots,p_k\}} (x \times \frac{C_i}{2} \times \frac{C_i}{2})}{\sum_{x \in \{1,2,3,5,7,\ldots,p_k\}} (x \times C_i \times C_i)}$$

$$= \frac{\frac{C_i^2}{2} + \frac{C_i^2}{4} \sum_{x \in \{1,2,3,5,7,\ldots,p_k\}} x}{C_i^2 \sum_{x \in \{1,2,3,5,7,\ldots,p_k\}} x}$$

$$= \frac{\frac{1}{2} + \frac{1}{4} \sum_{x \in \{1,2,3,5,7,\ldots,p_k\}} x}{\sum_{x \in \{1,2,3,5,7,\ldots,p_k\}} x} \tag{7}$$

$$\approx \frac{\frac{1}{2} + \frac{1}{4} \cdot \frac{p_k^2}{\ln(p_k)}}{\frac{p_k^2}{\ln(p_k)}}$$

$$= \frac{2\ln(p_k) + p_k^2}{4p_k^2}$$

With $p_k = 11$ (CODE-15%), EcoScale-Net requires only $\approx 26\%$ of the first-stage parameters of OS-CNN, and the gap widens in deeper layers due to the hierarchical reduction of $p_k^{(i)}$.

A $1 \times 1$ convolution recombines channels at the same timestamp and therefore contributes zero additional span to the receptive field (RF). For a sequence of kernels with lengths $\{l_i\}_{i=1}^n$ (stride 1, no dilation) the cumulative RF is $R = \sum_{i=1}^n l_i - (n-1)$. Hence, the dual $1 \times 1$ bottlenecks that frame every multi-kernel block in EcoScale-Net neither shrink nor reset temporal reach, while still enabling channel-wise projections and fusions.

**Table 1.** Experiment results on the ECG dataset. We also provide number of trainable parameters (M) and FLOPs (G) for each methods.

| Model | Param (M) | FLOPs (G) | Average | | | Exp-ML | | | Exp-BIN | | |
|---|---|---|---|---|---|---|---|---|---|---|---|
| | | | Pre | Rec | F1 | Pre | Rec | F1 | Pre | Rec | F1 |
| GRU [11] | 0.55 | 145.5 | 89.7 | 84.0 | 86.0 | 89.1 | 77.9 | 81.9 | 90.3 | 90.0 | 90.1 |
| Transformer [12] | 87.43 | 64.1 | 88.8 | 86.9 | 87.7 | 85.7 | 81.6 | 83.5 | 91.8 | 92.2 | 91.9 |
| ResNet [10] | 3.85 | 45.9 | 92.4 | 93.2 | 92.8 | 91.8 | 93.2 | 92.5 | 92.9 | 93.1 | 93.0 |
| InceptionTime [13] | 0.49 | 129.4 | - | - | - | 92.8 | 89.5 | 91.1 | - | - | - |
| ResBlk [14] | 6.78 | 124.4 | *93.6* | *94.0* | *93.8* | 92.8 | *93.8* | 93.2 | *94.4* | *94.1* | *94.3* |
| OS-CNN [6] | 84.83 | 22240.2 | - | - | - | 91.6 | 91.4 | 91.5 | - | - | - |
| ResU-Dense [15] | 7.20 | 278.6 | 92.8 | 93.7 | 93.2 | 91.8 | 93.6 | 92.6 | 93.8 | 93.8 | 93.8 |
| ResUNet-LC [16] | 9.98 | 3749.1 | 81.8 | 81.9 | 81.8 | <u>94.1</u> | 92.7 | *93.3* | 69.5 | 71.0 | 70.3 |
| **EcoScale-Net** | 8.55 | 66.9 | <u>94.4</u> | <u>94.4</u> | <u>94.3</u> | *93.6* | <u>94.2</u> | <u>93.9</u> | <u>95.1</u> | <u>94.5</u> | <u>94.7</u> |
| | | | +0.5 | +0.4 | +0.5 | −0.5 | +0.4 | +0.6 | +0.7 | +0.4 | +0.4 |

## 3  Experimental Results

### 3.1  Experimental Settings and Implementation Details

We conducted all experiments in Pytorch 2.1.2 and Python 3.11.5 on a NVIDIA GeForce RTX 4070 GPU and used a publicly available ECG dataset [9] for training and evaluation. Each record is represented as a $12 \times 4096$ signal; the characteristic period of $\sim 256$ samples guided the initial maximum prime kernel size $p_k$ in our architecture. To evaluate EcoScale-Net under different clinical use-cases, we defined *two* tasks, both using identical patient-level splits (90% train, 5% validation, and 5% test, stratified by patient ID to avoid leakage):

(1) **Positive-Only Multi-Label Classification (Exp-ML).** We retained only **positive** ECGs that contain at least one of the six target abnormalities {1dAVb, RBBB, LBBB, SB, AF, ST}. The goal is to predict the *subset* of abnormal labels present in each record. This protocol emphasizes detailed abnormality recognition while forcing the network to focus on pathological patterns without the overwhelming prevalence of normal signals.

(2) **Binary Normal/Abnormal Classification (Exp-BIN).** The full cohort—both normal (negative) and abnormal (positive) recordings—was used. A single binary label indicates whether *any* of the six disorders occurs. This setting reflects a real-world screening scenario in which the foremost question is *"Is this ECG normal?"*

We compared the proposed EcoScale-Net with five general signal classification models (GRU [11], Transformer [12], ResNet [10], InceptionTime [13], and OS-CNN [6]) and three ECG signal abnormal detection models (ResBlk [9], ResU-Dense [15], and ResUNet-LC [16]). Specifically, OS-CNN stacked three OS blocks with residual connections. All models were trained in an end-to-end manner using the AdamW [17] optimizer. The initial learning rate started from $10^{-4}$ and was decreased to $10^{-6}$ using the cosine annealing learning rate scheduler [18], and the training settings were set to a batch size of 64 and epochs of 50. For evaluation, we used three metrics (Precision, Recall, and F1-Score) to measure the performance of each model. In all tables, <u>Red</u> and ***Blue*** are the first and second best performance results, respectively.

**Table 2.** Win counts and average ranks for Precision, Recall, and F1 score for each label.

| Model | Win | Average Rank |
|---|---|---|
| GRU | 1 | 7.9 |
| Transformer | 0 | 8.4 |
| ResNet | 1 | 4.7 |
| InceptionTime | 1 | 5.2 |
| OS-CNN | 1 | 4.9 |
| ResBlk | 2 | 3.3 |
| ResU-Dense | 1 | 4.5 |
| ResUNet-LC | 4 | 3.1 |
| **EcoScale-Net (Ours)** | **8** | **2.2** |

## 3.2  Results Analysis

Table 1 compares eight models with the proposed EcoScale-Net on two complementary tasks derived from the same CODE-15% dataset: (i) a positive-only multi-label setting (**Exp-ML**) and (ii) a binary normal/abnormal setting that includes both negative and positive records (**Exp-BIN**).

EcoScale-Net achieves the best performance in both experimental configurations. In the positive-only multi-label task (Exp-ML) it achieves a F1-score of 93.9%, surpassing the next-strongest CNN baseline (ResUNet-LC) by 0.6% and the computationally intensive OS-CNN by 2.4%. When the problem is reduced to binary normal/abnormal screening (Exp-BIN), it again leads with 94.7% F1-score, maintaining a consistent margin over all eight models. These outcomes verify that the proposed hierarchical receptive-field cascade and dual $1 \times 1$ bottleneck scheme capture both local morphology and global rhythm cues more effectively than conventional single-scale or exhaustive multi-scale alternatives.

The accuracy gains do not come at the expense of efficiency. EcoScale-Net contains 8.6M parameters and 66.9GFLOPs, yielding a 90% parameter reduction and a 99% FLOP reduction relative to OS-CNN, while out-performing lightweight architectures such as InceptionTime by 2.8% in macro-F1. Moreover, it is at least $50\times$ leaner than U-shaped models (e.g., ResUNet-LC) that still fall short in accuracy, thereby establishing the state-of-the-art model for ECG analysis and enabling real-time inference on commodity GPUs and edge devices.

Robustness across diagnostic categories on Exp-ML is evidenced by the win-count statistics in Table 2: EcoScale-Net secures eight per-label victories and the highest mean rank (2.2) for precision, recall, and F1—double the win total of its closest competitor. This uniform superiority indicates that the architecture generalises beyond a single arrhythmia class, delivering clinically reliable predictions across heterogeneous cardiac conditions while satisfying stringent computational budgets.

**Table 3.** Ablation study for EcoScale-Net. C1D (1) and '*' denote a convolution 1D with kernel size 1 and the model without applying C1D (1), respectively.

| Model | OS Conv | C1D (1) | Performance | Param (M) | FLOPs (G) |
|---|---|---|---|---|---|
| Backbone | × | × | 92.5 | 3.85 | 45.9 |
| EcoScale-Net* | ✓ | × | 93.2 | 9.70 | 167.7 |
| **EcoScale-Net** | ✓ | ✓ | **93.9** | 8.55 | 66.9 |

## 3.3  Ablation Study

In this section, we conducted an ablation study on the abnormal signal classification for 12-lead ECG signals to demonstrate the effectiveness of the proposed module. As listed in Table 3, our approach, which utilized both OS Convolution (OS Conv) and convolution with kernel size 1 (C1D (1)) exhibited the best performance with reasonable computational complexity. We initially observed that the EcoScale-Net without C1D (1), achieved a 0.7% performance improvement compared to the backbone, but with significantly higher complexity, including a 60% and 72% increase in the number of parameters and FLOPs, respectively. Conversely, applying C1D (1) at each OS stage reduced the number of parameters by 1.2M and decreased FLOPs by 100G while achieving a 0.7% performance improvement. These results indicate that C1D (1) effectively models the dependencies of each receptive field, while mitigating the exponential increase in dimensions caused by channel concatenation.

## 4    Conclusion and Future Works

We have introduced EcoScale-Net, a hierarchical omni-scale convolutional network that attains complete receptive-field coverage for long 12-lead ECG sequences while curbing the quadratic cost growth of prior OS-CNNs through stage-wise kernel capping and dual convolutional bottlenecks. On the CODE-15% benchmark, EcoScale-Net delivered state-of-the-art macro-F1 scores— 93.9% for positive-only multi-label diagnosis and 94.7% for binary screening— using 90% fewer parameters and 99% fewer floating-point operations than the original OS-CNN, thereby establishing a new accuracy–efficiency Pareto frontier suitable for real-time, low-power clinical deployment.

Nevertheless, EcoScale-Net still faces several limitations that we are actively working to overcome. First, we will conduct comprehensive backbone-swap ablations and benchmark the model against additional lightweight architectures— such as MobileNet-v4-TS and MiniRocket—to verify the generality of our design. Second, we will validate the network on diverse public ECG datasets (PTB-XL, Chapman-SHA, and Shaoxing) to assess robustness across patient demographics, noise profiles, and recording hardware. In parallel, future work will extend the omni-scale paradigm to other biosignals, incorporate adaptive kernel selection, and enable on-device continual learning, thereby expanding the translational impact of EcoScale-Net in both clinical and resource-constrained environments.

**Acknowledgements.** This work was supported in part by Institute of Information and communications Technology Planning & Evaluation (IITP) grant funded by the Korea government (MSIT) (No. RS-2022-00155915, Artificial Intelligence Convergence Innovation Human Resources Development (Inha University).

**Disclosure of Interests.** The authors have no competing interests to declare that are relevant to the content of this article.

## References

1. Chung, C.T., et al.: Clinical significance, challenges and limitations in using artificial intelligence for electrocardiography-based diagnosis. Int. J. Arrhythmia **23**(1), 24 (2022)

2. Nam, J.-H., Syazwany, N.S., Kim, S.J., Lee, S.-C.: Modality-agnostic domain generalizable medical image segmentation by multi-frequency in multi-scale attention. In: Proceedings of the IEEE/CVF Conference on Computer Vision and Pattern Recognition, pp. 11480–11491 (2024)
3. Tan, J.H., et al.: Application of stacked convolutional and long short-term memory network for accurate identification of cad ECG signals. Comput. Biol. Med. **94**, 19–26 (2018)
4. Chen, Y.-J., Liu, C.L., Tseng, V.S., Hu, Y.F., Chen, S.A.: Large-scale classification of 12-lead ECG with deep learning. In: 2019 IEEE EMBS International Conference on Biomedical & Health Informatics (BHI), pp. 1–4. IEEE (2019)
5. Nam, J.H., Park, S.H., Kim, S.J., Lee, S.C.: Vizecgnet: visual ECG image network for cardiovascular diseases classification with multi-modal training and knowledge distillation. arXiv preprint arXiv:2408.02888 (2024)
6. Tang, W., Long, G., Liu, L., Zhou, T., Blumenstein, M., Jiang, J.: Omni-scale CNNs: a simple and effective kernel size configuration for time series classification. In: International Conference on Learning Representations (2022)
7. Chen, C., Jin, B., Che, C., Li, R.: OSGAN: omni scale and global-aware ECG arrhythmia diagnostic network. Biomed. Signal Process. Control **96**, 106602 (2024)
8. Lei, T., Li, J., Yang, K.: Time and frequency-domain feature fusion network for multivariate time series classification. Expert Syst. Appl. **252**, 124155 (2024)
9. Ribeiro, A.H., et al.: Code-15%: a large scale annotated dataset of 12-lead ECGs. Zenodo Jun **9** (2021)
10. He, K., Zhang, X., Ren, S., Sun, J.: Deep residual learning for image recognition. In: Proceedings of the IEEE Conference on Computer Vision and Pattern Recognition, pp. 770–778 (2016)
11. Chung, J., Gulcehre, C., Cho, K., Bengio, Y.: Empirical evaluation of gated recurrent neural networks on sequence modeling. In: NIPS 2014 Workshop on Deep Learning, December 2014 (2014)
12. Vaswani, A., et al.: Attention is all you need. In: Guyon, I., et al. (eds.) Advances in Neural Information Processing Systems, vol. 30. Curran Associates, Inc. (2017)
13. Fawaz, H.I., et al.: Inceptiontime: finding alexnet for time series classification. Data Mining Knowl. Discov. **34**(6), 1936–1962 (2020)
14. Ribeiro, A.H., et al.: Automatic diagnosis of the 12-lead ECG using a deep neural network. Nat. Commun. **11**(1), 1760 (2020)
15. Hwang, S., Cha, J., Heo, J., Cho, S., Park, Y.: Multi-label ECG abnormality classification using a combined resnet-densenet architecture with resu blocks. In: 2023 IEEE EMBS Special Topic Conference on Data Science and Engineering in Healthcare, Medicine and Biology, pp. 111–112 (2023)
16. Hwang, S., Cha, J., Heo, J., Cho, S., Park, Y.: Multi-label abnormality classification from 12-lead ECG using a 2D residual U-net. In: ICASSP 2024-2024 IEEE International Conference on Acoustics, Speech and Signal Processing (ICASSP), pp. 2265–2269. IEEE (2024)
17. Loshchilov, I., Hutter, F.: Decoupled weight decay regularization, arXiv preprint arXiv:1711.05101 (2017)
18. Loshchilov, I., Hutter, F.: SGDR: stochastic gradient descent with warm restarts, arXiv preprint arXiv:1608.03983 (2016)

# Impact of Clinical Image Quality on Efficient Foundation Model Finetuning


Yucheng Tang[1,2(✉)], Pawel Rajwa[3], Alexander Ng[3], Yipei Wang[1,2], Wen Yan[1,2], Natasha Thorley[4], Aqua Asif[3], Clare Allen[5], Louise Dickinson[5], Francesco Giganti[3,5], Shonit Punwani[4,5], Daniel C. Alexander[1,7], Veeru Kasivisvanathan[3,6], and Yipeng Hu[1,2]

[1] Hawkes Institute, University College London, London, UK
[2] Department of Medical Physics and Biomedical Engineering, University College London, London, UK
yucheng.tang.24@ucl.ac.uk
[3] Division of Surgery and Interventional Science, University College London, London, UK
[4] Centre of Medical Imaging, University College London, London, UK
[5] Department of Radiology, UCLH NHS Foundation Trust, London, UK
[6] Department of Urology, UCLH NHS Foundation Trust, London, UK
[7] Department of Computer Science, University College London, London, UK



**Abstract.** Foundation models in medical imaging have shown promising label efficiency, achieving high performance on downstream tasks using only a fraction of the annotated data otherwise required. In this study, we evaluate this potential in the context of prostate multiparametric MRI using ProFound, a recently developed domain-specific vision foundation model pretrained on large-scale prostate MRI datasets. We investigate the impact of variable image quality on the label-efficient finetuning, by quantifying the generalisability of the finetuned models. We conduct a comprehensive set of experiments by systematically varying the ratios of high- and low-quality images in the finetuning and evaluation sets. Our findings indicate that image quality distribution and its finetune-and-test mismatch significantly affect model performance. In particular: a) Varying the ratio of high- to low-quality images between finetuning and test sets leads to notable differences in downstream performance; and b) The presence of sufficient high-quality images in the finetuning set is critical for maintaining strong performance, whilst the importance of matched finetuning and testing distribution varies between different downstream tasks, such as automated radiology reporting and prostate cancer detection. Importantly, experimental results also show that, although finetuning requires significantly less labeled data compared to training from scratch when the quality ratio is consistent, this label efficiency is not independent of the image quality distribution. For example, we show cases that, without sufficient high-quality images in finetuning, finetuned models may fail to outperform those without pretraining. This, in turn, highlights the importance of assessing (and potentially aligning) image quality distributions between finetuning and deployment, and the need for quality standards in finetuning data for specific downstream tasks.




T. Chen et al. (Eds.): EMA4MICCAI 2025 Workshops, LNCS 16318, pp. 194–204, 2026.
https://doi.org/10.1007/978-3-032-13961-0_20

Using ProFound as a concrete example, this study demonstrates the value of quantifying image quality and its distribution in both finetuning and deployment to fully realise the data and compute efficiency benefits of foundation models.

**Keywords:** Foundation Model · Image Quality · Prostate MRI

## 1   Introduction

Foundation models have shown strong transferability and generalization in medical image analysis [25], and have been applied across different anatomical regions and imaging modalities [9], such as MultiTalent [20] for multi-organ segmentation in abdominal computed tomography (CT), SAM-Med3D [21], which adapts the Segment Anything Model [26] to 3D medical images, SegVol [5] for general CT segmentation tasks, and Adam [18] for organ identification in chest X-rays and retinal images. Based on these developments, some foundation model-based studies have emerged for prostate magnetic resonance imaging (MRI) related tasks, including cancer detection [22], modality classification [4], gland segmentation [10], and cancer segmentation [27]. However, despite their success, the systematic examination of how prostate MRI quality affects the transferability and performance of foundation models in downstream tasks remains underexplored. In clinical practice, where variability in prostate MRI quality is common across different centers, scanners, and scanning protocols [23], key questions arise: Can foundation models adapt effectively to data with varying quality levels? Does the transferability and performance of foundation models across image quality levels vary depending on the downstream tasks?

Previous work focused on the quality assessment of prostate MRIs, ranging from traditional feature-based approaches to deep learning-based quality classifiers [17]. These studies examined the clinical impact of T2-weighted (T2W) image quality on diagnostic outcomes, including cancer detection [11] and the evaluation of extraprostatic extension [12]. Subsequent studies applied the Prostate Imaging Quality Scoring System (PI-QUAL) [7], the international standard for evaluating prostate MRI quality, to multimodal prostate MRI scans [3] and explored the correlation between PI-QUAL scores and the detection rates of clinically significant prostate cancer at biopsy [2].

In this work, we analyze and reveal how prostate MRI quality affects the transferability and performance of finetuned foundation models across downstream tasks. Specifically, we utilize a publicly available, multi-task compatible prostate MRI foundation model, ProFound[1], and then fine-tune it using the PRIME dataset [1], a multi-institutional collection with PI-QUAL scores collected from 21 centers. We evaluated the finetuned model on four tasks: 1) Prostate imaging-reporting and data system (PI-RADS) score [19] 5-class classification (scores 1–5), 2) PI-RADS score binary classification ($\geq 3$ vs. $<3$), 3)

---

[1] https://github.com/pipiwang/ProFound.

PI-RADS score binary classification ($\geq$4 vs. <4), 4) Gleason score [6] binary classification ($\geq$3+4 vs. <3+4).

Our contributions are as follows: First, we curated the PRIME dataset from 21 centers, together with image quality PI-QUAL scoring. Second, after preprocessing of the data, with the image quality labels, radiological and histopathological disease labels, we finetuned the ProFound model using the preprocessed PRIME dataset across different downstream tasks. Furthermore, we compared and analyzed the generalisability of this independent data set by varying the ratios of high-quality and low-quality images used in both finetuning and testing, thus concluding the importance of quantifying image quality to the label efficiency due to foundation models.

## 2    Method

We utilize the ProFound-alpha model, a recently developed and released foundation model for prostate multiparametric MRI that was pretrained on large-scale datasets including PI-CAI [16], Prostate-X [16], as well as on other private datasets. It adopts a ConvNeXt V2 Tiny [24] backbone pretrained via masked autoencoding (MAE) [8] to learn generalizable imaging features. Model architecture and pretraining details are available in the official repository[9]. In addition, the ProFound repository provides finetuning code for different downstream tasks, which we used for finetuning in this study with the same hyperparameter configurations unless specified. The data preprocessing and further finetuning details are described in Sect. 2.1 and Sect. 2.2, respectively.

### 2.1    Data Preprocessing

The private PRIME dataset [1] contains 483 cases of prostate MRI with PI-QUAL scores assigned by expert radiologists (v2 [15]), including 452 cases of high quality (PI-QUAL $\geq$ 4, possible to rule out all significant lesions) and 31 cases of low quality (PI-QUAL < 4, not possible to rule in all significant lesions). We acknowledge that the dataset is imbalanced and relatively small, particularly for low-quality scans; however, this reflects the natural prevalence of high-quality imaging in clinical workflows. For the PRIME dataset used in finetuning, we applied standardized preprocessing to ensure spatial consistency across multi-center scans. First, from each case, we selected three image sequences: (1) the diffusion-weighted imaging (DWI) sequence with the highest b-value (typically b=2000), (2) the axial T2W image with the highest in-plane resolution, and (3) the corresponding apparent diffusion coefficient (ADC) map. The transverse T2W image was used as the spatial reference for subsequent imaging coordinate alignment and resampling. We then aligned the DWI and ADC maps to the T2W image reference using an inter-sequence coordinate transformation with SimpleITK library [13], ensuring consistent image origin, orientation, and direction across modalities. After alignment, images from the three modalities were resampled to a uniform voxel spacing of $0.5 \times 0.5 \times 1.0$ mm$^3$. Finally, each resampled volume was center-cropped and symmetrically zero-padded to a fixed spatial size of $224 \times 224 \times 64$ voxels to ensure consistent input sizes consistent with the pretrained ProFound model.

## 2.2  Foundation Model Finetuning for Downstream Tasks

Following the data preprocessing, we finetuned the ProFound foundation model on the processed data. The finetuning tasks are formulated as binary or multiclass classification problems to predict clinically relevant categories. Specifically, we address four downstream tasks: 1) multi-class classification of the PI-RADS scores into five categories corresponding to scores 1 through 5, aiming to stratify prostate lesions by their likelihood of clinically significant cancer; 2) binary classification of the PI-RADS scores, distinguishing cases with scores $\geq 3$ vs. $<$ 3, which is generally considered the threshold for suspicious lesions warranting further investigation; 3) binary classification of the PI-RADS scores, distinguishing cases with scores $\geq 4$ vs. $< 4$, which is considered the threshold for lesions at greater risk; and 4) binary classification of the Gleason scores, separating $\geq$ 3+4 from $<$ 3+4, which helps differentiate more aggressive prostate cancers that often demand active treatment from less aggressive cases.

Specifically, for each finetuning setting, a classification model is constructed by attaching a fully connected classification head, composed of two linear layers with ReLU activation, to the pretrained ConvNeXt V2 Tiny backbone. During finetuning, all model parameters are trainable. We apply layer-wise learning rate decay to the backbone, assigning smaller learning rates to layers closer to the input and higher rates to deeper layers. For supervision, we adopt the cross entropy loss as the loss function in finetuning stage, which is defined as in Eq. 1.

$$\mathcal{L}_{fine} = -\frac{1}{N} \sum_{n=1}^{N} \sum_{c=1}^{C} y_{n,c} \log\left(\frac{\exp(\hat{y}_{n,c})}{\sum_{k=1}^{C} \exp(\hat{y}_{n,k})}\right) \tag{1}$$

where $N$ is the number of samples, $C$ is the number of classes, $\hat{y}_{n,c}$ is the predicted logit for the $c$-th class of the $n$-th sample, and $y_{n,c}$ is the one-hot encoded ground truth label. This finetuning scheme enables the foundation model to adapt to the specific data and task while leveraging the pretrained spatial feature representations learned from large-scale data.

## 3  Experiments and Results

**Implementation Datails.** The ProFound model was pretrained for 800 epochs under a masked autoencoding framework with a mask ratio of 0.6, and we used the checkpoint of the ProFound model at the $800^{th}$ epoch for downstream finetuning. The finetuning process was conducted using PyTorch [14], and was run for 100 epochs on the preprocessed PRIME dataset with a batch size of 8, an input size of $224 \times 224 \times 64$, and a maximum learning rate of $1 \times 10^{-4}$ assigned to the deepest layer group. We adopted a layer-wise learning rate decay strategy with a decay factor of 0.9 applied to groups of three consecutive layers, where each shallower group receives a learning rate 0.9 times that of the next deeper group. All experiments were conducted on NVIDIA Quadro GV100 GPUs, each with 24 GB of memory.

**Finetuning Data Settings.** To evaluate the transferability and performance of the finetuned foundation model under different data quality scenarios, we adopted three data settings for finetuning: (1) Mixed-finetuned: using both high and low-quality data (180 high-quality and 16 low-quality cases), followed by affine augmentation to produce 540 cases in each group. The resulting model is referred to as the 'mixed-finetuned model' in the following text; (2) HQ-finetuned: using 180 high-quality cases augmented to 1080 cases. The resulting model is referred to as the 'HQ-finetuned model' in the following text; and (3) LQ-finetuned: using 16 low-quality cases augmented to 1080 cases. The resulting model is referred to as the 'LQ-finetuned model' in the following text. The affine transformation was applied jointly to all three modalities (T2W image, ADC, and DWI) of each patient case, using random rotation (up to $15°$) and translation (up to $0.15\,\mathrm{mm}$) while preserving spatial alignment.

**Testing Data Settings.** For testing, we fixed the size of the test set to 60 cases and varied the sampling ratio of high-quality to low-quality data at five levels: 14:1, 11:1, 8:1, 5:1, and 2:1. For each ratio, samples were drawn from the remaining cases not used in training. We performed five independent samplings per ratio and reported the average and standard deviation of evaluation metrics.

**Evaluation Metrics.** For binary classification tasks aimed at identifying clinically significant lesions (e.g., PI-RADS $\geq 3$ vs. $< 3$ or $\geq 4$ vs. $< 4$, Gleason score $\geq 3+4$ vs. $< 3+4$), we evaluated model performance using accuracy (ACC) and area under the ROC curve (AUC). For multi-class classification tasks (e.g., PI-RADS 1–5), we reported top-1 accuracy (T1-ACC) and AUC.

**PI-RADS Score 5-Class Classification.** As shown in Fig. 1(a), and Fig. 2(a), both the mixed-finetuned model and the HQ-finetuned model exhibit a decreasing performance across all three metrics as the proportion of low-quality data increases in the test set, with the HQ-finetuned model showing a significantly steeper decline due to the difference between the finetuning and testing data distributions. In contrast, the LQ-finetuned model demonstrates improved T1-ACC under these conditions, due to better alignment between its finetuning and testing data distributions. Despite these trends, the mixed-finetuned model consistently outperforms the LQ-finetuned model across all test settings, with statistical significance confirmed by paired t-tests ($p < 0.05$). Therefore, finetuning with a combination of high- and low-quality data is recommended to ensure better performance stability across variable test conditions.

**PI-RADS Score Binary Classification ($\geq$ 3 vs. <3).** As shown in Fig. 1(b), and Fig. 2(b), the mixed-finetuned model exhibits performance degradation as the proportion of low-quality data increases in the test set, while

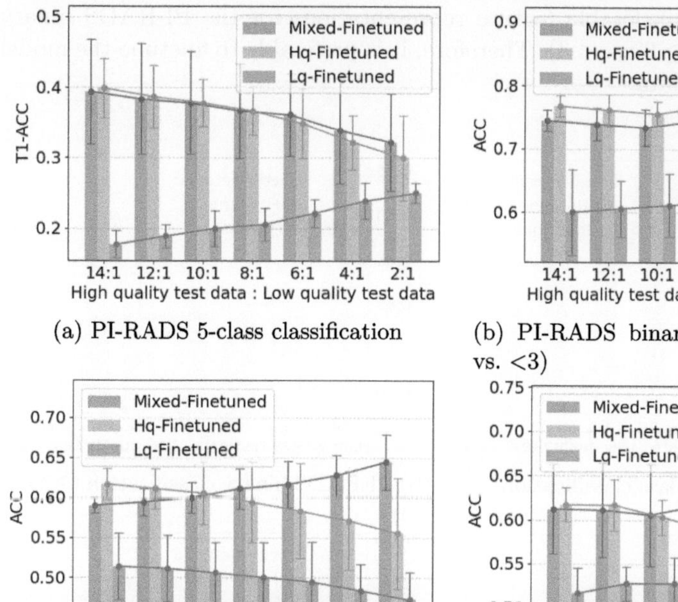
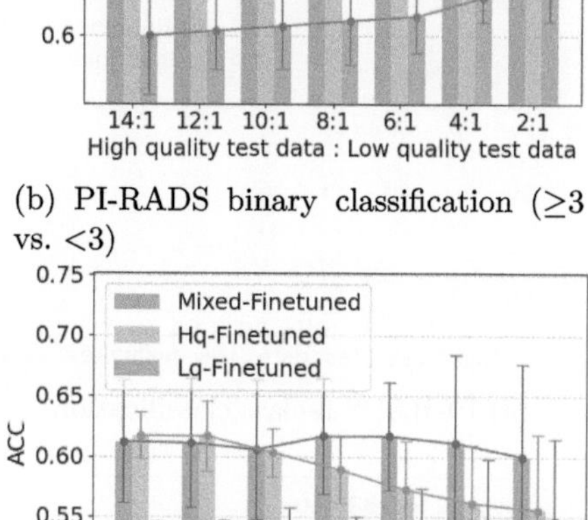

(a) PI-RADS 5-class classification

(b) PI-RADS binary classification ($\geq 3$ vs. $<3$)

(c) PI-RADS binary classification ($\geq 4$ vs. $<4$)

(d) Gleason score binary classification ($\geq 3+4$ vs. $<3+4$)

**Fig. 1.** Experimental results for the four downstream tasks. The evaluation metric is accuracy (and top 1 accuracy for 5-class classification). In the figures, the blue bars, line, and error bars represent the test accuracy (with standard deviation) of the foundation model finetuned on both high- and low-quality data. The orange elements represent the model finetuned on high-quality data only, and the green ones correspond to the model finetuned on low-quality data only. (Color figure online)

the LQ-finetuned model shows improved performance as the test set becomes increasingly dominated by low-quality data. These trends are similar to those observed in the PI-RADS 5-class classification task. Notably, the HQ-finetuned model maintains stable performance even as the proportion of low-quality data increases in the test set. Furthermore, in this task, the mixed-finetuned model only significantly outperforms the LQ-finetuned model when the test set contains a high-to-low quality ratio of at least 8:1, with statistical significance confirmed by paired t-tests ($p < 0.05$). As the test distribution becomes dominated by low-quality samples, the performance of finetuning on mixed data decreases quickly. In contrast, the HQ-finetuned model consistently outperforms the LQ-finetuned model across all test settings, with statistical significance ($p < 0.05$), and even surpasses the mixed-finetuned model under most conditions. This suggests that incorporating low-quality data during finetuning compromises the model's transferability and generalization ability, and that high-quality data alone provides more stable and transferable feature representations for the PI-RADS binary classification task ($\geq 3$ vs. $< 3$). Therefore, it is preferable to finetune the model using high-quality data.

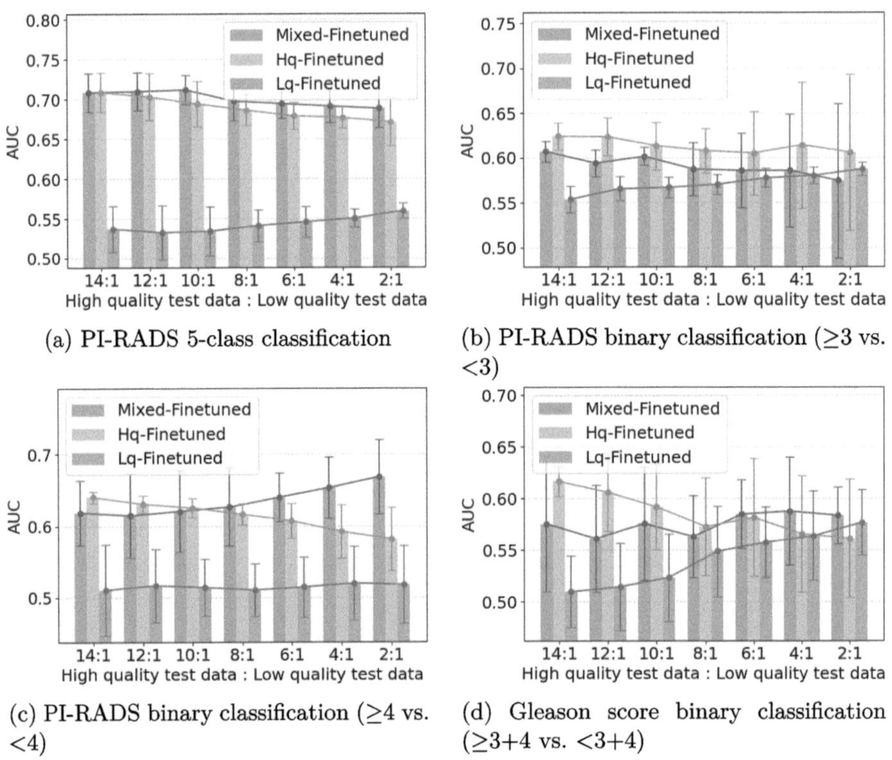

(a) PI-RADS 5-class classification

(b) PI-RADS binary classification ($\geq$3 vs. <3)

(c) PI-RADS binary classification ($\geq$4 vs. <4)

(d) Gleason score binary classification ($\geq$3+4 vs. <3+4)

**Fig. 2.** Experimental results for the four downstream tasks. The evaluation metric is AUC. Color and marker conventions are the same as in Fig. 1.

**PI-RADS Score Binary Classification ($\geq 4$ vs. <4).** The results of the PI-RADS binary classification task ($\geq 4$ vs. $< 4$) are shown in Fig. 1(c), and Fig. 2(c). Surprisingly, unlike other tasks, the mixed-finetuned model shows improved generalization as more low-quality data was added to the test set. In contrast, the LQ-finetuned model achieves very poor test metrics, indicating that it fails to generalize to test sets that contain mostly high-quality data. The HQ-finetuned model also shows performance degradation as the proportion of low-quality data increases due to the difference between finetuning and testing data distributions. Moreover, the mixed-finetuned model significantly outperforms the LQ-finetuned model across all test settings, and also outperforms the HQ-finetuned model when the high-to-low quality ratio is 2:1, with paired t-tests confirming statistical significance ($p < 0.05$). This suggests that, for the

PI-RADS binary classification task ($\geq$ 4 vs. < 4), it is important to include low-quality data along with high-quality data during training to cover the full range of image variability and improve model robustness.

**Gleason Score Binary Classification ($\geq$ 3+4 vs. <3+4).** The results of the Gleason score binary classification task ($\geq$ 3+4 vs. < 3+4) are shown in Fig. 1(d) and Fig. 2(d). The model finetuned on the mixed data demonstrates relatively stable generalization performance, showing limited sensitivity to increasing proportions of low-quality test data. In contrast, the HQ-finetuned and LQ-finetuned models perform well only within their respective familiar testing data distributions, but struggle to generalize across quality levels. Specifically, only when the high-to-low quality ratio in the test set exceeds 10:1, the HQ-finetuned model significantly outperforms the LQ-finetuned model, with statistical significance confirmed by paired t-tests (p < 0.05). Moreover, this task shows higher variance in performance compared to the others, suggesting less consistent predictions, due to the inherent subjectivity and complexity of Gleason grading. These findings indicate that, for the Gleason score binary classification task, both high- and low-quality finetuning data are necessary. While each quality-specific model performs well in its own testing data's quality level, their limited transferability highlights the need for finetuning data that spans the full levels of image quality to improve robustness.

**Comparisons with Models Without Pretrained Weights.** To investigate the transferability of the foundation model, we conducted experiments by training models from scratch, using randomly initialized weights but keeping the same model architecture and configurations as finetuning. Specifically, we trained models for the four tasks using the same datasets as in the finetuning setup, which demonstrated satisfactory performance in the experiments before. Experimental results demonstrate that models trained from scratch converge more slowly, typically requiring 15 to 20 epochs to reach convergence, in contrast to 5 to 10 epochs for finetuning models. Furthermore, training from scratch using mixed and high-quality-only datasets led to performance drops ranging from 7.72% to 16.77% in ACC and 2.63% to 9.38% in AUC across different tasks, training settings, and high-to-low quality test ratios (as used in the finetuning setup). These findings highlight the superior transferability of the foundation model, showing that its pretrained knowledge offers a strong initialization that not only speeds up convergence but also leads to consistently better performance across multiple classification tasks and varying data quality conditions. However, the results that support label efficiency are conditioned on consistent image quality ratios between models with and without pretraining. When comparing models with different imaging quality ratios, such gains in performance (and/or label efficiency) depend on the image quality distribution. For example, as more low quality images were included in the finetuning set, the average accuracy gain from pretraining (across different tasks and high-to-low quality test ratios) dropped from +12.55% with high-quality-only data to +8.34% with mixed data, and became negative (−0.31%) when using only low-quality data.

## 4    Conclusion and Discussion

In this work, we reveal the impact of prostate MRI quality on finetuning a foundation model. Our results show that models finetuned only on low-quality data consistently perform worse across all tasks as such data leads to irreversible information loss and artifact learning, degrading feature representations. This, in turn, disrupts clinical workflows and increases the risk of missed diagnoses and unnecessary biopsies. While including high-quality data in finetuning generally improves performance gain due to pretraining. Moreover, such an impact from image quality to downstream performance is also task-specific. Among them, Gleason score binary classification task suffers the most due to its reliance on fine microstructural features, whereas PI-RADS ($\geq$4 vs. <4) classification is comparatively robust, benefiting from more resilient texture-based cues. Adaptive fine-tuning may offer a potential solution to such task-specific challenges. Through the example of ProFound, our findings highlight that rigorous quantification of image quality and its distribution is critical to unlocking the full potential of foundation models in terms of data and computational efficiency. Future work will benefit from expanding both the task diversity (e.g., segmentation or report generation) and model tuning strategies (e.g., adapter-based fine-tuning or quality-aware sampling).

**Disclosure of Interests.** The authors have no competing interests to declare that are relevant to the content of this article.

## References


1. Asif, A., et al.: Comparing biparametric to multiparametric MRI in the diagnosis of clinically significant prostate cancer in biopsy-naive men (PRIME): a prospective, international, multicentre, non-inferiority within-patient, diagnostic yield trial protocol. BMJ Open **13**(4), e070280 (2023)
2. Brembilla, G., et al.: Impact of prostate imaging quality (PI-QUAL) score on the detection of clinically significant prostate cancer at biopsy. Eur. J. Radiol. **164**, 110849 (2023)
3. Cheng, Y., Zhang, L., Wu, X., Zou, Y., Niu, Y., Wang, L.: Impact of prostate MRI image quality on diagnostic performance for clinically significant prostate cancer (CSPCA). Abdom. Radiol. **49**(11), 4113–4124 (2024)
4. Denner, S., et al.: Fine-tuning vision foundation models for multi-modal prostate MR sequence classification. In: Medical Imaging with Deep Learning-Short Papers (2025)
5. Du, Y., Bai, F., Huang, T., Zhao, B.: Segvol: universal and interactive volumetric medical image segmentation. Adv. Neural. Inf. Process. Syst. **37**, 110746–110783 (2024)
6. Epstein, J.I.: An update of the gleason grading system. J. Urol. **183**(2), 433–440 (2010)
7. Giganti, F., et al.: Prostate imaging quality (PI-QUAL): a new quality control scoring system for multiparametric magnetic resonance imaging of the prostate from the precision trial. Eur. Urol. Oncol. **3**(5), 615–619 (2020)

8. He, K., Chen, X., Xie, S., Li, Y., Dollár, P., Girshick, R.: Masked autoencoders are scalable vision learners. In: Proceedings of the IEEE/CVF Conference on Computer Vision and Pattern Recognition, pp. 16000–16009 (2022)
9. Khan, W., Leem, S., See, K.B., Wong, J.K., Zhang, S., Fang, R.: A comprehensive survey of foundation models in medicine. IEEE Rev. Biomed. Eng. (2025)
10. Kim, H., Butoi, V.I., Dalca, A.V., Sabuncu, M.R.: Empirical analysis of a segmentation foundation model in prostate imaging. In: International Conference on Medical Image Computing and Computer-Assisted Intervention, pp. 140–150. Springer (2023)
11. Lin, Y., et al.: Deep learning-based T2-weighted MR image quality assessment and its impact on prostate cancer detection rates. J. Magn. Reson. Imaging $59(6)$, 2215–2223 (2024)
12. Lin, Y., et al.: Deep learning-based image quality assessment: impact on detection accuracy of prostate cancer extraprostatic extension on mri. Abdom. Radiol. $49(8)$, 2891–2901 (2024)
13. Lowekamp, B.C., Chen, D.T., Ibáñez, L., Blezek, D.: The design of simpleitk. Front. Neuroinform. $7$, 45 (2013)
14. Paszke, A.: Pytorch: an imperative style, high-performance deep learning library. arXiv preprint arXiv:1912.01703 (2019)
15. de Rooij, M., et al.: PI-QUAL version 2: an update of a standardised scoring system for the assessment of image quality of prostate MRI. Eur. Radiol. $34(11)$, 7068–7079 (2024)
16. Saha, A., et al.: Artificial intelligence and radiologists at prostate cancer detection in MRI—the PI-CAI challenge. In: Medical Imaging with Deep Learning, short paper track (2023)
17. Stępień, I., Oszust, M.: A brief survey on no-reference image quality assessment methods for magnetic resonance images. J. Imaging $8(6)$, 160 (2022)
18. Taher, M.R.H., Gotway, M.B., Liang, J.: Representing part-whole hierarchies in foundation models by learning localizability composability and decomposability from anatomy via self supervision. In: Proceedings of the IEEE/CVF Conference on Computer Vision and Pattern Recognition, pp. 11269–11281 (2024)
19. Turkbey, B., et al.: Prostate imaging reporting and data system version 2.1: 2019 update of prostate imaging reporting and data system version 2. Eur. Urol. $76(3)$, 340–351 (2019)
20. Ulrich, C., Isensee, F., Wald, T., Zenk, M., Baumgartner, M., Maier-Hein, K.H.: Multi-dataset approach to medical image segmentation: Multitalent. In: BVM Workshop, p. 78. Springer (2024)
21. Wang, H., et al.: Sam-med3d: towards general-purpose segmentation models for volumetric medical images. In: European Conference on Computer Vision, pp. 51–67. Springer (2025)
22. Wilson, P.F., et al.: Prostnfound: integrating foundation models with ultrasound domain knowledge and clinical context for robust prostate cancer detection. In: International Conference on Medical Image Computing and Computer-Assisted Intervention, pp. 499–509. Springer (2024)
23. Woernle, A., et al.: Picture perfect: the status of image quality in prostate MRI. J. Magn. Reson. Imaging $59(6)$, 1930–1952 (2024)
24. Woo, S., et al.: Convnext v2: co-designing and scaling convnets with masked autoencoders. In: Proceedings of the IEEE/CVF Conference on Computer Vision and Pattern Recognition, pp. 16133–16142 (2023)
25. Zhang, S., Metaxas, D.: On the challenges and perspectives of foundation models for medical image analysis. Med. Image Anal. $91$, 102996 (2024)

26. Zhang, Y., Shen, Z., Jiao, R.: Segment anything model for medical image segmentation: current applications and future directions. Comput. Biol. Med. 108238 (2024)
27. Zhang, Y., et al.: Generalist medical foundation model improves prostate cancer segmentation from multimodal MRI images. NPJ Digit. Med. **8**(1), 1–11 (2025)

# Continual Multiple Instance Learning for Hematologic Disease Diagnosis

Zahra Ebrahimi[1,2,3], Raheleh Salehi[1,4], Nassir Navab[5], Carsten Marr[1(✉)], and Ario Sadafi[1,5(✉)]

[1] Institute of AI for Health, Helmholtz Munich, Neuherberg, Germany
carsten.marr@helmholtz-munich.de
[2] TUM School of Computation, Information and Technology, Technical University Munich, Munich, Germany
[3] Faculty of Mathematics, Computer Science and Statistics, Ludwig-Maximilians-Universität München (LMU), Munich, Germany
[4] Institute of Chemical Epigenetics, Faculty of Chemistry and Pharmacy, Ludwig-Maximilians-Universität München (LMU), Munich, Germany
[5] Computer Aided Medical Procedures, Technical University of Munich, Munich, Germany
ario.sadafi@helmholtz-munich.de

**Abstract.** The dynamic environment of laboratories and clinics, with streams of data arriving on a daily basis, requires regular updates of trained machine learning models for consistent performance. Continual learning is supposed to help train models without catastrophic forgetting. However, state-of-the-art methods are ineffective for multiple instance learning (MIL), which is often used in single-cell-based hematologic disease diagnosis (e.g., leukemia detection). Here, we propose the first continual learning method tailored specifically to MIL. Our method is rehearsal-based over a selection of single instances from various bags. We use a combination of the instance attention score and distance from the bag mean and class mean vectors to carefully select which samples and instances to store in exemplary sets from previous tasks, preserving the diversity of the data. Using the real-world input of one month of data from a leukemia laboratory, we study the effectiveness of our approach in a class incremental scenario, comparing it to well-known continual learning methods. We show that our method considerably outperforms state-of-the-art methods, providing the first continual learning approach for MIL. This enables the adaptation of models to shifting data distributions over time, such as those caused by changes in disease occurrence or underlying genetic alterations.

**Keywords:** Continual learning · Multiple instance learning · Hematologic diseases · Microscopy

## 1 Introduction

Computer-aided diagnosis systems based on deep learning have achieved human-level performance in high-throughput analysis of large amounts of image data


T. Chen et al. (Eds.): EMA4MICCAI 2025 Workshops, LNCS 16318, pp. 205–214, 2026.
https://doi.org/10.1007/978-3-032-13961-0_21

[2,7,12,14]. Multiple instance learning (MIL) plays a central role in medical image analysis. In MIL, a bag of instances is collected from a patient, and a single diagnosis is associated with all of them. These instances can be single cells or histopathology tissue patches – on their own, they are normally insufficient to diagnose a patient, while together they can provide enough information for a reliable clinical conclusion.

In recent years, many methods have been developed for the diagnosis of haematologic diseases. For instance, Eckardt et al. proposed a method for the identification of acute promyelocytic leukemia (APL) [8] and acute myeloid leukemia (AML) with NPM1 mutation [7], based on single white blood cells microscopically imaged in a bone marrow smear. For detection of APL, Sidhom et al. [21] suggest an ensemble approach including both single instance and multiple instance level analysis. Attention-based MIL architectures provide an additional attention score indicating the most important instances that were used for the prediction. Focusing on single red blood cells, Sadafi et al. [18] proposed an approach for the diagnosis of hereditary hemolytic anemias from peripheral blood. Similarly, Hehr et al. [9] employed an attention-based MIL framework to classify genetic subtypes of AML.

With the huge stream of data arriving in laboratories on a daily basis, with the consistent changes observed in the data [20] regular updating of models is an ongoing task. However, training neural networks on new datasets can lead to forgetting previously learned tasks, an issue called catastrophic forgetting [10, 19]. Continual learning methods mitigate this problem in three different ways: (i) Augmenting the architecture of the model so that it has different sub-networks for every task; (ii) Regularizing updates of the weights of the network such that important weights are not updated while less important neurons contribute to learning the new task, e.g. via elastic weight consolidation (EWC) [11]; (iii) Rehearsal-based methods such as iCaRL [17] sample a few images from the previous tasks and augment the dataset with those, such that they minimize the model's forgetting. Derakhshani et al. [6] have recently benchmarked continual learning methods on several biomedical datasets, demonstrating the potential of rehearsal-based approaches such as iCaRL. However, these methods are not applicable to MIL architectures, since sampling a huge bag of instances from histopathology or cytology datasets is not practically feasible. To the best of our knowledge, so far, no mechanism of instance sampling exists for efficiently selecting only the most diagnostically relevant instances while discarding less informative ones, which often constitute the majority of a bag's content. This gap highlights the need for a continual learning approach specifically tailored to MIL, enabling models to adapt efficiently while preserving their diagnostic accuracy. Given that MIL has become a fundamental paradigm in computational pathology and cytology, where diagnoses rely on aggregating information from large sets of instances rather than single observations, developing an effective continual learning strategy for MIL is crucial to ensuring applicability in evolving clinical settings.

Recently, MICIL [16] introduced a multiple-instance class-incremental learning framework for skin cancer whole slide image analysis, highlighting the potential of integrating MIL with continual learning in medical imaging. However, MICIL primarily addresses large-scale whole slide images and relies on embedding-level distillation to retain WSI-level knowledge. In contrast, a major challenge in many diagnostic settings, including hematology and histopathology, lies in the efficient selection of diagnostically relevant instances from vast and often heterogeneous patient samples containing hundreds of instances. In hematology, for instance, a large fraction of single cells in a patient sample do not contribute to the final diagnosis. Efficient instance selection is therefore crucial to ensure that continual learning methods focus on the most relevant instances and utilize the rehearsal memory efficiently.

Here, we are proposing CoMIL, the first continual learning method specifically tailored to MIL architectures and datasets with single instance selection. Our suggested rehearsal-based continual learning method performs instance sampling based on the attention score and its distance from the class mean and bag mean vectors in the latent space, such that the characteristics of the bags and hallmark cells necessary for diagnosis are preserved. Source code is available at https://github.com/marrlab/contmil.

## 2   Methodology

### 2.1   Attention-Based MIL

Multiple instance learning methods operate on a bag of instances $B = \{I_1, \ldots, I_N\}$ to produce a single bag-level prediction $\hat{y}$ along with a set of attention scores $\alpha_i \in A$ for each instance. Attention-based MIL consists of three stages (see Fig. 1):

1. **Instance feature extraction:** For each instance $I_i$, a feature vector $h_i = \psi(I_i)$ is computed, where $\psi$ is the pretrained feature extractor.
2. **Attention weight computation:** The importance of each instance is estimated through an attention mechanism. Attention for instance $I_i$ is computed as:

$$\alpha_i = \frac{\exp\left\{w^\top \tanh(V h_i^\top)\right\}}{\sum_{j=1}^{N} \exp\left\{w^\top \tanh(V h_j^\top)\right\}}, \tag{1}$$

Where $V \in \mathbb{R}^{D \times d}$ is a trainable matrix that projects instance features $h_i \in \mathbb{R}^d$ into a $D$-dimensional attention space, and $w \in \mathbb{R}^D$ is a trainable vector that maps the transformed features to scalar attention scores.
3. **Bag-level aggregation:** The bag feature vector $z$ is computed as a weighted sum of the instance features:

$$z = \sum_{k=1}^{N} \alpha_k h_k, \tag{2}$$

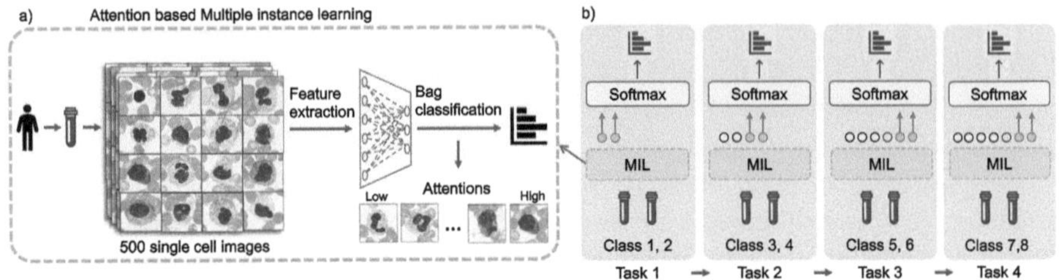


**Fig. 1.** A continual attention-based MIL scenario for hematologic disease diagnosis. a) From a blood probe, 500 single white blood cell images (instances) are taken for one patient (bag). After feature extraction and pooling, the bag classification probability and instance attentions are returned. b) Our dataset consists of 8 hematologic disease classes, and we have divided it into four tasks to evaluate our class incremental learning method.

Which aggregates information from the most relevant instances in the bag. This bag-level representation $z$ is then used for the final classification.

## 3  Evaluation

### 3.1  Problem Definition

At every step $t$ a training set $\mathcal{D}_t = \{B, y\}$ is provided such that $y_i \in C_t$ is a label from the set of new classes $C_t$ the classifier $f_t(.)$ is going to be trained on. The training involves updating model parameters $\theta_t$, having $\theta_{t-1}$ as the knowledge from the previous task. An exemplar set $\mathcal{X}_t$ is sampled at every step, containing bags with selected instances and stored in a limited amount of memory capable of holding $K$ instances. This set of samples is carried to the next step of continual learning and used for rehearsal of the previous knowledge during the training.

### 3.2  Training

At every step $t$, the training set $\mathcal{D}_t$ is augmented with the exemplar set $\mathcal{X}_t$. The model is initialized with the previously learned parameters $\theta_{t-1}$. The minimization is performed using a loss consisting of distillation and classification losses, defined as:

$$\mathcal{L}(\theta_t) = \mathcal{L}_{\text{cls}}(\theta_t) + \mathcal{L}_{\text{dist}}(\theta_t). \tag{3}$$

and a negative log likelihood loss for the classification loss. The distillation loss preserves the previous state of the model as much as possible and alleviates catastrophic forgetting. Having $\theta_{t-1}$ as the model parameters before the beginning of training step $t$, distillation loss is defined as

$$\mathcal{L}_{\text{dist}}(\theta_t) = \sum_{j \in C_{t-1}} \mathcal{S}(\hat{y}_j^{t-1})\log(\mathcal{S}(\hat{y}_j^t)) + (1 - \mathcal{S}(\hat{y}_j^{t-1}))\log(1 - \mathcal{S}(\hat{y}_j^t)) \qquad (4)$$

where $\forall (B_j) \in \mathcal{D}_t \cup \mathcal{X}_t$: $\hat{y}_j^{t-1} = f_{\text{MIL}}(B_j; \theta_{t-1})$ and $\hat{y}_i^t = f_{\text{MIL}}(B_j; \theta)$. $\mathcal{S}(.)$ is the sigmoid function and $C_{t-1}$ denotes the classes at $t - 1$.

### 3.3   Exemplar Set Selection

To rehearse the previously learned classes, a small number of instances can be carried between the tasks, as commonly done in rehearsal-based continual learning [1]. An exemplar set selection must be specifically tailored for MIL methods and carried out at the instance level. Using existing methods such as iCaRL [17] and keeping whole bags is memory-consuming and severely limits the number and diversity of the selected examples.

With a limited memory of $K$ instances and $|C_t|$ classes, a total of $m = \frac{K}{|C_T|}$ instances can be selected for each class. Considering that not all instances are equal in information value, one intuitive way of sampling is to keep instances with the highest attention in each bag. However, this method fails to preserve the bag structure, which is formed mainly by non-diagnostic instances and breaks the structure of the bag, leading to a shift in attention pooling outcome and hence the final classification (see Sect. 4 and Fig. 2).

Having all of the instances in all bags of any class $I_j \in B_j \in \mathcal{D}_c$ where $\mathcal{D}_c$ are all of the samples in the dataset belonging to class $c$. For every instance, the CoMIL instance value is defined as:

$$v_i = \alpha_i + \sqrt{(\psi(I_i; \theta_t) - \bar{B}_j)^2} + \sqrt{(\psi(I_i; \theta_t) - \bar{C})^2} \qquad (5)$$

where for every bag $B_j$ with a size of $N$, a bag mean is defined as $\bar{B}_j = \frac{1}{N}\sum_{i=1}^{N} I_i$ and a class mean is also defined as $\bar{C} = \frac{1}{M}\sum_{j=1}^{M} B_j$ where $M$ is the total number of bags in the class. $\alpha_i$ is the attention value the model has estimated for the instance.

After estimation of every CoMIL instance value, considering a memory capacity of $K$ instances and the fact that every instance occupies one unit of memory, a typical knapsack problem is formulated [15]. Here, the goal is to select items to fill the capacity while maximizing the amount of total value of the selected items. We decided to solve this problem with dynamic programming [5]. After selection of instances, they are organized back into their corresponding bags and stored in the exemplar set.

### 3.4   Exemplar Set Reduction

With the arrival of new classes, the amount of memory associated with each class decreases, and shrinking the exemplar sets is inevitable. If the old size of the memory for every class is $m' = \frac{K}{C_{t-1}}$ and the new memory size is $m = \frac{K}{C_t}$, the value for all of the instances are once more estimated using Eq. (5). This time, we shrink the bags by removing the least important instances. If a bag is empty, it will be completely removed from exemplar sets.

**Table 1.** Classes with training and test patient counts; the task number indicates when each class is introduced in the simulated continual learning process.

| | Training patients | Test patients | Task number |
| --- | --- | --- | --- |
| No disease evidence | 348 | 116 | 1 |
| Acute myeloid leukemia (AML) | 34 | 12 | 1 |
| Myelodysplastic syndrome (MDS) | 133 | 44 | 2 |
| Chronic myeloid leukaemia (CML) | 46 | 16 | 2 |
| Chronic lymphocytic leukemia (CLL) | 91 | 30 | 3 |
| Myeloproliferative neoplasms (MPN) | 192 | 64 | 3 |
| Chronic myelomonocytic leukemia (CMML) | 37 | 13 | 4 |
| Lymphoma (LYM) | 34 | 11 | 4 |

### 3.5    Dataset and Continual Learning Scenario

We are testing our method on a dataset with 1221 patient samples, each containing 500 microscopy single white cell images, resulting in more than 611,000 single cell images. There are 8 classes in the dataset, comprising patients with and without neoplastic changes (Table 1). In our class incremental experiment, we have defined 4 steps, where in each step, 2 new classes are introduced. We have divided the data into 75% training and 25% hold-out test sets in a stratified manner. Figure 1 shows the continual learning scenario and MIL architecture.

### 3.6    Baselines

To evaluate the performance of our continual learning method, we compare it against six different baselines: (i) Simple finetuning, a naive approach to the problem; (ii) Elastic Weight Consolidation (EWC) [11], a regularization-based solution for continual learning; (iii) iCaRL [17], an established rehearsal-based continual learning method; (iv) BIC [22], a bias correction method designed to mitigate the imbalance between old and new classes in incremental learning; (v) DER [24], a memory-efficient continual learning approach that combines knowledge distillation with replay strategies; and (vi) attention-based iCaRL, where instances are treated according to their attention value.

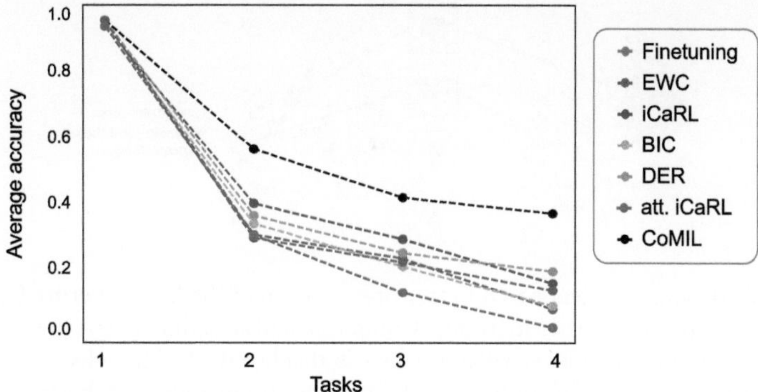


**Fig. 2.** Average accuracy of CoMIL on four steps of class increment learning experiment surpasses simple finetuning, elastic weight consolidation (EWC), iCaRL, Bias Correction (BIC), Dynamically Expandable Representation (DER), and iCaRL exemplar set sampling based on high attention cells of every bag (Attention iCaRL).

## 3.7 Implementation Details

Our MIL architecture consists of two networks. The first network is a ResNext [23], pretrained on the AML cytomorphology dataset [4,13] for the task of single leukocyte recognition [14], with its parameters frozen and used as a feature extractor. The MIL network has three layers of convolutions followed by a two-layer fully connected classifier. The attention module also has two fully connected layers. In our experiments, the model is trained for 20 epochs using a stochastic gradient descent optimizer. For iCaRL and all rehearsal-based experiments, the exemplar set size $K$ is set to 5000.

## 4   Results

In addition to the baselines, we conducted a comparison between our proposed method with an upper bound where the model has access to the complete datasets from previous tasks. The results are summarized in Table 2, which presents the average accuracy and average forgetting [3] of our CoMIL approach, as well as the baselines and the defined upper bound (UB). CoMIL consistently outperforms the baseline methods, indicating its superiority in handling multiple instance learning tasks. Figure 2 shows the average accuracy for four tasks defined in our class incremental learning experiment.

To gain a better understanding of the instance selection process within the bags, we plotted a UMAP embedding of the selected instances in Fig. 3. In the case of iCaRL, which lacks an instance selection mechanism, all 500 images in the bag are sampled (blue dots in Fig. 3 left). When using an attention-based selection method for iCaRL, only the 50 most important instances are selected (black dots, right). However, this selection is limited to diagnostic hallmark cells, and the original structure of the bag is lost, resulting in a shift in the bag feature

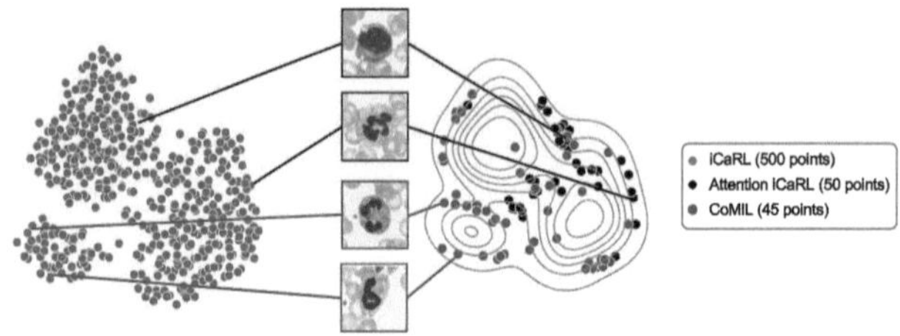


**Fig. 3.** CoMIL sampling leads to a better preservation of the bag structure for continual learning as compared to other methods. Comparison of sampling between three different methods on the instance level within a bag is displayed. iCaRL selects all instances, while attention-based iCaRL only keeps high-attention instances. A better distribution of sampling points is only done through our proposed approach. (Color figure online)

vector. Visually, rarely any point covers the third maximum in the KDE plot, probably containing mainly granulocytes (Fig. 3 middle images with pink frame).

**Table 2.** Average accuracy and average forgetting are reported for all methods on all four tasks and classes within each task. CoMIL method consistently outperforms other baselines of finetuning, elastic weight consolidation (EWC), iCaRL, Bias Correction (BIC), Dynamically Expandable Representation (DER), and attention-based iCaRL (att. iCaRL). The upper bound (UB) of problem assumes model access to all previous data.

| | Fine- tuning | EWC | iCaRL | BIC | DER | att. iCarl | CoMIL | UB |
|---|---|---|---|---|---|---|---|---|
| Acc.↑ | $45.2_{\pm0.1}$ | $46.0_{\pm0.1}$ | $49.9_{\pm0.1}$ | $45.3_{\pm0.2}$ | $49.4_{\pm0.2}$ | $43.1_{\pm0.3}$ | $\mathbf{61.3}_{\pm0.1}$ | $70.0_{\pm15.0}$ |
| For.↓ | $31.5_{\pm0.1}$ | $75.5_{\pm0.1}$ | $24.2_{\pm0.2}$ | $26.5_{\pm0.1}$ | $25.0_{\pm0.1}$ | $31.8_{\pm0.3}$ | $\mathbf{22.1}_{\pm0.2}$ | - |

Our proposed CoMIL instance selection method achieves a more uniform distribution of points, covering all of the sub-distributions in the KDE plot (pink dots). This emphasizes the effectiveness of our approach in preserving the diversity of the data and selecting representative instances for continual learning in MIL tasks.

To mitigate privacy concerns in medical data replay, our method can operate solely on pre-extracted, anonymized feature embeddings rather than raw images or identifiable patient data. The exemplar memory stores only these anonymized features, further minimizing re-identification risk. Additionally, patient data is excluded from single-cell images.

## 5   Conclusion

We proposed CoMIL, an approach to continual multiple instance learning, and showed its potential on a challenging hematologic disease diagnosis task. The proposed method is rehearsal-based and uses instance attention scores and distances from bag mean and class mean vectors as criteria to select samples and instances to store in exemplary sets from previous tasks.

We chose to use the knapsack method for instance sampling to provide a more versatile and adaptable approach for future developments, rather than relying on a simpler algorithm like the greedy method, which would only work for instances with equal cost. Our method allows for a range of possibilities, such as incorporating instances with varying costs, including higher costs for those that initiate a new bag, or adjusting costs to balance the selection of instances based on the difficulty or prevalence of a particular class. There are many exciting directions for future enhancements of our approach.

We evaluated our approach using real-world data from a leukemia laboratory, comprising over 600,000 single-cell images. In a class-incremental setting, CoMIL significantly outperformed established continual learning methods, demonstrating the effectiveness of the first continual learning approach tailored for MIL. This study marks an important step toward developing more efficient and accurate machine learning models for disease diagnosis in clinical and laboratory environments, where new data arrives daily and regular model updates are essential, making continual learning not just beneficial but necessary.

**Acknowledgement.** C.M. acknowledges funding from the European Research Council (ERC) under the European Union's Horizon 2020 research and innovation program (Grant Agreement No. 866411 & 101113551 & 101213822) and support from the High-tech Agenda Bayern.

**Disclosure of Interests.** The authors have no competing interests to declare that are relevant to the content of this article.

# References


1. Bagus, B., Gepperth, A.: An investigation of replay-based approaches for continual learning. In: 2021 International Joint Conference on Neural Networks (IJCNN), pp. 1–9. IEEE (2021)
2. Campanella, G., et al.: Clinical-grade computational pathology using weakly supervised deep learning on whole slide images. Nat. Med. **25**(8), 1301–1309 (2019)
3. Chaudhry, A., Rohrbach, M., Elhoseiny, M., Ajanthan, T., Torr, P.H.: Riemannian walk for incremental learning: understanding forgetting and intransigence. In: Proceedings of the European Conference on Computer Vision (ECCV), pp. 532–547 (2018)
4. Clark, K., et al.: The cancer imaging archive (tcia): maintaining and operating a public information repository. J. Digit. Imaging **26**, 1045–1057 (2013)
5. Cormen, T.H., Leiserson, C.E., Rivest, R.L., Stein, C.: Introduction to Algorithms, 2nd edn. The MIT Press, Cambridge (2001)
6. Derakhshani, M.M., et al.: Lifelonger: a benchmark for continual disease classification. In: Medical Image Computing and Computer Assisted Intervention–MICCAI 2022: 25th International Conference, Singapore, 18–22 September 2022, Proceedings, Part II, pp. 314–324. Springer, Cham (2022)

7. Eckardt, J.N., et al.: Deep learning detects acute myeloid leukemia and predicts npm1 mutation status from bone marrow smears. Leukemia **36**(1), 111–118 (2022)
8. Eckardt, J.N., et al.: Deep learning identifies acute promyelocytic leukemia in bone marrow smears. BMC Cancer **22**(1), 1–11 (2022)
9. Hehr, M., et al.: Explainable AI identifies diagnostic cells of genetic AML subtypes. PLOS Digit. Health **2**(3), e0000187 (2023). https://doi.org/10.1371/journal.pdig.0000187
10. Kemker, R., McClure, M., Abitino, A., Hayes, T., Kanan, C.: Measuring catastrophic forgetting in neural networks. In: Proceedings of the AAAI Conference on Artificial Intelligence, vol. 32 (2018)
11. Kirkpatrick, J., et al.: Overcoming catastrophic forgetting in neural networks. Proc. Natl. Acad. Sci. **114**(13), 3521–3526 (2017)
12. Van der Laak, J., Litjens, G., Ciompi, F.: Deep learning in histopathology: the path to the clinic. Nat. Med. **27**(5), 775–784 (2021)
13. Matek, C., Schwarz, S., Marr, C., Spiekermann, K.: A single-cell morphological dataset of leukocytes from AML patients and non-malignant controls (aml-cytomorphology_lmu). The Cancer Imaging Archive (TCIA) (2019)
14. Matek, C., Schwarz, S., Spiekermann, K., Marr, C.: Human-level recognition of blast cells in acute myeloid leukaemia with convolutional neural networks. Nat. Mach. Intell. **1**(11), 538–544 (2019)
15. Mathews, G.B.: On the partition of numbers. Proc. Lond. Math. Soc. **1**(1), 486–490 (1896)
16. Meseguer, P., Del Amor, R., Naranjo, V.: Micil: multiple-instance class-incremental learning for skin cancer whole slide images. Artif. Intell. Med. **152**, 102870 (2024)
17. Rebuffi, S.A., Kolesnikov, A., Sperl, G., Lampert, C.H.: icarl: incremental classifier and representation learning. In: Proceedings of the IEEE Conference on Computer Vision and Pattern Recognition, pp. 2001–2010 (2017)
18. Sadafi, A., et al.: Attention based multiple instance learning for classification of blood cell disorders. In: Martel, A.L., et al. (eds.) MICCAI 2020. LNCS, vol. 12265, pp. 246–256. Springer, Cham (2020). https://doi.org/10.1007/978-3-030-59722-1_24
19. Sadafi, A., et al.: A continual learning approach for cross-domain white blood cell classification. In: MICCAI Workshop on Domain Adaptation and Representation Transfer, pp. 136–146. Springer, Cham (2023)
20. Salehi, R., et al.: Unsupervised cross-domain feature extraction for single blood cell image classification. In: Medical Image Computing and Computer Assisted Intervention–MICCAI 2022: 25th International Conference, Singapore, 18–22 September 2022, Proceedings, Part III, pp. 739–748. Springer, Cham (2022)
21. Sidhom, J.W., et al.: Deep learning for diagnosis of acute promyelocytic leukemia via recognition of genomically imprinted morphologic features. NPJ Precis. Oncol. **5**(1), 38 (2021)
22. Wu, Y., et al.: Large scale incremental learning. In: Proceedings of the IEEE/CVF Conference on Computer Vision and Pattern Recognition, pp. 374–382 (2019)
23. Xie, S., Girshick, R., Dollár, P., Tu, Z., He, K.: Aggregated residual transformations for deep neural networks. In: Proceedings of the IEEE Conference on Computer Vision and Pattern Recognition, pp. 1492–1500 (2017)
24. Yan, S., Xie, J., He, X.: Der: dynamically expandable representation for class incremental learning. In: Proceedings of the IEEE/CVF Conference on Computer Vision and Pattern Recognition, pp. 3014–3023 (2021)

# MIP-Based Tumor Segmentation: A Radiologist-Inspired Approach


Romario Zarik[1(✉)] [ID], Nahum Kiryati[2] [ID], Michael Green[3] [ID],
Liran Domachevsky[3], and Arnaldo Mayer[3] [ID]

[1] School of Electrical and Computer Engineering, Tel Aviv University, Tel Aviv, Israel
`romariozarik@mail.tau.ac.il`
[2] Klachky Chair of Image Processing, School of Electrical and Computer
Engineering, Tel Aviv University, Tel Aviv, Israel
`nk@eng.tau.ac.il`
[3] Diagnostic Imaging, Sheba Medical Center, Affiliated with the Gray School of
Medicine, Tel Aviv University, Tel Aviv, Israel
`{liran.domachevsky,arnaldo.mayer}@sheba.health.gov.il`



**Abstract.** PET/CT imaging is the gold standard for tumor detection, offering high accuracy in identifying local and metastatic lesions. Radiologists often begin assessment with rotational Multi-Angle Maximum Intensity Projections (MIPs) from PET, confirming findings with volumetric slices. This workflow is time-consuming, especially in metastatic cases. Despite their clinical utility, MIPs are underutilized in automated tumor segmentation, where 3D volumetric data remains the norm. We propose an alternative approach that trains segmentation models directly on MIPs, bypassing the need to segment 3D volumes and then project. This better aligns the model with its target domain and yields substantial gains in computational efficiency and training time. We also introduce a novel occlusion correction method that restores MIP annotations occluded by high-intensity structures, improving segmentation. Using the autoPET 2022 Grand Challenge dataset, we evaluate our method against standard 3D pipelines in terms of performance and training/computation efficiency for segmentation and classification, and analyze how MIP count affects segmentation. Our MIP-based approach achieves segmentation performance on par with 3D ($\leq$1% Dice difference, 26.7% better Hausdorff Distance), while reducing training time (convergence time) by 55.8–75.8%, energy per epoch by 71.7–76%, and TFLOPs by two orders of magnitude, highlighting its scalability for clinical use. For classification, using 16 MIPs only as input, we surpass 3D performance while reducing training time by over 10$\times$ and energy consumption per epoch by 93.35%. Our analysis of the impact of MIP count on segmentation identified 48 views as optimal, offering the best trade-off between performance and efficiency.

**Keywords:** Positron Emission Tomography (PET) · Lesion Segmentation · Maximum Intensity projections (MIPs)





T. Chen et al. (Eds.): EMA4MICCAI 2025 Workshops, LNCS 16318, pp. 215–224, 2026.
https://doi.org/10.1007/978-3-032-13961-0_22

## 1   Introduction

Positron emission tomography (PET), combined with CT or MRI, has become an invaluable tool in cancer imaging, allowing the assessment of primary tumors and metastatic disease across the whole body. In PET imaging, a radiotracer consisting of a positron-emitting isotope bound to an organic ligand, such as Fluorodeoxyglucose (FDG), is intravenously injected. The photon pairs resulting from positron annihilation are recorded by a ring of detectors surrounding the body. Through tomographic reconstruction, a 3D distribution map of the tracer's physiological uptake is generated [3].

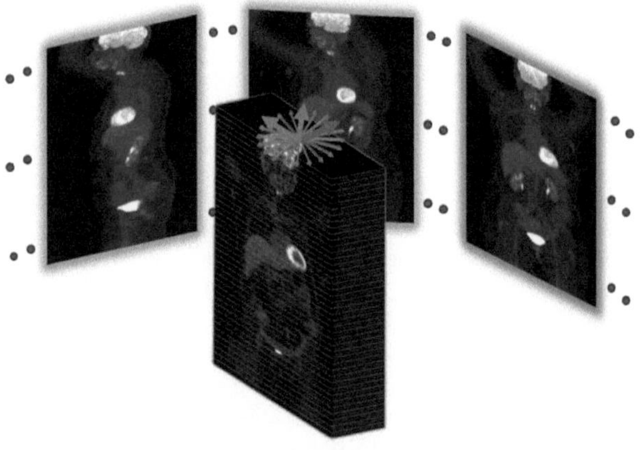

**Fig. 1.** Illustration of Multi-Angle Maximum Intensity Projections (MIPs) derived from the same 3D PET volume. Each MIP corresponds to a unique yaw angle, capturing different perspectives of the tumor. The figure presents three example MIPs generated at 0° (red), 45° (green), and 90° (cyan). (Color figure online)

To facilitate clinical assessment of a patient's PET scan, radiologists frequently use Multi-Angle Maximum Intensity Projections (MIPs), which are 2D images that capture the highest intensity values along each line of sight, making it easier to identify regions with increased tracer uptake. This technique enhances the visualization of structures with high radiotracer uptake, such as tumors, by providing a comprehensive overview of their distribution and intensity. By computing MIPs for different yaw angles, we obtain a series of 2D MIP images (see Fig. 1). Even before consulting patient history or indication, the initial review of a continuously rotating MIP is valuable in achieving an unbiased assessment, favoring a "gestalt" perception of the case [8].

Interpreting PET scans is a time-consuming process that often requires cross-referencing with CT or MRI. Automatically delineating potential tumors directly on the rotating MIPs can streamline this workflow by guiding radiologists to regions suspected of containing active lesions, thereby significantly reducing medical interpretation time.

Although deep learning has been applied to PET-CT for lesion detection and disease staging, most models treat PET as a slice-based modality, overlooking the benefits of rotated MIP images. A few recent studies have incorporated MIPs into their pipelines. For instance, Kawakami et al. [11] used a YOLOv2 detector on multi-orientation MIPs to identify physiological uptake and highlight suspect regions. Takahashi et al. [19] employed an Xception model on MIPs from multiple angles to improve breast cancer classification. In another study, Heiliger et al. [7] combined sagittal and coronal MIPs with a gating strategy to reduce false positives. Toosi et al. [21] extracted features from 72 MIPs and used them in a recurrence-free survival prediction pipeline for head and neck cancer.

While 3D volumetric segmentation remains the dominant paradigm, recent studies have begun exploring 2D projections to leverage their efficiency and complementary information. Constantino et al. [2] demonstrated that incorporating MIP representations can enhance 3D PET/CT segmentation for both FDG and PSMA tracers, and Toosi et al. [20] reconstructed volumetric segmentations from 2D MIPs, achieving state-of-the-art results on PSMA PET scans. Similarly, Wang et al. [23] introduced a "2.75D" approach, combining multiple 2D views to enrich 3D learning in data-limited scenarios. Building on these insights, our study focuses on direct segmentation of MIPs: we systematically analyze their standalone performance, evaluate how the number of MIPs impacts segmentation quality, and benchmark their efficiency against traditional 3D pipelines on FDG PET scans, which are widely used across cancer types.

Training directly on Multi-Angle Maximum Intensity Projections (MIPs) offers substantial advantages over conventional 3D volumetric segmentation. MIPs provide a computationally efficient representation of PET data; for instance, 16 views capture approximately 4% of the volumetric information (depending on resolution) while preserving critical lesion details. This compact format enables training on standard hardware with significantly lower memory and computational demands. Moreover, operating on 2D projections reduces training time and facilitates faster model development and deployment. The resulting lightweight models are more suitable for real-time clinical use. Importantly, aligning the model's input domain with radiologists' diagnostic perspective enhances the learning of clinically relevant features.

The major contributions of this work are as follows:

1. **Segmentation Performance Comparison:** We demonstrate that direct segmentation on MIPs (48 MIPs) achieves performance comparable to conventional 3D segmentation followed by MIP projection, while significantly reducing training time, energy consumption, and computational cost.
2. **Classification Performance Comparison:** To further highlight the effectiveness of MIPs, we show that a CNN trained on just 16 MIPs outperforms a 3D model in binary classification (healthy vs. non-healthy), achieving over 10× faster training and a significant reduction in energy use per epoch.

3. **Occlusion Correction for MIP Annotations:** We introduce a pre-processing method that corrects MIP annotations occluded by high-intensity structures, reducing false positives and improving segmentation accuracy.
4. **Impact of MIP Quantity and Angular Resolution:** We analyze the effect of varying the number of MIPs, equivalent to adjusting angular resolution or projection spacing, and identify 48 views as the optimal trade-off between segmentation performance and efficiency.

The remainder of this paper is organized as follows: Sect. 2 details our methodology, Sect. 3 describes the experimental setup and results, and Sect. 4 discusses conclusions, limitations, and future research directions.

## 2     Methods

### 2.1     Data Partitioning

**Data.** We used the open-source autoPET 2022 dataset [5], which includes 1,014 PET/CT scans from 900 patients diagnosed with lung cancer, lymphoma, melanoma, or confirmed as healthy (Table 1). Each case provides a 3D PET scan, CT scan, and tumor segmentation map. While MIPs can be generated for both PET and CT, we focused on PET MIPs, as they are standard for whole-body tumor assessment and enable a fair comparison with 3D PET-based segmentation. PET values were standardized to SUV units [4].

**Data Split.** We partitioned the dataset by setting aside 15% of the data as an independent test set for the final evaluation. The remaining 85% were used for 5-fold cross-validation, ensuring that each model was trained and validated on different subsets before being tested on the independent test set. To maintain consistency, we preserved the same class distribution across all splits.

**Table 1.** Distribution of cases across the four classes in the dataset

| Class | Negative (Healthy) | Lymphoma | Melanoma | Lung Cancer |
|---|---|---|---|---|
| Number of Cases | 513 | 145 | 188 | 168 |

### 2.2     MIP Generation

To generate MIPs for both PET images and their lesion annotations, we applied maximum-intensity projections along the anterior-posterior axis of the 3D data after rotating it around the superior-inferior (vertical/yaw) axis. Each MIP image, $F_k(i,j)$, is computed by taking the maximum intensity across the depth dimension $d$ for each pixel $(i,j)$ and MIP index $k$, as defined in Eq. 1:

$$F_k(i,j) = \max_d f_k(i,j,d) \tag{1}$$

where $F_k(i, j)$ represents the resulting MIP image for index $k$, and $f_k(i, j, d)$ denotes the 3D data after rotation by an angle of $k\Delta\Theta$. The MIP images were captured at equal angular increments, $\Delta\Theta$, spanning from 0 to 180° to ensure symmetry. The angular step size, $\Delta\Theta$, is given by Eq. 2:

$$\Delta\Theta(N) = \frac{180°}{N} \tag{2}$$

where $N$ is the number of MIPs created from the 3D data. Images from 180 to 360° were not captured, as they are mirror images of those in the 0–180° range. In our study, we generated MIP image sets in multiples of 16, ranging from 16 to 80 images, all derived from the 0–180° rotation range.

## 2.3   MIP Occlusion Correction

Projecting 3D annotations onto MIPs sometimes led to inconsistent labels due to occlusions by high-intensity structures. These occlusions occur when lesions and high-FDG-uptake organs (e.g., brain, heart, and kidneys) are aligned along the same viewing angle used to generate the MIP. As a result, high-intensity pixels from these organs can dominate the projection, obscuring tumor annotations and introducing false positives. To address this, we designed a three-step processing pipeline to generate a more accurate training set:

1. **Occlusion Detection**: For each labeled tumor (connected component) in the generated MIPs, we verified that at least 75% of the pixels labeled as tumor originated from tumors in the volumetric PET data. This verification was possible because the projection process allows us to trace each pixel back to its corresponding voxel in the 3D data.
2. **Annotation Splitting**: If a labeled tumor contained fewer than 75% tumor-originated pixels, we split the label to retain only the pixels confirmed to originate from the tumor.
3. **Low-Contrast Filtering**: Additional processing was applied to handle remnants of tumors with very low contrast, which were deemed undetectable by eye and subsequently removed from the annotations.

This process ensured that only accurate and visible tumor annotations were retained in the MIP images, as occluded tumors are generally considered undetectable by radiologists. Analysis of the annotations revealed that only 0.57% of tumors were excluded from all MIPs during this preprocessing step, accounting for just 0.09% of the original volumetric volume. These figures suggest that the GT was largely preserved. In our experiments, we utilize both the original GT MIPs (OR-MIPs) and the occlusion-corrected MIPs (OC-MIPs) during training.

## 2.4   Models and Implementation

**Models.** For semantic segmentation on MIPs, we employed Convolutional Neural Networks (CNNs) due to their flexibility and robustness across different numbers of MIPs. Among the CNN architectures evaluated, Attention U-Net [14] demonstrated the best performance and was therefore selected for all MIP-based segmentation experiments. For 3D volumetric segmentation, we implemented the training pipeline that ranked 5th in the autoPET 2022 Grand Challenge [7], which was based on a Swin-UNETR [6] architecture. Higher-ranked teams either did not share their code for reproducibility or relied on high-VRAM GPUs, which were not available to us. For classification, we used a CNN encoder followed by attention pooling to produce a fixed-size representation regardless of input shape. This was passed through a fully connected head ending with two output neurons for binary prediction.

**Implementation.** The implementation used the MONAI [1] and PyTorch [15] frameworks, with additional support from the original GitHub repositories of the models. All models were trained using a single 24GB RTX 3090 GPU. The code and preprocessing tools used in this study are publicly available in our GitHub repository[1].

### 2.5   Loss Function and Evaluation

**Loss Function.** Segmentation models were trained using Dice Loss [13], either alone or in combination with Cross-Entropy Loss [12], depending on the experimental setting. For classification, we used Cross-Entropy Loss exclusively.

**Evaluation.** We report Dice Score [17], IoU [10], and Hausdorff Distance (HD) [9] for segmentation; Accuracy, Precision, Recall [16], and F1-score [22] for classification; and convergence time (CT), time per epoch (TPE), and energy per epoch (EPE) for training efficiency. Convergence time is defined as the time taken to reach peak validation performance (Dice/Accuracy), with the corresponding weights used for final testing. Inference time and computational cost were measured using the time and ptflops [18] python packages, respectively. Costs are reported in teraflops (TFLOPs), where 1 TFLOP equals $10^{12}$ floating-point operations. MIP generation costs were included for fair evaluation.

## 3   Experiments and Results

### 3.1   MIPs vs. 3D

We compare lesion segmentation trained on 3D volumetric data (followed by maximum-intensity projection) to direct segmentation on MIPs. The 3D pipeline from [7] was adapted to use only the PET (SUV) channel, and its predictions were projected to MIPs for a shared 2-D evaluation domain.

All models were evaluated on the OR-MIPs dataset, which offers the fairest basis for comparison: once 3D predictions are projected, occlusions cannot be corrected as in OC-MIPs, so evaluating in a shared domain avoids bias against the 3D model. Results (Table 2) show comparable Dice scores across methods, with mean values within 1% of each other. Both MIP-based models achieved

---

[1] https://github.com/ZROM-GIT/MIP-Based-Tumor-Segmentation.

**Table 2.** Comparison results (mean ± standard deviation) of 3D-based and MIP-based models' segmentation performance and efficiency metrics. All trained models were tested on the OR-MIPs test set for the fairest comparison.

|  | Metric | 3D projected | OR-MIPs | OC-MIPs |
|---|---|---|---|---|
| Segment. | Dice (↑) | **0.597** ± 0.05 | 0.578 ± 0.01 | 0.591 ± 0.01 |
|  | IoU (↑) | **0.471** ± 0.04 | 0.452 ± 0.01 | 0.466 ± 0.01 |
|  | HD (↓) | 139.614 ± 8.42 | 102.813 ± 9.61 | **102.26** ± 9.53 |
| Efficiency | CT (hours, ↓) | 54.64 ± 19.22 | 24.14 ± 17.8 | **13.18** ± 4.1 |
|  | EPE ($\frac{\text{Wh}}{\text{epoch}}$, ↓) | 142.2 ± 79.1 | 40.22 ± 12.48 | **34.194** ± 4.7 |
|  | TFLOPs (↓) | 317.42 ± 144.05 | **0.97** ± 0.29 | **0.97** ± 0.29 |

better Hausdorff distances, indicating improved boundary accuracy. A one-sided Wilcoxon signed-rank test on fold-wise paired results (null: no difference; alternative: 3D is better) yielded p-values of 0.22 (OR-MIPs) and 0.5 (OC-MIPs), showing no statistical advantage for 3D.

In terms of efficiency, the OC-MIPs model reduced training time from 54.6 to 13.2 h (4.1× faster), energy per epoch from 142.2 to 34.2 Wh (4.2× lower), and TFLOPs from 317.4 to 0.97 (over 300× lower), demonstrating substantial gains in scalability and resource savings.

To further highlight the effectiveness of MIPs, we compare classification performance using identical CNN-based models with attention pooling and a FC head, trained on either 3D volumes or 16-angle MIPs (healthy vs. non-healthy). As shown in Table 3, MIP-based models outperform their 3D counterparts across most metrics, including accuracy (80.5% vs. 72.8%) and F1-score (86.4% vs. 82.3%). While the 3D models show slightly higher recall (91.9% vs. 89.5%), their large standard deviation suggests instability and less consistent performance. In terms of classification training efficiency, MIP-based training reduced training time by over 10× and energy consumption per epoch by 93.35%.

**Table 3.** Classification results (mean ± standard deviation) and training efficiency metrics of identical models trained on the 3D and 16 MIPs datasets.

|  | Metric | 3D Dataset | 16 MIPs Dataset |
|---|---|---|---|
| Classification | Accuracy (%, ↑) | 72.8 ± 3.2 | **80.5** ± 1.7 |
|  | Precision (%, ↑) | 75.4 ± 6.0 | **83.6** ± 3.3 |
|  | Recall (%, ↑) | **91.9** ± 8.8 | 89.5 ± 2.9 |
|  | F1-score (%, ↑) | 82.3 ± 1.2 | **86.4** ± 0.8 |
| Efficiency | CT (hours, ↓) | 44.7 ± 1.5 | **4.2** ± 0.2 |
|  | TPE ($\frac{\text{minutes}}{\text{epoch}}$, ↓) | 26.1 ± 0.59 | **1.45** ± 0.04 |
|  | EPE ($\frac{\text{Wh}}{\text{epoch}}$, ↓) | 70.7 ± 3.23 | **4.7** ± 0.1 |

## 3.2   Number of MIPs

To assess the impact of the number of MIPs on semantic lesion segmentation, we trained models on datasets with different MIP counts and evaluated them on a fixed test set with different MIP counts (see Fig. 2). This ensured a rigorous analysis while maintaining a fair comparison across different MIP configurations.

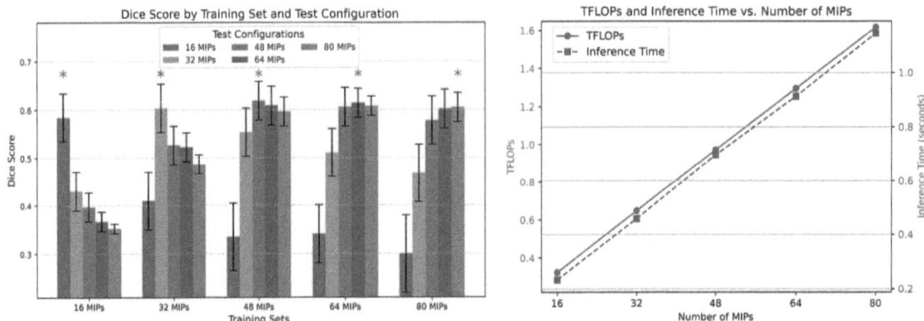

**Fig. 2.** (Left) Dice Scores for models trained/tested on X, Y $\in$ {16, 32, 48, 64, 80}. (Right) TFLOPs and inference time (seconds) vs. number of MIPs. Green (red) stars indicate statistically significant (insignificant) improvement of the highest bar over the second highest, based on a one-sided Wilcoxon signed-rank test.

Our results show that 48 MIPs yield the highest and most consistent Dice scores across all train/test combinations (Fig. 2). Models trained on 48 MIPs performed comparably even when tested on 64 or 80 MIPs, demonstrating both robustness and efficiency. For statistical analysis, a one-sided Wilcoxon signed-rank test was performed by pairing the highest and second-highest test MIPs datasets for each training set, with each pair corresponding to a shared training fold. This approach is appropriate as the test assumes a connection between the pairs; in this case, each pair was trained on the same data, differing only in the number of MIPs used during testing. The analysis revealed statistically significant results for the 16 and 32 MIPs training sets. In contrast, no statistical significance was observed for the training sets with the larger number of MIPs (48, 64, 80).

As shown in the right panel of Fig. 2, both TFLOPs and average inference time per case increase with the number of MIPs, as expected. Since Dice performance peaks and plateaus at 48 MIPs, we identify this configuration as the optimal trade-off between performance and efficiency.

## 4   Conclusions and Discussion

We focused and analyzed a radiologist-aligned approach that performs tumor segmentation directly on Multi-Angle MIPs, offering substantial efficiency gains without sacrificing accuracy. Compared to 3D volumetric segmentation, our

MIP-based models achieve similar Dice scores (within 1%) while reducing training time by up to 4.1×, energy per epoch by up to 4.2×, and TFLOPs by over 300×. Classification results further support the approach: using just 16 MIPs, we surpass 3D performance in accuracy and F1-score, with over 10× faster training and approximately 6.65% energy used. Our analysis shows that 48 MIPs offer the best trade-off between segmentation performance and efficiency. These results suggest MIP-based models are highly efficient and practical for clinical use, especially in resource-constrained settings.

Future work includes incorporating CT into MIPs by mapping corresponding CT voxels from projected PET voxels, and developing models that leverage MIP-specific structural priors. Additionally, [20] proposed MIP segmentation using diffusion models followed by 3D annotation reconstruction via OSEM in PSMA PET scans, a direction we plan to explore on FDG-PET data to enable fair comparisons in the 3D domain.

**Acknowledgements.** This work was supported by a grant from the Tel Aviv University Center for AI and Data Science (TAD).

**Disclosure of Interests.** The authors have no competing interests to declare that are relevant to the content of this article.

# References


1. Cardoso, M.J., et al.: Monai: an open-source framework for deep learning in healthcare. arXiv preprint arXiv:2211.02701 (2022)
2. Constantino, C.S., Oliveira, F.P., Machado, M., Vinga, S., Costa, D.C.: The use of maximum-intensity projections and deep learning adds value to the fully automatic segmentation of lesions avid for [18F] FDG and [68Ga] Ga-PSMA in PET/CT. J. Nucl. Med. **66**(5), 795–801 (2025)
3. Crişan, G., Moldovean-Cioroianu, N.S., Timaru, D.G., Andrieş, G., Căinap, C., Chiş, V.: Radiopharmaceuticals for pet and spect imaging: a literature review over the last decade. Int. J. Mol. Sci. **23**(9), 5023 (2022)
4. Fletcher, J., Kinahan, P.: PET/CT standardized uptake values (SUVs) in clinical practice and assessing response to therapy. NIH Public Access **31**(6), 496–505 (2010)
5. Gatidis, S., et al.: A whole-body FDG-PET/CT dataset with manually annotated tumor lesions. Sci. Data **9**(1), 601 (2022)
6. Hatamizadeh, A., Nath, V., Tang, Y., Yang, D., Roth, H.R., Xu, D.: Swin unetr: swin transformers for semantic segmentation of brain tumors in MRI images. In: International MICCAI Brainlesion Workshop, pp. 272–284. Springer, Cham (2021)
7. Heiliger, L., et al.: Autopet challenge: combining nn-unet with swin unetr augmented by maximum intensity projection classifier. arXiv preprint arXiv:2209.01112 (2022)
8. Hofman, M.S., Hicks, R.J.: How we read oncologic FDG PET/CT. Cancer Imaging **16**, 1–14 (2016)
9. Huttenlocher, D.P., Klanderman, G.A., Rucklidge, W.J.: Comparing images using the hausdorff distance. IEEE Trans. Pattern Anal. Mach. Intell. **15**(9), 850–863 (1993)

10. Jaccard, P.: Étude comparative de la distribution florale dans une portion des alpes et des jura. Bull. Soc. Vaudoise Sci. Nat. **37**, 547–579 (1901)
11. Kawakami, M., et al.: Development of combination methods for detecting malignant uptakes based on physiological uptake detection using object detection with pet-ct mip images. Front. Med. **7**, 616746 (2020)
12. Long, J., Shelhamer, E., Darrell, T.: Fully convolutional networks for semantic segmentation. In: Proceedings of the IEEE Conference on Computer Vision and Pattern Recognition, pp. 3431–3440 (2015)
13. Milletari, F., Navab, N., Ahmadi, S.A.: V-net: Fully convolutional neural networks for volumetric medical image segmentation. In: 2016 Fourth International Conference on 3D Vision (3DV), pp. 565–571. IEEE (2016)
14. Oktay, O., et al.: Attention u-net: learning where to look for the pancreas. arXiv preprint arXiv:1804.03999 (2018)
15. Paszke, A.: Pytorch: an imperative style, high-performance deep learning library. arXiv preprint arXiv:1912.01703 (2019)
16. Sokolova, M., Lapalme, G.: A systematic analysis of performance measures for classification tasks. Inf. Process. Manage. **45**(4), 427–437 (2009)
17. Sorensen, T.: A method of establishing groups of equal amplitude in plant sociology based on similarity of species content and its application to analyses of the vegetation on Danish commons. Biologiske skrifter **5**, 1–34 (1948)
18. Sovrasov, V.: ptflops: a flops counting tool for neural networks in pytorch framework (2018–2024). https://github.com/sovrasov/flops-counter.pytorch
19. Takahashi, K., et al.: Deep learning using multiple degrees of maximum-intensity projection for PET/CT image classification in breast cancer. Tomography **8**(1), 131–141 (2022)
20. Toosi, A., Harsini, S., Bénard, F., Uribe, C., Rahmim, A.: How to segment in 3D using 2D models: automated 3D segmentation of prostate cancer metastatic lesions on pet volumes using multi-angle maximum intensity projections and diffusion models. arXiv preprint arXiv:2407.18555 (2024)
21. Toosi, A., Shiri, I., Nasr, F., Zaidi, H., Rahmim, A.: Fully automated segmentation-free outcome prediction for head and neck cancer using multi-angle maximum intensity projections (ma-mips) of FDG-pet images (2024)
22. Van Rijsbergen, C.J.: Information Retrieval, 2nd edn. Newton (1979)
23. Wang, X., et al.: 2.75 d: boosting learning by representing 3d medical imaging to 2d features for small data. Biomed. Signal Process. Control **84**, 104858 (2023)

# Interpretability-Aware Pruning
## for Efficient Medical Image Analysis

Nikita Malik[1,2], Pratinav Seth[1(✉)], Neeraj K. Singh[1],
Chintan Chitroda[1], and Vinay K. Sankarapu[1]

[1] AryaXAI Alignment Lab, AryaXAI.com, Mumbai, India
`pratinav.seth@aryaxai.com`
[2] Manipal Institute of Technology, Manipal, India

**Abstract.** Deep learning has driven significant advances in medical image analysis, yet its adoption in clinical practice remains constrained by the large size and lack of transparency in modern models. Advances in interpretability techniques such as DL-Backtrace, Layerwise Relevance Propagation, and Integrated Gradients make it possible to assess the contribution of individual components within neural networks trained on medical imaging tasks. In this work, we introduce an interpretability-guided pruning framework that reduces model complexity while preserving both predictive performance and transparency. By selectively retaining only the most relevant parts of each layer, our method enables targeted compression that maintains clinically meaningful representations. Experiments across multiple medical image classification benchmarks demonstrate that this approach achieves high compression rates with minimal loss in accuracy, paving the way for lightweight, interpretable models suited for real-world deployment in healthcare settings (Code will be available at: https://github.com/ AryaXAI/interpretability-aware-pruning-healthcare).

**Keywords:** Model Pruning · Model Compression · Explainable AI (XAI) · Trustworthy AI in Healthcare · AI Alignment

## 1 Introduction

Deep learning has revolutionized numerous fields, with medical image analysis being a prominent beneficiary [17,26]. Convolutional Neural Networks (CNNs) and other deep architectures have demonstrated state-of-the-art performance across a spectrum of tasks, from disease detection and segmentation to diagnosis and prognosis. Despite their remarkable accuracy, the widespread adoption of these models in clinical settings is often hampered by two critical limitations: their inherent computational complexity and their "black-box" nature [6,15]. The former necessitates significant computational resources, making deployment challenging in environments with limited infrastructure, while the latter hinders trust and understanding among medical professionals who require transparent and explainable insights into model decisions.


T. Chen et al. (Eds.): EMA4MICCAI 2025 Workshops, LNCS 16318, pp. 225–235, 2026.
https://doi.org/10.1007/978-3-032-13961-0_23

To address these challenges, model compression techniques, particularly pruning, have emerged as a promising avenue [3,18]. Pruning aims to reduce the size and computational footprint of neural networks by removing redundant or less important parameters. Traditionally, pruning methods have relied on heuristics such as weight magnitude or Random removal [7,9,11]. While effective in reducing model size, these approaches often lack a direct connection to the model's decision-making process, potentially discarding parameters that contribute to critical features or interpretability.

This paper introduces an interpretability-aware pruning method that leverages advanced attribution techniques to guide the compression process. By integrating methods like Layer-wise Relevance Propagation (LRP) [20], DL Backtrace (DLB) [25], and Integrated Gradients (IG) [28], we compute importance scores for individual layers (and neurons), reflecting their contributions to the model's prediction. These scores then inform a targeted pruning strategy, allowing us to remove less relevant components while preserving the model's performance and enhancing its transparency. Our approach is particularly effective in identifying and removing individual neurons that are not crucial for model prediction, leading to significant lossless compression. We demonstrate the efficacy of our method on diverse medical imaging datasets, showcasing its potential to create efficient and interpretable deep learning models for real-world clinical applications.

## 2    Related Works

### 2.1    Model Pruning

Model pruning is a widely adopted technique for neural network compression, aiming to reduce model size and accelerate inference by eliminating redundant parameters. Pruning methods can be broadly categorized based on when and how the pruning is applied. Train-time pruning integrates the pruning process directly into the training phase [24,29], while post-training pruning, conversely, applies pruning techniques to a fully trained model as a separate step [3,12]. Our work focuses on a post-training approach where importance scores are computed on a trained model for individual layers and neurons [13]. It focuses on identifying and pruning individual neurons, which aligns with unstructured pruning at a conceptual level, but with an interpretability-guided selection.

### 2.2    Model Interpretability and Model Compression

Model Interpretability aims to make the decision-making processes of complex machine learning models more transparent and understandable. In critical domains such as healthcare, finance, and law enforcement, where AI-driven decisions can have significant ethical, legal, and societal implications, the ability to explain how AI systems arrive at their conclusions is paramount [1,2,8,10]. Beyond enhancing transparency and trust, Model Interpretability can also facilitate model compression. By identifying which components of a model—such as specific neurons, filters, or layers—are most influential in its predictions, it is possible to remove less critical parts without substantially affecting performance. This approach, often termed "pruning by explaining", leverages interpretability to guide the simplification of models, making them more efficient and suitable for deployment in resource-constrained environments [23].

To implement interpretability-aware pruning, we utilize several techniques that assess the contribution of different components within a neural network:

**Layer-wise Relevance Propagation (LRP):** LRP operates by propagating the prediction backward through the network, distributing a "relevance score" from the output layer down to the input features or intermediate neurons. A key property of LRP is its conservation principle, ensuring that the total relevance is preserved across layers. This allows for a quantitative measure of how much each neuron contributes to the final prediction, making it suitable for identifying less important components [19].

**DL-Backtrace (DLB):** DL-Backtrace is a model-agnostic method that assigns relevance scores across layers, revealing feature importance, information flow, and potential biases in predictions. A significant advantage of DLB is its independence from auxiliary models or baselines, ensuring consistent and deterministic interpretations across diverse architectures (MLPs, CNNs, LLMs) and data types (images, text, tabular data). This makes it a robust tool for our pruning strategy [25].

**Integrated Gradients (IG):** IG is a path-based explanation technique that quantifies the contribution of individual input features to a model's prediction. It works by integrating the gradients of the model output with respect to the input features along a straight-line path from a baseline input (e.g., a black image) to the actual input. IG is known for satisfying desirable axioms and can mitigate issues like saturation effects, providing less noisy and more complete explanations [28].

By applying these interpretability techniques, we can derive importance scores that inform our pruning strategy. This allows us to move beyond simple magnitude-based heuristics and instead focus on the functional importance of model components, leading to more efficient and interpretable models.


## 3    Methodology

Our proposed interpretability-aware pruning method integrates interpretability techniques with a targeted neuron removal strategy to achieve efficient and transparent model compression. The entire pruning process (as illustrated in Fig. 1) involves several key steps, from computing importance scores to iteratively pruning and evaluating the model.

### 3.1  Importance Score Computation

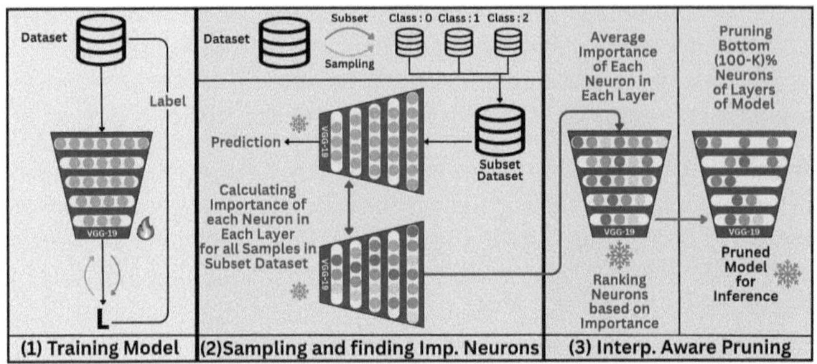



**Fig. 1.** Workflow for Interpretability-Aware Model Pruning: (1) Train the model on the dataset with labels, (2) Perform sampling and rank neurons based on their importance in each layer using subset datasets, (3) Prune the least important neurons (bottom (100-K)%) from each layer to create a compressed model for inference.

The foundation of our method lies in accurately quantifying the importance of individual neurons within the deep learning model. For this, we employ three distinct attribution methods: Layer-wise Relevance Propagation (LRP), DL Backtrace (DLB), and Integrated Gradients (IG). Each of these methods produces scores at the initial and intermediate feature levels. To approximate importance at the neuron level, we aggregate these importance values by summing across the channel dimension to obtain a per-neuron importance score aligned with the output of each feature map. This aggregation step helps to smooth out noise and provide a more stable measure of a neuron's overall importance.

### 3.2  Sample Selection for Importance Computation

To ensure that the computed importance scores are representative and robust, we utilize various sampling techniques to select 10 samples per class from the training set on which the importance scores are calculated. This addresses the potential for importance scores to vary across different inputs. The sampling techniques explored include:

**Confidence Sampling:** Selects samples for which the model has the highest prediction Confidence. This focuses on inputs where the model's decision is strong, potentially highlighting the most critical neurons.

**Random Sampling:** A Random selection of samples from each class is used. This provides a general overview of neuron importance across the dataset.

**Clustering-based Sampling:** Samples are grouped into clusters based on their features or model activations, and representatives from each cluster are selected. This ensures diversity in the chosen samples, covering different data distributions.

### 3.3   Pruning Strategy

Once the aggregated scores for all neurons are obtained, we proceed with the pruning process by identifying and removing the "bottom-most" neurons, i.e., those with the lowest scores, up to a specified pruning threshold. For each layer or the entire network, neurons are ranked across the entire network based on their aggregated scores. A predefined pruning rate determines the percentage of neurons with the lowest importance scores to be removed. Neurons falling below this threshold are considered low-importance and are pruned by setting their associated weights to zero. This effectively eliminates their contribution to the network's computation, aligning with an unstructured pruning strategy at the neuron level, driven by interpretability.

## 4   Experimental Setup

### 4.1   Datasets and Models

We utilized four medical imaging datasets, each with unique clinical contexts:

**MURA Dataset [22]:** A large-scale dataset of musculoskeletal radiographs from Stanford, comprising seven standard study types (e.g., elbow, wrist, shoulder), with each X-ray labeled as normal or abnormal.

**KVASIR Dataset [21]:** KVASIR is a collection of Endoscopic images of the gastrointestinal tract, categorized by anatomical landmarks (e.g., Z-line, pylorus) and pathological findings (e.g., esophagitis, polyps).

**CPN Dataset [16]:** The CPN (Common Peroneal Nerve) dataset focuses on diagnosing common peroneal nerve injuries in the lower limb. This dataset is used for classification tasks in nerve injury detection and related clinical scenarios.

**FETAL Planes Dataset [4]:** This dataset comprises high-resolution ultrasound images of fetal heads, highlighting regions such as the brain, cavum septum pellucidum (CSP), and lateral ventricles (LV), supporting both classification and detection tasks.

We applied our pruning methodology across three widely used architectures: VGG19 [27], ResNet50 [14], and Vision Transformer (ViT) [5]. Each model was trained in a supervised fashion on all datasets to establish a strong baseline. This process incorporated data augmentation techniques, learning rate schedulers, optimization algorithms, and loss functions, including Cross Entropy, to achieve optimal results.

### 4.2  Pruning Process and Evaluation

For each model and dataset, we followed the methodology outlined in Sect. 3. Importance scores were aggregated from a subset of samples obtained from the specified sampling techniques (most Confidence, Random, Clustering with 10 samples per class from the training set). Neurons with the lowest aggregated importance scores were pruned based on a defined pruning rate. We evaluated the models' accuracy and computational efficiency at various pruning rates, specifically observing the point of "lossless pruning" where accuracy is maintained despite significant compression. Although the importance score computation incurs a one-time overhead proportional to model size, this cost is theoretically justified by the resulting gains in post-pruning inference efficiency, thereby amplifying benefits in resource-limited clinical settings.

## 5  Results and Discussion

The results demonstrate the effectiveness of the proposed pruning methodology across different medical imaging datasets and model architectures. This section highlights core findings related to model resilience under high pruning rates, the impact of attribution methods, and the influence of sampling strategies. Table 1 and Fig. 2 summarize pruning performance across the experimental spectrum. Across all datasets and models, interpretability-guided pruning using LRP, DLB, and IG consistently enables high model compression while maintaining accuracy within a 5% margin, even at moderate pruning rates.

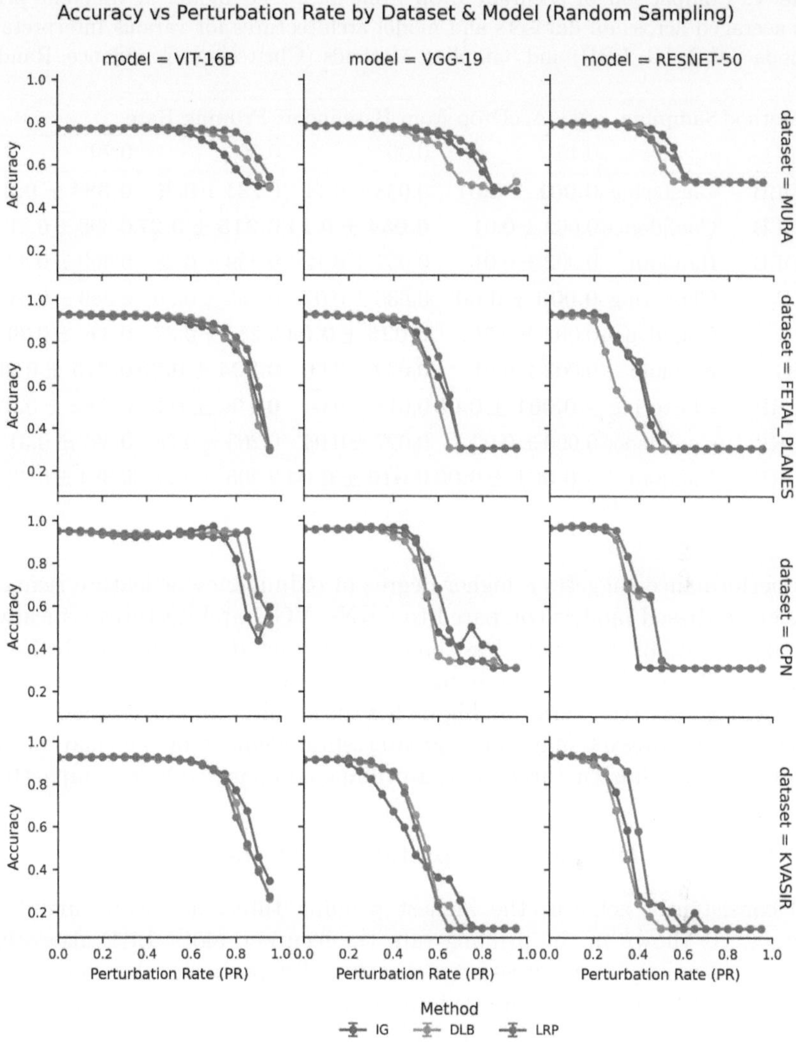

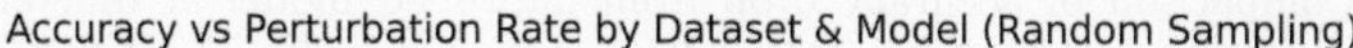

Accuracy vs Perturbation Rate by Dataset & Model (Random Sampling)

**Fig. 2.** Accuracy vs Pruning Rate across various Models (Vit, Resnet,Vgg) and Datasets (Mura, Fetal Planes, Cpn, Kvasir) using Various Attribution Methods (IG, DLB, LRP).

## 5.1   Model-Wise Observations

We observed across all datasets that, in most cases, ViTs seem to have the highest accuracy followed by Vgg and Resnet. Among the architectures, ViTs demonstrate exceptional robustness, consistently preserving performance even beyond 65–80% pruning. Notably, in certain configurations (e.g., CPN with LRP or DLB), ViTs withstand pruning rates of 85% with minimal degradation.

**Table 1.** Comparison of accuracy drop from unpruned model at different pruning rates averaged across all datasets and model architectures for various Interpretability Methods (DLB, IG, LRP) and Sampling Methods (Clustering, Confidence, Random).

| Method | Sampling | $\Delta(\downarrow)$AccDrop from Baseline at Pruning Rate | | | |
|---|---|---|---|---|---|
| | | 0.15 | 0.30 | 0.50 | 0.70 |
| DLB | Clustering | **0.001 ± 0.01** | 0.058 ± 0.11 | 0.234 ± 0.30 | **0.384 ± 0.31** |
| DLB | Confidence | 0.002 ± 0.01 | **0.054 ± 0.11** | **0.215 ± 0.27** | 0.398 ± 0.31 |
| DLB | Random | 0.002 ± 0.01 | 0.059 ± 0.12 | 0.239 ± 0.28 | 0.400 ± 0.32 |
| IG | Clustering | **0.000 ± 0.00** | 0.036 ± 0.07 | 0.255 ± 0.29 | 0.389 ± 0.31 |
| IG | Confidence | 0.002 ± 0.01 | **0.026 ± 0.04** | 0.253 ± 0.27 | 0.398 ± 0.30 |
| IG | Random | 0.002 ± 0.01 | 0.039 ± 0.06 | **0.224 ± 0.29** | **0.375 ± 0.30** |
| LRP | Clustering | **−0.001 ± 0.00** | 0.018 ± 0.04 | **0.196 ± 0.28** | **0.382 ± 0.33** |
| LRP | Confidence | 0.000 ± 0.00 | 0.027 ± 0.04 | 0.203 ± 0.28 | 0.397 ± 0.31 |
| LRP | Random | **−0.001 ± 0.00** | **0.016 ± 0.04** | 0.205 ± 0.27 | 0.384 ± 0.33 |

This performance suggests a higher degree of redundancy or feature richness in transformer-based models compared to CNNs. VGG architectures typically tolerate up to 50% pruning with less than 5% accuracy drop, whereas ResNets are comparatively sensitive, maintaining stability only up to 30% pruning in most settings. The observed variation highlights the architectural differences: residual connections in ResNet may cause greater entanglement of information across neurons, making unstructured neuron pruning comparatively less impactful.

## 5.2   Impact of Different Interpretability Methods

LRP consistently achieves the highest pruning thresholds while maintaining accuracy. As shown in the pruning rate vs. accuracy plots, LRP also achieves the lowest accuracy drop across pruning rates, slightly better than IG and DLB. This affirms LRP's strong conservation properties and robustness in identifying less important neurons followed by DLB and IG.

## 5.3   Impact of Different Sampling Strategies

Clustering-based sampling performs best on average across attribution methods, particularly noticeable at moderate pruning levels (30–50%). As shown in Table 1, LRP with Clustering shows the lowest drop, outperforming Random and Confidence-based alternatives. Confidence-based sampling performs competitively, particularly for IG and DLB, where it occasionally surpasses Random selection in maintaining model stability. Interestingly, in certain configurations (especially at lower pruning rates like 15–30%), a slight increase in accuracy is observed. This counterintuitive behavior arises because pruning also removes neurons that may have a negative or noisy influence on predictions. By discarding these misleading neurons, the model generalizes better, resulting in a net accuracy gain. The sampling strategy also influences pruning stability; while minor fine-tuning may be required for specific datasets, the overall framework remains robust across sampling choices. The observed high variance is expected as these results are averaged across different datasets and architectures; however, overall trends remain consistent.

## 6   Conclusion

In this work, we introduce an interpretability-aware pruning framework that leverages multiple interpretability techniques to guide the compression of deep neural networks used in medical image analysis. Instead of relying on traditional magnitude-based or heuristic pruning strategies, our method utilizes importance scores derived from model interpretability techniques, enabling a principled and transparent approach to model compression.

We evaluate our framework on four diverse medical imaging datasets— MURA, CPN, KVASIR, and Fetal Planes—across three representative architectures: VGG19, ResNet50, and VIT-16b. Our experiments demonstrate that the proposed method achieves substantial pruning rates (up to 80–85%) with minimal loss in accuracy. Notably, ViT-based models retained performance particularly well under compression, highlighting their potential for deployment in resource-constrained clinical environments. Among the interpretability techniques studied, Layer-wise Relevance Propagation (LRP) consistently enabled the highest pruning thresholds without degrading performance, followed by DL-Backtrace (DLB) and Integrated Gradients (IG). We also observed that the choice of sampling strategy significantly impacts pruning effectiveness: clustering-based sampling outperformed Confidence-based and Random strategies, achieving the most robust results. Interestingly, in certain settings, we observed improved accuracy after pruning, suggesting that interpretability-guided pruning may help eliminate redundant or noisy neurons, thereby improving generalization. This reinforces its dual role in facilitating both compression and performance enhancement.

Overall, our findings highlight that interpretability-guided pruning offers an effective pathway to building lightweight, interpretable, and potentially more robust AI systems—an essential step toward the safe and trustworthy deployment of AI systems in high-stakes domains such as healthcare.

## 7   Implications for Medical Image Analysis

Interpretability-aware pruning offers significant benefits for healthcare:

- **Efficiency:** Achieving 40–50% lossless pruning creates lightweight models with reduced memory and computation needs, enabling deployment on edge devices, mobile platforms, and clinics with limited resources, while speeding up diagnostic workflows.

- **Interpretability:** Pruning guided by interpretability methods links model compression with transparency, highlighting which neurons are critical and helping clinicians understand model decisions based on meaningful features.
- **Robustness:** Using diverse sampling methods to evaluate neuron importance ensures pruning preserves neurons important for varied inputs and edge cases, enhancing model reliability.

Although further empirical validation is needed, we hypothesize that pruning pre-trained models using region-specific, representative data could improve generalization at deployment. This approach may mitigate domain shift and preserve model reliability in real-world clinical settings.

**Disclosure of Interests.** The authors are affiliated with AryaXAI.com, part of Aurionpro Solutions Limited. DL-Backtrace was introduced by AryaXAI. The authors declare no further competing interests.

# References


1. Arrieta, A.B., et al.: Explainable artificial intelligence (XAI): concepts, taxonomies, opportunities and challenges toward responsible AI (2019). https://arxiv.org/abs/1910.10045
2. Atakishiyev, S., Salameh, M., Goebel, R.: Safety implications of explainable artificial intelligence in end-to-end autonomous driving (2025). https://arxiv.org/abs/2403.12176
3. Blalock, D., Ortiz, J.J.G., Frankle, J., Guttag, J.V.: What is the state of neural network pruning? In: Proceedings of Machine Learning and Systems, vol. 2, pp. 129–146 (2020)
4. Burgos-Artizzu, X.P., et al.: Evaluation of deep convolutional neural networks for automatic classification of common maternal fetal ultrasound planes. Sci. Rep. **10**(1), 10200 (2020)
5. Dosovitskiy, A., et al.: An image is worth $16 \times 16$ words: transformers for image recognition at scale. In: International Conference on Learning Representations (ICLR) (2021)
6. Esteva, A., et al.: Deep learning-enabled medical computer vision. NPJ Digit. Med. **4**(1), 5 (2021)
7. Frankle, J., Carbin, M.: The lottery ticket hypothesis: finding sparse, trainable neural networks. In: International Conference on Learning Representations (ICLR) (2019)
8. Fresz, B., et al.: The contribution of XAI for the safe development and certification of AI: an expert-based analysis (2024). https://arxiv.org/abs/2408.02379
9. Gale, T., Elsen, E., Hooker, S.: The state of sparsity in deep neural networks. arXiv preprint arXiv:1902.09574 (2019)
10. Gohel, P., Singh, P., Mohanty, M.: Explainable AI: current status and future directions (2021). https://arxiv.org/abs/2107.07045
11. Han, S., Pool, J., Tran, J., Dally, W.J.: Learning both weights and connections for efficient neural networks. In: Advances in Neural Information Processing Systems (NeurIPS) (2015)

12. Hassibi, B., Stork, D.G.: Second order derivatives for network pruning: optimal brain surgeon. In: Advances in Neural Information Processing Systems (NeurIPS), pp. 164–171 (1993)

13. Hatefi, S.M.V., Dreyer, M., Achtibat, R., Wiegand, T., Samek, W., Lapuschkin, S.: Pruning by explaining revisited: optimizing attribution methods to prune CNNs and transformers (2024). https://arxiv.org/abs/2408.12568

14. He, K., Zhang, X., Ren, S., Sun, J.: Deep residual learning for image recognition. In: Proceedings of the IEEE Conference on Computer Vision and Pattern Recognition, pp. 770–778 (2016)

15. Holzinger, A., Biemann, C., Pattichis, C.S., Kell, D.B.: What do we need to build explainable AI systems for the medical domain? arXiv preprint arXiv:1712.09923 (2017)

16. Kumar, S.: Covid19-Pneumonia-normal chest X-Ray images (2022)

17. Litjens, G., et al.: A survey on deep learning in medical image analysis. Med. Image Anal. **42**, 60–88 (2017)

18. Liu, Z., Sun, M., Zhou, T., Huang, G., Darrell, T.: Rethinking the value of network pruning. In: International Conference on Learning Representations (ICLR) (2019)

19. Montavon, G., Binder, A., Lapuschkin, S., Samek, W., Müller, K.: Layer-wise relevance propagation: an overview. In: Explainable AI (2019). https://api.semanticscholar.org/CorpusID:202579539

20. Montavon, G., Lapuschkin, S., Binder, A., Samek, W., Müller, K.R.: Explaining nonlinear classification decisions with deep taylor decomposition. Pattern Recogn. **65**, 211–222 (2017)

21. Pogorelov, K., et al.: Kvasir: a multi-class image dataset for computer aided gastrointestinal disease detection. In: Proceedings of the 8th ACM on Multimedia Systems Conference, pp. 164–169 (2017)

22. Rajpurkar, P., et al.: Mura: large dataset for abnormality detection in musculoskeletal radiographs. arXiv preprint arXiv:1712.06957 (2017)

23. Sabih, M., Hannig, F., Teich, J.: Utilizing explainable AI for quantization and pruning of deep neural networks. arXiv abs/2008.09072 (2020). https://api.semanticscholar.org/CorpusID:221186873

24. Sanh, V., Wolf, T., Rush, A.M.: Movement pruning: adaptive sparsity by fine-tuning. In: Advances in Neural Information Processing Systems, vol. 33, pp. 20378–20389 (2020)

25. Sankarapu, V.K., Chitroda, C., Rathore, Y., Singh, N.K., Seth, P.: Dlbacktrace: a model agnostic explainability for any deep learning models (2025). https://arxiv.org/abs/2411.12643

26. Shen, D., Wu, G., Suk, H.I.: Deep learning in medical image analysis. Annu. Rev. Biomed. Eng. **19**, 221–248 (2017)

27. Simonyan, K., Zisserman, A.: Very deep convolutional networks for large-scale image recognition. arXiv preprint arXiv:1409.1556 (2014)

28. Sundararajan, M., Taly, A., Yan, Q.: Axiomatic attribution for deep networks. In: Precup, D., Teh, Y.W. (eds.) Proceedings of the 34th International Conference on Machine Learning, ICML 2017, Sydney, NSW, Australia, 6–11 August 2017. Proceedings of Machine Learning Research, vol. 70, pp. 3319–3328. PMLR (2017). https://api.semanticscholar.org/CorpusID:16747630

29. Zhu, M., Gupta, S.: To prune, or not to prune: exploring the efficacy of pruning for model compression. In: International Conference on Learning Representations (ICLR) (2018)

# PeekNet: A Power and Efficiency-Enhanced Knowledge-Aware Network for Real-Time Capsule Endoscopy Image Classification

Krispian Lawrence[(✉)], Usha Goparaju, and Karunan Joseph

Equitable Technologies, Boston, USA
`{kris,usha.goparaju,karunan.joseph}@screenwithpeek.com`

**Abstract.** Wireless Capsule Endoscopy (WCE) enables non-invasive imaging of the gastrointestinal (GI) tract. However, it generates over 50,000 frames per exam, making full-frame transmission using radio frequency (RF) communication highly energy-consuming and bandwidth-inefficient. To overcome this, we introduce PeekNet a compact, low-power convolutional neural network tailored for on-device GI lesion classification in a resource-constrained environment. By enabling real-time analysis onboard the capsule, PeekNet allows only clinically relevant frames with high-confidence predictions to be transmitted, conserving energy and extending device longevity. The architecture combines grouped convolutions, parallel dilated branches, and lightweight attention to capture multi-scale context with minimal computational cost. In its fully quantized INT8 form, PeekNet fits within **337kB** of flash, executes in under **70ms**, and consumes significantly less energy per frame than Bluetooth Low-energy (BLE) transmission. We have evaluated on the Kvasir-Capsule dataset, it achieves **97.24%** accuracy using only **0.15M parameters**, outperforming conventional lightweight models. This work represents a critical step toward fully autonomous, privacy-preserving, and energy-efficient explainable AI integration in next-generation WCE systems.

**Keywords:** Capsule Endoscopy · Edge AI · Lightweight CNN · Inference · Embedded AI · Anomaly Detection · Explainable AI

## 1 Introduction

Colorectal cancer (CRC) remains the second leading cause of cancer-related mortality globally, where early detection can significantly improve survival outcomes [1]. Wireless Capsule Endoscopy (WCE) has become a pivotal diagnostic modality, offering full-tract gastrointestinal (GI) imaging in a non-invasive manner particularly valuable for regions inaccessible by conventional endoscopy like small bowel. As CRC incidence rises and screening guidelines broaden, WCE


T. Chen et al. (Eds.): EMA4MICCAI 2025 Workshops, LNCS 16318, pp. 236–246, 2026.
https://doi.org/10.1007/978-3-032-13961-0_24

is increasingly integrated into population-scale screening programs beyond its established roles in obscure GI bleeding and Crohn's disease monitoring [2,3]. However, current AI-assisted WCE workflows are typically post-hoc, requiring full-frame transmission to external workstations or cloud servers for offline analysis. This places significant strain on battery life, bandwidth, and storage. With each capsule producing tens of thousands of mostly non-informative frames, the process is inefficient and lacks real-time capability. The added latency also delays clinical feedback and limits scalability.

Edge AI integration in capsule endoscopy involves processing the frames on-device and transmitting only the AI flagged abnormalities in real-time. In capsule endoscopy, wireless data transfer is one of the most energy-hungry operations. Hence this particular approach of sending only the clinically significant AI flagged frames considerably reduces the power required for wireless data transfer. The saved energy can help the capsule to last longer and can be used for other tasks like on-device landmark detection avoiding the need to offload raw frames to servers for Location inference. This reduces latency, lowers server-side energy use and operational costs, and becomes increasingly beneficial as adoption scales. However, a major gap remains in AI models optimized for the visual complexity of GI imaging in the strict resource limits of embedded hardware. Fully harnessing Edge AI can transform capsule endoscopy from passive imaging into an autonomous, efficient, and scalable diagnostic tool. In a nutshell, our **key contributions** are: We introduce PeekNet (Power and Efficiency-Enhanced Knowledge-Aware Network), a domain-specialized lightweight model designed for real-time GI image analysis on ultra-low-power devices. Unlike generic mobile networks, PeekNet is purpose-built for embedded deployment, enabling fast, energy-efficient, and Explainable diagnostics directly on edge systems.

## 2   Related Work

Recent advances in deep learning have significantly improved disease detection in GI endoscopy, particularly through ensemble and CNN architectures. In [4], the authors evaluated the classification performance of multiple state-of-the-art models, including VGG16, ResNet, MobileNet and Xception, on the Kvasir dataset. [5] explored the recent advances in transfer learning, attention mechanisms, multi-modal learning, automated lesion detection. An edge-friendly diagnostic framework for WCE proposed in [6], integrates CNN-based lesion detection with energy-efficient hardware constraints. Similarly, [7] advanced semi-automated annotation pipelines using deep CNNs to reduce clinician burden in capsule endoscopy workflows. Our design philosophy aligns with recent directions emphasizing edge-aware, efficient AI for medical applications [8].

Lightweight CNNs are increasingly vital for medical image classification under resource constraints. MobileNet [9] and MobileNetV2 [10] introduced depthwise separable convolutions, reducing computation with minimal accuracy loss. ShuffleNet [11] advanced this via pointwise group convolutions and channel shuffle for real-time inference on low-power devices. ESPNetv2 [12]

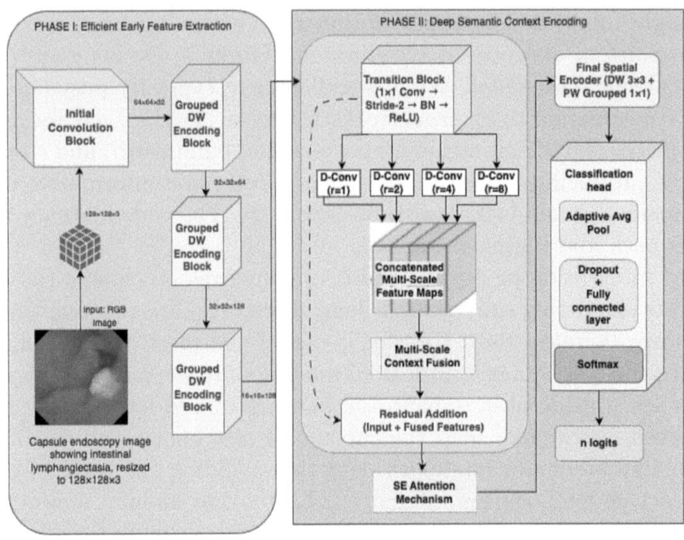


**Fig. 1.** Overview of the proposed two phase **PeekNet** architecture.

balanced speed and accuracy using spatial pyramid modules and depthwise dilated convolutions, while MCU-Net [13] achieved segmentation-level performance on sub-1MB models for microcontroller-class hardware. Though mainly tested on standard datasets, these efficient architectures are well-suited for edge-deployable frameworks like PeekNet. This design trend supports interpretable, low-latency, and energy-efficient medical AI. The shift from cloud-based inference to hardware-aware, on-device computation has driven the development of models tailored for real-time GI diagnostics. [14] introduced the Galar dataset with 3.5M annotated frames and proposed a CNN-HMM framework achieving 93% localization accuracy with  1M parameters for embedded deployment. [15] used transformers to model temporal patterns in WCE, showing self-attention's effectiveness despite spatial discontinuity. There is a limited research on Edge AI based architectures in capsule endoscopy. Hence, in this work, we aim to bridge that gap through efficient on-device intelligence.

## 3   Proposed Methodology

Deploying deep models within the extreme constraints of capsule-based systems remains an open challenge. Prior lightweight models offer promising FLOP reductions and fast inference, but they often fall short in real-world deployment on deeply embedded platforms particularly micro-controller-class devices with strict memory and power limits. Understanding the unique needs of capsule endoscopy, where diagnostic accuracy is paramount and compute/memory budgets are extremely tight, we designed PeekNet with a dual-phase architecture (Fig. 1) that strategically balances efficiency and representational capacity.

**Architecture Overview**: We have analyzed several existing lightweight architectures and identified a significant gap when it comes to deploying these architectures in the real world that consumes less power and is memory-efficient. Hence, we have taken inspiration from their strengths and proposed a custom architecture that integrates selected segments with targeted enhancements for real-time capsule endoscopy. The architecture is grounded in four core principles tailored for real-time capsule endoscopy. First, *modular efficiency*: lightweight, reusable blocks ensure scalable deployment across heterogeneous hardware. Second, *multi-scale representation*: diverse receptive fields that aid in capturing both fine-grained lesions and global anatomical context. Third, *channel-wise attention*: streamlined attention modules emphasize salient features with minimal computational cost. Finally, *resource-aware design*: the use of grouped convolutions, channel shuffling, etc., ensures low-latency inference and strict memory compliance, facilitating deployment on embedded diagnostic platforms.

**Phase I: Efficient Early Feature Extraction**: This phase of the network focuses on efficient early-stage encoding by replacing conventional downsampling and convolutional blocks with a sequence of grouped and shuffled convolutional units. It begins with a lightweight strided 3×3 convolution (the stem), followed by multiple blocks combining grouped pointwise convolutions and depthwise spatial filtering, as popularized in ShuffleNetV2 [16]. This structure substantially reduces computational cost without sacrificing spatial granularity. To mitigate the channel isolation effect inherent in grouped convolutions, we apply channel shuffling after each unit to enable inter-group communication and enrich feature diversity [16]. Our design adapts this mechanism for low-resolution (128×128) GI imagery, where large anatomical structures dominate. This allows us to widen the feature space early in the pipeline, capturing subtle pathological cues at minimal compute cost. Unlike off-the-shelf lightweight encoders, in our implementation we reparameterize the batch normalization and residual pathways to meet the strict latency and memory requirements of edge NPUs used in capsule endoscopy. Each stage is optimized for bandwidth efficiency and receptive field expansion, resulting in a compact but expressive front-end that preserves clinically relevant textures essential for early abnormality detection.

**Phase II: Deep Semantic Context Encoding**: To achieve high-level semantic abstraction under strict efficiency constraints, the second phase of our architecture leverages parallel dilated convolutional branches coupled with lightweight channel attention. Drawing inspiration from ESPNetv2 [12], we use dilation rates of 1,2,4,8 to process input at multiple receptive fields in parallel, enabling simultaneous capture of both fine-grained and global contextual cues, a critical need in medical imaging where diagnostic features are often distributed or subtle [12]. Unlike the deep sequential stacks that gather context gradually, our parallel dilation design provides faster multi-scale abstraction and improved gradient propagation. This is followed by Squeeze-and-Excitation (SE) modules that adaptively recalibrate channel-wise features, enhancing discriminative capacity while suppressing background noise [17]. Attention is applied only at deeper layers intentionally to avoid overfitting on low-level features. The output is then

**Table 1.** Accuracy and efficiency of classification models evaluated on the Kvasir dataset. All metrics are obtained from inference performed on an AWS cloud instance using the full-precision models.

| Model | Accuracy (%) | Params (M) | FLOPs | Model Size (MB) |
|---|---|---|---|---|
| ResNet18 | 98.86 | 11.18 | 1820.00 | 44.72 |
| EfficientNet | 98.67 | 4.03 | 408.93 | 16.12 |
| MobileNetV2 | 98.43 | 2.24 | 319.04 | 8.96 |
| ShuffleNetV2 | 94.54 | 1.27 | 151.38 | 5.08 |
| ESPNetv2 | 97.41 | 1.24 | 28.37 | 4.96 |
| **PeekNet (Ours)** | **97.42** | **0.15** | **20.99** | **0.78** |

aggregated via global average pooling, regularized with dropout ($p = 0.2$), and fed to a fully connected layer for classification. The model supports both 14-class and binary classification settings flexibly by adjusting the dimensionality.

**Experimental Setup**: We evaluated on the publicly available Kvasir-Capsule dataset [18] benchmark of over 117,000 clinically labeled wireless capsule endoscopy frames spanning 14 GI categories, including polyps, ulcers, angiectasia, and mucosal inflammation. Kvasir-Capsule was chosen for its high-quality annotations, clinical relevance, and broad GI class coverage specific to capsule endoscopy. Other datasets primarily focus on colonoscopy or lack similar diversity. Future work will explore broader dataset evaluations for generalizability. We explored two classification settings: (i) multi-class prediction over all 14 labels, and (ii) binary classification (normal vs. abnormal) to emulate clinical triage. Images are resized to 128ÃŮ128 and normalized using ImageNet statistics. No balancing is applied to preserve natural class imbalance. Standard augmentations (horizontal flip, affine transforms, and brightness/contrast jitter) are used during training. All models are deployed on the Arm Corstone-300 (Cortex-M55 & Ethos-U55), an architecture of low-power edge hardware with 8MB flash, 2 MB SRAM, and 512 KB TCM [20]. Metrics (latency, memory, and power) are recorded from real-time inference on 128ÃŮ128 grayscale inputs. Models are trained in PyTorch with FP32 precision, then exported to ONNX and converted to TensorFlow for post-training INT8 quantization via TFLite using representative calibration data. The quantized models utilize Arm Ethos-U Vela compiler [19], applying operator fusion, memory tiling, and scheduling tailored to the Ethos-U55. The final binary is integrated into device firmware by converting it into a C Array. Runtime results reflect full on-device inference using CMSIS-NN (Cortex Microcontroller Software Interface Standard - Neural Network) and Vela-optimized scheduling

## 4   Results and Analysis

We benchmarked **PeekNet** against a broad spectrum of state-of-the-art models, including high-capacity server-side networks (ResNet18, EfficientNet-B0)

**Table 2.** Class-wise precision, recall, and F1-score for PeekNet (quantized) on the Kvasir validation set.

| Metric | Polyp | Lymph-angiecta-sia | Normal Mucosa | Reduced Mucosal View | Pylorus | Foreign Body | Erosion | Angiec-tasia | Ulcer |
|---|---|---|---|---|---|---|---|---|---|
| **Precision** | 0.99 | 0.99 | 0.98 | 0.98 | 0.90 | 0.92 | 0.88 | 0.98 | 0.92 |
| **Recall** | 0.93 | 0.91 | 0.99 | 0.96 | 0.90 | 0.92 | 0.69 | 0.89 | 0.96 |
| **F1-Score** | 0.97 | 0.95 | 0.99 | 0.97 | 0.90 | 0.92 | 0.77 | 0.94 | 0.94 |

**Table 3.** Class-wise precision, recall, and F1-score comparison across ResNet18, EfficientNetB0, and MobileNetV2 on the Kvasir validation set.

| Class | Polyp | | | Lymphangiectasia | | | Normal Mucosa | | |
|---|---|---|---|---|---|---|---|---|---|
| Metric | ResNet18 | EffNetB0 | MobileNetV2 | ResNet18 | EffNetB0 | MobileNetV2 | ResNet18 | EffNetB0 | MobileNetV2 |
| Precision | 1.00 | 1.00 | 1.00 | 0.95 | 0.98 | 0.94 | 0.99 | 1.00 | 0.99 |
| Recall | 1.00 | 1.00 | 1.00 | 0.97 | 0.99 | 0.98 | 0.98 | 0.99 | 1.00 |
| F1-Score | 1.00 | 1.00 | 1.00 | 0.96 | 0.98 | 0.96 | 0.99 | 0.99 | 0.99 |
| **Class** | Reduced Mucosal View | | | Pylorus | | | Foreign Body | | |
| **Metric** | ResNet18 | EffNetB0 | MobileNetV2 | ResNet18 | EffNetB0 | MobileNetV2 | ResNet18 | EffNetB0 | MobileNetV2 |
| Precision | 0.97 | 0.98 | 0.99 | 0.87 | 0.95 | 0.97 | 0.99 | 0.97 | 0.96 |
| Recall | 0.98 | 0.96 | 0.94 | 0.96 | 0.96 | 0.92 | 0.95 | 0.96 | 0.96 |
| F1-Score | 0.97 | 0.97 | 0.97 | 0.91 | 0.96 | 0.95 | 0.97 | 0.96 | 0.96 |
| **Class** | Erosion | | | Angiectasia | | | Ulcer | | |
| **Metric** | ResNet18 | EffNetB0 | MobileNetV2 | ResNet18 | EffNetB0 | MobileNetV2 | ResNet18 | EffNetB0 | MobileNetV2 |
| Precision | 0.79 | 0.85 | 0.87 | 0.99 | 0.94 | 0.98 | 0.97 | 0.99 | 0.99 |
| Recall | 0.89 | 0.88 | 0.89 | 0.98 | 0.98 | 0.96 | 0.95 | 0.95 | 0.96 |
| F1-Score | 0.84 | 0.87 | 0.88 | 0.98 | 0.96 | 0.97 | 0.96 | 0.97 | 0.98 |

and edge-optimized architectures (MobileNetV2, ESPNetv2). Table 1 shows that PeekNet achieves a classification accuracy of **97.24%** on the Kvasir-Capsule dataset with just **0.15M parameters** and **20.99 MMACs**, offering over **90×** reduction in compute compared to ResNet18 with only a minor drop in accuracy. Unlike scaled-down variants of existing models, PeekNet is a task-specific architecture co-designed for real-time, low-power gastrointestinal screening. Its fully quantized form occupies **337KB of flash 6× smaller than ESPNetv2** and **20× smaller than MobileNetV2** enabling deployment on microcontroller-class hardware. Table 2 and Table 3 further show strong per-class F1 performance across clinically significant GI findings, including *polyp* (0.97–1.00), *ulcer* (0.94–0.98), and *lymphangiectasia* (0.95–0.98), underscoring the robustness of PeekNet and baseline CNN models for lesion detection and their utility in colorectal cancer screening and general GI triage.

**Explainability and Visual Attribution**: Explainability is paramount in medical AI, where trust, accountability, and clinical validation are essential for real-world adoption. In the context of capsule endoscopy where physicians rely on subtle spatial and textural cues to identify abnormalities the ability of an AI model to provide visual explanations for its predictions is critical. As illus-

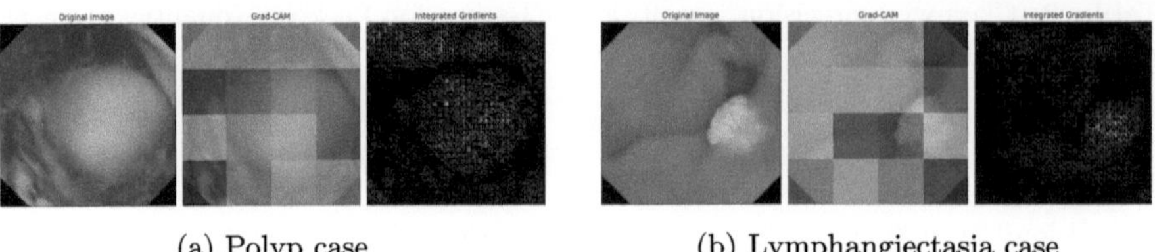

(a) Polyp case                    (b) Lymphangiectasia case

**Fig. 2.** Explainability visualizations using Grad-CAM and Integrated Gradients.

**Table 4.** Model efficiency and energy comparison

(a)Pre- vs Post-Quantization of the model on the cloud

| Metric | FP32 | INT8 |
|---|---|---|
| Accuracy (%) | 97.42 | 97.24 |
| Model Size (KB) | 786 | 337 |
| Inference Time (ms) | 9.72 | **1.77** |

(b) Energy per Frame: AI on Edge vs BLE Transmission

| Mode | T (ms) | I (mA) | E (mJ) |
|---|---|---|---|
| Edge Inference | 70 | 43 | **9.03** |
| BLE @ 200kbps | 655.36 | 20 | 39.32 |
| BLE @ 400kbps | 327.68 | 20 | 19.66 |

trated in Fig. 2, our PeekNet model generates semantically aligned and anatomically meaningful attributions via Grad-CAM [22] and Integrated Gradients. For instance, in the polyp example, the model localizes the lesion boundary accurately, while in lymphangiectasis, the focus aligns with vascular dilation and textural irregularities. These heatmaps confirm that PeekNet is not a black-box classifier, but a feature-aware system whose decisions can be interrogated and validated.

**Ablation Study:** PeekNet's architecture reflects strategic balance of performance, efficiency, and deployability, guided by rigorous ablation studies. **PeekNet-B** (with deeper ShuffleNet units in deeper layers too) improves accuracy by +0.274% but increases parameters (+13%), model size (+17%), and FLOPs (+22.8%). **PeekNet-C** (adds SE+ECA attention and dilated paths) offers marginal accuracy gains over the baseline but underperforms PeekNet-B, suggesting diminishing returns. These results validate PeekNet as a carefully optimized design shaped by empirical analysis and practical deployment constraints.

**Edge Inference Performance**: To validate the deployment suitability of PeekNet, we present an in-depth hardware-aware analysis covering model quantization, energy efficiency, memory utilization, and operator execution. As shown in Table 4 (a), INT8 quantization reduces inference latency by over 5× (from 9.72 ms to 1.77 ms) and compresses the model size from 786 KB to 337 KB, while preserving nearly the same accuracy (97.24%). This highlights the effectiveness of post-training quantization for low-power inference without compromising diagnostic fidelity. Figure 3 aComponent-wise memory allocation, visualized in Fig. 4 a, shows balanced utilization across weights, activations, and buffers, staying well within the SRAM budget. Figure 4 bdepicts that the majority of execu-

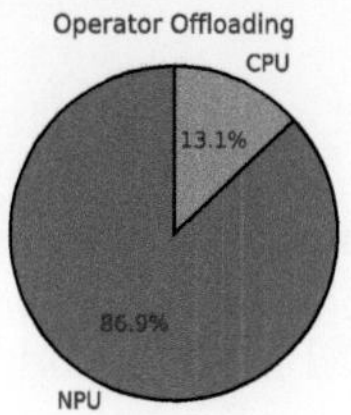
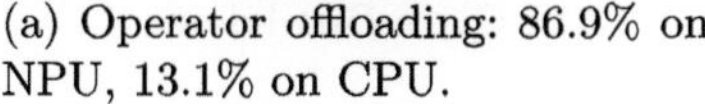


(a) Operator offloading: 86.9% on NPU, 13.1% on CPU.

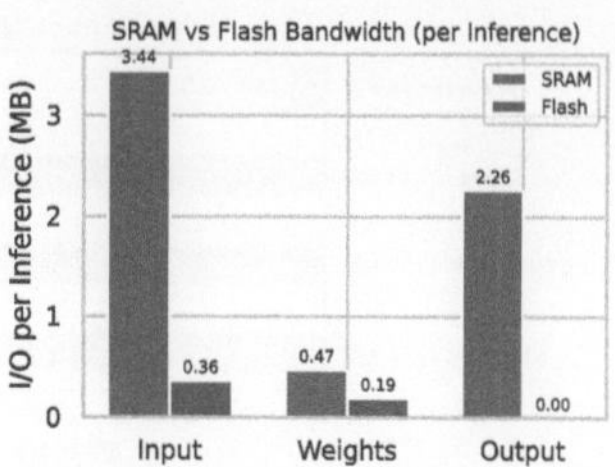


(b) Per-inference SRAM vs Flash I/O (MB) from Vela Compiler logs.

**Fig. 3.** Hardware profiling of the quantized PeekNet model.

tion cycles are efficiently handled by the NPU, with minimal CPU or DMA overhead. This optimised cycle distribution demonstrates that PeekNet is not just a light-weight architecture but also tightly aligned with the hardware accelerator stack, ensuring predictable runtime and power consumption behaviour. Considering all the above parameters, these results strongly support PeekNet as a principled, hardware-aligned solution for real-time AI inference in embedded medical systems, delivering robust accuracy, low latency, and ultra-low energy consumption without exceeding microcontroller-class constraints. Notably, PeekNet surpasses the model of [23], the prior work targeting edge based capsule endoscopy delivering higher accuracy with significantly lower compute and memory, making it far more deployable on embedded hardware.

**Power Estimation:** Conventional WCE systems typically use sub-GHz RF for transmission [24], which, although comparable in-capsule power, relies on external receiver modules that significantly increase overall energy usage. To quantify the benefits of on-device inference, we compare energy consumption for edge AI and BLE-based wireless transmission using hardware-measured current profiles and realistic bitrate assumptions. The quantized PeekNet model executes on Arm Corstone-300 hardware, drawing $43\,\mathrm{mA}$ over $70\,\mathrm{ms}$ at $3.0\,\mathrm{V}$, yielding an inference energy of $E_{\mathrm{infer}} = 3.0 \times 43\,\mathrm{mA} \times 0.070\,\mathrm{s} = \mathbf{9.03}\,\mathrm{mJ}$. In contrast, transmitting a $128{\times}128$ grayscale frame ($16\,\mathrm{KB} = 131072$ bits) over BLE at $200\,\mathrm{kbps}$ (TX current $= 20\,\mathrm{mA}$) takes $t_{\mathrm{tx@200}} = 131072/200000 = 0.655\,\mathrm{s}$, consuming $E_{\mathrm{BLE@200}} = 3.0 \times 20\,\mathrm{mA} \times 0.655\,\mathrm{s} = \mathbf{39.3}\,\mathrm{mJ}$. At $400\,\mathrm{kbps}$, $t_{\mathrm{tx@400}} = 0.328\,\mathrm{s}$, and $E_{\mathrm{BLE@400}} = 3.0 \times 20\,\mathrm{mA} \times 0.328\,\mathrm{s} = \mathbf{19.68}\,\mathrm{mJ}$ [25] as shown in Table 4 (b). In both cases, wireless transmission consumes significantly more energy than inference. These findings showcase that, regardless of wireless modality (BLE or RF), performing AI inference at the edge offers superior energy efficiency, making it essential for battery-powered medical systems.

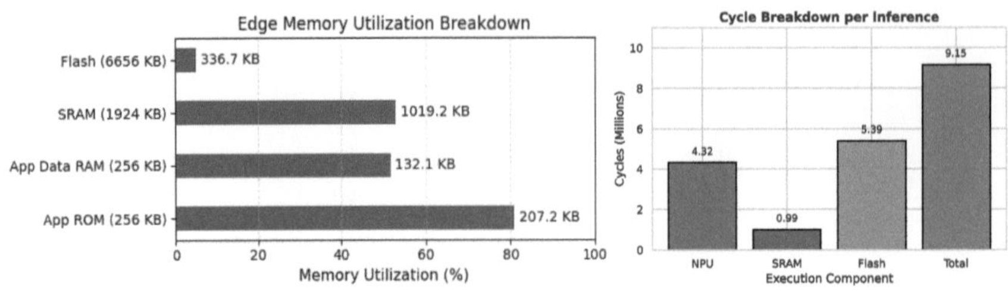

(a) Component-level Memory Breakdown    (b) Cycle Breakdown

**Fig. 4.** Detailed memory and execution breakdown of PEEKNET on Cortex-M55.

## 5    Conclusion

We introduced **PeekNet**, an optimized architecture for real-time gastrointestinal image classification on resource-constrained edge devices. Unlike the retrofitted general-purpose CNNs, PeekNet is explicitly designed for microcontroller-class hardware to achieve both efficiency and accuracy. Evaluated on the Kvasir-Capsule dataset, PeekNet delivers **97.24% accuracy** using just **0.15M parameters** and **20.99M MACs**, with sub-**70 ms** inference on a Cortex-M55 MCU. Its quantized version fits within **337KB** of flash and consumes significantly less energy than BLE transmission demonstrating the feasibility of real-time, on-device AI in low-power medical applications. As per the authors' knowledge, PeekNet represents one of the most *computationally efficient* models to date for capsule endoscopy. Extensive hardware profiling and class-wise validation confirm its clinical reliability and deployment readiness. While the model has not yet been tested on actual capsule endoscopy hardware, integration and validation on real-world devices is planned for future work to further assess deployment viability. Future work will explore superpixel-guided attention and adaptive frame selection to further reduce inference time and energy use [26]. This study highlights the impact of hardware-aware model design in enabling practical, high-performance optimal-cost edge AI for medical diagnostics.

## References


1. Siegel, R.L., Miller, K.D., Wagle, N.S., Jemal, A.: Cancer statistics, 2023. CA: a cancer J. Clin., **73**(1), 17–48 (2023). https://doi.org/10.3322/caac.21763
2. Liao, Z., Gao, R., Xu, C., Li, Z.S.: Indications and detection, completion, and retention rates of small-bowel capsule endoscopy: a systematic review. Gastroint. Endoscopy **71**(2), 280–286 (2010). https://doi.org/10.1016/j.gie.2009.09.031
3. Cao, Q., et al.: Robotic wireless capsule endoscopy: recent advances and upcoming technologies. Nat. Commun. **15**(1), 4597 (2024)
4. Dheir,I.M., Abu-Naser, S.S.: Classification of anomalies in gastrointestinal tract using deep learning. Int. J. Academic Eng. Res. (IJAER) **6**(3), 15–28 (2022). https://philpapers.org/rec/DHECOA

5. Habe, T.T., Haataja, K., Toivanen, P.: Review of deep learning performance in wireless capsule endoscopy images for GI disease classification. F1000Res **13**, 201 (2024). https://doi.org/10.12688/f1000research.145950.1, PMID: 39464781, PMCID: PMC11503939

6. Qin, K., et al.: Convolution neural network for the diagnosis of wireless capsule endoscopy: a systematic review and meta-analysis. Surg. Endosc. **36**(1), 16–31 (2021). https://doi.org/10.1007/s00464-021-08689-3

7. Namikawa, K., et al.: Utilizing artificial intelligence in endoscopy: a clinician's guide. Expert Rev. Gastroenterol. Hepatol., **14**(8), 689–706 (2020). https://doi.org/10.1080/17474124.2020.1779058

8. Gong, E.J., Bang, C.S., Lee, J.J.: Edge artificial intelligence device in real-time endoscopy for classification of gastric neoplasms: development and validation study. Biomimetics, **9**(12), 783 (2024). https://doi.org/10.3390/biomimetics9120783

9. Howard, A.G., et al.: MobileNets: efficient convolutional neural networks for mobile vision applications. arXiv preprint arXiv:1704.04861 (2017)

10. Sandler, M., Howard, A., Zhu, M., Zhmoginov, A., Chen, L.C.: MobileNetV2: inverted residuals and linear bottlenecks. In: Proceedings of the IEEE Conference on Computer Vision and Pattern Recognition (CVPR), pp. 4510–4520 (2018)

11. Zhang, X., Zhou, X., Lin, M., Sun, J.: ShuffleNet: an extremely efficient convolutional neural network for mobile devices. In: Proceedings of the IEEE Conference on Computer Vision and Pattern Recognition (CVPR), pp. 6848–6856 (2018)

12. Mehta, S., Rastegari, M., Caspi, A., Shapiro, L., Hajishirzi, H.: ESPNetv2: a lightweight, power efficient, and general purpose convolutional neural network. In: Proceedings of the IEEE/CVF Conference on Computer Vision and Pattern Recognition (CVPR), pp. 9190–9200 (2019)

13. Lin, J., Chen, W.M., Gan, C., Han, S.: MCUNetV2: memory-efficient patch-based inference for tiny deep learning. arXiv preprint arXiv:2204.08655 (2022)

14. Le Floch, M., Weber, R., Schröder, M., et al.: Advancing video capsule endoscopy with Edge AI: the galar multi-label dataset and efficient on-device inference models. Endoscopy Int. Open (2025). https://www.thieme-connect.com/products/ejournals/html/10.1055/s-0045-1805505

15. Tang, S., et al.: Transformer-based multi-task learning for classification and segmentation of gastrointestinal tract endoscopic images. Comput. Biol. Med. **157**, 106723 (2023). https://doi.org/10.1016/j.compbiomed.2023.106723

16. Ma, N., Zhang, X., Zheng, H. T., Sun, J.: Shufflenet v2: practical guidelines for efficient CNN architecture design. In: Proceedings of the European Conference on Computer Vision (ECCV), pp. 116–131 (2018).

17. Hu, J., Shen, L., Sun, G.: Squeeze-and-excitation networks. In: 2018 IEEE/CVF Conference on Computer Vision and Pattern Recognition, Salt Lake City, pp. 7132–7141 (2018). https://doi.org/10.1109/CVPR.2018.00745

18. Li, J., Feng, S., Ren, Y., et al.: Energy-aware embedded AI for gastrointestinal video capsule diagnostics. Bioengineering, **12**(6), 613 (2023). https://www.mdpi.com/2306-5354/12/6/613

19. Smedsrud, P.H., Thambawita, V., Hicks, S.A., et al.: Kvasir-Capsule, a video capsule endoscopy dataset. Sci. Data **8**, 142 (2021). https://doi.org/10.1038/s41597-021-00920-z

20. Millar, J., Huang, Y., Sethi, S., Haddadi, H., Madhavapeddy, A.: Benchmarking Ultra-Low-Power $\mu$NPUs. arXiv preprint arXiv:2503.22567 (2025). https://arxiv.org/abs/2503.22567

21. Arm Vela Compiler - https://developer.arm.com/documentation/109267/0102/Tool-support-for-the-Arm-Ethos-U-NPU/Ethos-U-Vela-compiler

22. Selvaraju, R.R., Cogswell, M., Das, A., Vedantam, R., Parikh, D., Batra, D.: Grad-CAM: visual explanations from deep networks via gradient-based localization. In: Proceedings of the IEEE International Conference on Computer Vision (ICCV) (2017)
23. Sahafi, A., Wang, Y., Rasmussen, C.L.M., et al.: Edge artificial intelligence wireless video capsule endoscopy. Sci. Rep. **12**, 13723 (2022). https://doi.org/10.1038/s41598-022-17502-7
24. Fontana, S., et al.: State of the art on advancements in wireless capsule endoscopy telemetry: a systematic approach. IEEE Open J. Antennas Propagation (2024)
25. Bulić, P., Kojek, G., Biasizzo, A.: Data transmission efficiency in bluetooth low energy versions. Sensors **19**(17), 3746 (2019). https://doi.org/10.3390/s19173746
26. Avelar, P.H.C., Tavares, A.R., da Silveira, T.L., Jung, C.R., Lamb, L.C.: Superpixel image classification with graph attention networks. In: 2020 33rd SIBGRAPI Conference on Graphics, Patterns and Images, pp. 203–209 (2020). https://doi.org/10.1109/SIBGRAPI51738.2020.00035, https://ieeexplore.ieee.org/document/9265983

# Efficient Foundation Model Pre-training on Mixed Retina Images from Similar Modalities


Boxuan Li[1], Yukun Zhou[2,3]([✉]), André Altmann[1,3], and Pearse A Keane[2]

[1] Department of Medical Physics and Biomedical Engineering, University College London, London, United Kingdom
[2] Institute of Ophthalmology, University College London, London, United Kingdom
`yukun.zhou.19@ucl.ac.uk`
[3] Hawkes Institute, University College London, London, United Kingdom



**Abstract.** Foundation models have demonstrated transformative potential across diverse domains, yet their development often requires extensive datasets and computational resources, necessitating efficient pre-training strategies. In this work, we hypothesise that introducing medical images from similar modalities can serve as an efficient way for data augmentation, potentially alleviating the stress of collecting substantial data and computational resources. We present RETFusion, a retinal foundation model pre-training on mixed retinal images from similar modalities, and evaluate it on extensive experiments. Specifically, we mix fundus fluorescein angiography (FFA) images, a modality with high contrast for lesion detection but rarely collected, with color fundus photography (CFP), commonly collected but with low contrast, for foundation model pre-training. The model is evaluated on clinically relevant applications with both FFA and CFP images. The results demonstrate that, although pre-trained on light data and computational resources, RETFusion achieved competitive performance in the CFP task compared to the state-of-the-art model RETFound and performed best in FFA tasks. Our findings suggest that pre-training on mixed data from similar modalities offers a practical and efficient solution for foundation model development in resource-constrained scenarios. The RETFusion code is available at: https://github.com/a-yayaya/RETFusion.

**Keywords:** Foundation model · Fluorescein Angiography · Diabetic Retinopathy


## 1 Introduction

Foundation models, pre-trained on large-scale datasets, can be adapted to diverse tasks and have shown promising performance [5]. In medical AI, models like GET [8] and Prov-GigaPath [19] demonstrate their potential in clinically relevant applications. RETFound, a typical example in ophthalmology, [21] was pre-trained on 1.6 million retinal images and showed good adaptability in ocular disease diagnosis and systemic condition prediction. However, the development of foundation models faces two major challenges: substantial computational costs and data scarcity. Collecting large-scale, real-world clinical data for medical foundation model pre-training is even more challenging.

Recent advances like DeepSeek [3] show that efficient pre-training can achieve comparable performance as state-of-the-art models like GPT-4 [1] and Claude-3.5-Sonnet [2] but require significantly less resources. Additionally, certain techniques like data augmentation [16], and data synthesis [4] have been proposed to release the stress of collecting large volumes of data and enrich data representations. However, few methods investigate the similarity across modalities in medical imaging and explicitly leverage such similarity in modeling.

Medical images across modalities sometimes show high similarity. For instance, fluorescein angiography images (FFA) and color fundus photographs (CFP) capture similar retinal areas and exhibit identical anatomical structures including the vasculature and optic disc. FFA provides high-contrast visualization between retinal vasculature and background, highlighting lesions for diabetic retinopathy (DR), a condition expected to affect 191 million people by 2030 [13,17,20]. Despite this efficiency, FFA images are not clinically routinely collected because they require an invasive intravenous dye injection and carry risks of adverse effects ranging from mild skin discoloration to severe anaphylaxis [12]. In contrast, CFP is non-invasive, rapid, and cost-effective [14], yet its limited contrast often hinders the detection of subtle DR pathologies such as microaneurysms and haemorrhages [9]. Given that CFP and FFA share similarities in imaging retinal structures (e.g. vasculature and optic disc), mixing images from these modalities straightforwardly increases the image quantity and potentially enriches the data representations.

Inspired by these observations, we hypothesize that mixing medical images from similar modalities can be regarded as an effective form of data augmentation. This enables efficient foundation model pre-training, which not only helps the model learn to process multi-modal inputs, but also achieves comparable or even better performance than pre-training on a single modality—while using significantly less data and computational resources. To validate it, we propose RETFusion, a foundational model that was pre-trained on a mixture of FFA images and CFP. In self-supervised pre-training, RETFusion learns abundant features on mixed images from two similar modalities. RETFusion achieves competitive performance in detecting diabetic retinopathy with FFA and CFP, while substantially reducing resource demands (e.g. 20% of images and 1.4% of computational resources compared to RETFound). Our findings suggest the benefits of mixing medical images from similar modalities, working as an efficient way to advance the efficiency of foundation model development, a critical yet underexplored area in medical AI.

## 2   Methodology

Figure 1 illustrates the overall workflow for constructing and applying RETFusion. Initially, RETFusion is pre-trained via self-supervised learning using a balanced set of CFP and FFA images randomly sampled from the AlzEye dataset. Subsequently, the model is fine-tuned on specific downstream tasks through supervised learning, followed by internal and external evaluations.

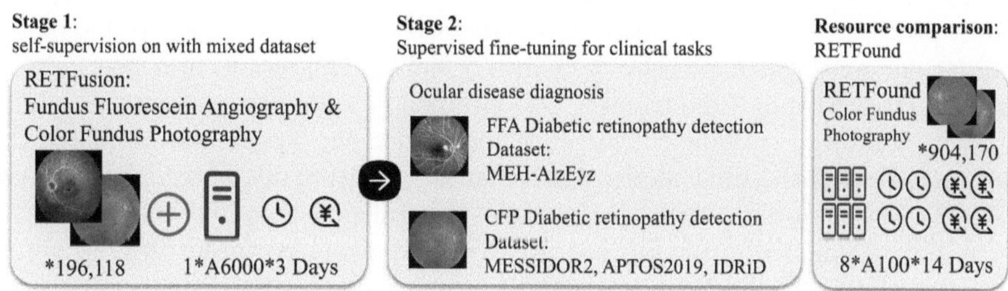


**Fig. 1. Overview of RETFusion. Stage 1 (Pre-training):** Self-supervised learning is performed on a mixture of FFA and CFP (98,059 images each) using a single NVIDIA A6000 GPU (24G) for 3 days. **Stage 2 (Fine-tuning):** The pre-trained model is fine-tuned to downstream tasks: one stream for diabetic retinopathy (DR) diagnosis using FFA images, and another for DR diagnosis using CFP datasets. Compared to RETFound, which requires 904,170 CFP images and eight A100 GPUs (40G each) for 14 days, RETFusion achieves competitive diagnostic performance with significantly reduced data and computational resources.

In order to highlight the benefits of pre-training on mixed images, we evaluate the RETFusion performance and compare it with multiple baseline models that share the same model architectures of vision transformer (ViT) [7]. As shown in Table 1, the differences between RETFusion and compared baselines are solely on the pre-training data. All methods are pre-trained on ImageNet-1k (Step 0). IMG has not been pre-trained on any retinal images. RETFound and FFAM are pre-trained on CFP and FFA images, respectively. CFP*-FFA is successively pre-trained on CFP and FFA images. CFP*-Fusion is first pre-trained on CFP images followed by pre-training on a mixture of CFP and FFA images. RETFusion is directly pre-trained on a mixture of CFP and FFA images after being pre-trained on ImageNet-1k.

## 3   Experimental

### 3.1   Datasets

We obtained pre-training data from the AlzEye dataset [18], which comprises 6,261,931 images collected from 353,157 patients between 2008 and 2018. To ensure demographic diversity, images were selected using stratified random sampling across age, sex, imaging devices, and temporal periods. From this larger dataset, we randomly sampled a balanced subset of 196,118 unlabeled images, evenly split between FFA (98,059 images) and CFP (98,059 images).

For DR classification tasks, we used images labeled according to the five-stage International Clinical DR Severity Scale. Specifically, we utilized 9,152 labeled FFA images and three publicly available CFP datasets: APTOS 2019 (3,662 images from India), IDRiD [15] (517 images from India), and MESSIDOR2 [6] (1,744 images from France). Consistent labeling across datasets enabled robust model pre-training and evaluation across diverse CFP sources. For internal model evaluation, we divided patient data into training, validation, and test subsets using a 55:15:30 split. The training set optimized model parameters, the validation set monitored training convergence and guided checkpoint selection, and the test set assessed the final model performance. Additionally, external validation datasets were employed to evaluate model generalization comprehensively.

Across all datasets, images are preprocessed using AutoMorph [22], which removes the image background without retinal information. The images are resized to $256 \times 256$ pixels. The pre-training process involves data augmentations, including random cropping, horizontal flipping, and image normalization, to enhance pre-training diversity.

**Table 1. Pre-training steps of RETFusion and baseline methods.** All methods share the same architecture and differ only in pre-training data. Step 0 uses ImageNet-1K (1.4M images). Step 1 and Step 2 use retinal datasets. **Note:**"Step 1 = X, Step 2 = None" is equivalent to "Step 1 = None, Step 2 = X". CFP* uses ~900k CFP images. CFP and CFP* are non-overlapping subsets drawn from the same dataset.

|        | IMG      | RETFound | FFAM     | CFP*-FFA | CFP*-Fusion | RETFusion  |
|--------|----------|----------|----------|----------|-------------|------------|
| Step 0 | ImageNet | ImageNet | ImageNet | ImageNet | ImageNet    | ImageNet   |
| Step 1 | None     | None     | None     | CFP*     | CFP*        | None       |
| Step 2 | None     | CFP*     | FFA      | FFA      | CFP & FFA   | CFP & FFA  |

## 3.2   Implementations

We use the Masked Autoencoder as the pre-training approach [10], with a masking ratio of 75%. An AdamW optimizer with layer-wise learning rate decay is included. The learning rate increases to $1 \times 10^{-3}$ over the first 15 epochs and then follows a cosine annealing schedule. The model is pre-trained for 100 epochs in total. At this stage, the ViT-large encoder is pre-trained alongside a lightweight decoder to reconstruct masked regions, enabling the model to learn robust representations from unlabeled data.

For downstream tasks, we retain only the ViT-large encoder to extract feature embeddings from retinal images, removing the decoder used during pre-training.

A multilayer perceptron is then attached to map these embeddings to disease class probabilities, with the output layer size corresponding to the number of disease categories. DR severity grading is formulated as a standard multi-class classification task, employing cross-entropy loss with label smoothing to mitigate potential overfitting.

Training uses a batch size of 16 over 50 epochs. The learning rate is initially ramped up from 0 to $5 \times 10^{-4}$ during the first 10 epochs, after which it is gradually reduced to $1 \times 10^{-6}$ using cosine annealing. After each epoch, we evaluate the model's performance on the validation set using the area under the receiver operating characteristic curve (AUROC) and the area under the precision-recall curve (AUPRC). The checkpoint with the highest AUROC on the validation set is retained for the final evaluation on the test set.

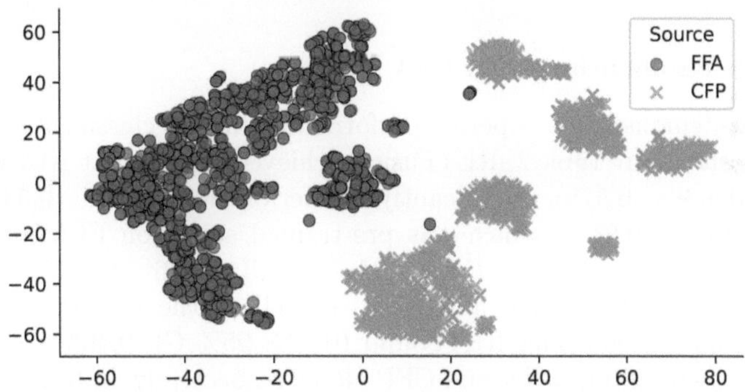

**Fig. 2. t-SNE visualization of feature embeddings** extracted by RETFusion. FFA images (blue) and CFP images (orange) form distinct clusters, indicating that the two modalities retain different feature representations.

## 4   Result

### 4.1   T-SNE Visualization

To understand how RETFusion perceives FFA and CFP images, we extracted feature embeddings with model encoders and applied t-distributed stochastic neighbor embedding (t-SNE) for dimensionality reduction and visualization (Fig. 2). Each point represents a single image, with blue color indicating FFA images and orange for CFP. The two modalities form distinct clusters, demonstrating their difference in feature embeddings. This collectively wider range of feature distribution likely trained the model to learn more general representations, equally working in parallel with data augmentation.

**Table 2.** Performance of pre-trained models on the FFA diabetic retinopathy classification task. P-values are derived from the Mann–Whitney U test, indicating the statistical significance of AUPRC comparisons between RETFusion and each baseline model. Both RETFound and CFP*-Fusion were trained on more than 900k images, while RETFusion was trained on fewer than 200k images.

| Model | AUPRC (95% CI) | AUROC (95% CI) | p-value (AUPRC) |
|---|---|---|---|
| IMG | 0.487 (0.469, 0.505) | 0.802 (0.796, 0.809) | 0.012 |
| FFAM | 0.543 (0.525, 0.561) | 0.830 (0.820, 0.840) | 0.012 |
| CFP*-FFA | 0.524 (0.496, 0.553) | 0.803 (0.790, 0.817) | 0.019 |
| CFP*-Fusion | 0.534 (0.519, 0.549) | 0.809 (0.804, 0.814) | 0.012 |
| RETFound | 0.427 (0.405, 0.448) | 0.754 (0.742, 0.767) | 0.012 |
| RETFusion | **0.568 (0.559, 0.578)** | **0.832 (0.829, 0.834)** | — |

## 4.2   DR Classification with FFA Images

RETFusion demonstrates superior performance in DR classification with FFA images. As shown in Table 2, RETFusion achieved the highest AUPRC of 0.568 (95% CI: 0.559 – 0.578), significantly outperforming FFAM (0.543; 95% CI: 0.525 – 0.561; p=0.018), which was pre-trained solely on FFA images. RETFusion also surpassed CFP*-FFA (0.524; 95% CI: 0.496 – 0.553), a model pre-trained sequentially on CFP and FFA, as well as the baselines IMG (0.487; 95% CI: 0.469 – 0.505) and RETFound (0.427; 95% CI: 0.405 – 0.448), which were pre-trained on ImageNet and CFP alone, respectively. In terms of AUROC, RETFusion achieved the highest score of 0.832 (95% CI: 0.827 – 0.837), slightly outperforming FFAM's 0.830 (95% CI: 0.820 – 0.840) and significantly exceeding RETFound's 0.754 (95% CI: 0.742 – 0.767). These results highlight the efficacy of RETFusion in DR classification on FFA images, likely integrating the complementary information from CFP and FFA images, even when pre-trained on a smaller dataset. This demonstrates RETFusion's potential as a robust and efficient solution for disease diagnosis based on FFA images.

## 4.3   Internal Evaluation for DR Classification with CFP Images

Under internal validation (Table 3), RETFusion demonstrated competitive performance across all three CFP datasets. On MESSIDOR2, RETFound achieved the highest AUROC of 0.884 (95% CI: 0.879 – 0.889), showing no significant difference (p=0.143) compared to RETFusion (0.877; 95% CI: 0.869 – 0.886). On IDRiD, RETFound significantly outperformed RETFusion (0.792; 95% CI: 0.785 – 0.799)(p=0.012). On APTOS2019, CFP*-Fusion achieved the highest AUROC of 0.946 (95% CI: 0.943 – 0.949), showing no significant performance compared to RETFusion with AUROC of 0.943 (95% CI: 0.939 – 0.947)(p=0.296). The AUPRC performance showed a similar trend, with RETFusion approximating the performance of RETFound and CFP*-Fusion across the three datasets. Notably, both CFP*-Fusion and RETFound were pre-trained on more than 900k

**Table 3.** Internal validation performance on DR classification with color fundus photography datasets. Both RETFound and CFP*-Fusion were trained on more than 900k images, while RETFusion was trained on fewer than 200k images. P-values (Mann–Whitney U test) indicate the significance of difference between RETFusion and the best-performing methods.

| Model | MESSIDOR2 (95% CI) | IDRiD (95% CI) | APTOS2019 (95% CI) |
|---|---|---|---|
| AUROC | | | |
| IMG | 0.824 (0.807, 0.840) | 0.760 (0.741, 0.779) | 0.894 (0.890, 0.898) |
| FFAM | 0.661 (0.635, 0.687) | 0.553 (0.517, 0.589) | 0.846 (0.837, 0.854) |
| CFP*-FFA | 0.734 (0.724, 0.744) | 0.623 (0.589, 0.656) | 0.880 (0.876, 0.884) |
| CFP*-Fusion | 0.881 (0.878, 0.884) | 0.802 (0.796, 0.808) | **0.946 (0.943, 0.949)** |
| RETFound | **0.884 (0.879, 0.889)** | **0.822 (0.812, 0.833)** | 0.943 (0.941, 0.946) |
| RETFusion | 0.877 (0.869, 0.886) | 0.792 (0.785, 0.799) | 0.943 (0.939, 0.947) |
| p-value | 0.143 | 0.012 | 0.296 |
| AUPRC | | | |
| IMG | 0.481 (0.438, 0.523) | 0.449 (0.412, 0.487) | 0.679 (0.661, 0.698) |
| FFAM | 0.302 (0.293, 0.312) | 0.275 (0.245, 0.306) | 0.457 (0.443, 0.471) |
| CFP*-FFA | 0.332 (0.319, 0.345) | 0.347 (0.310, 0.383) | 0.517 (0.496, 0.538) |
| CFP*-Fusion | 0.667 (0.658, 0.676) | 0.469 (0.459, 0.478) | **0.732 (0.728, 0.736)** |
| RETFound | **0.670 (0.651, 0.689)** | **0.497 (0.475, 0.518)** | 0.726 (0.720, 0.733) |
| RETFusion | 0.615 (0.558, 0.671) | 0.469 (0.459, 0.479) | 0.713 (0.701, 0.725) |
| p-value | 0.021 | 0.012 | 0.021 |

CFP images, while RETFusion used only 98,059 CFP images alongside 98,059 FFA images. These results highlight RETFusion's data efficiency, achieving performance comparable to RETFound and CFP*-Fusion despite using significantly fewer resources.

### 4.4 External Evaluation for DR Classification with CFP Images

We fine-tuned the model to one DR dataset and externally tested it on the other two (Table 4). RETFusion achieved the highest AUROC in two cases and remained highly competitive in the others. Specifically, when fine-tuned on APTOS2019 and evaluated on MESSIDOR2, RETFusion outperformed all models with an AUROC of 0.739 (95% CI: 0.720 – 0.758), slightly surpassing RETFound (0.738; 95% CI: 0.726 – 0.751) and CFP*-Fusion (0.727; 95% CI: 0.717 – 0.737). When fine-tuned on IDRiD and tested on APTOS2019, RETFusion and CFP*-Fusion both achieved the highest AUROC of 0.788, outperforming RETFound (0.755; 95% CI: 0.746 – 0.764). In other scenarios, such as fine-tuning on MESSIDOR2 and testing on APTOS2019 or IDRiD, RETFound achieved the best performance, closely followed by RETFusion. When fine-tuned on APTOS2019 and evaluated on IDRiD, RETFound achieved the

**Table 4.** Performance in external evaluation of DR classification. The model was fine-tuned on one DR dataset and tested on the other two datasets. Abbreviations: F = Fine-tune, T = Test, M = MESSIDOR2, A = APTOS2019, ID = IDRiD

| Metric | F | T | CFP*-Fusion | RETFound | RETFusion |
|---|---|---|---|---|---|
| AUROC | M | A | 0.800 (0.791, 0.808) | **0.808 (0.797, 0.818)** | 0.785 (0.764, 0.806) |
| AUROC | M | ID | 0.765 (0.758, 0.772) | **0.785 (0.767, 0.804)** | 0.727 (0.708, 0.746) |
| AUROC | A | M | 0.727 (0.717, 0.737) | 0.738 (0.726, 0.751) | **0.739 (0.720, 0.758)** |
| AUROC | A | ID | 0.721 (0.705, 0.737) | **0.822 (0.812, 0.833)** | 0.804 (0.791, 0.817) |
| AUROC | ID | M | 0.766 (0.752, 0.780) | **0.824 (0.809, 0.838)** | 0.803 (0.793, 0.814) |
| AUROC | ID | A | 0.788 (0.773, 0.803) | 0.755 (0.746, 0.764) | **0.788 (0.772, 0.803)** |
| AUPRC | M | A | 0.490 (0.479, 0.502) | **0.492 (0.481, 0.504)** | 0.414 (0.389, 0.440) |
| AUPRC | M | ID | 0.425 (0.401, 0.449) | **0.464 (0.427, 0.501)** | 0.394 (0.373, 0.414) |
| AUPRC | A | M | 0.482 (0.458, 0.507) | 0.502 (0.473, 0.532) | **0.516 (0.502, 0.529)** |
| AUPRC | A | ID | 0.403 (0.376, 0.429) | **0.497 (0.475, 0.518)** | 0.512 (0.491, 0.532) |
| AUPRC | ID | M | 0.428 (0.412, 0.445) | **0.508 (0.489, 0.527)** | 0.479 (0.460, 0.498) |
| AUPRC | ID | A | 0.445 (0.431, 0.458) | 0.419 (0.406, 0.432) | **0.453 (0.429, 0.478)** |

highest AUROC (0.822), while RETFusion (0.804) outperformed CFP*-Fusion (0.790). In terms of AUPRC, RETFusion exhibited a performance trend similar to AUROC, often matching or exceeding RETFound and CFP*-Fusion. Models such as FFAM and CFP*-FFA, which did not include CFP images in their stage 2 pre-training, are excluded from the table due to consistently poor performance.

### 4.5  Comparison on Development Efficiency

RETFusion demonstrates significant improvements in both data and computational efficiency, compared to baseline models such as RETFound. Specifically, RETFusion uses only 98,059 images from each modality, less than 20% of the data used by CFP*-Fusion (successively trained on 900k CFP images and 196k mixed images). However, RETFusion exhibited comparable or even better performance in certain evaluations. In terms of computational resources, RETFusion consumes around 1.4% of the GPU resources required by RETFound. For instance, pre-training RETFound used eight A100 GPUs over 14 days, whereas RETFusion was pre-trained using a single A6000 GPU over 3 days. By substantially reducing data and computational requirements, RETFusion provides a practical and efficient option for medical imaging analysis.

## 5  Conclusion and Discussion

This work presents RETFusion, a foundation model pre-trained on a mixture of FFA and CFP retinal images. By treating CFP as an effective modality-level augmentation for FFA, RETFusion learns complementary representations and achieves state-of-the-art performance in FFA tasks, while preserving competitive performance on CFP downstream tasks. These results support our hypothesis that mixing images from similar medical modalities serves as an efficient form of data augmentation, enabling strong model performance with significantly reduced data and computational requirements.

Despite promising results, RETFusion currently faces two key limitations. Firstly, although externally validated on CFP datasets, it lacks external validation on FFA images, which is essential for ensuring robustness across diverse populations, imaging devices, and acquisition protocols. Secondly, RETFusion has thus far been evaluated only on two specific retinal imaging modalities, and its applicability to other ophthalmic imaging methods, such as optical coherence tomography, or broader medical imaging domains, has yet to be explored.

Future work will likely proceed along two primary directions. First, since RETFusion is architecture-agnostic and currently adopts MAE mainly for fair comparison with RETFound, future versions can readily incorporate alternative self-supervised learning approaches such as DINO v2 [11]. Second, we plan to extend RETFusion to three-dimensional medical imaging tasks, such as optical coherence tomography, to assess its generalizability in more complex spatial domains.

**Acknowledgments.** Yukun Zhou is funded by Wellcome Award 318987/Z/24/Z. Pearse A. Keane is supported by a UK Research & Innovation Future Leaders Fellowship (MR/T019050/1) and The Rubin Foundation Charitable Trust.

**Disclosure of Interests.** The authors have no competing interests to declare that are relevant to the content of this article.

# References


1. Achiam, J., et al.: Gpt-4 technical report. arXiv preprint arXiv:2303.08774 (2023)
2. Anthropic: Claude 3 model card (2023). https://assets.anthropic.com/m/61e7d27f8c8f5919/original/Claude-3-Model-Card.pdf. Accessed: 21-Jan-2025
3. Bi, X., et al.: Deepseek LLM: Scaling open-source language models with longtermism. arXiv preprint arXiv:2401.02954 (2024)
4. Black, M.J., Patel, P., Tesch, J., Yang, J.: Bedlam: a synthetic dataset of bodies exhibiting detailed lifelike animated motion. In: Proceedings of the IEEE/CVF Conference on Computer Vision and Pattern Recognition, pp. 8726–8737 (2023)
5. Bommasani, R., et al.: On the opportunities and risks of foundation models. arXiv preprint arXiv:2108.07258 (2021)
6. Decencière, E., et al.: Feedback on a publicly distributed image database: The messidor database. Image Anal. Stereol. **33**, 231–234 (2014). https://api.semanticscholar.org/CorpusID:56390811
7. Dosovitskiy, A.: An image is worth 16x16 words: Transformers for image recognition at scale. arXiv preprint arXiv:2010.11929 (2020)
8. Fu, X., et al.: A foundation model of transcription across human cell types. Nature pp. 1–9 (2025)

9. Gao, Z., et al.: Automatic interpretation and clinical evaluation for fundus fluorescein angiography images of diabetic retinopathy patients by deep learning. Br. J. Ophthalmol. **107**(12), 1852–1858 (2023)
10. He, K., Chen, X., Xie, S., Li, Y., Dollár, P., Girshick, R.: Masked autoencoders are scalable vision learners. In: Proceedings of the IEEE/CVF Conference on Computer Vision and Pattern Recognition, pp. 16000–16009 (2022)
11. Jose, C., et al.: Dinov2 meets text: A unified framework for image-and pixel-level vision-language alignment. In: Proceedings of the Computer Vision and Pattern Recognition Conference, pp. 24905–24916 (2025)
12. Leila, L.: Adverse effects of fluorescein angiography (2006)
13. Novotny, H.R., Alvis, D.L.: A method of photographing fluorescence in circulating blood in the human retina. Circulation **24**(1), 82–86 (1961)
14. Panwar, N., et al.: Fundus photography in the 21st century–a review of recent technological advances and their implications for worldwide healthcare. Telemedicine and e-Health **22**(3), 198–208 (2016)
15. Porwal, P., et al.: Idrid: Diabetic retinopathy-segmentation and grading challenge. Med. Image Anal. **59**, 101561 (2020)
16. Rebuffi, S.A., Gowal, S., Calian, D.A., Stimberg, F., Wiles, O., Mann, T.A.: Data augmentation can improve robustness. Adv. Neural. Inf. Process. Syst. **34**, 29935–29948 (2021)
17. Ting, D.S.W., Cheung, G.C.M., Wong, T.Y.: Diabetic retinopathy: global prevalence, major risk factors, screening practices and public health challenges: a review. Clin. Exp. Ophthal. **44**(4), 260–277 (2016)
18. Wagner, S.K., et al.: Cohort profile: Alzeye: longitudinal record-level linkage of ophthalmic imaging and hospital admissions of 353 157 patients in london, UK. BMJ Open **12**(3) (2022)
19. Xu, H., et al.: A whole-slide foundation model for digital pathology from real-world data. Nature, pp. 1–8 (2024)
20. Yau, J.W., et al.: Global prevalence and major risk factors of diabetic retinopathy. Diabetes Care **35**(3), 556–564 (2012)
21. Zhou, Y., et al.: A foundation model for generalizable disease detection from retinal images. Nature **622**(7981), 156–163 (2023)
22. Zhou, Y., Wagner, S.K., Keane, P.A., et al.: Automorph: automated retinal vascular morphology quantification via a deep learning pipeline. Transl. Vision Sci. Technol. **11**(7), 12–12 (2022)

# niiv: Interactive Self-supervised Neural Implicit Isotropic Volume Reconstruction


Jakob Troidl[1(✉)], Yiqing Liang[2], Johanna Beyer[1], Mojtaba Tavakoli[3], Johann Danzl[3], Markus Hadwiger[4], Hanspeter Pfister[1], and James Tompkin[2]

[1] Harvard University, Cambridge, USA
jakob.troidl@gmail.com
[2] Brown University, Providence, USA
[3] IST Austria, Klosterneuburg, Austria
[4] KAUST, Thuwal, Saudi Arabia



**Abstract.** Three-dimensional (3D) microscopy data is often anisotropic with significantly lower resolution (up to $8\times$) along the $z$ axis than along the $xy$ axes. Computationally generating plausible isotropic resolution from anisotropic imaging data would benefit the visual analysis of large-scale volumes. This paper proposes niiv, a self-supervised method for isotropic reconstruction of 3D microscopy data that can quickly produce images at arbitrary output resolutions. The representation embeds a learned latent code within a neural field that describes the implicit higher-resolution isotropic image region. We use an attention-guided latent interpolation approach, which allows flexible information exchange over a local latent neighborhood. Under isotropic volume assumptions, we self-supervise this representation on low-/high-resolution lateral image pairs to reconstruct an isotropic volume from low-resolution axial images. We evaluate our method on simulated and real anisotropic electron (EM) and light microscopy (LM) data. Compared to diffusion-based baselines, niiv shows improved reconstruction quality ($+1$ dB PSNR) and is over three orders of magnitude faster ($1,000\times$) to infer. Specifically, niiv reconstructs a $128^3$ voxel volume in $2/10$ th of a second, renderable at varying (continuous) high resolutions for display. Our code is available at https://github.com/jakobtroidl/niiv-miccai.


**Keywords:** Volume Reconstruction · Neural Fields · Self-Supervised

## 1 Introduction

3D imaging data is ubiquitous in scientific domains such as biology or material sciences. However, many imaging modalities like 3D electron microscopy (EM) or light microscopy (LM) have limited axial ($z$) resolution due to physical sectioning of tissue slices or optical limitations. Thus, resolution is typically much higher in the lateral directions than in the axial direction (Fig. 1a).


© The Author(s), under exclusive license to Springer Nature Switzerland AG 2026
T. Chen et al. (Eds.): EMA4MICCAI 2025 Workshops, LNCS 16318, pp. 257–267, 2026.
https://doi.org/10.1007/978-3-032-13961-0_26

Downstream tasks like interactive visual analysis would benefit from high-resolution isotropic volumes, but these can be extremely costly or impossible to obtain. Several computational methods attempt to generate isotropically resolved volumes [5,8,11,21,30,31,34,35]. Some approaches [30,31] require specific shape priors, such as exact point spread functions (PSFs), which are difficult to measure in practice. Machine learning approaches like *diffusion* can model complex data distributions but require copious training data and are slow to infer [11,21]—requiring multiple minutes or even hours to reconstruct a small isotropic volume.

At the same time, anisotropic imaging volumes grow in size every year, containing terabytes [27,36] or even petabytes [24] of imaging data. Reconstructing isotropic volumes is typically an offline postprocess after image acquisition, but with increasing data sizes this becomes infeasible. For instance, Lee et al. [12] take up to three minutes to reconstruct a $128^3$ voxel volume. Instead, isotropic volumes should be reconstructed on-demand and locally at interactive rates from anisotropic data for visual inspection. Faster neural implicit reconstruction approaches are either supervised [5] or rely on bilinear latent interpolation [34] with fixed averaging, thus limiting the field of view per queried latent.

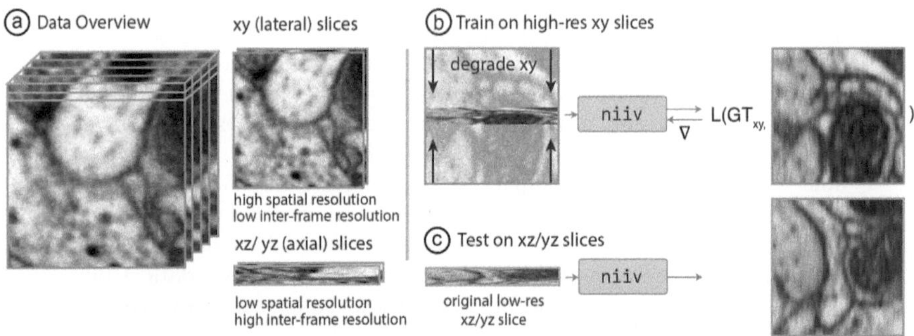


**Fig. 1. Workflow.** (a) Lateral ($xy$) slices in anisotropic volumes have a high spatial but low inter-frame resolution, while axial ($xz/yz$) slices have a low spatial but high inter-frame resolution. (b) Thus, **niiv** is trained to predict high-resolution lateral slices from artificially downsampled input. (c) **niiv** infers isotropic volumes at test time by predicting high-resolution axial ($xz/yz$) slices from their low-resolution counterparts.

Thus, we propose an interactive self-supervised method to reconstruct isotropic volumes from anisotropic data, which also enables learnt latent interpolation using a local attention mechanism. Building on recent advances in neural field representations [10,19,25,32], our model uses a super-resolution encoder [14] to relate a low-resolution axial slice to a plausible high-resolution image via a latent space [2,3]. A multi-layer perceptron (MLP) decodes a set of latent codes into a high-resolution axial slice sample, with local attention-guided latent interpolation creating an output image at any pixel resolution (Fig. 2). Both encoder and decoder are trained end-to-end on simulated anisotropic slices by downsampling isotropic lateral slices (Fig. 1b). Inference is fast, requiring only $2/10$ th of a second to generate a $128^3$ voxel volume, allowing interactive isotropic visual inspection.

For validation, we compare niiv against bilinear upsampling and three current self-supervised methods, including two neural-field [25,34], and one diffusion-based approach [12]. Our approach shows quality improvements over all and quantitative improvements by +1 dB over the diffusion model. We demonstrate this through peak-signal-to-noise ratio (PSNR) computations in a sweep of a frequency-clipped Fourier domain, which offers a more robust metric than pixel-wise PSNR to noise in the training data. For computational efficiency, niiv is $1,000\times$ faster than the diffusion model, $666\times$ faster than the SIREN baseline considering volume-specific pertaining times and achieves similar inference speeds to Zhang et al. [34].

## 2   Related Work

**Isotropic Volume Reconstruction.** Recent self-supervised approaches [12, 13,15,21] train 2D diffusion models to learn the distribution of high-resolution lateral images. During reconstruction, they use low-resolution axial slices as priors for the backward diffusion process to predict missing volume information. While diffusion models achieve high-quality results, their usability is limited by compute-intensive training and time-consuming inference. In contrast, our approach improves reconstruction quality while inferencing three orders of magnitude faster than the diffusion baseline [12]. Recently, Zhang et al. [34] also use neural representations for anisotropic volume reconstruction with bilinear latent interpolation. Our approach additionally enables learning latent interpolation through a local attention mechanism. Deng et al. [4] learns a degradation model that generates realistic low-resolution, high-resolution training pairs. These pairs are used to train a reconstruction model like Iso-Net-2 [31]. Both models are trained independently, leading to complex training setups. On the other hand, supervised approaches [5,8] show high-quality results but are challenging to use in practice since isotropic volumes are required at training time. Other methods use video transformers [7], optical flow field interpolation [1], or standard ConvNets [31,35], which are limited to a specific output pixel resolution, whereas niiv can be decoded at any resolution.

**Neural Implicit Super-Resolution.** Encoding spatial information through implicit neural representations (INR) [20,32] has proven to be useful in areas, such as inverse graphics [19,25], shape representation [9,26,33], video encoding [10], and super resolution [2,3,5,18,34,35]. Our approach builds upon local implicit image functions (LIIF) [2], which allows the sampling of images at arbitrary resolution while retaining high-quality visual details. Critically, our approach differs from related approaches [34,35] by using attention guided latent refinement mechanism that enables learnt feature interpolation over a local latent neighborhood (Fig. 2).

## 3   Methodology

**Problem Statement.** Given a sampling of a volume $V$ with isotropic $xy$ axes and anisotropic $z$ axis, we aim to learn a model $g$ that reconstructs an isotropic $z$ sampling of a volume $\tilde{V}$ purely by self-supervision. We assume that the volume sampling contains a physical medium whose distribution of material can be effectively modeled by observing local statistics of the $xy$ samplings. Given the low-resolution anisotropic slice $I_i^{x \times z}$ as input, $g$ must reconstruct a plausible high-resolution isotropic $xz$ slice $\tilde{I}_i^{x \times \alpha z}$, where $i$ denotes a slice from the input volume sampling and $\alpha$ is the axial anisotropy factor (e.g., 8). Then, $\tilde{V}$ is constructed by stacking predicted high-resolution slices $\tilde{V} = \{\tilde{I}_0, ..., \tilde{I}_n\}$. The same approach applies equally to both $xz$ and $yz$ slices.

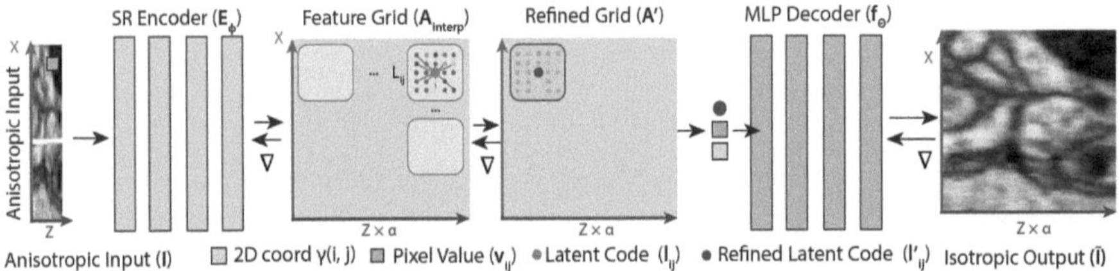


**Fig. 2. Model overview.** A super-resolution encoder $E_\phi$ [14] embeds the anisotropic input slice into latent codes placed within a 2D spatially-referenced grid $A$. $A$ is bilinearly interpolated ($A_\text{interp}$) at output coordinates and subsequently refined using local attention ($A'$). We predict a pixel value in the output by querying $A'$ at its coordinate $(i, j)$ and concatenating the resulting latent code $l'_{ij}$ (green) with the positionally encoded coordinate $(i, j)$ (yellow) and the value at $(i, j)$ in the input (beige). The decoding function $f_\theta$, parametrized by an MLP, predicts the respective pixel value.

**INR with Learned Latent Interpolation.** Our hybrid neural field [32] uses latent codes within a 2D space to encode the high-resolution slice. First, a convolutional super-resolution encoder $E_\phi$ with parameters $\phi$ embeds a low-resolution axial slice $I \in \mathbb{R}^{x \times z}$ into a 2D referenced $d$-dimensional latent grid $A \in \mathbb{R}^{x \times z \times d}$, of latent codes $l$. Next, we bilinearly interpolate $A$ at the desired output coordinates, such that $A_\text{interp} \in \mathbb{R}^{x \times (z\alpha) \times d}$. Next, we locally refine $A_\text{interp}$ by attending each latent $l_{ij} \in A_\text{interp}$ to its local neighborhood $L_{ij}$ (Fig. 2). We name refined latent codes $l'_{ij}$, and the refined latent grid $A'$.

$$L_{ij} = \{l_{i+m,j+n}\}_{m,n\in\{-k,...,0,...,k\}}, k \in \mathbb{N} \tag{1}$$

$$l'_{ij} = \text{Attn}(l_{ij}, L_{ij}) = \sigma\left(\frac{l_{ij}W_Q(L_{ij}W_K)^T}{\sqrt{D}}\right) L_{ij}W_V \in \mathbb{R}^d \tag{2}$$

$W_Q$, $W_K$, $W_V$ and $D$ define the attention mechanism's trainable weight matrices and dimensionality, respectively [29]. $\sigma$ represents the softmax function.

Finally, a MLP decoder $f_\theta$ with parameters $\theta$ (Fig. 2) produces reconstructed image intensities $\tilde{I}$ at an output pixel coordinate $(x, y)$:

$$\tilde{I}(i, j) = f_\theta\left([l'_{ij}, v_{ij}, \gamma(i, j)]\right). \tag{3}$$

$(x, y)$ is encoded using a 2-band frequency basis $\gamma(i, j)$, and $v_{ij}$ is the pixel value obtained by bilinearly interpolating $I$ at $(i, j)$. Thus, niiv can adapt flexibly to the requirements of interactive display across devices, unlike other approaches [8, 31]. $E_\phi$ and $f_\theta$ are shared between volumes in the training and test dataset. We use the mean absolute error loss function (MAE) during training.

**Simulating Axial Degradation.** During training, we use artificially degraded $xy$ images $I_{\mathrm{d}}^{\mathrm{xy}}$ as model inputs and supervise outputs with the respective high-resolution $xy$ slices $I_{\mathrm{gt}}^{\mathrm{xy}}$. We apply a function $d$ that aims to simulate degradation along the $z$ axis such that $d(I_{\mathrm{gt}}^{\mathrm{xy}}) = I_{\mathrm{d}}^{\mathrm{xy}}$. Here, we define $d$ as an average pooling operator. In principle, other degradation models [4,6,12] can be applied based on the specific application and imaging domain.

## 4    Evaluating Reconstructions with Noisy Ground Truth

Evaluating niiv brings challenges, as only noisy ground truth exists, leading to uninformative PSNR values (Fig. 3a). Thus, a method that perfectly reconstructs lateral slices is overfitting to the noise; this is especially problematic in low-data regimes with powerful data-fitting models [12]. We wish to assess the reconstruction of biological structures despite the noise. Prior research has addressed this problem by downscaling the data to diminish noise [8] at the cost of sacrificing resolution.

We propose calculating the PSNR in the Fourier domain where it is easier to separate high-frequency components of signals [6] such as noise (Fig. 3b), where we vary a cutoff frequency $f_{cutoff}$ (Fig. 3c) across a range of values to observe the quality across frequencies. For example, if a method only achieves a greater PSNR than another at high $f_{cutoff}$ but not at low $f_{cutoff}$, then it is likely overfitting the noise. Given Parseval's theorem [22] and the unitary nature of the Fourier transform $\mathcal{F}$, we can directly compute the PSNR in the frequency domain, sidestepping the inverse transformation to the spatial domain.

$$PSNR(I, I_{\mathrm{pred}}) = PSNR(\mathcal{F}I, \mathcal{F}I_{\mathrm{pred}}). \tag{4}$$

We now incorporate the clipping operation in the Fourier domain, denoted by a low-pass operator $L$ that discards frequencies above $f_{cutoff}$. Given the above relationship, we receive

$$PSNR(\mathcal{F}^{-1}L\,\mathcal{F}I, \mathcal{F}^{-1}L\,\mathcal{F}I_{\mathrm{pred}})) = PSNR(L\,\mathcal{F}I, L\,\mathcal{F}I_{\mathrm{pred}}). \tag{5}$$

That is, we can transform both images into the Fourier domain, apply the clipping operation via $L$, and then compute the PSNR directly in Fourier space. For more details, please refer to the supplement.

## 5   Experiments

### 5.1   Data and Implementation Details

We demonstrate the effectiveness of our approach on the publicly available FlyEM Hemibrain [23], FAFB [36] EM datasets and also ablate against LM approaches like LICONN [28] (Fig. 5b). While the Hemibrain contains the central brain region of Drosophila melanogaster imaged at isotropic $8 \times 8 \times 8$ nm pixel resolution, we downsample the data to $8\times$ anisotropy along the $z$-axis through average pooling. FAFB shows the entire brain of a female adult fruit fly at naturally $5\times$ anisotropic $8 \times 8 \times 40$ nm pixel resolution. We randomly sample 400 subvolumes ($128^3$ pixels in the Hemibrain and $130^3$ pixels in FAFB) and separate them into training ($N = 350$) and test datasets ($N = 50$). All metrics are reported on entire volumes rather than individual images. Our method is implemented in PyTorch, and all tests were performed on a single NVIDIA RTX 3090 Ti GPU. All experiments use the EDSR [14] super-resolution encoder without upsampling modules, six residual blocks, and 64-dimensional output features. The MLP is five layers deep, each 256 neurons wide. We train our model for 900

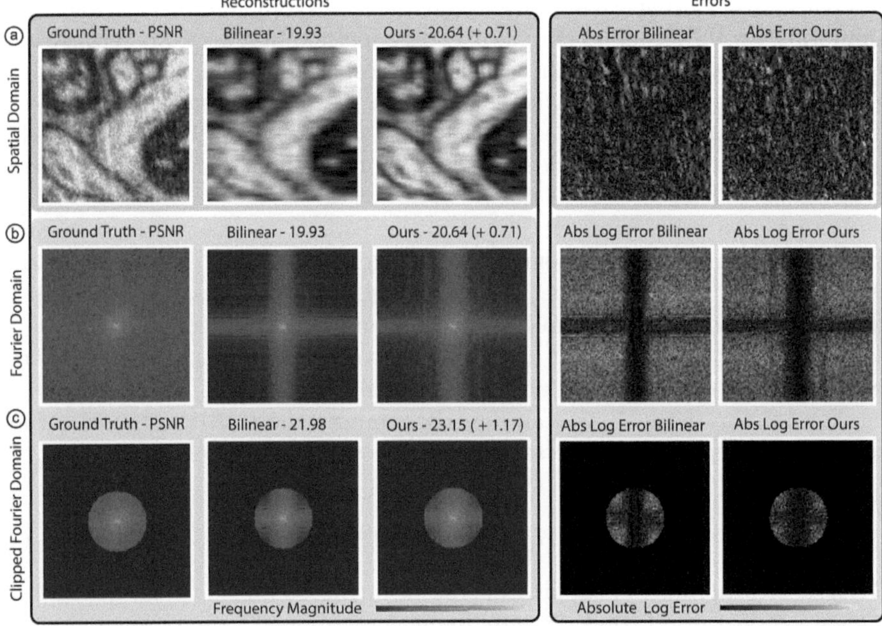


**Fig. 3. Fourier space separates incorrect from correctly reconstructed frequencies.** (a) In the spatial domain, reconstruction errors are randomly distributed for the baseline and our reconstruction. (b) Visualizing errors in the Fourier domain (right column) separates erroneous (bright) and correctly reconstructed frequencies (dark). (c) By cropping the Fourier domain's high frequencies, the PSNR is not perturbed by frequencies corresponding to noise, yielding more informative PSNR values.

**Table 1.** Hemibrain Evaluation. We report clipped Fourier PSNR (CF PSNR) with $f_{cutoff} = 25$, regular PSNR, and SSIM. We differentiate between volume-specific pretraining time and inference time (Pre/Infer). The best scores are shown in bold.

| Hemibrain Data | CF PSNR ↑ | PSNR ↑ | SSIM ↑ | Time (Pre/Infer) ↓ | VRAM (GB) |
|---|---|---|---|---|---|
| Nearest | 23.16 | 20.42 | 0.50 | – | – |
| Bilinear | 23.53 | 20.92 | 0.51 | – | – |
| SIREN [25] | 19.55 | 18.24 | 0.34 | (150 s/0.003 s) | 3.9 |
| Diffusion EM [12] | 23.24 | 20.65 | 0.56 | (-/264 s) | 3.9 |
| Zhang et al. [34] | 24.86 | 21.63 | **0.57** | **(-/0.113 s)** | 3.4 |
| Ours | **25.06** | **21.72** | **0.57** | (-/0.225 s) | 3.9 |

epochs using the Adam optimizer and a learning rate of $5 \times 10^{-5}$. We will make all code and data publicly available upon acceptance of this work.

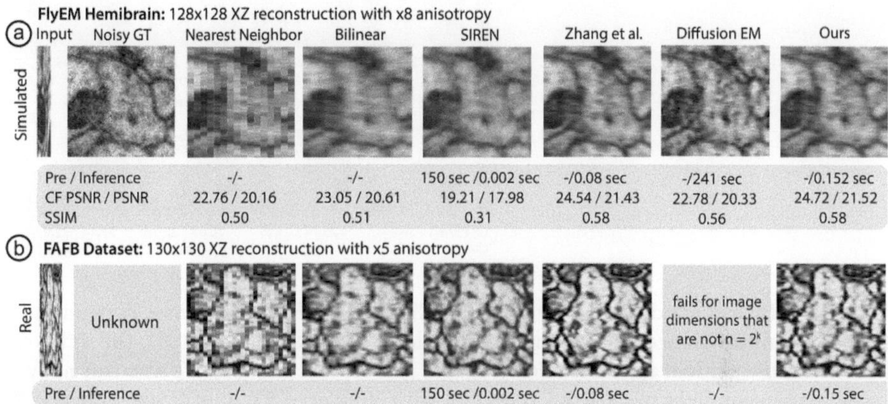


**Fig. 4. Qualitative comparison of simulated (a) and real (b) anisotropic data.** We achieve up to three orders of magnitude faster inference compared to diffusion baselines [12] and other neural implicit approaches like SIREN [25] while also reconstructing smaller structures with higher fidelity.

## 5.2   Qualitative and Quantitative Comparison

To showcase our method's suitability for interactive reconstruction, we capped the GPU memory usage at 4 GB for all methods, reflecting a mid-tier laptop's capacity. Within this constraint, our approach significantly outperforms the diffusion baseline, delivering inference speeds up to three orders of magnitude faster (0.225 vs. 264 s) for an anisotropy reconstruction task with anisotropy $\alpha = 8$ on

$128^3$ volumes (Hemibrain). The advantage is due to Diffusion-EM's slow iterative inference process and the need to enforce frame-by-frame consistency for the probabilistic reconstruction process by conditioning each slice inference on a latent code retrieved from the previous slice, prohibiting batch processing. We also outperform SIREN [25] as it requires separate pretraining for each subvolume, leading to costly inference on unseen data (Table 1). Additionally, we achieve better qualitative results (CF PSNR, PSNR, SSIM) than Zhang et al. [34], while being slightly slower due to the additional computations required to compute attention-based latent interpolation. Comparing reconstruction quality, in contrast to the baselines, our model can reconstruct fine details (Fig. 4a) with sharp edges (Fig. 4b). While the diffusion results visually look sharp, small details are often reconstructed incorrectly, explaining the lower metric scores. Diffusion EM also fails for volume sizes, not in $\{2^i\}$ (Fig. 4b).

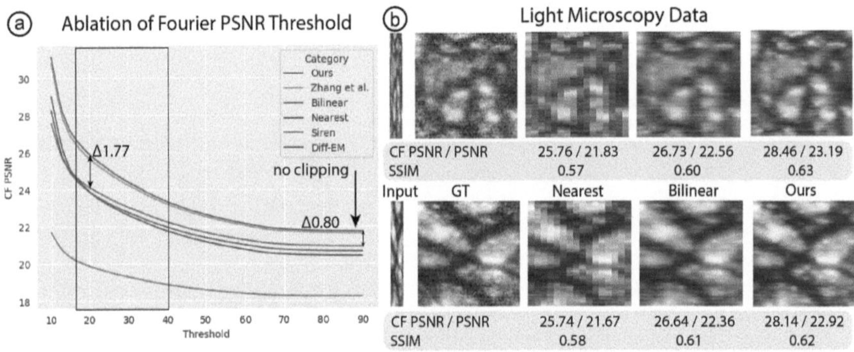


**Fig. 5. Ablation studies.** (a) While the unclipped PSNR in the Fourier domain shows no significant difference between our approach and the baselines ($\Delta 0.6$), the difference becomes more evident for thresholds $f_{cutoff} \in [14, 40]$ ($\Delta 1.63$). (b) We also test **niiv** on recent expansion light microscopy data [28] with simulated $8\times$ anisotropy. $f_{cutoff} = 25$.

### 5.3  Ablation Studies

**Fourier PSNR.** We tested the effect of the Fourier clipping threshold on the PSNR (Fig. 5a). If no clipping threshold is applied, the PSNR of our method and the baselines are low and close together due to the random image noise in the ground truth data. However, the black box (Fig. 5a) indicates a clipping window in Fourier space where image quality differences for the SIREN, Diff-EM, and Bilinear baselines are more accurately represented through the PSNR.

**Data Modality.** We use a recent, near isotropic voxel-size ($9.7 \times 9.7 \times 13$ nm) expansion LM dataset [28] of a mammalian hippocampus and simulate $8\times$ anistropy using average pooling as a degradation model (Fig. 5b). Next, we train on 350 randomly sampled volumes and reconstruct 50 unseen $128^3$ voxel test volumes at isotropic voxel size. Figure 5b shows input and GT images and also compares our results with nearest- and bilinear interpolation. We find that niiv produces sharper images compared to bilinear interpolation also for LM data.

## 6   Conclusions and Future Work

Interactive isotropic rendering of anisotropic data is useful for large-scale data visual inspection tasks. Thus, we demonstrate that neural fields and encoder-based superresolution representations are promising for fast and flexible self-supervised volume reconstruction. We propose three avenues for future work. First, integrating machine-learning elements like our approach into low-power Web-based image-rendering tools such as neuroglancer [16] or Viv [17] would rapidly deploy these advances. Second, future work should investigate whether latent image representations express higher-level, semantically interpretable morphological features, as these could be useful in downstream tasks such as tissue classification. Third, developing more accurate physics-based axial degradation models will help to improve the simulation of anisotropic training slices.

**Acknowledgements.** This work was supported by NIH grants 1U01NS132158 and R01HD104969. We thank the reviewers for their constructive feedback.

## References

1. Carata, L., Shao, D., Hadwiger, M., Groeller, E.: Improving the visualization of electron-microscopy data through optical flow interpolation. In: Proceedings of the 27th Spring Conference on Computer Graphics, pp. 103–110 (2011)
2. Chen, Y., Liu, S., Wang, X.: Learning Continuous Image Representation with Local Implicit Image Function (2020)
3. Chen, Z., et al.: VideoINR: learning video implicit neural representation for continuous space-time super-resolution. In: CVPR (2022)
4. Deng, S., et al.: Isotropic reconstruction of 3D EM images with unsupervised degradation learning. In: Martel, A.L., et al. (eds.) MICCAI 2020. LNCS, vol. 12265, pp. 163–173. Springer, Cham (2020). https://doi.org/10.1007/978-3-030-59722-1_16
5. Fang, W., et al.: CycleINR: cycle implicit neural representation for arbitrary-scale volumetric super-resolution of medical data. In: CVPR, pp. 11631–11641 (2024)
6. Fritsche, M., Gu, S., Timofte, R.: Frequency separation for real-world super-resolution. In: ICCVW, pp. 3599–3608. IEEE (2019)
7. He, J., et al.: IsoVEM: isotropic reconstruction for volume electron microscopy based on transformer. Technical report, Biophysics (2023)
8. Heinrich, L., et al.: Deep learning for isotropic super-resolution from non-isotropic 3D electron microscopy. In: MICCAI, pp. 135–143. Springer, Cham (2017)
9. Hendriks, T., Vilanova, A., Chamberland, M.: Implicit neural representation of multi-shell constrained spherical deconvolution for continuous modeling of diffusion MRI. Imaging Neurosci. (2025)

10. Kim, S., Yu, S., Lee, J., Shin, J.: Scalable neural video representations with learnable positional features. Adv. Neural. Inf. Process. Syst. **35**, 12718–12731 (2022)
11. Lee, J., Jin, K.H.: Local Texture Estimator for Implicit Representation Function (2021), publisher: arXiv Version Number: 6
12. Lee, K., Jeong, W.K.: Reference-Free Isotropic 3D EM Reconstruction using Diffusion Models (2023)
13. Lee, K., Jeong, W.K.: Reference-free axial super-resolution of 3D microscopy images using implicit neural representation with a 2D diffusion prior. In: International Conference on Medical Image Computing and Computer-Assisted Intervention, pp. 593–602. Springer, Cham (2024)
14. Lim, B., Son, S., Kim, H., Nah, S., Mu Lee, K.: Enhanced deep residual networks for single image super-resolution. In: Proceedings of the IEEE Conference on Computer Vision and Pattern Recognition Workshops, pp. 136–144 (2017)
15. Lu, C., et al.: EMDiffuse: a diffusion-based deep learning method augmenting ultrastructural imaging and volume electron microscopy. Cell Biol. (2023)
16. Maitin-Shepard, J., Baden, A., Silversmith, W., Perlman, E., et al.: google/neuroglancer (2021)
17. Manz, T., Gold, I., et al.: Viv: multiscale visualization of high-resolution multiplexed bioimaging data on the web. Nat. Methods **19**(5), 515–516 (2022)
18. McGinnis, J., et al.: Single-subject multi-contrast MRI super-resolution via implicit neural representations. In: MICCAI, pp. 173–183. Springer, Cham (2023)
19. Mildenhall, B., Srinivasan, P.P., Tancik, M., Barron, J.T., Ramamoorthi, R., Ng, R.: Nerf: representing scenes as neural radiance fields for view synthesis. Commun. ACM **65**(1), 99–106 (2021)
20. Molaei, A., et al.: Implicit neural representation in medical imaging: a comparative survey. In: ICCVW, pp. 2381–2391 (2023)
21. Pan, M., et al.: DiffuseIR: diffusion models for isotropic reconstruction of 3D microscopic images. In: Greenspan, H., et al. (eds.) MICCAI, vol. 14229, pp. 323–332 (2023)
22. Parseval, M.A.: Mémoire sur les séries et sur l'intégration complète d'une équation aux différences partielles linéaires du second ordre, à coefficients constants. Mém. prés. par divers savants, Acad. des Sciences, Paris, (1) **1**, 638–648 (1806)
23. Scheffer, L.K., Xu, C.S., Januszewski, M., et al.: A connectome and analysis of the adult Drosophila central brain. eLife **9**, e57443 (2020)
24. Shapson-Coe, A., Januszewski, M., Berger, D.R., Pope, A., Wu, Y., et al.: A petavoxel fragment of human cerebral cortex reconstructed at nanoscale resolution. Science **384** (2024)
25. Sitzmann, V., Martel, J., Bergman, A., Lindell, D., Wetzstein, G.: Implicit neural representations with periodic activation functions. Adv. Neural. Inf. Process. Syst. **33**, 7462–7473 (2020)
26. Sitzmann, V., Rezchikov, S., Freeman, B., Tenenbaum, J., Durand, F.: Light field networks: neural scene representations with single-evaluation rendering. In: Advances in Neural Information Processing Systems, vol. 34, pp. 19313–19325 (2021)
27. Takemura, S., Hayworth, K.J., Huang, G.B., et al.: A connectome of the male drosophila ventral nerve cord, pp. 2023–06 (2023)
28. Tavakoli, M.R., Lyudchik, J., et al.: Light-microscopy based dense connectomic reconstruction of mammalian brain tissue. Technical report, Neuroscience (2024)
29. Vaswani, A., et al.: Attention is all you need. In: NeurIPS, vol. 30 (2017)
30. Weigert, M., Müller, A., et al.: Content-aware image restoration: pushing the limits of fluorescence microscopy. Nat. Methods **15**(12), 1090–1097 (2018)

31. Weigert, M., Royer, L., Jug, F., Myers, G.: Isotropic reconstruction of 3D fluorescence microscopy images using convolutional neural networks. In: MICCAI, pp. 126–134. Springer, Cham (2017)
32. Xie, Y., et al.: Neural fields in visual computing and beyond. Comput. Graph. Forum (2022)
33. Yariv, L., Gu, J., Kasten, Y., Lipman, Y.: Volume rendering of neural implicit surfaces. In: Advances in Neural Information Processing Systems, vol. 34, pp. 4805–4815. Curran Associates, Inc. (2021)
34. Zhang, H., et al.: Self-supervised arbitrary scale super-resolution framework for anisotropic MRI. In: ISBI, pp. 1–5. IEEE (2023)
35. Zhao, C., Dewey, B.E., Pham, D.L., Calabresi, P.A., Reich, D.S., Prince, J.L.: SMORE: a self-supervised anti-aliasing and super-resolution algorithm for MRI using deep learning. IEEE TMI **40**(3), 805–817 (2021)
36. Zheng, Z., et al.: A complete electron microscopy volume of the brain of adult Drosophila melanogaster. Cell **174**(3), 730–743 (2018)

# RARE-UNet: Resolution-Aligned Routing Entry for Adaptive Medical Image Segmentation

Simon Winther Albertsen, Hjalte Svaneborg Bjørnstrup,
and Mostafa Mehdipour Ghazi[(⊠)]

Pioneer Centre for Artificial Intelligence, Department of Computer Science,
University of Copenhagen, Copenhagen, Denmark
`ghazi@di.ku.dk`

**Abstract.** Accurate segmentation is crucial for clinical applications, but existing models often assume fixed, high-resolution inputs and degrade significantly when faced with lower-resolution data in real-world scenarios. To address this limitation, we propose RARE-UNet, a resolution-aware multi-scale segmentation architecture that dynamically adapts its inference path to the spatial resolution of the input. Central to our design are multi-scale blocks integrated at multiple encoder depths, a resolution-aware routing mechanism, and consistency-driven training that aligns multi-resolution features with full-resolution representations. We evaluate RARE-UNet on two benchmark brain imaging tasks for hippocampus and tumor segmentation. Compared to standard UNet, its multi-resolution augmented variant, and nnUNet, our model achieves the highest average Dice scores of 0.84 and 0.65 across resolution, while maintaining consistent performance and significantly reduced inference time at lower resolutions. These results highlight the effectiveness and scalability of our architecture in achieving resolution-robust segmentation. The codes are available at: https://github.com/simonsejse/RARE-UNet.

**Keywords:** Medical Image Segmentation · Brain Imaging · U-Net ·
Multi-Resolution · Augmentation

## 1 Introduction

Accurate segmentation in magnetic resonance imaging (MRI) is vital for clinical workflows, supporting tasks from developmental studies to diagnosis and treatment planning. As multi-institutional neuroimaging efforts grow [1,2], there is an increasing need for robust segmentation methods that generalize across heterogeneous MRI scans with varying acquisition protocols. Yet, most deep learning

---

**Supplementary Information** The online version contains supplementary material available at https://doi.org/10.1007/978-3-032-13961-0_27.


T. Chen et al. (Eds.): EMA4MICCAI 2025 Workshops, LNCS 16318, pp. 268–277, 2026.
https://doi.org/10.1007/978-3-032-13961-0_27

models, especially UNet variants [3–8], assume fixed input resolution and spatial shape, an assumption rarely valid in real-world clinical data.

In practice, resolution and quality vary due to differences in scanners, protocols, and patient-specific factors. This variability is common in real-world clinical settings and large-scale studies, where scans are acquired under non-standardized conditions and often exhibit inconsistent resolution, noise levels, or structural clarity. Multi-center datasets introduce variability due to diverse voxel spacing and anisotropic resolutions. Standard pipelines often rely on pre-processing to enforce shape consistency, but such operations can degrade image quality, e.g., resampling may lose small structures or introduce blur or artifacts. Over-padding can also skew predictions toward background regions.

We propose RARE-UNet, a resolution-adaptive extension of the UNet tailored for efficient segmentation of variable-resolution brain MRI. The core idea is a set of multi-scale blocks (MSBs), which allow inputs to enter the encoder at depths matched to their spatial resolution. While prior multi-input multi-scale networks [9,10] have been successfully employed in image restoration tasks, their focus is on fusing visual features for improved quality. Moreover, multi-scale segmentation networks, designed to enhance receptive field diversity, do not process multi-resolution inputs [11]. In contrast, our approach is designed for semantic segmentation and introduces a resolution-aligned entry mechanism within a single UNet architecture, reusing features across scales. Rather than processing all inputs through full or parallel branches, our model adapts dynamically to input resolution, enabling only the semantically relevant network pathway, and enforces deep supervision and cross-scale consistency for robust anatomical delineation. Low-resolution inputs are injected directly into deeper layers to leverage semantic representations, optimizing computational efficiency.

This approach eliminates the need for heavy pre-processing and aligns feature abstraction levels with input fidelity. During inference, a lightweight resolution-based routing mechanism selects the appropriate MSB, enabling efficient, adaptive processing. Our contributions are as follows: (1) We introduce a novel UNet variant with resolution-aware MSBs for resolution-adaptive segmentation using a single shared architecture. (2) We propose a deep supervision strategy where each resolution path contributes to the loss, combined with a scale consistency loss to align features across scales. (3) We present an efficient inference-time routing mechanism that activates only relevant encoder layers based on input resolution, reducing preprocessing and compute costs. (4) We conduct extensive experiments on 3D brain MRI datasets showing improved segmentation accuracy and robustness across diverse resolutions, while offering significant computational savings and outperforming baseline UNets and nnUNet [12].

## 2    Methods

### 2.1    RARE-UNet Architecture

Unlike prior multi-scale designs that primarily fuse features at the decoder stage, RARE-UNet introduces scale-awareness directly at the input level. As shown in

Fig. 1, our model is built upon a standard 3D UNet backbone with an encoder-decoder structure, skip connections, and a shared bottleneck. The core innovation lies in the introduction of multi-scale gateway blocks, serving as resolution-aware routing entry points at different encoder depths. This design enables the model to accept both full- and downsampled-resolution inputs routed to appropriate depths without the need for global resampling or shape adjustment.

For example, a full-resolution input enters the network at the first encoder layer (depth 0), while coarser inputs (e.g., 1/2, 1/4, or 1/8 scale) bypass the early encoders and are injected directly via MSBs at deeper layers. This routing strategy not only preserves image fidelity but also avoids redundant computations for low-resolution scans. Each resolution path has its own dedicated segmentation head, allowing for independent predictions and supervision. RARE-UNet thus provides a unified and efficient framework for processing variable-resolution inputs through a shared encoder-decoder network, adapting computation dynamically to input scale while retaining the structural advantages of UNet.

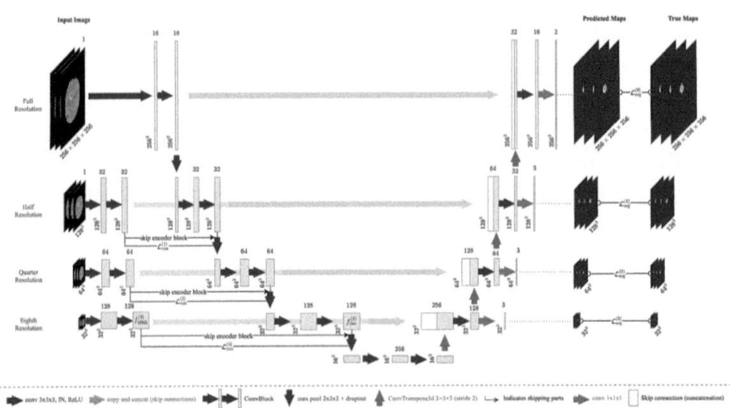

**Fig. 1.** Overview of the RARE-UNet architecture. The model extends a standard 3D UNet with multi-scale blocks, serving as resolution-aware entry points at various encoder depths. Full-resolution inputs are processed from the first encoder layer, while low-resolution inputs (e.g., 1/2, 1/4, 1/8 scale) are routed to deeper blocks. Each path shares the same bottleneck and proceeds through a resolution-aligned decoder with dedicated segmentation heads. The example shown uses four resolution levels, but the architecture can be scaled deeper or shallower depending on the input size and available computational resources.

## 2.2  Multi-scale Gateway Blocks

The gateway blocks enable resolution-adaptive processing by routing inputs at different scales into the UNet at corresponding encoder depths. An example is shown for MSB1 in the Supplementary Material. A 1/2-resolution input enters at depth 1 via MSB1, which transforms it into a feature map $f_{\text{MSB}}^{(1)}$ that aligns in shape and semantics with the standard encoder output $f_{\text{enc}}^{(1)}$. To ensure this alignment, we apply a mean squared error (MSE) consistency loss between these representations during training. The MSB output is then used both as the skip connection and as the input to deeper layers (from depth 2 onward). A resolution-specific segmentation head (a $1 \times 1 \times 1$ convolution) generates the prediction for this path, in contrast to the shared final head used by the full-resolution stream.

***Training.*** During training, inputs are downsampled by factors of $2^d$ to create lower-resolution versions. Each version follows a path through the network appropriate to its resolution. The full-resolution input is processed through the entire encoder-decoder pipeline, storing intermediate encoder outputs as targets for training MSBs. Each downsampled input enters via its corresponding MSB (e.g., MSB2 for 1/4 scale), which generates features that approximate what the encoder would produce at that depth. These features are passed through the remaining encoder layers, the bottleneck, and decoder blocks up to their resolution level. The segmentation loss is computed separately for each output using resolution-specific heads. This setup allows the model to learn consistent representations across scales, enabling it to generalize to varying input resolutions without requiring resampling, separate models, or fusion schemes.

***Inference.*** At inference time, the input image size is rounded to the nearest matching resolution level. Full-resolution inputs follow the standard encoder path; low-resolution inputs are routed through the corresponding MSBs, skipping shallower encoder and decoder layers. The segmentation is produced using the head specific to that resolution. This resolution-aware routing reduces unnecessary computation and allows the model to adapt to a range of input sizes without modification to the network or input shape.

### 2.3   Loss Function

***Segmentation Loss.*** Each resolution path produces a segmentation output, compared against a downsampled version of the ground truth using nearest-neighbor interpolation to preserve label structure. We compute a weighted combination of cross-entropy and soft Dice loss at each depth $d$, given by $\mathcal{L}_{\text{seg}}^{(d)} = \alpha \, \mathcal{L}_{\text{CE}}^{(d)} + (1 - \alpha) \, \mathcal{L}_{\text{Dice}}^{(d)}$, where $\alpha \in [0, 1]$ is initially set to 0.5 in our experiments. The total segmentation loss is the average over active resolution paths.

***Consistency Loss.*** To align feature representations across scales, we introduce a consistency loss between the MSB output $f_{\text{MSB}}^{(d)}$ and the corresponding encoder feature $f_{\text{enc}}^{(d)}$ using MSE: $\mathcal{L}_{\text{con}}^{(d)} = \|f_{\text{MSB}}^{(d)} - f_{\text{enc}}^{(d)}\|_2^2$. These are averaged across all MSB levels to obtain $\mathcal{L}_{\text{con}}$. The final training loss is a weighted sum of segmentation and consistency terms: $\mathcal{L}_{\text{total}} = \mathcal{L}_{\text{seg}} + \lambda_{\text{con}} \cdot \mathcal{L}_{\text{con}}$, where the regularization factor $\lambda_{\text{con}}$ is initially set to 1 in our experiments.

# 3  Experiments and Results

## 3.1  Data

We evaluate our model on two publicly available brain imaging datasets: BraTS [13,14] (484 labeled 4D scans) and VUMC [15] (260 labeled 3D scans). These datasets were preprocessed and resampled to $1\,\mathrm{mm}^3$ isotropic resolution as part of the Medical Segmentation Decathlon [16], corresponding to the first and fourth tasks (brain tumor and hippocampus segmentation). For hippocampus segmentation, volumes were cropped or padded to a fixed size of $32{\times}64{\times}32$ voxels. For tumor segmentation, we used $256{\times}256{\times}128$ volumes. Each dataset was randomly split into 80% training/validation and 20% testing. Intensity normalization involved clipping voxel values to the [0.5, 99.5] percentile range and stretching the contrast in the [0, 1] range. A detailed description of both datasets and pre-processing steps is provided in the Supplementary Material.

## 3.2  Experimental Setup

We evaluate RARE-UNet against three baselines: (1) a standard 3D UNet, (2) a UNet trained with multi-resolution input augmentation (UNet+Aug), and (3) nnUNet, a state-of-the-art self-configuring framework that automatically adapts pre-processing, augmentation, patch size, batch size, and other training settings to each dataset. To ensure a fair and controlled comparison focused solely on architectural and algorithmic differences, we disabled optional features such as deep supervision and aggressive data augmentation in all UNet variants. All models share similar architectural choices, unless otherwise specified.

To isolate the effect of our multi-scale architecture from that of resolution diversity during training, we implemented the UNet+Aug variant, which randomly receives either full-resolution or downsampled inputs with a 50% chance. The downsampling factor is randomly selected from $1/2, 1/4, 1/8$, corresponding to different encoder depths. These inputs are then zero-padded or upsampled to the original resolution, ensuring consistency with the ground-truths and preventing the model from learning to simulate resolution variation through pre-processing.

We assess segmentation accuracy using the Dice Similarity Coefficient (DSC). We used Weights & Biases [17] to track training and validation metrics, including loss functions and segmentation performance across scales. To simulate multi-resolution inputs, we downsample each scan using linear interpolation at scales of $1/2$, $1/4$, and $1/8$ of the original resolution. For UNet-based models, low-resolution inputs are either padded (Pad) or upsampled (Up) to match the original resolution, consistent with their respective training protocols. For each dataset and model, we report DSC at the full resolution and each downsampled scale, along with the average DSC across all resolutions.

## 3.3  Results

***Hippocampus Segmentation.*** Table 1 reports the Dice scores on the hippocampus segmentation test set. Our RARE-UNet consistently outperforms all baselines across downsampled resolutions, while remaining competitive with state-of-the-art models at full resolution. As expected, UNet variants with upsampling generally outperform those with zero-padding when handling low-resolution inputs. Besides, nnUNet achieves the highest DSC at full resolution, consistent with its extensive auto-configuration and preprocessing pipeline.

More specifically, when considering average performance across all resolutions, our model achieves an average DSC of 0.84, which is approximately 0.25 higher than nnUNet, demonstrating better robustness to varying input resolutions. Additionally, RARE-UNet exhibits lower standard deviation across scales, indicating greater consistency and generalization. Notably, the performance gap becomes more pronounced at lower resolutions, where baseline models experience a significant drop in accuracy, while RARE-UNet maintains stable performance.

Interestingly, the U-Net trained with resolution augmentation and upsampling achieves performance comparable to RARE-UNet at certain scales. However, it is important to note that this approach does not yield architectural adaptivity or efficiency. While it exposes the model to resolution variability during training, it still relies on a fixed architecture and incurs the same computational cost regardless of input resolution. In contrast, RARE-UNet offers dynamic resolution-aware processing with reduced complexity for lower-resolution.

These results highlight the scalability and resolution-adaptive capabilities of our architecture for volumetric medical image segmentation. Qualitative results are shown in Fig. 2, where segmentation outputs are visualized for a sample test scan. The differences between methods are subtle at full resolution, though the proposed model better preserves structural detail across resolutions. Detailed per-class segmentation accuracies are provided in the Supplementary Material.

**Table 1.** Comparison of test DSCs (mean $\pm$ SD) for hippocampus segmentation at multiple resolutions. The best results per resolution are highlighted. The proposed model achieves high accuracy and low variance across scales.

| Method | Scale 1 | Scale 1/2 | Scale 1/4 | Scale 1/8 | Overall |
|---|---|---|---|---|---|
| UNet–Pad | 0.874 $\pm$ 0.037 | 0.034 $\pm$ 0.033 | 0.000 $\pm$ 0.000 | 0.000 $\pm$ 0.000 | 0.227 $\pm$ 0.374 |
| UNet–Up | 0.874 $\pm$ 0.037 | 0.848 $\pm$ 0.058 | 0.776 $\pm$ 0.083 | 0.334 $\pm$ 0.150 | 0.708 $\pm$ 0.219 |
| UNet+Aug–Pad | 0.871 $\pm$ 0.034 | 0.213 $\pm$ 0.034 | 0.066 $\pm$ 0.026 | 0.000 $\pm$ 0.000 | 0.287 $\pm$ 0.345 |
| UNet+Aug–Up | 0.871 $\pm$ 0.034 | 0.860 $\pm$ 0.039 | 0.822 $\pm$ 0.069 | **0.789** $\pm$ 0.131 | 0.835 $\pm$ 0.032 |
| nnUNet–Pad | **0.880** $\pm$ 0.032 | 0.819 $\pm$ 0.045 | 0.529 $\pm$ 0.097 | 0.030 $\pm$ 0.062 | 0.564 $\pm$ 0.336 |
| nnUNet–Up | **0.880** $\pm$ 0.032 | 0.820 $\pm$ 0.067 | 0.597 $\pm$ 0.106 | 0.055 $\pm$ 0.085 | 0.588 $\pm$ 0.325 |
| RARE-UNet | 0.869 $\pm$ 0.032 | **0.862** $\pm$ 0.037 | **0.835** $\pm$ 0.063 | 0.785 $\pm$ 0.134 | **0.838** $\pm$ 0.033 |

***Brain Tumor Segmentation.*** Table 2 reports the DSCs on the brain tumor test set across multiple resolutions. As expected, nnUNet achieves the highest accuracy at full resolution (0.71), followed closely by UNet and our proposed RARE-UNet (0.69). However, at lower resolutions, RARE-UNet consistently outperforms all baselines. Notably, our model achieves the highest average

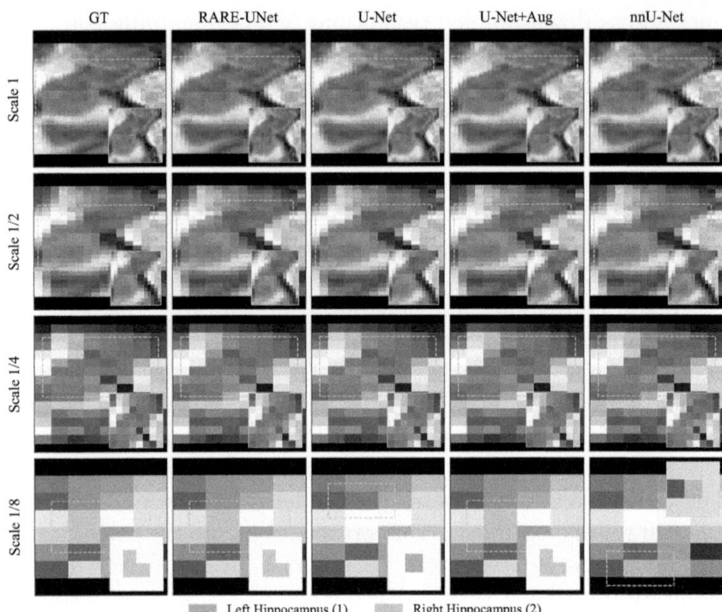



**Fig. 2.** Qualitative comparison of hippocampus segmentation results on a sample test scan. Axial slices are shown for each model to highlight differences in anatomical delineation per scale.

DSC across all scales (0.65), surpassing nnUNet (0.61) and other alternatives. Additionally, RARE-UNet exhibits the smallest variation in performance across resolutions, demonstrating greater stability and robustness to input scale.

The superior performance of nnUNet at full resolution may be partially attributed to its patch-based strategy, which enables more memory-efficient processing of high-resolution volumes. This design typically increases training sample diversity and enhances robustness by mitigating translational variances, factors particularly beneficial in non-symmetric and anatomically variable tasks such as tumor segmentation. However, such patch-based approaches require additional post-processing (e.g., Gaussian smoothing) to correct boundary artifacts, which may impact both efficiency and precision in multi-scale contexts. More quantitative and qualitative results are included in the Supplementary Material.

***Model Efficiency.*** In addition to segmentation accuracy, we assess the computational efficiency of each model by measuring the average inference time over 10 runs on the test set for both tasks. Figure 3 illustrates the trade-offs among inference time, segmentation accuracy, and model complexity (number of parameters) for the hippocampus and brain tumor segmentation tasks. Although we aligned the number of filters and parameters across models for a fair comparison, minor differences in model size persisted, likely due to architectural variations such as different convolutional blocks or implicit optimization strategies.

**Table 2.** Comparison of test DSCs (mean ± SD) for brain tumor segmentation at multiple resolutions. The best results per resolution are highlighted. The proposed model achieves high accuracy and low variance across scales.

| Method | Scale 1 | Scale 1/2 | Scale 1/4 | Scale 1/8 | Overall |
|---|---|---|---|---|---|
| UNet–Pad | <u>0.699</u> ± 0.154 | 0.208 ± 0.124 | 0.176 ± 0.114 | 0.066 ± 0.062 | 0.287 ± 0.244 |
| UNet–Up | <u>0.699</u> ± 0.154 | <u>0.677</u> ± 0.151 | 0.620 ± 0.133 | 0.493 ± 0.134 | 0.622 ± 0.080 |
| UNet+Aug–Pad | 0.688 ± 0.144 | 0.072 ± 0.058 | 0.033 ± 0.038 | 0.046 ± 0.094 | 0.210 ± 0.277 |
| UNet+Aug–Up | 0.688 ± 0.144 | 0.673 ± 0.139 | <u>0.627</u> ± 0.118 | <u>0.509</u> ± 0.119 | <u>0.624</u> ± 0.070 |
| nnUNet–Pad | **0.712** ± 0.152 | 0.670 ± 0.152 | 0.583 ± 0.128 | 0.399 ± 0.125 | 0.591 ± 0.120 |
| nnUNet–Up | **0.712** ± 0.152 | 0.660 ± 0.155 | 0.595 ± 0.140 | 0.452 ± 0.145 | 0.605 ± 0.097 |
| RARE-UNet | 0.693 ± 0.159 | **0.693** ± 0.154 | **0.652** ± 0.138 | **0.567** ± 0.162 | **0.651** ± 0.052 |

RARE-UNet achieves stable performance across resolutions with significantly reduced inference time, stemming from its multi-input architecture that efficiently leverages lower-resolution inputs without sacrificing quality. In brain tumor segmentation, as the spatial resolution is halved, RARE-UNet achieves a 4 times speedup without a noticeable drop in accuracy. This efficiency gain arises because halving each spatial dimension reduces the number of voxel-wise computations by a factor of 1/8, while the number of channels doubles per encoder stage ($2 \times 1/8$), resulting in a favorable efficiency-accuracy trade-off.

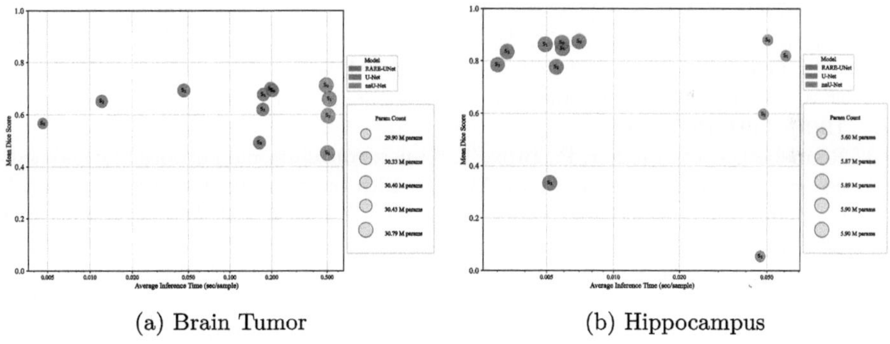

(a) Brain Tumor          (b) Hippocampus

**Fig. 3.** Trade-off between segmentation accuracy, inference time, and model complexity for different methods across multiple resolutions. For clarity, only the upsampling variants of the UNet baselines and nnUNet are shown, as they consistently outperformed their padding counterparts. S0 through S4 denote image resolutions from no scaling to scale 4 (1/8 of the original resolution).

## 4    Conclusion

We proposed a resolution-aware architecture for medical image segmentation, capable of maintaining high performance across a wide range of input image resolutions. Unlike standard UNets, our model incorporates multi-resolution branches supervised by both segmentation and consistency losses to promote resolution-robust feature learning. We demonstrated the effectiveness of our method on two benchmark datasets, showing that RARE-UNet achieves competitive accuracy at full resolution and outperforms state-of-the-art baselines at reduced resolutions, especially when compared to nnUNet. Our method also offers improved inference efficiency through its dynamic parameter scaling with input resolution, achieving significant speed-ups without compromising segmentation accuracy. This makes the proposed approach promising for real-world clinical workflows, where image resolution may vary due to protocols or hardware limitations.

**Acknowledgments.** This project is supported by the Pioneer Centre for AI, funded by the Danish National Research Foundation (grant number P1).

**Disclosure of Interests.** The authors have no competing interests in the paper.

## References

1. Jack, C.R., Jr., et al.: Overview of ADNI MRI. Alzheimer's Dementia **20**(10), 7350–7360 (2024)
2. Marcus, D.S., Wang, T.H., Parker, J., Csernansky, J.G., Morris, J.C., Buckner, R.L.: Open access series of imaging studies (OASIS): cross-sectional MRI data in young, middle aged, nondemented, and demented older adults. J. Cogn. Neurosci. **19**(9), 1498–1507 (2007)
3. Ronneberger, O., Fischer, P., Brox, T.: U-net: convolutional networks for biomedical image segmentation. In: MICCAI 2015: 18th International Conference, Munich, Germany, 5–9 October 2015, Proceedings, Part III 18, pp. 234–241. Springer, Cham (2015)
4. Zhou, Z., Rahman Siddiquee, M.M., Tajbakhsh, N., Liang, J.: Unet++: a nested u-net architecture for medical image segmentation. In: Deep Learning in Medical Image Analysis and Multimodal Learning for Clinical Decision Support: MICCAI Workshops on DLMIA and ML-CDS, pp. 3–11. Springer, Cham (2018)
5. Zhou, Z., Siddiquee, M.M.R., Tajbakhsh, N., Liang, J.: Unet++: redesigning skip connections to exploit multiscale features in image segmentation. IEEE Trans. Med. Imaging **39**(6), 1856–1867 (2019)
6. Huang, H., et al.: Unet 3+: a full-scale connected unet for medical image segmentation. In: ICASSP, pp. 1055–1059. IEEE (2020)
7. Ibtehaz, N., Rahman, M.S.: MultiResUNet: rethinking the u-net architecture for multimodal biomedical image segmentation. Neural Netw. **121**, 74–87 (2020)
8. Azad, R., et al.: Medical image segmentation review: the success of u-net. IEEE Trans. Pattern Anal. Mach. Intell. (2024)

9. Cho, S.J., Ji, S.W., Hong, J.P., Jung, S.W., Ko, S.J.: Rethinking coarse-to-fine approach in single image deblurring. In: Proceedings of the IEEE/CVF International Conference on Computer Vision, pp. 4641–4650 (2021)
10. Lin, Z., et al.: Image defogging based on multi-input and multi-scale UNet. SIViP **17**(4), 1143–1151 (2023)
11. Chen, L.C., Papandreou, G., Kokkinos, I., Murphy, K., Yuille, A.L.: Deeplab: semantic image segmentation with deep convolutional nets, atrous convolution, and fully connected CRFs. IEEE Trans. Pattern Anal. Mach. Intell. **40**(4), 834–848 (2017)
12. Isensee, F., Jaeger, P.F., Kohl, S.A., Petersen, J., Maier-Hein, K.H.: nnU-Net: a self-configuring method for deep learning-based biomedical image segmentation. Nat. Methods **18**(2), 203–211 (2021)
13. Bakas, S., et al.: Advancing the cancer genome atlas glioma MRI collections with expert segmentation labels and radiomic features. Sci. Data **4**(1), 1–13 (2017)
14. Bakas, S., et al.: Identifying the best machine learning algorithms for brain tumor segmentation, progression assessment, and overall survival prediction in the BRATS challenge. arXiv preprint arXiv:1811.02629 (2018)
15. Simpson, A.L., et al.: A large annotated medical image dataset for the development and evaluation of segmentation algorithms. arXiv preprint arXiv:1902.09063 (2019)
16. Antonelli, M., et al.: The medical segmentation decathlon. Nat. Commun. **13**(1), 4128 (2022)
17. Biewald, L.: Experiment tracking with weights and biases (2020). Software available from https://wandb.com

# Graph-Based LLM over Semi-Structured Population Data for Dynamic Policy Response

Daqian Shi[1]([⊠]), Xiaolei Diao[2], Jinge Wu[1], Honghan Wu[1,3], Xiongfeng Tang[4], Felix Naughton[5], and Paulina Bondaronek[1]([⊠])

[1] Institute of Health Informatics, UCL, London, UK
`Daqian.shi@ucl.ac.uk`
[2] School of Electronic Engineering and Computer Science, QMUL, London, UK
[3] School of Health and Wellbeing, University of Glasgow, London, UK
[4] The Second Norman Bethune Hospital of Jilin University, Changchun, China
[5] School of Health Sciences, University of East Anglia, Norwich, UK

**Abstract.** Timely and accurate analysis of population-level data is crucial for effective decision-making during public health emergencies such as the COVID-19 pandemic. However, the massive input of semi-structured data, including structured demographic information and unstructured human feedback, poses significant challenges to conventional analysis methods. Manual expert-driven assessments, though accurate, are inefficient, while standard NLP pipelines often require large task-specific labeled datasets and struggle with generalization across diverse domains. To address these challenges, we propose a novel graph-based reasoning framework that integrates large language models with structured demographic attributes and unstructured public feedback in a weakly supervised pipeline. The proposed approach dynamically models evolving citizen needs into a need-aware graph, enabling population-specific analyses based on key features such as age, gender, and the Index of Multiple Deprivation. It generates interpretable insights to inform responsive health policy decision-making. We test our method using a real-world dataset, and preliminary experimental results demonstrate its feasibility. This approach offers a scalable solution for intelligent population health monitoring in resource-constrained clinical and governmental settings.

**Keywords:** LLM Agent · Need-aware Graph · Population Data Analysis · Policy Response

## 1 Introduction

Timely and accurate analysis of population-level data is essential for effective decision-making during public health emergencies such as the COVID-19 pandemic [6]. As governments and healthcare systems seek to understand the evolving needs and behaviors of citizens, they have to find evidence from vast volumes of semi-structured data stream [17]. This includes structured demographic

© The Author(s), under exclusive license to Springer Nature Switzerland AG 2026
T. Chen et al. (Eds.): EMA4MICCAI 2025 Workshops, LNCS 16318, pp. 278–288, 2026.
https://doi.org/10.1007/978-3-032-13961-0_28

records, such as age, gender, and socioeconomic indicators, and unstructured human feedback drawn from sources like community surveys, public helplines, and social media platforms [16]. These multimodal, asynchronous data streams hold potential insights for targeting interventions, allocating resources, and shaping policies [7]. However, traditional approaches for interpreting such complex data landscapes are increasingly proving inadequate in dynamic and resource-constrained environments.

Manual, expert-driven assessment pipelines are often considered the gold standard due to their domain-informed accuracy and context sensitivity. Yet, these processes are inherently slow, labor-intensive, and impractical for handling real-time or large-scale feedback during health crises [15]. In contrast, automated natural language processing (NLP) systems can process unstructured data at scale but face significant limitations: they typically require task-specific labeled datasets, are rigid in adapting to new or domain-shifted content, and often fail to capture the nuanced and evolving concerns of heterogeneous populations [1]. Consequently, many valuable signals in public feedback go underutilized, leading to critical blind spots in healthcare response strategies, particularly when timely local insights are needed to protect vulnerable groups [26].

To address these challenges, we propose a graph-based large language model (LLMs) framework designed to integrate and analyze semi-structured population data in a dynamic, weakly supervised manner. At the core of our system is a hybrid framework that connects structured demographic attributes with unstructured human feedback through graph representations. By leveraging the reasoning capabilities of LLMs in conjunction with a need-aware graph, our method enables fine-grained, interpretable, and temporally adaptive analysis of public sentiment and needs. Noting that the construction of the graph adopts a pipeline that combines automatic knowledge extraction with expert validation. Therefore, the proposed method requires only minimal task-specific supervision, avoiding the high cost of large-scale manual annotation. Our contributions are threefold:

1. We introduce a novel graph-based LLM analyzing framework that integrates structured and unstructured population data to support dynamic policy response.
2. We develop a pipeline that allows for interpretable, need-aware insights with minimal reliance on manually labeled datasets.
3. We run the proposed method on a real-world dataset as a case study, demonstrating its potential for effective population health monitoring in resource-constrained clinical and governmental contexts.

## 2   Related Work

### 2.1   Unstructured Population Data Analysis

Early public-health surveillance relied on rule-based or lexicon-based sentiment engines such as VADER, which score text with handcrafted lexical heuristics and polarity intensifiers [12]. These systems are quick to deploy but brittle when confronted with concept drift. Traditional machine-learning pipelines that paired TF-IDF features with linear classifiers showed similar limitations on COVID-19 tweets [5]. Moreover, topic modeling techniques such as Latent Dirichlet Allocation (LDA) have been employed to identify major topics in large-scale pandemic-related discussions by clustering textual content to uncover the public's primary concerns [24]. Bondaronek et al. propose a human-in-the-loop Structural Topic Modeling approach that can efficiently analyze free-text feedback from 37,914 UK adults to extract actionable themes, offering rapid, scalable insights to inform improvements in the NHS Test & Trace service [3]. However, systems employing unsupervised clustering algorithms still face several limitations, such as the continued need for manual effort to interpret and label the resulting clusters. Moreover, the labeling process tends to be subjective, making it challenging to generate in-depth and consistent analytical insights.

Simultaneously, lightweight n-gram logistic regression classifiers have proven effective in rapidly detecting symptom mentions or misinformation in real-time Twitter streams, offering a fast and reasonably accurate alternative under constrained computational resources [8]. Transformer models pretrained on outbreak corpora provide richer context. COVID-Twitter-BERT (CT-BERT) is trained on 160 million pandemic-related tweets and improves classification accuracy by 10–30 percent over general BERT [14]. Nevertheless, supervised fine-tuning remains label hungry, and domain shift degrades performance as vocabulary evolves. In summary, these limitations highlight a critical research gap: current approaches to analyzing public feedback often require predefined output targets and substantial manual annotation, yet there remains a lack of effective methods for generating deep insights without heavy reliance on human-labeled data.

### 2.2  Graph-Based LLM for Unstructured Data Analysis

Recent studies have explored the integration of large language models (LLMs) with graph-based reasoning algorithms to enhance factual reliability and depth of inference across various free text datasets [19,27]. For instance, K-BERT incorporates knowledge graphs into BERT by injecting triples into the self-attention mechanism, using entity relationships to constrain contextual encoding and thereby strengthen reasoning capabilities [13]. KEPLER jointly optimizes language modeling and knowledge embedding objectives, improving few-shot relation extraction without requiring additional fine-tuning data [20]. Extending this approach, CoLAKE constructs a lexical knowledge graph to unify entity-level and lexical-level contexts during masked language model training [18].

In the healthcare domain, DR. KNOWS retrieves UMLS knowledge paths as prompts for LLMs, significantly improving diagnostic F1 scores on electronic health record data [9]. MedRAG combines retrieval-augmented generation with a diagnostic knowledge graph to reduce misdiagnoses on the DDXPlus benchmark [28]. These systems demonstrate strong reasoning capabilities by leveraging LLMs' understanding of unstructured data, further enhanced by the integration of structured knowledge graphs, which support deeper factual inference.

Additionally, they offer potential to reduce annotation demands through semi-supervised approaches [21]. However, adapting these techniques to the deep analysis of population-level needs requires further design considerations, such as integrating discussions with population-level metadata and addressing temporal dynamics to capture evolving public needs over time [10].

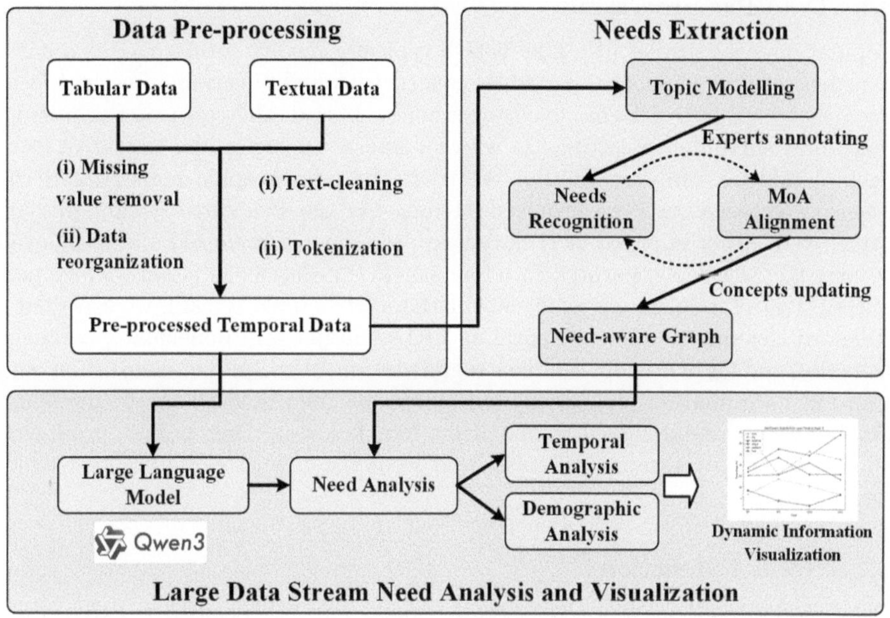


**Fig. 1.** The overall demonstration of our proposed framework for analyzing semi-structured large population data-stream.

## 3  The Proposed Method

This study introduces a novel graph-based LLM analyzing framework that integrates structured demographic features with unstructured public feedback in a weakly supervised pipeline. Citizen needs are dynamically modeled as a need-aware graph, enabling population-specific analysis along key features such as age, gender, and the Index of Multiple Deprivation (IMD). Figure 1 depicts the complete framework, which is organized into three tightly coupled modules: (i) **data pre-processing**, (ii) **needs extraction**, and (iii) **large language-model need analysis and visualization**. Given streams of tabular (demographic) and textual (feedback) data, we first perform unified pre-processing to obtain a clean, time-stamped corpus. We then extract needs by identifying latent issue categories and aligning them with a library of Mechanism of Actions (MoA).

The resulting signals populate an evolving need-aware graph. A lightweight local LLM consumes graph-enhanced inputs to score current needs. Finally, temporal and demographic analytics generate deep insights that are presented visually, thereby informing responsive health-policy decision-making. We detail each module accordingly in the rest of this section.

### 3.1   Data Pre-processing

Population-level studies of public health typically involve *semi-structured* data: machine-readable demographic tables coexist with highly variable free-text feedback that captures citizens' lived experience. This dual-stream design mirrors real-world surveillance settings in which numeric registries and narrative feedback should be analyzed jointly. We treat the demographic registry and the free-text corpus as two synchronized streams. For the *structured* stream, missing values were either imputed or removed; records were anonymized and re-indexed by user ID. Age was separated into four bands (18–29, 30–39, 40–49, 50+), producing strata for subgroup analysis. For the *unstructured* stream, we executed a standard cleaning pipeline: removal of URLs, emojis, and boilerplate; language detection and lower-casing; sentence segmentation; Word piece tokenization; and stop-word elimination [23]. Each text entry was then linked back to its demographic vector and assigned to one of the four follow-up time points, producing a harmonized, time-stamped dataset that feeds the downstream graph construction module.

### 3.2   Needs Extraction

The pre-processed unstructured text is passed into the needs-extraction module, which identifies the demands articulated by citizens [4], maps them to the behavioural-science ontology of MoA, and writes the results into a continuously updated need-aware graph that provides structural context for subsequent LLM reasoning. The workflow proceeds as follows.

- **Stage1: Topic modelling**. We apply Latent Dirichlet Allocation (LDA) [2] to the unlabelled corpus. The number of topics is tuned to the setting that minimises held-out perplexity (typically around ten in our data). LDA yields coarse themes, such as *medicine shortage* or *feelings of isolation*, without requiring manual annotation.
- **Stage2: Needs recognition**. Domain experts inspect each topic's top tokens and representative documents, then assign a concise *need label* drawn from a seed lexicon (e.g. *hygiene needs, food needs, mental-health support*). A lightweight rule set maps topic distributions to these labels, producing pseudo-tags that serve as weak supervision for recognition.
- **Stage3: MoA alignment**. The labelled snippets are matched to our in-house MoA ontology[1]. A local LLM Qwen-1.7B then proposes the most relevant

---

[1] The Mechanisms of Action (MoA) ontology is a behaviour-science taxonomy that organizes intervention techniques by the psychological or environmental mechanisms through which they operate.

MoA concept for each recognized need[2]. If a need has been encountered before, its dictionary entry is retained; otherwise, the newly detected need and its MoA mapping are appended to the seed lexicon. By updating the lexicon and graph in this online manner, the system continuously improves recognition quality while keeping the need-aware graph current as new data flows in.

We initiate a five-layer sub-graph and continuously enrich it as fresh information arrives. Formally, at time step $t$ we maintain:

$$\mathcal{G}_t = (\mathcal{V}_t, \mathcal{E}_t), \quad \mathcal{V}_t = \mathcal{C} \cup \mathcal{N}_t \cup \mathcal{O}_t \cup \mathcal{B} \cup \mathcal{I},$$

where the vertex sets correspond to the following five semantic layers:

- **Category** $\mathcal{C}$: high-level domains such as *Need* or *Obstacle*.
- **Need** $\mathcal{N}_t$: concrete demands extracted from text (e.g. *food needs*).
- **Obstacle** $\mathcal{O}_t$: stated barriers that hinder fulfilment (e.g. *no nearby site*).
- **COM-B** $\mathcal{B}$: behavioural determinants that link each obstacle to the Capability-Opportunity-Motivation model.
- **BCIO class** $\mathcal{I}$: Behaviour Change Intervention Ontology nodes specifying evidence-based techniques applicable to the needâĂŞobstacle pair.

Edges in $\mathcal{E}_t$ encode hierarchical *is-a* or *belongs-to* relations and inherit timestamps from the originating documents. As new feedback streams in, stages 2 and 3 run online; the resulting node increments $\Delta \mathcal{V}_t$ and edge increments $\Delta \mathcal{E}_t$ update the graph according to

$$\mathcal{V}_{t+1} = \mathcal{V}_t \cup \Delta \mathcal{V}_t, \quad \mathcal{E}_{t+1} = \mathcal{E}_t \cup \Delta \mathcal{E}_t.$$

This incremental scheme keeps the graph current and supplies structural constraints for the downstream LLM, which draws on the graph to produce interpretable, population-related inferences.

### 3.3 Dynamic Need Analysis and Visualization

The outputs of the need-aware graph and LLM reasoning feed a *dynamic analysis module* that quantifies how needs evolve over time and how they differ across population subgroups. Two complementary components are implemented. We deploy the locally hosted LLM Qwen 3 [25] as the core inference engine for this module. Its outputs drive the dynamic analysis, quantifying how needs shift over time and how they differ across population segments. The reasoning is constrained by the need-aware graph [22], so the model concentrates on three aspects: identifying needs, diagnosing their underlying causes, and suggesting potential solutions. The findings are delivered in two complementary formats to support dynamic policy response: (i) a concise natural-language report that summarizes the key needs and recommended interventions, and (ii) visual dashboards that display

---

[2] The alignment can also be performed manually when expert oversight is required.

the quantifiable elements, such as need prevalence and sentiment trajectories, in a graphical form.

**Temporal Analysis.** For every time window $t$ we compute the prevalence of a need $n$ as: $P_{n,t} = \frac{\text{count}(n,t)}{\sum_{n'} \text{count}(n',t)}$, where $\text{count}(n,t)$ is the number of documents in which the LLM assigns need $n$ the highest score. Plotting $P_{n,t}$ as a line chart reveals shifts in public attention. For instance, early in the pandemic, peaks appear for *virus transmission* and *personal protection*, whereas later windows highlight *employment insecurity* and *family dynamics*. We also attach sentiment trajectories by running a BERT-based emotion classifier fine-tuned on social-media text [11], allowing us to observe whether concern about, e.g., remote schooling is predominantly negative or neutral as the crisis unfolds.

**Demographic Analysis.** The same need scores are stratified by demographic attributes (age band, gender, IMD decile). For each subgroup $d$ we compute $P_{n,t}^{(d)}$ analogously and visualise disparities. For instance, we find that women report *mental-health support* needs 1.4 times more frequently than men during the six-month follow-up, while low-IMD respondents exhibit persistently lower *living satisfaction* concerns.

## 4   Experimental Observations

We test the proposed framework via a workable case study, drawing on a longitudinal corpus collected from 1,045 UK residents during the COVID-19 pandemic [3]. The dataset spans twenty-four months and couples structured descriptors, age, gender, and the Index of Multiple Deprivation (IMD), with repeated, open-ended survey responses. Each participant contributed text at four follow-up points (3, 6, 12, 24 months), yielding 3,812 timestamped documents. Our main observations are summarized below.

### 4.1   Temporal Analysis

Applying LDA to the 3,812 time-stamped responses revealed five coherent thematic clusters that recur throughout the corpus: (1) *Mental Health and Emotions*, (2) *Physical Health and Behaviours*, (3) *Economy and Work*, (4) *Coping Strategies and Positive Behaviours*, and (5) *Constraints and Control*. Although these themes persisted across the full 24-month observation window, their relative prevalence changed substantially from wave to wave:

- **0–3 months.** Many respondents expressed concerns about infection and difficulties obtaining essential supplies. At the same time, individuals began to mention topics such as online meetings and the purchase of virtual exercise classes. These accounts reflect residents' psychological anxiety and sense of lack of control during the early phase of the pandemic.

- **6 months.** As the healthcare system stabilized, discussions shifted towards employment instability and income loss, highlighting the escalating economic impact of the pandemic. Mentions of business closures and furlough anxieties increase. On a positive note, respondents also talked about spending time with family and engaging in outdoor physical activities.
- **12–24 months.** In the medium and longer term, discussions about isolation and restrictions gradually decreased. Some narratives focused on family gatherings, fitness routines, and healthy eating. Explicit fears of infection and anxiety about shortages of medical resources diminished over time; however, concerns related to mental health remained a prominent topic.

Sentiment trajectories exhibited a comparable but more nuanced arc. The BERT-based classifier indicated a sharp spike in negative affect, fear, anger, and confusion during the first survey wave; this declined steadily as respondents acclimatized to public-health measures, only to rebound when extended restrictions and economic setbacks compounded stress six months later. Conversely, positive sentiment showed a modest uptick during the strictest lockdown, fueled by reports of mutual aid, online social events, and the adoption of new coping routines such as home-exercise challenges. By the final wave, the corpus was dominated by neutral or emotionally fatigued language, phrases expressing resignation, boredom, or "pandemic burnout", signalling widespread habituation to the emerging "new normal" and a dampening of both positive and negative emotional extremes.

## 4.2   Demographic Analysis

- **Gender.** Women reported *Health and Emotional Stress* needs more frequently than men, especially in the first 6 months, the topic related to caregiving duties is also mentioned more frequently; men more often highlighted work-related stress and financial uncertainty.
- **Age.** Respondents aged 18âĂŞ29 exhibited the highest anxiety over disrupted education and career prospects, with a pronounced spike in social-relationship concerns at months 3 and 12. The $50+$ cohort mentions more worries about accessing routine healthcare for chronic conditions at months 6 and 24.
- **Socioeconomic status (IMD).** Participants in the 1–5 IMD consistently expressed elevated stress over employment and basic needs; their references to *Economy and Work* are higher than those with the higher-IMD groups.

These subgroup patterns confirm that COVID-19 has magnified pre-existing social inequalities. Mental-health trajectories and perceived needs are conditioned not only by the crisis timeline but also by intersecting demographic factors, underscoring the value of our need-aware, graph-constrained analysis for targeted policy response.

## 5   Conclusion and Future Work

Our study demonstrates that a graph-enhanced, weakly supervised LLM pipeline can capture the temporal evolution and demographic heterogeneity of pandemic-related needs and emotions, offering actionable insights for responsive public-health planning. By linking unstructured feedback to a behaviour-science ontology and visualising subgroup trajectories, we show that citizen concerns shift from acute infection anxiety to longer-term psychosocial and economic challenges, with marked variations by age, gender, and socioeconomic status. These findings underscore the importance of continuously monitoring population-level feedback to support timely, equitable interventions and to design policies that are both adaptive and inclusive. However, it should be noted that we also identified traces of inherent stereotypes in the results, which reveal certain intrinsic biases in AI-driven population analysis. While this demonstrates the capabilities of the proposed approach, it also highlights the limitations of the current work. Since the primary focus of our study is to establish a robust pipeline for analyzing user needs and perspectives, further validation and refinement of the results through domain experts will become the main focus of our subsequent work.

Our future work will focus on several directions. On the one hand, we plan to leverage large, expert-validated knowledge graphs to further strengthen behavioral and psychological interpretations of user needs and actions. On the other hand, we will further explore human-in-the-loop paradigms, emphasizing how domain experts, following initial analyses, can generate deeper and more robust insights, thereby enhancing the interpretability of analytical outcomes.

**Acknowledgments.** This research is supported by the Wellcome Trust (Project No.300252/Z/23/Z). This work was also supported by the UK's Medical Research Council (Project No. MR/S004149/1, MR/X030075/1).

**Disclosure of Interests.** The authors have no competing interests to declare that are relevant to the content of this article.

# References


1. Alon, Y., Naimi, E., Levin, C., Videl, H., Saban, M.: Leveraging natural language processing to elucidate real-world clinical decision-making paradigms: a proof of concept study. J. Biomed. Inform., 104829 (2025)
2. Blei, D.M., Ng, A.Y., Jordan, M.I.: Latent Dirichlet allocation. J. Mach. Learn. Res. **3**(Jan), 993–1022 (2003)
3. Bondaronek, P., Papakonstantinou, T., Stefanidou, C., Chadborn, T.: User feedback on the NHS test & trace service during COVID-19: the use of machine learning to analyse free-text data from 37,914 England adults. Public Health Pract. **6**, 100401 (2023)
4. Bondaronek, P., Li, J., Potts, H.W.: Public understanding and expectations of digital health evidence generation: focus group study. JMIR Formative Res. **9**, e56523 (2025)
5. Boon-Itt, S., Skunkan, Y.: Public perception of the COVID-19 pandemic on Twitter: sentiment analysis and topic modeling study. JMIR Public Health Surveill. **6**(4), e21978 (2020). https://doi.org/10.2196/21978
6. Chen, J., See, K.C.: Artificial intelligence for COVID-19: rapid review. J. Med. Internet Res. **22**(10), e21476 (2020)

7. Consoli, S., et al.: An epidemiological knowledge graph extracted from the world health organization's disease outbreak news. Sci. Data **12**(1), 1–19 (2025)

8. Didi, Y., Walha, A., Wali, A.: COVID-19 tweets classification based on a hybrid word embedding method. Big Data Cogn. Comput. **6**(2), 58 (2022)

9. Gao, Y., Li, R., Caskey, J., Dligach, D., Afshar, M.: Leveraging medical knowledge graphs into large language models for diagnosis prediction: design and application study. JMIR AI **2**(4), e58670 (2023). https://doi.org/10.2196/58670

10. Hall, K., Chang, V., Jayne, C.: A review on natural language processing models for COVID-19 research. Healthc. Analytics **2**, 100078 (2022)

11. Hoang, M., Bihorac, O.A., Rouces, J.: Aspect-based sentiment analysis using BERT. In: Proceedings of the 22nd Nordic Conference on Computational Linguistics, pp. 187–196 (2019)

12. Hutto, C., Gilbert, E.: VADER: a parsimonious rule-based model for sentiment analysis of social media text. In: Proceedings of ICWSM, pp. 216–225 (2014)

13. Liu, W., Zhou, P., Zhao, Z., Wang, Z., Ju, Q., Deng, H., Wang, P.: K-BERT: enabling language representation with knowledge graph. In: Proceedings of the AAAI Conference on Artificial Intelligence, vol. 34, pp. 2901–2908 (2020)

14. Müller, M., Salathé, M., Kummervold, P.E.: COVID-Twitter-BERT: a natural language processing model to analyse COVID-19 content on Twitter. Front. Artif. Intell. **6**, 1023281 (2023)

15. Sarker, A., et al.: Natural language processing for digital health in the era of large language models. Yearb. Med. Inform. **33**(01), 229–240 (2024)

16. Shakeri Hossein Abad, Z., et al.: Digital public health surveillance: a systematic scoping review. NPJ Digit. Med. **4**(1), 41 (2021)

17. Shi, B., Huang, W., Dang, Y., Zhou, W.: Leveraging social media data for pandemic detection and prediction. Human. Soc. Sci. Commun. **11**(1), 1–18 (2024)

18. Sun, T., et al.: COLAKE: contextualized language and knowledge embedding. In: Proceedings of the 28th International Conference on Computational Linguistics, pp. 3660–3670 (2020)

19. Wang, R., et al.: K-adapter: infusing knowledge into pre-trained models with adapters. In: Findings of the Association for Computational Linguistics: ACL-IJCNLP 2021, pp. 1405–1418 (2021)

20. Wang, X., Gao, T., Zhu, Z., Zhang, Z., Liu, Z., Li, J., Tang, J.: KEPLER: A unified model for knowledge embedding and pre-trained language representation. Trans. Assoc. Comput. Linguist. **9**, 176–194 (2021). https://doi.org/10.1162/tacl_a_00360

21. White, B.K., et al.: Informing social media analysis for public health: a cross-sectional survey of professionals. Arch. Public Health **82**(1), 1 (2024)

22. Wu, J., Kim, Y., Shi, D., Cliffton, D., Liu, F., Wu, H.: SLaVA-CXR: small language and vision assistant for chest X-ray report automation. arXiv preprint: arXiv:2409.13321 (2024)

23. Wu, J., Shi, D., Hasan, A., Wu, H.: KnowLab at RadSum23: comparing pre-trained language models in radiology report summarization. In: Proceedings of the Annual Meeting of the Association for Computational Linguistics, pp. 535–540. ACL (2023)

24. Xue, J., Chen, J., Chen, C., Zheng, C., Li, S., Zhu, T.: Public discourse and sentiment during the covid 19 pandemic: using latent Dirichlet allocation for topic modeling on twitter. PLoS ONE **15**(9), e0239441 (2020)

25. Yang, A., et al.: Qwen3 technical report. arXiv preprint: arXiv:2505.09388 (2025)

26. Yang, N., et al.: Sudden death of COVID-19 patients in Wuhan, China: a retrospective cohort study. J. Glob. Health **11**, 05006 (2021)

27. Yasunaga, M., Ren, H., Yu, W., Seo, M., Leskovec, J.: QA-GNN: reasoning with language models and knowledge graphs for question answering. In: Proceedings of NAACL, pp. 535–546 (2021)
28. Zhao, X., Liu, S., Yang, S.Y., Miao, C.: MedRAG: enhancing retrieval-augmented generation with knowledge graph-elicited reasoning for healthcare copilot. In: Proceedings of the ACM on Web Conference 2025, pp. 4442–4457 (2025)

# Neural Cellular Automata for Weakly Supervised Segmentation of White Blood Cells


Michael Deutges[1], Chen Yang[2], Raheleh Salehi[1,3], Nassir Navab[4],
Carsten Marr[1(✉)], and Ario Sadafi[1,4(✉)]

[1] Institute of AI for Health, Helmholtz Zentrum München – German Research Center
for Environmental Health, Neuherberg, Germany
`{carsten.marr,ario.sadafi}@helmholtz-munich.de`
[2] TUM School of Computation, Information and Technology,
Technical University Munich, Munich, Germany
[3] Institute of Chemical Epigenetics, Faculty of Chemistry and Pharmacy,
Ludwig Maximilian University, Munich, Germany
[4] Computer Aided Medical Procedures, Technical University of Munich,
Munich, Germany



**Abstract.** The detection and segmentation of white blood cells in blood smear images is a key step in medical diagnostics, supporting various downstream tasks such as automated blood cell counting, morphological analysis, cell classification, and disease diagnosis and monitoring. Training robust and accurate models requires large amounts of labeled data, which is both time-consuming and expensive to acquire. In this work, we propose a novel approach for weakly supervised segmentation using neural cellular automata (NCA-WSS). By leveraging the feature maps generated by NCA during classification, we can extract segmentation masks without the need for retraining with segmentation labels. We evaluate our method on three white blood cell microscopy datasets and demonstrate that NCA-WSS significantly outperforms existing weakly supervised approaches. Our work illustrates the potential of NCA for both classification and segmentation in a weakly supervised framework, providing a scalable and efficient solution for medical image analysis.

**Keywords:** Neural Cellular Automata · Weakly Supervised Segmentation · White Blood Cells


## 1 Introduction

The segmentation of white blood cells (WBCs) in blood smear images plays a crucial role in medical diagnostics and treatment. Accurate segmentation of WBCs enable a range of downstream applications, including automated blood cell counting, morphological analysis, and disease diagnosis. These analyses are particularly relevant for hematologic disorders such as leukemia, where abnormalities in WBC morphology, size, and distribution serve as key diagnostic indicators [15].



T. Chen et al. (Eds.): EMA4MICCAI 2025 Workshops, LNCS 16318, pp. 289–298, 2026.
https://doi.org/10.1007/978-3-032-13961-0_29

Manual segmentation remains the gold standard in clinical practice due to its accuracy, but it is labor-intensive, time-consuming, and subject to inter- and intra-observer variability. To address these challenges, automated segmentation methods have gained increasing attention as a means to improve efficiency, consistency, and scalability. However, traditional deep learning-based segmentation models rely on pixel-wise annotations, which are costly and time-consuming to obtain, limiting their applicability in real-world medical settings.

This has motivated the development of weakly supervised approaches that aim to infer segmentation masks from less expensive or already available annotations, such as image-level class labels [5,8,9,16–18,20,22]. These approaches are particularly valuable in medical imaging, where acquiring fully annotated datasets is costly and time-consuming.

A common strategy for weakly supervised segmentation is to leverage class activation maps (CAMs) [23], which highlight the most discriminative regions of an image for a given class. Methods such as GradCAM [14] and attention-based approaches [6,18] have been widely used to localize objects within an image. However, these methods often struggle with capturing complete object structures, as they primarily focus on the most salient features and may fail to capture the full extent of a white blood cell.

An additional challenge for existing approaches in white blood cell segmentation is the poor generalization across different datasets and clinical settings. Variations in microscope scanners, staining protocols, and lighting conditions, can introduce significant domain shifts [13]. These shifts make it difficult for models trained on one dataset to perform well on another.

Recently, neural cellular automata (NCA) have emerged as a promising class of models for various tasks, demonstrating strong generalization capabilities by leveraging self-organizing behaviour through iterative update rules [1,3,11]. This behavior enables NCA to learn robust, spatially structured representations that are less sensitive to domain shifts [1]. Additionally, NCA models are highly parameter-efficient while maintaining strong performance, making them well-suited for applications with limited resources.

NCA provide a powerful mechanism for iterative feature extraction by modeling spatial interactions between pixels [1,21]. Unlike conventional models, NCA dynamically refine local representations over multiple iterations, allowing the emergence of structured feature maps. This property enables the extraction of high-quality segmentation masks without the need for explicit supervision.

Here, we propose a novel weakly supervised NCA approach for white blood cell segmentation. Our method extracts segmentation masks from NCA-generated feature maps using principal component analysis [2] and is evaluated on two diverse datasets. To assess the robustness of our approach, we further examine its cross-domain performance across three datasets, demonstrating its generalizability in different data distributions. To foster reproducible research, we publish our source code at https://github.com/marrlab/NCA-WSS.

## 2    Methods

We propose a weakly supervised segmentation approach where we first train an NCA-based classifier using image-level labels and then apply a feature-based segmentation strategy to localize white blood cells. In the following, we describe the details of our NCA architecture, classification framework, and segmentation mask extraction process.

### 2.1    NCA Backbone

NCA operate through iterative local updates, where each cell $c \in \mathbf{R}^n$ adjusts its state based on its (e.g. $3 \times 3$) neighborhood $N_c$. In image processing tasks, a cell corresponds to a pixel across all feature channels. The NCA update rule consists of two main functions:

- The perception function $f_p$ aggregates local information using two convolutional filters.
- The update function $f_u$ processes the perception output through a two-layer fully connected network with ReLU activations.

The computed update is stochastically applied to the cell state at time $t$

$$c^{t+1} = c^t + \delta f_u(f_p(N_c)), \tag{1}$$

where $\delta$ is a binary variable acting as a regularization method that ensures only a random subset of cells are updated per iteration.

At time step $t$, the full state of all cells forms a feature representation $S_t \in \mathbf{R}^{H \times W \times n}$, which evolves over multiple iterations. Here, $H$, $W$, and $n$ are height, width and number of channels. The NCA update function can be expressed as

$$\mathrm{NCA}_\phi : \mathbf{R}^{H \times W \times n} \to \mathbf{R}^{H \times W \times n} \tag{2}$$

where $\phi$ represents the learnable parameters of the perception and update functions.

### 2.2    Classification Architecture

Following NCA-based feature extraction, we aggregate the feature maps into a single vector for classification. Specifically, we apply average pooling across the spatial dimensions to obtain a compact representation

$$\mathrm{pool} : \mathbf{R}^{H \times W \times n} \to \mathbf{R}^n. \tag{3}$$

The pooled feature vector is then passed through a fully connected network to predict class probabilities. By training the model end-to-end, the NCA learns to extract informative, structured features that are effective for classification (Fig. 1).

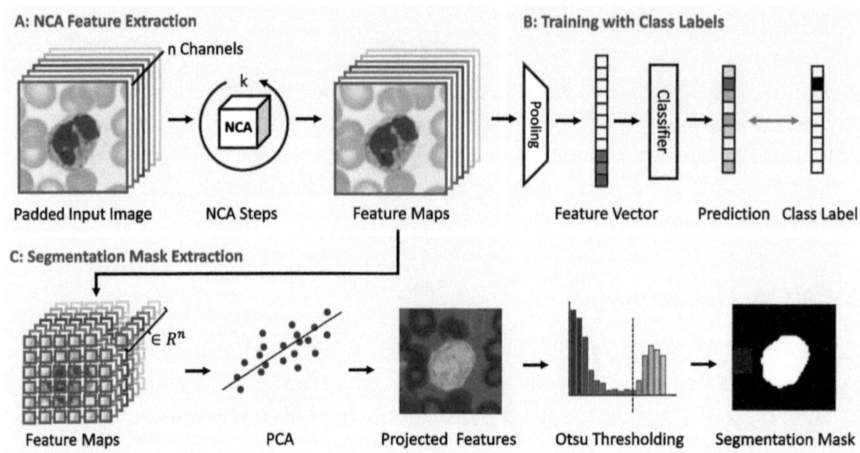



**Fig. 1.** Weakly Supervised Segmentation using Neural Cellular Automata (NCA-WSS) uses feature maps to identify WBCs in image patches. **A:** Feature maps are generated through the iterative local updates of the NCA. **B:** A class prediction is obtained by pooling NCA-generated feature maps, followed by a fully connected network. **C:** We extract segmentation masks by projecting the NCA features onto their first principal component, followed by Otsu thresholding to generate the binary mask.

## 2.3  Segmentation Mask Extraction

Given an NCA-processed image with feature maps $S \in \mathbf{R}^{H \times W \times n}$, we treat each cell (i.e., each pixel across all $n$ feature channels) as a point in an $n$-dimensional space. We apply principal component analysis (PCA) [2] to extract the principal direction of variance. Specifically, we compute the covariance matrix $\Sigma$ of the feature vectors across all spatial locations:

$$\Sigma = \frac{1}{HW} \sum_{i,j} (S_{i,j} - \bar{S})(S_{i,j} - \bar{S})^T, \tag{4}$$

where $\bar{S} \in \mathbf{R}^n$ is the mean of the NCA-cells. The first principal component $v_1 \in \mathbf{R}^n$ is obtained by solving

$$v_1 = \arg \max_{v, \|v\|=1} v^T \Sigma v. \tag{5}$$

We then project each feature vector onto $v_1$ to form a response map

$$P_{i,j} = v_1^T S_{i,j}, \quad \forall (i,j) \in H \times W. \tag{6}$$

This projection enhances high-variance regions, which correspond to informative structures within the WBC, while reducing background variations.

To obtain a binary segmentation mask, we apply Otsu's thresholding [12] to $P$, selecting the optimal threshold $\tau^*$ that minimizes intra-class variance

$$\tau^* = \arg\min_{\tau} \left( \omega_1(\tau)\sigma_1^2(\tau) + \omega_2(\tau)\sigma_2^2(\tau) \right), \tag{7}$$

where $\omega_1, \omega_2$ and $\sigma_1^2, \sigma_2^2$ are the class probabilities and variances for pixels below and above the threshold $\tau$, respectively. The final segmentation mask is given by

$$M_{i,j} = \mathbf{1}_{\{P_{i,j} > \tau^*\}}. \tag{8}$$

This approach effectively combines the extracted feature representations learned by the classification model, which allows for segmentation without requiring annotations for segmentation.

## 3    Experiments and Results

### 3.1    Datasets

We train our method using two datasets of white blood cell microscopy images, Raabin [4] and Matek19 [10]. Images in both datasets are annotated with segmentation masks and class labels. Additionally, we collect an internal, independent dataset with segmentation masks but without class labels, serving as an extra test set to evaluate the generalizability of our weakly supervised segmentation method (Fig. 2).

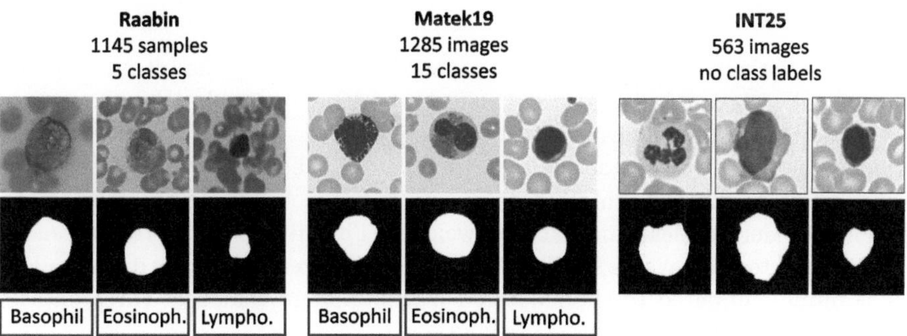


**Fig. 2.** Example images from the three white blood cell datasets used in this study. For each sample, we display the original blood smear image with its corresponding ground truth segmentation mask and class label below.

*Raabin* [4] is a diverse dataset of white blood cell images covering five classes. The images are captured using different cameras and microscopes to ensure variability. For our experiments, we use a subset of 1,145 images that includes expert annotated segmentation masks.

*Matek19* [10] contains white blood cell images collected from 200 patients at the Munich University Hospital, with some images originating from patients diagnosed with acute myeloid leukemia. The dataset includes 15 distinct white blood cell classes, annotated by medical experts. For our experiments, we use a subset of 1,285 images that include both segmentation masks and class labels.

*INT25* is our in-house dataset, consisting of 563 microscopy images including segmentation masks but no class labels. As a result, this dataset is used exclusively for evaluating segmentation performance in the cross domain experiment.

### 3.2  Implementation Details

**Model Parameters.** Our NCA backbone consists of 32 channels and a hidden layer of size 32. We iterate for 32 update steps before applying average pooling. The classifier network has a hidden layer of size 128.

**Training Parameters.** We optimize the model using an Adam optimizer with a learning rate of $10^{-4}$ and betas set to (0.9, 0.999). Learning rate decay is applied via an exponential scheduler with a decay rate of 0.9999. The model is trained using focal loss [7] with a batch size of 32. During training, we augment the images with random rotation and flips. We train for 256 epochs on the Raabin dataset and 128 epochs on Matek19. All experiments are conducted with five fold cross validation.

### 3.3  Quantitative Results

We evaluate the performance of our proposed method using the Intersection over Union (IoU) metric on the two datasets Matek19 and Raabin. For comparison, we include several baselines from a recently published study [9] where the authors trained the models in a federated learning setup using class labels. In contrast, our method trains on a single dataset and tests on the same set, without the benefit of federated learning's shared weights. This difference in training should not be expected to have an advantage due to the limited amount of data available for training compared to the federated learning setup that uses three datasets simultaneously.

Table 1 shows the IoU scores of the proposed NCA-WSS approach compared with the mentioned baselines when trained on both datasets.

To further assess generalization, we conduct a cross-domain experiment where we train on one dataset and test on the other two. Our method still achieves significantly superior performance compared to the baselines, even in this cross-domain setting. This result suggests that our model has good generalization capabilities, enabling it to perform well on unseen domains. Table 2 shows the in-domain and cross-domain performances.

**Table 1.** Our NCA-based weakly supervised segmentation significantly outperforms existing approaches in terms of IoU scores on both datasets. Mean and standard deviation are computed from five independent runs.

| Method | Backbone | IoU Raabin | IoU Matek19 |
|---|---|---|---|
| AuxSegNet [19] | ResNet38 | $37.2 \pm 0.9$ | $44.1 \pm 0.1$ |
| SEAM [18] | ResNet38 | $33.6 \pm 0.5$ | $41.0 \pm 0.7$ |
| EPS [5] | ResNet101 | $36.7 \pm 0.4$ | $45.7 \pm 0.8$ |
| Luo et al. [8] | VGG16 | $36.9 \pm 0.4$ | $41.9 \pm 0.4$ |
| CDA [16] | ResNet38 | $37.2 \pm 0.2$ | $43.5 \pm 0.4$ |
| MCTformer [20] | ResNet38 | $37.0 \pm 0.8$ | $44.8 \pm 0.5$ |
| Wang et al. [17] | VGG16 | $31.9 \pm 0.9$ | $38.9 \pm 0.2$ |
| CONTA [22] | ResNet38 | $33.8 \pm 0.7$ | $40.6 \pm 0.5$ |
| FL-W3S [9] | ResNet38 | $39.8 \pm 0.5$ | $47.0 \pm 1.6$ |
| **NCA WSS** | **NCA** | $\mathbf{49.6 \pm 1.8}$ | $\mathbf{82.6 \pm 2.0}$ |

**Table 2.** Our NCA-based weakly supervised segmentation generalizes well to unseen domains. Mean and standard deviation of IoU scores are computed from five independent runs.

| Train | Test | | |
|---|---|---|---|
| | Raabin | Matek19 | INT25 |
| Raabin | $49.6 \pm 1.8$ | $64.9 \pm 1.4$ | $27.6 \pm 6.1$ |
| Matek19 | $55.1 \pm 2.0$ | $82.6 \pm 2.0$ | $63.7 \pm 4.3$ |

## 3.4   Discussion

In contrast to the existing approaches, our method fundamentally differs by leveraging the unique features extracted by the NCA backbone, which are then robustly combined using PCA (Fig. 3).

The NCA extracts localized features from the input image, focusing on discriminative information guided by the training with class labels. These features allow the model to effectively differentiate between cellular structures. Rather than directly relying on the absolute values of individual features, we use PCA to identify regions of high variance that typically correspond to the key structures within the white blood cell, such as the nucleus and cytoplasm.

By applying PCA, our model dampens the influence of background noise and non-informative variations, ensuring that only the most informative and stable features are used for segmentation. This focus on the most prominent features in terms of variance, rather than raw pixel values, contributes significantly to the higher IoU scores observed in our experiments, particularly in cross-domain scenarios.

These results highlight the robustness and effectiveness of our approach for weakly supervised semantic segmentation of WBCs, even when compared to

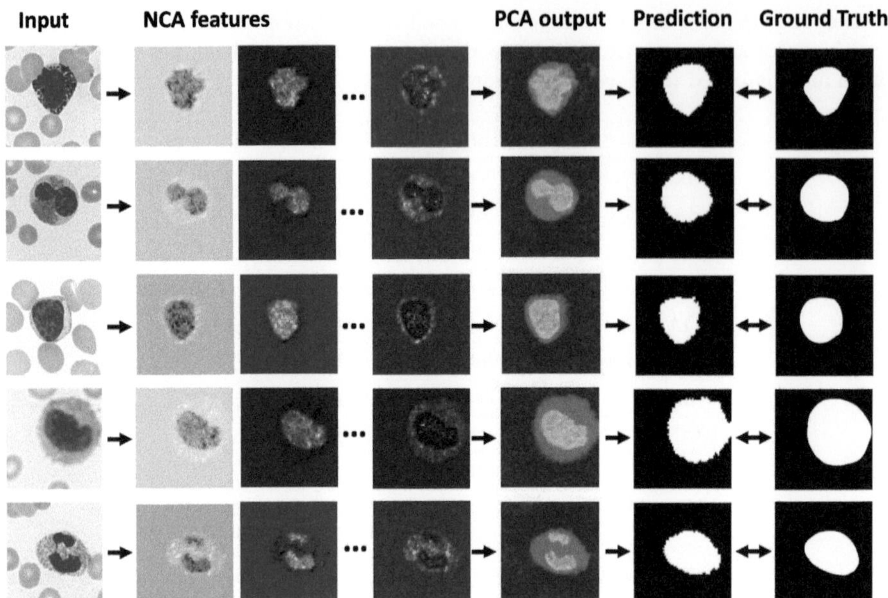



**Fig. 3.** Example of the extracted features and generated masks. The unique features learned by the NCA backbone allow for accurate segmentation of white blood cells. PCA highlights regions of high variance that correspond to the most relevant features within the cell, while filtering out noise.

state-of-the-art methods. Despite being trained on only a single dataset at a time, our method significantly outperforms all baselines trained using a federated learning scheme with three datasets, demonstrating its effectiveness even with limited training data.

## 4   Conclusion

In this work, we proposed a novel method for weakly-supervised segmentation of white blood cells, leveraging the unique capabilities of NCA combined with PCA. Our approach stands out by extracting highly localized and discriminative features through NCA, which are then robustly aggregated using PCA to obtain segmentation masks from a classification model without retraining.

Our experiments on three datasets demonstrate the effectiveness of our method in both in-domain and cross-domain scenarios, achieving superior segmentation results when compared to several baseline approaches. The robustness and high accuracy of our method highlight its potential for real-world applications in medical image analysis, where labeled segmentation data is scarce.

This work opens up new avenues for further improvements in weakly-supervised learning, and future efforts will explore extending the method to more complex segmentation tasks and broader datasets.

**Acknowledgment.** C.M. acknowledges funding from the European Research Council (ERC) under the European Union's Horizon 2020 research and innovation program (Grant Agreement No. 866411 & 101113551 & 101213822) and support from the Hightech Agenda Bayern.

**Disclosure of Interests.** The authors have no competing interests to declare that are relevant to the content of this article.

# References


1. Deutges, M., Sadafi, A., Navab, N., Marr, C.: Neural cellular automata for lightweight, robust and explainable classification of white blood cell images. In: International Conference on Medical Image Computing and Computer-Assisted Intervention, pp. 693–702. Springer (2024)
2. Jolliffe, I.T.: Principal Component Analysis for Special Types of Data. Springer (2002)
3. Kalkhof, J., González, C., Mukhopadhyay, A.: Med-NCA: robust and lightweight segmentation with neural cellular automata. In: International Conference on Information Processing in Medical Imaging, pp. 705–716. Springer (2023)
4. Kouzehkanan, Z.M., et al.: A large dataset of white blood cells containing cell locations and types, along with segmented nuclei and cytoplasm. Sci. Rep. **12**(1), 1123 (2022)
5. Lee, S., Lee, M., Lee, J., Shim, H.: Railroad is not a train: saliency as pseudo-pixel supervision for weakly supervised semantic segmentation. In: Proceedings of the IEEE/CVF Conference on Computer Vision and Pattern Recognition, pp. 5495–5505 (2021)
6. Li, K., Wu, Z., Peng, K.C., Ernst, J., Fu, Y.: Tell me where to look: guided attention inference network. In: Proceedings of the IEEE Conference on Computer Vision and Pattern Recognition, pp. 9215–9223 (2018)
7. Lin, T.Y., Goyal, P., Girshick, R., He, K., Dollár, P.: Focal loss for dense object detection. IEEE Trans. Pattern Anal. Mach. Intell. **42**(2), 318–327 (2020). https://doi.org/10.1109/TPAMI.2018.2858826
8. Luo, W., Yang, M.: Learning saliency-free model with generic features for weakly-supervised semantic segmentation. In: Proceedings of the AAAI Conference on Artificial Intelligence, vol. 34, pp. 11717–11724 (2020)
9. Madni, H.A., Umer, R.M., Zottin, S., Marr, C., Foresti, G.L.: FL-W3S: cross-domain federated learning for weakly supervised semantic segmentation of white blood cells. Int. J. Med. Inform., 105806 (2025)
10. Matek, C., Schwarz, S., Spiekermann, K., Marr, C.: Human-level recognition of blast cells in acute myeloid leukaemia with convolutional neural networks. Nat. Mach. Intell. **1**(11), 538–544 (2019)
11. Mordvintsev, A., Randazzo, E., Niklasson, E., Levin, M.: Growing neural cellular automata. Distill **5**(2), e23 (2020)
12. Otsu, N., et al.: A threshold selection method from gray-level histograms. Automatica **11**(285–296), 23–27 (1975)
13. Salehi, R., et al.: Unsupervised cross-domain feature extraction for single blood cell image classification. In: International Conference on Medical Image Computing and Computer-Assisted Intervention, pp. 739–748. Springer (2022)

14. Selvaraju, R.R., Cogswell, M., Das, A., Vedantam, R., Parikh, D., Batra, D.: GRAD-CAM: visual explanations from deep networks via gradient-based localization. In: 2017 IEEE International Conference on Computer Vision (ICCV), pp. 618–626 (2017). https://doi.org/10.1109/ICCV.2017.74
15. Shahzad, M., et al.: Blood cell image segmentation and classification: a systematic review. PeerJ Comput. Sci. **10**, e1813 (2024)
16. Su, Y., Sun, R., Lin, G., Wu, Q.: Context decoupling augmentation for weakly supervised semantic segmentation. In: Proceedings of the IEEE/CVF International Conference on Computer Vision, pp. 7004–7014 (2021)
17. Wang, X., Liu, S., Ma, H., Yang, M.H.: Weakly-supervised semantic segmentation by iterative affinity learning. Int. J. Comput. Vision **128**, 1736–1749 (2020)
18. Wang, Y., Zhang, J., Kan, M., Shan, S., Chen, X.: Self-supervised equivariant attention mechanism for weakly supervised semantic segmentation. In: Proceedings of the IEEE/CVF Conference on Computer Vision and Pattern Recognition, pp. 12275–12284 (2020)
19. Xu, L., Ouyang, W., Bennamoun, M., Boussaid, F., Sohel, F., Xu, D.: Leveraging auxiliary tasks with affinity learning for weakly supervised semantic segmentation. In: Proceedings of the IEEE/CVF International Conference on Computer Vision, pp. 6984–6993 (2021)
20. Xu, L., Ouyang, W., Bennamoun, M., Boussaid, F., Xu, D.: Multi-class token transformer for weakly supervised semantic segmentation. In: Proceedings of the IEEE/CVF Conference on Computer Vision and Pattern Recognition, pp. 4310–4319 (2022)
21. Yang, C., Deutges, M., Navab, N., Sadafi, A., Marr, C.: Hierarchical neural cellular automata for lightweight microscopy image classification. In: International Conference on Information Processing in Medical Imaging. Springer (2025)
22. Zhang, D., Zhang, H., Tang, J., Hua, X.S., Sun, Q.: Causal intervention for weakly-supervised semantic segmentation. In: Advances in Neural Information Processing Systems, vol. 33, pp. 655–666 (2020)
23. Zhou, B., Khosla, A., Lapedriza, A., Oliva, A., Torralba, A.: Learning deep features for discriminative localization. In: Proceedings of the IEEE Conference on Computer Vision and Pattern Recognition, pp. 2921–2929 (2016)

# EndoSfM3D: Learning to 3D Reconstruct Any Endoscopic Surgery Scene Using Self-supervised Foundation Model


Changhao Zhang[1]([✉]), Matthew J. Clarkson[1], and Mobarak I. Hoque[1,2]

[1] Department of Medical Physics and Biomedical Engineering, UCL Hawkes Institute and University College London, London, UK
{changhao.zhang.24,m.clarkson}@ucl.ac.uk, mobarak.hoque@manchester.ac.uk
[2] Division of Informatics, Imaging and Data Sciences, The University of Manchester, Manchester, UK



**Abstract.** 3D reconstruction of endoscopic surgery scenes plays a vital role in enhancing scene perception, enabling AR visualization, and supporting context-aware decision-making in image-guided surgery. A critical yet challenging step in this process is the accurate estimation of the endoscope's intrinsic parameters. In real surgical settings, intrinsic calibration is hindered by sterility constraints and the use of specialized endoscopes with continuous zoom and telescope rotation. Most existing methods for endoscopic 3D reconstruction do not estimate intrinsic parameters, limiting their effectiveness for accurate and reliable reconstruction. In this paper, we integrate intrinsic parameter estimation into a self-supervised monocular depth estimation framework by adapting the Depth Anything V2 (DA2) model for joint depth, pose, and intrinsics prediction. We introduce an attention-based pose network and a Weight-Decomposed Low-Rank Adaptation strategy for efficient fine-tuning of DA2. Our method is validated on the SCARED and C3VD public datasets, demonstrating superior performance compared to recent state-of-the-art approaches in self-supervised monocular depth estimation and 3D reconstruction. Code and model weights can be found in project repository: https://github.com/MOYF-beta/EndoSfM3D.

**Keywords:** Foundation model · Self-supervised learning · 3D reconstruction


## 1 Introduction

Depth estimation plays a crucial role in minimally invasive endoscopic surgery by supporting precise navigation, accurate 3D surface reconstruction, and realistic augmented-reality visualization [8,31]. Achieving reliable depth estimation in surgical scenes, however, is difficult due to complex anatomical structures, limited illumination, and texture-sparse regions [23]. Classical multi-view geometry techniques such as Structure from Motion (SfM) [21] and Simultaneous


© The Author(s), under exclusive license to Springer Nature Switzerland AG 2026
T. Chen et al. (Eds.): EMA4MICCAI 2025 Workshops, LNCS 16318, pp. 299–309, 2026.
https://doi.org/10.1007/978-3-032-13961-0_30

Localization and Mapping (SLAM) [14] often fail under such conditions. Deep learning approaches have shown strong performance for depth estimation in natural images [5,26], but obtaining large-scale, high-quality surgical depth ground truth for supervised learning is constrained by data privacy, security, and clinical expertise requirements. Consequently, self-supervised learning (SSL) approaches have gained attention, where depth predictions are guided by geometric consistency across video frames [4,18]. Shao *et al.* [23] addressed illumination inconsistencies in endoscopic depth estimation using appearance flow. Yang *et al.* [28] proposed a compact architecture integrating CNN and Transformer modules to reduce model complexity. Zeinoddin *et al.* [30] employed the pre-trained Depth Anything V2 model with Parameter-Efficient Fine-Tuning (PEFT) for surgical depth estimation, while Cui *et al.* [9] adopted a pre-trained DinoV2 encoder with a novel Dynamic Vector-Based Low-Rank Adaptation (DV-LoRA) strategy. However, in the aforementioned studies, researchers have predominantly focused on the accuracy of monocular depth estimation, often overlooking a critical factor for its application to 3D reconstruction.

Unlike conventional imaging environments, endoscopic camera calibration remains particularly challenging due to dynamically changing imaging parameters during surgery. Optical zooming causes continuous variation in intrinsic parameters such as focal length, principal point, and distortion coefficients, making traditional calibration methods unreliable [3]. In addition, telescope rotation in oblique-viewing endoscopes alters projection geometry and extrinsic pose relationships, introducing further calibration instability [10]. Manual endoscope manipulation compounds these issues through hand tremorinduced errors and inconsistent positioning [1]. These challenges are further intensified by surgical constraints such as limited field of view, occlusions, and sterility requirements [16]. Despite advances in modeling and calibration, achieving robust and accurate estimation under continuous zoom and rotation remains an open problem with substantial clinical relevance. In this work, we observe that the re-projection loss used in SfM-based self-supervised learning can be extended to jointly optimize the intrinsic parameter matrix, offering an alternative route for precise intrinsic estimation.

Our key contributions can be summarized as follows: (1) We integrate intrinsic parameter estimation into the AF-SfM self-supervised monocular depth estimation framework by adapting the Depth Anything V2 (DA2) model for *joint prediction* of depth, pose, and intrinsics, addressing a critical limitation in endoscopic 3D reconstruction where sterility constraints and specialized endoscopes hinder traditional calibration. (2) We introduce two key architectural innovations: an attention-based pose network and a Weight-Decomposed Low-Rank Adaptation (DoRA) [15] strategy for efficient fine-tuning of DA2, optimizing parameter efficiency while maintaining representation capacity. (3) Validation on the SCARED and C3VD datasets demonstrates state-of-the-art performance, achieving best-reported AbsRel scores of **0.050** (SCARED) and **0.058** (C3VD) for depth estimation, outperforming recent methods in self-supervised endoscopic reconstruction on depth estimation accuracy, and accurate intrinsic prediction with error of less than **2%** on critical intrinsic parameter focal length $(f_x, f_y)$ and less than 10% on principal point coordinate $(c_x, c_y)$.

## 2   Method

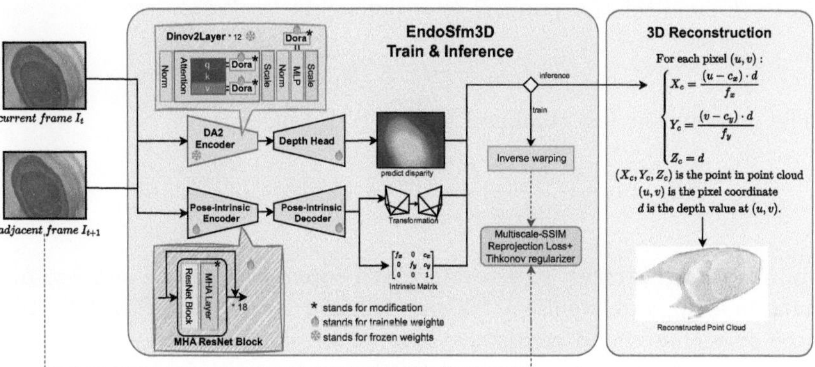


**Fig. 1.** Illustration of the proposed EndoSfM3D framework. A ViT-based encoder and DPT-like decoder pre-trained from Depth Anything V2 [27] are used for depth estimation. Weight-Decomposed Low-Rank Adaptation (DoRA) is applied to the feature extractor for parameter-efficient fine-tuning (PEFT). A ResNet-based Pose Encoder with multi-head attention layers extracts SfM features shared between two frames for transformation and intrinsic estimation. Both depth and pose networks are trained using the reprojection loss from MonoDepth2 [12] and the Tikhonov regularizer from AF-SfMLearner [23].

### 2.1   Preliminaries

**Weight-Decomposed Low-Rank Adaptation (DoRA)**   [15]. DoRA was proposed to enhance the fine-tuning efficiency of foundation models by decoupling the weight matrix into directional and magnitude components. It is motivated by the intuition that directional updates capture task-specific feature orientations while magnitude adjustments regulate their intensities, enabling more precise adaptation. DoRA achieves parameter-efficient tuning by decomposing each pre-trained weight matrix into a directional matrix and a trainable magnitude vector, combined with low-rank updates. Specifically, for a pre-trained weight matrix $W_0 \in \mathbb{R}^{d \times k}$, DoRA reformulates the computation as:

$$h = \left( \frac{V}{||V||} \odot g \right) x + BAx = \left( \frac{W_0 + \Delta V}{||W_0 + \Delta V||} \odot g \right) x + BAx \qquad (1)$$

where $V = W_0 + \Delta V$ represents the directional component with $||\cdot||$ denoting L2 normalization, $g \in \mathbb{R}^d$ is a learnable magnitude vector, and $B \in \mathbb{R}^{d \times r}, A \in \mathbb{R}^{r \times k}$ are low-rank matrices $(r \ll \min(d, k))$. Only $\Delta V$, $g$, $A$, and $B$ are updated during training, while the original weights $W_0$ remain frozen.

**Self-supervised Depth, Ego-Motion, and Intrinsic Estimation.** Self-supervised methods for depth and ego-motion estimation leverage view synthesis as a supervisory signal. Given consecutive frames $I_t$ (target) and $I_s$ (source), the core objective is to minimize the photometric error between $I_t$ and the warped source image $I_{s \to t}$. The warping operation $\pi$ uses estimated depth $z$, camera intrinsics $K$, and relative pose $(R, t)$ as defined in Eq. 7:

$$I_{s \to t} = \pi\left(z, K, R, t, I_s\right) \tag{2}$$

The photometric loss combines L1 and SSIM metrics:

$$\mathcal{L}_p = \alpha \frac{1 - \mathrm{SSIM}\left(I_t, I_{s \to t}\right)}{2} + (1 - \alpha)\left\|I_t - I_{s \to t}\right\|_1 \tag{3}$$

**Tikhonov Regularizer.** To stabilize self-supervised depth and ego-motion learning in endoscopy, we use a Tikhonov regularizer $\mathcal{R}_k$ following [23]. It incorporates smoothness and consistency priors, helping to address the problem's ill-posed nature. The regularizer is defined as:

$$\mathcal{R}_k = \lambda_1 \mathcal{L}_{rs} + \lambda_2 \mathcal{L}_{ax} \tag{4}$$

Compared with Af-SfMLearner's Tikhonov regularizer [23], we removed Edge-Aware Smoothness Loss $\mathcal{L}_{es}$, as it's redundant and harmful to powerful pre-trained depth model We describe the first two components below:

*(a) Residual-Based Smoothness Loss $\mathcal{L}_{rs}$* This term enforces smoothness in the predicted appearance flow $\mathbf{C}_\delta$, while preserving edges near high photometric differences (e.g., specular regions). It is defined as, where $\mathbf{p} = (u, v)$ is the coordinate of pixel:

$$\mathcal{L}_{rs} = \sum_{\mathbf{p}} |\nabla \mathbf{C}_\delta(\mathbf{p})| \cdot e^{-\nabla |I^t(\mathbf{p}) - I^{s \to t}(\mathbf{p})|} \tag{5}$$

The exponential term reduces smoothness penalties in areas with strong brightness changes.

*(b) Auxiliary Loss $\mathcal{L}_{ax}$* This loss aligns the appearance flow with optical flow to ensure consistency with motion cues:

$$\mathcal{L}_{ax} = \sum_{\mathbf{p}} \mathbf{V}(\mathbf{p}) \cdot \Phi\left(I^{s \to t}(\mathbf{p}), I^t(\mathbf{p}) + \mathbf{C}_\delta(\mathbf{p})\right) \tag{6}$$

Here, $\Phi(\cdot)$ measures photometric error, and $\mathbf{V}(\mathbf{p})$ masks out occluded regions. This encourages $\mathbf{C}_\delta$ to follow realistic motion patterns.

### 2.2  Proposed Framework: EndoSfM3D

As illustrated in Fig. 1, The EndoSfM3D fine-tune the Depth Anything V2 model into an Endoscope foundation model for accurate depth estimation. The framework includes three main components: DepthNet, Pose-Intrinsics Net, and a semi-supervised training system based on EndoSfM3D we proposed. DepthNet predicts depth from the reference frame using a ViT-based encoder (pre-trained with Depth Anything V2) and a DPT-like decoder. Pose-Intrinsics Net predicts motion and camera parameters from the same input, sharing a ResNet encoder with two output heads. EndoSfM3D uses predicted depth, motion, and camera parameters to reproject frames and optimize the model by comparing reprojected and reference frames, thus getting the self-supervised training loss. In EndoSfM3D, compared with original AF-SfMLearner [23] which introduced multiple regularizer to enhance the depth estimation, we only kept smoothness of optic flow and disparity, removed other constrains since a powerful pretrained depth model no longer need them. In optimizer, we utilize $Loss = \mathcal{L}_p + \mathcal{R}_k$ where $\mathcal{L}_p$ and $\mathcal{R}_k$ are defined by we utilize $Loss = \mathcal{L}_p + \mathcal{R}_k$ where $\mathcal{L}_p$ and $\mathcal{R}_k$ are defined by (3) and (4).

**Pretrained Foundation Models for Depth.** Foundation Models generally refer to powerful pre-trained models trained on extensive amounts of data which enable them to exhibit strong generalization capabilities across multiple tasks and scenarios. Dense Prediction Transformer (DPT) [20] is a depth estimation foundation model based on Vision Transformer (ViTs). DINOv2 [17] is a semantic foundation model suitable for many vision tasks including depth estimation with separate decode decoders. In this work, we aim to adapt Depth Anything [27], which is a depth estimation foundation model trained on large-scale labeled and unlabeled data, to endoscopic scenes.

**Pose-Intrinsics Net.** The architecture employs a ResNet-18 backbone, optimized for computational efficiency and feature extraction in endoscopic applications, processing pairs of consecutive frames for pose estimation. Multi-Head Attention (MHA) modules are integrated after each ResNet block (layer1layer4), enabling spatial relationship learning across feature resolutions of 64, 128, 256, and 512 channels. Each MHA module uses 8 attention heads, where Query, Key, and Value matrices are generated via $1 \times 1$ convolutions on ResNet outputs. Each head processes $channel_{dim}/8$ channels, focusing attention on spatially relevant regions.

Feature extraction occurs in two stages: standard ResNet blocks initially process features, followed by MHA modules with residual connections. These modules apply layer normalization and self-attention, with outputs added to input features via residuals. This design simultaneously captures spatial attention patterns critical for both ego-motion and intrinsic parameter prediction. The component takes consecutive frames as input, predicting 6DoF ego-motion and camera intrinsics through separate heads. These predictions—combined with depth estimates—enable pixel-wise 3D re-projection through geometric reprojection. The re-projection formula is as follows:

$$z^{'}p^{'} = KRK^{-1}zp + Kt, \tag{7}$$

where K refers to the intrinsic matrix given by $K = \begin{vmatrix} f_x & 0 & x_0 \\ 0 & f_y & y_0 \\ 0 & 0 & 1 \end{vmatrix}$, $p$ and $p'$ are pixel coordinates before and after the transformation of rotation matrix $R$ and translation vector $t$; $z$ and $z'$ are corresponding depths. Previous work [13] has demonstrated that given Eq. (7), no $\tilde{K}$ and $\tilde{R}$ exist such that $\tilde{K}\tilde{R}\tilde{K}^{-1} = KRK^{-1}$ leading the estimation of $K$, $R$ and $t$ to converge simultaneously. Therefore, the ego-motion head and the intrinsic parameters head share the same encoder.

### 2.3 Experiment and Results

**Dataset and Implementation Details.** We trained and validated our model on two datasets: SCARED [2] and C3VD [7]. SCARED contains 35 porcine abdominal endoscopy videos (22,950 frames) with depth, pose, and intrinsic ground truth, using Shao et al.'s split [23]. C3VD provides 22 synthetic colon model sequences (10,015 frames) with comprehensive ground truth annotations, following Paruchuri et al.'s split [19]. During training, we employ the Adam optimizer with an initial learning rate of $1 \times 10^{-4}$, which decays to $1 \times 10^{-5}$ after 10 epochs, and train all models for 20 epochs with batch size 12. The training loss is given by $Loss = \mathcal{L}_p + \mathcal{R}_k$ where $\mathcal{L}_p$ and $\mathcal{R}_k$ are defined by we utilize $Loss = \mathcal{L}_p + \mathcal{R}_k$ where $\mathcal{L}_p$ and $\mathcal{R}_k$ are defined by (3) and (4) respectively. respectively.

**Table 1.** Quantitative depth estimation comparison on SCARED and C3VD datasets. Bold reflect the best result.

| | Method | Year | AbsRel↓ | SqRel↓ | Rmse↓ | RmseLog↓ |
|---|---|---|---|---|---|---|
| SCARED | Fang et al. [11] | 2020 | 0.078 | 0.794 | 6.794 | 0.109 |
| | Monodepth2 [12] | 2019 | 0.069 | 0.577 | 5.546 | 0.094 |
| | Endo-SfM [18] | 2021 | 0.062 | 0.606 | 5.726 | 0.093 |
| | AF-SfMLearner [23] | 2022 | 0.059 | 0.435 | 4.925 | 0.082 |
| | DARES [30] | 2024 | 0.052 | 0.356 | 4.483 | 0.073 |
| | EndoDAC [9] | 2024 | 0.052 | 0.362 | **4.464** | 0.073 |
| | Endo-FASt3r [29] | 2025 | 0.051 | **0.354** | 4.480 | – |
| | **EndoSfM3D (Ours)** | – | **0.050** | 0.389 | 4.749 | **0.070** |
| C3VD | AF-SfMLearner [23] | 2022 | 0.086 | 0.358 | – | 0.104 |
| | Col3D-MTL [24] | 2023 | 0.109 | 0.386 | **3.052** | 0.131 |
| | **EndoSfM3D (Ours)** | – | **0.058** | **0.333** | 4.413 | **0.076** |

**Depth Estimation.** The proposed method is compared with several SOTA self-supervised and supervised methods [6,9,11,12,18,22–25,28,30], and Depth Anything [27] model, all results corresponding to the trained dataset comes from their paper's result. During training, we utilized 2 datasets: C3VD and

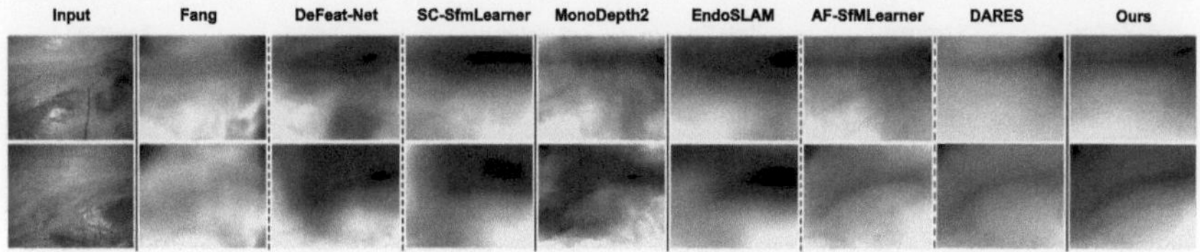

**Fig. 2.** Results comparison on SCARED for previous researches and our results.

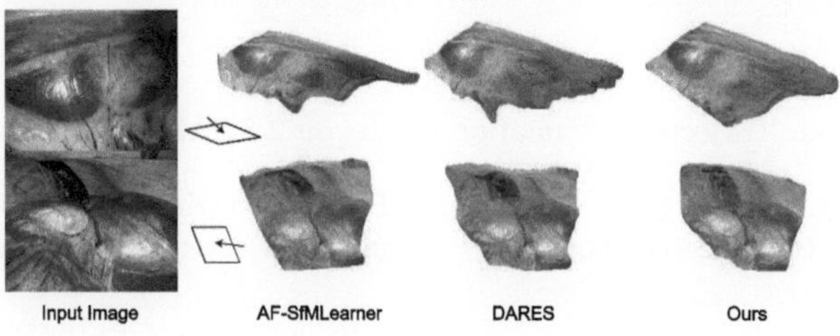


**Fig. 3.** Comparison of 3D reconstruction results using AF-SfMLearner [23], DARES [30], and our method.

SCARED. The quantitative results for depth comparison is shown on Table 1, our method have SOTA performance on both dataset(on Abs Rel). Figure 2 shows the qualitative depth comparison between our method and other methods. Figure 3 shows several 3D reconstruction qualitative results comparison on DARES dataset, we can observe the corresponding 3D reconstruction precisely reflect the structure of organs in our method, and getting more reasonable result on the edge of images.

**Pose and Intrinsics Estimation.** Two sequences of SCARED dataset are selected followed [9, 12, 18, 23, 29, 30] for evaluation of pose and intrinsic estimation. Pose estimation is evaluated on 2 sequences separately while intrinsic estimation is evaluated with a weighted average percentage error on two sequences. The results are presented in Tables 2 and 3. Table 2 shows our proposed method obtains satisfactory performances on pose estimation with or without given intrinsic parameters, with Fig. 4 shows the qualitative results on 2 SCARED sequence to confirm the overall accuracy of pose estimation. Our proposed method can also estimate accurate camera intrinsic parameters with error of less than **2%** on critical intrinsic parameter focal length $(f_x, f_y)$ and less than 10% on principal point coordinate $(c_x, c_y)$.

**Ablation Study.** Table 4 presents the ablation results. We progressively enabled the proposed components, including LoRA/DoRA integration, variations of MHA layers in the Pose-Intrinsics Net, and intrinsic parameter prediction, while monitoring performance changes. The results show consistent improvements with each modification, indicating that the proposed architectural choices contribute effectively to performance. Moreover, the inclusion of intrin-

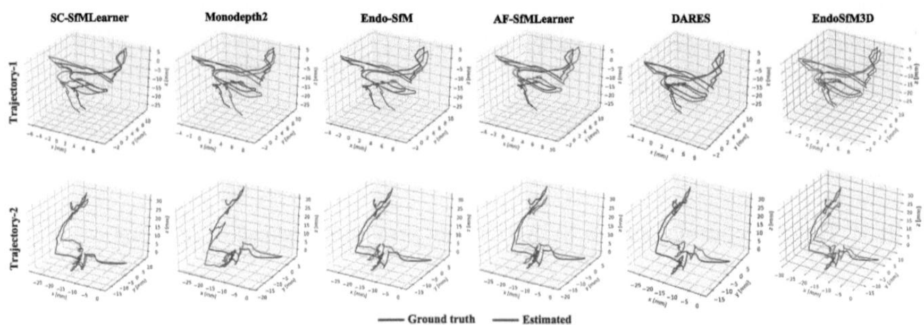



**Fig. 4.** Trajectory estimation results on 2 SCARED sequences.

**Table 2.** Quantitative pose estimation comparison on two selected sequences.

| Method | Year | ATE ↓ (Seq.1) | ATE ↓ (Seq.2) |
|---|---|---|---|
| Monodepth2 [12] | 2019 | 0.0769 | 0.0554 |
| Endo-SfM [18] | 2021 | 0.0759 | 0.0500 |
| AF-SfMLearner [23] | 2022 | 0.0742 | 0.0478 |
| EndoFASt3r [29] | 2025 | **0.0702** | **0.0438** |
| **EndoSfM3D(Ours)** | - | 0.0791 | 0.0529 |

**Table 3.** Intrinsic estimation comparison on two selected C3VD sequences.

| Intrinsics | GT | Seq 1 Error | Seq 2 Error |
|---|---|---|---|
| $f_x$ | 769.24 | 0.68 % | 1.56% |
| $f_y$ | 769.24 | 0.69 % | 1.62% |
| $c_x$ | 679.54 | 7.73 % | 5.42% |
| $c_y$ | 543.97 | 10.92% | 0.80% |

**Table 4.** Ablation study on DARES dataset comparing depth estimation variants. Underlined methods denote framework adaptations; bold/underlined results indicate best/second-best performance.

| Depth | Pose | Intrinsic | AbsRel↓ | SqRel↓ | Rmse↓ | RmseLog↓ |
|---|---|---|---|---|---|---|
| LoRA | ResNet | Fixed | 0.0523 | 0.383 | 4.6635 | 0.076 |
| LoRA | ResNet | Predicted | 0.0527 | 0.436 | 4.9580 | 0.079 |
| LoRA | MHA ResNet | Fixed | 0.0509 | 0.387 | 4.6837 | 0.074 |
| DoRA | MHA ResNet | Fixed | **0.0501** | **0.357** | **4.511** | 0.072 |
| DoRA | MHA ResNet | Predicted | 0.0504 | 0.389 | 4.749 | **0.070** |

sic prediction has a minimal effect on overall accuracy, confirming its stability within the framework.

## 3 Conclusion

In this work, we introduced EndoSfM3D, a self-supervised framework that unifies depth, pose, and intrinsic parameter estimation for endoscopic 3D reconstruction. The method addresses a long-standing challenge in surgical vision by enabling accurate intrinsic calibration through geometric consistency within monocular video, removing the need for physical calibration targets. Experiments on multiple endoscopic datasets show that EndoSfM3D achieves reliable depth and motion estimation while maintaining stable intrinsic predictions under zoom and rotation. This joint optimization enables accurate 3D scene reconstruction from standard surgical videos and extends the practicality of self-supervised learning to real clinical environments. Future work will focus on improving temporal consistency, domain generalization across different endoscope types, and integration with real-time image-guided surgery systems to enhance clinical applicability.

**Acknowledgments.** This work was supported in whole, or in part, by the Engineering and Physical Sciences Research Council (EPSRC) under grants [EP/W00805X/1]. For the purpose of open access, the author has applied a CC BY public copyright licence to any author accepted manuscript version arising from this submission.

**Disclosure of Interests.** The authors have no competing interests to declare that are relevant to the content of this article.

# References


1. Al-Obaidi, A., et al.: Effective calibration of an endoscope to an optical tracking system for medical augmented reality. Int. J. Comput. Assist. Radiol. Surg. **12**(9), 1619–1628 (2017)
2. Allan, M., et al.: Stereo correspondence and reconstruction of endoscopic data challenge. arXiv preprint: arXiv:2101.01133 (2021)
3. An, P., et al.: Two-point calibration method for a zoom camera with an approximate focal-invariant radial distortion model. J. Opt. Soc. Am. A **38**(4), 504–514 (2021)
4. Arampatzakis, V., Pavlidis, G., Mitianoudis, N., Papamarkos, N.: Monocular depth estimation: a thorough review. IEEE Trans. Pattern Anal. Mach. Intell. (2023)
5. Bhat, S.F., Alhashim, I., Wonka, P.: LocalBins: improving depth estimation by learning local distributions. In: European Conference on Computer Vision, pp. 480–496. Springer (2022)
6. Bian, J., et al.: Unsupervised scale-consistent depth and ego-motion learning from monocular video. In: Advances in Neural Information Processing Systems, vol. 32 (2019)
7. Bobrow, T.L., Golhar, M., Vijayan, R., Akshintala, V.S., Garcia, J.R., Durr, N.J.: Colonoscopy 3D video dataset with paired depth from 2D–3D registration. Med. Image Anal. **90**, 102956 (2023)
8. Collins, T., et al.: Augmented reality guided laparoscopic surgery of the uterus. IEEE Trans. Med. Imaging **40**(1), 371–380 (2020)
9. Cui, B., Islam, M., Bai, L., Wang, A., Ren, H.: EndoDAC: efficient adapting foundation model for self-supervised depth estimation from any endoscopic camera. In: International Conference on Medical Image Computing and Computer-Assisted Intervention, pp. 208–218. Springer (2024)
10. Eppenga, R., et al.: An improved camera model for oblique-viewing laparoscopes: high reprojection accuracy independent of telescope rotation. Phys. Med. Biol. **68**(18), 185007 (2023)
11. Fang, Z., Chen, X., Chen, Y., Gool, L.V.: Towards good practice for CNN-Based monocular depth estimation. In: Proceedings of the IEEE Winter Conference on Applications of Computer Vision, pp. 1091–1100 (2020)

12. Godard, C., Mac Aodha, O., Firman, M., Brostow, G.J.: Digging into self-supervised monocular depth estimation. In: Proceedings of the IEEE/CVF International Conference on Computer Vision, pp. 3828–3838 (2019)
13. Gordon, A., Li, H., Jonschkowski, R., Angelova, A.: Depth from videos in the wild: unsupervised monocular depth learning from unknown cameras. In: Proceedings of the IEEE/CVF International Conference on Computer Vision, pp. 8977–8986 (2019)
14. Grasa, O.G., Bernal, E., Casado, S., Gil, I., Montiel, J.: Visual slam for handheld monocular endoscope. IEEE Trans. Med. Imaging **33**(1), 135–146 (2013)
15. Liu, S.Y., et al.: DoRA: weight-decomposed low-rank adaptation. In: Forty-first International Conference on Machine Learning (2024)
16. Mountney, P., et al.: Endoscopic camera calibration and its application in laparoscopic surgery. In: MICCAI 2011, LNCS. vol. 6891, pp. 473–480 (2011)
17. Oquab, M., et al.: DINOv2: learning robust visual features without supervision. arXiv preprint: arXiv:2304.07193 (2023)
18. Ozyoruk, K.B., et al.: EndoSLAM dataset and an unsupervised monocular visual odometry and depth estimation approach for endoscopic videos. Med. Image Anal. **71**, 102058 (2021)
19. Paruchuri, A., et al.: Leveraging near-field lighting for monocular depth estimation from endoscopy videos. In: European Conference on Computer Vision, pp. 473–491. Springer (2024)
20. Ranftl, R., Bochkovskiy, A., Koltun, V.: Vision transformers for dense prediction. In: Proceedings of the IEEE/CVF International Conference on Computer Vision, pp. 12179–12188 (2021)
21. Rattanalappaiboon, S., Bhongmakapat, T., Ritthipravat, P.: Fuzzy zoning for feature matching technique in 3D reconstruction of nasal endoscopic images. Comput. Biol. Med. **67**, 83–94 (2015)
22. Recasens, D., Lamarca, J., Fácil, J.M., Montiel, J., Civera, J.: Endo-depth-and-motion: reconstruction and tracking in endoscopic videos using depth networks and photometric constraints. IEEE Robot. Autom. Lett. **6**(4), 7225–7232 (2021)
23. Shao, S., et al.: Self-supervised monocular depth and ego-motion estimation in endoscopy: appearance flow to the rescue. Med. Image Anal. **77**, 102338 (2022)
24. Solano, P.E.C., Bulpitt, A., Subramanian, V., Ali, S.: Multi-task learning with cross-task consistency for improved depth estimation in colonoscopy. Med. Image Anal. **99**, 103379 (2025)
25. Spencer, J., Bowden, R., Hadfield, S.: DeFeat-Net: general monocular depth via simultaneous unsupervised representation learning. In: Proceedings of the IEEE/CVF Conference on Computer Vision and Pattern Recognition, pp. 14402–14413 (2020)
26. Sun, L., Bian, J.W., Zhan, H., Yin, W., Reid, I., Shen, C.: SC-DepthV3: robust self-supervised monocular depth estimation for dynamic scenes. IEEE Trans. Pattern Anal. Mach. Intell. (2023)
27. Yang, L., et al.: Depth anything V2. In: Advances in Neural Information Processing Systems, vol. 37, pp. 21875–21911 (2024)
28. Yang, Z., Pan, J., Dai, J., Sun, Z., Xiao, Y.: Self-supervised lightweight depth estimation in endoscopy combining CNN and transformer. IEEE Trans. Med. Imaging (2024)
29. Zeinoddin, M.S., et al.: Endo-FAST3r: endoscopic foundation model adaptation for structure from motion. arXiv preprint: arXiv:2503.07204 (2025)

30. Zeinoddin, M.S., et al.: DARES: depth anything in robotic endoscopic surgery with self-supervised vector-lora of the foundation model. arXiv preprint: arXiv:2408.17433 (2024)
31. Zhang, P., et al.: Real-time navigation for laparoscopic hepatectomy using image fusion of preoperative 3D surgical plan and intraoperative indocyanine green fluorescence imaging. Surg. Endosc. **34**, 3449–3459 (2020)

# WeakSupCon: Weakly Supervised Contrastive Learning for Encoder Pre-training

Bodong Zhang[1,2]([envelope]) [iD], Hamid Manoochehri[1,2] [iD], Xiwen Li[2] [iD], Beatrice S. Knudsen[3] [iD], and Tolga Tasdizen[1,2] [iD]

[1] Department of Electrical and Computer Engineering, University of Utah, Salt Lake City, UT, USA
bodong.zhang@utah.edu
[2] Scientific Computing and Imaging Institute, University of Utah, Salt Lake City, UT, USA
[3] Department of Pathology, University of Utah, Salt Lake City, UT, USA

**Abstract.** Weakly supervised multiple instance learning (MIL) is a challenging task given that only bag-level labels are provided, while each bag typically contains multiple instances. This topic has been extensively studied in histopathological image analysis, where labels are usually available only at the whole slide image (WSI) level, while each WSI could be divided into thousands of small image patches for training. The dominant MIL approaches focus on feature aggregation and take fixed patch features as inputs. However, weakly supervised feature representation learning in MIL settings is always neglected. Those features used to be generated by self-supervised learning methods that do not utilize weak labels, or by foundation encoders pre-trained on other large datasets. In this paper, we propose a novel weakly supervised feature representation learning method called Weakly Supervised Contrastive Learning (WeakSupCon) that utilizes bag-level labels. In our method, we employ multi-task learning and define distinct contrastive losses for samples with different bag labels. Our experiments demonstrate that the features generated using WeakSupCon with limited computing resources significantly enhance MIL classification performance compared to self-supervised approaches across three datasets. Our WeakSupCon code is available at https://github.com/BzhangURU/Paper_WeakSupCon.

**Keywords:** Contrastive Learning · Multiple Instance Learning · Weakly Supervised Learning · Histopathological Images

## 1 Introduction

Deep learning has been widely utilized in medical image analysis, particularly for histopathological image classification tasks. Traditional deep learning-based image classification requires training on a large dataset in a fully supervised


T. Chen et al. (Eds.): EMA4MICCAI 2025 Workshops, LNCS 16318, pp. 310–319, 2026.
https://doi.org/10.1007/978-3-032-13961-0_31

manner, where each image is assigned a label during training. However, this requirement poses significant challenges in the medical domain, as labeling a vast number of images demands substantial effort from experts. To address this issue, multiple instance learning (MIL) [11,14,18] methods have been proposed to enable weakly supervised training, thereby reducing the burden.

In multiple instance learning (MIL), instead of assigning labels at the instance level, labels are provided at the bag level. Each bag contains multiple instances. A bag is labeled as positive if it contains at least one positive instance and is labeled as negative if all instances within it are negative. The MIL framework is particularly useful in histopathological image classification, where labels are assigned only at the whole slide image (WSI) level. Typically, each slide can be divided into thousands of patches, which serve as inputs for deep learning models. A slide is considered a positive slide if a portion of its patches are positive.

Due to computational constraints and the need to ensure the stability of MIL models under weak supervision, image patches are typically encoded into fixed embedded features before applying MIL methods. In attention-based MIL (AB-MIL) [9], an attention-based operator is introduced to assign different attention weights to patches within a bag. The final representation of a bag (slide) is obtained as a weighted sum of the feature embeddings from its instances (patches). The attention mechanism enables the model to identify key instances that contribute to the slide-level labels, thereby making a greater impact on the embedded features of slides during MIL training. Double-Tier Feature Distillation Multiple Instance Learning (DTFD-MIL) [18] further enhances AB-MIL by introducing the concept of pseudo-bags to artificially increase the number of training bags. Each bag is split into a certain number of pseudo-bags, and instances are randomly assigned to these pseudo-bags.

While the MIL structure directly influences MIL classification results, the quality of patch feature embeddings is crucial for the success of MIL classification. These features encapsulate the characteristics of instances in a way that facilitates learning the relationships between instances and the overall bag label. High-quality embedded features ensure that the aggregation process captures relevant patterns, thereby contributing effectively to bag-level classification. Although ImageNet pre-trained encoders are commonly used to generate patch features [18], the fact that ImageNet consists of natural images introduces a domain shift when these encoders are applied to histopathological images. An alternative way is to generate features by foundation models pre-trained on large histopathological images. [1,15] However, those foundation models are also pre-trained on histopathological datasets from other resources, which still introduces domain shifts to some extent. In this paper, we try to explore more effective approaches to pre-train encoders on local training datasets. Self-supervised contrastive learning [3,4,12,16,17] is a powerful method for pre-training encoders without the need for labels. Different views of the same sample are generated through image augmentation. Positive pairs are defined when two views originate from the same original sample, whereas negative pairs are formed when they come from different original samples. The contrastive loss function aims to minimize the distance between positive pairs while maximizing the distance between negative pairs. In SimCLR [2], given a batch of N samples, each sample is augmented twice, resulting in a total of 2N samples. The contrastive loss term between features from sample i and sample j is defined as:

$$\ell_{i,j} = -\log \frac{\exp(sim(z_i, z_j)/\tau)}{\sum_{k=1}^{2N} \mathbf{1}_{[k \neq i]} \exp(sim(z_i, z_k)/\tau)} \tag{1}$$

where $sim(u, v) = u^{\top} v / \|u\| \|v\|$, $z_i$ and $z_j$ form a positive pair when they originate from the same original sample. An example of the distribution of learned features through self-supervised contrastive learning can be found in Fig. 1 (a).

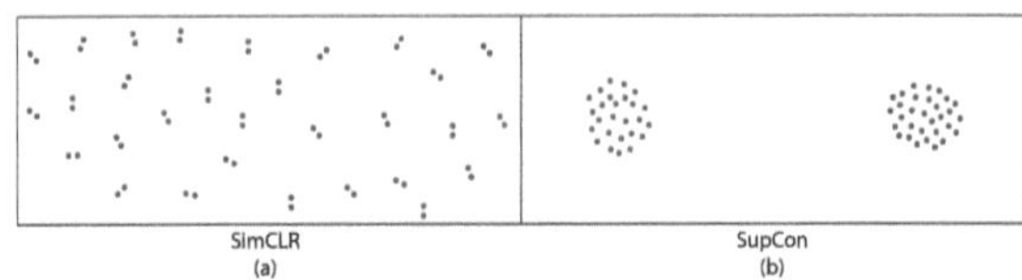

**Fig. 1.** Example of feature distributions after pre-training on (a) SimCLR and (b) SupCon. Different colors represent samples with different labels.

Supervised contrastive learning (SupCon) [10] extends the self-supervised contrastive approach to a fully supervised setting by utilizing instance-level labels. The loss function is defined as:

$$\mathcal{L}^{sup} = \sum_{i \in I} \frac{-1}{|P(i)|} \sum_{p \in P(i)} \log \frac{\exp(z_i \cdot z_p/\tau)}{\sum_{a \in A(i)} \exp(z_i \cdot z_a/\tau)} \tag{2}$$

where $z_i$ and $z_p$ form a positive pair if they originate from samples that share the same label, $A(i)$ is the set of all samples except $i$, while $P(i)$ only contains samples that share the same label. $\tau$ is a temperature hyperparameter. SupCon has also been evaluated in transfer learning experiments on CIFAR-10, CIFAR-100, and ImageNet, where the encoder pre-trained with SupCon was frozen, and an additional classification layer was appended to perform classification training on the same dataset. Results [10] have demonstrated that SupCon outperforms self-supervised contrastive learning and even traditional end-to-end training using cross-entropy loss [13]. Figure 1 (b) demonstrates the ideal distribution of learned features after SupCon pre-training. Despite these promising results, the SupCon method that requires instance-level supervision still faces theoretical challenges in MIL settings, where only bag-level labels are available.

## 2   Method

Inspired by Supervised Contrastive Learning (SupCon), rather than pursuing a complex end-to-end multiple instance learning (MIL) solution, we propose

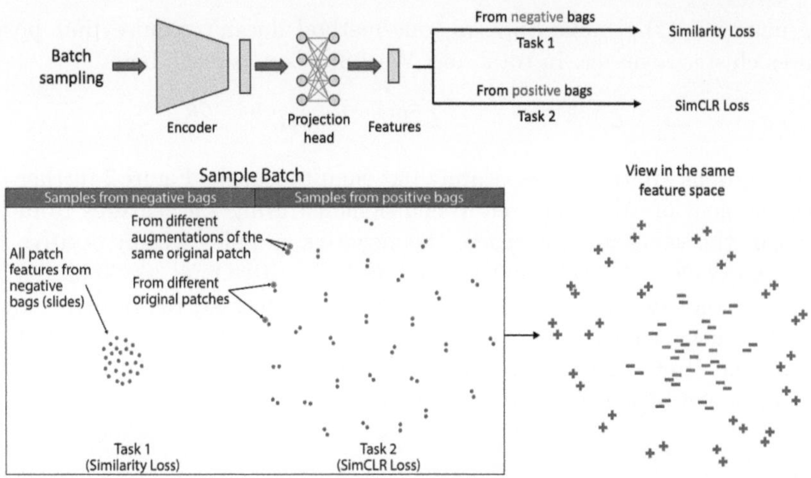


**Fig. 2.** Main idea of WeakSupCon. The samples in a batch are divided into distinct contrastive learning tasks based on their bag labels. Different colors denote different bag labels, while the symbols '+' and '-' indicate the actual instance labels.

weakly supervised contrastive learning (WeakSupCon) to enhance encoder pre-training by transitioning from a self-supervised to a weakly supervised approach.

In our method, we treat all image patches within negative bags as negative samples based on the definition of negative bags. However, determining the true labels of patches within positive bags in pre-training is challenging, as they contain both positive and negative samples. To address this, we propose a multi-task learning approach that assigns different tasks to patch instances based on their bag labels. Figure 2 illustrates the main concept of WeakSupCon. For each training batch during pre-training, we split samples into separate groups based on their bag labels. In the negative group, we apply a supervised version of the contrastive learning task to minimize the distances among all features from samples with negative bag labels. In detail, we introduce a Similarity Loss by taking only the positive pair component from the SupCon Loss (2) to maximize the similarity among all the features from negative bags, as described below:

$$\mathcal{L}^{Similarity} = \sum_{i \in Neg} \frac{-1}{|Neg|} \sum_{j \in Neg, j \neq i} z_i \cdot z_j / \tau \tag{3}$$

where $Neg$ represents the negative group. In the positive group, we apply self-supervised contrastive learning (SimCLR) by defining the loss as follows:

$$\mathcal{L}^{SimCLR} = \sum_{i \in Pos} \ell_{i,p(i)} \tag{4}$$

where $Pos$ represents the positive group, $p(i)$ denotes another feature generated from same original sample as $i$ but with a different augmentation, $\ell_{i,p(i)}$ is defined as in equation (1). Unlike SupCon, our method doesn't require that positive features cluster together. In total, our WeakSupCon loss will be:

$$\mathcal{L}^{WeakSupCon} = \mathcal{L}^{Similarity} + \mathcal{L}^{SimCLR} \tag{5}$$

The two groups are trained separately but simultaneously. Figure 2 further illustrates the goal of WeakSupCon. When demonstrating the features from both groups in the same feature space, the negative samples within positive bags tend to move closer to the negative samples in negative bags, as Similarity Loss encourages the clustering of negative samples. In contrast, the positive samples in positive bags tend to move further away from negative samples due to the effect of the SimCLR loss. This separation makes MIL models more likely to locate or assign higher attention weights to positive samples.

## 3   Experiments

### 3.1   Datasets

We conducted experiments on three datasets, including Camelyon16 dataset [6,7], renal vein thrombosis (RVT) dataset, and kidney metastasis dataset. The Camelyon16 is a public dataset designed for slide-level classification between normal slides and metastatic cancer slides in lymph nodes, with 270 slides in the training set. The remaining two datasets are our institutional datasets that are available with data transfer agreements by contacting the authors.

In the renal vein thrombosis (RVT) dataset, case-level (patient-level) labels are provided instead of slide-level labels like in the Camelyon16 dataset, with each case usually containing multiple slides. The task is to predict the presence of RVT. The dataset consists of 74/12/18 negative cases and 31/8/11 positive cases in the training, validation, and test sets, respectively. In total, the training set contains 862 slides. We generated 1,518,872 patches with negative bag labels and 695,439 patches with positive bag labels in the training set for pre-training.

The kidney metastasis dataset contains only case-level labels as well, with the goal of predicting metastasis. The training set consists of 15 negative cases and 42 positive cases. The validation set includes 10 negative cases and 26 positive cases. The test set contains 13 negative cases and 33 positive cases. In the training set, the negative cases provide 107 slides, from which 383,725 patches were generated. The positive cases provide 393 slides, with 930,939 generated patches.

Among the datasets, the proportion of positive regions in positive slides varies significantly. In Camelyon16, it is estimated that less than 10% of the foreground area in a positive slide contains cancerous regions [11,14], whereas in the RVT dataset, positive regions occupy a much larger proportion in the positive slides.

### 3.2   Experiment Settings

We first pre-trained encoders by feature representation learning with various contrastive learning settings, including self-supervised learning (SimCLR, MoCo v3), supervised learning (SupCon), and weakly supervised learning (our Weak-SupCon). For SupCon pre-training, all patch samples in positive bags were assigned positive pseudo-labels. Due to the limit of our computing resources, we used a batch size of 512. Compared to ResNet18 [8], we found that using ViT-tiny [5] as the backbone was challenging across all contrastive learning settings. ResNet18 achieved around 10% accuracy advantage in downstream MIL tasks in all settings. Consequently, we adopted ResNet18 as the backbone for all models.

After encoder pre-training, we extracted features for all patches in the training, validation, and test sets and evaluated different encoder models using DTFD-MIL, considering its high performance and popularity. We set the number of pseudo-bags to 5 for the Camelyon16 dataset and to 30 for the remaining two datasets to leverage the large number of positive patches in each bag. For comparison, we also generated features by pathology foundation models pre-trained on extremely large datasets, including Prov-GigaPath [15] and UNI2-h [1].

Our experiments were conducted on NVIDIA RTX A6000 GPUs. Each epoch requires approximately 35 GB of GPU memory and 2 h. The memory and running time of WeakSupCon are similar to SimCLR and SupCon. We repeated each MIL experiment three times to get balanced accuracy, accuracy, and AUC. Our code is available at github.com/BzhangURU/Paper_WeakSupCon

**Table 1.** Comparison between our WeakSupCon model and other contrastive learning approaches, including self-supervised contrastive learning models (MoCo v3, SimCLR) and supervised contrastive learning model (SupCon).

| Encoder | Balanced acc | Accuracy | AUC |
|---|---|---|---|
| MIL Results on Camelyon16 dataset | | | |
| MoCo v3 | $0.9051 \pm 0.0200$ | $0.9199 \pm 0.0195$ | $0.9238 \pm 0.0050$ |
| SimCLR | $0.8928 \pm 0.0050$ | $0.9095 \pm 0.0089$ | $0.9130 \pm 0.0048$ |
| SupCon | $0.8760 \pm 0.0191$ | $0.9018 \pm 0.0161$ | $0.8792 \pm 0.0077$ |
| WeakSupCon | $\mathbf{0.9265 \pm 0.0036}$ | $\mathbf{0.9431 \pm 0.0044}$ | $\mathbf{0.9694 \pm 0.0018}$ |
| MIL Results on renal vein thrombosis (RVT) dataset | | | |
| MoCo v3 | $0.7012 \pm 0.0466$ | $0.7241 \pm 0.0345$ | $0.7610 \pm 0.0556$ |
| SimCLR | $0.6785 \pm 0.0239$ | $0.7012 \pm 0.0526$ | $0.7592 \pm 0.0466$ |
| SupCon | $0.7281 \pm 0.0368$ | $0.7356 \pm 0.0527$ | $0.8266 \pm 0.0304$ |
| WeakSupCon | $\mathbf{0.8014 \pm 0.0130}$ | $\mathbf{0.8046 \pm 0.0199}$ | $\mathbf{0.8771 \pm 0.0177}$ |
| MIL Results on kidney metastasis dataset | | | |
| MoCo v3 | $0.8633 \pm 0.0135$ | $0.8261 \pm 0.0000$ | $0.8982 \pm 0.0048$ |
| SimCLR | $0.8939 \pm 0.0000$ | $0.8478 \pm 0.0000$ | $0.9192 \pm 0.0088$ |
| SupCon | $0.8858 \pm 0.0000$ | $\mathbf{0.8696 \pm 0.0000}$ | $0.9176 \pm 0.0016$ |
| WeakSupCon | $\mathbf{0.9091 \pm 0.0000}$ | $\mathbf{0.8696 \pm 0.0000}$ | $\mathbf{0.9277 \pm 0.0016}$ |

## 3.3    Experiment Results

Table 1 presents the results from different encoder pre-training models across the three datasets. It is worth noting that the SupCon and our WeakSupCon are based on SimCLR, with modifications to the contrastive loss functions. As a result, it provides a fair comparison among different contrastive loss designs in MIL tasks. Overall, our WeakSupCon method achieves the best performance across all three datasets. Interestingly, SupCon performs worse than SimCLR on the Camelyon16 dataset but outperforms SimCLR on the RVT dataset. This discrepancy can be attributed to the proportion of positive patches within positive slides. In Camelyon16, fewer than 10% of patches in tumor slides contain actual tumor regions, leading to poor pseudo-labeling in SupCon. In contrast, WeakSupCon does not assign pseudo-labels to patches in tumor slides. Instead, it allows the loss functions to automatically cluster negative samples while enabling positive samples to generate more distinct features. In the RVT dataset, where a larger percentage of patches contain positive regions, the pseudo-labeling in SupCon is more accurate. The superior performance of SupCon in the RVT dataset also underscores the potential of contrastive learning in a supervised setting compared to its self-supervised counterpart. On the kidney metastasis dataset, we observed that the accuracies are the same across three runs for all contrastive learning models, probably due to the small number of cases on the test set and the robust feature representations produced by contrastive learning.

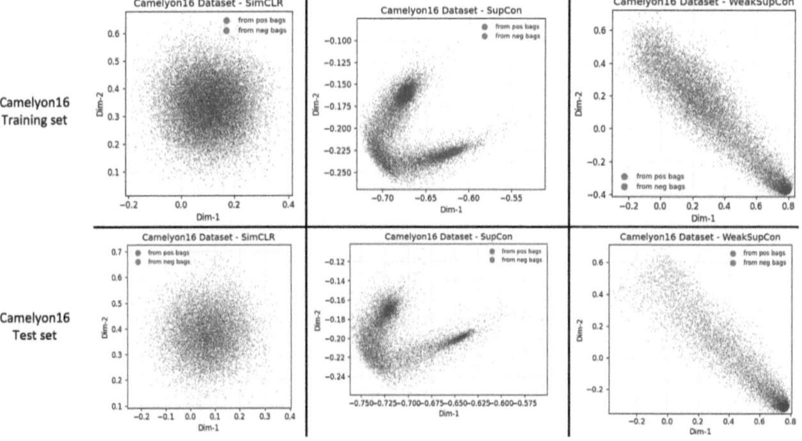

**Fig. 3.** PCA visualization of feature distributions on the Camelyon16 dataset after pre-training on the training set. The features were downsampled from the whole training set or test set for better visualization.

To better visualize the learned features from different models after encoder pre-training, we applied principal component analysis (PCA) to reduce the features to two dimensions on the Camelyon16 dataset. The feature distributions after pre-training by SimCLR, SupCon, and WeakSupCon can be found in Fig. 3. Based on these figures, even though the features pre-trained by a self-supervised learning method like SimCLR demonstrate large variations, indicating an abundant amount of information, the distribution differences between features from negative and positive bags are not obvious, which introduces challenges in downstream classification. The features pre-trained by SupCon show distinct distributions between negative bags and positive bags in the training set. However, the unavoidable errors caused by incorrect pseudo-labels lead to overfitting and affect generalization, especially for datasets with only a small portion of positive instances in positive bags. Consequently, as shown in the figures, SupCon fails to produce distinct feature distributions between negative and positive bags in the test set of the Camelyon16, and the features are totally mixed. Moreover, the variations of these features are much smaller compared to those from SimCLR, only varying between -0.75 and -0.5 in the first dimension in the Camelyon16 training set, as illustrated in Fig. 3. In contrast, our WeakSupCon first generates distinct feature distributions between negative bags and positive bags by assigning different loss functions according to the bag labels. The Similarity loss encourages instance features with negative labels to cluster, while the SimCLR loss encourages features with positive labels to exhibit greater variation, enabling these features to receive higher attention in downstream MIL tasks. The variations of features are even greater than those obtained by SimCLR, with values ranging between -0.3 and 0.8 in the first dimension in the Camelyon16 dataset. In WeakSupCon, the features from positive bags and negative bags also appear more mixed in the Camelyon16 test set than in the training set. However, this does not necessarily indicate that the model is not generalizing well. In fact, all patches from the test set are new to the model, and more than 90% of patches from positive bags are actually negative. As a result, those patches will theoretically mix with negative patches from negative bags. In theory, if a sample from positive bag (a red dot) is closer to green dots, it is more likely that the sample is also negative. What we only expect to see is that a small portion of patches from positive bags do not mix with patches from negative bags, and those patches are likely the true positive patches in the positive bags.

We also compared our WeakSupCon with foundation models. As shown in Table 2, WeakSupCon always significantly outperforms the ImageNet pre-trained backbone, highlighting the importance of feature encoders for downstream MIL tasks. Additionally, two state-of-the-art pathology foundation models were included in the experiments. We found that WeakSupCon pre-trained on just one GPU outperforms Prov-GigaPath and UNI2-h in most cases, despite that they were pre-trained on more than 1.3 billion or 200 million pathology patches using much more powerful computing resources and substantially larger backbones.

**Table 2.** Comparison between our WeakSupCon model and foundation models, including state-of-the-art pathology foundation models (Prov-GigaPath and UNI2-h).

| Encoder | Balanced acc | Accuracy | AUC |
|---|---|---|---|
| MIL Results on Camelyon16 dataset | | | |
| ImageNet pre-trained | $0.8034 \pm 0.0211$ | $0.8346 \pm 0.0119$ | $0.8530 \pm 0.0186$ |
| Prov-GigaPath | $\mathbf{0.9469}\pm0.0036$ | $\mathbf{0.9586}\pm0.0044$ | $0.9757 \pm 0.0009$ |
| UNI2-h | $0.9461 \pm 0.0032$ | $0.9561 \pm 0.0044$ | $\mathbf{0.9782}\pm0.0016$ |
| WeakSupCon | $0.9265 \pm 0.0036$ | $0.9431 \pm 0.0044$ | $0.9694 \pm 0.0018$ |
| MIL Results on renal vein thrombosis (RVT) dataset | | | |
| ImageNet pre-trained | $0.6330 \pm 0.0238$ | $0.6322 \pm 0.0199$ | $0.6280 \pm 0.0480$ |
| Prov-GigaPath | $0.7096 \pm 0.0140$ | $0.7126 \pm 0.0199$ | $0.7576 \pm 0.0101$ |
| UNI2-h | $0.6524 \pm 0.0229$ | $0.5977 \pm 0.0199$ | $0.6229 \pm 0.0191$ |
| WeakSupCon | $\mathbf{0.8014}\pm0.0130$ | $\mathbf{0.8046}\pm0.0199$ | $\mathbf{0.8771}\pm0.0177$ |
| MIL Results on kidney metastasis dataset | | | |
| ImageNet pre-trained | $0.7848 \pm 0.0291$ | $0.7246 \pm 0.0251$ | $0.8415 \pm 0.0142$ |
| Prov-GigaPath | $0.8862 \pm 0.0076$ | $0.8478 \pm 0.0218$ | $0.9192 \pm 0.0178$ |
| UNI2-h | $0.8889 \pm 0.0175$ | $0.8406 \pm 0.0251$ | $0.9161 \pm 0.0185$ |
| WeakSupCon | $\mathbf{0.9091}\pm0.0000$ | $\mathbf{0.8696}\pm0.0000$ | $\mathbf{0.9277}\pm0.0016$ |

# 4    Conclusion

In this paper, we propose Weakly Supervised Contrastive Learning (WeakSupCon) for encoder pre-training by leveraging bag-level labels. The features learned through WeakSupCon further enhance downstream MIL performance compared to self-supervised contrastive learning, highlighting the potential for more accurate medical diagnosis under limited training labels and computing resources.

**Acknowledgments.** The experiments were funded by NIH/NCI 1R21CA277381, DoD HT94252410186, and Department of Veterans Affairs I01CS002622. We also acknowledge the support of the Computational Oncology Research Initiative (CORI) at the Huntsman Cancer Institute, ARUP Laboratories, and the Department of Pathology at the University of Utah.

**Disclosure of Interests.** The authors have no competing interests to declare that are relevant to the content of this article.

# References

1. Chen, R.J., et al.: Towards a general-purpose foundation model for computational pathology. Nat. Med. **30**(3), 850–862 (2024). https://doi.org/10.1038/s41591-024-02857-3

2. Chen, T., Kornblith, S., Norouzi, M., Hinton, G.: A simple framework for contrastive learning of visual representations. In: Iii, H.D., Singh, A. (eds.) Proceedings of the 37th International Conference on Machine Learning. Proceedings of Machine Learning Research, vol. 119, pp. 1597–1607. PMLR (2020)

3. Chen, T., Kornblith, S., Swersky, K., Norouzi, M., Hinton, G.: Big self-supervised models are strong semi-supervised learners. arXiv [cs.LG] (2020)

4. Chen, X., Xie, S., He, K.: An empirical study of training self-supervised vision transformers. In: 2021 IEEE/CVF International Conference on Computer Vision (ICCV). IEEE (2021). https://doi.org/10.1109/iccv48922.2021.00950

5. Dosovitskiy, A., et al.: An image is worth 16x16 words: transformers for image recognition at scale. arXiv preprint: arXiv:2010.11929 (2020)

6. Ehteshami Bejnordi, B., et al.: CAMELYON16 - grand challenge (2023). https://camelyon16.grand-challenge.org/Data/. Accessed 15 Dec 2023

7. Ehteshami Bejnordi, B., et al.: Diagnostic assessment of deep learning algorithms for detection of lymph node metastases in women with breast cancer. JAMA **318**(22), 2199–2210 (2017). https://doi.org/10.1001/jama.2017.14585

8. He, K., Zhang, X., Ren, S., Sun, J.: Deep residual learning for image recognition, pp. 770–778. arXiv [cs.CV] (2015)

9. Ilse, M., Tomczak, J., Welling, M.: Attention-based deep multiple instance learning. In: Dy, J., Krause, A. (eds.) Proceedings of the 35th International Conference on Machine Learning. Proceedings of Machine Learning Research, vol. 80, pp. 2127–2136. PMLR (2018)

10. Khosla, P., et al.: Supervised contrastive learning. arXiv [cs.LG] (2020)

11. Li, B., Li, Y., Eliceiri, K.W.: Dual-stream multiple instance learning network for whole slide image classification with self-supervised contrastive learning. arXiv [cs.CV] (2020)

12. Manoochehri, H., Zhang, B., Knudsen, B., Tasdizen, T.: SRA: a novel method to improve feature embedding in self-supervised learning for histopathological images. In: Medical Imaging with Deep Learning-Short Papers (2025)

13. Shannon, C.E.: The mathematical theory of communication. 1963. MD Comput. **14**(4), 306–317 (1997)

14. Shao, Z., et al.: TransMIL: transformer based correlated multiple instance learning for whole slide image classification. arXiv [cs.CV] (2021)

15. Xu, H., et al.: A whole-slide foundation model for digital pathology from real-world data. Nature **630**(8015), 181–188 (2024). https://doi.org/10.1038/s41586-024-07441-w

16. Zhang, B., Knudsen, B., Sirohi, D., Ferrero, A., Tasdizen, T.: Stain based contrastive co-training for histopathological image analysis. In: Workshop on Medical Image Learning with Limited and Noisy Data, pp. 106–116. Springer (2022)

17. Zhang, B., et al.: CLASS-M: adaptive stain separation-based contrastive learning with pseudo-labeling for histopathological image classification. Med. Image Anal., 103711 (2025)

18. Zhang, H., et al.: DTFD-MIL: double-tier feature distillation multiple instance learning for histopathology whole slide image classification. In: Proceedings of the IEEE/CVF Conference on Computer Vision and Pattern Recognition, pp. 18802–18812 (2022)

# DetSAM: A Joint Detection-and-Segmentation Learning Framework for Multi-class Surgical Instrument Segmentation


Jingsong Wang[1], Rui Song[2], Yibin Li[2], Max Q.-H. Meng[3,4], and Zhe Min[2,5(✉)]

[1] School of Mathematics, Shandong University, Jinan, China
[2] School of Control Science and Engineering, Shandong University, Jinan, China
minzhe@sdu.edu.cn
[3] Department of Electronic and Electrical Engineering, Southern University of Science and Technology, Shenzhen, China
[4] Department of Electronic Engineering, The Chinese University of Hong Kong, Hong Kong, China
[5] UCL Hawkes Institute, and Department of Medical Physics and Biomedical Engineering, University College London, London, UK



**Abstract.** The Segment Anything Model (SAM) is a powerful foundational model designed to generalize and automate image segmentation tasks. However, when directly applied to surgical images, SAM encounters several critical challenges including the imaging disparities between natural and medical images, its reliance on high-quality prompts, and the lack of support for multi-class segmentation. To address these limitations, we propose a novel approach Detection-SAM (DetSAM), which integrates a detection module with SAM. By leveraging the output of a detection module as a prompt for each individual class, fully automatic multi-class surgical instrument segmentation can be realized. Meanwhile, we also design a block-wise fine-tuned image encoder to extract image features. We have validated DetSAM on two standard public benchmark datasets (i.e., Endovis2017 and Endovis2018), achieving Ch_IoU scores of 77.53% and 76.61% respectively, surpassing existing state-of-the-art (SOTA) methods. The superior performances underscore the effectiveness of combining our detection module and SAM for surgical instrument segmentation. The code is available at: https://github.com/JingsongWang04/DetSAM

**Keywords:** SAM · Instrument segmentation · Semantic segmentation


## 1 Introduction

Computer-assisted surgery plays a critical role in advancing modern medicine. It enables surgical automation and establishes the prerequisite basis for various downstream applications, such as surgical phase assessment [4], surgical



T. Chen et al. (Eds.): EMA4MICCAI 2025 Workshops, LNCS 16318, pp. 320–329, 2026.
https://doi.org/10.1007/978-3-032-13961-0_32

instrument segmentation [16,17], and tumor segmentation [15,22]. The advent of foundational vision segmentation models SAM [12] and SAM 2 [18] has catalyzed significant research interest in their adaptation for downstream medical applications, emerging as a prominent focus in contemporary computer-assisted intervention studies. Researchers have developed various medical image segmentation methods based on SAM [12], involving different modalities such as CT, MRI, pathological images, colonoscopic images, and endoscopic images [25]. These methods also encompass techniques like zero-shot validation [21], parameter-efficient fine-tuning [25], and full fine-tuning [14]. However, it is demonstrated in [21] that when applied to surgical instrument segmentation, SAM [12] exhibits limited zero-shot generalization capability due to instrument overlap, blur, and shadow in surgical scenes, necessitating domain-specific fine-tuning for this specialized task.

The application of SAM [12] to surgical instrument segmentation necessitates addressing the following two issues. First, multiple surgical instruments often appear in surgical scenes simultaneously [7], so the model needs to be capable of multi-class segmentation. However, SAM [12] is inherently designed for single-class segmentation. Second, the segmentation performance of SAM [12] is highly dependent on the prompt information provided by users. However, in real surgical scenarios, manually acquiring high-quality prompts is not only time-consuming but also requires sufficient professional knowledge [20]. To address these issues, we propose a novel joint-detection-and-segmentation framework Detection-SAM (DetSAM), which integrates SAM [12] with the detection module for multi-class surgical instrument segmentation.

**Contributions. 1)** We innovatively propose DetSAM, a unified framework that utilizes multi-class bounding box information generated by the detection module as prompts for the downstream segmentation task. **2)** We develop a lightweight block-wise fine-tuning strategy to effectively adapt the SAM image encoder for surgical domains, while preserving its superior feature extraction capabilities. **3)** We have conducted extensive experiments and ablation studies, demonstrating DetSAM's superior performances over state-of-the-art approaches, especially in semantic segmentation scenarios.

## 2   Related Work

In this section, we review state-of-the-art methods for surgical instrument segmentation and broadly classify them into three categories.

**Temporal Consistency Based Methods.** ISINet [7] is an instance-based surgical instrument segmentation network via a temporal consistency module. TraSeTR [26] uses tracking signals and a contrastive query mechanism to achieve precise segmentation. These methods are specifically designed for surgical video sequences and may experience performance degradation when dealing with individual frames.

**Large-scale Model Based Methods.** SurgicalSAM [23], which is based on SAM, provides category prompts to a prototype-based category prompt

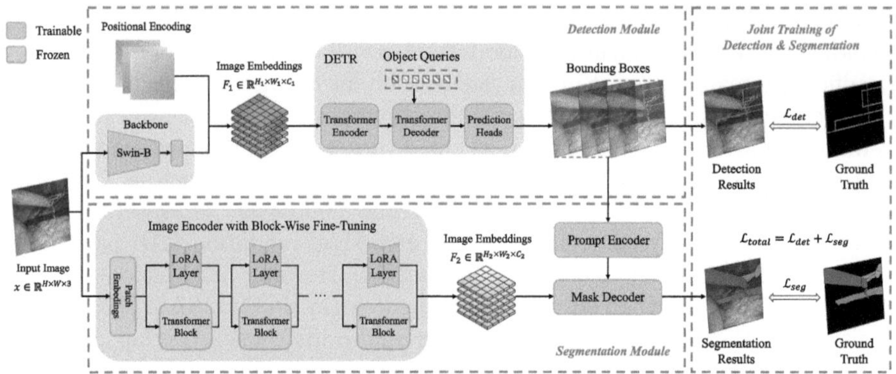

**Fig. 1.** Overall architecture of DetSAM.

encoder. Text-Promptable-SIS [27], based on pre-trained Vision-Language Models (VLMs), requires text prompts that include the names of the instruments and their additional attributes.

**Detection Based Methods.** S3Net [3] is a two-stage segmentation framework based on Mask R-CNN [8], which consists of a Region Proposal Network (RPN) [19] for detection. Surgical-DeSAM [20] streamlines the segmentation process by removing the image encoder of SAM [12] and directly utilizing the output from the DETR [5] encoder as the feature input for the SAM mask decoder. However, it is demonstrated in Sect. 4 that Surgical-DeSAM [20] has weaker recognition and response to object contours compared to our DetSAM that employs fine-tuning on the pre-trained SAM [12] image encoder. For a fair comparison with Surgical-DeSAM [20], we adopted SAM [12] instead of SAM 2 [18] for the experiments to validate the superiority of our framework.

## 3    Method

We propose DetSAM, an integrated detection-and-segmentation architecture for surgical instrument segmentation, as shown in Fig. 1. DetSAM integrates SAM's [12] image feature extraction with DETR's [5] object detection capabilities, leveraging DETR-generated prompt to enhance focus on target regions and improve segmentation accuracy and robustness.

### 3.1    Image Encoder with Block-Wise Fine-Tuning

The Low-Rank Adaptation (LoRA) [9] fine-tuning strategy is applied to the image encoder of DetSAM to achieve efficient feature extraction. For each Transformer block in the image encoder, the weight matrix of the projection layer $\mathbf{W} \in \mathbb{R}^{C_{\text{out}} \times C_{\text{in}}}$ is decomposed into two low-rank matrices $\mathbf{A} \in \mathbb{R}^{r \times C_{\text{in}}}$ and $\mathbf{B} \in \mathbb{R}^{C_{\text{out}} \times r}$, where $r \in \mathbb{N}$ represents the rank of the low-rank adjustment matrix, and satifies $r \ll \min\{C_{\text{in}}, C_{\text{out}}\}$. The original weight matrix update is approximated as $\hat{\mathbf{W}} = \mathbf{W} + \mathbf{BA}$. Here, $\hat{\mathbf{W}}$ denotes the updated weight matrix, and $\mathbf{BA}$ represents the low-rank adjustment matrix.

We apply LoRA [9] to the projection layers of the query and value while retaining the original projection layer of the key. According to SAMed [25], this approach achieves better performance than fine-tuning the projection layers of the query, key and value simultaneously. Therefore, The process of LoRA [9] fine-tuning in DetSAM can be represented as shown in Eqs. (1) to (4):

$$\text{Att}(\mathbf{Q}, \mathbf{K}, \mathbf{V}) = \text{Softmax}\left(\frac{\mathbf{Q}\mathbf{K}^T}{\sqrt{d_k}} + \mathbf{B}\right)\mathbf{V}, \tag{1}$$

$$\mathbf{Q} = \hat{\mathbf{W}}_q\mathbf{F} = \mathbf{W}_q\mathbf{F} + \mathbf{B}_q\mathbf{A}_q\mathbf{F}, \tag{2}$$

$$\mathbf{K} = \mathbf{W}_k\mathbf{F}, \tag{3}$$

$$\mathbf{V} = \hat{\mathbf{W}}_v\mathbf{F} = \mathbf{W}_v\mathbf{F} + \mathbf{B}_v\mathbf{A}_v\mathbf{F}. \tag{4}$$

where $\mathbf{Q} \in \mathbb{R}^{N \times d_q}$, $\mathbf{K} \in \mathbb{R}^{N \times d_k}$, and $\mathbf{V} \in \mathbb{R}^{N \times d_v}$ are the query, key and value matrices respectively, with $N \in \mathbb{R}$ representing the number of tokens and $d_q \in \mathbb{R}$, $d_k \in \mathbb{R}$, $d_v \in \mathbb{R}$ representing the dimensions of the query, key and value vectors. $\mathbf{W}_q \in \mathbb{R}^{d \times d_q}$, $\mathbf{W}_k \in \mathbb{R}^{d \times d_k}$ and $\mathbf{W}_v \in \mathbb{R}^{d \times d_v}$ are the original frozen projection layers from SAM, with $d$ refers to the total dimensionality of the input features, while $\mathbf{A}_q \in \mathbb{R}^{r \times d_q}$, $\mathbf{B}_q \in \mathbb{R}^{d_q \times r}$, $\mathbf{A}_v \in \mathbb{R}^{r \times d_v}$ and $\mathbf{B}_v \in \mathbb{R}^{d_v \times r}$ are the trainable LoRA [9] parameters.

Through this block-wise fine-tuning approach, we retain the pre-trained performance of SAM [12] while fine-tuning for surgical instrument segmentation using only a small number of parameters.

### 3.2   Detection and Segmentation Integrated Architecture

In this section, we will elaborate on the detection and segmentation modules of DetSAM.

**Detection Module.** Given an input image $\mathbf{x} \in \mathbb{R}^{H \times W \times 3}$, we first extract its feature embeddings $\mathbf{F}_1 \in \mathbb{R}^{H_1 \times W_1 \times C_1}$ using the Swin-B network based on Swin Transformer [13], where $H_1$ and $W_1$ are the spatial resolutions, and $C_1$ is the number of channels. Then, the feature embeddings $\mathbf{F}_1$ along with the learnable object queries $\mathbf{Q} \in \mathbb{R}^{N_{\text{query}} \times C_1}$ are processed through multiple Transformer blocks in DETR [5] to generate outputs class predictions $\hat{\mathbf{Y}} \in \mathbb{R}^{N_{\text{query}} \times K}$ and bounding box coordinates $\hat{\mathbf{B}} \in \mathbb{R}^{N_{\text{query}} \times 4}$, where $K \in \mathbb{R}$ denotes the number of classes and $N_{\text{query}} \in \mathbb{R}$ represents the number of object queries.

**Segmentation Module.** The input image $\mathbf{x}$ is fed into the block-wise fine-tuned image encoder described previously to generate feature representation $\mathbf{F}_2 \in \mathbb{R}^{H_2 \times W_2 \times C_2}$. Meanwhile, the prompt encoder encodes the bounding boxes $\hat{\mathbf{Y}}$ into prompt embeddings $\mathbf{P} \in \mathbb{R}^{N_{bbox} \times D}$, where $N_{bbox} \in \mathbb{R}$ is the number of selected bounding boxes and $D$ is the dimension of the embeddings. The mask decoder processes the bounding box prompts $\mathbf{P}$ for each category separately while integrating the image feature embeddings $\mathbf{F}_2$ to generate multi-class segmentation masks $\mathbf{M} \in \mathbb{R}^{H \times W \times K}$.

Through the combination of the detection and segmentation module, our method not only achieves full automation of surgical instrument segmentation, but also extends SAM's [12] binary segmentation to multi-class segmentation.

### 3.3   Joint Training of Detection and Segmentation

We define the total loss function $\mathcal{L}_{\text{total}}$ as a linear combination of detection loss $\mathcal{L}_{\text{det}}$ and segmentation loss $\mathcal{L}_{\text{seg}}$ to jointly optimize both tasks.

The detection loss $\mathcal{L}_{\text{det}}$ is similar to that in DETR [5], consisting of the cross-entropy loss $\mathcal{L}_{\text{cls}}$, the Generalized IoU loss $\mathcal{L}_{\text{giou}}$, and the L1 loss $\mathcal{L}_{\text{L1}}$. The segmentation loss $\mathcal{L}_{\text{seg}}$ is composed of binary cross-entropy loss $\mathcal{L}_{\text{bce}}$ and Dice loss $\mathcal{L}_{\text{dice}}$. The variables $\mathcal{L}_{\text{total}}$, $\mathcal{L}_{\text{det}}$, and $\mathcal{L}_{\text{seg}}$ can be represented shown as follows

$$\mathcal{L}_{\text{total}} = \mathcal{L}_{\text{det}} + \mathcal{L}_{\text{seg}}, \tag{5}$$

$$\mathcal{L}_{\text{det}} = \lambda_{\text{cls}}\mathcal{L}_{\text{cls}} + \lambda_{\text{giou}}\mathcal{L}_{\text{giou}} + \lambda_{\text{L1}}\mathcal{L}_{\text{L1}}, \tag{6}$$

$$\mathcal{L}_{\text{seg}} = \lambda_{\text{bce}}\mathcal{L}_{\text{bce}} + \lambda_{\text{dice}}\mathcal{L}_{\text{dice}}, \tag{7}$$

where $\lambda_{\text{cls}} \in \mathbb{R}$, $\lambda_{\text{giou}} \in \mathbb{R}$, $\lambda_{\text{L1}} \in \mathbb{R}$, $\lambda_{\text{bce}} \in \mathbb{R}$, and $\lambda_{\text{dice}} \in \mathbb{R}$ are the coefficients of $\mathcal{L}_{\text{cls}}$, $\mathcal{L}_{\text{giou}}$, $\mathcal{L}_{\text{L1}}$, $\mathcal{L}_{\text{bce}}$, and $\mathcal{L}_{\text{dice}}$ respectively.

## 4   Experiments and Results

### 4.1   Datasets and Evaluation

Our method was evaluated on the EndoVis17 [2] and EndoVis18 [1] datasets, both widely-used benchmarks for endoscopic surgery. For EndoVis17 [2], sequences 1âĂŞ8 were used for training, and sequences 9âĂŞ10 for validation. For EndoVis18 [1], we followed the partitioning scheme from ISINet [7], using sequences 2, 5, 9, and 15 for validation and the rest for training. In the evaluation, we assess the performance using the Challenge IoU (Ch_IoU) metric as proposed in [2], as well as the ISINet IoU (ISI_IoU) and mean class IoU (mcIoU) metrics introduced in [7].

### 4.2   Implementation Details

The segmentation component of DetSAM uses Vit_B model for SAM [12]. For fine-tuning, the rank of LoRA [9] layers is empirically set to 4 [9]. The weights of the loss function are set to $\lambda_{\text{cls}} = 1.0$, $\lambda_{\text{giou}} = 2.0$, $\lambda_{\text{L1}} = 5.0$, $\lambda_{\text{bce}} = 20.0$, and $\lambda_{\text{dice}} = 1.0$. Training is performed for 150 epochs using the Adam optimizer with a learning rate of $1 \times 10^{-5}$ for the backbone and $1 \times 10^{-4}$ for other components.

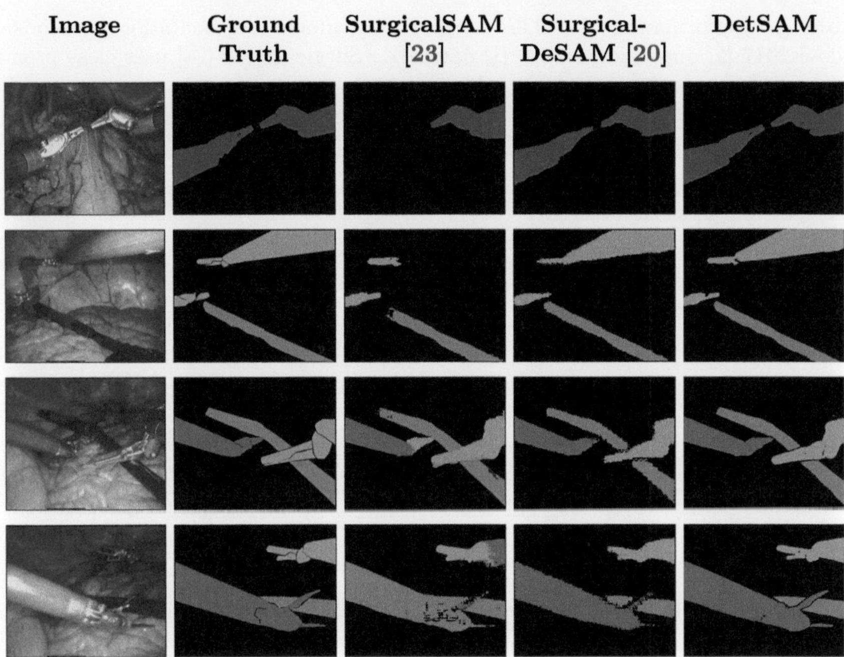


**Fig. 2.** Comparison of segmentation performances between DetSAM and other methods.

## 4.3   Comparsions with State-of-the-Art Methods

**Quantitative Analysis.** We compared DetSAM with the current state-of-the-art methods on Endovis2017 [2] and Endovis2018 [1] datasets. The results, shown in Table 1, demonstrate that DetSAM achieves SOTA performance on both datasets. On the Endovis2017 [2] dataset, DetSAM achieves a Ch_IoU of 77.53%, an ISI_IoU of 74.73%, and an mcIoU of 45.97%, representing improvements of 1.69%, 1.64% on Ch_IoU and ISI_IoU respectively compared to the previous SOTA methods. On the Endovis2018 dataset, DetSAM attains a Ch_IoU of 76.61%, an ISI_IoU of 75.59%, and an mcIoU of 53.66%, representing improvements of 0.41%, 1.57%, and 5.89% respectively.

**Qualitative Analysis.** We conducted a qualitative comparison on the Endovis2017 [2] dataset with Surgical-DeSAM [20] and SurgicalSAM [23]. Figure 2 illustrates the segmentation results of these methods, where the first two rows represent segmentation outcomes in non-overlapping cases, and the last two rows depict results in overlapping cases.

In non-overlapping scenarios, DetSAM demonstrates higher precision in delineating the contours of surgical instruments compared to both Surgical-SAM [23] and Surgical-DeSAM [20]. The superior performance of DetSAM in detail processing stems from its fine-tuning strategy based on SAM's [12] pretrained image encoder, in contrast to Surgical-DeSAM [20] which employs an

**Table 1.** Performance of SOTA surgical instrument segmentation methods on Endovis2017 [2] and Endovis2018 [1] datasets. *SurgicalSAM [23] uses class prompts during the inference process and is therefore **not** included in the comparison of best performance.

| Dataset | Method | Ch_IoU | ISI_IoU | mcIoU |
|---|---|---|---|---|
| Endovis17 | TernausNet [10] | 35.27 | 12.67 | 10.17 |
| | MF-TAPNet [11] | 37.35 | 13.49 | 10.77 |
| | ISINet [7] | 55.62 | 52.20 | 28.96 |
| | TraSeTR [26] | 60.40 | 65.20 | 36.79 |
| | S3Net [3] | 72.54 | 71.99 | **46.55** |
| | SurgicalSAM* [23] | 69.94 | 69.94 | 67.03 |
| | Surgical-DeSAM [20] | 75.84 | 73.09 | 45.44 |
| | **Ours** | **77.53** | **74.73** | 45.97 |
| Endovis18 | TernausNet [10] | 46.22 | 39.87 | 14.19 |
| | MF-TAPNet [11] | 67.87 | 39.14 | 24.68 |
| | ISINet [7] | 73.03 | 70.97 | 40.21 |
| | TraSeTR [26] | 76.20 | – | 47.77 |
| | S3Net [3] | 75.81 | 74.02 | 42.58 |
| | SurgicalSAM* [23] | 80.33 | 80.33 | 58.87 |
| | Surgical-DeSAM [20] | 74.89 | 73.16 | 50.21 |
| | **Ours** | **76.61** | **75.59** | **53.66** |

image encoder trained from scratch. In overlapping scenarios, compared to SurgicalSAM [23] and Surgical-DeSAM [20], DetSAM not only accurately identifies different categories of surgical instruments in overlapping scenarios, but also maintains good responsiveness to the edges of the instruments.

## 4.4   Ablation Studies

We conducted ablation studies on Endovis2017 [2] dataset to evaluate the performance of our block-wise fine-tuned image encoder and compare it with other image encoders: **1)** the original pre-trained SAM [12] image encoder; **2)** the fully fine-tuned MobileSAM [24] image encoder and **3)** our image encoder with block-wise fine-tuning. Among them, methods 1) and 3) are based on the image encoder of SAM's [12] ViT-B version, while method 2) is based on the lightweight encoder of Tiny-ViT [6], and other experimental settings remain the same. Figure 3 illustrates the qualitative comparison results of these methods, and Table 2 presents the comparison results on the three metrics.

The results in Table 2 show that the SAM image encoder fine-tuned with LoRA [9] achieved performance improvements of 5.43%, 5.16%, and 1.73% in Ch_IoU, ISI_IoU, and mcIoU respectively, compared to the pre-trained SAM image encoder. Figure 3 demonstrates that the block-wise fine-tuned SAM [12]

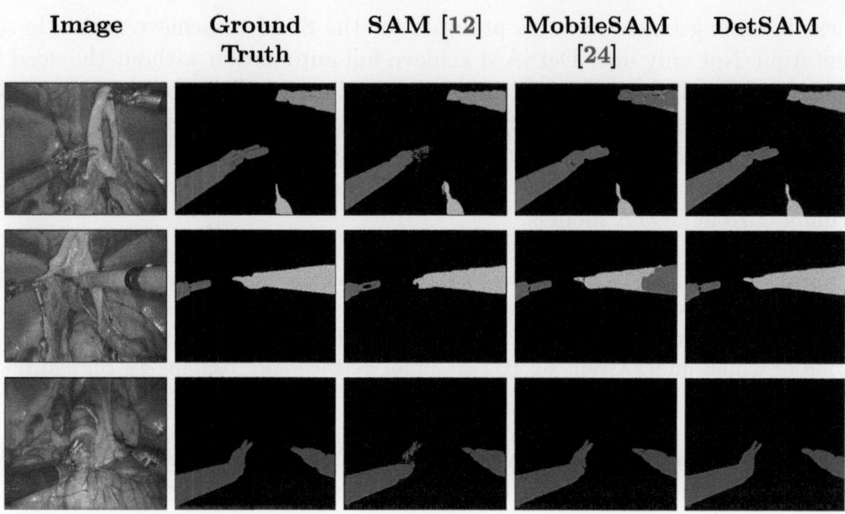



**Fig. 3.** Ablation studies on fine-tuning methods of image encoder.

**Table 2.** Comparison of different fine-tuning methods.

| Method | Ch_IoU | ISI_IoU | mcIoU | Params |
|---|---|---|---|---|
| SAM [12] (Frozen) | 72.10 | 69.57 | 44.10 | – |
| MobileSAM [24] (Trainable) | 76.36 | 73.50 | 44.47 | 6.07 M |
| **Ours** | **77.53** | **74.73** | **45.83** | **0.15M** |

image encoder is capable of segmenting the contour of the instrument head completely, compared to the un-fine-tuned version.

MobileSAM [24] employs a lightweight Tiny-ViT [6] encoder, significantly reducing computational costs while maintaining performance comparable to SAM [12]. As shown in Table 2, compared to the fully fine-tuned MobileSAM [24], our block-wise fine-tuning method showed improvements in all evaluation metrics and required far fewer parameters. Figure 3 shows that when MobileSAM [24] is used as an image encoder, it may produce segmentation parts outside the bounding box of an instrument, thereby causing the problem of segmentation overlap. This demonstrates that our block-wise fine-tuning is a superior approach for adapting the SAM [12] image encoder, achieving high performance with a minimal number of parameters.

## 5   Conclusions

In this paper, we propose DetSAM, a novel architecture that integrates detection and segmentation for surgical instrument segmentation. By leveraging DETR for object detection, we predict categories and bounding boxes for instruments.

These bounding boxes serve as prompts for the SAM to achieve semantic segmentation. Not only does DetSAM achieve full automation without the need for prompts during inference, but it also extends the architecture of SAM to enable multi-class segmentation, thereby breaking through the limitation of SAM's original capability to perform only binary segmentation tasks. DetSAM exhibits superior generalization on the EndoVis2017 and EndoVis2018 datasets, outperforming current SOTA models.

**Acknowledgments.** This work was supported in part by the National Natural Science Fund for Excellent Young Scientists Fund Program (Overseas) under Grant 22IAA01849. This work was also supported by the National Natural Science Foundation of China under Grant 62303275, Jinan Science and Technology Bureau under Grant 202333011.

**Disclosure of Interests.** The authors have no competing interests to declare that are relevant to the content of this article.

# References


1. Allan, M., et al.: 2018 robotic scene segmentation challenge. arXiv preprint: arXiv:2001.11190 (2020)
2. Allan, M., et al.: 2017 robotic instrument segmentation challenge. arXiv preprint: arXiv:1902.06426 (2019)
3. Baby, B., et al.: From forks to forceps: a new framework for instance segmentation of surgical instruments. In: Proceedings of the IEEE/CVF Winter Conference on Applications of Computer Vision, pp. 6191–6201 (2023)
4. Bai, L., et al.: Multimodal graph representation learning for robust surgical workflow recognition with adversarial feature disentanglement. Inf. Fus., 103290 (2025)
5. Carion, N., Massa, F., Synnaeve, G., Usunier, N., Kirillov, A., Zagoruyko, S.: End-to-end object detection with transformers. In: European Conference on Computer Vision, pp. 213–229. Springer (2020)
6. Dosovitskiy, A., et al.: An image is worth 16x16 words: transformers for image recognition at scale. arXiv preprint: arXiv:2010.11929 (2020)
7. González, C., Bravo-Sánchez, L., Arbelaez, P.: ISINet: an instance-based approach for surgical instrument segmentation. In: International Conference on Medical Image Computing and Computer-Assisted Intervention, pp. 595–605. Springer (2020)
8. He, K., Gkioxari, G., Dollár, P., Girshick, R.: Mask R-CNN. In: Proceedings of the IEEE International Conference on Computer Vision, pp. 2961–2969 (2017)
9. Hu, E.J., et al.: LoRA: low-rank adaptation of large language models. ICLR **1**(2), 3 (2022)
10. Iglovikov, V., Shvets, A.: TernausNet: U-Net with vgg11 encoder pre-trained on ImageNet for image segmentation. arXiv preprint: arXiv:1801.05746 (2018)
11. Jin, Y., Cheng, K., Dou, Q., Heng, P.A.: Incorporating temporal prior from motion flow for instrument segmentation in minimally invasive surgery video. In: Medical Image Computing and Computer Assisted Intervention–MICCAI 2019: 22nd International Conference, Shenzhen, China, 13–17 October 2019, Proceedings, Part V 22, pp. 440–448. Springer (2019)

12. Kirillov, A., et al.: Segment anything. In: Proceedings of the IEEE/CVF International Conference on Computer Vision, pp. 4015–4026 (2023)

13. Liu, Z., et al.: Swin transformer: hierarchical vision transformer using shifted windows. In: Proceedings of the IEEE/CVF International Conference on Computer Vision, pp. 10012–10022 (2021)

14. Ma, J., He, Y., Li, F., Han, L., You, C., Wang, B.: Segment anything in medical images. Nat. Commun. **15**(1), 654 (2024)

15. Min, Z., et al.: Segmentation versus detection: development and evaluation of deep learning models for prostate imaging reporting and data system lesions localisation on bi-parametric prostate magnetic resonance imaging. CAAI Trans. Intell. Technol. (2024)

16. Min, Z., Lai, J., Ren, H.: Innovating robot-assisted surgery through large vision models. Nat. Rev. Electr. Eng., 1–14 (2025)

17. Min, Z., Song, R., Li, C., Luo, J.: Advances in modern intelligent surgery: from computer-aided diagnosis to medical robotics (2025)

18. Ravi, N., et al.: SAM 2: segment anything in images and videos. arXiv preprint: arXiv:2408.00714 (2024)

19. Ren, S., He, K., Girshick, R., Sun, J.: Faster R-CNN: towards real-time object detection with region proposal networks. In: Advances in Neural Information Processing Systems, vol. 28 (2015)

20. Sheng, Y., Bano, S., Clarkson, M.J., Islam, M.: Surgical-DeSAM: decoupling SAM for instrument segmentation in robotic surgery. Int. J. Comput. Assist. Radiol. Surg. **19**(7), 1267–1271 (2024)

21. Wang, A., Islam, M., Xu, M., Zhang, Y., Ren, H.: Sam meets robotic surgery: an empirical study on generalization, robustness and adaptation. In: International Conference on Medical Image Computing and Computer-Assisted Intervention, pp. 234–244. Springer (2023)

22. Yan, W., et al.: A semi-supervised prototypical network for prostate lesion segmentation from multimodality MRI. Phys. Med. Biol. **70**(8), 085020 (2025)

23. Yue, W., Zhang, J., Hu, K., Xia, Y., Luo, J., Wang, Z.: SurgicalSAM: efficient class promptable surgical instrument segmentation. In: Proceedings of the AAAI Conference on Artificial Intelligence, vol. 38, pp. 6890–6898 (2024)

24. Zhang, C., et al.: Faster segment anything: towards lightweight SAM for mobile applications. arXiv preprint: arXiv:2306.14289 (2023)

25. Zhang, K., Liu, D.: Customized segment anything model for medical image segmentation. arXiv preprint: arXiv:2304.13785 (2023)

26. Zhao, Z., Jin, Y., Heng, P.A.: TraSeTR: track-to-segment transformer with contrastive query for instance-level instrument segmentation in robotic surgery. In: 2022 International Conference on Robotics and Automation (ICRA), pp. 11186–11193. IEEE (2022)

27. Zhou, Z., Alabi, O., Wei, M., Vercauteren, T., Shi, M.: Text promptable surgical instrument segmentation with vision-language models. In: Advances in Neural Information Processing Systems, vol. 36, pp. 28611–28623 (2023)

# Debunking Optimization Myths in Federated Learning for Medical Image Classification


Youngjoon Lee[1], Hyukjoon Lee[2], Jinu Gong[3], Yang Cao[4], and Joonhyuk Kang[1(✉)]

[1] School of Electrical Engineering, KAIST, Daejeon, South Korea
{yjlee22,jkang}@kaist.ac.kr
[2] AI Group, AMD, Santa Clara, USA
[3] Department of Applied AI, Hansung University, Seoul, South Korea
[4] Department of Computer Science, Institute of Science Tokyo, Tokyo, Japan



**Abstract.** Federated Learning (FL) is a collaborative learning method that enables decentralized model training while preserving data privacy. Despite its promise in medical imaging, recent FL methods are often sensitive to local factors such as optimizers and learning rates, limiting their robustness in practical deployments. In this work, we revisit vanilla FL to clarify the impact of edge device configurations, benchmarking recent FL methods on colorectal pathology and blood cell classification tasks. We numerically show that the choice of local optimizer and learning rate has a greater effect on performance than the specific FL method. Moreover, we find that increasing local training epochs can either enhance or impair convergence, depending on the FL method. These findings indicate that appropriate edge-specific configuration is more crucial than algorithmic complexity for achieving effective FL.

**Keywords:** Medical AI · Federated Learning · Device Configuration


## 1 Introduction

In recent years, medical imaging has undergone significant advancements, enhancing both diagnostic accuracy and the range of clinical applications in various domains of healthcare [1,23]. These improvements have largely resulted from the widespread adoption of deep learning techniques, which leverage large-scale, high-quality datasets to train powerful neural networks [5,29]. However, in many real-world medical scenarios, stringent privacy regulations and institutional governance severely restrict the direct sharing of sensitive data across organizations [10,14,24]. To address this challenge, Federated Learning (FL) [19] has emerged as a promising decentralized learning paradigm that allows collaborative model training without the need to transmit raw data [7,17]. By ensuring

---

Y. Lee—Work done while a visiting student at Science Tokyo.



T. Chen et al. (Eds.): EMA4MICCAI 2025 Workshops, LNCS 16318, pp. 330–339, 2026.
https://doi.org/10.1007/978-3-032-13961-0_33

that data remain localized at the source, FL offers a privacy-preserving solution that aligns well with legal and ethical constraints in medical AI development [4,15] (Fig. 1).

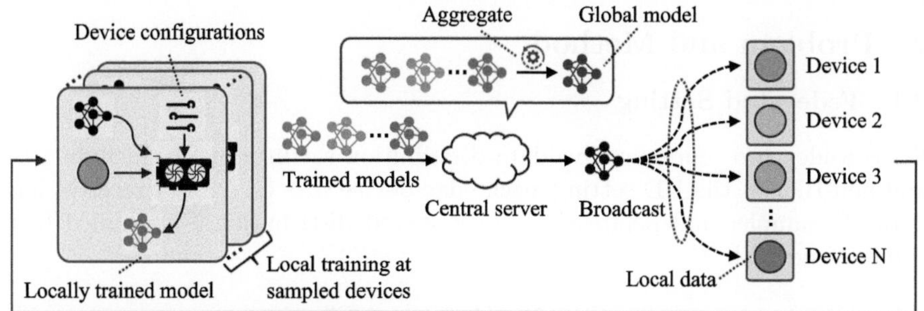


**Fig. 1.** Illustration of general FL process. In each global epoch, selected edge devices train locally using their own data and configurations (e.g., local optimizer, local learning rate, local epochs). Updated models are sent to the server for aggregation, and the new global model is broadcast back to all devices.

FL provides several key advantages that make it particularly well-suited for healthcare-related applications [11]. First, FL preserves data sovereignty by enabling institutions to retain complete control over their datasets while contributing to the global model [25]. Additionally, this method allows for the development of more generalizable models by leveraging diverse datasets [21]. Furthermore, FL reduces the computational and storage burden on individual institutions by distributing the training process across multiple participants [8]. Thus, FL emerges as an effective and scalable solution for developing secure, collaborative, and inclusive medical AI systems [20].

However, many recent FL methods have introduced complex optimization pipelines that exhibit a strong dependence on the careful tuning of algorithm-specific hyperparameters [13]. These methods rely heavily on carefully tuned hyperparameters, regularization factors, and aggregation techniques, sensitive to variations in data distribution and network conditions [9]. Moreover, deploying FL systems in practical environments introduces additional variability through individual edge device configurations. In detail, differences in the choice of local optimizers and learning rates can significantly influence convergence behavior and model performance.

In this work, we revisit the effectiveness of vanilla FL—namely, the original approach based on simple model averaging—within the context of medical imaging. We conduct comprehensive experiments on a representative medical imaging dataset using recent FL methods, including vanilla FL. Our numerical results demonstrate that vanilla FL performs comparably to more sophisticated methods across a wide range of federated training conditions. Despite diverse local optimizers, learning rates, and local epoch settings, relative performance rankings remain stable. Therefore, we numerically show that the effectiveness of FL in practice depends strongly on the appropriate selection of local training configurations.

## 2   Problem and Method

### 2.1   Federated Setting

We consider two representative data distribution settings in FL, including IID and non-IID. In the IID setting, each edge device $n \in \{1, \ldots, N\}$ receives local data $\mathcal{D}^n$ sampled independently from a shared distribution $\mathcal{P}$, assumed to be standard normal:

$$x \sim \mathcal{P} = \mathcal{N}(0, I), \quad \forall x \in \mathcal{D}^n, \; \forall n. \tag{1}$$

In contrast, in the non-IID setting, we model label distribution heterogeneity using a Dirichlet distribution as [16]. Let $\mathcal{Y} = \{1, \ldots, C\}$ be the set of class labels. For each device $n$, a label distribution vector $\mathbf{p}^n = (p_1^n, \ldots, p_C^n)$ is drawn from a Dirichlet distribution:

$$\mathbf{p}^n \sim \mathrm{Dir}(\alpha), \quad \alpha > 0. \tag{2}$$

Then, the local dataset $\mathcal{D}^n$ is constructed by sampling data conditioned on the assigned label proportions $\mathbf{p}^n$. Note that, smaller values of $\alpha$ result in higher label skew, where each device is likely to contain samples from only a few classes. This setting reflects real-world data heterogeneity, which induces client drift and thereby hinders effective training in FL.

### 2.2   General FL Process

The goal of FL is to learn a global model $w \in \mathbb{R}^d$ by minimizing the aggregated objective function $F(w) := \frac{1}{N} \sum_{n=1}^{N} F_n(w)$. Each local objective $F_n(w)$ is defined over edge device $n$'s private dataset $\mathcal{D}^n$ as $F_n(w) := \frac{1}{|\mathcal{D}^n|} \sum_{x \in \mathcal{D}^n} f(w; x)$, where $f(w; x)$ denotes the loss evaluated on sample $x$.

At the beginning of each global epoch $g_e$, the central server broadcasts the current global model $w^{g_e}$ to all $N$ edge devices. Then, the server randomly selects a subset of devices $\mathcal{S}_{g_e} \subset \{1, \ldots, N\}$ to participate in federated training during the global epoch. Each selected edge device $n \in \mathcal{S}{g_e}$ initializes its local model to $w^{g_e}$ and trains locally using the optimizer EdgeOpt($\cdot$) for $l_e$ steps with local learning rate $\eta_l$:

$$w_n^{g_e, l_e} = \mathrm{EdgeOpt}(w^{g_e}, \mathcal{D}^n, \eta_l, l_e). \tag{3}$$

After completing local training, each participating device sends its updated model $w_n^{g_e, l_e}$ to the central server. The server aggregates these updates using a server-side optimizer ServerOpt($\cdot$), which may incorporate weighting schemes or other update rules:

$$w^{g_e+1} = \text{ServerOpt}(\{w_n^{g_e,le}\}_{n \in \mathcal{S}_{g_e}}). \tag{4}$$

This procedure repeats for $g_e = 1, \ldots, G$, until convergence [18] or a predefined number of global epochs $G$ is reached. The dynamics of federated training depend on device-specific configurations, including local optimizer, $\eta_l$, and $l_e$, as well as the optimization behavior defined by EdgeOpt($\cdot$) and ServerOpt($\cdot$).

**Table 1.** Top-1 test accuracy (%) and corresponding sub-optimal $g_e$ of FL methods under IID and non-IID settings. The vanilla FL achieves performance comparable to recent FL methods. Here, peak-$g_e$ denotes the global epoch at which each method reaches its peak accuracy.

| Method | Colorectal Pathology Task | | | | Blood Cell Task | | | |
|---|---|---|---|---|---|---|---|---|
| | IID | | non-IID | | IID | | non-IID | |
| | Acc. (%) | Peak-$g_e$ | Acc. (%) | Peak-$g_e$ | Acc. (%) | Peak-$g_e$ | Acc. (%) | Peak-$g_e$ |
| FedAvg | 95.02 | 52.7 | 93.88 | 90.3 | 96.91 | 94.3 | 92.69 | 95.7 |
| FedDyn | 95.17 | 30.7 | 94.58 | 79.3 | 97.82 | 77.7 | 96.89 | 94.7 |
| FedSAM | 95.21 | 65.7 | 94.09 | 83.0 | 96.99 | 97.7 | 93.57 | 94.0 |
| FedSpeed | 95.38 | 36.0 | 94.73 | 81.7 | 97.94 | 88.0 | 97.16 | 87.0 |
| FedSMOO | 95.37 | 70.3 | 94.81 | 73.0 | 97.99 | 87.0 | 97.15 | 91.7 |
| FedGamma | 93.66 | 71.3 | 89.79 | 70.7 | 96.65 | 98.0 | 93.49 | 99.3 |

# 3  Experiment and Results

## 3.1  Experiment Setting

To check the robustness of FedAvg, we conduct experiments on a colorectal pathology [12] and blood cell [3] image classification task under federated settings. In detail, all edge devices employ ConvNeXtV2 [30] as local AI model, and we compare FedAvg with recent FL methods including FedDyn [2], FedSAM [22], FedSpeed [28], FedSMOO [27], and FedGamma [6]. To simulate the non-IID setting, we distribute samples across $N = 100$ edge devices with $\alpha = 0.1$. At each $g_e$, a subset of $M = 10$ devices is randomly selected to participate in training. All experiments are run with 3 random seeds, and training is accelerated using AMD Instinct MI300X GPUs [26], supported by AMD Developer Cloud credits.

**FL Method Comparison: IID vs. Non-IID.** To investigate whether FedAvg can achieve competitive performance compared to recent FL methods, we evaluate under both IID and non-IID label distributions. As shown in Table 1, all methods attain similar top-1 test accuracy, with only marginal differences across settings. Under the IID setting, FedAvg achieves 95.02% and 96.91% accuracy on the Colorectal Pathology and Blood Cell tasks, respectively—only 0.36% and 1.03% below the best-performing methods (FedSpeed and FedSMOO). In terms of convergence, FedAvg requires 52.7 and 94.3 global epochs, whereas FedDyn and FedSpeed converge fastest with 30.7 and 77.7 epochs, respectively.

Under the non-IID setting, FedAvg achieves 93.88% on Colorectal and 92.69% on Blood Cell, falling 0.93% and 4.47% short, with FedSMOO and FedSpeed being the top performers for each task. Moreover, FedAvg shows strong stability: on the Colorectal task, it outperforms FedGamma by 4.09%, and on the Blood Cell task, it surpasses FedGamma by 3.20%, while also converging up to 25 epochs earlier. Overall, the results indicate that the choice of FL algorithm has only a limited effect on the performance.

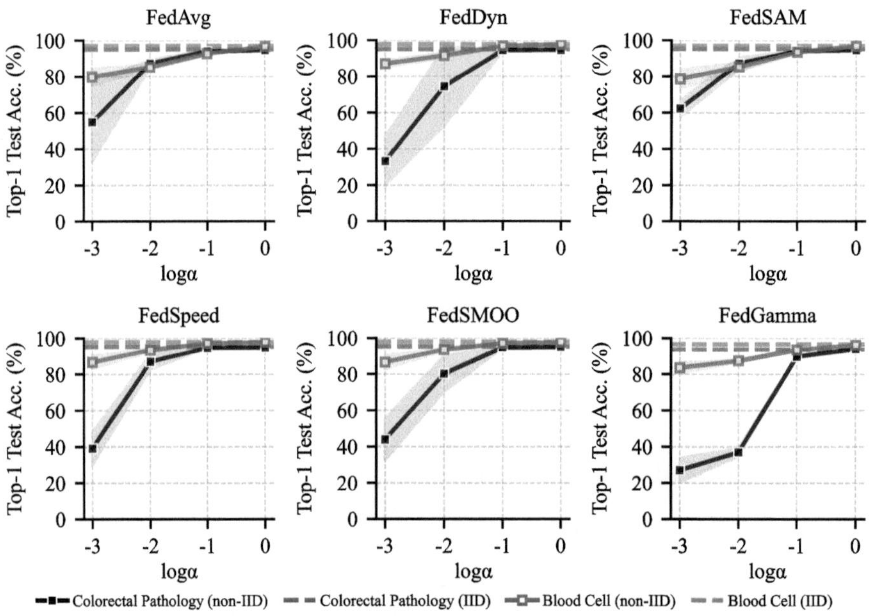



**Fig. 2.** Top-1 test accuracy (%) of FL methods under varying Dirichlet $\alpha$ values, which control the degree of label heterogeneity. While all methods improve as $\alpha$ increases, their robustness at low $\alpha$ varies significantly.

**Impact of Non-IID Degree.** To analyze the impact of label distribution skew on FL performance, we adjust the Dirichlet $\alpha$ parameter to simulate varying degrees of non-IID conditions. When $\alpha$ becomes larger and label distributions are more balanced, results in consistent performance gains across all FL methods, as shown in Fig. 2. This trend persists across both medical imaging tasks, indicating that the degree of data heterogeneity strongly influences model performance. Although some methods exhibit slightly better robustness than others, the overall shift in performance is largely driven by the change in $\alpha$.

In the colorectal task, FedAvg improves dramatically from 54.87% at $\alpha = 0.001$ to 94.65% at $\alpha = 1.0$, closely tracking FedSAM, which rises from 62.29% to 94.66%. Even methods like FedGamma, which struggle under high heterogeneity (27.12% at $\alpha = 0.001$), recover to over 93% as $\alpha$ increases. For the blood cell task, the best-performing methods—FedSpeed and FedSMOO—reach above 97.7% at $\alpha = 1.0$, improving from around 86.6% at $\alpha = 0.001$. Meanwhile, FedDyn shows a narrower gain, rising from 87.02% to 97.70%, suggesting limited responsiveness to distribution shift. FedAvg, although simpler, steadily narrows the gap as heterogeneity decreases. Collectively, these results imply that adapting to non-IID severity is often more consequential than the specific FL algorithm employed.

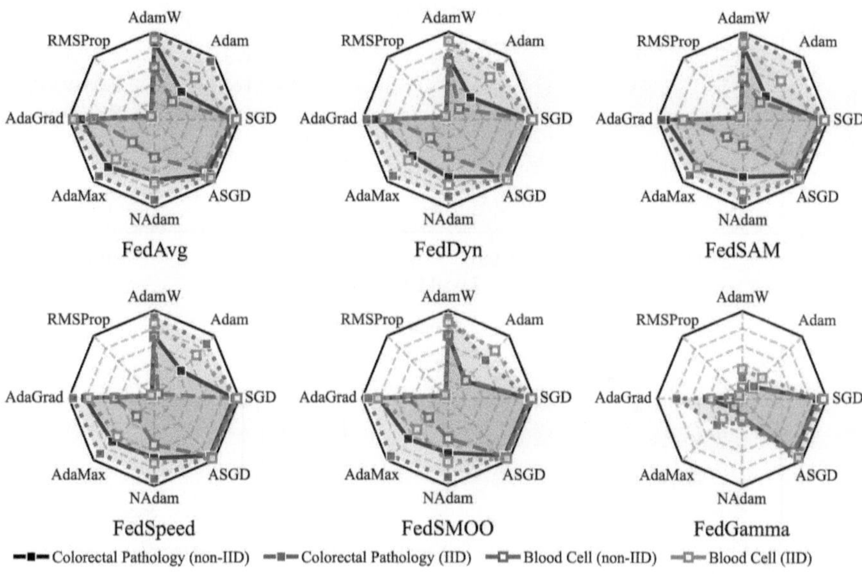

**Fig. 3.** Top-1 test accuracy (%) of FL methods evaluated under representative local optimizers at the edge device. The choice of local optimizer substantially impacts FL performance more than optimization variations.

**Impact of Local Optimizers.** To examine how local optimizer choice affects federated training performance, we evaluate FL methods across commonly used optimizers. As shown in Fig. 3, optimizer choice leads to greater performance variation than the specific FL algorithm itself. FedAvg shows relatively steady behavior, but its accuracy still drops from over 93% with SGD to as low as

20% with RMSProp. In contrast, methods like FedDyn and FedGamma exhibit sharp fluctuations, particularly under Adam and AdamW. These results highlight the critical role of optimizer stability in federated training, particularly under heterogeneous data distributions.

When trained with SGD, all methods achieve strong performance, with Fed-Speed and FedSMOO exceeding 94% in both the colorectal pathology and blood cell tasks. However, under Adam, FedDyn drops to 45.10% in the colorectal task and 29.68% in the blood cell task, while FedGamma falls below 32% in both. While AdaGrad yields more consistent results—FedAvg achieves 87.85% and 75.61% in the two tasks respectively—RMSProp consistently underperforms, producing sub-20% accuracy across the board. Among stable alternatives, ASGD performs well overall, with FedSAM and FedDyn both exceeding 90% in the colorectal task. Overall, the local optimizer selection has a greater impact on performance than the choice of FL method.

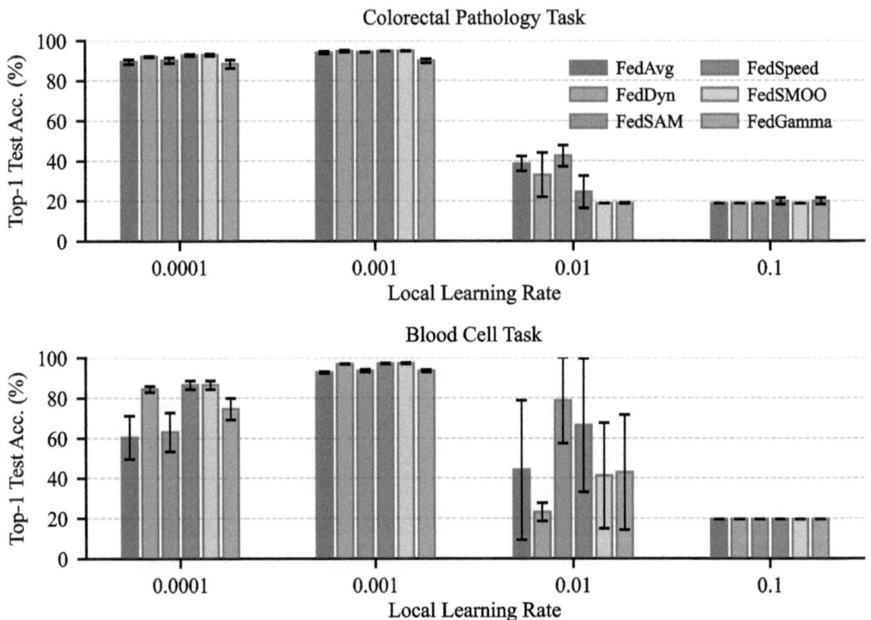


**Fig. 4.** Top-1 test accuracy (%) of FL methods evaluated under various local learning rates. Improper local learning rate selection can significantly degrade FL performance. The error bars denote the standard deviation over 3 independent runs.

**Impact of Local Learning Rate.** To investigate how the local learning rate influences model performance, we evaluate FL methods across three representative values: 0.0001, 0.001, 0.01, and 0.1. At $\eta_l = 0.001$, all methods exhibit stable and high accuracy, demonstrating reliable convergence, as shown in Fig. 4. However, as $\eta_l$ increases to 0.01, performance variation across methods becomes more pronounced. This trend is further exacerbated at 0.1, where most methods collapse to below 20% accuracy regardless of task. These observations indicate that higher learning rates destabilize training, particularly in FL methods sensitive to local updates.

At $\eta_l = 0.001$, FedSMOO and FedSpeed achieve the highest accuracies in the blood cell task, both exceeding 97.1%, while FedDyn reaches 96.89%. When increasing $\eta_l$ to 0.01, FedSAM remains relatively robust, achieving 78.73% in the blood cell task and 42.46% in the colorectal task. In contrast, FedSMOO and FedSpeed drop sharply to 18.64% and 24.37%, respectively, in the colorectal task. This instability becomes universal at $\eta_l = 0.1$, where all methods flatten to around 19.47% in the blood cell task. These results confirm that high learning rates impede convergence, underscoring the importance of carefully tuning $\eta_l$ to avoid performance degradation.

**Table 2.** Top-1 test accuracy (%) difference and corresponding global epoch difference between each FL method and FedAvg across different local epochs. The presented values represent mean differences relative to FedAvg.

| Method | Colorectal Pathology Task | | | | | | Blood Cell Task | | | | | |
|---|---|---|---|---|---|---|---|---|---|---|---|---|
| | $l_e = 1$ | | $l_e = 5$ | | $l_e = 20$ | | $l_e = 1$ | | $l_e = 5$ | | $l_e = 20$ | |
| | $\delta_{Acc.}$ | $\delta_{g_e}$ | $\delta_{Acc.}$ | $\delta_{g_e}$ | $\delta_{Acc.}$ | $\delta_{g_e}$ | $\delta_{Acc.}$ | $\delta_{g_e}$ | $\delta_{Acc.}$ | $\delta_{g_e}$ | $\delta_{Acc.}$ | $\delta_{g_e}$ |
| FedDyn | +2.69 | −9.0 | +0.04 | −12.7 | +0.17 | −18.3 | +14.41 | +0.3 | +1.11 | −21.3 | +0.10 | −43.7 |
| FedSAM | +1.09 | −1.7 | +0.02 | −0.3 | −0.17 | +12.7 | +0.24 | −1.0 | +0.14 | +0.7 | −0.08 | −8.7 |
| FedSpeed | +3.30 | −4.7 | +0.24 | +5.7 | −0.48 | −16.7 | +13.85 | +0.3 | +1.16 | −6.3 | −0.01 | −28.3 |
| FedSMOO | +3.52 | +1.0 | +0.43 | +22.7 | −0.39 | −36.3 | +13.87 | +0.3 | +1.18 | −20.3 | +0.09 | −33.3 |
| FedGamma | +1.20 | − | −0.70 | +35.0 | −3.46 | −11.0 | +6.03 | − | −0.53 | +1.0 | −1.72 | −15.7 |

**Ablation Study.** To check the effect of local training duration, we evaluate performance for $l_e \in \{1, 5, 20\}$ using SGD with $\eta_l = 0.001$, as shown in Table 2. In particular, increasing $l_e$ generally improves accuracy for FedAvg, reaching 95.22% at $l_e = 20$, while also reducing required global epochs at $l_e = 5$. FedDyn benefits from more frequent local updates at $l_e = 1$, showing the largest accuracy gains of +2.69% and +14.41% in the colorectal and blood cell tasks, respectively. In contrast, FedGamma consistently degrades with longer local training, dropping by −3.46% and −1.72% at $l_e - 20$ while requiring fewer global epochs. FedSMOO and FedSpeed show similar trends: both improve moderately at $l_e = 5$ in both tasks, but their accuracy declines at $l_e = 20$, despite converging faster than FedAvg. In conclusion, longer local training can either benefit or impair performance, highlighting the need for adaptive and well-calibrated $l_e$ settings.

## 4    Conclusion

In this work, we show that FL performance is more sensitive to edge-specific hyperparameters than to the underlying federated optimization strategy. Through comprehensive experiments, we show that local optimizers and local learning rates impact performance and convergence more than the choice of FL method. Moreover, the heightened sensitivity of recent FL methods to these hyperparameters raises concerns regarding their robustness, reproducibility, and deployability in practical settings. These results highlight the need for FL methods that are not only theoretically sound but also resilient to variations in device-level configurations.

**Acknowledgments.** This research was partly supported by the Institute of Information & Communications Technology Planning & Evaluation (IITP)-ITRC (Information Technology Research Center) grant funded by the Korea government (MSIT) (IITP-2025-RS-2020-II201787, contribution rate: 50%) and (IITP-2025-RS-2023-00259991, contribution rate: 50%).

**Disclosure of Interests.** The authors have no competing interests to declare relevant to this article's content.

## References


1. Abouelmehdi, K., Beni-Hessane, A., Khaloufi, H.: Big healthcare data: preserving security and privacy. J. Big Data **5**(1), 1–18 (2018)
2. Acar, D.A.E., Zhao, Y., Matas, R., Mattina, M., Whatmough, P., Saligrama, V.: Federated learning based on dynamic regularization. In: Proceedings of the ICLR, Vienna, Austria (2021)
3. Acevedo, A., Merino, A., Alférez, S., Molina, Á., Boldú, L., Rodellar, J.: A dataset of microscopic peripheral blood cell images for development of automatic recognition systems. Data Brief **30** (2020)
4. Antunes, R.S., André da Costa, C., Küderle, A., Yari, I.A., Eskofier, B.: Federated learning for healthcare: systematic review and architecture proposal. ACM Trans. Intell. Syst. Technol. **13**(4), 1–23 (2022)
5. Bisio, I., et al.: Ai-enabled internet of medical things: architectural framework and case studies. IEEE Internet Things Mag. **8**(2), 121–128 (2025)
6. Dai, R., et al.: FedGamma: federated learning with global sharpness-aware minimization. IEEE Trans. Neural Netw. Learn. Syst. **35**(12), 17479–17492 (2024)
7. Ding, J., Tramel, E., Sahu, A.K., Wu, S., Avestimehr, S., Zhang, T.: Federated learning challenges and opportunities: an outlook. In: Proceedings of the IEEE ICASSP, Marina Bay, Singapore (2022)
8. Guan, H., Yap, P.T., Bozoki, A., Liu, M.: Federated learning for medical image analysis: a survey. Pattern Recognit. (2024)
9. Houssein, E.H., Sayed, A.: Boosted federated learning based on improved particle swarm optimization for healthcare IoT devices. Comput. Biol. Med. **163** (2023)
10. Joshi, M., Pal, A., Sankarasubbu, M.: Federated learning for healthcare domain-pipeline, applications and challenges. ACM Trans. Comput. Healthc. **3**(4), 1–36 (2022)

11. Kairouz, P., McMahan, H.: Advances and open problems in federated learning. Found. Trends Mach. Learn. **14** (2021)

12. Kather, J.N., et al.: Predicting survival from colorectal cancer histology slides using deep learning: a retrospective multicenter study. PLoS Med.**16**(1) (2019)

13. Lee, Y., Gong, J., Choi, S., Kang, J.: Revisit the stability of vanilla federated learning under diverse conditions. In: Proceedings of the MICCAI, Daejeon, Republic of Korea (2025)

14. Lee, Y., Park, S., Ahn, J.H., Kang, J.: Accelerated federated learning via greedy aggregation. IEEE Commun. Lett. **26**(12), 2919–2923 (2022)

15. Lee, Y., Park, S., Kang, J.: Fast-convergent federated learning via cyclic aggregation. In: Proceedings of the IEEE ICIP, Kuala Lumpur, Malaysia (2023)

16. Li, Q., Diao, Y., Chen, Q., He, B.: Federated learning on non-IID data silos: an experimental study. In: Proceedings of the IEEE ICDE, Kuala Lumpur, Malaysia (2022)

17. Li, T., Sahu, A.K., Talwalkar, A., Smith, V.: Federated learning: challenges, methods, and future directions. IEEE Signal Process. Mag. **37**(3), 50–60 (2020)

18. Li, X., Huang, K., Yang, W., Wang, S., Zhang, Z.: On the convergence of FedAvg on non-IID data. In: Proceedings of the ICLR, Virtual Event, Ethiopia (2020)

19. McMahan, B., Moore, E., Ramage, D., Hampson, S., y Arcas, B.A.: Communication-efficient learning of deep networks from decentralized data. In: Proceedings of the AISTAT, Fort Lauderdale, USA (2017)

20. Nguyen, D.C., et al.: Federated learning for smart healthcare: a survey. ACM Comput. Surv. **55**(3), 1–37 (2022)

21. Pfitzner, B., Steckhan, N., Arnrich, B.: Federated learning in a medical context: a systematic literature review. ACM Trans. Internet Technol. **21**(2), 1–31 (2021)

22. Qu, Z., Li, X., Duan, R., Liu, Y., Tang, B., Lu, Z.: Generalized federated learning via sharpness aware minimization. In: Proceedings of the ICML, Baltimore, USA (2022)

23. Rajpurkar, P., Chen, E., Banerjee, O., Topol, E.J.: Ai in health and medicine. Nat. Med. **28**(1), 31–38 (2022)

24. Rauniyar, A., et al.: Federated learning for medical applications: a taxonomy, current trends, challenges, and future research directions. IEEE Internet Things J. **11**(5), 7374–7398 (2024)

25. Rieke, N., et al.: The future of digital health with federated learning. NPJ Digit. Med. **3**(1), 119 (2020)

26. Smith, A., et al.: AMD instinct$^{\text{TM}}$ mi300x accelerator: packaging and architecture co-optimization. In: IEEE Symposium on VLSI Circuits, Hawaii, USA (2024)

27. Sun, Y., Shen, L., Chen, S., Ding, L., Tao, D.: Dynamic regularized sharpness aware minimization in federated learning: approaching global consistency and smooth landscape. In: Proceedings of the ICML, Hawaii, USA (2023)

28. Sun, Y., Shen, L., Huang, T., Ding, L., Tao, D.: FedSpeed: larger local interval, less communication round, and higher generalization accuracy. In: Proceedings of the ICLR, Kigali, Rwanda (2023)

29. Whang, S.E., Roh, Y., Song, H., Lee, J.G.: Data collection and quality challenges in deep learning: a data-centric AI perspective. VLDB J. **32**(4), 791–813 (2023)

30. Woo, S., et al.: ConvNext v2: co-designing and scaling convnets with masked autoencoders. In: Proceedings of the IEEE/CVF CVPR, Vancouver, Canada (2023)

# A Staining Variability-Aware Semi-supervised Framework for H&E-to-IHC Virtual Staining

Baoshun Wang, Weiping Lin, Shen Liu, Yihuang Hu, and Liansheng Wang[✉]

Department of Computer Science, School of Informatics, Xiamen University,
Xiamen, China
{bswang,wplin,liushen,huyihuang}@stu.xmu.edu.cn, lswang@xmu.edu.cn

**Abstract.** Supervised virtual staining methods achieve high accuracy when trained on large-scale paired data. However, paired H&E-to-IHC images are extremely scarce. Furthermore, staining variations caused by differences in staining protocols and scanning equipment introduce irrelevant discrepancies that further hinder model performance. The scarcity of paired data and staining variations across institutions represent two major challenges in virtual staining. To address these issues, we propose a staining variability-aware semi-supervised framework. The semi-supervised approach leverages a small number of paired H&E-IHC image pairs along with more unlabeled H&E images to enhance model performance. Furthermore, the staining variability-aware perturbation method simulates staining differences across institutions and staining batches. These two strategies improve the robustness, generalizability, and overall staining consistency of the model. Our method further unlocks the potential of supervised approaches when paired data is limited. Experimental results demonstrate that our method significantly improves virtual staining performance. The code will be available.

**Keywords:** Virtual staining · Semi-supervised learning · Staining variability

## 1 Introduction

Traditional pathological staining is both time-consuming and labor-intensive, placing a significant burden on pathologists. Moreover, its complex and prolonged procedures may lead to delays in patient treatment. To address these limitations, virtual staining has emerged as a deep learning-based alternative, transforming images stained with one dye into another without additional physical staining. Compared to traditional methods, virtual staining improves efficiency, consistency, and cost-effectiveness while reducing contamination risks [2,7,16]. It has achieved remarkable success in various pathological staining tasks, such as MxIF to H&E [3], FFPE to H&E [5,11,15], and H&E to IHC [9,13,14].

© The Author(s), under exclusive license to Springer Nature Switzerland AG 2026
T. Chen et al. (Eds.): EMA4MICCAI 2025 Workshops, LNCS 16318, pp. 340–349, 2026.
https://doi.org/10.1007/978-3-032-13961-0_34

Virtual staining methods can be categorized as supervised (e.g., Pix2pix [6], Pix2pixHD [19]) and unsupervised (e.g., CycleGAN [22], CUT [12]) based on the use of paired images. Supervised methods offer high precision but require large, well-aligned paired datasets. Unsupervised methods learn mappings from unpaired data, providing greater flexibility and broader applicability but often suffer from lower accuracy and artifacts, limiting their clinical reliability.

Given these limitations, semi-supervised methods offer a promising alternative by leveraging both labeled and unlabeled data to enhance model performance. They bridge the gap between supervised and unsupervised learning, reducing reliance on large paired datasets while maintaining high accuracy. Inspired by this, virtual staining can be improved by incorporating a small amount of paired data with a larger set of unpaired images, balancing accuracy and data efficiency while enhancing model robustness. Several studies have investigated the use of semi-supervised learning in virtual staining [8,20] or virtual immunohistochemical detection [21].

However, these studies either rely on additional supervision or do not directly generate target domain images. Meanwhile, a core objective of virtual staining is accurate color transformation from the source to the target domain. However, staining variations across institutions and staining batches often disrupt model training, a challenge that becomes more pronounced when paired samples are scarce. Unfortunately, most semi-supervised learning studies have overlooked this issue.

To address these challenges, we propose a staining variability-aware semi-supervised framework for virtual staining. Specifically, we integrate the classic semi-supervised learning framework, Mean Teacher [17], with virtual staining models, enabling the model to leverage a larger set of source domain images despite limited paired data. We introduce perturbations in the teacher model to simulate staining variations across institutions and batches. Extensive experiments on our carefully curated, well-aligned dataset demonstrate the effectiveness of our approach under varying proportions of paired data. Our contributions are as follows: (1) We introduce a staining variability-aware perturbation strategy to address staining variations in H&E images, enhancing model generalization and robustness. (2) We propose a novel semi-supervised virtual staining method, achieving superior performance with minimal paired data and additional source domain images. This is the first integration of Mean Teacher with virtual staining, significantly reducing reliance on large-scale paired datasets while improving staining performance.

## 2   Method

We propose a semi-supervised virtual staining method aware of staining variability. Figure 1 provides an overview of our method. We integrate the Mean Teacher framework into virtual staining models, utilizing both labeled (paired images) and unlabeled data (source domain images only) to enhance model generalization. Additionally, we introduce staining variability-aware perturbations to the teacher model, enabling it to better capture pathology image staining variations, thereby significantly improving model robustness.

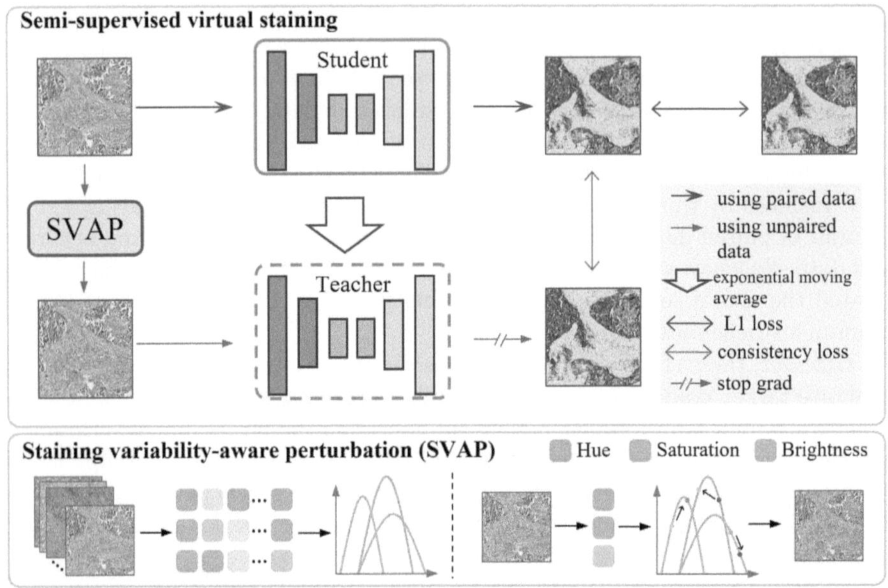


**Fig. 1.** Overview. Virtual staining models combined with Mean Teacher are trained using a small amount of labeled data (paired images) and more unlabeled data (source domain images only). The input images to the teacher model undergo staining variability-aware perturbation.

## 2.1 Virtual Staining with Mean Teacher

Mean Teacher is a semi-supervised learning framework consisting of a student model, which is actively trained, and a teacher model, which provides stable guidance. The teacher model is an auxiliary model that provides stable pseudo-labels to guide the student. The teacher's parameters are updated as the exponential moving average (EMA) of the student's parameters, which is formulated by Eq. 1. Here $\alpha$ is the EMA decay rate, and $\theta_t, \theta_s$ represent the teacher and student model parameters, respectively. The teacher model serves as a denoised version of the student, offering more stable predictions for consistency learning.

$$\theta_t \leftarrow \alpha\theta_t + (1 - \alpha)\theta_s \tag{1}$$

In virtual staining, labeled data refers to paired images, where the target domain image serves as the supervision for the corresponding source domain image. Unlabeled data consists of only source domain images, without paired target domain supervision. In our approach, both the student and teacher models utilize the generator from Pix2pixHD (or Pix2pix), denoted by $\mathcal{G}_s$ and $\mathcal{G}_t$, respectively. When training, $D_p = \{(x_p, y_p) \mid x_p \in \mathcal{X}, y_p \in \mathcal{Y}\}$ provides supervised training signals, while $D_u = \{x_u \mid x_u \in \mathcal{X}\}$ enables semi-supervised learning through consistency regularization.

**For paired samples**, the student model is optimized using two loss functions. The reconstruction loss (L1 Loss) ensures pixel-wise alignment with the ground truth stained image, which is given by Eq. 2.

$$\mathcal{L}_{recon} = \mathbb{E}_{(x_p, y_p)} \|\mathcal{G}_s(x_p) - y_p\|_1 \tag{2}$$

The adversarial loss is utilized to train the generator using a discriminator $\mathcal{D}$ to produce realistic stain appearances, which is defined in Eq. 3

$$\mathcal{L}_{GAN} = \mathbb{E}_{y_p}[\log(1 - \mathcal{D}(\mathcal{G}_s(x_p)))] + \mathbb{E}_{y_p}[log(\mathcal{D}(y_p))] \tag{3}$$

**For unpaired samples** $x_u \in D_u$, ground truth stained images are unavailable. Instead, the teacher model $\mathcal{G}_t$ generates pseudo-labels $\tilde{y}_u$ from perturbation-augmented version of $x_u$. To ensure consistency between the student and teacher outputs, we constrain the consistency between the output of $\mathcal{G}_s$ and pseudo-labels from the teacher model by:

$$\mathcal{L}_{cl} = \mathbb{E}_{x_u} \|\mathcal{G}_s(x_u) - \mathcal{G}_t(\mathcal{T}(x_u))\|_1 \tag{4}$$

where $\mathcal{T}(\cdot)$ is the proposed staining variability-aware perturbation, which will be detailed in the following section.

## 2.2   Staining Variability-Aware Perturbation

To enhance the teacher model's ability to learn robust features, we introduce a staining variability-aware perturbation method for H&E images, designed to address staining variability caused by differences across institutions and staining batches. Since virtual staining primarily focuses on color transformation, it is highly sensitive to such variations, which can mislead the model into learning irrelevant features, thus compromising its robustness and generalization. We first construct empirical distributions of hue (H), saturation (S), and brightness (B) from a large set of H&E-stained image patches and then perturb images within these distributions to simulate realistic staining variability.

Specifically, the processing of H, S, and B follows the same approach. For simplicity, we illustrate the process using H as an example. First, we extract $H$ values from each image patch and estimate their distributions via kernel density estimation (KDE):

$$P_H(h) = \frac{1}{N\sigma} \sum_{i=1}^{N} \mathcal{K}(\frac{h - h_i}{\sigma}) \tag{5}$$

where $h_i$ are the sampled values from image pixels, $\mathcal{K}$ is the Gaussian kernel and $\sigma$ is the bandwidth, which is selected via Silverman's rule to optimize the trade-off between bias and variance.

For a given H&E image with extracted mean H value $H_{ori}$, perturbations are applied by sampling from the corresponding distributions:

$$\Delta H \sim \mathcal{N}(0, \sigma_H) \tag{6}$$

where $\sigma_H$ represents the standard deviations of the estimated distributions. The perturbed H is formulated as:

$$H^{'} = max(H_l, min(H_{ori} + \Delta H, H_r)) \tag{7}$$

where $H_l$ and $H_r$ are used to constrain $H^{'}$ within the range of the distribution. Finally, $(H^{'}, S^{'}, B^{'})$ is used to generate a perturbed image for the teacher model.

This approach explicitly models staining variability to enhance robustness, ensuring that perturbations remain within the natural range observed in real-world data. This prevents the introduction of unrealistic or artificial alterations that could mislead the model.

## 3    Experiments

**Datasets.** We collected the H2I4HER2 dataset, which consists of IHC-stained images specifically used for HER2 scoring and processed with the 4B5 antibody [18]. This dataset is strictly registered at the paired level. Since H&E and IHC-stained WSIs were obtained from serial sections, we first manually screened WSIs, retaining only those with highly similar contours. We then applied image registration [4] and cropped non-overlapping $1024 \times 1024$ pixel patches. Given that even minor misalignment at the WSI level can be amplified at the patch level, we conducted an additional visual inspection to remove misaligned patch pairs. As a result, we obtained a total of 3,206 H&E-IHC image pairs, with 2,632 pairs allocated for training and 574 pairs for testing. Additionally, MIST-HER2 [9] and BCI [10] are used as external datasets, and some H&E images from the IHC4BC [1] dataset are incorporated for unsupervised training.

**Evaluation Metrics.** We used two groups of evaluation metrics. The first includes conventional image quality metrics such as Structural Similarity Index (SSIM) and Peak Signal-to-Noise Ratio (PSNR). The second relies on deep image features, incorporating Fréchet Inception Distance (FID), Kernel Inception Distance (KID), and Deep Image Structure and Texture Similarity (DISTS). These feature-based metrics assess high-level perceptual differences beyond pixel-wise accuracy.

**Implementation Details.** Our method was implemented using PyTorch 2.0, and all experiments were conducted on a server with eight RTX 3090 GPUs. The EMA decay rate $\alpha$ was set to 0.999. The warm-up stage lasts for 60 epochs, during which only paired data were used for training, while the total number of training epochs was set to 100.

**Comparison with Baselines.** Our method is compatible with various supervised virtual staining models, enabling them to leverage additional unlabeled

**Table 1.** Comparison between our method and the baseline. D1, D2, and D3 represent H2I4HER2, MIST-HER2, and BCI, respectively. Models are trained on the training set of D1 and evaluated on the test sets of all three datasets. When $\beta = 0.25$, the baseline uses only 25% of the paired samples, while Ours additionally incorporates the remaining 75% of samples (H&E images only). When $\beta = 1.00$, Ours includes $m$ H&E images from IHC4BC, where $m$ is 50% of the training set size of D1.

| $\beta$ | Dataset | Method | Pix2pixHD | | | | | Pix2pix | | | | |
|---|---|---|---|---|---|---|---|---|---|---|---|---|
| | | | PSNR | SSIM | FID | KID | DISTS | PSNR | SSIM | FID | KID | DISTS |
| 0.25 | D1 | Baseline | 18.34 | 0.3339 | 151.88 | 0.1485 | 0.3223 | 17.85 | 0.3564 | 73.07 | 0.0453 | 0.2848 |
| | | w/ ours | 18.74 | 0.3628 | 106.45 | 0.0937 | 0.3163 | 18.11 | 0.3707 | 72.23 | 0.0480 | 0.3005 |
| | D2 | Baseline | 13.78 | 0.2122 | 187.52 | 0.1596 | 0.3857 | 13.54 | 0.2158 | 62.01 | 0.0305 | 0.3326 |
| | | w/ ours | 13.87 | 0.2207 | 164.16 | 0.1396 | 0.3791 | 13.75 | 0.2235 | 59.80 | 0.0293 | 0.3455 |
| | D3 | Baseline | 14.97 | 0.3923 | 187.21 | 0.1918 | 0.3257 | 14.92 | 0.4159 | 79.21 | 0.0552 | 0.3284 |
| | | w/ ours | 15.18 | 0.4006 | 167.21 | 0.1493 | 0.3027 | 15.23 | 0.4314 | 76.91 | 0.0530 | 0.3252 |
| 0.50 | D1 | Baseline | 18.28 | 0.3363 | 108.80 | 0.0970 | 0.2858 | 17.88 | 0.3165 | 69.58 | 0.0422 | 0.2875 |
| | | w/ ours | 18.43 | 0.3619 | 79.49 | 0.0531 | 0.2782 | 18.13 | 0.3449 | 69.43 | 0.0435 | 0.2915 |
| | D2 | Baseline | 13.63 | 0.2072 | 164.03 | 0.1305 | 0.3635 | 13.70 | 0.1912 | 67.67 | 0.0375 | 0.3510 |
| | | w/ ours | 13.88 | 0.2457 | 138.42 | 0.1105 | 0.3213 | 13.97 | 0.2073 | 62.12 | 0.0317 | 0.1131 |
| | D3 | Baseline | 15.02 | 0.3911 | 169.73 | 0.1648 | 0.3170 | 14.89 | 0.3610 | 92.80 | 0.0704 | 0.3430 |
| | | w/ ours | 15.43 | 0.4334 | 109.09 | 0.0792 | 0.2989 | 15.12 | 0.3984 | 81.02 | 0.0568 | 0.3390 |
| 0.75 | D1 | Baseline | 18.39 | 0.3321 | 87.68 | 0.0660 | 0.2807 | 17.75 | 0.3241 | 69.24 | 0.0413 | 0.2870 |
| | | w/ ours | 18.39 | 0.3421 | 84.98 | 0.0584 | 0.2741 | 18.14 | 0.3454 | 68.33 | 0.0413 | 0.2868 |
| | D2 | Baseline | 13.83 | 0.2041 | 148.10 | 0.1089 | 0.3674 | 13.81 | 0.1804 | 60.73 | 0.0278 | 0.3514 |
| | | w/ ours | 13.88 | 0.2339 | 133.64 | 0.1006 | 0.3351 | 14.02 | 0.2069 | 59.08 | 0.0272 | 0.3418 |
| | D3 | Baseline | 15.11 | 0.3855 | 195.85 | 0.2042 | 0.3242 | 15.11 | 0.3577 | 76.15 | 0.0537 | 0.3423 |
| | | w/ ours | 15.41 | 0.4147 | 123.91 | 0.0982 | 0.3000 | 15.34 | 0.4065 | 75.32 | 0.0513 | 0.3255 |
| 1.00 | D1 | Baseline | 18.33 | 0.3498 | 88.19 | 0.0647 | 0.2696 | 18.16 | 0.3623 | 68.50 | 0.0414 | 0.2496 |
| | | w/ ours | 18.51 | 0.3488 | 84.26 | 0.0605 | 0.2748 | 18.28 | 0.3592 | 68.36 | 0.0409 | 0.2848 |
| | D2 | Baseline | 14.08 | 0.2255 | 143.14 | 0.1042 | 0.3540 | 13.90 | 0.1755 | 64.73 | 0.0327 | 0.3486 |
| | | w/ ours | 14.52 | 0.2376 | 128.49 | 0.9037 | 0.3157 | 14.33 | 0.2344 | 61.25 | 0.0308 | 0.3823 |
| | D3 | Baseline | 15.47 | 0.4162 | 135.26 | 0.1141 | 0.3044 | 15.13 | 0.3423 | 85.92 | 0.0603 | 0.3458 |
| | | w/ ours | 15.63 | 0.4399 | 126.76 | 0.1068 | 0.2864 | 15.44 | 0.4116 | 73.91 | 0.0497 | 0.3297 |

**Table 2.** Robustness analysis models under small perturbations. The metric is *SSIM_R*

| $\beta$ | Pix2pix | | | | Pix2pixHD | | | |
|---|---|---|---|---|---|---|---|---|
| | 0.25 | 0.50 | 0.75 | 1.00 | 0.25 | 0.50 | 0.75 | 1.00 |
| Baseline | 0.5096 | 0.5038 | 0.5190 | 0.5756 | 0.4381 | 0.4617 | 0.4765 | 0.4930 |
| w/ ours | 0.5743 | 0.5360 | 0.5481 | 0.5838 | 0.5002 | 0.4991 | 0.5109 | 0.5136 |

data for enhanced performance. We evaluate it on Pix2pix and Pix2pixHD using the H2I4HER2 dataset. From the training set of the H2I4HER2 dataset, a subset of samples is randomly selected as paired data (with a ratio of $\beta$), while the remaining samples use only H&E images for unsupervised training. The results are presented in Table 1. In most cases, our method significantly outperforms the baseline on both internal and external test sets. To further improve performance, we conduct fully supervised training using all paired samples from H2I4HER2 while incorporating additional H&E images from other datasets for unsupervised training. This also leads to a notable performance improvement on external test sets, indicating improved generalization ability. We found that Pix2PixHD underperforms Pix2Pix in certain cases. Due to its larger number of model parameters, Pix2PixHD tends to overfit when paired data is limited. Our method effectively mitigates this issue, as evidenced by the significant performance improvement on external test sets. Figure 2 provides a visual comparison of generated images, showing that our method produces more accurate and consistent stain transformations while better preserving histological details.

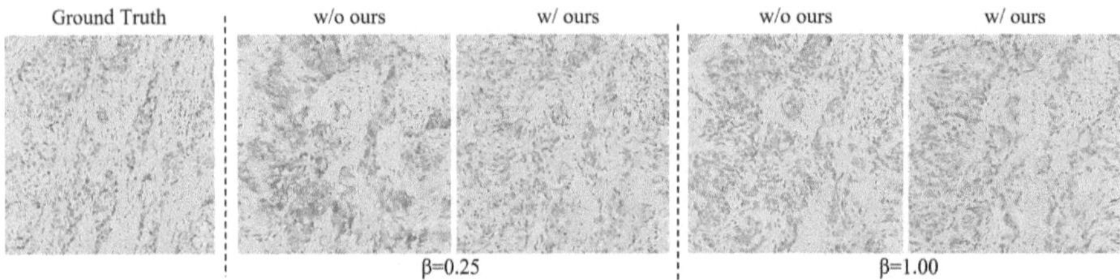


**Fig. 2.** Visual comparison of generated images.

**Model Output Consistency Analysis.** We conducted robustness analysis experiments to assess the model's consistency under minor perturbations. Given an H&E image, we generate a perturbed version by adjusting its hue and saturation within a defined range. Both images are then processed by the trained virtual staining model, producing two corresponding IHC images. The Structural Similarity Index (SSIM) between them is computed for all test set images, and the average SSIM, denoted as $SSIM\_R$, quantifies the model's robustness. A higher $SSIM\_R$ indicates greater stability against perturbations. Table 2 presents these results, showing that models trained with our method achieve improved robustness.

**Ablation Study.** The effectiveness of integrating Mean Teacher has been validated in Table 1. Here, we further assess the impact of SVAP through ablation experiments, comparing our full method with two alternatives: (1) removing staining variability-aware perturbation entirely and (2) replacing it with random color perturbations. As shown in Table 3, our method outperforms both alternative settings, demonstrating the superiority of the proposed staining variability-aware perturbation (SVAP).

**Table 3.** Ablation study on the effect of SVAP using the Pix2PixHD model.

|  | PSNR | SSIM | FID | KID | DISTS | SSIM_R |
| --- | --- | --- | --- | --- | --- | --- |
| SVAP | 18.43 | 0.3619 | 79.49 | 0.0531 | 0.2782 | 0.3972 |
| w/o SVAP | 18.32 | 0.3482 | 93.01 | 0.0711 | 0.2883 | 0.3908 |
| random | 18.27 | 0.3541 | 89.14 | 0.0653 | 0.2916 | 0.4048 |

**Effectiveness of Increasing Unlabeled Data.** To investigate the impact of additional unlabeled data on model performance, we progressively expand the training set with external samples. Assuming the H2I4HER2 dataset contains $M$ paired samples, we introduce additional unlabeled data (H&E images) from the IHC4BC dataset in quantities of $0.5M$, $1.0M$, and $2.0M$. As shown in Fig. 3, increasing the number of unlabeled samples consistently improves performance on the external test set. However, there is a slight decline in performance on the internal test set. This can be attributed to the baseline model's potential reliance on dataset-specific spurious correlations, which may benefit the internal test set. By incorporating our method, the model learns more generalized features, reducing its dependence on these spurious correlations, thus leading to a slight performance decrease on the internal test set.

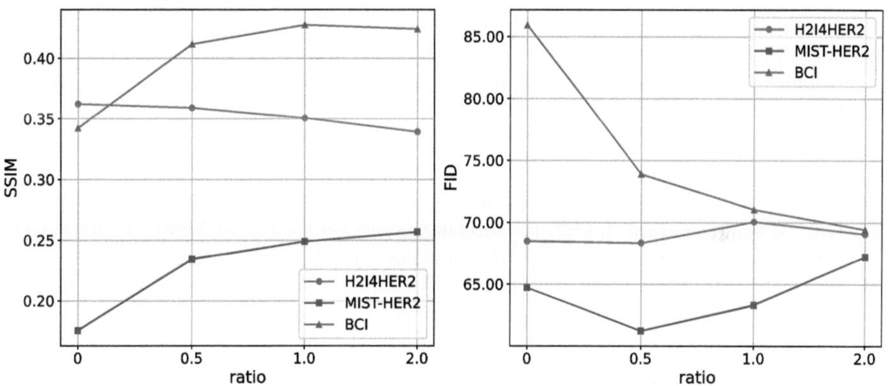

**Fig. 3.** Performance of the model with increasing amounts of external unlabeled data from the IHC4BC dataset.

## 4   Conclusion

In this study, we propose a staining variability-aware semi-supervised framework for virtual staining, integrating Mean Teacher and staining variability-aware perturbation (SVAP) with existing supervised models to enhance their performance. Our method requires only additional H&E images, which are readily available in clinical practice, to improve model robustness and generalization. By introducing SVAP in the teacher model, we effectively model staining differences across institutions and staining batches, reducing their adverse impact on training and improving the model's ability to generate consistent stain transformations. Experiments with increasing unlabeled data show that the model continues to benefit as more H&E images are incorporated. Overall, our framework provides a practical and effective way to unlock the full potential of supervised virtual staining models with minimal additional data requirements, making it a scalable solution for real-world pathology applications.

**Acknowledgments.** This work was supported by National Natural Science Foundation of China (Grant No. 62371409) and Fujian Provincial Natural Science Foundation of China (Grant No. 2023J01005)

**Disclosure of Interests.** The authors have no competing interests to declare that are relevant to the content of this article.

# References


1. Akbarnejad, A., Ray, N., Barnes, P.J., Bigras, G.: Predicting Ki67, ER, PR, and HER2 statuses from H&E-stained breast cancer images. arXiv preprint arXiv:2308.01982 (2023)
2. Bai, B., Yang, X., Li, Y., Zhang, Y., Pillar, N., Ozcan, A.: Deep learning-enabled virtual histological staining of biological samples. Light: Sci. Appl. **12**(1), 57 (2023)
3. Bao, S., Hin, H.: Alleviating tiling effect by random walk sliding window in high-resolution histological whole slide image synthesis. Med. Imaging Deep Learn. (2023)
4. Gatenbee, C.D., et al.: Virtual alignment of pathology image series for multi-gigapixel whole slide images. Nat. Commun. **14**(1), 4502 (2023)
5. Hu, Y., et al.: Boosting FFPE-to-he virtual staining with cell semantics from pre-trained segmentation model. In: International Conference on Medical Image Computing and Computer-Assisted Intervention, pp. 67–76. Springer (2024)
6. Isola, P., Zhu, J.Y., Zhou, T., Efros, A.A.: Image-to-image translation with conditional adversarial networks. In: Proceedings of the IEEE Conference on Computer Vision and Pattern Recognition, pp. 1125–1134 (2017)
7. Latonen, L., Koivukoski, S., Khan, U., Ruusuvuori, P.: Virtual staining for histology by deep learning. Trends Biotechnol. (2024)
8. Lee, K.C., Che, H., Kim, J., Bae, D., Horstmeyer, R., Lee, S.A.: Semi-supervised virtual staining for high-throughput and label-free histopathology. In: Conference on Lasers and Electro-Optics/Pacific Rim, p. We2G_2. Optica Publishing Group (2024)
9. Li, F., Hu, Z., Chen, W., Kak, A.: Adaptive supervised patchnce loss for learning H&E-to-IHC stain translation with inconsistent groundtruth image pairs. In: International Conference on Medical Image Computing and Computer-Assisted Intervention, pp. 632–641. Springer (2023)
10. Liu, S., Zhu, C., Xu, F., Jia, X., Shi, Z., Jin, M.: BCI: breast cancer immunohistochemical image generation through pyramid pix2pix. In: Proceedings of the IEEE/CVF Conference on Computer Vision and Pattern Recognition, pp. 1815–1824 (2022)

11. Ma, J., Chen, H.: Efficient supervised pretraining of swin-transformer for virtual staining of microscopy images. IEEE Trans. Med. Imaging (2023)

12. Park, T., Efros, A.A., Zhang, R., Zhu, J.Y.: Contrastive learning for unpaired image-to-image translation. In: Computer Vision–ECCV 2020: 16th European Conference, Glasgow, UK, 23–28 August 2020, Proceedings, Part IX 16, pp. 319–345. Springer (2020)

13. Pati, P., et al.: Accelerating histopathology workflows with generative AI-based virtually multiplexed tumour profiling. Nat. Mach. Intell. 1–17 (2024)

14. Peng, Q., et al.: Advancing H&E-to-IHC virtual staining with task-specific domain knowledge for her2 scoring. In: International Conference on Medical Image Computing and Computer-Assisted Intervention, pp. 3–13. Springer (2024)

15. Rana, A., et al.: Use of deep learning to develop and analyze computational hematoxylin and eosin staining of prostate core biopsy images for tumor diagnosis. JAMA Netw. Open **3**(5), e205111–e205111 (2020)

16. Salvi, M., et al.: Computational synthesis of histological stains: a step toward virtual enhanced digital pathology. Int. J. Imaging Syst. Technol. **34**(5), e23165 (2024)

17. Tarvainen, A., Valpola, H.: Mean teachers are better role models: weight-averaged consistency targets improve semi-supervised deep learning results. Adv. Neural Inf. Process. Syst. **30** (2017)

18. Van Der Vegt, B., De Bock, G.H., Bart, J., Zwartjes, N.G., Wesseling, J.: Validation of the 4B5 rabbit monoclonal antibody in determining HER2/neu status in breast cancer. Mod. Pathol. **22**(7), 879–886 (2009)

19. Wang, T.C., Liu, M.Y., Zhu, J.Y., Tao, A., Kautz, J., Catanzaro, B.: High-resolution image synthesis and semantic manipulation with conditional GANs. In: Proceedings of the IEEE Conference on Computer Vision and Pattern Recognition, pp. 8798–8807 (2018)

20. Zeng, B., et al.: Semi-supervised PR virtual staining for breast histopathological images. In: International Conference on Medical Image Computing and Computer-Assisted Intervention, pp. 232–241. Springer (2022)

21. Zhou, S., et al.: Uncertainty-assisted virtual immunohistochemical detection on morphological staining via semi-supervised learning. Opt. Lasers Eng. **184**, 108657 (2025)

22. Zhu, J.Y., Park, T., Isola, P., Efros, A.A.: Unpaired image-to-image translation using cycle-consistent adversarial networks. In: Proceedings of the IEEE International Conference on Computer Vision, pp. 2223–2232 (2017)

# Counterfactual Augmentation for Long-Tailed Multi-label Chest X-Ray Classification


Seungin Baek and Jitae Shin$^{(\boxtimes)}$

Department of Electrical and Computer Engineering, Sungkyunkwan University,
Suwon, Republic of Korea
back1101@g.skku.edu, jtshin@skku.edu



**Abstract.** Medical multi-label classification is hampered by two intertwined data pathologies: a surfeit of "clean" images that contain no positive findings and extreme label imbalance in which clinically critical diseases appear only a handful of times. Together, these factors bias conventional CNNs toward a conservative decision boundary that overwhelmingly predicts no finding, leaving rare conditions severely underrepresented in the learned feature space. We propose Counterfactual Variational autoencoder Augmentation (COVA), a lightweight pipeline that trains a variational auto-encoder on the full training set and then counterfactually edits latent codes of negative or head-class images to synthesize realistic examples of tail diseases. Each generated sample carries ground-truth labels by construction and is re-inserted into the training pool without modifying the backbone architecture or loss function. Evaluated on a de-identified chest-X-ray benchmark with 112,120 images and 14 disease labels (tail-to-head ratio $\approx$ 1:98), COVA lifts the average area under receiver-operating-characteristic curve(AUROC) from 0.799 to 0.840 ($+4.1\,\%p$) over a strong baseline that combines a randomized augmentation policy (RandAugment) with class-weighted loss. To our knowledge, this is the first study to exploit counterfactual image synthesis for data augmentation in medical multi-label classification. These findings show that label-aware generative augmentation can meaningfully reduce false negatives and improve reliability in medical multi-label settings without additional annotation cost.

**Keywords:** Multi-label classification · Data augmentation ·
Variational auto-encoder


## 1 Introduction

Computer-aided diagnosis is increasingly cast as a *multi-label* prediction task: a single chest radiograph must be screened for dozens of possible findings that can co-occur or be mutually exclusive [13,16]. Unfortunately, two intertwined data pathologies undermine reliable training. First, the majority of images are clinically normal (no finding). Second, the abnormal subset follows a long-tail distribution in which life-threatening yet rare disorders appear only a handful of times.


© The Author(s), under exclusive license to Springer Nature Switzerland AG 2026
T. Chen et al. (Eds.): EMA4MICCAI 2025 Workshops, LNCS 16318, pp. 350–359, 2026.
https://doi.org/10.1007/978-3-032-13961-0_35

Under such imbalance, standard convolutional neural networks (CNNs) skew toward the dominant normal class, leaving rare conditions under-represented in the learned feature space. Re-weighting strategies such as Focal Loss, Asymmetric Loss (adopted as the classification loss in this study), and LDAM Loss have been proposed [2,15,17]. These loss functions down-weight gradients from easy head-class samples, thereby amplifying the learning signal for tail classes. Mini-batch re-sampling [26] and SMOTE-style over-sampling [3,6] further increase the exposure of minority classes. In addition, loss-based methods such as Class-Balanced Loss [6] and the two-stage Decoupled Training (DC-T) paradigm [14] mitigate class imbalance by reweighting or resampling, yet they treat each label independently and thus fail to capture clinically prevalent label co-occurrence patterns. Consequently, when a rare finding appears alongside several common ones, the learning signal for the rare label remains weak and inter-label interactions are ignored.

However, all of these techniques merely re-weight or re-arrange existing observations; they cannot create new minority examples. Consequently, the overwhelming prevalence of "no-finding" radiographs continues to bias the decision boundary. Pixel-level augmentation schemes such as Mixup, CutMix, and Copy–Paste [9,24,25] enrich diversity, yet in multi-label radiography they often disrupt label fidelity when a rare lesion occupies only a small region [7]. Generative models—Generative Adversarial Networks (GANs), Variational Autoencoders (VAEs), and diffusion networks—can synthesize high-fidelity images [8,22]; nevertheless, naive sampling still yields few usable instances of rare disorders and may hallucinate spurious findings [1]. The outstanding challenge, therefore, is to generate tail-class images on demand while guaranteeing clinically consistent labels. Our work retains the benefits of asymmetric loss for imbalance-aware classification and couples it with a counterfactual VAE generator that supplies the missing minority examples. Latent spaces of VAEs are approximately linear: semantic attributes can be toggled by simple vector arithmetic. If a VAE is trained on the full dataset, we can counterfactually edit a normal image's latent code to insert a specific rare pathology, thereby creating a realistic exemplar whose ground-truth label vector is known by construction.

Our COVA pipeline (Fig. 1) operates on-the-fly during downstream training: whenever a no-finding image enters a mini-batch, we record its label cardinality; we then feed the same image to the encoder with a new target label vector— either a single under-represented disease or a multi-label combination sampled from the empirical co-occurrence distribution; conditioned on this new label, the conditional VAE (cVAE) re-samples a latent code and immediately decodes it into a high-fidelity counterfactual radiograph; finally, we discard the original normal image and retain only the freshly synthesized, label-consistent sample in the mini-batch.

This study makes three key contributions. We introduce a counterfactual augmentation framework that learns and mimics real-world medical statistics, generating patient-specific radiographs that preserve anatomy while selectively toggling rare findings. Next, we present a data-driven, two-stage strategy in which one stage balances infrequent single-label cases and the other synthesizes multi-label images in proportion to their empirical co-occurrence, thereby capturing both rarity and clinical co-morbidity. Finally, we carry out comprehensive ablation experiments on the ChestX-ray14 dataset—comparing a baseline trained on original data, the baseline augmented with single-label counterfactuals, the baseline augmented with multi-label counterfactuals, and a full COVA configuration that combines both approaches—to show that deliberate counterfactual editing, rather than generic generative noise, accounts for most of the observed AUROC improvement and to provide reproducible guidelines for imbalance-aware medical-image augmentation. To the best of our knowledge, COVA is the first plug-and-play framework to enable on-demand, counterfactually consistent augmentation specifically for extreme imbalance in medical multi-label classification.

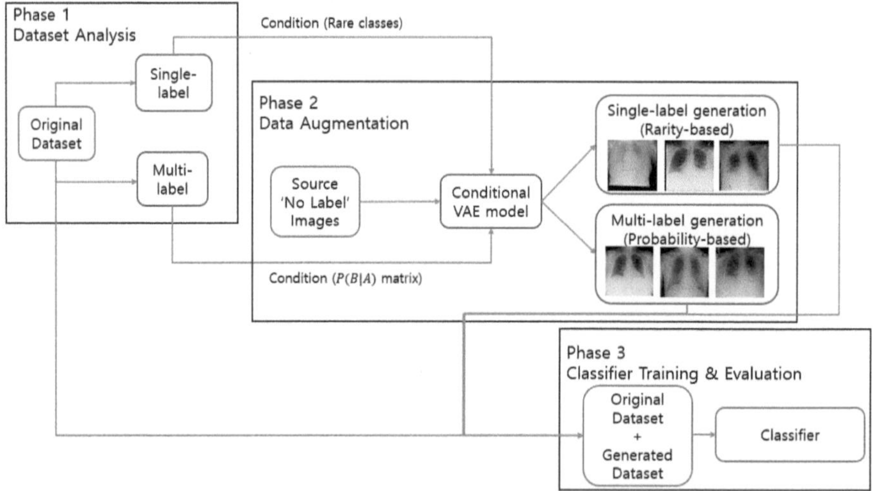


**Fig. 1.** ChestX-ray14 label-cardinality distribution before augmentation, in the set of counterfactuals generated by COVA, and in the final augmented training pool. See Sect. 2 for the generation procedure.

## 2 Method

### 2.1 Overview

Our pipeline unfolds in three stages—dataset analysis, counterfactual image generation, and classifier training (see Fig. 1): we first analyze the label distribution and co-occurrence statistics of the original dataset; next, guided by these statistics, we use a cVAE to synthesize single- and multi-label counterfactual images; finally, we train a classifier on the augmented set and assess the effectiveness of the approach through comprehensive experiments.

**Table 1.** LabelâĂŞcardinality distribution *before* and *after* COVA augmentation.

| # Positive labels | Original | | Generated | | Augmented |
|---|---|---|---|---|---|
| | Count | Ratio (%) | Count | Ratio (%) | Count |
| 0 | 50,500 | 58.4 | 0 | 0.0 | 50,500 |
| 1 | 22,971 | 26.6 | 6,776 | 64.1 | 29,747 |
| 2 | 9,285 | 10.7 | 2,739 | 25.9 | 12,024 |
| 3 | 2,898 | 3.3 | 854 | 8.1 | 3,752 |
| 4 | 675 | 0.8 | 200 | 1.9 | 875 |
| $\geq 5$ | 195 | 0.2 | 0 | 0.0 | 195 |
| *Total* | 86,524 | 100 | 10,569 | 100 | 97,093 |

## 2.2  Dataset Analysis

The original ChestX-ray14 training split is highly skewed not only in class frequency but also in label cardinality Table 1). A majority of images (58.4%) contain no positive findings, while only 15.0% exhibit two or more concurrent abnormalities. To facilitate multi-label augmentation, we computed the co-occurrence probability between disease labels. For each pair of diseases $A$ and $B$, the conditional probability $P(B|A)$ is defined as:

$$P(B|A) = \frac{N(A \cap B)}{N(A)} \tag{1}$$

where $N(A \cap B)$ is the number of images labeled with both $A$ and $B$, and $N(A)$ is the number of images labeled with $A$. The resulting co-occurrence matrix $\mathbf{C}$, where $C_{i,j} = P(L_j|L_i)$ for label $L_i$ and $L_j$, was used to guide the sampling of realistic multi-label combinations during augmentation. We also analyzed the empirical distribution of the number of labels per image, which was later used to match the label count distribution in the generated multi-label images (see Fig. 2). All radiographs were down-sampled from the original 1024 × 1024 to 224 × 224 before being fed to both the cVAE and the classifier.

## 2.3  Counterfactual Image Generation

The cVAE consists of an encoder $q_\phi(\mathbf{z}|\mathbf{x}, \mathbf{y})$ and a decoder $p_\theta(\mathbf{x}|\mathbf{z}, \mathbf{y})$, where $\mathbf{x}$ denotes the input image, $\mathbf{y}$ is the target label vector, and $\mathbf{z}$ is the latent variable. The cVAE is trained to maximize the following evidence lower bound (ELBO):

$$\mathcal{L}_{cVAE} = \mathbb{E}_{q_\phi(\mathbf{z}|\mathbf{x},\mathbf{y})}\left[\log p_\theta(\mathbf{x}|\mathbf{z}, \mathbf{y})\right] - D_{KL}\left(q_\phi(\mathbf{z}|\mathbf{x}, \mathbf{y})\|p(\mathbf{z})\right) \tag{2}$$

where $D_{KL}$ denotes the Kullback-Leibler divergence. For counterfactual generation, we first encode a "No Finding" image $\mathbf{x}_{NF}$ to obtain its latent representation $\mathbf{z}_{NF}$. We then decode $\mathbf{z}_{NF}$ conditioned on a target label vector $\mathbf{y}_{target}$ to synthesize a counterfactual image:

$$\mathbf{x}_{CF} = p_\theta(\mathbf{x}|\mathbf{z}_{NF}, \mathbf{y}_{target}) \tag{3}$$

**Single-Label Augmentation.** For the six least frequent classes, we generated single-label counterfactual images by setting $\mathbf{y}_{\text{target}}$ to the one-hot vector of the chosen class; the number of synthetic images for each of these classes was matched one-for-one with its original sample count.

**Multi-label Augmentation.** To mimic the real-world label distribution, we sampled multi-label vectors $\mathbf{y}_{target}$ according to the empirical distribution of label counts and the co-occurrence matrix $\mathbf{C}$ described in Sect. 2. For each sampled $\mathbf{y}_{target}$, we generated a counterfactual image using the same procedure as above.

### 2.4   Classifier Training and Evaluation

To evaluate our augmentation strategy, we train a TResNet-M classifier [18] pre-trained on ImageNet via the timm library. The network is optimized with AdamW while minimizing the Asymmetric Loss (ASL), which down-weights easy negative examples and retains informative positive gradients—an approach well suited to long-tailed, multi-label data. Following the official ChestX-ray14 protocol, we randomly split train_val_list.txt into training and validation subsets at a 9:1 ratio, and keep test_list.txt untouched for final evaluation.

## 3   Experiment Results

### 3.1   Experimental Setup

All experiments were carried out on a workstation equipped with a single A100 GPU and 16 GB of system RAM. For data partitioning, we retained the official test_list.txt for final evaluation and randomly divided train_val_list.txt into training and validation subsets in a 9:1 ratio. Unless stated otherwise, the classifier was fine-tuned for 30 epochs with a batch size of 16 using the AdamW optimizer and an initial learning rate of $3 \times 10^{-4}$; early stopping was triggered when the validation loss failed to improve. When Asymmetric Loss was employed, we fixed the focusing parameters at $\gamma^+ = 0$ and $\gamma^- = 4$. Model performance was quantified as the mean class-wise area under the receiver-operating-characteristic curve (AUROC) across all 14 pathologies; for brevity, we refer to AUROC simply as AUC throughout the manuscript.

**Table 2.** AUC comparisons of COVA with existing methods on the ChestX-Ray14 dataset. The 14 pathologies are atelectasis (atel), cardiomegaly (card), effusion (effu), infiltration (infi), mass, nodule (nodu), pneumonia (pne1), pneumothorax (pne2), consolidation (cons), edema (edem), emphysema (emph), fibrosis (fibr), pleural thickening (pt) and hernia (hern). Bolded numbers are the best results.

| Method | atel | card | effu | infi | mass | nodu | pne1 | pne2 | cons | edem | emph | fibr | pt | hern | Mean |
|---|---|---|---|---|---|---|---|---|---|---|---|---|---|---|---|
| U–DCNN [21] | 0.700 | 0.810 | 0.759 | 0.661 | 0.693 | 0.669 | 0.658 | 0.799 | 0.703 | 0.805 | 0.833 | 0.786 | 0.684 | 0.872 | 0.745 |
| DR-DNN [19] | 0.766 | 0.801 | 0.797 | 0.751 | 0.760 | 0.741 | 0.778 | 0.800 | 0.787 | 0.820 | 0.773 | 0.765 | 0.759 | 0.748 | 0.775 |
| LSTM-Net [23] | 0.772 | 0.904 | 0.859 | 0.695 | 0.792 | 0.717 | 0.713 | 0.841 | **0.788** | **0.882** | 0.829 | 0.767 | 0.765 | 0.914 | 0.798 |
| AGCL [20] | 0.756 | 0.887 | 0.819 | 0.689 | 0.814 | 0.755 | 0.729 | 0.850 | 0.728 | 0.848 | 0.906 | 0.818 | 0.765 | 0.875 | 0.803 |
| CheXNet [16] | 0.769 | 0.885 | 0.825 | 0.694 | 0.824 | 0.759 | 0.715 | 0.852 | 0.745 | 0.842 | 0.906 | 0.821 | 0.766 | 0.901 | 0.807 |
| DNet [11] | 0.767 | 0.883 | 0.828 | **0.709** | 0.821 | 0.758 | 0.731 | 0.846 | 0.745 | 0.835 | 0.895 | 0.818 | 0.761 | 0.896 | 0.807 |
| CRAL [10] | 0.781 | 0.880 | 0.829 | 0.702 | 0.834 | 0.773 | 0.729 | 0.857 | 0.754 | 0.850 | 0.908 | 0.830 | 0.778 | 0.917 | 0.816 |
| DualCheXN [4] | 0.784 | 0.888 | 0.831 | 0.705 | 0.838 | 0.796 | 0.727 | **0.876** | 0.746 | 0.852 | 0.942 | **0.837** | 0.796 | 0.912 | 0.823 |
| CheXGCN [5] | **0.786** | 0.893 | 0.832 | 0.699 | **0.840** | **0.800** | 0.739 | **0.876** | 0.751 | 0.850 | **0.944** | 0.834 | 0.795 | 0.929 | 0.826 |
| **COVA (Ours)** | 0.783 | **0.907** | **0.838** | 0.705 | 0.831 | 0.796 | **0.790** | **0.876** | 0.748 | 0.851 | 0.942 | 0.830 | **0.802** | **0.935** | **0.840** |

## 3.2 Quantitative Results

Table 2 compares our singleâĂŞimage classifier with four representative multi-label models that report average AUC on the standard ChestX-ray14 split. Our counterfactual-augmented pipeline achieves a AUC of 0.840, outperforming every prior method. Per-label analysis (Table 2) shows that our counterfactual augmenter consistently improves AUC on the rare findings, while the performance of the remaining classes remains virtually unchanged. In short, the method strengthens tail-class recognition without compromising head- or mid-frequency accuracy, demonstrating that counterfactual synthesis works in harmony with Asymmetric Loss.

## 3.3 Qualitative Results

Figure 2 shows examples of counterfactual images generated by our method. The synthesized images exhibit realistic anatomical structures and plausible disease patterns, demonstrating the effectiveness of our cVAE-based augmentation.

## 3.4 Ablation Study

We evaluated four configurations (Table 3)—Baseline (training on the original set only); Single (the Baseline augmented with single-label counterfactuals); Multi (the Baseline augmented with multi-label counterfactuals); and Full (the Single configuration further augmented with multi-label counterfactuals). Adding single-label counterfactuals lifted the mean AUC from 0.799 to 0.816, whereas using only multi-label images achieved 0.818. Combining both types of counterfactuals produced the best result, 0.840, highlighting their complementary benefits. These findings confirm that our two-stage counterfactual augmentation strategy effectively enhances both precision and overall classification performance.

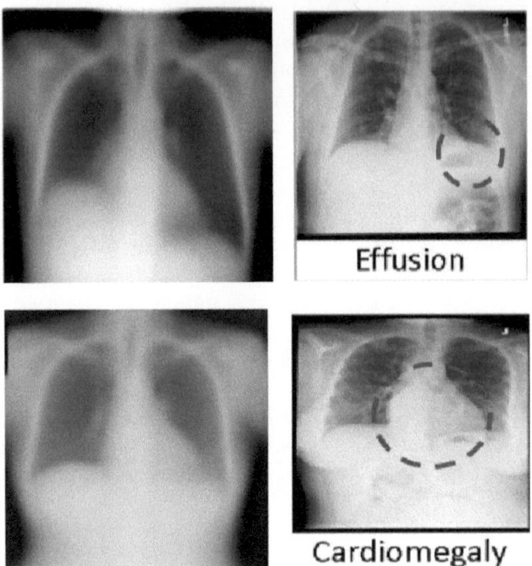


**Fig. 2. Left:** Counterfactual chest X-ray synthesized by our cVAE for the target finding. **Right:** Representative radiographic pattern for the same label provided on the official dataset website. Images are shown at $224 \times 224$, the native resolution used for training; original radiographs are $1024 \times 1024$.

**Table 3.** Ablation study on ChestX-ray14 (AUC per class). The abbreviation for label is in Table 2. Bolded numbers are the best results.

| Method | atel | card | effu | infi | mass | nodu | pne1 | pne2 | cons | edem | emph | fibr | pt | hern | Mean |
|---|---|---|---|---|---|---|---|---|---|---|---|---|---|---|---|
| Baseline | 0.763 | 0.878 | 0.824 | 0.680 | 0.802 | 0.744 | 0.683 | 0.856 | 0.734 | 0.846 | 0.899 | 0.813 | 0.780 | 0.896 | 0.799 |
| Single-label only | 0.769 | 0.899 | 0.826 | 0.685 | 0.801 | 0.753 | 0.784 | 0.857 | 0.743 | 0.844 | 0.940 | 0.821 | 0.772 | 0.933 | 0.816 |
| Multi-label only | 0.782 | 0.880 | 0.833 | **0.718** | 0.822 | 0.781 | 0.719 | 0.861 | **0.748** | 0.847 | 0.924 | 0.812 | 0.800 | 0.924 | 0.818 |
| **Full** | **0.783** | **0.907** | **0.838** | 0.705 | **0.831** | **0.796** | **0.790** | **0.876** | **0.748** | **0.851** | **0.942** | **0.830** | **0.802** | **0.935** | **0.840** |

## 4    Discussion

Our experiments demonstrate that counterfactual image augmentation using cVAE leads to consistent improvements in AUC over the baseline. Notably, the inclusion of multi-label counterfactual images further enhances classification performance, highlighting the importance of modeling real-world label co-occurrence.

Despite these promising results, several limitations remain. First, because our cVAE is trained with a pixel-wise reconstruction loss, the synthesized images often appear over-smoothed or blurry, so delicate disease patterns may be partially obscured; more expressive generative objectives could mitigate this artifact. Second, the overall quality of generated images is inherently constrained by the capacity of the cVAE model and the diversity of the training data, meaning some rare or complex findings are still not faithfully reproduced. Third, our evaluation is limited to a single dataset (NIH ChestX-ray14), so additional benchmarks are needed to confirm generalisability. Finally, we have not yet assessed the clinical interpretability of the generated images, which warrants further investigation.

## 5  Conclusion

In this work, we proposed a two-stage counterfactual image augmentation framework for multi-label medical image classification. By leveraging a cVAE, we generated both single-label and multi-label counterfactual images that preserve patient-specific anatomical features and reflect the statistical properties of the original dataset. Our intelligent augmentation strategy, guided by label rarity and co-occurrence probabilities, led to consistent improvements in AUC over the baseline. Comprehensive ablation studies further demonstrated the effectiveness of each component of our approach. Our findings suggest that counterfactual augmentation is a practical and effective solution for addressing class imbalance and label sparsity in medical imaging. We believe that our method can be readily integrated into existing clinical AI pipelines to enhance diagnostic performance, especially for rare disease classes.

Future research could explore the use of more advanced generative models (e.g., diffusion models [12]), domain adaptation to other imaging modalities, and human-in-the-loop evaluation with radiologists. We also plan to compare cVAE with latent-diffusion-based counterfactuals to mitigate blurriness. Additionally, integrating uncertainty estimation and explainability techniques could further enhance the clinical utility of counterfactual augmentation.

**Acknowledgment.** This work was supported by the BK21 FOUR Project.

## References


1. Bozorgtabar, B., et al.: Informative sample generation using class aware generative adversarial networks for classification of chest xrays. Comput. Vis. Image Underst. **184**, 57–65 (2019)
2. Cao, K., Wei, C., Gaidon, A., Arechiga, N., Ma, T.: Learning imbalanced datasets with label-distribution-aware margin loss. In: Advances in Neural Information Processing Systems, vol. 32 (2019)
3. Chawla, N.V., Bowyer, K.W., Hall, L.O., Kegelmeyer, W.P.: SMOTE: synthetic minority over-sampling technique. J. Artif. Intell. Res. **16**, 321–357 (2002)
4. Chen, B., Li, J., Guo, X., Lu, G.: DualCheXNet: dual asymmetric feature learning for thoracic disease classification in chest x-rays. Biomed. Signal Process. Control **53**, 101554 (2019)
5. Chen, B., Li, J., Lu, G., Yu, H., Zhang, D.: Label co-occurrence learning with graph convolutional networks for multi-label chest x-ray image classification. IEEE J. Biomed. Health Inform. **24**(8), 2292–2302 (2020)

6. Cui, Y., Jia, M., Lin, T.Y., Song, Y., Belongie, S.: Class-balanced loss based on effective number of samples. In: Proceedings of the IEEE/CVF Conference on Computer Vision and Pattern Recognition, pp. 9268–9277 (2019)
7. Durand, T., Mehrasa, N., Mori, G.: Learning a deep convnet for multi-label classification with partial labels. In: Proceedings of the IEEE/CVF conference on computer vision and pattern recognition, pp. 647–657 (2019)
8. Frid-Adar, M., Diamant, I., Klang, E., Amitai, M., Goldberger, J., Greenspan, H.: GAN-based synthetic medical image augmentation for increased CNN performance in liver lesion classification. Neurocomputing **321**, 321–331 (2018)
9. Ghiasi, G., et al.: Simple copy-paste is a strong data augmentation method for instance segmentation. In: Proceedings of the IEEE/CVF Conference on Computer Vision and Pattern Recognition, pp. 2918–2928 (2021)
10. Guan, Q., Huang, Y., Zhong, Z., Zheng, Z., Zheng, L., Yang, Y.: Diagnose like a radiologist: attention guided convolutional neural network for thorax disease classification. arXiv preprint arXiv:1801.09927 (2018)
11. Gündel, S., Grbic, S., Georgescu, B., Liu, S., Maier, A., Comaniciu, D.: Learning to recognize abnormalities in chest X-rays with location-aware dense networks. In: Vera-Rodriguez, R., Fierrez, J., Morales, A. (eds.) CIARP 2018. LNCS, vol. 11401, pp. 757–765. Springer, Cham (2019). https://doi.org/10.1007/978-3-030-13469-3_88
12. Ho, J., Jain, A., Abbeel, P.: Denoising diffusion probabilistic models. Adv. Neural. Inf. Process. Syst. **33**, 6840–6851 (2020)
13. Irvin, J., et al.: CheXpert: a large chest radiograph dataset with uncertainty labels and expert comparison. In: Proceedings of the AAAI Conference on Artificial Intelligence, vol. 33, pp. 590–597 (2019)
14. Kang, B., et al.: Decoupling representation and classifier for long-tailed recognition. arXiv preprint arXiv:1910.09217 (2019)
15. Lin, T.Y., Goyal, P., Girshick, R., He, K., Dollár, P.: Focal loss for dense object detection. In: Proceedings of the IEEE International Conference on Computer Vision, pp. 2980–2988 (2017)
16. Rajpurkar, P., et al.: CheXNet: radiologist-level pneumonia detection on chest X-rays with deep learning. arXiv preprint arXiv:1711.05225 (2017)
17. Ridnik, T., et al.: Asymmetric loss for multi-label classification. In: Proceedings of the IEEE/CVF International Conference on Computer Vision, pp. 82–91 (2021)
18. Ridnik, T., Lawen, H., Noy, A., Ben Baruch, E., Sharir, G., Friedman, I.: TResNet: high performance GPU-dedicated architecture. In: proceedings of the IEEE/CVF Winter Conference on Applications of Computer Vision, pp. 1400–1409 (2021)
19. Shen, Y., Gao, M.: Dynamic routing on deep neural network for thoracic disease classification and sensitive area localization. In: Shi, Y., Suk, H.-I., Liu, M. (eds.) MLMI 2018. LNCS, vol. 11046, pp. 389–397. Springer, Cham (2018). https://doi.org/10.1007/978-3-030-00919-9_45
20. Tang, Y., Wang, X., Harrison, A.P., Lu, L., Xiao, J., Summers, R.M.: Attention-guided curriculum learning for weakly supervised classification and localization of thoracic diseases on chest radiographs. In: Shi, Y., Suk, H.-I., Liu, M. (eds.) MLMI 2018. LNCS, vol. 11046, pp. 249–258. Springer, Cham (2018). https://doi.org/10.1007/978-3-030-00919-9_29
21. Wang, X., Peng, Y., Lu, L., Lu, Z., Bagheri, M., Summers, R.M.: ChestX-ray8: hospital-scale chest X-ray database and benchmarks on weakly-supervised classification and localization of common thorax diseases. In: Proceedings of the IEEE Conference on Computer Vision and Pattern Recognition, pp. 2097–2106 (2017)

22. Wolleb, J., Bieder, F., Sandkühler, R., Cattin, P.C.: Diffusion models for medical anomaly detection. In: Wang, L., Dou, Q., Fletcher, P.T., Speidel, S., Li, S. (eds.) MICCAI 2022. LNCS, vol. 13438, pp. 35–45. Springer, Cham (2022). https://doi.org/10.1007/978-3-031-16452-1_4
23. Yao, L., Poblenz, E., Dagunts, D., Covington, B., Bernard, D., Lyman, K.: Learning to diagnose from scratch by exploiting dependencies among labels. arXiv preprint arXiv:1710.10501 (2017)
24. Yun, S., Han, D., Oh, S.J., Chun, S., Choe, J., Yoo, Y.: CutMix: regularization strategy to train strong classifiers with localizable features. In: Proceedings of the IEEE/CVF International Conference on Computer Vision, pp. 6023–6032 (2019)
25. Zhang, H., Cisse, M., Dauphin, Y.N., Lopez-Paz, D.: mixup: beyond empirical risk minimization. arXiv preprint arXiv:1710.09412 (2017)
26. Zhou, B., Cui, Q., Wei, X.S., Chen, Z.M.: BBN: bilateral-branch network with cumulative learning for long-tailed visual recognition. In: Proceedings of the IEEE/CVF conference on computer vision and pattern recognition, pp. 9719–9728 (2020)

# Domain-Incremental Continual Learning for Robust Surgical Tool Segmentation

Gokul Adethya, N. Nitish[(✉)], Raghavan Balanathan, and K. Sitara

Department of Computer Science and Engineering, National Institute of Technology, Tiruchirappalli, Tiruchirappalli, India
`nitish2k03@gmail.com, sitara@nitt.edu`

**Abstract.** Robust segmentation of surgical tools is essential to improve robot-assisted surgery, but is affected by challenging visual scenes such as smoke, bleeding, and low light. Deep learning models cannot be generalized to such diverse domains, typically suffering from catastrophic forgetting and data privacy issues. To overcome this, we present a Domain-Incremental Continual Learning (CL) framework for robust and privacy-preserving segmentation of surgical tools. We construct our solution based on Segment Anything Model 2 (SAM2) and utilize parameter-efficient Low-Rank Adaptation (LoRA) for domain-specific adaptation learning. The foundation of our solution is a K-Means clustering strategy on CLIP embeddings that dynamically selects the appropriate LoRA adapter for the current visual domain, isolating domain knowledge, and avoiding forgetting. We perform a rigorous evaluation on the challenging SegSTRONG-C endoscopic video dataset. Our findings show that our solution is substantially better than CL baselines at segmentation accuracy as well as knowledge retention, presenting a promising path to reliable and adaptive AI for real-world surgical procedures. The code is made public at https://github.com/DonWick32/image-segmentation.

**Keywords:** surgical tool segmentation · continual learning · privacy · catastrophic forgetting

## 1 Introduction

Robot-assisted surgery has improved surgical practice to be more accurate and less invasive through platforms such as the da Vinci Surgical System [4]. Its success mostly relies on computer vision, i.e., instrument segmentation for real-time decision, navigation, and possible autonomous capabilities [11]. Real surgical environments introduce image corruptions such as bleeding, smoke, and low lighting that can compromise model robustness, such as SegSTRONG-C dataset's photo-realistic corruptions [3].

---

G. Adethya, N. Nitish and R. Balanathan—Equal contribution.

Deep learning models like U-Net [15], DeepLabv3+ [2], and foundation models like Segment Anything Model (SAM) [6] have demonstrated good instrument-segmentation performance. Clinical use is hindered by domain shifts across institutions, modalities, and patient-cohorts [18,19], data privacy constraints, and catastrophic forgetting upon sequential model updating [7,18]. Computationally costly retraining is required frequently, and models fail to generalize to new situations.

Continual Learning (CL) allows models to learn from new data without forgetting previously acquired knowledge [7,17,18]. Domain-Incremental Learning (DIL), particularly important in medical imaging, allows adaptation to varied clinical environments without domain labels at test time as depicted in Fig. 1 [16]. Existing CL approaches face challenges for difficult segmentation: regularization-based methods like LwF [8] trade off too much performance to retain past knowledge and resist new learning; replay buffers pose privacy concerns; and dynamic architectures are too resource-intensive for large models like SAM. Among regularization methods, we choose LwF alone due to its competitive performance and minimal compute overhead, unlike others which are more demanding.

Besides, we employ Low-Rank Adaptation (LoRA) [5], which offers an effective fine-tuning approach that maintains capacity while keeping important resource requirements minimal.

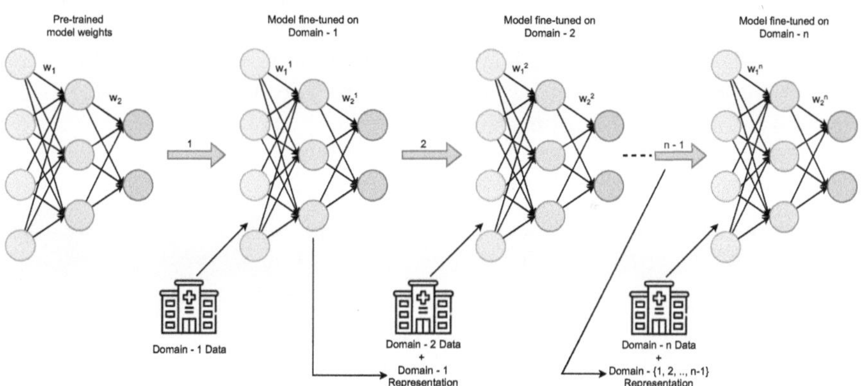


**Fig. 1.** The DIL framework, illustrating step-by-step adaptation to new domains with retention of knowledge learned previously.

Driven by the imperative of having a robust, adaptive, and privacy-aware solution to surgical segmentation, we summarize our contributions as follows: 1) We present a continual learning framework that integrates a prompted Segment Anything Model 2 (SAM2) [14] pipeline with LoRA to facilitate efficient adaptation across varied visual domains, with particular emphasis on frequent corruptions observed in surgical videos. 2) We develop a lightweight and privacy-aware adaptation process that integrates LoRA with k-means clustering of domain-specific features to inform domain-specific model adjustments, resulting in better performance while preserving data privacy. 3) We perform experiments on the SegSTRONG-C dataset [3] to compare our solution to the LwF method. Our experiments demonstrate superior segmentation accuracy across varied corruption domains along with a noteworthy reduction in catastrophic forgetting, thereby establishing the efficacy of our proposed solutions for robust surgical tool segmentation.

## 2   Method

We introduce a robust surgical instrument segmentation approach optimized for domain adaptation in real-world surgical environments. At its core is a CL model based on SAM2, adapted seamlessly with LoRA. For fine-tuning cost saving, LoRA is used only for the query and value projections of SAM2's image encoder's last two transformer blocks.

As shown in Fig. 2, the initial base model $(M)$ is first trained on an initial domain $(D_1)$, which represents the data distribution of a specific hospital and surgical condition (e.g., smoke), thus producing model $M_1$. The model then learns in succession to accommodate subsequent domains $(D_2, \ldots, D_n)$ with a CL strategy that preserves performance on all previously encountered distributions, under the privacy assumption that earlier data remain undisclosed. To illustrate an extreme distribution shift, we treat each SegStrong-C corruption as its own domain. In reality, however, domain shifts tend to produce mixed distributions rather than entirely discrete ones. The final model $(M_n)$ is then employed for inference on unseen test data.

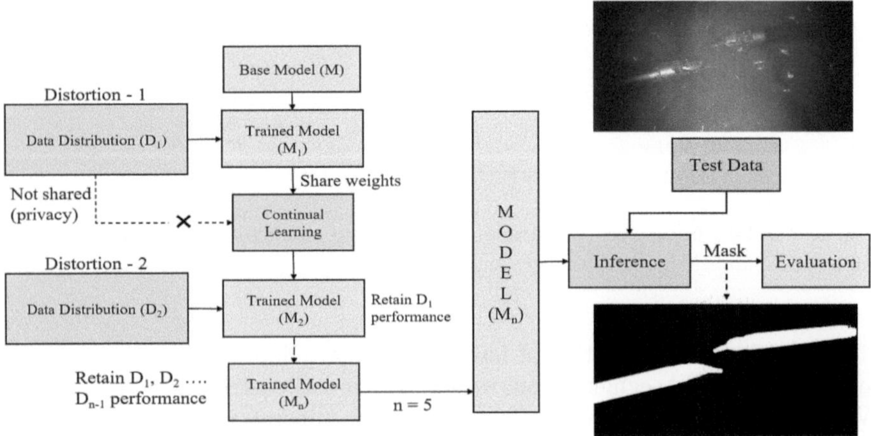


**Fig. 2.** The proposed CL pipeline, where a model is sequentially adapted across multiple hospital-specific data distributions $(D_1 \rightarrow D_n)$ without forgetting prior knowledge, for final inference.

Our approach, described in Sect. 2.2, uses separate LoRA adapters per domain, which are dynamically selected during inference via feature-based domain detection. This is in contrast to baseline approaches like sequential fine-tuning and LwF (Sect. 2.1).

## 2.1   Continual Learning Strategies

To accommodate changing surgical conditions (e.g., smoke, bleeding, lighting), we consider each type of visual corruption as its own domain and apply CL techniques that freeze the SAM2 backbone and learn only LoRA adapters at the query and value projections of the image encoder's last two transformer blocks. As baselines, we used Naive sequential fine-tuning, where one LoRA adapter is fine-tuned on all domains, and LwF [8], which uses knowledge distillation to retain previous knowledge.

## 2.2   Adaptive LoRA with Domain Identification (K-Means + CLIP)

Apart from LoRA-based adaptation, our main method trains a per-domain LoRA adapter for each domain, separates domain-specific knowledge and avoids catastrophic forgetting by design. LoRA (rank 8) is applied only to the query and value projections of the last two transformer blocks of the image encoder. This configuration adds around 60K trainable parameters which is less than 1% of the size of the whole model. To enable efficient training and inference, we only save and load the LoRA parameters with custom functions. During inference, the test domain is determined through a K-Means clustering of CLIP-derived features, and the respective pre-trained adapter is dynamically loaded.

---

**Algorithm 1.** Domain-Specific LoRA Adapter Training

---

1: **Input:** Pre-trained model with frozen weights, Feature Encoder $E$ (CLIP), Set of domains $D = \{D_1, \ldots, D_T\}$.
2: **Output:** Set of trained LoRA adapters $\Phi = \{\phi_1, \ldots, \phi_T\}$, Set of domain centroids $C = \{c_1, \ldots, c_T\}$.
3: Initialize empty sets $\Phi \leftarrow \emptyset$ and $C \leftarrow \emptyset$.
4: **for** $t = 1$ to $T$ **do**
5:     Initialize a new LoRA adapter $\phi_t$.
6:     Train $\phi_t$ on all data $(x_i, y_i) \in D_t$ by minimizing the task loss $\mathcal{L}_{\text{task}}$.
7:     Store the trained adapter: $\Phi \leftarrow \Phi \cup \{\phi_t\}$.
8:     Compute the domain centroid $c_t$ by averaging feature embeddings $E(x_i)$ for all $x_i \in D_t$.
9:     Store the centroid: $C \leftarrow C \cup \{c_t\}$.
10: **end for**
11: **return** $\Phi, C$.

---

At offline training (Algorithm 1), we learn an adapter $\phi_t$ per domain $D_t$ on the task loss $\mathcal{L}_{\text{task}}$ (see Sect. 2.3). To enable the detection of a domain, we calculate a centroid $c_t$ per domain by averaging Contrastive Language-Image Pre-training (CLIP) [12] (Base) model's feature embeddings from its video frames. The collection of learned adapters $\Phi$ and centroids $C$ is cached.

During inference (Algorithm 2, depicted in Fig. 3), a CLIP embedding $e_{\text{test}}$ is sampled from the test video and compared to all centroids $c_t$ using cosine similarity. The adapter $\phi_k$ of the closest domain is then loaded into the frozen SAM2 for final segmentation.

---

**Algorithm 2.** Adaptive LoRA Adapter Selection during Inference

---

1: **Input:** Test sample $x_{\text{test}}$, Feature Encoder $E$ (CLIP), Pre-trained model (SAM2), Stored adapters $\Phi$, Stored centroids $C$.
2: **Output:** Predicted segmentation mask $y_{\text{pred}}$.
3: Extract feature embedding for the test sample: $e_{\text{test}} \leftarrow E(x_{\text{test}})$.
4: Identify best matching domain index: $k \leftarrow \arg\max_{t \in \{1,\ldots,T\}} \text{similarity}(e_{\text{test}}, c_t)$.
5: Retrieve the corresponding adapter: $\phi_{\text{best}} \leftarrow \phi_k \in \Phi$.
6: Load the adapter $\phi_{\text{best}}$ into SAM2.
7: Generate segmentation mask with a forward pass: $y_{\text{pred}} \leftarrow \text{model\_forward}(x_{\text{test}})$.
8: **return** $y_{\text{pred}}$.

---

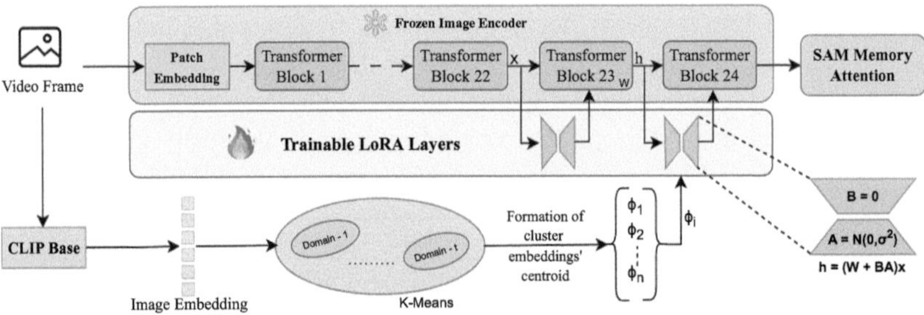


**Fig. 3.** Adaptive LoRA selection by K-Means and CLIP. A CLIP embedding selects the domain-specific LoRA adapter ($\phi_i$) to be injected into the frozen SAM2 encoder during inference.

## 2.3   Segmentation Loss Function

The training of each LoRA adapter is guided by a composite loss function computed on a per-frame basis to optimize spatial segmentation accuracy. The task-specific loss $\mathcal{L}_{\text{task}}$ for a single frame combines Focal Loss ($\mathcal{L}_{\text{focal}}$) [9], Dice Loss ($\mathcal{L}_{\text{dice}}$) [10], and Intersection over Union (IoU) Loss ($\mathcal{L}_{\text{iou}}$) [13], weighted by coefficients $\lambda_1, \lambda_2, \lambda_3$:

$$\mathcal{L}_{\text{task}} = \lambda_1 \mathcal{L}_{\text{focal}} + \lambda_2 \mathcal{L}_{\text{dice}} + \lambda_3 \mathcal{L}_{\text{iou}} \tag{1}$$

## 3   Experiments

**Dataset and Setup:** Experiments were conducted on SegSTRONG-C [3], a MICCAI EndoVis'24 challenge benchmark. It includes stereo videos ($1920\times1080$ resolution, 10 fps) with real-world corruptions. As the corruption domains required for our task are present only in the official test and validation splits, we utilized the validation set (3 sequences) for training, and the test set (3 sequences) was split into 1 for validation and 2 for testing, forming a 3:1:2 split. Five domains were utilized for CL experiments: Smoke, Bleeding, Low Brightness, Background Change, and Regular, training the model sequentially in this provided order.

**Training Setup:** The model was trained in PyTorch on 6 T V100 GPUs with SAM 2.1 Hiera Base Plus. Input clips had a maximum of 4 frames with a skip of up to 3. We employed the AdamW optimizer with a learning rate of $1 \times 10^{-4}$ and a batch size of 2 per GPU. Each domain was trained for 5 epochs with the composite loss of Eq. 1, with $\lambda_1 = 20$, $\lambda_2 = 1$, and $\lambda_3 = 1$. The point prompts required for SAM2 are sampled from the ground truth of the first frame alone during training. For LwF, the knowledge distillation weight $\lambda_{KD}$ was chosen to be 0.1.

**Evaluation:** Performance on segmentation was evaluated using mean Intersection over Union (mIoU) and mean Dice Similarity Coefficient (mDSC). For a comparison of forgetting during CL, we used the Forgetting Score $(F_t)$ from Chaudhry et al. [1], a measure performance loss on earlier domains after training on subsequent ones. It is calculated by averaging the drop between the peak performance on a task and its performance after training is complete. A lower $F_t$ score indicates less forgetting and is therefore better.

## 4   Results

**Forgetting Analysis.** We measured forgetting by tracking mIOU on previously learned domains as the model progressed through the sequence: Smoke $\rightarrow$ Blood $\rightarrow$ Low Brightness $\rightarrow$ BG Change $\rightarrow$ Regular. As can be seen in Fig. 4, Naive Sequential Fine-tuning experienced the greatest forgetting, with accuracy on Smoke decreasing by $-0.27$ after training on the BG Change domain. LwF reduced forgetting to an extent, reducing the decrease on Smoke to $-0.106$, leveraging the regularization effect of knowledge distillation. The best performance was attained by the K-Means CL method, which utilized domain-specific LoRA adapters and prevented interference with previous domains to the greatest extent, having the lowest forgetting overall. Such success, however, depends on accurate domain identification at test time.

**Segmentation Accuracy Comparison.** Table 1 shows the final mIoU and mDSC scores averaged over test videos per domain after CL. Both LwF and K-Means CL outperformed the Naive baseline, reducing catastrophic forgetting and improving segmentation accuracy. K-Means CL, which uses domain-specific

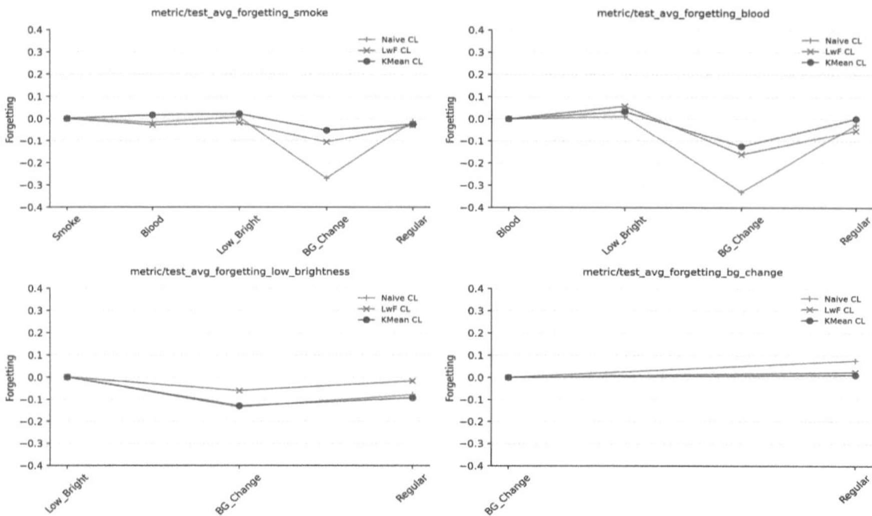

**Fig. 4.** Forgetting curves (IOU) for previously learned domains during sequential adaptation. Each subplot shows performance on a specific past domain.

adapters selected via CLIP-based identification, achieved the best overall performance by preserving domain-specific knowledge. Though it underperformed on Low Brightness and Regular (uncorrupted) domains, it remained robust in challenging ones like Smoke and Blood. On the Regular domain, performance differences between methods were minimal, suggesting that with clear visual input, even the Naive method performs well, making CL less crucial.

**Table 1.** Mean IoU and DSC Scores across Domains for different CL Methods.

| CL Method | Metric | Smoke | Blood | Low Brightness | BG Change | Regular |
|---|---|---|---|---|---|---|
| Naive CL | mIoU | 0.495 | 0.350 | 0.033 | 0.809 | 0.834 |
|  | mDSC | 0.600 | 0.466 | 0.052 | 0.884 | 0.907 |
| K-Means CL (Ours) | mIoU | **0.725** | **0.542** | 0.084 | **0.876** | 0.838 |
|  | mDSC | **0.828** | **0.684** | 0.133 | **0.933** | 0.910 |
| LwF CL [8] | mIoU | 0.672 | 0.489 | **0.091** | 0.864 | **0.853** |
|  | mDSC | 0.780 | 0.640 | **0.144** | 0.923 | **0.919** |

To illustrate these differences, Fig. 5 depicts segmentation masks in the Smoke domain. Naive CL method masks are error-prone on previously learned domains. The K-Means CL method has a higher likelihood of producing better-looking and more stable segmentations and accurately detecting tool boundaries even after extreme corruptions due to domain-specific adapters. LwF possesses a moderate quality level.

**Table 2.** Average Inference Time per Frame (Milliseconds).

| Hardware Configuration | Model Inference (ms) |
|---|---|
| NVIDIA Tesla V100 GPU | ~95 |
| NVIDIA GeForce RTX 4060 (Desktop) | ~133 |
| Intel Ultra 7 155H | ~7000 |

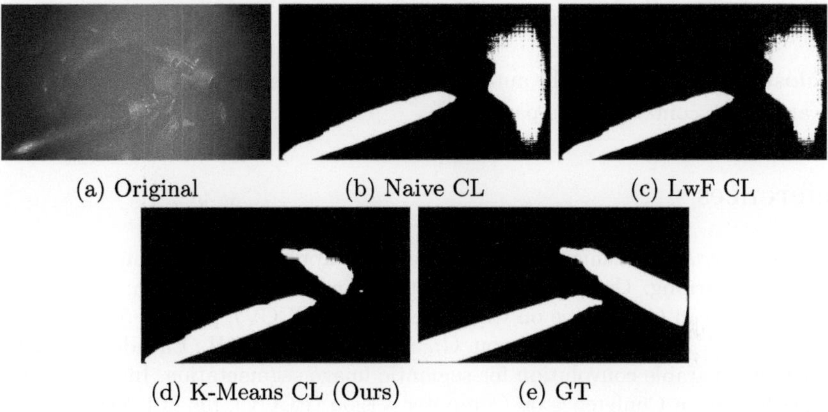

(a) Original                    (b) Naive CL                    (c) LwF CL

(d) K-Means CL (Ours)                    (e) GT

**Fig. 5.** Qualitative comparison of segmentation masks on the Smoke domain.

**Inference Time Analysis.** We measured the average time to process one video frame (Table 2). The frame rate of the SegSTRONG-C dataset is 10 fps (100ms per frame). The model that is inferenced includes SAM2 with the pre-loaded LoRA adapter. High-performance GPUs (V100) can compute at levels that satisfy the 10 fps requirement. Consumer-grade GPUs (RTX 4060) are close, and inference on the CPU is too slow and of no value in real-time. The K-Means CL approach, involving adapter loading and inference, is feasible for deployment on appropriate GPU hardware.

## 5   Conclusion

In this paper, we presented a paradigm for CL for robust surgical tool segmentation across domain shifts, employing SAM2 with LoRA adapters. In this setup, the K-Means + CLIP method was most effective, sustaining performance across domains via domain-specific adapters and minimizing forgetting. As mentioned earlier, SAM2 still requires a point prompt for the first frame which could be automated using models to generate bounding boxes. Moreover, we treat each SegStrong-C corruption as its own domain to illustrate extreme shifts, but real-world distributions are mixed and merit further study. Our method is currently validated only on SegStrong-C, which limits the generalizability of the findings and highlights the need for evaluation on additional datasets. Lastly, a federated-learning extension that jointly optimizes adapters across institutions without sharing raw data could enable truly decentralized, privacy-preserving deployment.

**Acknowledgments.** We acknowledge National Supercomputing Mission (NSM) for providing computing resources of 'PARAM Porul' at National Institute of Technology, Tiruchirappalli, which is implemented by C-DAC and supported by the Ministry of Electronics and Information Technology (MeitY) and Department of Science and Technology (DST), Government of India.

**Disclosure of Interests.** The authors have no competing interests to declare that are relevant to the content of this paper.

# References


1. Chaudhry, A., Dokania, P.K., Ajanthan, T., Torr, P.H.: Riemannian walk incremental learning: Understanding forgetting and intransigence. In: Proceedings of the European Conference on Computer Vision (ECCV), pp. 532–547 (2018)
2. Chen, L.C., Zhu, Y., Papandreou, G., Schroff, F., Adam, H.: Encoder-decoder with atrous separable convolution for semantic image segmentation. In: Proceedings of the European Conference on Computer Vision (ECCV), pp. 801–818 (2018)
3. Ding, H., et al.: SegSTRONG-C: segmenting surgical tools robustly on non-adversarial generated corruptions–an EndoVis' 24 challenge. arXiv preprint arXiv:2407.11906 (2024)
4. Herrera, K., Quach, T., Phillips, E.: Robotic assisted surgery: a theoretical approach to perceived workload and non-verbal and verbal communication. Proceedings of the Human Factors and Ergonomics Society Annual Meeting, vol. 67, pp. 2378–2381 (2023)
5. Hu, E.J., et al.: LoRA: low-rank adaptation of large language models. In: International Conference on Learning Representations (ICLR) (2022)
6. Kirillov, A., et al.: Segment anything. In: Proceedings of the IEEE/CVF International Conference on Computer Vision, pp. 4015–4026 (2023)
7. Li, R., Ye, J., Huang, Y., Jin, W., Xu, P., Guo, L.: A continuous learning approach to brain tumor segmentation: integrating multi-scale spatial distillation and pseudo-labeling strategies. Front. Oncol. **13**, 1247603 (2024)
8. Li, Z., Hoiem, D.: Learning without forgetting. IEEE Trans. Pattern Anal. Mach. Intell. **40**(12), 2935–2947 (2017)
9. Lin, T.Y., Goyal, P., Girshick, R., He, K., Dollár, P.: Focal loss for dense object detection. In: Proceedings of the IEEE International Conference on Computer Vision (ICCV), pp. 2980–2988 (2017)
10. Milletari, F., Navab, N., Ahmadi, S.A.: V-net: fully convolutional neural networks for volumetric medical image segmentation. In: 2016 Fourth International Conference on 3D Vision (3DV), pp. 565–571 (2016)
11. Qian, C., Ren, H.: Deep reinforcement learning in surgical robotics: enhancing the automation level. In: Handbook of Robotic Surgery, pp. 89–102 (2025)
12. Radford, A., et al.: Learning transferable visual models from natural language supervision. In: International Conference on Machine Learning, pp. 8748–8763 (2021)

13. Rahman, M.A., Wang, Y.: Optimizing intersection-over-union in deep neural networks for image segmentation. In: International Symposium on Visual Computing, pp. 234–244 (2016)
14. Ravi, N., et al.: SAM 2: segment anything in images and videos. arXiv preprint arXiv:2408.00714 (2024)
15. Ronneberger, O., Fischer, P., Brox, T.: U-net: convolutional networks for biomedical image segmentation. In: Navab, N., Hornegger, J., Wells, W.M., Frangi, A.F. (eds.) MICCAI 2015. LNCS, vol. 9351, pp. 234–241. Springer, Cham (2015). https://doi.org/10.1007/978-3-319-24574-4_28
16. Volpi, R., Larlus, D., Rogez, G.: continual adaptation of visual representations via domain randomization and meta-learning. In: Proceedings of the IEEE/CVF Conference on Computer Vision and Pattern Recognition, pp. 4443–4453 (2021)
17. Wang, L., Zhang, X., Su, H., Zhu, J.: A comprehensive survey of continual learning: Theory, method and application. IEEE Trans. Pattern Anal. Mach. Intell. (2024)
18. Xu, M., Islam, M., Bai, L., Ren, H.: Privacy-preserving synthetic continual semantic segmentation for robotic surgery. IEEE Trans. Med. Imaging (2024)
19. Zhang, X., et al.: Progressive test time energy adaptation for medical image segmentation. arXiv preprint arXiv:2503.16616 (2025)

# Author Index





T. Chen et al. (Eds.): EMA4MICCAI 2025 Workshops, LNCS 16318, pp. 371–373, 2026.
https://doi.org/10.1007/978-3-032-13961-0